IDEAS AND PATTERNS
FOR
WRITING

IDEAS AND PATTERNS FOR WRITING

CARLE B. SPOTTS
Ohio State University

HOLT, RINEHART AND WINSTON, INC.
New York · Chicago · San Francisco · Toronto

PREFACE

Users of *Ideas and Patterns for Writing* may not agree whether a collection of readings such as this should be useful mainly as a stimulus to ideas—ideas that will get themselves recorded with some freshness in student themes—or whether they should serve primarily as models or patterns. Both these aims have been given about equal weight in selecting the contents of this book. Each essay chosen had to convince me that it would serve first (or perhaps second) as a kind of pattern which the student could use to improve his own craft, and second (or perhaps first) as a stimulus or challenge to the student's ideas on a given subject. (I once thought of calling the book Gadflies and Models.)

Fringe benefits from these readings undoubtedly will accrue: expanded ideas and vocabulary, improved reading skills, and, as Frost would say, "some little stay against confusion." And these gains are not to be scorned. Clear thinking and all the language arts are interrelated and support each other.

The selections may be taken in any order. However, "Chapter 1, English in business, the Professions, and Social Life" in the first table of contents should prove especially useful at the beginning of the course. It should help motivate those students who enter college composition with serious, though silent, questioning of the necessity of more required English. The essays in it by the anonymous editor at General Electric, and the essays by Arnold Bennett, Helen Keller, and Lewis Mumford should make the student see communication as something much more human and vital than mere etiquette of language. The sayer, as Emerson reminded us, is the whole man. To be articulate is to be human.

The types of writing covered and the subject areas included are varied. No article, however, requires specialized technical knowledge in fields other than composition, nor is it intended to provide such knowledge except incidentally. (We teachers of composition sometimes need to be reminded that we should, in all modesty, allow teachers in other departments to do their share in providing the student with a well-rounded education.)

Six of the chapters (Contents I) contain articles dealing with the subject fields that teachers of composition and literature are most expert in. In addition to "Chapter 1, English in Business, the Professions, and Social

v

39222

Life," the following chapters contain articles in the English area: "Chapter 5, Grammar and Usage: What Is Good English?"; "Chapter 6, Some Principles of Writing: Style"; "Chapter 7, Science and Scientific Thinking" (deduction, induction, fallacies, evidence); "Chapter 11, Mass Communication"; "Chapter 12, Literature and the Fine Arts."

A generous proportion of other articles deal with problems of the student as a member of a family ("Crabbed Age and Youth"), of a college community, and of organized government.

Each of the seventy selections, mostly expository and mostly dealing with ideas, has (1) a headnote on the author and the article, (2) questions on the content and form of the article, and (3) questions on the vocabulary (in context), and (4) theme suggestions. This part of the book, it is hoped, will save time for the busy teacher and be especially helpful for the beginning teacher.

Since every student can learn something of the narrative art from well-written fiction and something of the real economy and power of words from poetry, I have included a few short stories and poems where they fit into the topics of the chapters.

C. B. S.

Ohio State University
December 1966

CONTENTS I

(Arranged by themes under the two major rhetorical types)

INTRODUCTORY CHAPTER

CHAPTER 1. *English in Business, the Professions, and Social Life*   3

  General Electric Bulletin   Why Study English?   3
  Arnold Bennett   Seeing Life   10
  Helen Keller   The Most Important Day   13
  Lewis Mumford   The Miracle of Language   16

PART I

Emphasis on Images: Narration and Description

CHAPTER 2. *Seeing and Reporting Experiences*   25

  Paul Gallico   The Feel   25
  Henry David Thoreau   The Battle of the Ants   34
           The Loon   37
  Hilaire Belloc   The Mowing of a Field   39
  Jack Kerouac   On the Road with Memère   43
  Carl Sandburg   The Assassination of Lincoln   50
  Herman Melville   The Encantadas or Enchanted Isles   59
  Katherine Anne Porter   The Grave   62
  Robert Browning   Meeting at Night   69
  Robert Frost   A Hillside Thaw   70
           The Road Not Taken   72
           The White-Tailed Hornet   73

CHAPTER 3. *The Character Sketch*   76

  John Earle   A Child   76
  Sir Thomas Overbury   A Melancholy Man   77
  Thomas Jefferson   The Character of Washington   79

Marshall Fishwick   The Man in the White Marble Toga   81
Robert Browning   My Last Duchess   90
Eudora Welty   Why I Live at the P.O.   92

CHAPTER 4. *Town and Country*   104

Mark Twain   Florida, Missouri, and the Quarles' Farm   104
                 Hannibal, Missouri   112
Phyllis McGinley   Suburbia, of Thee I Sing   114
E. B. White   Here Is New York   122
Carl Sandburg   Chicago   131

PART II

Emphasis on Ideas: Exposition and Argument

CHAPTER 5. *Grammar and Usage: What Is Good English?*   135

Paul Roberts   The Future of Grammar   135
Bergen Evans   But What's a Dictionary For?   139
James Sledd   The Lexicographer's Easy Chair   151
Granville Hicks   The Right Word to Write   154

CHAPTER 6. *Some Principles of Writing: Style*   159

John Mason Brown   Pleasant Agony   159
Frank Sullivan   The Cliché Expert Reveals Himself in His
                 True Colors   164
Malcolm Cowley   Sociological Habit Patterns in Linguistic
                 Transmogrification   169
W. Somerset Maugham   Lucidity, Simplicity, Euphony   174

CHAPTER 7. *Science and Scientific Thinking*   183

Thomas Henry Huxley   The Method of Scientific
                         Investigation   183
Bertrand Russell   Galileo   190
Robert Gorham Davis   Logic and Logical Fallacies   200
Marchette Chute   Getting at the Truth   211

CHAPTER 8. On Getting an Education   *218*

   Sir Francis Bacon   Of Studies   218
   Thomas Fuller   Four Kinds of Students   221
   Samuel H. Scudder   In the Laboratory with Agassiz   222
   Mortimer J. Adler   How to Mark a Book   227
   Edmund S. Morgan   What Every Yale Freshman
                        Should Know   232
   John Ciardi   The Unfading Beauty: A Well-Filled Mind 238

CHAPTER 9. Crabbed Age and Youth   *247*

   Sir Francis Bacon   Of Youth and Age   247
   Louis Reik   War of the Generations   249
   Alfred Kazin   The Kitchen   256
   William S. White   Old Junior's Progress—From Prep
                        School to Severance Pay   261
   Thomas B. Morgan   Teen-Age Heroes: Mirrors of
                        Muddled Youth   267
   Lord Chesterfield   Letters to His Son   280
   Willa Cather   Paul's Case   288
   Carl Sandburg   A Father to His Son   306
   W. B. Yeats   A Prayer for My Daughter   307

CHAPTER 10. College Life   *311*

   James H. S. Bossard and Eleanor Stoker Boll
      Campus Marriages—For Better or For Worse   311
   James Thurber   Courtship Through the Ages   318
   Frances Gray Patton   The Man Jones   323
   Eugene Youngert   College Athletics: Their Pressure on
                        High Schools   341
   Henry Steele Commager   Give the Games Back
                        to the Students   348

CHAPTER 11. Mass Communication   *356*

   Vance Packard   The Ad and the Id   356
   Eric Sevareid   A Cub Reporter Becomes Disillusioned   365

Robert M. Hutchins   The Gigantic Task Ahead   371
Arnold J. Toynbee   Television: The Lion That Squeaks   374
Ernest van den Haag   Reflections on Mass Culture   380

CHAPTER 12. *Literature and the Fine Arts*   388

Maxwell Anderson   Whatever Hope We Have   388
Robert Frost   from The Figure a Poem Makes   395
Aaron Copland   The Creative Process in Music   397
Frank Lloyd Wright   Modern Architecture:
                              The Cardboard House   404
A. E. Housman   Terence, This Is Stupid Stuff   417

CHAPTER 13. *Government and the Individual*   421

George Orwell   Shooting an Elephant   421
John Milton   Areopagitica   429
Arthur M. Schlesinger   Extremism in American Politics   432
Eric Sevareid   The Dark of the Moon   442
W. H. Auden   The Unknown Citizen   444

CONTENTS II

(*Arranged by rhetorical types and modes of development. The introductory essays in Chapter 1 are not listed here. Other selections are listed as main entries only once.*)

I. NARRATIVE: FACT

Jack Kerouac On the Road with Memère	43
Carl Sandburg The Assassination of Lincoln	50
Henry David Thoreau The Battle of the Ants	34
The Loon	37

II. NARRATIVE: FICTION

Willa Cather Paul's Case	288
Frances Gray Patton The Man Jones	323
Katherine Anne Porter The Grave	62
Eudora Welty Why I Live at the P.O.	92

III. DESCRIPTION OF PERSONS

John Earle A Child	76
Thomas Jefferson The Character of Washington	79
Marshall Fishwick The Man in the White Marble Toga	81
Alfred Kazin The Kitchen	256
Robert Browning My Last Duchess	90
W. H. Auden The Unknown Citizen	444

IV. DESCRIPTION OF PLACES

Mark Twain Florida, Missouri, and the Quarles' Farm	104
Hannibal, Missouri	112
Herman Melville The Encantadas or Enchanted Isles	59
E. B. White Here Is New York	122
Phyllis McGinley Suburbia, of Thee I Sing	114
Carl Sandburg Chicago	13J

V. DESCRIPTION OF ACTION

Paul Gallico   The Feel   25
Hilaire Belloc   The Mowing of a Field   39
Robert Browning   Meeting at Night   69
Robert Frost   A Hillside Thaw   70
                 The Road Not Taken   72
                 The White-Tailed Hornet   73

VI. THE RIGHT WORD

Bergen Evans   But What's a Dictionary For?   139
James Sledd   The Lexicographer's Easy Chair   151
Granville Hicks   The Right Word to Write   154
Paul Roberts   The Future of Grammar   135

VII. STYLE: DICTION AND SENTENCE STRUCTURE

John Mason Brown   Pleasant Agony   159
Malcolm Cowley   Sociological Habit Patterns in Linguistic
                   Transmogrification   169
Frank Sullivan   The Cliché Expert Reveals Himself in His
                   True Colors   164
W. Somerset Maugham   Lucidity, Simplicity, Euphony   174

VIII. CLASSIFICATION, DIVISION, ANALYSIS

Thomas Fuller   Four Kinds of Students   221
Sir Francis Bacon   Of Studies   218
Louis Reik   War of the Generations   249
Maxwell Anderson   Whatever Hope We Have   388
John Ciardi   The Unfading Beauty: A Well-Filled Mind   238
Edmund S. Morgan   What Every Yale Freshman
                     Should Know   232

IX. PROCESS OR PROCEDURE

Mortimer J. Adler   How to Mark a Book   227

Aaron Copland   The Creative Process in Music   397
Samuel H. Scudder   In the Laboratory with Agassiz   222

X. COMPARISON AND CONTRAST

Sir Francis Bacon   Of Youth and Age   247
Lord Chesterfield   Letters to His Son   280
Eric Sevareid   The Dark of the Moon   442

XI. EXAMPLE AND ILLUSTRATION

James Thurber   Courtship Through the Ages   318
Eric Sevareid   A Cub Reporter Becomes Disillusioned   365
Arthur M. Schlesinger   Extremism in American Politics   432
George Orwell   Shooting an Elephant   421
Thomas B. Morgan   Teen-Age Heroes: Mirrors of
                                 Muddled Youth   267
William S. White   Old Junior's Progress—From Prep School
                                 to Severance Pay   261
Vance Packard   The Ad and the Id   356
A. E. Housman   Terence, This Is Stupid Stuff   417

XII. FIGURE AND SYMBOL

Robert Frost   from The Figure a Poem Makes   395
Carl Sandburg   A Father to His Son   306
W. B. Yeats   A Prayer for My Daughter   307
(See also *W. H. Auden*, The Unknown Citizen, p. 444; *Carl
Sandburg*, Chicago, p. 131; *Herman Melville*, The Encantadas
or Enchanted Isles, p. 59; the three *Robert Frost* poems, pp. 70–
73; *Robert Browning*, Meeting at Night, p. 69.)

XIII. ARGUMENT IN THEORY AND PRACTICE

A. Theory
Bertrand Russell   Galileo   190
Thomas Henry Huxley   The Method of Scientific Investigation   183

Robert Gorham Davis   Logic and Logical Fallacies   200
Marchette Chute   Getting at the Truth   211
B. Practice
Eugene Youngert   College Athletics: Their Pressure on
                                High Schools   341
Henry Steele Commager   Give the Games Back
                                to the Students   348
Robert M. Hutchins   The Gigantic Task Ahead   371
Arnold J. Toynbee   Television: The Lion That Squeaks   374
Ernest van den Haag   Reflections on Mass Culture   380

XIV. DEFINITION

Sir Thomas Overbury   A Melancholy Man   77
Frank Lloyd Wright   Modern Architecture:
                                The Cardboard House   404
(See also *Vance Packard*, The Ad and the Id, p. 356; *Bergen
Evans*, But What's a Dictionary For? p. 139; *Thomas Henry
Huxley*, The Method of Scientific Investigation, p. 183; *Robert
Gorham Davis*, Logic and Logical Fallacies, p. 200; *Marchette
Chute*, Getting at the Truth, p. 211; *Henry Steele Commager*,
Give the Games Back to the Students, p. 348.)

Introductory Chapter

1 | ENGLISH IN BUSINESS,
THE PROFESSIONS,
AND SOCIAL LIFE

WHY STUDY ENGLISH?

General Electric Bulletin

[1] If what Peter Drucker says is true, and we believe it is, you had better do something about your English.

[2] Mr. Drucker wrote an article for the May, 1952, FORTUNE called "How to Be an Employee." He said that the ability to express ideas in writing and in speaking heads the list of requirements for success.

[3] "As soon as you move one step up from the bottom, your effectiveness depends on your ability to reach others through the spoken or written word. And the further away your job is from manual work, the larger the organization of which you are an employee, the more important it will be that you know how to convey your thoughts in writing or speaking. In the very large organizations, whether it is the government, the large business corporation, or the Army, this ability to express oneself is perhaps the most important of all the skills a man can possess."

[4] It pleases us at General Electric to go on record as supporters of Mr. Drucker's statement. We know, of course, that there are many skills and personal qualifications leading to success. There is no doubt in our minds, for example, that you should have a genuine desire to exchange your best efforts in your employer's behalf for the chance to tackle increasingly more important, more challenging, and more rewarding as-

Reprinted with the permission of the General Electric Company.

signments. We think that you should be able to look a fellow employee, including your boss, in the eye; that you should be reasonably neat and clean.

[5] But right now we have much to say about English.

[6] The top engineer upstairs is on the telephone. He says to us: "Right before my eyes is a brief report made out by one of our young engineers. I have to guess what the fellow is driving at. I'm no English shark, but I find myself getting a little angry when I see four sentences tied together into one with commas. He has *principle* for *principal,* and he has also misspelled *accommodate* and *Cincinnati.* What if some of this fellow's bad sentences get into the hands of our customers?"

[7] We sympathize, and we say somewhat lamely that it's up to him to suggest that the fellow hire a tutor.

[8] The top engineer is wound up. "At the last meeting of our Association, representatives of all the major companies complained about the way their younger men were putting down their words—and futures—on paper. Can't someone tell us what to do?"

[9] We reach for an answer.

[10] "When boys and girls began avoiding mathematics like the plague," we remind him, "we began printing facts. It is now our duty and privilege to beat the drums for English! Our motives are partly selfish, because we want American business to succeed even more than it has in the past. But our motive is more than self-interest. We know because we rub shoulders with people, at work and in the community, that a solid background in English is prerequisite to happiness and well-being. Without a reasonably good command of English—as a means of communication—and without knowledge of what the best minds of all time have put into print, we are not educated for personal happiness, apart from the job, or for personal success in the exciting business of making a living."

[11] "But I thought all boys and girls took English in high school and college?"

[12] "Yes, they have put in their time. Their teachers have spread the feast, but some of them haven't been very hungry. Perhaps they will listen to us. Their teachers can tell them a thousand times that English is important, but they will say, 'Teacher means well, but she's trying to sell us on the importance of her subject.' Perhaps when a manufacturer of turbines, generators, jet engines, lamps, room air coolers, toasters, refrigerators, and 200,000 other electrical products says English is of tremendous importance, they will listen. After all, English is almost as important as math in our business, isn't it?"

[13] The engineer's answer is deliberately emphatic: "Change the word *almost* to *just,* and, brother, you've said a mouthful! Tell them that English is important to them—and to us—because very soon their ability

to read and to know and to remember what they have read, and to speak and to write well, will make all the difference, whether they and we or some other company of their career choice will succeed together."

[14] At one time or another, all of us try our hand at writing.

[15] A group of engineers applies the new principle to the development of a revolutionary type of gadget. The results of this effort are summed up in a typewritten report to the head of their department. The report is then mimeographed for the benefit of others in the organization.

[16] The company prepares to put the new product on the market. Writers prepare literature describing its virtues, or explaining how to use it and keep it in working order.

[17] This is indeed useful writing. No piece of company business can begin, progress, and achieve its purpose without the use of words. Writing, together with reading, is as much an integral part of the electrical manufacturing business (or any business) as your bones are part of your body.

[18] Every day in your future you will be called upon to speak and write, and when you open your mouth, or write a letter or report, you will be advertising your progress and your potential worth.

[19] Here is a verbatim extract from a laboratory notebook:

[20] "Curt flew into the cloud, and I started the dispenser in operation. I dropped about three pounds (of dry ice) and then swung around and headed south.

[21] "About this time I looked toward the rear and was thrilled to see long streamers of snow falling from the base of the cloud through which we had just passed. I shouted to Curt to swing around, and as we did so we passed through a mass of glistening snow crystals! We made another run through a dense portion of the unseeded cloud, during which time I dispensed about three more pounds of crushed dry ice. . . . This was done by opening the window and letting the suction of the passing air remove it. We then swung west of the cloud and observed draperies of snow which seemed to hang for 2-3000 feet below us and noted the cloud drying up rapidly, very similar to what we observe in the cold box in the laboratory. . . . While still in the cloud as we saw the glinting crystals all over, I turned to Curt, and we shook hands as I said, 'We *did* it!' Needless to say, we were quite excited."

[22] This extract is from the laboratory notebook of Vincent J. Schaefer. It is of historical significance because it describes the first artificial snow making outside the General Electric Research Laboratory. Without such record, other men could not have understood the purpose, procedure, and effect; would not have had a starting point from which to take off on their own investigations.

[23] Since its beginning in 1900, the Research Laboratory has published

nearly 2000 papers in technical journals, and these have recorded new facts, new basic discoveries, and new theories. Many are recognized the world over as classics, and are cited as authoritative references in their fields. Some opened up wholly new fields for exploration. Others cast new light on known phenomena. Some disclosed new tools for research.

[24] But the recording of ideas and facts is not confined only to the engineering and scientific laboratories. Each year, thousands of General Electric mechanics, stenographers, accountants, and others write down their suggestions for improving company products and procedures. To each whose suggestion is adopted is given a certain amount of money, but we suspect that the real gain—for company and employee—is the focusing of attention upon those persons who can think of a better way and who can tell about it with words on paper.

[25] We thought little of it at the time, but one night several of us were visiting over the back fence, and a college boy, home for the summer, joined us. He told us how he was enjoying his summer job as helper on a General Electric truck. We asked him who his boss was and how he liked him. He gave us the name and said, simply, "I like him very much. He is a well-spoken man." We think that you, too, if you will stop to think, prefer well-spoken men and women.

[26] You will probably grant that General Electric knows a thing or two about its various specialties, but you may question whether our expertness extends to the English part of the education field. Let's get off the hook directly: your English teacher has probably forgotten more about the teaching of English than we will ever know. As a matter of fact, if someday your employer finds you wobbly in English, he will be critical of you, not some long-suffering teacher or parent.

[27] One of our business colleagues, who would hate us if we gave away his name, has an interesting background. Early in his growing-up years, he dropped schooling so he could earn enough money to buy a Stutz roadster. Eight years later, after working in a shoe factory, another powerful desire took possession of him. He wanted a Harvard degree. For one year he studied all the specified high school subjects; he read everything he could lay his hands on. Then he took all the required high school examinations and passed them with an average of 95 per cent. At Harvard, he kept on reading everything he could squeeze into four years' time. To make a long story short, he's now doing better than all right.

[28] Attitude makes all the difference!

[29] If you are one of those "dese" and dose" guys, and if it "don't make no sense" to you that your school and your employer "wants" you to become a literate person, all the teaching skill and the modern facilities can't win you over.

[30] Did you ever hear of a mental block? It's a massive barrier in your mind, but like the Maginot Line, it can be penetrated.

[31] That block may be mathematics or history or spelling or perhaps a feeling that no one likes you or something else. Do you remember how you learned to swim? You had flailed the water and sunk like a stone. But then a fortunate stroke propelled you forward, and now it doesn't occur to you when you dive off the board that you may not be able to swim to shore.

[32] Too, your mind may be blocked because you imagine all well-read, literate persons are precious, prissy characters who go around spouting Shakespeare. There may be a few of those people, but that is not Shakespeare's fault. We are just realistic eneough to believe that some of the master poet's gracious writing style will rub off on you. We know that in a sense we became a part of what we read, and that what we call writing style is born from our unconscious attempt to imitate what we like.

[33] We hope it has occurred to you that English extends beyond a single classroom; that your success or failure in your other classrooms is largely due to your ability to read, to understand, to speak, and to write. English is just as all-embracing in a business organization. Whether we are at drafting board, desk, machine, or calling on customers, we are involved more or less in communication.

[34] We say that English—especially to American boys and girls—is an easy language to learn. Making English behave may be a little troublesome. You can play safe by writing dull little sentences, and they, of course, are less frustrating to the reader than involved wrong sentences. But since the sentence you write or speak is what the reader or listener uses as a criterion in judging you, it is good sense to learn how to become its master.

[35] We know from our experience at General Electric that too many of our younger employees say to themselves before spreading their wings for a flight with words: "But if I write that report the way I *feel* it should be written, my boss will think that I am a child." If an engineer, for example, is testing an insulating material and it chars and smells like burned string beans, we can think of no reason why he should not say so.

[36] Our business world needs young people whose minds are packed with facts, but with the boldness of imagination to release them in a form that is easy and pleasant to take.

[37] We have on our desk copies of the GENERAL ELECTRIC REVIEW and the SCIENTIFIC AMERICAN—both written for thousands of top-flight engineers and scientists. The editors of both magazines know that factual reporting is necessary so that their readers, who are so bril-

liantly expert in many fields, will have confidence in the authority of their articles. But they know, too, that men and women, whatever their job or profession, are willing to begin and stay with an article only if it is well-written. Only you can guess how many books and articles you have thrown aside after tasting the first few paragraphs. Everyone who reads and listens is so very human.

[38] Without interested readers, whether the magazine is SCHOLAS-TIC or SCIENTIFIC AMERICAN, its survival depends upon the skill and labor-of-love that editors and authors lavish upon it. Your survival, too, as the adult you are aiming to be, depends upon your ability, desire, and courage to put your best foot forward in a world that will judge you by your words as well as your actions.

[39] Who is the next most important man or woman in your life? We aren't thinking of the next prom date, but an understanding person who is sitting at a desk studying a filled-in application blank. Whether he's a college admissions or an employment officer, he hopes he is so right before saying *yes* or *no*.

[40] Can you live up to your expressed desires? Will you fit in? Have you enough preparation, enough intellectual background? Can your brain direct your hands in performing skills? Can you stand the pace of competition? Can you accept responsibility? Will you worry a workaday problem, like a dog with a bone, till you have conquered it—and then brace yourself for a tougher assignment?

[41] If what you have said on the application blank shows a glimmer of hope, you are brought in for a personal interview. This can be rough going if you haven't habituated yourself to accurate and well-organized expression.

[42] The interviewer across the desk from you has been charged by his college or company to weigh your worth; he has accepted the responsibility of determining the future of the organization he represents—any good organization is but the lengthened shadow of qualified men.

[43] Your job interests. Your participation in school activities. Your subject preferences. Your hobbies. Your ambitions. These and many other topics are brought forward for you to discuss.

[44] The minutes speed by. You summon up the skills of presentation you have practiced in English and other classes. It strikes you, as you talk, that in neither writing nor speaking can you conceal your inadequacies.

[45] As you move up the success ladder, what you write and what you say will determine in part your rate of climb. It is neither too early nor too late to become practiced in the art of communication; certainly not too late to accumulate background through reading experiences. . . .

[46] We pause and listen to the unceasing whine of a motor across the yard. In the distance three green-gray columns of smoke are rushing upward from three yellow-brick chimneys. We see them as symbols of mechanical might controlled by the will, the wit, and the intelligence of earnest men. And these men, adventurers and pioneers of industry, can move ahead with their plans, because their own thought processes have been built upon such logical disciplines as history and math—and English!

QUESTIONS AND COMMENT ON FORM AND CONTENT

1. Note the unique, challenging beginning. It gives the reader the impression of listening in on an informal talk. It has the additional merit of plunging directly into the main point of the article: Why Study English?

2. What devices are used throughout the article to hold the reader's attention and to give him the feeling of informality and of the direct speaking of one employee to other employees? Be specific.

3. If you have not already done so, comment on the paragraphing and the informal diction. Can you justify the sentence fragments in paragraph 43?

4. Reread the last paragraph of the essay. Comment on its effectiveness as a concluding paragraph.

5. What does Mr. Drucker say about the importance of English? Do you agree? How can a good writing style be developed? See paragraph 32.

6. What other arguments for good English do the authors of this article use? Can they be applied to other businesses and the professions?

VOCABULARY: WHAT DO THE ITALICIZED WORDS MEAN?

. . . your mind may be *blocked* (32)[1]

[1] Number in parentheses refers to paragraph number.

You imagine all . . . *literate* persons are *precious, prissy* characters (32)
. . . the listener uses [this] as a *criterion* in judging you (34)

THEME SUGGESTIONS

Why I Had (Have) a Mental Block against English
The Need for Effective English in _____ (Name the occupation)
My Greatest Weakness in English
Mr. _____ Was a Well-Spoken Man

SEEING LIFE

Arnold Bennett

Although he is better known as a British novelist, Arnold Bennett (1867-1931) also wrote many brilliant articles on political and literary subjects. "Seeing Life" is from a discussion on writing.

[1] A young dog, inexperienced, sadly lacking in even primary education, ambles and frisks along the footpath of Fulham Road, near the mysterious gates of a Marist convent. He is a large puppy, on the way to be a dog of much dignity, but at present he has little to recommend him but that gawky elegance, and that bounding gratitude for the gift of life, which distinguish the normal puppy. He is an ignorant fool. He might have entered the convent of nuns and had a fine time, but instead he steps off the pavement into the road, the road being a vast and interesting continent imperfectly explored. His confidence in his nose, in his agility, and in the goodness of God is touching, absolutely painful to witness. He glances casually at a huge, towering vermilion construction that is whizzing towards him on four wheels, preceded by a glint of brass and a whisp of steam; and then with disdain he ignores it as less important than a mere speck of odorous matter in the mud. The next instant he is lying inert in the mud. His confidence in the goodness of God had been misplaced. Since the beginning of time God had ordained him a victim.

[2] An impressive thing happens. The motor-bus reluctantly slackens and stops. Not the differential brake, nor the foot-brake, has arrested the motor-bus, but the invisible brake of public opinion, acting by administrative transmission. There is not a policeman in sight. Theoretically, the motor-bus is free to whiz onward in its flight to the paradise of Shoreditch, but in practice it is paralysed by dread. A man in brass buttons and a stylish cap leaps down from it, and the blackened demon who sits on its neck also leaps down from it, and they move gingerly towards the puppy. A little while ago the motor-bus might have overturned a human cyclist or so, and proceeded nonchalant on its way. But now even a puppy requires a post-mortem: such is the force of public opinion aroused. Two policemen appear in the distance.

[3] "A street accident" is now in being, and a crowd gathers with calm joy and stares, passive and determined. The puppy offers no sign whatever; just lies in the road. Then a boy, destined probably to a great future by reason of his singular faculty of initiative, goes to the puppy and car-

ries him by the scruff of the neck, to the shelter of the gutter. Relinquished by the boy, the lithe puppy falls into an easy horizontal attitude, and seems bent upon repose. The boy lifts the puppy's head to examine it, and the head drops back wearily. The puppy is dead. No cry, no blood, no disfigurement! Even no perceptible jolt of the wheel as it climbed over the obstacle of the puppy's body! A wonderfully clean and perfect accident!

[4] The increasing crowd stares with beatific placidity. People emerge impatiently from the bowels of the throbbing motor-bus and slip down from its back, and either join the crowd or vanish. The two policemen and the crew of the motor-bus have now met in parley. The conductor and the driver have an air at once nervous and resigned; their gestures are quick and vivacious. The policemen, on the other hand, indicate by their slow and huge movements that eternity is theirs. And they could not be more sure of the conductor and the driver if they had them manacled and leashed. The conductor and the driver admit the absolute dominion of the elephantine policemen; they admit that before the simple will of the policemen inconvenience, lost minutes, shortened leisure, docked wages, count as less than naught. And the policemen are carelessly sublime, well knowing that magistrates, jails, and the very Home Secretary on his throne—yes, and a whole system of conspiracy and perjury and brutality—are at their beck in case of need. And yet occasionally in the demeanour of the policemen towards the conductor and the driver there is a silent message that says: "After all, we, too, are working men like you, over-worked and under-paid and bursting with grievances in the service of the pitiless and dishonest public. We, too, have wives and children and privations and frightful apprehensions. We, too, have to struggle desperately. Only the awful magic of these garments and of the garter which we wear on our wrists sets an abyss between us and you." And the conductor writes and one of the policemen writes, and they keep on writing while the traffic makes beautiful curves to avoid them.

[5] The still increasing crowd continues to stare in the pure blankness of pleasure. A close-shaved, well-dressed, middle-aged man, with a copy of *The Sportsman* in his podgy hand, who has descended from the motor-bus, starts stamping his feet. "I was knocked down by a taxi last year," he says fiercely. "But nobody took no notice of *that!* Are they going to stop here all the blank morning for a blank tyke?" And for all his respectable appearance, his features become debased, and he emits a jet of disgusting profanity and brings most of the Trinity into the thunderous assertion that he has paid his fare. Then a man passes wheeling a muck-cart. And he stops and talks a long time with the other uniforms, because he, too, wears vestiges of a uniform. And the crowd never moves nor ceases to stare. Then the new arrival stoops and picks up the unclaimed,

masterless puppy, and flings it, all soft and yielding, into the horrid mess of the cart, and passes on. And only that which is immortal and divine of the puppy remains behind, floating perhaps like an invisible vapour over the scene of the tragedy.

[6] The crowd is tireless, all eyes. The four principals still converse and write. Nobody in the crowd comprehends what they are about. At length the driver separates himself, but is drawn back, and a new parley is commenced. But everything ends. The policemen turn on their immense heels. The driver and conductor race towards the motor-bus. The bell rings, the motor-bus, quite empty, disappears snorting round the corner into Walham Green. The crowd is now lessening. But it separates with reluctance, many of its members continuing to stare with intense absorption at the place where the puppy lay or the place where the policemen stood. An appreciable interval elapses before the "street accident" has entirely ceased to exist as a phenomenon.

[7] The members of the crowd follow their noses, and during the course of the day remark to acquaintances:

[8] "Saw a dog run over by a motor-bus in the Fulham Road this morning! Killed dead!"

[9] And that is all they do remark. That is all they have witnessed. They will not, and could not, give intelligible and interesting particulars of the affair (unless it were as to the breed of the dog or the number of the bus-service). They have watched a dog run over. They analyse neither their sensations nor the phenomenon. They have witnessed it whole, as a bad writer uses a *cliché*. They have observed—that is to say, they have really seen—nothing.

QUESTIONS AND COMMENT ON FORM AND CONTENT

1. List some effective words and phrases used in describing the puppy in paragraph 1.

2. How do the policemen treat the conductor and the driver? What characteristics give the policemen and the motormen and the garbage man some sense of kinship? Are any of them described?

3. How does the crowd behave? What is Bennett's final assertion about the members of the crowd?

4. Was the story written to illustrate how unobservant and inarticulate most people are? Does the title foreshadow this purpose?

5. Name some specific details Arnold Bennett puts into the story—details that the crowd would not think of recording. Be specific.

6. Is there a minor theme of religion or philosophy running through the story? Remember that the dog was about to enter a convent at the beginning of the scene.

VOCABULARY: WHAT DO THE ITALICIZED WORDS MEAN?

. . . proceeded *nonchalant* on its way (2)
. . . puppy requires a *post-mortem* (2)
. . . a crowd gathers . . . , *passive* and determined (3)
The increasing crowd stares with *beatific placidity*. (4)
. . . sets an *abyss* between us and you (4)
. . . a copy in his *podgy* hand (5)

THEME SUGGESTIONS

An Accident
I Wore a Uniform
How a Uniform Affects Civilians
Observation and Writing

THE MOST IMPORTANT DAY

Helen Keller

Helen Keller (1880-   ), author, lecturer, humanitarian, was born in Tuscumbia, Alabama, and became blind and deaf at the age of nineteen months. Through the efforts of her teacher Anne Sullivan she was taught to speak. She was graduated from Radcliffe with honors in 1904 and is the author of The Story of My Life *(1903),* The World I Live In *(1908), and* Helen Keller's Journal, 1936--1937 *(1938). Our selection is from* The Story of My Life.

[1] The most important day I remember in all my life is the one on which my teacher, Anne Mansfield Sullivan, came to me. I am filled with wonder when I consider the immeasurable contrast between the two lives which it connects. It was the third of March, 1887, three months before I was seven years old.

[2] On the afternoon of that eventful day, I stood on the porch, dumb, expectant. I guessed vaguely from my mother's signs and from the hurrying to and fro in the house that something unusual was about to happen, so I went to the door and waited on the steps. The afternoon sun penetrated the mass of honeysuckle that covered the porch, and fell on my upturned face. My fingers lingered almost unconsciously on the familiar leaves and blossoms which had just come forth to greet the sweet southern spring. I did not know what the future held of marvel or sur-

prise for me. Anger and bitterness had preyed upon me continually for weeks and a deep languor had succeeded this passionate struggle.

[3] Have you ever been at sea in a dense fog, when it seemed as if a tangible white darkness shut you in, and the great ship, tense and anxious, groped her way toward the shore with plummet and sounding-line, and you waited with beating heart for something to happen? I was like that ship before my education began, only I was without compass or sounding-line, and had no way of knowing how near the harbour was. "Light! give me light!" was the wordless cry of my soul, and the light of love shone on me in that very hour.

[4] I felt approaching footsteps. I stretched out my hand as I supposed to my mother. Some one took it, and I was caught up and held close in the arms of her who had come to reveal all things to me, and, more than all things else, to love me.

[5] The morning after my teacher came she led me into her room and gave me a doll. The little blind children at the Perkins Institution had sent it and Laura Bridgman had dressed it; but I did not know this until afterward. When I had played with it a little while, Miss Sullivan slowly spelled into my hand the word "d-o-l-l." I was at once interested in this finger play and tried to imitate it. When I finally succeeded in making the letters correctly I was flushed with childish pleasure and pride. Running downstairs to my mother I held up my hand and made the letters for doll. I did not know that I was spelling a word or even that words existed; I was simply making my fingers go in monkey-like imitation. In the days that followed I learned to spell in this uncomprehending way a great many words, among them *pin, hat, cup* and a few verbs like *sit, stand* and *walk.* But my teacher had been with me several weeks before I understood that everything has a name.

[6] One day, while I was playing with my new doll, Miss Sullivan put my big rag doll into my lap also, spelled "d-o-l-l" and tried to make me understand that "d-o-l-l" applied to both. Earlier in the day we had had a tussle over the words "m-u-g" and "w-a-t-e-r." Miss Sullivan had tried to impress it upon me that "m-u-g" is *mug* and "w-a-t-e-r" is *water,* but I persisted in confounding the two. In despair she had dropped the subject for the time, only to renew it at the first opportunity. I became impatient at her repeated attempts and, seizing the new doll, I dashed it upon the floor. I was keenly delighted when I felt the fragments of the broken doll at my feet. Neither sorrow nor regret followed my passionate outburst. I had not loved the doll. In the still, dark world in which I lived there was no strong sentiment or tenderness. I felt my teacher sweep the fragments to one side of the hearth, and I had a sense of satisfaction that the cause of my discomfort was removed. She brought me my hat,

and I knew I was going out into the warm sunshine. This thought, if a wordless sensation may be called a thought, made me hop and skip with pleasure.

[7] We walked down the path to the well-house, attracted by the fragance of the honeysuckle with which it was covered. Some one was drawing water and my teacher placed my hand under the spout. As the cool stream gushed over one hand she spelled into the other the word *water,* first slowly, then rapidly. I stood still, my whole attention fixed upon the motions of her fingers. Suddenly I felt a misty consciousness as of something forgotten—a thrill of returning thought; and somehow the mystery of language was revealed to me. I knew then that "w-a-t-e-r" meant the wonderful cool something that was flowing over my hand. That living word awakened my soul, gave it light, hope, joy, set it free! There were barriers still, it is true, but barriers that could in time be swept away.

[8] I left the well-house eager to learn. Everything had a name, and each name gave birth to a new thought. As we returned to the house every object which I touched seemed to quiver with life. That was because I saw everything with the strange, new sight that had come to me. On entering the door I remembered the doll I had broken. I felt my way to the hearth and picked up the pieces. I tried vainly to put them together. Then my eyes filled with tears; for I realized what I had done, and for the first time I felt repentance and sorrow.

[9] I learned a great many new words that day. I do not remember what they all were; but I do know that *mother, father, sister, teacher* were among them—words that were to make the world blossom for me, "like Aaron's rod, with flowers." It would have been difficult to find a happier child than I was as I lay in my crib at the close of that eventful day and lived over the joys it had brought me, and for the first time longed for a new day to come.

QUESTIONS AND COMMENT ON FORM AND CONTENT

1. How does Miss Keller describe her condition before she was able to communicate with others through language?

2. *Water* seems to have been the word that gave her the clue to language as communication. How did this come about? What effect did it have on her personality?

3. How important is communication to man?

4. Why is solitary confinement considered so severe as punishment that it is seldom continued for any considerable period of time today? Why do people talk when they have nothing to say?

5. Would you expect that further improvement of language would add to desirable personality traits? Can we think without language? Can we think better with language? Explain.

VOCABULARY: WHAT DO THE ITALICIZED WORDS MEAN?

. . . a deep *languor* had *succeeded* this passionate struggle (2)
. . . a *tangible* white darkness (3)
. . . a *consciousness* as of something forgotten (7)

THEME SUGGESTIONS

Compulsive Talk
Language and Feeling
Language and Behavior
See also theme topics following Mumford's "The Miracle of Language."

THE MIRACLE OF LANGUAGE

Lewis Mumford

Lewis Mumford (1895–   ) has done his most distinguished writing in language, literature, architecture, and American cultural history.

[1] The growth of conscious purpose and self-direction—all that is implied in the historic concepts of the soul and the person—was made possible by man's special skill in interpreting his own nature and working his experiences into a meaningful and valuable whole, upon which he could draw for future actions and operations. That skill rests upon a special aptitude, embedded in man's very physiology: the ability to form and transmit symbols. Man's most characteristic social trait, his possession of an extra-organic environment and a super-organic self, which he transmits from generation to generation without using the biological mechanism of heredity, is dependent upon his earlier conquest of the word.

[2] During the last century this essential fact about man's nature has been obscured by the false assumption that man is primarily a "tool-using animal." Carlyle called him that long before Bergson suggested that the term Homo Faber, Man the Maker, should replace Homo Sapiens.

From *The Conduct of Life,* copyright 1951 by Lewis Mumford. Reprinted by permission of Harcourt, Brace & World, Inc.

But man is not essentially distinguished from his animal relatives either by the fact that he lives in groups or performs physical work with tools. Man is first and foremost the self-fabricating animal: the only creature who has not rested content with his biological form or with the dumb repetitions of his animal role. The chief source of this particular form of creativity was not fire, tools, weapons, machines, but two subjective instruments far older than any of these: the dream and the word.

[3] Without dwelling on the function of symbolization, one cannot begin to describe the nature of man or plumb the deepest spring of his creativeness. That is why I pass over many other attributes, fully taken into account today by anthropology and psychology, to dwell on man's role as interpreter. Language, the greatest of all human inventions, is the most essential key to the truly human. When words fail him, as we find in the few authenticated cases of wild children reared without the benefit of human society, man is an animal without a specific life-plan, compelled to imitate the wolfish habits of the animal in whose brood he has been suckled and reared.

[4] One can, of course, only speculate on the way in which man invented and perfected the various tools of symbolization. But in the primary instance of speech, the word was made possible by changes in the bodily organs including the larynx, the tongue, the teeth, and not least the creation of mobile lips: in the earliest skulls identifiable as man, the anatomists find the speech centers already relatively well developed. The enlargement of man's powers, through his quicker ability to learn by trial and correction, demanded a special instrument for dealing with the multitude of sensations and meanings, suggestions and demands, that impinged upon him. Every sensation, as Adelbert Ames has experimentally demonstrated, is a prognostic directive to action: hence even the simplest stimulus must be interpreted, for whether we accept it or reject it depends not only upon its own nature but upon our purposes and predispositions and proposals. Even the purest sensation must be translated and re-ordered, before the organism will in fact see it, hear it, or answer it. In that response, the entire organism co-operates; and what is actually seen or heard or felt is only what makes sense in terms of the organism's immediate purpose or its historic plan of development.

[5] At every moment of his waking existence, man senses, interprets, proposes, acts in a single unified response: but between the starting point and the end, the intermediate steps of interpretation and planful reorganization are critical, for it is here that error, miscalculation, and frustration may intervene. With the development of language, man created an instrument of interpretation that gave him a way of traversing the largest possible field of life. What he took in of the world expressed his own nature: what he expressed of himself partook of the nature of the

world; for it is only in thought that organism and environment can be separated.

[6] Now other creatures than man respond to immediate signals: the snarl of a dog has meaning for another dog, and the upraised white tail of a doe tells the fawns, as plainly as words, "Follow me!" But man, at a critical moment in his development, began to invent signs, in the form of audible words, which represent an event or a situation even when they are not present. By this act of detachment and abstraction, man gained the power of dealing with the non-present, the unseen, the remote, and the internal: not merely his visible lair and his daily companions, but his ancestors and his descendents and the sun and the moon and the stars: eventually the concepts of eternity and infinity, of electron and universe: he reduced a thousand potential occasions in all their variety and flux to a single symbol that indicated what was common to all of them.

[7] Similarly, by kindred means, man was able to give form to and project his inner world, otherwise hidden and private: by words, images, related sounds, it became part of the public world, and thus an "object." This extraordinary laborsaving device, for extracting, condensing, and preserving the most complicated kinds of events, was perhaps another manifestation of the creative uses if his exuberance and vital proliferation. Man's possession of a "useless instrument," his voice-producing organs, with their wide range of tones, plus a love of repetition, which one observes in the fullest degree in infants, opened up playful possibilities. If man is an inventor or an artist, the first object of his interest is his own body: he falls in love with his own organs long before he seeks to master the outside world.

[8] "We must never forget," the distinguished philologist Jespersen once observed, "that the organs of speech . . . are one of mankind's most treasured toys, and that not only children but also grown people in civilized as well as savage communities, find amusement in letting their vocal cords and tongue and lips play all sorts of games." Out of this original organic overflow, man found, too, a way to shape a meaningful, orderly world: the world realized in language, music, poesy, and directed thought. The gift of tongues is the greatest of all gifts: in the beginning was the Word.

[9] Speech, human speech, affected a miraculous transformation in human society: by such magic Prospero tamed Caliban and released Ariel. Speech, at first probably inseparable from gesture, exclamatory, disjointed, structureless, purely emotive, laid the foundation for a more complex mechanism of abstractions, the independent structure of language itself: and with language, human culture as an extra-organic activity, no longer wholly dependent upon the stability and continuity of the physical

body and its daily environment, became possible. This broke through the boundaries of time and place that limit animal associations.

[10] In the behavior of that perpetual primitive, the human infant, we can follow the original transition from babble to the involuntary reproduction of facial movements, from private gurglings for self-satisfaction to public demands in which a particular tone will be evoked to bring forth a particular response from the mother: the offer of a breast, the production of a dry diaper, the removal of a pricking pin, the reassurance of human companionship. Much of the intercourse between mother and child is the expression, on both sides, of feeling: tenderness, joy, rage, anxiety. Beyond doubt, the introjection and projection of feeling were basic to the whole achievement of language; a point often overlooked by pragmatic or rationalist interpretations.

[11] In the instances of wild children nurtured by animals, we can verify this interpretation: for the ability to form words seems to disappear altogether when the infant's earliest vocalizings are not encouraged by similar vocalizing on the part of those who look after him. With the loss of language man also loses the facility for more complex forms of human behavior; though some of his organic capacities become intensified to animal sharpness, in an extra-sensitive nose or in muscular endurance, the veritably human touch remains absent: above all, the wild child forfeits the capacity to understand or communicate human feeling, thus becoming inferior, not only to other human beings, but to the dog or cat, who have had the benefit of human association, and who have learned the gestures and tones by which human feelings are expressed. Negatively, there is still another way of understanding the specifically human role of language: for psychologists have found that deaf-mutism, even when combated with skillful care, is a greater handicap to intelligence than blindness. Speech, even though accompanied by blindness, opens the path of social cooperation.

[12] In his attempt to associate intelligence with the special faculty for dealing with the geometrical, the mechanical, the non-living, Henri Bergson curiously underestimated the formative effect of language and over-stressed the part played by physical tools and mechanical aptitudes, for he perversely interpreted speech as being lamed by man's rational preoccupation with static objects. On the contrary, language developed far more rapidly and effectively than mechanical tools; and it was probably in origin primarily a means of representing labile feelings and attitudes, the least geometrical part of man's experience. The most important thing for a human being to know, from infancy onward, is whether he is welcome or unwelcome, whether he is being loved and cherished and protected or hated and feared; and the give-and-take of

speech, with all its modulation of color and tone, provides these essential clues. Language was not invented by philosophers seeking truth or by scientists seeking to understand the processes of nature, nor yet by mechanics seeking to shape a more adequate tool; nor was it created by methodical bookkeepers seeking to make an inventory of the contents of the world. Language was the outcome of man's need to affirm solidarity with his own kind. Because it was a prime organ, not only of social co-operation, but of sympathetic and dramatic insight, it helped to control and direct all human behavior.

[13] In time, no doubt, language lent itself to many other uses besides communion and fellowship: it gave rise to a sense of "thatness" as well as "we-ness" and furthered causal insight into processes and relationships. Not least, language was a means whereby subjective reactions became externalized, and objective facts became internalized: thus it favored constant intercourse and traffic between the public world and the private world. In every sense, then, speech was man's prime instrument for sharing his private world with his fellows and for bringing the public world home to himself, though in time it was supplemented by the symbols and significants of the other arts. He who could speak the language could be trusted: every word was a password, indicating friend or foe, in-group or out-group; and these practices linger on in establishing identity right down to our own day. The practical and rational offices of language, which now seem to us all-important, must for long have been purely incidental.

[14] The complicated structure, the grammatical and logical subtletv, and the immense variety of even primitive languages drive one to believe that a large part of man's creative activity, perhaps for hundreds of thousands of years, must have concerned itself almost exclusively with the development of intelligible speech, and with secondary means of symbolization through the visual arts; for painting, too, in the Aurignacian caves, shows an exquisite perfection that argues a prolonged period of unremitting effort. No machine that man invented before the twentieth century compares in complexity and refinement with the simplest of human languages. No wonder this superorganic structure transformed the terms of man's self-development.

[15] Beavers can build dams: bees can construct efficient dwellings: the meanest bird has still a surer mechanism for flying and landing than man has yet achieved. But no other creature has come within sight of man in the arts of symbolic communication. Mainly through language man has created a second world, more durable and viable than the immediate flux of experience, more rich in possibilities than the purely material habitat of any other creature. By the same agent, he has reduced the vastness and overpowering multiplicity of his environment to human

dimensions: abstracting from its totality just so much as he could handle and control. The very formal qualities of words served as an instrument for understanding and directing the everlasting flow of things: it is because the structure of language and logic is relatively static (Parmenides and Plato) that the unceasing changes and processes of the natural world (Heraclitus) can be interpreted. If meanings changed as quickly as events, no event would have a meaning.

[16] Let us make no mistake then: language is far more basic than any other kind of tool or machine. Through man's overdeveloped forebrain and his overflowing sensory-emotional responses, he came into contact with an ever-enlarging field of action; and through language, he found an economic way of dealing with this complexity and turning every state and activity to the service of meaning. So essential is language to man's humanness, so deep a source is it of his own creativity, that it is by no means an accident in our time that those who have tried to degrade man and enslave him have first debased and misused language, arbitrarily turning meanings inside out. Civilization itself, from the most primitive stage onward, moves toward the continuous creation of a common social heritage, transcending all the peculiarities of race and environment and historic accident, shared over ever wider reaches of space and time. This heritage, apart from environmental modifications, such as roads, canals, and cities, is transmitted largely in symbolic form; and by far the greater part of its symbolization is in spoken and written language. Contrary to the proverb, words make a greater difference than sticks and stones: they are more durable too.

QUESTIONS AND COMMENT ON FORM AND CONTENT

1. What is Mumford's theme or thesis in this essay? Does the title suggest it? Is the first sentence the topic sentence of the first paragraph or does it express the aim of the entire essay?

2. What is meant by *symbols* in connection with language? Does Mumford agree that man is essentially a tool-using animal?

3. Explain and comment on "Man is first and foremost a self-fabricating animal."

4. To what extent are the tongue, the lips, the teeth and the larynx organs of speech? Have they other uses?

5. Compare the snarl or bark of a dog with the speech of man. What can we learn, according to Mumford, from the few authentic cases of children brought up without benefit of speech?

6. The author says, "Language was the outcome of man's need to affirm solidarity with his own kind." What does *solidarity* as used here mean? Does the statement have implications as to the comparative importance of language

for business and language for social purposes? Which is more basic to human personality and happiness?

7. Comment on the following statement:

> So essential is language to man's humanness, so deep a source is it of his own creativity, that it is by no means an accident in our time that those who have tried to degrade man and enslave him have first debased and misused language, arbitrarily turning meanings inside out.

VOCABULARY: WHAT DO THE ITALICIZED WORDS MEAN?

. . . the ability to form and transmit *symbols* (1)
Man is first and foremost a *self-fabricating* animal. (2)
. . . a complex mechanism of *abstractions* (9)
. . . the structure of language . . . is *relatively static* (15)

THEME SUGGESTIONS

Why People Talk
Men and Parrots
Language and Civilization
Language and Propaganda
Language for Solidarity

PART I

EMPHASIS ON IMAGES
Narration and Description

---

2 | SEEING AND REPORTING

EXPERIENCES

THE FEEL

Paul Gallico

Paul Gallico (1897-   ) is best known as a sports writer, though he has also written novels and short stories.

[1] A child wandering through a department store with its mother is admonished over and over again not to touch things. Mother is convinced that the child only does it to annoy or because it is a child, and usually hasn't the vaguest inkling of the fact that Junior is "touching" because he is a little blotter soaking up information and knowledge, and "feel" is an important adjunct to seeing. Adults are exactly the same, in a measure, as you may ascertain when some new gadget or article is produced for inspection. The average person says: "Here, let me see that," and holds out his hand. He doesn't mean "see," because he is already seeing it. What he means is that he wants to get it into his hands and feel it so as to become better acquainted.

[2] As suggested in the foregoing chapter, I do not insist that a curiosity and capacity for feeling sports is necessary to be a successful writer, but it is fairly obvious that a man who has been tapped on the chin with five fingers wrapped up in a leather boxing glove and propelled by the arm of an expert knows more about that particular sensation than one who has not, always provided he has the gift of expressing himself. I once inquired

of a heavyweight prizefighter by the name of King Levinsky, in a radio interview, what it felt like to be hit on the chin by Joe Louis, the King having just acquired that experience with rather disastrous results. Levinsky considered the matter for a moment and then reported: "It don't feel like nuttin'," but added that for a long while afterwards he felt as though he were "in a transom."

[3] I was always a child who touched things and I have always had a tremendous curiosity with regard to sensation. If I knew what playing a game felt like, particularly against or in the company of experts, I was better equipped to write about the playing of it and the problems of the men and women who took part in it. And so, at one time or another, I have tried them all, football, baseball, boxing, riding, shooting, swimming, squash, handball, fencing, driving, flying, both land and sea planes, rowing, canoeing, skiing, riding a bicycle, ice-skating, roller-skating, tennis, golf, archery, basketball, running, both the hundred-yard dash and the mile, the high jump and shot put, badminton, angling, deep-sea, stream-, and surf-casting, billiards and bowling, motorboating and wrestling, besides riding as a passenger with the fastest men on land and water and in the air, to see what it felt like. Most of them I dabbled in as a youngster going through school and college, and others, like piloting a plane, squash, fencing, and skiing, I took up after I was old enough to know better, purely to get the feeling of what they were like.

[4] None of these things can I do well, but I never cared about becoming an expert and besides, there wasn't time. But there is only one way to find out accurately human sensations in a ship two or three thousand feet up when the motor quits, and that is actually to experience that gone feeling at the pit of the stomach and the sharp tingling of the skin from head to foot, followed by a sudden amazing sharpness of vision, clear-sightedness, and coolness that you never knew you possessed as you find the question of life or death completely in your own hands. It is not the "you" that you know, but somebody else, a stranger who noses the ship down, circles, fastens upon the one best spot to sit down, pushes or pulls buttons to try to get her started again, and finally drops her in, safe and sound. And it is only by such experience that you learn likewise of the sudden weakness that hits you right at the back of the knees after you have climbed out and started to walk around her and that comes close to knocking you flat as for the first time since the engine quit its soothing drone you think of destruction and sudden death.

[5] Often my courage has failed me and I have flunked completely, such as the time I went up to the top of the thirty-foot Olympic diving-tower at Jones Beach, Long Island, during the competitions, to see what it was like to dive from that height, and wound up crawling away from the edge on hands and knees, dizzy, scared, and a little sick, but with a

wholesome respect for the boys and girls who hurled themselves through the air and down through the tough skin of the water from that awful height. At other times sheer ignorance of what I was getting into has led me into tight spots such as the time I came down the Olympic ski run from the top of Kreuzeck, six thousand feet above Garmisch-Partenkirchen, after having been on skis but once before in snow and for the rest had no more than a dozen lessons on an indoor artificial slide in a New York department store. At one point my legs, untrained, got so tired that I couldn't stem (brake) any more, and I lost control and went full tilt and all out, down a three-foot twisting path cut out of the side of the mountain, with a two-thousand-foot abyss on the left and the mountain itself on the right. That was probably the most scared I have ever been, and I scare fast and often. I remember giving myself up for lost and wondering how long it would take them to retrieve my body and whether I should be still alive. In the meantime the speed of the descent was increasing. Somehow I was keeping my feet and negotiating turns, how I will never know, until suddenly the narrow patch opened out into a wide, steep stretch of slope with a rise at the other end, and *that* part of the journey was over.

[6] By some miracle I got to the bottom of the run uninjured, having made most of the trip down the icy, perpendicular slopes on the flat of my back. It was the thrill and scare of a lifetime, and to date no one has been able to persuade me to try a jump. I know when to stop. After all, I am entitled to rely upon my imagination for something. But when it was all over and I found myself still whole, it was also distinctly worth while to have learned what is required of a ski runner in the breakneck *Abfahrt* or downhill race, or the difficult *slalom*. Five days later, when I climbed laboriously (still on skis) halfway up that Alp and watched the Olympic downhill racers hurtling down the perilous ice-covered, and nearly perpendicular *Steilhang*, I knew that I was looking at a great group of athletes who, for one thing, did not know the meaning of the word "fear." The slope was studded with small pine trees and rocks, but half of the field gained precious seconds by hitting that slope all out, with complete contempt for disaster rushing up at them at a speed often better than sixty miles an hour. And when an unfortunate Czech skidded off the course at the bottom of the slope and into a pile of rope and got himself snarled up as helpless as a fly in a spider's web, it was a story that I could write from the heart. I had spent ten minutes getting myself untangled after a fall, *without* any rope to add to the difficulties. It seems that I couldn't find where my left leg ended and one more ski than I originally donned seemed to be involved somehow. Only a person who has been on those fiendish runners knows the sensation.

[7] It all began back in 1922 when I was a cub sportswriter and consumed with more curiosity than was good for my health. I had seen my

first professional prizefights and wondered at the curious behavior of men under the stress of blows, the sudden checking and the beginning of a little fall forward after a hard punch, the glazing of the eyes and the loss of locomotor control, the strange actions of men on the canvas after a knockdown as they struggled to regain their senses and arise on legs that seemed to have turned into rubber. I had never been in any bad fist fights as a youngster, though I had taken a little physical punishment in football, but it was not enough to complete the picture. Could one think under those conditions?

[8] I had been assigned to my first training-camp coverage, Dempsey's at Saratoga Springs, where he was preparing for his famous fight with Luis Firpo. For days I watched him sag a spar boy with what seemed to be no more than a light cuff on the neck, or pat his face with what looked like no more than a caressing stroke of his arm, and the fellow would come all apart at the seams and collapse in a useless heap, grinning vacuously or twitching strangely. My burning curiosity got the better of prudence and a certain reluctance to expose myself to physical pain. I asked Dempsey to permit me to box a round with him. I had never boxed before, but I was in good physical shape, having just completed a four-year stretch as a galley slave in the Columbia eight-oared shell.

[9] When it was over and I escaped through the ropes, shaking, bleeding a little from the mouth, with rosin dust on my pants and a vicious throbbing in my head, I knew all that there was to know about being hit in the prize-ring. It seems that I had gone to an expert for tuition. I knew the sensation of being stalked and pursued by a relentless, truculent professional destroyer whose trade and business it was to injure men. I saw the quick flash of the brown forearm that precedes the stunning shock as a bony, leather-bound fist lands on cheek or mouth. I learned more (partly from photographs of the lesson, viewed afterwards, one of which shows me ducked under a vicious left hook, an act of which I never had the slightest recollection) about instinctive ducking and blocking than I could have in ten years of looking at prizefights, and I learned, too, that as the soldier never hears the bullet that kills him, so does the fighter rarely, if ever, see the punch that tumbles blackness over him like a mantle, with a tearing rip as though the roof of his skull were exploding, and robs him of his senses.

[10] There was just that—a ripping in my head and then sudden blackness, and the next thing I knew, I was sitting on the canvas covering of the ring floor with my legs collapsed under me, grinning idiotically. How often since have I seen that same silly, goofy look on the faces of dropped fighters—and understood it. I held onto the floor with both hands, because the ring and the audience outside were making a complete clockwise revolution, came to a stop, and then went back again counter-clock-

wise. When I struggled to my feet, Jack Kearns, Dempsey's manager, was counting over me, but I neither saw nor heard him and was only conscious that I was in a ridiculous position and that the thing to do was to get up and try to fight back. The floor swayed and rocked beneath me like a fishing dory in an off-shore swell, and it was a welcome respite when Dempsey rushed into a clinch, held me up, and whispered into my ear: "Wrestle around a bit, son, until your head clears." And then it was that I learned what those little lovetaps to the back of the neck and the short digs to the ribs can mean to the groggy pugilist more than half knocked out. It is a murderous game, and the fighter who can escape after having been felled by a lethal blow has my admiration. And there, too, I learned that there can be no sweeter sound than the bell that calls a halt to hostilities.

[11] From that afternoon on, also, dated my antipathy for the spectator at prizefights who yells: "Come on, you bum, get up and fight! Oh, you big quitter! Yah yellow, yah yellow!" Yellow, eh? It is all a man can do to get up after being stunned by a blow, much less fight back. But they do it. And how a man is able to muster any further interest in a combat after being floored with a blow to the pit of the stomach will always remain to me a miracle of what the human animal is capable of under stress.

[12] Further experiments were less painful, but equally illuminating. A couple of sets of tennis with Vinnie Richards taught me more about what is required of a top-flight tournament tennis player than I could have got out of a dozen books or years of reporting tennis matches. It is one thing to sit in a press box and write caustically that Brown played uninspired tennis, or Black's court covering was faulty and that his frequent errors cost him the set. It is quite another to stand across the net at the back of a service court and try to get your racket on a service that is so fast that the ear can hardly detect the interval between the sound of the server's bat hitting the ball and the ball striking the court. Tournament tennis is a different game from week-end tennis. For one thing, in average tennis, after the first hard service has gone into the net or out, you breathe a sigh of relief, move up closer and wait for the cripple to come floating over. In big-time tennis second service is practically as hard as the first, with an additional twist on the ball.

[13] It is impossible to judge or know anything about the speed of a forehand drive hit by a champion until you have had one fired at you, or, rather, away from you, and you have made an attempt to return it. It is then that you first realize that tennis is played more with the head than with the arms and the legs. The fastest player in the world cannot get to a drive to return it if he hasn't thought correctly, guessed its direction, and anticipated it by a fraction of a second.

[14] There was golf with Bob Jones and Gene Sarazen and Tommy

Armour, little Cruickshank and Johnny Farrell, and Diegel and other pro-
fessionals; and experiments at trying to keep up in the water with Johnny
Weissmuller, Helene Madison, and Eleanor Holm, attempts to catch football passes thrown by Benny Friedman. Nobody actually plays golf until
he has acquired the technical perfection to be able to hit the ball accurately, high, low, hooked or faded and placed. And nobody knows what
real golf is like until he has played around with a professional and seen
him play, not the ball, but the course, the roll of the land, the hazards,
the wind, and the texture of the greens and the fairways. It looks like
showmanship when a top-flight golfer plucks a handful of grass and lets
it flutter in the air, or abandons his drive to march two hundred yards
down to the green and look over the situation. It isn't. It's golf. The average player never knows or cares whether he is putting with or across the
grain of a green. The professional *always* knows. The same average player
standing on the tee is concentrating on getting the ball somewhere on the
fairway, two hundred yards out. The professional when preparing to drive
is actually to all intents and purposes playing his *second* shot. He means
to place his drive so as to open up the green for his approach. But you
don't find that out until you have played around with them when they are
relaxed and not competing, and listen to them talk and plan attacks on
holes.

[15] Major-league baseball is one of the most difficult and precise of
all games, but you would never know it unless you went down on the
field and got close to it and tried it yourself. For instance the distance between pitcher and catcher is a matter of twenty paces, but it doesn't seem
like enough when you don a catcher's mitt and try to hold a pitcher with
the speed of Dizzy Dean or Dazzy Vance. Not even the sponge that catch-
ers wear in the palm of the hand when working with fast-ball pitchers,
and the bulky mitt are sufficient to rob the ball of shock and sting that
lames your hand unless you know how to ride with the throw and kill
some of its speed. The pitcher, standing on his little elevated mound,
looms up enormously over you at that short distance, and when he ties
himself into a coiled spring preparatory to letting fly, it requires all your
self-control not to break and run for safety. And as for the things they
can do with a baseball, those major-league pitchers. . . . One way of
finding out is to wander down on the field an hour or so before game-
time when there is no pressure on them, pull on the catcher's glove and
try to hold them.

[16] I still remember my complete surprise the first time I tried catching
for a real curve-ball pitcher. He was a slim, spidery left-hander of the
New York Yankees, many years ago, by the name of Herb Pennock. He
called that he was going to throw a fast breaking curve and warned me
to expect the ball at least two feet outside the plate. Then he wound up

and let it go, and that ball came whistling right down the groove for the center of the plate. A novice, I chose to believe what I saw and not what I heard, and prepared to catch it where it was headed for, a spot which of course it never reached, because just in front of the rubber, it swerved sharply to the right and passed nearly a yard from my glove. I never had a chance to catch it. That way, you learn about the mysterious drop, the ball that sails down the alley chest high but which you must be prepared to catch around your ankles because of the sudden dip it takes at the end of its passage as though someone were pulling it down with a string. Also you find out about the queer fade-away, the slow curve, the fast in- and out-shoots that seem to be timed almost as delicately as shrapnel, to burst, or rather break, just when they will do the most harm—namely, at the moment when the batter is swinging.

[17] Facing a big-league pitcher with a bat on your shoulder and trying to hit his delivery is another vital experience in gaining an understanding of the game about which you are trying to write vividly. It is one thing to sit in the stands and scream at a batsman: "Oh, you bum!" for striking out in a pinch, and another to stand twenty yards from that big pitcher and try to make up your mind in a hundredth of a second whether to hit at the offering or not, where to swing and when, not to mention worrying about protecting yourself from the consequences of being struck by the ball that seems to be heading straight for your skull at an appalling rate of speed. Because, if you are a big-league player, you cannot very well afford to be gun-shy and duck away in panic from a ball that swerves in the last moment and breaks perfectly over the plate, while the umpire calls: "Strike!" and the fans jeer. Nor can you afford to take a crack on the temple from the ball. Men have died from that. It calls for undreamed-of niceties of nerve and judgment, but you don't find that out until you have stepped to the plate cold a few times during batting practice or in training quarters, with nothing at stake but the acquisition of experience, and see what a fine case of the jumping jitters you get. Later on, when you are writing your story, your imagination, backed by the experience, will be able to supply a picture of what the batter is going through as he stands at the plate in the closing innings of an important game, with two or three men on base, two out, and his team behind in the scoring, and fifty thousand people screaming at him.

[18] The catching and holding of a forward pass for a winning touchdown on a cold, wet day always make a good yarn, but you might get an even better one out of it if you happen to know from experience about the elusive qualities of a hard, soggy, mud-slimed football rifled through the air, as well as something about the exquisite timing, speed, and courage it takes to catch it on a dead run, with two or three 190-pound men reaching for it as your fingers touch it.

[19] Any football coach during a light practice will let you go down the field and try to catch punts, the long, fifty-yard spirals and the tricky, tumbling end-over-enders. Unless you have had some previous experience, you won't hang on to one out of ten, besides knocking your fingers out of joint. But if you have any imagination, thereafter you will know that it calls for more than negligible nerve to judge and hold that ball and even plan to run with it, when there are two husky ends bearing down at full speed, preparing for a head-on tackle.

[20] In 1932 I covered my first set of National Air Races, in Cleveland, and immediately decided that I had to learn how to fly to find out what that felt like. Riding as a passenger isn't flying. Being up there all alone at the controls of a ship is. And at the same time began a series of investigations into the "feel" of the mechanized sports to see what they were all about and the qualities of mentality, nerve, and physique they called for from their participants. These included a ride with Gar Wood in his latest and fastest speedboat, *Miss America X*, in which for the first time he pulled the throttle wide open on the Detroit River straightaway; a trip with the Indianapolis Speedway driver Cliff Bergere, around the famous brick raceway; and a flip with Lieutenant Al Williams, one time U.S. Schneider Cup race pilot.

[21] I was scared with Wood, who drove me at 127 miles an hour, jounced, shaken, vibrated, choked with fumes from the exhausts, behind which I sat hanging on desperately to the throttle bar, which after a while got too hot to hold. I was on a plank between Wood and his mechanic, Johnson, and thought that my last moment had come. I was still more scared when Cliff Bergere hit 126 on the Indianapolis straightaway in the tiny racing car in which I was hopelessly wedged, and after the first couple of rounds quite resigned to die and convinced that I should. But I think the most scared I have ever been while moving fast was during a ride I took in the cab of a locomotive on the straight, level stretch between Fort Wayne, Indiana, and Chicago, where for a time we hit 90 miles per hour, which of course is no speed at all. But nobody who rides in the comfortable Pullman coaches has any idea of the didoes cut up by a locomotive in a hurry, or the thrill of pelting through a small town, all out and wide open, including the crossing of some thirty or forty frogs and switches, all of which must be set right. But that wasn't sport. That was just plain excitement.

[22] I have never regretted these researches. Now that they are over, there isn't enough money to make me do them again. But they paid me dividends, I figured. During the great Thompson Speed Trophy race for land planes at Cleveland in 1935, Captain Roscoe Turner was some eight or nine miles in the lead in his big golden, low-wing speed monoplane. Suddenly, coming into the straightaway in front of the grandstands, buzz-

ing along at 280 miles an hour like an angry hornet, a streamer of thick, black smoke burst from the engine cowling and trailed back behind the ship. Turner pulled up immediately, using his forward speed to gain all the altitude possible, turned and got back to the edge of the field, still pouring out that evil black smoke. Then he cut his switch, dipped her nose down, landed with a bounce and a bump, and rolled up to the line in a perfect stop. The crowd gave him a great cheer as he climbed out of the oil-spattered machine, but it was a cheer of sympathy because he had lost the race after having been so far in the lead that had he continued he could not possibly have been overtaken.

[23] There was that story, but there was a better one too. Only the pilots on the field, all of them white around the lips and wiping from their faces a sweat not due to the oppressive summer heat, knew that they were looking at a man who from that time on, to use their own expression, was living on borrowed time. It isn't often when a Thompson Trophy racer with a landing speed of around eighty to ninety miles an hour goes haywire in the air, that the pilot is able to climb out of the cockpit and walk away from his machine. From the time of that first burst of smoke until the wheels touched the ground and stayed there, he was a hundred-to-one shot to live. To the initiated, those dreadful moments were laden with suspense and horror. Inside that contraption was a human being who any moment might be burned to a horrible, twisted cinder, or smashed into the ground beyond all recognition, a human being who was cool, gallant, and fighting desperately. Every man and woman on the field who had ever been in trouble in the air was living those awful seconds with him in terror and suspense. I, too, was able to experience it. That is what makes getting the "feel" of things distinctly worthwhile.

QUESTIONS AND COMMENT ON FORM AND CONTENT

1. Paul Gallico might have written an article about his varied experiences in sports. Would it have had unity?

2. Does this article have a higher unity? What is the theme or controlling purpose? Is it hinted at in the title?

3. The first paragraph describes a child ("a little blotter") and its mother in a department store. Is it only an interesting experience to get the reader's ear, or does it further the purpose of the article? Explain.

4. Can you find a paragraph in the entire article in which the theme or thesis is not expressly stated?

5. How does the author avoid making himself the hero?

6. Which one of his descriptions of experiences in sports (boxing, baseball, diving, and the like) succeeds best in giving you the "feel" of the sport? How is the vividness achieved? What senses are appealed to?

7. How do you account for the long sentences? See, for example, the second sentence of the first paragraph or the first sentence of the second paragraph or the sentence used in paragraph 18. Does the humorous description remind you of a sports article? Technically, what kinds of sentences are the long ones? Is ornate language characteristic of the sports page?

VOCABULARY: WHAT DO THE ITALICIZED WORDS MEAN?

. . . a child is *admonished* not to touch things (1)
. . . felt as though he was "in a *transom*" (2)
. . . *stalked* and pursued by a relentless, *truculent* . . . destroyer (9)
. . . felled by a *lethal* blow (10)
. . . my *antipathy* for the spectator (11)

THEME SUGGESTIONS

Tell one of your own somewhat hazardous experiences as a beginner in such a sport as diving, skating, skiing. Try to give the reader the "feel" of it.
Writing and Experience

THE BATTLE OF THE ANTS

FROM "WALDEN"_____*Henry David Thoreau*

Henry David Thoreau (1817-1862) is best known as a naturalist, some might say supernaturalist. His most notable writing Walden or Life in the Woods *remains an American classic. He was born and spent most of his life in Concord, Massachusetts, home of Ralph Waldo Emerson and other notable writers.*

[1] One day when I went out to my wood-pile, or rather my pile of stumps, I observed two large ants, the one red, the other much larger, nearly half an inch long, and black, fiercely contending with one another. Having once got hold, they never let go, but struggled and wrestled and rolled on the chips incessantly. Looking farther, I was surprised to find that the chips were covered with such combatants, that it was not a *duellum,* but a *bellum,* a war between two races of ants, the red always pitted against the black, and frequently two red ones to one black. The legions of these Myrmidons covered all the hills and vales in my woodyard, and the ground was already strewn with the dead and dying, both red and black. It was the only battle which I have ever witnessed, the only battlefield I ever trod while the battle was raging; internecine war; the red republi-

cans on the one hand, and the black imperialists on the other. On every side they were engaged in deadly combat, yet without any noise that I could hear, and human soldiers never fought so resolutely. I watched a couple that were fast locked in each other's embraces, in a little sunny valley amid the chips, now at noon-day prepared to fight till the sun went down, or life went out. The smaller red champion had fastened himself like a vice to his adversary's front, and through all the tumblings on that field never for an instant ceased to gnaw at one of his feelers near the root, having already caused the other to go by the board; while the stronger black one dashed him from side to side, and, as I saw on looking nearer, had already divested him of several of his members. They fought with more pertinacity than bulldogs. Neither manifested the least disposition to retreat. It was evident that their battle-cry was "Conquer or die." In the meanwhile there came along a single red ant on the hill-side of this valley, evidently full of excitement, who either had despatched his foe, or had not yet taken part in the battle; probably the latter, for he had lost none of his limbs; whose mother had charged him to return with his shield or upon it. Or perchance he was some Achilles, who had nourished his wrath apart, and had now come to avenge or rescue his Patroclus. He saw this unequal combat from afar,—for the blacks were nearly twice the size of the red,—he drew near with rapid pace till he stood on his guard within half an inch of the combatants; then, watching his opportunity, he sprang upon the black warrior, and commenced his operations near the root of his right fore-leg, leaving the foe to select among his own members; and so there were three united for life, as if a new kind of attraction had been invented which put all other locks and cements to shame. I should not have wondered by this time to find that they had their respective musical bands stationed on some eminent chip, and playing their national airs the while, to excite the slow and cheer the dying combatants. I was myself excited somewhat even as if they had been men. The more you think of it, the less the difference. And certainly there is not the fight recorded in Concord history, at least, if in the history of America, that will bear a moment's comparison with this, whether for the numbers engaged in it, or for the patriotism and heroism displayed. For numbers and for carnage it was an Austerlitz or Dresden. Concord Fight! Two killed on the patriots' side, and Luther Blanchard wounded! Why here every ant was a Buttrick,—"Fire! for God's sake fire!"—and thousands shared the fate of Davis and Hosmer. There was not one hireling there. I have no doubt that it was a principle they fought for, as much as our ancestors, and not to avoid a three-penny tax on their tea; and the results of this battle will be as important and memorable to those whom it concerns as those of the battle of Bunker Hill, at least.

[2] I took up the chip on which the three I have particularly described

were struggling, carried it into my house, and placed it under a tumbler on my window-sill, in order to see the issue. Holding a microscope to the first-mentioned red ant, I saw that, though he was assiduously gnawing at the near fore-leg of his enemy, having severed his remaining feeler, his own breast was all torn away, exposing what vitals he had there to the jaws of the black warrior, whose breast-plate was apparently too thick for him to pierce; and the dark carbuncles of the sufferer's eyes shone with ferocity such as war only could excite. They struggled half an hour longer under the tumbler, and when I looked again the black soldier had severed the heads of his foes from their bodies, and the still living heads were hanging on either side of him like ghastly trophies at his saddle-bow, still apparently as firmly fastened as ever, and he was endeavoring with feeble struggles, being without feelers and with only the remnant of a leg, and I know not how many other wounds, to divest himself of them; which at length, after an hour more, he accomplished. I raised the glass, and he went off over the window-sill in that crippled state. Whether he finally survived that combat, and spent the remainder of his days in some Hotel des Invalides, I do not know; but I thought that his industry would not be worth much thereafter. I never learned which party was victorious nor the cause of the war; but I felt for the rest of that day as if I had had my feelings excited and harrowed by witnessing the struggle, the ferocity and carnage, of a human battle before my door.

QUESTIONS AND COMMENT ON FORM AND CONTENT

1. Thoreau describes this battle in two rather long paragraphs, the first one containing over seven hundred words. On what basis was the division made? If he were writing this article for a popular magazine of today and wished, therefore, to break the first paragraph into three or four units, where could the breaks be made? Would the paragraphs still have logical unity?

2. Thoreau is famous for his style. A novice might write Thoreau's first sentence like this: "One day I went out to my wood-pile, or rather my pile of stumps. There I observed two large ants. The one was red and the other black. The black one was much larger than the red one. It was half an inch long. The red and black ants were fiercely fighting." How did Thoreau work these details smoothly into one sentence? Notice, too, the variety in the length of sentences. For example, near the middle of the first paragraph, read the long sentence that begins, "The smaller red champion. . . ." and then the three short sentences that follow. What is the effect of the change in type of sentence? Is it like resting after a long struggle? A pause in the battle? The sentence that follows the three short ones continues in the longer, narrative style.

3. What details and word choices are used to give us the feeling that this is a battle between armies on an ancient battlefield? Does the comparison of ants with men make the description more interesting? More heroic?

VOCABULARY: WHAT DO THE ITALICIZED WORDS MEAN?

. . . rolled on the chips *incessantly* (1)
. . . it was not a *duellum*, but a *bellum* (1)
The *legions* of these *Myrmidons* (1)
. . . *internecine* war (1)
. . . fastened himself . . . to his *adversary's* front (1)
. . . *divested* him of several of his *members* (1)
. . . with more *pertinacity* than bulldogs (1)
. . . who either had *despatched* his foe (1)
. . . he was some *Achilles* . . . come to . . . rescue his *Patroclus* (1)
. . . placed it under a tumbler . . . to see the *issue* (2)
. . . he was *assiduously* gnawing at the fore-leg (2)
. . . my feelings excited and *harrowed* (2)
. . . witnessing . . . the ferocity and *carnage* (2)

THEME SUGGESTIONS

Relate a fight you have seen between dogs, cats, or other animals.
Describe a foolish quarrel between friends, perhaps one in which you partic-
ipated. Use some dialogue.
Ants and Men

THE LOON

FROM "WALDEN"———*Henry David Thoreau*

As I was paddling along the north shore one very calm October afternoon, for on such days especially they [loons] settle on to the lakes, like
the milkweed down, having looked in vain over the pond for a loon, suddenly one, sailing out from the shore toward the middle a few rods in
front of me, set up his wild laugh and betrayed himself. I pursued with a
paddle and he dived, but when he came up I was nearer than before. He
dived again but I miscalculated the direction he would take, and we
were fifty rods apart when he came to the surface this time, for I had
helped to widen the interval; and again he laughed long and loud, and
with more reason than before. He maneuvered so cunningly that I could
not get within half a dozen rods of him. Each time, when he came to the
surface, turning his head this way and that, he coolly surveyed the water
and the land, and apparently chose his course so that he might come up
where there was the widest expanse of water and at the greatest distance

from the boat. It was surprising how quickly he made up his mind and put his resolve into execution. He led me at once to the widest part of the pond, and could not be driven from it. While he was thinking one thing in his brain, I was endeavoring to divine his thought in mine. It was a pretty game, played on the smooth surface of the pond, a man against a loon. Suddenly your adversary's checker disappears beneath the board, and the problem is to place yours nearest to where his will appear again. Sometimes he would come up unexpectedly on the opposite side of me, having apparently passed directly under the boat. So long-winded was he and so unweariable, that when he had swum farthest he would immediately plunge again, nevertheless; and then no wit could divine where in the deep pond, beneath the smooth surface, he might be speeding his way like a fish, for he had time and ability to visit the bottom of the pond in its deepest part. It is said that loons have been caught in the New York lakes eighty feet beneath the surface, with hooks set for trout,—though Walden is deeper than that. How surprised must the fishes be to see this ungainly visitor from another sphere speeding his way amid their schools! Yet he appeared to know his course as surely under water as on the surface, and swam much faster there. Once or twice I saw a ripple where he approached the surface, just put his head out to reconnoitre, and instantly dived again. I found that it was as well for me to rest on my oars and wait his reappearing as to endeavor to calculate where he would rise; for again and again, when I was straining my eyes over the surface one way, I would suddenly be startled by his unearthly laugh behind me. But why, after displaying so much cunning, did he invariably betray himself the moment he came up by that loud laugh? Did not his white breast enough betray him? He was indeed a silly loon, I thought. I could commonly hear the splash of the water when he came up, and so also detected him. But after an hour he seemed as fresh as ever, dived as willingly and swam yet farther than at first. It was surprising to see how serenely he sailed off with unruffled breast when he came to the surface, doing all the work with his webbed feet beneath. His usual note was this demoniac laughter, yet somewhat like that of a water-fowl; but occasionally, when he had balked me most successfully and come up a long way off, he uttered a long-drawn unearthly howl, probably more like that of a wolf than any bird; as when a beast puts his muzzle to the ground and deliberately howls. This was his looning,—perhaps the wildest sound that is ever heard here, making the woods ring far and wide. I concluded that he laughed in derision of my efforts, confident of his own resources. Though the sky was by this time overcast, the pond was so smooth that I could see where he broke the surface when I did not hear him. His white breast, the stillness of the air, and the smoothness of the water were all against him. At length, having come up fifty rods off, he uttered one of those prolonged howls, as if calling on the god of loons to aid him, and immediately there came a wind from the east, and rippled the surface, and filled the whole air with misty rain, and I was impressed as if it were the prayer of the loon answered, and his god was angry with me; and so I left him disappearing far away on the tumultuous surface.

QUESTIONS AND COMMENT ON FORM AND CONTENT

1. Again we have a very long paragraph. Is it unified? Write a comprehensive topic sentence for it.
2. Why did Thoreau think that the loon was deliberately playing a game with him? In what three ways did the loon reveal himself?
3. With what game did he compare this one? Did the loon actually outguess Thoreau? Was the laugh really in ridicule of Thoreau's efforts or was it a spontaneous one at having found safety?
4. What connotations does the word *loon* have? How does Thoreau use this connotation?
5. We say that a loon laughs, a cat says "meow," a dog says "bow-wow," and the like. Do people speaking other languages agree with us?

VOCABULARY: WHAT DO THE ITALICIZED WORDS MEAN?

. . . like the milkweed *down*
. . . no wit could *divine* where . . . he might be
. . . this *demoniac* laughter
When he had *balked* me most successfully

THEME SUGGESTIONS

If you have played such a game with a fly, moth, dog, kitten, fish, squirrel, rabbit, fox, or other animal, tell about the experience, following Thoreau's detailed manner. Did the animal seem to enjoy keeping the game exciting? Was he sure of his powers? Was this a form of communication?

THE MOWING OF A FIELD

Hilaire Belloc

Hilaire Belloc (1870-1953), though born in France, was graduated from Balliol College, Oxford, and became a British citizen. He was the author

From *Hills and the Sea*, by Hilaire Belloc. Used by permission of Methuen & Co., Ltd.

of novels, poems, essays, and books on history. His name is often associated with another great English essayist, his close friend G. K. Chesterton.

[1] When I got into the long grass the sun was not yet risen, but there were already many colors in the eastern sky, and I made haste to sharpen my scythe, so that I might get to the cutting before the dew should dry. Some say that it is best to wait till all the dew has risen, so as to get the grass quite dry from the very first. But, though it is an advantage to get the grass quite dry, yet it is not worth while to wait till the dew has risen. For, in the first place, you lose many hours of work (and those are the coolest), and next—which is more important—you lose that great ease and thickness in cutting which comes of the dew. So I at once began to sharpen my scythe.

[2] There is an art also in the sharpening of the scythe, and it is worth describing carefully. Your blade must be dry, and that is why you will see men rubbing the scythe-blade with grass before they whet it. Then also your rubber must be quite dry, and on this account it is a good thing to lay it on your coat and keep it there during all your day's mowing. The scythe you stand upright, with the blade pointing away from you, and put your left hand firmly on the back of the blade, grasping it; then you pass the rubber first down one side of the blade-edge and then down the other, beginning near the handle and going on to the point and working quickly and hard. When you first do this you will, perhaps, cut your hand; but it is only at first that such an accident will happen to you.

[3] To tell when the scythe is sharp enough this is the rule. First the stone clangs and grinds against the iron harshly; then it rings musically to one note; then, at last, it purrs as though the iron and stone were exactly suited. When you hear this, your scythe is sharp enough; and I, when I heard it that June dawn, with everything quite silent except the birds, let down the scythe and bent myself to mow.

[4] When one does anything anew, after so many years, one fears very much for one's trick or habit. But all things once learnt are easily recoverable, and I very soon recovered the swing and power of the mower. Mowing well and mowing badly—or rather not mowing at all—are separated by very little; as is also true of writing verse, of playing the fiddle, and of dozens of other things, but of nothing more than of believing. For the bad or young or untaught mower without tradition, the mower Promethean, the mower original and contemptuous of the past, does all these things: He leaves great crescents of grass uncut. He digs the point of the scythe hard into the ground with a jerk. He loosens the handles and even the fastening of the blade. He twists the blade with his blunders, he blunts the blade, he chips it, dulls it, or breaks it clean off at the tip. If any one is standing by he cuts him in the ankle. He sweeps up into the

air wildly, with nothing to resist his stroke. He drags up earth with the grass, which is like making the meadow bleed. But the good mower who does things just as they should be done and have been for a hundred thousand years, falls into none of these fooleries. He goes forward very steadily, his scythe-blade just barely missing the ground, every grass falling; the swish and rhythm of his mowing are always the same.

[5] So great an art can only be learnt by continual practice; but this is worth writing down, that, as in all good work, to know the thing with which you work is the core of the affair. Good verse is best written on good paper with an easy pen, not with a lump of coal on a whitewashed wall. The pen thinks for you; and so does the scythe mow for you if you treat it honorably and in a manner that makes it recognize its service. The manner is this. You must regard the scythe as a pendulum that swings, not as a knife that cuts. A good mower puts no more strength into his stroke than into his lifting. Again, stand up to your work. The bad mower, eager and full of pain, leans forward and tries to force the scythe through the grass. The good mower, serene and able, stands as nearly straight as the shape of his scythe will let him, and follows up every stroke closely, moving his left foot forward. Then also let every stroke get well away. Mowing is a thing of ample gestures, like drawing a cartoon. Then, again, get yourself into a mechanical and repetitive mood: be thinking of anything at all but your mowing and be anxious only when there seems some interruption to the monotony of the sound. In this, mowing should be like one's prayers—all of a sort and always the same, and so made that you can establish a monotony and work them, as it were, with half your mind: that happier half, the half that does not bother.

[6] In this way, when I had recovered the art after so many years, I went forward over the field, cutting lane after lane through the grass, and bringing out its most secret essences with the sweep of the scythe until the air was full of odours. At the end of every lane I sharpened my scythe and looked back at the work done, and then carried my scythe down again upon my shoulder to begin another. So, long before the bell rang in the chapel above me—that is, long before six o'clock, which is the time for the *Angelus*—I had many swathes already lying in order parallel like soldiery; and the high grass yet standing, making a great contrast with the shaven part, looked dense and high. As it says in the *Ballad of Val-ès-Dunes*, where

> The tall son of the Seven Winds
> Came riding out of Hither-hythe,

and his horse-hoofs (you remember) trampled into the press and made a gap in it, and his sword (as you know)

> . . . was like a scythe
> In Arcus when the grass is high
> And all the swathes in order lie,
> And there's the bailiff standing by
> A-gathering of the tithe.

[7] So I mowed all that morning, till the houses awoke in the valley, and from some of them rose a little fragrant smoke, and men began to be seen.

QUESTIONS AND COMMENT ON FORM AND CONTENT

1. Is Belloc mainly interested in teaching us how to whet a scythe and mow a field of grass so that we can do it, or is he trying to give us an experience, to see what life was like to Belloc, the mower, who is carrying on this age-old work? Is this essay, then, mainly expository or descriptive? Would a different purpose have made a quite different essay?

2. What are some words used to describe the sounds made in sharpening a mowing scythe? Do any of them suggest the sound itself, that is, are any of them onomatopoetic? What kind of sound does the scythe make as it moves through the grass?

3. How does Belloc include verse writing and especially tradition and believing in his essay without leaving his subject?

4. How does he describe "the bad or young or untaught mower without tradition, the mower Promethean, the mower original and contemptuous of the past"? (paragraph 4) Does the simple sentence structure, much of it parallel, add to the effectiveness?

5. In his description of the good mower is there anything to suggest that in the back of his mind he was also thinking of the good life? (paragraph 5)

6. Why is a simple Anglo-Saxon word choice and simple sentence structure especially appropriate for this sort of writing?

7. From this short selection would you classify Belloc as a conservative, liberal, or radical in his attitude toward morals, customs, and beliefs?

8. In the sentence "He drags up earth with the grass, which is like making the meadow bleed," what common process probably suggested the simile?

VOCABULARY: WHAT DO THE ITALICIZED WORDS MEAN?

. . . the mower *Promethean* (4)
I had many *swathes* already lying in order (6)
A-gathering of the *tithe* (6)

THEME SUGGESTIONS

Write a theme or paragraph in which you contrast the good and bad golfer, tennis-player, or skater, carpenter sawing a board or driving a nail, housewife getting a meal for company or cutting up a chicken, or the like. You may follow Belloc's pattern of the good and bad mower. Which does he describe first? Why?

ON THE ROAD WITH MEMÈRE

Jack Kerouac

Expressing joy, despair, pessimism, and occasionally, a ray of hope, Jack Kerouac (1933?-   ) is perhaps the leading spokesman of the so-called "beat generation."

[1] My widowed mother's name is now "Memère"—nickname for Grandma in Québecois—since her grandson, my nephew, calls her that. It is 1957. I am still an itinerant; Memère and I are going from Florida to try to settle down in San Francisco, our meager belongings following us slowly in a moving van.

[2] Here we are in Florida with two tickets to California, standing waiting for the bus to New Orleans, where we'll change for El Paso and Los Angeles. It's hot in May in Florida. I long to get out and go west beyond the East Texas Plain, to that high plateau and on over the Divide to dry Arizona and beyond. Poor Memère is standing there absolutely dependent on me. I wonder what my father is saying in Heaven. "That crazy Ti Jean is carting her 3,000 miles in wretched buses just for a dream he's had about a new life near a holy pine tree."

[3] There's hardly anything in the world, or at least in America, more miserable than a transcontinental bus trip with limited means. More than three days and three nights wearing the same clothes, bouncing around into town after town; even at three in the morning, when you've finally fallen asleep, there you are being bounced over the railroad tracks of a town, and all the lights are turned on bright to reveal your raggedness and weariness in the seat. To do that, as I'd done so often as a strong young man, is bad enough; but to have to do that when you're a sixty-two-year-old lady . . . yet Memère is more cheerful than I, and she devises a terrific trick to keep us in fairly good shape—aspirins with Coke three times a day to calm the nerves.

[4] From mid-Florida we roll in the late afternoon over orange-grove hills toward the Tallahassee and Mobile of morning, no prospect of New Orleans till noon and already fair exhausted. Such an enormous country, you realize when you cross it on buses, the dreadful stretches between equally dreadful cities, all of them looking the same when seen from the bus of woes, the never-get-there bus stopping everywhere, and worst of all the string of fresh enthusiastic drivers every two or three hundred miles warning everyone to relax and be happy.

[5] Sometimes during the night I look at my poor sleeping mother cruelly crucified there in the American night because of no-money, no-hope-of-money, no-family, no-nothing—just myself, the stupid son of plans all compacted of eventual darkness. God, how right Hemingway was when he said there was no remedy for life. No remedy but in my mind. I raise a fist to Heaven, promising that I shall bull-whip the first bum who makes fun of human hopelessness. I know it's ridiculous to pray to my father, that hunk of dung in a grave, yet I pray to him anyway. What else shall I do? Sneer? Shuffle papers on a desk and burp with rationality?

[6] I say that we shall all be reborn with the Only One, that we will not be ourselves any more but simply the Companions of the Only One, and that's what makes me go on, and my mother too. She has her rosary in the bus, don't deny her that, that's *her* way of stating the fact. If there can't be love among men, let there be love at least between men and God. Human courage is an opiate, but opiates are human too. If God is an opiate, so am I. Therefore eat me. Therefore *eat me*. *Eat* the night, the long desolate American night between Sanford and Shlamford and Blamford and Crapford, eat the blood in the ground, the dead Indians, the dead pioneers, the dead Fords and Pontiacs, the dead Mississippis, the dead arms of forlorn hopelessness washing underneath. Who are men that they can insult men? I'm talking about human helplessness in the darkness of birth and death, and asking, "What is there to laugh about in that?" "How can you be *clever* in a meatgrinder?" "Who makes fun of misery?"

[7] There's my mother, a hunk of flesh that didn't ask to be born, sleeping restlessly, dreaming hopefully, beside her son who also didn't ask to be born, thinking desperately, praying hopelessly, in a bouncing vehicle going from nowhere to nowhere.

[8] When Memère wakes up in the middle of the night and groans, my heart breaks. The bus goes belumping over back lots of Crapford to pick up one package in a dawn station. Groans everywhere, all the way to the back seats where black sufferers suffer no less because their skin is black.

[9] And there's just no hope anywhere because we're all disunited and ashamed. The only thing to do is be like mother: patient, believing, careful, bleak, self-protective, glad for little favors, suspicious of great favors,

make it your own way, hurt no one, mind your own business and make your compact with God. For God is our Guardian Angel, and this is a fact that's only proven when proof exists no more.

[10] The bus arrives in New Orleans at noon, and we have to disembark with all our tangled luggage and wait four hours for the El Paso express, so Memère and I decide to investigate New Orleans and stretch our legs. In my mind I imagine a big glorious lunch in a Latin Quarter restaurant among grillwork balconies and palms, but when we find such a restaurant, near Bourbon Street, the prices on the menu are so high that we have to walk out sheepishly.

[11] Just for the hell of it Memère and I decide to walk into a New Orleans saloon that has an oyster bar. And there by God she has the time of her life drinking wine, eating oysters on the half shell with *piquante* and yelling crazy conversations with the old Italian oyster man. He gives her a free wine. "Are you married, ey?" No, he's not married, and would she like some clams now, maybe steamed? And they exchange names and addresses but later never write. Memère is all excited at being in famous New Orleans at last, and when we walk around she buys pickaninny dolls and praline candies and packs them in our luggage to send as presents to my sister. A relentless hope. Just like my father, she won't let anything discourage her. I walk sheepishly by her side. And she's been doing this for sixty-two years; at the age of fourteen there she was, at dawn, walking to the shoe factory to work till six that evening, till Saturday evening, seventy-two-hour week, all gleeful in anticipation of that pitiful Saturday night in old New Hampshire, and Sunday when there'd be popcorn and swings and singing.

[12] We get back on the El Paso bus after an hour standing in line in blue bus fumes, loaded with presents and luggage, talking to everybody, and off we roar north and then across the Louisiana plains, sitting in front again, feeling gay and rested now, partly because I've bought a little pint of port wine to nip us along.

[13] "I don't care what anybody says," says Memère, pouring a nip into her ladylike portable shot glass, "a little drink never hurt nobody!" I agree, ducking down beneath the range of the driver's rearview mirror and gulping a snort. Off we go to Lafayette. Where to our amazement we hear the local people talking French exactly as we do in Québecois. The Cajuns are only Acadians. But there's no time, the bus is already leaving for Texas.

[14] In reddish dusk, we're rolling across the Texas plains, talking and drinking, but soon the pint runs out, and poor Memère's sleeping again, just a hopeless baby in the world, and all that distance yet to go. And when we get there, what? Liberty, and Houston, and Sealy, the dull bus

stops, the sighs, the endlessness of it, only halfway across the continent, another night of sleeplessness ahead and another one later, and still another one.

[15] We are finally bashing down the Rio Grande Valley into the wink of El Paso night, all 900 *miserere* miles of Texas behind us, both of us, both of us completely bushed and numb with tiredness. I realize there's nothing to do but leave the bus and get a hotel suite and a good night's sleep before going on to California more than another thousand bumpy miles.

[16] In the meantime I will show my mother Mexico across the little bridge to Juarez.

[17] Everybody knows what it feels like after two days of vibration on wheels to suddenly lie in still beds on still ground and sleep. Right next to the bus station I got a hotel suite and went out to buy chicken-in-the-basket while Memère washed up. She was having a big adventurous trip, visiting New Orleans and staying in hotel suites ($4.50) and going to Mexico for the first time tomorrow. We drank another port pint, ate the chicken and slept like logs.

[18] In the morning, with eight hours till bus time, we sallied forth strong. I made her walk the mile to the Mexican bridge for exercise. We paid three cents each and went over.

[19] Immediately we were among Indians in an Indian earth. Among the smells of mud, chickens, Chihuahua dust, lime peels, horses, straw, Indian weariness. The strong smell of cantinas, beer, dank. The smell of the market. And the sight of beautiful old Spanish churches rising in the sun with all their woeful, majestical Maria Guadalupes and Crosses and cracks in the walls.

[20] "O, Ti Jean! I want to go in that church and light a candle to Papa!"

[21] When we go in we see an old man kneeling in the aisle with his arms outstretched in penitence—a *penitente*. Hours like that he kneels, old *serape* over his shoulder, old shoes, hat on the church floor, raggedy old white beard.

[22] "O, Ti Jean, what's he done that he's so sad for? I can't believe that old man has ever done anything really bad!"

[23] "He's a *penitente*," I tell her in French. "He's a sinner and he doesn't want God to forget him."

[24] "*Pauvre bonhomme!*" And I see a woman turn and look at Memère thinking she said "Pobrecito," which is exactly what she said anyway.

[25] But the most pitiful sight suddenly in the old Juarez church is a shawled woman, all dressed in black, barefooted, with a baby in her arms,

advancing slowly on her knees up the aisle to the altar. "What has happened *there?*" cries my mother amazed. "That poor li'l mother had done no wrong! Is it her husband who's in prison? She's carrying that little baby! Is *she* a penitent *too?* That little baby is a penitent? She's got him all wrapped up in a little ball in her shawl!"

[26] "I don't know why."

[27] "Where's the priest that he don't bless her? There's nobody here but that poor little mother and that poor old man! This is the church of Mary?"

[28] "This is the church of Maria de Guadalupe. A peasant found a shawl in Guadalupe, Mexico, with her face imprinted on it."

[29] "And they pray to Marie? But that poor young mother is only halfway to the altar. She comes slowly on her knees all quiet. Aw, but these are good people, the *Indians,* you say?"

[30] "*Oui.*" Indians just like the American Indians, but here the Spaniards did not destroy them. In French: "*Ici les Espagnols sont mariés avec les Indiens.*"

[31] "*Pauvre monde!* They believe in God just like us! I didn't know that, Ti Jean! I never saw anything like this!" We crept up to the altar and lit candles and put dimes in the church box to pay for the wax. Memère made a prayer to God and did the sign of the cross. The Chihuahua desert blew dust into the church, the little mother was still advancing on her knees with the infant quietly asleep in her arms. Memère's eyes blurred with tears. Now she understood Mexico and why I had come there so often even though I'd get sick of dysentery or lose weight or get pale. "*C'est du monde qu'ils ont du coeur!*" she whispered—these are people who have heart!

[32] "*Oui.*"

[33] She put a dollar in the church machine, hoping it would do some good somehow. She never forgot that afternoon: in fact even today she still adds a prayer for the little mother with the child, crawling to the altar on her knees: "There was something was wrong in her life. Her husband, or maybe her baby was sick. We'll never know. But I will always pray for that little woman. Ti Jean, when you took me there you showed me something I'd never believed I'd *ever* see."

[34] Meanwhile the old man *penitente* still knelt there, arms outspread. All your Zapatas and Castros come and go, but the Old Penitence is still there and will always be there, like Coyotl Old Man in the Navajo Mountains and Mescalero foothills up north.

[35] It was also very funny to be in Mexico with my mother, for when we came out of the church of Santa Maria we sat in the park to rest and enjoy the sun, and next to us sat an old Indian in his shawl, with

his wife, saying nothing, looking straight ahead, on their big visit to Juarez from the hills of the desert out beyond. Come by bus or burro.

[36] Memère offered them a cigarette. At first the old Indian was afraid, but finally he took a cigarette. She offered him one for his wife, in Québecois French, so he took it, puzzled. The old lady never looked at Memère. They knew we were American tourists, but never tourists like these. The old man slowly lighted his cigarette and looked straight ahead.

[37] Memère asked: "They're afraid to talk?"

[38] "They don't know what to do. They never meet anybody. They came from the desert. They don't even speak Spanish, just Indian. Say Chihuahua!"

[39] Memère said "Chihuahua" and the old man grinned at her, and the old lady smiled. "Good-by," said Memère as we left.

[40] We went wandering across the sweet little park full of children and ice cream and balloons, and came to a strange man with birds in a cage, who yelled for our attention.

[41] "What does he want?"

[42] "Fortune! His birds will tell your fortune. We give him one peso and his little bird grabs a slip of paper and your fortune's written on it."

[43] "Okay! Seenyor!" The little bird beaked up a slip of paper from a pile, of papers and handed it to the man. The man with his little mustache and gleeful eyes opened it. It read as follows:

> You will have goods fortuna with one who is your son who love you. Say the bird.

[44] He gave the little paper to us laughing.

[45] "Now," said Memère as we walked arm in arm through the streets of Old Juarez, "how could that silly bird know I have a son, or *anything* about me? Phew, there's a lot of dust around here!" That million-million-grained desert blew dust along the doors. "Can you explain me that? And the little bird knew all that? Hah? That guy with the mustache doesn't know us. His little bird knew everything."

[46] She had the slip of paper in her purse.

[47] "And the little bird picked out the paper with his crazy face! Ah, but the people are poor here, eh?"

[48] "Yes, but the government is taking care of that a lot now. Used to be there were families sleeping on the sidewalk wrapped in newspapers. And girls sold themselves for twenty cents. They have a good government since Aleman, Cardenas, Cortines. . . ."

[49] "The poor little bird of Mexica! And the little mother! I can always say I've seen Mexica!" She pronounced it "Mexica." I think because of the little mother.

QUESTIONS AND COMMENT ON FORM AND CONTENT

1. The telling of a trip in unselected detail is usually boring. In "The Golden Honeymoon," a short story, Ring Lardner satirizes a talkative old man who tells in monotonous detail about a trip to Florida: "We reached North Philadelphia at 4:03 P.M. and we reached West Philadelphia at 4:14, but did not go into Broad Street. We reached Baltimore at 6:30 and Washington, D.C., at 7:25." How, in general, does Kerouac avoid such monotony?

2. Although this essay was published in 1965, Kerouac says, "It is 1957. I am still an itinerant." The essay continues to use the present tense for most of the descriptions. Does this add to the reality of it?

3. What is the general impression given of the many towns they pass through?

4. What is the impression given of taking a transcontinental trip on a bus?

5. What kind of person does the author picture himself to be? How does he introduce his beliefs about life?

6. What kind of person is Memère? How are her character, personality, and beliefs brought out? How does the trip into Mexico help to reveal her character? Which of the following characters in Mexico affected her most profoundly: the *penitente,* the little mother with her child, the old Indian and his wife, the man who told fortunes with birds?

7. Comment on the style.

8. Why is the essay divided into five parts?

VOCABULARY: WHAT DO THE ITALICIZED WORDS MEAN?

I am still an *itinerant.* (1)
. . . plans all *compacted* of eventual darkness (5)
The bus goes *belumping* (8)
. . . make your *compact* with God (9)
. . . port wine to *nip* us along (12)
. . . finally *bashing* down the Rio Grande Valley (15)
. . . into the *wink* of El Paso night (15)

THEME SUGGESTIONS

A Trip with _____
Grandfather (Grandmother) and I

THE ASSASSINATION OF LINCOLN

Carl Sandburg

Carl Sandburg (1878-   ), American poet and biographer, was born in Galesburg, Illinois, lived in various parts of the Midwest, including Chicago, and has remained close to the thought and idiom of the people. His biography of Lincoln (1926-1939) was written from material collected over a period of thirty years. Our selection is from Volume Four of The War Years.

[1] The play proceeds, not unpleasant, often stupid, sprinkled with silly puns, drab and aimless dialogue, forced humor, characters neither truly English nor truly American nor fetching as caricatures. The story centers around the Yankee lighting his cigar with an old will, burning the document to ashes and thereby throwing a fortune of $400,000 away from himself into the hands of an English cousin. The mediocre comedy is somewhat redeemed by the way the players are doing it. The audience agrees it is not bad. The applause and laughter say the audience is having a good time.

[2] Mrs. Lincoln sits close to her husband, at one moment leaning on him fondly, suddenly realizing they are not alone, saying with humor, "What will Miss Harris think of my hanging on to you so?" and hearing his: "She won't think anything about it."

[3] From the upholstered rocking armchair in which Lincoln sits he can see only the persons in the box with him, the players on the stage, and any persons offstage on the left. The box on the opposite side of the theatre is empty. With the box wall at his back and the closely woven lace curtains at his left arm, he is screened from the audience at his back and from the musicians in the orchestra pit, which is below and partly behind him.

[4] The box has two doors. Sometimes by a movable cross partition it is converted into two boxes, each having its door. The door forward is locked. For this evening the President's party has the roominess and convenience of double space, extra armchairs, side chairs, and a small sofa. In the privacy achieved he is in sight only of his chosen companions, the actors he has come to see render a play, and the few people who may be offstage to the left.

[5] This privacy however has a flaw. It is not as complete as it seems. A few feet behind the President is the box door, the only entry to the

box unless by a climb from the stage. In this door is a small hole, bored that afternoon to serve as a peephole—from the outside. Through this peephole it is the intention of the Outsider who made it with a gimlet to stand and watch the President, then at a chosen moment to enter the box. This door opens from the box on a narrow hallway that leads to another door which opens on the balcony of the theatre.

[6] Through these two doors the Outsider must pass in order to enter the President's box. Close to the door connecting with the balcony two inches of plaster have been cut from the brick wall of the narrow hallway. The intention of the Outsider is that a bar placed in this cut-away wall niche and then braced against the panel of the door will hold that door against intruders, will serve to stop anyone from interference with the Outsider while making his observations of the President through the gimleted hole in the box door.

[7] At either of these doors, the one to the box or the one to the hallway, it is the assigned duty and expected responsibility of John F. Parker to stand or sit constantly and without fail. A Ward Lamon or an Eckert on his duty would probably have noticed the gimleted hole, the newly made wall niche, and been doubly watchful. If Lincoln believes what he told Crook that afternoon, that he trusted the men assigned to guard him, then as he sits in the upholstered rocking armchair in the box he believes that John F. Parker in steady fidelity is just outside the box door, in plain clothes ready with the revolver Pendel at the White House had told him to be sure to have with him.

[8] In such a trust Lincoln is mistaken. Whatever dim fog of thought or duty may move John F. Parker in his best moments is not operating tonight. His life habit of never letting trouble trouble him is on him this night; his motive is to have no motive. He has always got along somehow. Why care about anything, why really care? He can always find good liquor and bad women. You take your fun as you find it. He can never be a somebody, so he will enjoy himself as a nobody—though he can't imagine how perfect a cipher, how completely the little end of nothing, one John F. Parker may appear as the result of one slack easygoing hour.

[9] "The guard . . . acting as my substitute," wrote the faithful Crook later, "took his position at the rear of the box, close to an entrance leading into the box. . . . His orders were to stand there, fully armed, and to permit no unauthorized person to pass into the box. His orders were to stand there and protect the President at all hazards. From the spot where he was thus stationed, this guard could not see the stage or the actors; but he could hear the words the actors spoke, and he became so interested in them that, incredible as it may seem, he quietly deserted his post of duty, and walking down the dimly-lighted side aisle, deliberately took a seat."

[10] The custom was for a chair to be placed in the narrow hallway for the guard to sit in. The doorkeeper Buckingham told Crook that such a chair was provided this evening for the accommodation of the guard. "Whether Parker occupied it at all, I do not know," wrote Crook. "Mr. Buckingham is of the impression that he did. If he did, he left it almost immediately, for he confessed to me the next day that he went to a seat, so that he could see the play." The door to the President's box is shut. It is not kept open so that the box occupants can see the guard on duty.

[11] Either between acts or at some time when the play was not lively enough to suit him or because of an urge for a pony of whiskey under his belt, John F. Parker leaves his seat in the balcony and goes down to the street and joins companions in a little whiff of liquor—this on the basis of a statement of the coachman Burns, who declared he stayed outside on the street with his carriage and horses, except for one interlude when "the special police officer [meaning John F. Parker] and the footman of the President [Forbes] came up to him and asked to take a drink with them; which he did."

[12] Thus circumstance favors the lurking and vigilant Outsider who in the afternoon gimleted a hole in the door of the President's box and cut a two-inch niche in a wall to brace a bar against a door panel and hold it against interference while he should operate.

[13] The play goes on. The evening and the drama are much like many other evenings when the acting is pleasant enough, the play mediocre and so-so, the audience having no thrills of great performance but enjoying itself. The most excited man in the house, with little doubt, is the orchestra leader, Withers. He has left the pit and gone backstage, where, as he related, "I was giving the stage manager a piece of my mind. I had written a song for Laura Keene to sing. When she left it out I was mad. We had no cue, and the music was thrown out of gear. So I hurried round on the stage on my left to see what it was done for."

[14] And of what is Abraham Lincoln thinking? As he leans back in this easy rocking chair, where does he roam in thought? If it is life he is thinking about, no one could fathom the subtle speculations and hazy reveries resulting from his fifty-six years of adventures drab and dazzling in life. Who had gone farther on so little to begin with? Who else as a living figure of republican government, of democracy, in practice, as a symbol touching freedom for all men—who else had gone farther over America, over the world? If it is death he is thinking about, who better than himself might interpret his dream that he lay in winding sheets on a catafalque in the White House and people were wringing their hands and crying "The President is dead!"—who could make clear this dream better than himself? Furthermore if it is death he is thinking about, has he not philosophized about it and dreamed about it and considered him-

self as a mark and a target until no one is better prepared than he for any sudden deed? Has he not a thousand times said to himself, and several times to his friends and intimates, that he must accommodate himself to the thought of sudden death? Has he not wearied of the constructions placed on his secret night ride through Baltimore to escape a plot aimed at his death? Has he not laughed to the overhead night stars at a hole shot in his hat by a hidden marksman he never mentioned even to his boon companion Hill Lamon? And who can say but that Death is a friend, and who else should be more a familiar of Death than a man who has been the central figure of the bloodiest war ever known to the Human Family—who else should more appropriately and decently walk with Death? And who can say but Death is a friend and a nurse and a lover and a benefactor bringing peace and lasting reconciliation? The play tonight is stupid. Shakespeare would be better. "Duncan is in his grave . . . he sleeps well."

[15] Yes, of what is Abraham Lincoln thinking? Draped before him in salute is a silk flag of the Union, a banner of the same design as the one at Independence Hall in Philadelphia in February of '61 which he pulled aloft saying, "I would rather be assassinated on this spot than surrender it," saying the flag in its very origins "gave promise that in due time the weights would be lifted from the shoulders of all men, and that all should have an equal chance." Possibly his mind recurs for a fleeting instant to that one line in his letter to a Boston widow woman: "the solemn pride that must be yours to have laid so costly a sacrifice upon the altar of freedom." Or a phrase from the Gettysburg speech: "we here highly resolve that these dead shall not have died in vain."

[16] Out in a main-floor seat enjoying the show is one Julia Adelaide Shephard, who wrote a letter to her father about this Good Friday evening at the theatre. "Cousin Julia has just told me," she reported, "that the President is in yonder right hand private box so handsomely decked with silken flags festooned over a picture of George Washington. The young and lovely daughter of Senator Harris is the only one of his party we see as the flags hide the rest. But we know Father Abraham is there like a Father watching what interests his children, for their pleasure rather than his own. It had been announced in the papers he would be there. How sociable it seems like one family sitting around their parlor fire. Everyone has been so jubilant for days that they laugh and shout at every clownish witticism such is the excited state of the public mind. One of the actresses whose part is that of a very delicate young lady talks about wishing to avoid the draft when her lover tells her not to be alarmed 'for there is to be no more draft' at which the applause is loud and long. The American cousin has just been making love to a young lady who says she'll never marry but for love but when her mother and herself find out that he has

lost his property they retreat in disgust at the left hand of the stage while the American cousin goes out at the right. We are waiting for the next scene."

[17] And the next scene?

[18] The next scene is to crash and blare and flare as one of the wildest, one of the most inconceivably fateful and chaotic, that ever stunned and shocked a world that heard the story.

[19] The moment of high fate was not seen by the theatre audience. Only one man saw that moment. He was the Outsider. He was the one who had waited and lurked and made his preparations, planning and plotting that he should be the single and lone spectator of what happened. He had come through the outer door into the little hallway, fastened the strong though slender bar into the two-inch niche in the brick wall, and braced it against the door panel. He had moved softly to the box door and through the little hole he had gimleted that afternoon he had studied the box occupants and his Human Target seated in an upholstered rocking armchair. Softly he had opened the door and stepped toward his prey, in his right hand a one-shot brass derringer pistol, a little eight-ounce vest-pocket weapon winged for death, in his left hand a steel dagger. He was cool and precise and timed his every move. He raised the derringer, lengthened his right arm, ran his eye along the barrel in a line with the head of his victim less than five feet away—and pulled the trigger.

[20] A lead ball somewhat less than a half-inch in diameter crashed into the left side of the head of the Human Target, into the back of the head, in a line with and three inches from the left ear. "The course of the ball was obliquely forward toward the right eye, crossing the brain in an oblique manner and lodging a few inches behind that eye. In the track of the wound were found fragments of bone, which had been driven forward by the ball, which was embedded in the anterior lobe of the left hemisphere of the brain."

[21] For Abraham Lincoln it was lights out, good night, farewell and a long farewell to the good earth and its trees, its enjoyable companions, and the Union of States and the world Family of Man he had loved. He was not dead yet. He was to linger in dying. But the living man could never again speak nor see nor hear nor awaken into conscious being.

[22] Near the prompt desk offstage stands W. J. Ferguson, an actor. He looks in the direction of a shot he hears, and sees "Mr. Lincoln lean back in his rocking chair, his head coming to rest against the wall which stood between him and the audience . . . well inside the curtains"—no struggle or move "save in the slight backward sway."

[23] Of this the audience in their one thousand seats know nothing.

[24] Major Rathbone leaps from his chair. Rushing at him with a knife is a strange human creature, terribly alive, a lithe wild animal, a

tiger for speed, a wildcat of a man bareheaded, raven-haired—a smooth sinister face with glaring eyeballs. He wears a dark sack suit. He stabs straight at the heart of Rathbone, a fast and ugly lunge. Rathbone parries it with his upper right arm, which gets a deep slash of the dagger. Rathbone is staggered, reels back. The tigerish stranger mounts the box railing. Rathbone recovers, leaps again for the stranger, who feels the hand of Rathbone holding him back, slashes again at Rathbone, then leaps for the stage.

[25] This is the moment the audience wonders whether something unusual is happening—or is it part of the play?

[26] From the box railing the Strange Man leaps for the stage, perhaps a ten-foot fall. His leap is slightly interrupted. On this slight interruption the Strange Man in his fine calculations had not figured. The draped Union flag of silk reaches out and tangles itself in a spur of one riding-boot, throwing him out of control. He falls to the stage landing on his left leg, breaking the shinbone a little above the instep.

[27] Of what he has done the audience as yet knows nothing. They wonder what this swift, raven-haired, wild-eyed Strange Man portends. They see him rush across the stage, three feet to a stride, and vanish. Some have heard Rathbone's cry "Stop that man!" Many have seen a man leap from a front seat up on the stage and chase after the weird Stranger, crying "Stop that man!"

[28] It is a peculiar night, an odd evening, a little weird, says the audience to itself. The action is fast. It is less than half a minute since the Strange Man mounted the box railing, made the stage, and strode off.

[29] Offstage between Laura Keene and W. J. Ferguson he dashes at breakneck speed, out of an entrance, forty feet to a little door opening on an alley. There stands a fast bay horse, a slow-witted chore boy nicknamed John Peanuts holding the reins. He kicks the boy, mounts the mare; hoofs on the cobblestones are heard but a few moments. In all it is maybe sixty or seventy seconds since he loosed the one shot of his eight-ounce brass derringer.

[30] Whether the Strange Man now riding away on a fast bay horse had paused a moment on the stage and shouted a dramatic line of speech, there was disagreement afterward. Some said he ran off as though every second of time counted and his one purpose was escape. Others said he faced the audience a moment, brandished a dagger still bloody from slashing Rathbone, and shouted the State motto of Virginia, the slogan of Brutus as he drove the assassin's knife into imperial Caesar: "*Sic semper tyrannis*"—"Thus be it ever to tyrants." Miss Shephard and others believed they heard him shriek as he brandished the dagger: "The South is avenged!" Others: "The South shall be free!" "Revenge!" "Freedom!"

[31] Some said the lights went out in the theatre, others adding the

detail that the assassin had stabbed the gasman and pulled the lever, throwing the house into darkness. Others a thousand miles from the theatre said they saw the moon come out from behind clouds blood-red. It is a night of many eyewitnesses, shaken and moaning eyewitnesses.

[32] The audience is up and out of its one thousand seats, standing, moving. Panic is in the air, fear over what may happen next. Many merely stand up from their seats, fixed and motionless, waiting to hear what has happened, waiting to see what further is to happen. The question is spoken quietly or is murmured anxiously—"What is it? What has happened?" The question is bawled with anger, is yelled with anguish—"For God's sake, what is it? What has happened?"

[33] A woman's scream pierces the air. Some say afterward it was Mrs. Lincoln. The scream carries a shock and a creeping shiver to many hearing it. "He has shot the President!" Miss Shephard looks from the main floor toward the box and sees "Miss Harris wringing her hands and calling for water." There are moanings "No, for God's sake, it can't be true—no! no! for God's sake!"

[34] Men are swarming up to the edge of the stage, over the gas-jet footlights onto the stage. The aisles fill with people not sure where to go; to leave would be safe, but they want to know what has happened, what else they may see this wild night. Men are asking whether some God-damned fool has for sure tried to shoot the President. Others take it as true. The man who ran across the stage did it. There are cries: "Kill him! Shoot him!" On the stage now are policemen, army officers, soldiers, besides actors and actresses in make-up and costume. Cries for "Water! water!" Cries for "A surgeon! a surgeon!" Someone brings water. It is passed up to the box.

[35] An army surgeon climbs to the stage and is lifted up and clambers over the railing into the box. Some two hundred soldiers arrive to clear the theatre. The wailing and the crazy chaos let down in the emptying playhouse—and flare up again in the street outside, where some man is accused of saying he is glad it happened, a sudden little mob dragging him to a lamppost with a ready rope to hang him when six policemen with clubs and drawn revolvers manage to get him away and put him in jail for safekeeping.

[36] Mrs. Lincoln in the box has turned from the railing, has turned from where she saw the wild-eyed raven-haired man vanish off the stage, sees her husband seated in the rocking chair, his head slumped forward. Never before has she seen her husband so completely helpless, so strangely not himself. With little moaning cries she springs toward him and with her hands keeps him from tumbling to the floor. Major Rathbone has shouted for a surgeon, has run out of the box into the narrow hallway,

and with one arm bleeding and burning with pain he fumbles to unfasten the bar between wall and door panel. An usher from the outside tries to help him. They get the bar loose. Back of the usher is a jam of people, He holds them back, allowing only one man to enter.

[37] This is a young-looking man, twenty-three years old, with mustache and sideburns, Charles A. Leale, assistant surgeon, United States Volunteers, who had left the army General Hospital at Armory Square, where he was in charge of the wounded commissioned officers' ward, saying he would be gone only a short time. Rathbone shows Dr. Leale his bleeding arm, "beseeching me to attend to his wound," related Leale later. "I placed my hand under his chin, looking into his eyes an almost instantaneous glance revealed the fact that he was in no immediate danger, and in response to appeals from Mrs. Lincoln and Miss Harris, who were standing by the high-backed armchair in which President Lincoln sat, I went immediately to their assistance, saying I was a United States army surgeon."

[38] Leale holds Mrs. Lincoln's outstretched hand while she cries piteously: "Oh, Doctor! Is he dead? Can he recover? Will you take charge of him? Do what you can for him. Oh, my dear husband!" He soothes her a little, telling her he will do all that can possibly be done.

[39] The body in the chair at first scrutiny seems to be that of a dead man, eyes closed, no certainty it is breathing. Dr. Leale with help from others lifts the body from the chair and moves it to a lying position on the floor. He holds the head and shoulders while doing this, his hand meeting a clot of blood near the left shoulder. Dr. Leale recalls seeing a dagger flashed by the assassin on the stage and the knife wound of Rathbone, and now supposes the President has a stab wound. He has the coat and shirt slit open, thinking to check perhaps a hemorrhage. He finds no wounds. He lifts the eyelids and sees evidence of a brain injury. He rapidly passes the separated fingers of both hands through the blood-matted hair of the head, finding a wound and removing a clot of blood, which relieves pressure on the brain and brings shallow breathing and a weak pulse. "The assassin," Leale commented later . . . "had evidently planned to shoot to produce instant death, as the wound he made was situated within two inches of the physiological point of selection, when instant death is desired."

[40] Dr. Leale bends over, puts a knee at each side of the body, and tries to start the breathing apparatus, attempts to stimulate respiration by putting his two fingers into the throat and pressing down and out on the base of the tongue to free the larynx of secretion. Dr. Charles Sabin Taft, the army surgeon lifted from the stage into the box, now arrives. Another physician, Dr. Albert F. A. King, arrives. Leale asks them each to

manipulate an arm while he presses upward on the diaphragm and else-where to stimulate heart action. The body responds with an improvement in the pulse and the irregular breathing.

[41] Dr. Leale is sure, however, that with the shock and prostration the body has undergone, more must now be done to keep life going. And as he told it later: "I leaned forcibly forward directly over his body, thorax to thorax, face to face, and several times drew in a long breath, then forcibly breathed directly into his mouth and nostrils, which expanded his lungs and improved his respirations. After waiting a moment I placed my ear over his thorax and found the action of the heart improving. I arose to the erect kneeling posture, then watched for a short time and saw that the President could continue independent breathing and that instant death would not occur. I then pronounced my diagnosis and prognosis: 'His wound is mortal; it is impossible for him to recover.'"

QUESTIONS AND COMMENT ON FORM AND CONTENT

1. The Lincoln party is in the box at Ford's Theatre as the scene presented above begins. Sandburg had been using the past tense, but now changes to present tense. Which is more common in novels, biographies, and short stories? How do you account for the change here?

2. Sandburg describes the play and the reaction of the audience. He does not say, "The audience is having a good time." He says, "The applause and laughter say the audience is having a good time." Which is better? Which would be classified as fact and which as opinion?

3. Suspense begins with paragraph 5. Why does Sandburg call this assassin the "Outsider" and later the "Strange Man" when everybody, certainly including Sandburg, knows it was John Wilkes Booth?

4. As in much of his poetry, Sandburg uses folk idiom or folk clichés here and there in this tragic scene. What are some folk sayings used in paragraph 8?

5. Explain the allusion to a play of Shakespeare: "The play tonight is stupid, Shakespeare would be better. 'Duncan is in his grave . . . he sleeps well.'"

6. What does the inclusion of small, intimate, relatively unimportant details add to the narrative? What is the effect of dialogue? What is the effect of representing what Lincoln might have been thinking?

7. How does Sandburg prepare for the main scene—the actual assassination starting with paragraph 14?

8. Does Sandburg, as a historian, seem to have sufficient facts to tell the story in detail? How does he handle contradictory testimony?

9. How do you account for the contradictory testimony of eyewitnesses?

10. Quotations may be introduced in various ways. How does Sandburg introduce them? Give some examples. Also note the punctuation.

VOCABULARY: WHAT DO THE ITALICIZED WORDS MEAN?

. . . characters neither truly English . . . nor *fetching* as *caricatures* (1)
. . . the play *mediocre* and *so-so* (13)
. . . a man bareheaded, *raven-haired,* a smooth *sinister* face (24)
I then *pronounced* my *diagnosis* and *prognosis* (41)

THEME SUGGESTIONS

Write a theme telling of some important or exciting happening. Prepare for the climax by introducing suspense and setting the stage. Use some dialogue, imaginary or real, quoting witnesses.

A Moment's Negligence

THE ENCANTADAS OR ENCHANTED ISLES

Herman Melville

Herman Melville (1819-1891), American novelist, poet, and short story writer, is remembered principally for his Moby Dick. Billy Budd *and other short stories have recently found new appreciation. Melville wrote principally about his early adventures as a sailor. At one time he lived with the cannibals of the Marquesas Islands in the South Seas.*

[1] Take five-and-twenty heaps of cinders dumped here and there in an outside city lot; imagine some of them magnified into mountains, and the vacant lot of the sea; and you will have a fit idea of the general aspect of the Encantadas, or Enchanted Isles. A group rather of extinct volcanoes than of isles; looking much as the world at large might, after a penal conflagration.

[2] It is to be doubted whether any spot of earth can, in desolateness, furnish a parallel to this group. Abandoned cemeteries of long ago, old cities by piecemeal tumbling to their ruin, these are melancholy enough; but, like all else which has but once been associated with humanity, they still awaken in us some thoughts of sympathy, however sad. Hence, even the Dead Sea, along with whatever other emotions it may at times inspire, does not fail to touch in the pilgrim some of his less unpleasurable feelings.

[3] And as for solitariness; the great forests of the north, the expanses of unnavigated waters, the Greenland ice-fields, are the profoundest of

solitudes to a human observer; still the magic of their changeable tides and seasons mitigates their terror; because, though unvisited by men, those forests are visited by the May; the remotest seas reflect familiar stars even as Lake Erie does; and in the clear air of a fine Polar day, the irradiated, azure ice shows beautifully as malachite.

[4] But the special curse, as one may call it, of the Encantadas, that which exalts them in desolation above Idumea and the Pole, is, that to them change never comes; neither the change of seasons nor of sorrows. Cut by the Equator, they know not autumn, and they know not spring; while already reduced to the lees of fire, ruin itself can work little more upon them. The showers refresh the deserts; but in these isles, rain never falls. Like split Syrian gourds left withering in the sun, they are cracked by an everlasting drought beneath a torrid sky. "Have mercy upon me," the wailing spirit of the Encantadas seems to cry, "and send Lazarus that he may dip the tip of his finger in water and cool my tongue, for I am tormented in this flame."

[5] Another feature in these isles is their emphatic uninhabitableness. It is deemed a fit type of all-forsaken overthrow, that the jackal should den in the wastes of weedy Babylon; but the Encantadas refuse to harbor even the outcasts of the beasts. Man and wolf alike disown them. Little but reptile life is here found: tortoises, lizards, immense spiders, snakes, and that strangest anomaly of outlandish nature, the *aguano*. No voice, no low, no howl is heard; the chief sound of life here is a hiss.

[6] On most of the isles where vegetation is found at all, it is more ungrateful than the blankness of Aracama. Tangled thickets of wiry bushes, without fruit and without a name, springing up among deep fissures of calcined rock, and treacherously masking them; or a parched growth of distorted cactus trees.

[7] In many places the coast is rock-bound or more properly, clinker-bound; tumbled masses of blackish or greenish stuff like the dross of an iron-furnace, forming dark clefts and caves here and there, into which a ceaseless sea pours a fury of foam; overhanging them with a swirl of gray, haggard mist, amidst which sail screaming flights of unearthly birds heightening the dismal din. However calm the sea without, there is no rest for these swells and those rocks; they lash and are lashed, even when the outer ocean is most at peace with itself. On the oppressive, clouded days, such as are peculiar to this part of the watery Equator, the dark, vitrified masses, many of which raise themselves among white whirlpools and breakers in detached and perilous places off the shore, present a most Plutonian sight. In no world but a fallen one could such lands exist. . . .

[8] Nor would the appellation, enchanted, seem misapplied in still another sense. For concerning the peculiar reptile inhabitant of these wilds —whose presence gives the group its second Spanish name, Galápagos—

concerning the tortoises found here, most mariners have long cherished a superstition, not more frightful than grotesque. They earnestly believe that all wicked sea-officers, more especially commodores and captains, are at death (and, in some cases, before death) transformed into tortoises; thenceforth dwelling upon these hot aridities, sole solitary lords of Asphaltum.

[9] Doubtless, so quaintly dolorous a thought was orignally inspired by the woe-begone landscape itself; but more particularly, perhaps, by the tortoises. For, apart from their strictly physical features, there is something strangely self-condemned in the appearance of these creatures. Lasting sorrow and penal hopelessness are in no animal form so suppliantly expressed as in theirs; while the thought of their wonderful longevity does not fail to enhance the impression.

[10] Nor even at the risk of meriting the charge of absurdly believing in enchantments, can I restrain the admission that sometimes, even now, when leaving the crowded city to wander out July and August among the Adirondack Mountains, far from the influences of towns and proportionally nigh to the mysterious ones of nature; when at such times I sit me down in the mossy head of some deep-wooded gorge, surrounded by prostrate trunks of blasted pines and recall, as in a dream, my other and far-distant rovings in the baked heart of the charmed isles; and remember the sudden glimpses of dusky shells, and long languid necks protruded from the leafless thickets; and again have beheld the vitreous inland rocks worn down and grooved into deep ruts by ages and ages of the slow draggings of tortoises in quest of pools of scanty water; I can hardly resist the feeling that in my time I have indeed slept upon evilly enchanted ground.

[11] Nay, such is the vividness of my memory, or the magic of my fancy, that I know not whether I am not the occasional victim of optical delusion concerning the Galápagos. For, often in scenes of social merriment, and especially at revels held by candle-light in old-fashioned mansions, so that shadows are thrown into the further recesses of an angular and spacious room, making them put on a look of haunted undergrowth of lonely woods, I have drawn the attention of my comrades by my fixed gaze and sudden change of air, as I have seemed to see, slowly emerging from those imagined solitudes, and heavily crawling along the floor, the ghost of a gigantic tortoise, with "Memento . . ." burning in live letters upon his back.

QUESTIONS AND COMMENT ON FORM AND CONTENT

1. The first paragraph gives us a general view of the Encantadas. How does Melville accomplish this?

2. What single word is the key to the second paragraph? The third? The

fourth? The fifth? With what are the Encantadas compared and contrasted? What is the chief sound? What does it suggest?

3. Quote some phrases from paragraph 7 describing the sea, the mist, and the birds. Do they all tend to reflect the mood or feeling that the isles are under an evil spell or enchantment or curse? What is a Plutonian sight?

4. In the last two paragraphs Melville uses two scenes to contrast with the enchanted isles. What are they?

5. What characteristics of turtles are stressed? Do these qualities make them a symbol of the isles? What superstition is there about them? What is the meaning of "Memento . . ."? (See *memento mori.*)

6. Note that the concluding paragraph becomes, like the conclusion of an oration, quite elevated in tone. Read it aloud. How is this accomplished? Consider rhythm, word choice, type of sentence.

VOCABULARY: WHAT DO THE ITALICIZED WORDS MEAN?

. . . after a *penal conflagration* (1)
. . . the *profoundest of solitudes* (3)
. . . the *irradiated azure* ice (3)
. . . dark *vitrified* masses (7)
. . . a superstition more frightful than *grotesque* (8)
. . . so *quaintly dolorous* a thought (9)
. . . hopelessness are in no animal form so *suppliantly* expressed (9)

THEME SUGGESTIONS

Describe a scene familiar to you. Select three or four key words appropriately applied to it. Try to suggest mood, total impression.

THE GRAVE

Katherine Anne Porter

Katherine Anne Porter (1897-   ) was born in Texas and spent her youth there and in Louisiana. Later she lived in various parts of the world including the South, New York City, Europe, and Mexico. Although she began writing stories when quite young, and writing became her absorbing occupation throughout her life, she did not attempt publication until she was thirty. "I ran my scales," she said, "for fifteen years before trying to sell a story." Throughout her career she has aimed at the highest perfection in the short stories and novel she has published. Fame came to her with Flowering Judas and Other Stories (*1930, 1935*). *Her other most distinguished volumes are* Pale Horse, Pale Rider (*1939*), The Leaning Tower and Other Stories (*1944*), *and* Ship of Fools (*1962*), *a novel begun in 1932.*

[1] The grandfather, dead for more than thirty years, had been twice disturbed in his long repose by the constancy and possessiveness of his widow. She removed his bones first to Louisiana and then to Texas as if she had set out to find her own burial place, knowing well she would never return to the places she had left. In Texas she set up a small cemetery in a corner of her first farm, and as the family connection grew, and oddments of relations came over from Kentucky to settle, it contained at last about twenty graves. After the grandmother's death, part of her land was to be sold for the benefit of certain of her children, and the cemetery happened to lie in the part set aside for sale. It was necessary to take up the bodies and bury them again in the family plot in the big new public cemetery, where the grandmother had been buried. At last her husband was to lie beside her for eternity, as she had planned.

[2] The family cemetery had been a pleasant small neglected garden of tangled rose bushes and ragged cedar trees and cypress, the simple flat stones rising out of uncropped sweet-smelling wild grass. The graves were lying open and empty one burning day when Miranda and her brother Paul, who often went together to hunt rabbits and doves, propped their twenty-two Winchester rifles carefully against the rail fence, climbed over and explored among the graves. She was nine years old and he was twelve.

[3] They peered into the pits all shaped alike with such purposeful accuracy, and looking at each other with pleased adventurous eyes, they said in solemn tones: "These were graves!" trying by words to shape a special, suitable emotion in their minds, but they felt nothing except an agreeable thrill of wonder: they were seeing a new sight, doing something they had not done before. In them both there was also a small disappointment at the entire commonplaceness of the actual spectacle. Even if it had once contained a coffin for years upon years, when the coffin was gone a grave was just a hole in the ground. Miranda leaped into the pit that had held her grandfather's bones. Scratching around aimlessly and pleasurably as any young animal, she scooped up a lump of earth and weighed it in her palm. It had a pleasantly sweet, corrupt smell, being mixed with cedar needles and small leaves, and as the crumbs fell apart, she saw a silver dove no larger than a hazel nut, with spread wings and a neat fan-shaped tail. The breast had a deep round hollow in it. Turning it up to the fierce sunlight, she saw that the inside of the hollow was cut in little whorls. She scrambled out, over the pile of loose earth that had

fallen back into one end of the grave, calling to Paul that she had found something, he must guess what. . . . His head appeared smiling over the rim of another grave. He waved a closed hand at her. "I've got something too!" They ran to compare treasures, making a game of it, so many guesses each, all wrong, and a final showdown with opened palms. Paul had found a thin wide gold ring carved with intricate flowers and leaves. Miranda was smitten at sight of the ring and wished to have it. Paul seemed more impressed by the dove. They made a trade, with some little bickering. After he had got the dove in his hand, Paul said, "Don't you know what this is? This is a screw head for a *coffin!* . . . I'll bet nobody else in the world has one like this!"

[4] Miranda glanced at it without covetousness. She had the gold ring on her thumb; it fitted perfectly. "Maybe we ought to go now," she said, "maybe one of the niggers 'll see us and tell somebody." They knew the land had been sold, the cemetery was no longer theirs, and they felt like trespassers. They climbed back over the fence, slung their rifles loosely under their arms—they had been shooting at targets with various kinds of firearms since they were seven years old—and set out to look for the rabbits and doves or whatever small game might happen along. On these expeditions Miranda always followed at Paul's heels along the path, obeying instructions about handling her gun when going through fences; learning how to stand it up properly so it would not slip and fire unexpectedly; how to wait her time for a shot and not just bang away in the air without looking, spoiling shots for Paul, who really could hit things if given a chance. Now and then, in her excitement at seeing birds whizz up suddenly before her face, or a rabbit leap across her very toes, she lost her head, and almost without sighting she flung her rifle up and pulled the trigger. She hardly ever hit any sort of mark. She had no proper sense of hunting at all. Her brother would be often completely disgusted with her. "You don't care whether you get your bird or not," he said. "That's no way to hunt." Miranda could not understand his indignation. She had seen him smash his hat and yell with fury when he had missed his aim. "What I like about shooting," said Miranda, with exasperating inconsequence, "is pulling the trigger and hearing the noise."

[5] "Then, by golly," said Paul, "whyn't you go back to the range and shoot at bulls-eyes?"

[6] "I'd just as soon," said Miranda, "only like this, we walk around more."

[7] "Well, you just stay behind and stop spoiling my shots," said Paul, who, when he made a kill, wanted to be certain he had made it. Miranda, who alone brought down a bird once in twenty rounds, always claimed as her own any game they got when they fired at the same moment. It was tiresome and unfair and her brother was sick of it.

[8] "Now, the first dove we see, or the first rabbit, is mine," he told her. "And the next will be yours. Remember that and don't get smarty."

[9] "What about snakes?" asked Miranda idly. "Can I have the first snake?"

[10] Waving her thumb gently and watching her gold ring glitter, Miranda lost interest in shooting. She was wearing her summer roughing outfit: dark blue overalls, a light blue shirt, a hired-man's straw hat, and thick brown sandals. Her brother had the same outfit except his was a sober hickory-nut color. Ordinarily Miranda preferred her overalls to any other dress, though it was making rather a scandal in the countryside, for the year was 1903, and in the back country the law of female decorum had teeth in it. Her father had been criticized for letting his girls dress like boys and go careering around astride barebacked horses. Big sister Maria, the really independent and fearless one, in spite of her rather affected ways, rode at a dead run with only a rope knotted around her horse's nose. It was said the motherless family was running down, with the Grandmother no longer there to hold it together. It was known that she had discriminated against her son Harry in her will, and that he was in straits about money. Some of his old neighbors reflected with vicious satisfaction that now he would probably not be so stiffnecked, nor have any more high-stepping horses either. Miranda knew this, though she could not say how. She had met along the road old women of the kind who smoked corn-cob pipes, who had treated her grandmother with most sincere respect. They slanted their gummy old eyes side-ways at the granddaughter and said, "Ain't you ashamed of yoself, Missy? It's against the Scriptures to dress like that. Whut yo Pappy thinkin about?" Miranda, with her powerful social sense, which was like a fine set of antennae radiating from every pore of her skin, would feel ashamed because she knew well it was rude and ill-bred to shock anybody, even bad-tempered old crones, though she had faith in her father's judgment and was perfectly comfortable in the clothes. Her father had said, "They're just what you need, and they'll save your dresses for school. . . ." This sounded quite simple and natural to her. She had been brought up in rigorous economy. Wastefulness was vulgar. It was also a sin. These were truths; she had heard them repeated many times and never once disputed.

[11] Now the ring, shining with the serene purity of fine gold on her rather grubby thumb, turned her feelings against her overalls and sockless feet, toes sticking through the thick brown leather straps. She wanted to go back to the farmhouse, take a good cold bath, dust herself with plenty of Maria's violet talcum powder—provided Maria was not present to object, of course—put on the thinnest, most becoming dress she owned, with a big sash, and sit in a wicker chair under the trees. . . . These things were not all she wanted, of course; she had vague stirrings of de-

sire for luxury and a grand way of living which could not take precise form in her imagination but were founded on family legend of past wealth and leisure. These immediate comforts were what she could have, and she wanted them at once. She lagged rather far behind Paul, and once she thought of just turning back without a word and going home. She stopped, thinking that Paul would never do that to her, and so she would have to tell him. When a rabbit leaped, she let Paul have it without dispute. He killed it with one shot.

[12] When she came up with him, he was already kneeling, examining the wound, the rabbit trailing from his hands. "Right through the head," he said complacently, as if he had aimed for it. He took out his sharp, competent bowie knife and started to skin the body. He did it very cleanly and quickly. Uncle Jimbilly knew how to prepare the skins so that Miranda always had fur coats for her dolls, for though she never cared much for her dolls she liked seeing them in fur coats. The children knelt facing each other over the dead animal. Miranda watched admiringly while her brother stripped the skin away as if he were taking off a glove. The flayed flesh emerged dark scarlet, sleek, firm; Miranda with thumb and finger felt the long fine muscles with the silvery flat strips binding them to the joints. Brother lifted the oddly bloated belly. "Look," he said, in a low amazed voice. "It was going to have young ones."

[13] Very carefully he slit the thin flesh from the center ribs to the flanks, and a scarlet bag appeared. He slit again and pulled the bag open, and there lay a bundle of tiny rabbits, each wrapped in a thin scarlet veil. The brother pulled these off and there they were, dark gray, their sleek wet down lying in minute even ripples, like a baby's head just washed, their unbelievably small delicate ears folded close, their little blind faces almost featureless.

[14] Miranda said, "Oh, I want to *see*," under her breath. She looked and looked—excited but not frightened, for she was accustomed to the sight of animals killed in hunting—filled with pity and astonishment and a kind of shocked delight in the wonderful little creatures for their own sakes, they were so pretty. She touched one of them ever so carefully, "Ah, there's blood running over them," she said and began to tremble without knowing why. Yet she wanted most deeply to see and to know. Having seen, she felt at once as if she had known all along. The very memory of her former ignorance faded, she had always known just this. No one had ever told her anything outright, she had been rather unobservant of the animal life around her because she was so accustomed to animals. They seemed simply disorderly and unaccountably rude in their habits, but altogether natural and not very interesting. Her brother had spoken as if he had known about everything all along. He may have seen all this before. He had never said a word to her, but she knew now a part at least

of what he knew. She understood a little of the secret, formless intuitions in her own mind and body, which had been clearing up, taking form, so gradually and so steadily she had not realized that she was learning what she had to know. Paul said cautiously, as if he were talking about something forbidden: "They were just about ready to be born." His voice dropped on the last word. "I know," said Miranda, "like kittens. I know, like babies." She was quietly and terribly agitated, standing again with her rifle under her arm, looking down at the bloody heap. "I don't want the skin," she said, "I won't have it." Paul buried the young rabbits again in their mother's body, wrapped the skin around her, carried her to a clump of sage bushes, and hid her away. He came out again at once and said to Miranda, with an eager friendliness, a confidential tone quite unusual in him, as if he were taking her into an important secret on equal terms: "Listen now. Now you listen to me, and don't ever forget. Don't you ever tell a living soul that you saw this. Don't tell a soul. Don't tell Dad because I'll get into trouble. He'll say I'm leading you into things you ought not to do. He's always saying that. So now don't you go and forget and blab out sometime the way you're always doing. . . . Now, that's a secret. Don't you tell."

[15] Miranda never told, she did not even wish to tell anybody. She thought about the whole worrisome affair with confused unhappiness for a few days. Then it sank quietly into her mind and was heaped over by accumulated thousands of impressions, for nearly twenty years. One day she was picking her path among the puddles and crushed refuse of a market street in a strange city of a strange country, when without warning, plain and clear in its true colors as if she looked through a frame upon a scene that had not stirred nor changed since the moment it happened, the episode of that far-off day leaped from its burial place before her mind's eye. She was so reasonlessly horrified she halted suddenly staring, the scene before her eyes dimmed by the vision back of them. An Indian vendor had held up before her a tray of dyed sugar sweets, in the shapes of all kinds of small creatures: birds, baby chicks, baby rabbits, lambs, baby pigs. They were in gay colors and smelled of vanilla, maybe. . . . It was a very hot day and the smell in the market, with its piles of raw flesh and wilting flowers, was like the mingled sweetness and corruption she had smelled that other day in the empty cemetery at home: the day she had remembered always until now vaguely as the time she and her brother had found treasure in the opened graves. Instantly upon this thought the dreadful vision faded, and she saw clearly her brother, whose childhood face she had forgotten, standing again in the blazing sunshine, again twelve years old, a pleased sober smile in his eyes, turning the silver dove over and over in his hands.

QUESTIONS AND COMMENT ON FORM AND CONTENT

1. For Miss Porter the theme and the characters are most important in what she calls the "art" story. For her a complicated plot with its suspense and resolution is not necessary. Does "The Grave" illustrate this theory?

2. What is the theme? Does the title "The Grave" apply only to the actual graves in the family cemetery? Could it apply also to the incidents in paragraph 14 and in paragraph 15? Note the use of the words *buried* and *burial* in these paragraphs.

3. Miss Porter has said that now and again "thousands of memories converge, harmonize, arrange themselves around a central idea in a coherent form, and I write a story." Does this seem to describe "The Grave"? Could our minds be thought of as the "graves" of our memories?

4. After you are thoroughly acquainted with the characters of a story, Miss Porter thinks you should "tell their story with all the truth and tenderness and severity you are capable of." Which meaning of *severity* is she using? (See the various meanings in a dictionary.) Has she treated the characters also with truth and tenderness? Give examples.

5. What differences do we see in Miranda and Paul as hunters and as children already imitating adults?

6. Point out the use of description in the story. Are there any scenes that would especially impress themselves upon Miranda's memory? Why is the story from paragraph 10 to the end mainly Miranda's story?

7. Look again at the final sentence of the story, a compound-complex one. What are the two independent or main clauses? What would you call the other parts? How are they related to the main clauses? Read the sentence aloud, noting the rhythm and parallelism. Does this sentence give an effective curtain effect to the story?

8. Rewrite the following passage in fewer words, and compare your version with Miss Porter's in paragraph 3: They ran to compare treasures and they decided to make a game of it. Each was given so many guesses as to what the other had found. But all the guesses were wrong. He could not guess what she had found and she could not guess what he had found. Finally with opened palms each showed his treasure.

VOCABULARY: WHAT DO THE ITALICIZED WORDS MEAN?

. . . *oddments* of relations came over (1)
. . . said Miranda, with *exasperating inconsequence* (4)
. . . law of female *decorum* had *teeth* (10)
. . . he was in *straits* about money (10)
. . . secret, formless *intuitions* (14)

THEME SUGGESTIONS

Tell an episode from your own early experience that has come back to you recently. Try, like Miss Porter, to tell it with "truth, tenderness, and severity." Buried in My Memory

MEETING AT NIGHT

Robert Browning

Robert Browning (1812-1889), husband of Elizabeth Barrett Browning, is recognized as an eminent Victorian poet. His poems that follow illustrate how essential description is to poetry. Poetry that fails to paint a picture is usually little more than moralizing in verse or mere versifying. Prose writers can learn much about vividness, euphony, and economy of language from great poetry.

> The grey sea and the long black land;
> And the yellow half-moon large and low;
> And the startled little waves that leap
> In fiery ringlets from their sleep,
> As I gain the cove with pushing prow,
> And quench its speed i' the slushy sand.
>
> Then a mile of warm sea-scented beach;
> Three fields to cross till a farm appears;
> A tap at the pane, the quick sharp scratch
> And blue spurt of a lighted match,
> And a voice less loud, through its joys and fears,
> Than the two hearts beating each to each!

QUESTIONS AND COMMENT ON FORM AND CONTENT

1. What is the position of the observer?
2. Was Browning setting down accurately what he saw or what he seemed to see in using the words *grey, black, large* in lines 1 and 2? Explain your answer.
3. Explain the use of the words *startled* and *fiery ringlets* in lines 3 and 4.
4. Note the effect of alliteration in lines 5 and 6. Does *slushy sand* also suggest the sound of a boat coming to shore? What is such use of language called?

5. Does *sharp scratch* suggest the sound of the action?

6. Note the economy of words used to describe the meeting of husband and wife.

THEME SUGGESTIONS

Poetry and Prose

What the Prose Writer Can Learn from the Poet

Economy, Euphony, and Vividness in Poetry

A HILLSIDE THAW

Robert Frost

In the three poems that follow, Robert Frost (1874-1963) recalls and reports experiences with a conciseness, vividness, reality, and an imagination that few prose writers can achieve, but from which most prose writers can learn. As Frost says in "The Figure a Poem Makes," a poem "begins in delight [the delight of recalling an experience] and ends in wisdom," not a great piece of wisdom necessarily, but some bit of whimsical, unifying or enlightening observation, some "stay against confusion."

Notably, his experiences become our experiences, even to the exact words he uses to describe them. Thus, while he makes us more aware of the beauty or poignancy of life, he adds to our capacity to communicate to or with others.

> To think to know the country and not know
> The hillside on the day the sun lets go
> Ten million silver lizards out of snow!
> As often as I've seen it done before
> I can't pretend to tell the way it's done.
> It looks as if some magic of the sun
> Lifted the rug that bred them on the floor
> And the light breaking on them made them run.
> But if I thought to stop the wet stampede,
> And caught one silver lizard by the tail,
> And put my foot on one without avail,
> And threw myself wet-elbowed and wet-kneed

In front of twenty others' wriggling speed,—
In the confusion of them all aglitter,
And birds that joined in the excited fun
By doubling and redoubling song and twitter,
I have no doubt I'd end by holding none.

It takes the moon for this. The sun's a wizard
By all I tell; but so's the moon a witch.
From the high west she makes a gentle cast
And suddenly, without a jerk or twitch,
She has her spell on every single lizard.
I fancied when I looked at six o'clock
The swarm still ran and scuttled just as fast.
The moon was waiting for her chill effect.
I looked at nine: the swarm was turned to rock
In every lifelike posture of the swarm,
Transfixed on mountain slopes almost erect.
Across each other and side by side they lay.
The spell that so could hold them as they were
Was wrought through trees without a breath of storm
To make a leaf, if there had been one, stir.
It was the moon's: she held them until day,
One lizard at the end of every ray.
The thought of my attempting such a stay!

QUESTIONS AND COMMENT ON FORM AND CONTENT

1. How does the speaker try unsuccessfully to stop the lizards, let loose by this wizard, the sun? Does he have any helpers? What in reality are the lizards?
2. What stops the "lizards" and turns them (apparently without effort) to rock?
3. Sometimes we use the word *metaphor* for any figure of speech, but we may distinguish *metaphor* from *simile*. What is the difference? How much of this poem could be called an extended metaphor?
4. From reading this poem what could we tell about the writer of it?

THEME SUGGESTIONS

Economy of Words in Poetry
Poetry and Imagination

THE ROAD NOT TAKEN

Robert Frost

Two roads diverged in a yellow wood,
And sorry I could not travel both
And be one traveler, long I stood
And looked down one as far as I could
To where it bent in the undergrowth;

Then took the other, as just as fair,
And having perhaps the better claim,
Because it was grassy and wanted wear,
Though as for that the passing there
Had worn them really about the same,

And both that morning equally lay
In leaves no step had trodden black.
Oh, I kept the first for another day!
Yet knowing how way leads on to way,
I doubted if I should ever come back.

I shall be telling this with a sigh
Somewhere ages and ages hence:
Two roads diverged in a wood, and I—
I took the one less traveled by,
And that has made all the difference.

QUESTIONS AND COMMENT ON FORM AND CONTENT

1. As we read the title and first two stanzas of this poem, we take the choice of roads as a literal one, though the fact that the traveler is sorry he could not travel both may make us suspicious of a deeper, broader meaning. Where in the poem does our suspicion become a certainty that the road is only a symbol of the road of life?

2. The flag, the cross, the hearth, the pen, the sword, and the like may be used literally or as symbols. What is a symbol?

3. Is it important to know whether this choice for Frost meant a choice of

being a poet rather than a farmer, millworker, or teacher? Is it more pertinent that the poem has universal application to people's choices?

4. Having made a choice, should one ordinarily look back "with a sigh"?

5. For the experience that led to the poem see Lawrance Thompson's *Selected Letters of Robert Frost*, xiv-xv.

THEME SUGGESTIONS

Choices: Their Importance
I Chose ——————
No Second Choice
Simplicity in Frost's Poetry
Symbolism in Poetry: Some Examples

THE WHITE-TAILED HORNET

Robert Frost

The while-tailed hornet lives in a balloon
That floats against the ceiling of the woodshed.
The exit he comes out at like a bullet
Is like the pupil of a pointed gun.
And having power to change his aim in flight,
He comes out more unerring than a bullet.
Verse could be written on the certainty
With which he penetrates my best defense
Of whirling hands and arms about the head
To stab me in the sneeze-nerve of a nostril.
Such is the instinct of it I allow.
Yet how about the insect certainty
That in the neighborhood of home and children
Is such an execrable judge of motives
As not to recognize in me the exception
I like to think I am in everything—
One who would never hang above a bookcase
His Japanese crepe-paper globe for trophy?
He stung me first and stung me afterward.

He rolled me off the field head over heels,
And would not listen to my explanations.

That's when I went as visitor to his house.
As visitor at my house he is better.
Hawking for flies about the kitchen door,
In at one door perhaps and out another,
Trust him then not to put you in the wrong.
He won't misunderstand your freest movements.
Let him light on your skin unless you mind
So many prickly grappling feet at once.
He's after the domesticated fly
To feed his thumping grubs as big as he is.
Here he is at his best, but even here—
I watched him where he swooped, he pounced, he struck;
But what he found he had was just a nailhead.
He struck a second time. Another nailhead.
'Those are just nailheads. Those are fastened down.'
Then disconcerted and not unannoyed,
He stooped and struck a little huckleberry
The way a player curls around a football.
'Wrong shape, wrong color, and wrong scent,' I said.
The huckleberry rolled him on his head.
At last it was a fly. He shot and missed;
And the fly circled round him in derision.
But for the fly he might have made me think
He had been at his poetry, comparing
Nailhead with fly and fly with huckleberry:
How like a fly, how very like a fly.
But the real fly he missed would never do;
The missed fly made me dangerously skeptic.

Won't this whole instinct matter bear revision?
Won't almost any theory bear revision?
To err is human, not to, animal.
Or so we pay the compliment to instinct,
Only too liberal of our compliment
That really takes away instead of gives.
Our worship, humor, conscientiousness
Went long since to the dogs under the table.
And served us right for having instituted
Downward comparisons. As long on earth
As our comparisons were stoutly upward

With gods and angels, were men at least,
But little lower than the gods and angels.
But once comparisons were yielded downward,
Once we began to see our images
Reflected in the mud and even dust,
'Twas disillusion upon disillusion.
We were lost piecemeal to the animals,
Like people thrown out to delay the wolves.
Nothing but fallibility was left us,
And this day's work made even that seem doubtful.

QUESTIONS AND COMMENT ON FORM AND CONTENT

1. Select details here that make the hornet and his balloon seem like real experiences. How is this reality attained? How much is dependent upon observation and how much upon imagination?

2. Is it true only of hornets that when they visit us their behavior is different from their behavior when we visit them?

3. What is meant by saying, "But for the fly he might have made me think/ He had been at his poetry. . . ."? How important is figurative language to good poetry? When is figurative language appropriate and effective in prose?

4. What is the concluding thought about the animal's instinctive behavior? Is this thought (like the moral in some second-rate poems) dragged in or does it seem to be a thought logically suggested by the actions of the hornet? Frost has insisted that the poet himself is not fully aware of the outcome of a poem. "No surprise for the writer, no surprise for the reader."

THEME SUGGESTIONS

The Instinct of Animals
I Observe a Fly
Hosts or Visitors
Frost's Kind of Fooling

A CHILD

John Earle

John Earle (1601?-1665) was for more than twenty years associated with Oxford as student and teacher. His Microcosmography *(1628), added to over the years, had at the time of his death seventy-eight characters. The word* character *as used here refers to a type or stereotype, though some individual may unknowingly have sat for the portrait. Originally the word* character *referred to a style of writing. See the pun on this meaning in the first sentence of "A Child."*

A child is a man in a small letter, yet the best copy of Adam before he tasted of Eve or the apple; and he is happy whose small practice in the world can only write his character. He is nature's fresh picture newly drawn in oil, which time, and much handling, dims and defaces. His soul is yet a white paper unscribbled with observations of the world, wherewith, at length, it becomes a blurred notebook. He is purely happy, because he knows no evil, nor hath made means by sin to be acquainted with misery. He arrives not at the misery of being wise, nor endures evils to come, by foreseeing them. He kisses and loves all, and, when the smart of the rod is past, smiles on his beater. Nature and his parents alike dandle him, and tice[1] him on with a bait of sugar to a draught of wormwood. He plays yet, like a young 'prentice the first day, and is not come to his task of melancholy. All the language he speaks yet is tears, and they

[1] Entice.

serve him well enough to express his necessity. His hardest labour is his tongue, as if he were loth to use so deceitful an organ; and he is best company with it when he can but prattle. We laugh at his foolish sports, but his game is our earnest; and his drums, rattles, and hobby-horses, but the emblems and mocking of man's business. His father hath writ him as his own little story, wherein he reads those days that he cannot remember, and sighs to see what innocence he has out-lived. The older he grows, he is a stair lower from God; and, like his first father, much worse in his breeches. He is the Christian's example, and the old man's relapse; the one imitates his pureness, and the other falls into his simplicity. Could he put off his body with his little coat, he had got eternity without a burden, and exchanged but one heaven for another.

QUESTIONS AND COMMENT ON FORM AND CONTENT

1. To what extent is the child's mind like "a white paper unscribbled with observations of the world. . . ."? Later John Locke in his *Essay Concerning Human Understanding* (1690) made much of the child's mind as a blank piece of paper. Compare the child's mind with that of an animal.
2. What is Earle's fanciful reason for the child's difficulty with language?
3. What is the meaning of the following statements?
   a. ". . . his game is our earnest;"
   b. "He is the Christian's example, and the old man's relapse;"

VOCABULARY: WHAT DO THE ITALICIZED WORDS MEAN?

Nature and his parents alike *dandle* him
. . . *loth* to use so deceitful an organ

THEME SUGGESTIONS

A Twentieth-Century Child
A Child-Centered Home
My Earliest Recollections

A MELANCHOLY MAN

Sir Thomas Overbury

In the second edition of his poem A Wife, *Sir Thomas Overbury (1581-1613) added twenty-one* Characters, *some written by him, some, admittedly, by his friends. The melancholy, thoughtful, or philosophical man was a favorite "character." In poetry Milton's "Il Penseroso" presents such a type. Shakespeare's character Hamlet is a still more famous example.*

A melancholy man is a strayer from the drove: one that nature made sociable, because she made him man, and a crazed disposition hath altered. Impleasing to all, as all to him; straggling thoughts are his content, they make him dream waking, there's his pleasure. His imagination is never idle, it keeps his mind in a continual motion, as the poise[1] the clock: he winds up his thoughts often, and as often unwinds them; Penelope's web thrives faster. He'll seldom be found without the shade of some grove, in whose bottom a river dwells. He carries a cloud in his face, never fair weather: his outside is framed to his inside, in that he keeps a decorum, both unseemly. Speak to him; he hears with his eyes; ears follow his mind, and that's not at leisure. He thinks business, but never does any: he is all contemplation, no action. He hews and fashions his thoughts, as if he meant them to some purpose; but they prove unprofitable, as a piece of wrought timber to no use. His spirits and the sun are enemies; the sun bright and warm, his humor black and cold: variety of foolish apparitions people his head, they suffer him not to breathe, according to the necessities of nature; which makes him sup up a draught of as much air at once, as would serve at thrice. He denies nature her due in sleep, and over-pays her with watchfulness: nothing pleaseth him long, but that which pleaseth his own fantasies: they are the consuming evils, and evil consumptions that consume him alive. Lastly he is a man only in show, but comes short of the better part; a whole reasonable soul, which is a man's chief preëminence, and sole mark from creatures sensible.

QUESTIONS AND COMMENT ON FORM AND CONTENT

1. Explain "strayer from the drove." Do the words *introvert* or *dreamer* apply to this type of man?
2. What is meant by
    a. "Penelope's web thrives faster."
    b. "Speak to him; he hears with his eyes; ears follow his mind, and that's not at leisure."
    c. ". . . and sole mark from creatures sensible."

VOCABULARY: WHAT DO THE ITALICIZED WORDS MEAN?

. . . he keeps a *decorum*, both *unseemly*
. . . his *humor* black and cold
. . . variety of foolish *apparitions*

[1] One of the weights in a clock.

THEME SUGGESTIONS

Society and Solitude
A Dreamer
A Cynic
A Romantic
A Beatnik
Oral or written report: Edwin Arlington Robinson's "Miniver Cheevy"

THE CHARACTER OF WASHINGTON

Thomas Jefferson

Thomas Jefferson (1743-1826) selected for his epitaph, "Here was buried Thomas Jefferson, author of the Declaration of Independence, the statute of Virginia for religious freedom, and father of the University of Virginia." He was also Secretary of State under Washington (1789-94), Vice-President (1797-1801), and President (1801-1809). The selection below is from a letter to Dr. Walter Jones.

Monticello, January 2, 1814.

[1] I think I knew General Washington intimately and thoroughly; and were I called on to delineate his character, it should be in terms like these.

[2] His mind was great and powerful, without being of the very first order; his penetration strong, though not so acute as that of a Newton, Bacon, or Locke; and as far as he saw, no judgment was ever sounder. It was slow in operation, being little aided by invention or imagination, but sure in conclusion. Hence the common remark of his officers, of the advantage he derived from councils of war, where hearing all suggestions, he selected whatever was best; and certainly no general ever planned his battles more judiciously. But, if deranged during the course of the action, if any member of his plan was dislocated by sudden circumstances, he was slow in re-adjustment. The consequence was that he often failed in the field, and rarely against an enemy in station, as at Boston and New York. He was incapable of fear, meeting personal dangers with the calmest unconcern. Perhaps the strongest feature in his character was prudence, never acting until every circumstance, every consideration, was maturely weighed; refraining if he saw a doubt, but, when once decided, going through with his purpose, whatever obstacles opposed. His integrity was most pure, his justice the most inflexible I have ever known, no

motives of interest or consanguinity, of friendship or hatred, being able to bias his decision. He was, indeed, in every sense of the words, a wise, a good, and a great man. His temper was naturally high toned; but reflection and resolution had obtained a firm and habitual ascendency over it. If ever, however, it broke its bonds, he was most tremendous in his wrath. In his expenses he was honorable, but exact; liberal in contributions to whatever promised utility; but frowning and unyielding on all visionary projects and all unworthy projects and all unworthy calls on his charity. His heart was not warm in its affections; but he exactly calculated every man's value, and gave him a solid esteem proportioned to it. His person, you know, was fine, his stature exactly what one would wish, his deportment easy, erect and noble; the best horseman of his age, and the most graceful figure that could be seen on horseback. Although in the circle of his friends, where he might be unreserved with safety, he took a free share in conversation, his colloquial talents were not above mediocrity, possessing neither copiousness of ideas, nor fluency of words. In public, when called on for a sudden opinion, he was unready, short, and embarrassed. Yet he wrote readily, rather diffusely, in an easy and correct style. This he had acquired by conversation with the world, for his education was merely reading, writing, and common arithmetic, to which he added surveying at a later day. His time was employed in action chiefly, reading little, and that only in agriculture and English history. His correspondence became necessarily extensive, and, with journalizing his agricultural proceedings, occupied most of his leisure hours within doors. On the whole, his character was, in its mass, perfect, in nothing bad, in few points indifferent; and it may truly be said, that never did nature and fortune combine more perfectly to make a man great, and to place him in the same constellation with whatever worthies have merited from man an everlasting remembrance. For his was the singular destiny and merit of leading the armies of his country successfully through an arduous war, for the establishment of its independence; of conducting its councils through the birth of a government, new in its forms and principles, until it had settled down into a quiet and orderly train; and of scrupulously obeying the laws through the whole of his career, civil and military, of which the history of the world furnishes no other example. . . .

QUESTIONS AND COMMENT ON FORM AND CONTENT

1. Jefferson says that Washington's mind "was great and powerful, without being of the very first order." What would "very first order" mean to Jefferson?

2. Though Jefferson knew Washington well, he does not rely entirely on his personal opinion. How does he support such statements as the following? Is the support also opinion, or is it factual?

a. His mind was "slow in operation, being little aided by invention or imagination, but sure in conclusion."

b. He was fearless.

c. He was prudent.

d. "His integrity was most pure. . . ."

e. He had a high temper.

f. "His person . . . was fine."

g. ". . . his colloquial talents were not above mediocrity."

3. Jefferson's conclusion begins with the words "On the whole. . . ." What further proof does he give of these generalizations?

4. Comment on Jefferson's style as used in letter writing. Is his selection of words simple or learned? Formal or informal? Is there evidence of a classical education?

VOCABULARY: WHAT DO THE ITALICIZED WORDS MEAN?

His mind was . . . not so *acute* as that of a Newton (2)

. . . no motives of interest or *consanguinity* (2)

. . . his *colloquial* talents were not above *mediocrity* (2)

Yet he wrote readily, rather *diffusely* (2)

. . . place him in the same *constellation* (2)

THEME SUGGESTIONS

Analyze some person whom you have known quite well.

THE MAN IN THE WHITE MARBLE TOGA

Marshall Fishwick

Marshall Fishwick (1923-   ) is an American historian, author of numerous books and articles, including American Heroes: Myth and Reality. *Much of his writing has dealt with the South. The article that follows first appeared in the* Saturday Review, *February 20, 1960.*

[1] He is still first in everything. His aloof alabaster face stares at us from monuments, paintings, coins, and postage stamps. Towns named after him are everywhere. Beds he slept in are relics, stones he stepped on are sacred, battles he lost are victories. But who amongst us really loves him? George Washington is the Man in the White Marble Toga.

[2] Let the super-salesmen of the happiness cult in our times take note.

Reprinted by permission of the author and of the *Saturday Review*.

The father of our country did not have the quick smile and neat phrase which we are all urged to cultivate. He kept his distance, and few men called him George. We visit his tomb today not so much to pay our respects to a man as to visit a shrine. His body may be at Mount Vernon, but his spirit looks down from Mount Olympus.

[3] This seems all the more incredible when we piece together what is known of the living Washington. In him there burned a hell which, when freed, seared the souls of those in his path. He was the soldier who wanted news "on the spur of speed, for I am all impatience"; the man who cursed his troops when they ran "like the wild bears of the mountains." He was the young buck who once danced for three hours without a pause, and the country boy whose stories about jackasses were decidedly Rabelaisian. There was hotter blood in Washington's veins than the dames of the DAR dream of. The godlike Washington was all man.

[4] Charles Lee, who was the target for some of Washington's most magnificent profanity, was one of the few men who begrudged the Virginian's fame. "He has long been in a state of divinity," Lee wrote his sister in 1792, "but of late the legality of his apotheosis begins to be questioned." Lee was right about the apotheosis, wrong about its legality. The judgment of the people, the final court of appeal, was nearly unanimous. Washington's prestige after Cornwallis's surrender was greater than that of the United States. "Know the intimate character of Washington himself," William Carlos Williams has said, "and you will know practically all there is to understand about the beginnings of the American Republic."

[5] Even during his life people referred to him as a "demigod." In 1800 a Pennsylvania farmer wrote "Washington's Ankunft in Elisium," depicting the general strolling around heaven, chatting with Brutus, Alexander, and Columbus. When Paul Svinin visited America a few years later, he wrote in his diary: "Every American considers it his sacred duty to have a likeness of Washington in his home, just as we have the image of God's saints." All this in the so-called Age of Reason, which was dedicated to a rationalistic view of nature and humanity.

[6] The nineteenth century felt the same way—and even more intensely. "I cannot write or speak the name of Washington without a contraction and dilation of the heart, if I do it irreverently," confessed John Neal. For Catherine Maria Sedgwick the very name "conjured up a sentiment resembling the awe of the pious Israelite when he approached the ark of the Lord." The Reverend J. N. Danforth likened Washington to Jesus, and his mother to an earlier Mary. The pronoun "Him" was capitalized in accounts of Washington's life. Only the Protestant ethos saved him from canonization.

[7] The worship of Washington jumped oceans with ease. In France,

Napoleon Bonaparte ordered a week of national mourning when Washington died. Alfieri and Botta in Italy, Byron and Thackeray in England, and Kosciusko in Poland knelt at Washington's image. Translations of the "Farewell Address" girdled the world. The modest squire of Mount Vernon became world-famous, and his legend supported a structure international in design and craftsmanship.

[8] Many historic factors help explain this phenomenon. Washington was capable, aristocratic, commanding; he had the look of greatness. He lived at a time, and participated in events, which aroused the heroic. His incredible patience and tenacity personified the colonies' noble but difficult task. He refused to usurp either military or civilian power. When the times that tried men's souls were past, he returned to the land.

[9] By his own efforts, George Washington won his place as father of his country. But it was not he who added the toga. That was the work of many who admired him, but who never called him George. History, biography, oratory, journalism, poetry, art, and fiction played their part. We can be more specific. Six men—Parson Mason Weems, Jared Sparks, Gilbert Stuart, Jean Antoine Houdon, Sol Bloom, and Douglas Southall Freeman—are the chief architects of the marbleized figure who broods like a Greek god over our culture. Without their words, pigment, stone, and strategy, he would not be what he has become.

[10] Weems was the nineteenth son of a Scotch immigrant. Preacher, bookseller, fiddler, keeper of the public pulse, he emerged as the poor man's Plutarch. Best known for his life of Washington, he also did biographies of Benjamin Franklin, William Penn, and Francis Marion. Studying great men made his "bosom heave with emotions unutterable, while the tear of delicious admiration swelled in my eyes." When he got to Washington, the tears became a torrent. His temperament and experience were highly susceptible. He took naturally to praising famous men fervently in his sermons and stump speeches. While he probably had met the general and had been a collector of Washington items, this hardly justified his conferring upon himself the rectorship of Mount Vernon Parish, particularly since there was none of that name. He just was not the type of man to be bound by the tyranny of facts, even when they were covered with clerical garb.

[11] When Washington died in 1799, hundreds of sketches and sermons came from the presses. The one that most clearly set the pattern for future eulogy was Weems's "History of the Life, Death, Virtues, and Exploits of General Washington," published in 1800. It was seldom a hard book to come by. Responsive to the law of supply and demand, Weems revised and fattened his work frequently; the fifth edition, issued in 1806, consisted of 250 pages. Sales continued strong long after Weems's death. In 1921 the seventy-ninth successful edition appeared.

[12] Anticipating Horatio Alger, Weems made the Washington saga a formalized success story. "Here was a proper rise for you," he gloated when Washington snared the rich widow Custis. In the fifth edition he introduced the cherry tree story (the most persistent single legend in American history), the cabbage story, and the wild colt story. Even if many of his tales were concocted, one feels that scientific historians have been unduly severe to this mixer of mythology, musketballs, and the backwoods. Shame on Allan Nevins for saying, as he does in the *Encyclopedia of Social Science*, that Weems "long exercised a deplorable influence upon popular history."

[13] Weems worked in the super-historical realm. There were and are two Washingtons. Weems concerned himself with the invented one. Of course his Washington was very different from the one born and reared in Virginia; he was bound to be. Americans of yesteryear who read Weems weren't concerned with the accuracy of the portrait. They read with their hearts. Many cried when they came to the account of Washington's death:

> Swift on angel's wings the brightening Saint ascended; while voices more than human were warbling through the happy region and hymning the great procession towards the gates of heaven. His glorious coming was seen from afar off; and myriads of mighty angels hastened forth with golden harps, to welcome the honoured stranger.

Let those who question such zeal bow their heads in silence.

[14] No attempt at subtlety lurks in Weems's words. His essential achievement can be stated in three words. He got across. He made intelligible the type of hero young America craved, and he had a virtue thoroughgoing historians lacked: he was readable. Common men appreciated this so much that when Weems died they made up legends about him, just as he had done about Washington. Tall tales concerning his life are still making the rounds in the South.

[15] The work of Jared Sparks raises fundamental questions. How much should historic truth be doctored to encourage heroic legend? Where does obligation to truth stop and poetic license begin? Should we attribute to great men what they actually said or did, or what they should have said and done? How deep should the editor's pencil dig? Jared Sparks is the Pontius Pilate of American historians.

[16] Raised on a small Connecticut farm, Sparks (1789-1866) soon displayed a brilliance that eventually made him president of Harvard and a Washington scholar almost literally beyond compare. He read Virgil at the rate of a hundred lines a day after less than eight weeks' schooling. When Harvard's President Kirkland reviewed Sparks's college record he

concluded, "Sparks is not only a man, but a man and a half." After a try at the ministry, Jared worked on the *North American Review*. There he developed a concern for history and documents that affected the rest of his life. He became our first highly efficient collector and editor of documents. The face of Washington he moulded into a death mask of perfection.

[17] With his assistant, Samuel Eliot, Sparks made many changes and deletions in the Washington manuscripts. "Old Put" became General Putnam, and naughty phrases disappeared. The Washington who finally emerged had no vices and no temper; he belonged to the ages.

[18] The French sculptor Jean Antoine Houdon was shrewd enough to realize that this was the Washington he must put into stone. So we have him, with a column of thirteen rods under his left hand, and the moldboard of a plow under the column. Here is the Cincinnatus of the West. This Washington you will meet not only in Virginia's state Capitol, where the original stands, but also in London's Trafalgar Square, Chicago's Art Institute, and Tokyo's Embassy Gardens, where there are copies. The image has world dimensions.

[19] As for the face itself, the one we know is Gilbert Stuart's. His Lansdown and Athenaeum portraits stare out at us from books, stamps, tablets, advertisements, and dollar bills. During the 1932 Washington Bicentennial, poster-sized reproductions of Stuart's portrait were sent to every American schoolroom. The Washington most of us know is this one.

[20] And the reason we know it so well is that the late Sol Bloom, the energetic and indefatigable New York Congressman, made it his life work. Retiring as a millionaire to public service in 1923, he represented the Riverside Drive district of Manhattan until his death in 1949.

[21] Sol Bloom's bizarre bills and his fist fights in Congress were nothing compared to his hero-making. In 1930 he became associate director of the George Washington Bicentennial Commission. His coequal on the Commission, U. S. Grant III, grandson of the general who made a name for himself by sticking it out on a battle line all winter, did not persist as his namesake had. He left Bloom in sole control. The new commander not only filled the breach; he spilled all over the wall. Before Congress knew what had happened, he organized a nine-month celebration, nailed down an appropriation of $338,000, and hired a staff of 125. During the legislative recess he devoted, in one way or another, fifteen hours a day to Washington. Millions of printed pieces jammed the nation's letter boxes. Tons of Washington badges, buttons, and busts went on sale. Sol even took over, with Washington's help, Mother's day, Memorial Day, Independence Day, and Goethe's birthday. Finally he set up his own radio station, with an antenna on top of the Washington Monument. Never has one man said so much about Washington to so many. As Will Rogers

wrote in a letter to Bloom, "You are the only guy who ever made a party run nine months, and you did it in dry times, too. You made the whole country Washington conscious."

[22] A newspaper cartoon pictured Sol in a Continental uniform, with the caption, "First in War, First in Peace, First in Bicentennial Publicity." One columnist thought Bloom was getting to look more and more like Washington. A Republican Senator replied there was little cause for alarm just as long as Washington didn't start to look like Sol Bloom.

[23] To no one's surprise, Bloom's offer of $500 for any Washington-publicizing idea that had escaped him went unclaimed. Bloom knew why. "I have taught more real American history in the last twenty years to more students than anyone in the United States," he claimed. Even those who would quibble with the Congressman's definition of "real American history" must concede that no one else has ever done more for Washington. Weems, Sparks, Stuart, and Houdon will have to move over and make room for Sol Bloom.

[24] In our own day, Douglas Southall Freeman has turned the quintet into a sextet. This Virginia gentleman, long-time editor of the Richmond *News Leader,* has published the nearest approximation to a "definitive" life of Washington, the last volume of which has just been released posthumously. It is too early to evaluate Freeman's contribution, but it is certain that this Virginia gentleman—writing about Virginia's best-known gentleman—has done a sympathetic, detailed, and heroic biography. Despite all the scholarly trimming and unusual documentation (Freeman has said that his model is Boswell's "Life of Johnson"), this is the old drum-and-trumpet history in modern dress; and it comes off very well. Washington is as untarnished as ever.

[25] Washington's reputation has of course declined in some periods. When the Jeffersonians were forming the party that swamped the Federalists, the President was one of their primary targets. Freneau, Bache, Madison, and many others attacked him; the Jay Treaty of 1795 brought strong protests. Another low point occurred after the Civil War. Lincoln emerged after his martyrdom as the national symbol of unity and greatness. The South found a new idol in the defeated yet untarnished Lee. Washington was temporarily discarded. The most serious attack came in the 1920's. William E. Woodward's "George Washington: The Image and the Man" (1926) was the debunker's major sally, portraying a vain, ordinary, and undemocratic man, "almost as impersonal at the top of the government as a statue on top of a monument would have been."

[26] Strange that Woodward, aware of this haughty impersonality, should launch a pea-shooter attack against a marble man.

[27] His ammunition did not penetrate. Coolidge, whose monosyllabic, granite-block answers made him something of a folk hero in his own

right, disposed of the debunkers in a few words. When asked if they could destroy George Washington, he looked out of the White House window. "Washington's monument is still here," he said.

[28] Washington's aloofness preserves his reputation, but it also minimizes his warm-blooded, human side. There was fire and venom and drama enough in the real Washington. Think of Washington at Newburgh in 1783 when confronted by the impetuous document of his officers who felt mistreated by the Continental Congress. "Gentlemen, you will permit me to put on my spectacles, for I have not only grown gray, but almost blind in the service of my country," he said. Not a man felt, after that simple statement, that he should complain.

[29] Recall the directions Washington's step-grandson gave a visitor at Mount Vernon. "You will meet with an old gentleman riding alone, in plain, drab clothes, a broad-brimmed white hat, a hickory switch in his hand, and carrying an umbrella with a long staff, which is attached to his saddle bow. That is General Washington."

[30] Legends are the slowly perfected fruit from a shoot of imagination grafted onto a tree of fact, a blur and blend of what was and what should have been. Some of those about Washington can be attributed to specific sources. We know that Parson Weems invented the cherry tree story and the tale about a Quaker named Potts finding Washington praying fervently in the snow-covered woods near Valley Forge. But historical research (which proved that Weems first used the Valley Forge prayer story in the *Federalist* for March 12, 1804) cannot kill the image. The praying Washington remains fixed in the stone of the New York Sub-Treasury Building and indelible on millions of stamps. All the scholars put together cannot erase the prayer legend.

[31] To no single source can be attributed the notions that Washington, like Saul of old, stood head and shoulders above most of his countrymen (actually he was shorter than Thomas Jefferson, whom we seldom think of as tall); that he was a man apart, with no real friends, and too heavy a burden to smile; that he concealed a deep, unrequited passion for a haughty colonial beauty; that he carved his initials on Natural Bridge and a score of other landmarks; or that he slept in almost every house of colonial America.

[32] More elaborate are stories of Washington's miraculous escapes from danger. One has an Indian chief turning to his men during the Braddock rout and saying, "Mark yon tall and daring warrior? He is not of the red coat tribe. He hath an Indian's wisdom and his warriors fight as we do—himself alone is exposed. Quick, let your aim be certain, and he will die!" But no Indian bullet can find him. "It is in vain," concludes the chief. "The Great Spirit protects that man and guides his life." What miracle story of medieval times could be more marvelous?

[33] Some legends flatly insist that Washington was protected by the gods. His mother is said to have had a prophetic dream in which young George saved the house (symbolically the Republic) from destruction by flames. Like other favorites of the gods, Washington allegedly had a sword with special properties. Samuel Woodworth asserted in "The Champion of Freedom" (1816) that this blade would bring forth a message from beyond the grave, that in times of crises it would "flash and brandish itself, arousing the living characters to action." Just as King Arthur is supposed to turn up to announce the millennium, just as Charlemagne is scheduled to reappear when his great white beard thrice encircles the stone table before him in Untersburg, so Washington is expected to make a return engagement in order to fulfill legendary requirements.

[34] In all these tales Washington epitomizes the traits of which young America was fondest: virtue, idealism, and piety. His flaws seem pale when held up against this central proposition; he was willing to stake his life and fortune on his high principles, to take up without question a task others could not perform. This is the basis of his real fame and "second fictional life." The South was particularly proud of this antebellum planter class. "How much more delightful to an undebauched mind," Washington wrote to Arthur Young in 1788, "is the task of making improvements on the earth than all the vain glories which can be acquired from ravaging it." Even the Republicans, out of sympathy with Federalist policies, were in accord with Washington's agrarian sympathies. Jefferson opposed him, but never stopped respecting him. "Washington was indeed, in every way," he wrote in 1814, "a wise, a good, and a great man."

[35] The blue cloth fades, and the white marble remains. In one of his more puckish moments, Nathaniel Hawthorne asked if anyone had ever seen Washington nude. "It is inconceivable," Hawthorne concluded. "He had no nakedness, but was born with his clothes on, and his hair powdered, and made a stately bow on his first appearance in the world."

[36] Men in gray flannel suits may learn a lot from the story of the man in the white marble toga. It is not by bending to every whim and request that we achieve real popularity, or by following every popular cause that we become great. There are times to smile, and times to scowl; to confuse the occasions is an act of cowardice. Washington lacked many of the attributes of some heads of chambers of commerce and multi-echelon organizations. The one thing he never lacked, even when he was in error or defeat, was *integrity*. To have men like Weems, Sparks, Stuart, Houdon, Bloom, and Freeman behind him was a tre-

mendous help. But Washington never looked back to see just who was behind him, or which way opportunism pointed. That is why he became father of his country.

[37] That same country, and the men who guide its destiny today, might well ponder his story.

QUESTIONS AND COMMENT ON FORM AND CONTENT

1. What do *white, marble,* and *toga* suggest to us about Washington? The title is derived from the novel, *The Man in the Gray Flannel Suit,* referred to in paragraph 36. Does this suggest a stereotype—a formalized figure? Comment on the rhythmical style of the first paragraph. How is this effect produced? Explain "His body may be at Mount Vernon but his spirit looks down from Mount Olympus."

2. The introductory part of the essay deals with Washington's reputation. Where does the explanation of this reputation begin? What are the causes of the hero worship?

3. How does the author establish the point that Parson Weems is not to be trusted for facts? Why was Weems's book so popular? What literary devices does Weems use to get the oratorical effect of the part quoted in paragraph 13?

4. What are the topic sentences of paragraphs 3, 5, 6, and 7? How, in general, are they developed?

5. What is the source of the following figure of speech? Does it seem appropriate or inappropriate? "The new commander [Bloom] not only filled the breach; he spilled all over the wall." (paragraph 21)

6. How are legends defined in paragraph 30? Does the metaphor make the definition clear?

7. Does Mr. Fishwick feel that he has succeeded in demolishing the man in the white marble toga and in setting up the man in the blue faded cloth? What does blue faded cloth represent?

8. The author ends as he began in paragraph 2 with a kind of moral. What is it? Was it desirable to include this moral? How does the author introduce and justify its inclusion?

VOCABULARY: WHAT DO THE ITALICIZED WORDS MEAN?

. . . boy whose stories about jackasses were *Rabelaisian* (3)
. . . legality of his *apotheosis* (4)
. . . only the Protestant *ethos* saved him from *canonization* (6)
. . . approximation to a *definitive* life of Washington (24)
Washington *epitomizes* the traits of . . . young America (34)
The one thing he never lacked . . . was *integrity.* (36)

THEME SUGGESTIONS

"How much should historic truth be doctored to encourage heroic legend?" (See paragraph 15) If you plan to be a teacher (elementary, secondary, or college), what should you say about Washington, Lord Byron, Walt Whitman, Richard Wagner and the like? "How deep should the editor's pencil dig?" Does something depend on the age and experience of the reader?

The Responsibility of the Historian (Teacher, Editor, etc.)
Legends: Davy Crockett (the American Cowboy, the American Indian, etc.)
Why Legends Are Popular

MY LAST DUCHESS

Robert Browning

Robert Browning (1812-1889) is noted for his dramatic monologues.

That's my last Duchess painted on the wall,
Looking as if she were alive. I call
That piece a wonder, now: Frà Pandolf's[1] hands
Worked busily a day, and there she stands.
Will't please you sit and look at her? I said
"Frà Pandolf" by design, for never read
Strangers like you that pictured countenance,
The depth and passion of its earnest glance,
But to myself they turned (since none puts by
The curtain I have drawn for you, but I)
And seemed as they would ask me, if they durst,
How such a glance came there; so, not the first
Are you to turn and ask thus. Sir, 'twas not
Her husband's presence only, called that spot
Of joy into the Duchess' cheek; perhaps
Frà Pandolf chanced to say, "Her mantle laps
Over my lady's wrist too much," or "Paint
Must never hope to reproduce the faint
Half-flush that dies along her throat." Such stuff
Was courtesy, she thought, and cause enough
For calling up that spot of joy. She had
A heart—how shall I say?—too soon made glad,
Too easily impressed; she liked whate'er
She looked on, and her looks went everywhere.

[1] An imaginary painter, a monk.

Sir, 'twas all one! My favour at her breast,
The dropping of the daylight in the West,
The bough of cherries some officious fool
Broke in the orchard for her, the white mule
She rode with round the terrace—all and each
Would draw from her alike the approving speech,
Or blush, at least. She thanked men,—good! but thanked
Somehow—I know not how—as if she ranked
My gift of a nine-hundred-years-old name
With anybody's gift. Who'd stoop to blame
This sort of trifling? Even had you skill
In speech—(which I have not)—to make your will
Quite clear to such an one, and say, "Just this
Or that in you disgusts me; here you miss,
Or there you exceed the mark"—and if she let
Herself be lessoned so, nor plainly set
Her wits to yours, forsooth, and made excuse
—E'en then would be some stooping; and I choose
Never to stoop. Oh, sir, she smiled, no doubt,
Whene'er I passed her; but who passed without
Much the same smile? This grew; I gave commands;
Then all smiles stopped together. There she stands
As if alive. Will't please you rise? We'll meet
The company below, then. I repeat,
The Count your master's known munificence
Is ample warrant that no just pretence
Of mine for dowry will be disallowed;
Though his fair daughter's self, as I avowed
As starting, is my object. Nay, we'll go
Together down, sir. Notice Neptune, though,
Taming a sea-horse, thought a rarity,
Which Claus of Innsbruck cast in bronze for me!

QUESTIONS AND COMMENT ON FORM AND CONTENT

1. In this monologue, who is talking to whom? In addition to talking about "my last duchess" what other important business does the speaker discuss?

2. What is the action or movement of the characters in the poem?

3. When a person talks about others, he reveals much of his own character. How does each item and the action of the poem contribute to the complete picture of duke and duchess?

4. What adjectives can be used to describe the duke? the duchess?

5. What is the meaning of the following?
    a. "Then all smiles stopped together."
    b. "Nay, we'll go together down, sir."

VOCABULARY: WHAT DO THE ITALICIZED WORDS MEAN?

. . . your master's known *munificence*
Is *ample warrant* that no just *pretence*
Of mine for *dowry* will be *disallowed.*

THEME SUGGESTIONS

Write a monologue in which a person reveals unknowingly most of his weaknesses. He or she could be speaking disparagingly about someone who is morally and intellectually superior, or a child could be telling how old-fashioned and stupid his parents are.

WHY I LIVE AT THE P.O.

Eudora Welty

Eudora Welty (1909-   ) was born in Jackson, Mississippi, and although she has lived in other sections of the country, she writes mostly about the Mississippi farmlands, forests, and small towns. She has received various prizes for her short stories. Her collections of short stories include A Curtain of Green *(1941),* The Wide Net *(1943),* Delta Wedding *(1946), and* The Golden Apples *(1949).*

I was getting along fine with Mama, Papa-Daddy and Uncle Rondo until my sister Stella-Rondo just separated from her husband and came back home again. Mr. Whitaker! Of course I went with Mr. Whitaker first, when he first appeared here in China Grove, taking "Pose Yourself" photos, and Stella-Rondo broke us up. Told him I was one-sided. Bigger on one side than the other, which is a deliberate, calculated falsehood: I'm the same. Stella-Rondo is exactly twelve months to the day younger than I am and for that reason she's spoiled.

She's always had anything in the world she wanted and then she'd throw it away. Papa-Daddy gave her this gorgeous Add-a-Pearl necklace when she was eight years old and she threw it away playing baseball when she was nine, with only two pearls.

So as soon as she got married and moved away from home the first thing she did was separate! From Mr. Whitaker! This photographer with the popeyes she said she trusted. Came home from one of those towns up in Illinois and to our complete surprise brought this child of two.

Mama said she like to made her drop dead for a second. "Here you had this marvelous blonde child and never so much as wrote your mother a word about it," says Mama. "I'm thoroughly ashamed of you." But of course she wasn't.

Stella-Rondo just calmly takes off this *hat,* I wish you could see it. She says, "Why, Mama, Shirley-T's adopted, I can prove it."

"How?" says Mama, but all I says was, "H'm!" There I was over the hot stove, trying to stretch two chickens over five people and a completely unexpected child into the bargain, without one moment's notice.

"What do you mean—'H'm!'?" says Stella-Rondo, and Mama says, "I heard that, Sister."

I said that oh, I didn't mean a thing, only that whoever Shirley-T. was, she was the spit-image of Papa-Daddy if he'd cut off his beard, which of course he'd never do in the world. Papa-Daddy's Mama's papa and sulks.

Stella-Rondo got furious! She said, "Sister, I don't need to tell you you got a lot of nerve and always did have and I'll thank you to make no future reference to my adopted child whatsoever."

"Very well," I said. "Very well, very well. Of course I noticed at once she looks like Mr. Whitaker's side too. That frown. She looks like a cross between Mr. Whitaker and Papa-Daddy."

"Well, all I can say is she isn't."

"She looks exactly like Shirley Temple to me," says Mama, but Shirley-T. just ran away from her.

So the first thing Stella-Rondo did at the table was turn Papa-Daddy against me.

"Papa-Daddy," she says. He was trying to cut up his meat. "Papa-Daddy!" I was taken completely by surprise. Papa-Daddy is about a million years old and's got this long-long beard. "Papa-Daddy, Sister says she fails to understand why you don't cut off your beard."

So Papa-Daddy l-a-y-s down his knife and fork! He's real rich. Mama says he is, he says he isn't. So he says, "Have I heard correctly? You don't understand why I don't cut off my beard?"

"Why," I says, "Papa-Daddy, of course I understand, I did not say any such of a thing, the idea!"

He says, "Hussy!"

I says, "Papa-Daddy, you know I wouldn't any more want you to cut off your beard than the man in the moon. It was the farthest thing from my mind! Stella-Rondo sat there and made that up while she was eating breast of chicken."

But he says, "So the postmistress fails to understand why I don't cut off my beard. Which job I got you through my influence with the government. 'Bird's nest'—is that what you call it?"

Not that it isn't the next to smallest P.O. in the entire state of Mississippi.

I says, "Oh, Papa-Daddy," I says, "I didn't say any such of a thing, I never dreamed it was a bird's nest, I have always been grateful though this is the next to smallest P.O. in the state of Mississippi, and I do not enjoy being referred to as a hussy by my own grandfather."

But Stella-Rondo says, "Yes, you did say it too. Anybody in the world could of heard you, that had ears."

"Stop right there," says Mama, looking at *me*.

So I pulled my napkin straight back through the napkin ring and left the table.

As soon as I was out of the room Mama says, "Call her back, or she'll starve to death," but Papa-Daddy says, "This is the beard I started growing on the Coast when I was fifteen years old." He would of gone on till nightfall if Shirley-T. hadn't lost the Milky Way she ate in Cairo.

So Papa-Daddy says, "I am going out and lie in the hammock, and you can all sit here and remember my words: I'll never cut off my beard as long as I live, even one inch, and I don't appreciate it in you at all." Passed right by me in the hall and went straight out and got in the hammock.

It would be a holiday. It wasn't five minutes before Uncle Rondo suddenly appeared in the hall in one of Stella-Rondo's flesh-colored kimonos, all cut on the bias, like something Mr. Whitaker probably thought was gorgeous.

"Uncle Rondo!" I says. "I didn't know who that was! Where are you going?"

"Sister," he says, "get out of my way, I'm poisoned."

"If you're poisoned stay away from Papa-Daddy," I says. "Keep out of the hammock. Papa-Daddy will certainly beat you on the head if you come within forty miles of him. He thinks I deliberately said he ought to cut off his beard after he got me the P.O., and I've told him and told him and told him, and he acts like he just don't hear me. Papa-Daddy must of gone stone deaf."

"He picked a fine day to do it then," says Uncle Rondo, and before you could say "Jack Robinson" flew out in the yard.

What he'd really done, he'd drunk another bottle of that prescription. He does it every single Fourth of July as sure as shooting, and it's horribly expensive. Then he falls over in the hammock and snores. So he insisted on zigzagging right on out to the hammock, looking like a half-wit.

Papa-Daddy woke up with this horrible yell and right there without moving an inch he tried to turn Uncle Rondo against me. I heard every word he said. Oh, he told Uncle Rondo I didn't learn to read till I was eight years old and he didn't see how in the world I ever got the mail put up at the P.O., much less read it all, and he said if Uncle Rondo could only fathom the lengths he had bone to get me that job! And he said on the other hand he thought Stella-Rondo had a brilliant mind and deserved credit for getting out of town. All the time he was just lying there swinging as pretty as you please and looping out his beard, and poor Uncle Rondo was *pleading* with him to slow down the hammock, it was making him as dizzy as a witch to watch it. But that's what Papa-Daddy likes about a hammock. So Uncle Rondo was too dizzy to get turned against me for the time being. He's Mama's only brother and is a good case of a one-track mind. Ask anybody. A certified pharmacist.

Just then I heard Stella-Rondo raising the upstairs window. While she was married she got this peculiar idea that it's cooler with the windows shut and locked. So she has to raise the window before she can make a soul hear her outdoors.

So she raises the window and says, "*Oh!*" You would have thought she was mortally wounded.

Uncle Rondo and Papa-Daddy didn't even look up, but kept right on with what they were doing. I had to laugh.

I flew up the stairs and threw the door open! I says, "What in the wide world's the matter, Stella-Rondo? You mortally wounded?"

"No," she says, "I am not mortally wounded but I wish you would do me the favor of looking out that window there and telling me what you see."

So I shade my eyes and look out the window.

"I see the front yard," I says.

"Don't you see any human beings?" she says.

"I see Uncle Rondo trying to run Papa-Daddy out of the hammock," I says. "Nothing more. Naturally, it's so suffocating-hot in the house, with all the windows shut and locked, everybody who cares to stay in their right mind will have to go out and get in the hammock before the Fourth of July is over."

"Don't you notice anything different about Uncle Rondo?" asks Stella-Rondo.

"Why, no, except he's got on some terrible-looking flesh-colored contraption I wouldn't be found dead in, is all I can see," I says.

"Never mind, you won't be found dead in it, because it happens to be part of my trousseau, and Mr. Whitaker took several dozen photographs of me in it," says Stella-Rondo. "What on earth could Uncle Rondo *mean* by wearing part of my trousseau out in the broad open daylight without saying so much as 'Kiss my foot,' *knowing* I only got home this morning after my separation and hung my negligee up on the bathroom door, just as nervous as I could be?"

"I'm sure I don't know, and what do you expect me to do about it?" I says. "Jump out the window?"

"No, I expect nothing of the kind. I simply declare that Uncle Rondo looks like a fool in it, that's all," she says. "It makes me sick to my stomach."

"Well, he looks as good as he can," I says. "As good as anybody in reason could." I stood up for Uncle Rondo, please remember. And I said to Stella-Rondo, "I think I would do well not to criticize so freely if I were you and came home with a two-year-old child I had never said a word about, and no explanation whatever about my separation."

"I asked you the instant I entered this house not to refer one more time to my adopted child, and you gave me your word of honor you would not," was all Stella-Rondo would say, and started pulling out every one of her eyebrows with some cheap Kress tweezers.

So I merely slammed the door behind me and went down and made some green-tomato pickle. Somebody had to do it. Of course Mama had turned both the niggers loose; she always said no earthly power could hold one anyway on the Fourth of July, so she wouldn't even try. It turned out that Jaypan fell in the lake and came within a very narrow limit of drowning.

So Mama trots in. Lifts up the lid and says, "H'm! Not very good for your Uncle Rondo in his precarious condition, I must say. Or poor little adopted Shirley-T. Shame on you!"

That made me tired. I says, "Well, Stella-Rondo had better thank her lucky stars it was her instead of me came trotting in with that very peculiar-looking child. Now if it had been me that trotted in from Illinois and brought a peculiar-looking child of two, I shudder to think of the reception I'd of got, much less controlled the diet of an entire family."

"But you must remember, Sister, that you were never married to Mr. Whitaker in the first place and didn't go up to Illinois to live," says Mama, shaking a spoon in my face. "If you had I would of been just as overjoyed to see you and your little adopted girl as I was to see Stella-Rondo, when you wound up with your separation and came on back home."

"You would not," I says.

"Don't contradict me, I would," says Mama.

But I said she couldn't convince me though she talked till she was blue in the face. Then I said, "Besides, you know as well as I do that that child is not adopted."

"She most certainly is adopted," says Mama, stiff as a poker.

I says, "Why, Mama, Stella-Rondo had her just as sure as anything in this world, and just too stuck up to admit it."

"Why, Sister," said Mama. "Here I thought we were going to have a pleasant Fourth of July, and you start right out not believing a word your own baby sister tells you!"

"Just like Cousin Annie Flo. Went to her grave denying the facts of life," I remind Mama.

"I told you if you ever mentioned Annie Flo's name I'd slap your face," says Mama, and slaps my face.

"All right, you wait and see," I says.

"I," says Mama, "I prefer to take my children's word for anything when it's humanly possible." You ought to see Mama, she weighs two hundred pounds and has real tiny feet.

Just then something perfectly horrible occurred to me.

"Mama," I says, "can that child talk?" I simply had to whisper! "Mama, I wonder if that child can be—you know—in any way? Do you realize," I says, "that she hasn't spoken one single, solitary word to a human being up to this minute? This is the way she looks," I says, and I looked looked like this.

Well, Mama and I just stood there and stared at each other. It was horrible!

"I remember well that Joe Whitaker frequently drank like a fish," says Mama. "I believed to my soul he drank *chemicals.*" And without another word she marches to the foot of the stairs and calls Stella-Rondo.

"Stella-Rondo? O-o-o-o-o! Stella-Rondo!"

"What?" says Stella-Rondo from upstairs. Not even the grace to get up off the bed.

"Can that child of yours talk?" asks Mama.

Stella-Rondo says, "Can she what?"

"Talk! Talk!" says Mama. "Burdyburdyburdyburdy!"

So Stella-Rondo yells back, "Who says she can't talk?"

"Sister says so," says Mama.

"You didn't have to tell me, I know whose word of honor don't mean a thing in his house," says Stella-Rondo.

And in a minute the loudest Yankee voice I ever heard in my life yells out, "OE'm Pop-OE the Sailor-r-r-r Ma-a-an!" and then somebody jumps up and down in the upstairs hall. In another second the house would of fallen down.

"Not only talks, she can tap-dance!" calls Stella-Rondo. "Which is more than some people I won't name can do."

"Why, the little precious darling thing!" Mama says, so surprised. "Just as smart as she can be!" Starts talking baby talk right there. Then she turns on me. "Sister, you ought to be thoroughly ashamed! Run up-stairs this instant and apologize to Stella-Rondo and Shirley-T."

"Apologize for what?" I says. "I merely wondered if the child was nor-mal, that's all. Now that she's proved she is, why, I have nothing further to say."

But Mama just turned on her heel and flew out, furious. She ran right upstairs and hugged the baby. She believed it was adopted. Stella-Rondo hadn't done a thing but turn her against me from upstairs while I stood there helpless over the hot stove. So that made Mama, Papa-Daddy and the baby all on Stella-Rondo's side.

Next, Uncle Rondo.

I must say that Uncle Rondo has been marvelous to me at various times in the past and I was completely unprepared to be made to jump out of my skin, the way it turned out. Once Stella-Rondo did something perfectly horrible to him—broke a chain letter from Flanders Field—and he took the radio back he had given her and gave it to me. Stella-Rondo was furious! For six months we all had to call her Stella instead of Stella-Rondo, or she wouldn't answer. I always thought Uncle Rondo had all the brains of the entire family. Another time he sent me to Mam-moth Cave, with all expenses paid.

But this would be the day he was drinking that prescription, the Fourth of July.

So at supper Stella-Rondo speaks up and says she thinks Uncle Rondo ought to try to eat a little something. So finally Uncle Rondo said he would try a little cold biscuits and ketchup, but that was all. So *she* brought it to him.

"Do you think it wise to disport with ketchup in Stella-Rondo's flesh-colored kimono?" I says. Trying to be considerate! If Stella-Rondo couldn't watch out for her trousseau, somebody had to.

"Any objections?" asks Uncle Rondo, just about to pour out all the ketchup.

"Don't mind what she says, Uncle Rondo," says Stella-Rondo. "Sister has been devoting this solid afternoon to sneering out my bedroom win-dow at the way you look."

"What's that?" says Uncle Rondo. Uncle Rondo has got the most ter-rible temper in the world. Anything is liable to make him tear the house down if it comes at the wrong time.

So Stella-Rondo says, "Sister says, 'Uncle Rondo certainly does look like a fool in that pink kimono!'"

Do your remember who it was really said that?

Uncle Rondo spills out all the ketchup and jumps out of his chair and tears off the kimono and throws it down on the dirty floor and puts his foot on it. It had to be sent all the way to Jackson to the cleaners and re-pleated.

"So that's your opinion of your Uncle Rondo, is it?" he says. "I look like a fool, do I? Well, that's the last straw. A whole day in this house with nothing to do, and then to hear you come out with a remark like that behind my back!"

"I didn't say any such of a thing, Uncle Rondo," I says, "and I'm not saying who did, either. Why, I think you look all right. Just try to take care of yourself and not talk and eat at the same time," I says. "I think you better go lie down."

"Lie down my foot," says Uncle Rondo. I ought to of known by that he was fixing to do something perfectly horrible.

So he didn't do anything that night in the precarious state he was in —just played Casino with Mama and Stella-Rondo and Shirley-T. and gave Shirley-T. a nickel with a head on both sides. It tickled her nearly to death, and she called him "Papa." But at 6:30 A.M. the next morning, he threw a whole five-cent package of some unsold one-inch firecrackers from the store as hard as he could into my bedroom and they every one went off. Not one bad one in the string. Anybody else, there'd be one that wouldn't go off.

Well, I'm just terribly susceptible to noise of any kind, the doctor has always told me I was the most sensitive person he had ever seen in his whole life, and I was simply prostrated. I couldn't eat! People tell me they heard it as far as the cemetery, and old Aunt Jep Patterson, that had been holding her own so good, thought it was Judgment Day and she was going to meet her whole family. It's usually so quiet here.

And I'll tell you it didn't take me any longer than a minute to make up my mind what to do. There I was with the whole entire house on Stella-Rondo's side and turned against me. If I have anything at all I have pride.

So I just decided I'd go straight down to the P.O. There's plenty of room there in the back, I says to myself.

Well! I made no bones about letting the family catch on to what I was up to. I didn't try to conceal it.

The first thing they knew, I marched in where they were all playing Old Maid and pulled the electric oscillating fan out by the plug, and everything got real hot. Next I snatched the pillow I'd done the needle-point on right off the davenport from behind Papa-Daddy. He went "Ugh!" I beat Stella-Rondo up the stairs and finally found my charm bracelet in her bureau drawer under a picture of Nelson Eddy.

"So that's the way the land lies," says Uncle Rondo. There he was, piecing on the ham. "Well, Sister, I'll be glad to donate my army cot if you got any place to set it up, providing you'll leave right this minute and let me get some peace." Uncle Rondo was in France.

"Thank you kindly for the cot and 'peace' is hardly the word I would select if I had to resort to firecrackers at 6:30 A.M. in a young girl's bedroom," I says back to him. "And as to where I intend to go, you seem to forget my position as postmistress of China Grove, Mississippi," I says. "I've always got the P.O."

Well, that made them all sit up and take notice.

I went out front and started digging up some four-o'clocks to plant around the P.O.

"Ah-ah-ah!" says Mama, raising the window. "Those happen to be my four-o'clocks. Everything planted in that star is mine. I've never known you to make anything grow in your life."

"Very well," I says. "But I take the fern. Even you, Mama, can't stand there and deny that I'm the one watered that fern. And I happen to know where I can send in a box top and get a packet of one thousand mixed seeds, no two the same kind free."

"Oh, where?" Mama wants to know.

But I says, "Too late. You 'tend to your house, and I'll 'tend to mine. You hear things like that all the time if you know to listen to the radio. Perfectly marvelous offers. Get anything you want free."

So I hope to tell you I marched in and got that radio, and they could of all bit a nail in two, especially Stella-Rondo, that it used to belong to, and she well knew she couldn't get it back, I'd sue for it like a shot. And I very politely took the sewing-machine motor I helped pay the most on to give Mama for Christmas back in 1929, and a good big calendar, with the first aid remedies on it. The thermometer and the Hawaiian ukulele certainly were rightfully mine, and I stood on the stepladder and got all my watermelon-rind preserves and every fruit and vegetable I'd put up, every jar. Then I began to pull the tacks out of the bluebird wall vases on the archway to the dining room.

"Who told you you could have those, Miss Priss?" says Mama, fanning as hard as she could.

"I bought 'em and I'll keep track of 'em," I says. "I'll tack 'em up one on each side of the post-office window, and you can see 'em when you come to ask me for your mail, if you're so dead to see 'em."

"Not I! I'll never darken the door to that post office again if I live to be a hundred," Mama says. "Ungrateful child! After all the money we spent on you at the Normal."

"Me either," says Stella-Rondo. "You can just let my mail lie there and *rot,* for all I care. I'll never come and relieve you of a single, solitary piece."

"I should worry," I says. "And who you think's going to sit down and write you all those big fat letters and postcards, by the way? Mr. Whitaker? Just because he was the only man ever dropped down in China Grove and you got him—unfairly—is he going to sit down and write you a lengthy correspondence after you come home giving no rhyme nor reason whatsoever for your separation and no explanation for the presence of that child? I may not have your brilliant mind, but I fail to see it."

So Mama says, "Sister, I've told you a thousand times that Stella-Rondo simply got homesick, and this child is far too big to be hers," and she says, "Now, why don't you all just sit down and play Casino?"

Then Shirley-T. sticks out her tongue at me in this perfectly horrible way. She has no more manners than the man in the moon. I told her she was going to cross her eyes like that some day and they'd stick.

"It's too late to stop me now," I says. "You should have tried that yesterday. I'm going to the P.O. and the only way you can possibly see me is to visit me there."

So Papa-Daddy says, "You'll never catch me setting foot in that post office, even if I should take a notion into my head to write a letter some place." He says, "I won't have you reachin' out of that little old window with a pair of shears and cuttin' off any beard of mine. I'm too smart for you!"

"We all are," says Stella-Rondo.

But I said, "If you're so smart, where's Mr. Whitaker?"

So then Uncle Rondo says, "I'll thank you from now on to stop reading all the orders I get on postcards and telling everybody in China Grove what you think is the matter with them," but I says, "I draw my own conclusions and will continue in the future to draw them." I says, "If people want to write their inmost secrets on penny postcards, there's nothing in the wide world you can do about it, Uncle Rondo."

"And if you think we'll ever *write* another postcard you're sadly mistaken," says Mama.

"Cutting off your nose to spite your face then," I says. "But if you're all determined to have no more to do with the US mail, think of this: What will Stella-Rondo do now, if she wants to tell Mr. Whitaker to come after her?"

"Wah!" says Stella-Rondo. I knew she'd cry. She had a conniption fit right there in the kitchen.

"It will be interesting to see how long she holds out," I says. "And now —I am leaving."

"Good-bye," says Uncle Rondo.

"Oh, I declare," says Mama, "to think that a family of mine should quarrel on the Fourth of July, or the day after, over Stella-Rondo leaving old Mr. Whitaker and having the sweetest little adopted child! It looks like we'd all be glad!"

"Wah!" says Stella-Rondo, and has a fresh conniption fit.

"*He* left *her*—you mark my words," I says. "That's Mr. Whitaker. I know Mr. Whitaker. After all, I knew him first. I said from the beginning he'd up and leave her. I foretold every single thing that's happened."

"Where did he go?" asks Mama.

"Probably to the North Pole, if he knows what's good for him," I says.

But Stella-Rondo just bawled and wouldn't say another word. She flew to her room and slammed the door.

"Now look what you've gone and done, Sister," says Mama. "You go apologize."

"I haven't got time, I'm leaving," I says.

"Well, what are you waiting around for?" asks Uncle Rondo.

So I just picked up the kitchen clock and marched off, without saying "Kiss my foot" or anything, and never did tell Stella-Rondo goodbye.

There was a nigger girl going along on a little wagon right in front.

"Nigger girl," I says, "come help me haul these things down the hill, I'm going to live in the post office."

Took her nine trips in her express wagon. Uncle Rondo came out on the porch and threw her a nickel.

And that's the last I've laid eyes on any of my family or my family laid eyes on me for five solid days and nights. Stella-Rondo may be telling the most horrible tales in the world about Mr. Whitaker, but I haven't heard them. As I tell everybody, I draw my own conclusions.

But oh, I like it here. It's ideal, as I've been saying. You see, I've got everything cater-cornered, the way I like it. Hear the radio? All the war news. Radio, sewing machine, book ends, ironing board and that great big piano lamp—peace, that's what I like. Butter-bean vines planted all along the front where the strings are.

Of course, there's not much mail. My family are naturally the main people in China Grove, and if they prefer to vanish from the face of the earth, for all the mail they get or the mail they write, why, I'm not going to open my mouth. Some of the folks here in town are taking up for me and some turned against me. I know which is which. There are always people who will quit buying stamps just to get on the right side of Papa-Daddy.

But here I am, and here I'll stay. I want the world to know I'm happy.

And if Stella-Rondo should come to me this minute, on bended knees, and *attempt* to explain the incidents of her life with Mr. Whitaker, I'd simply put my fingers in both my ears and refuse to listen.

QUESTIONS AND COMMENT ON FORM AND CONTENT

1. We know from the title and the first line that this story is told by one of the characters. It could have been told by some invisible third person who sees everything and who might even read the minds of the characters. What advantages and disadvantages result from having one of the characters (usually, as here, an important one) tell the story? How would this story differ if told by Stella-Rondo, by Mama, or by one of the other characters, including Mr. Whitaker? What point of view is most commonly used in novels and short stories? Would it be good to have part of the story told one way and part another way?

2. In telling the story, Sister reveals or exposes herself as well as the others. How do we form an estimate of character in real life? Is the process the same in fiction? Here we see the other characters only through the report of Sister. Do you think she is a fair and accurate reporter?

3. Why did Miss Welty have the story begin just as Stella-Rondo returns home with a child? How had Sister gotten along with the family before Stella-Rondo returned? Does this have any implications for the future if Stella-Rondo gets a letter from Mr. Whitaker and goes back to him? How much time elapses in the story? Why didn't Miss Welty give us some earlier scenes resulting from the rivalry for the love of Mr. Whitaker?

4. Much of the effectiveness of a story, as Edgar Allan Poe pointed out, depends upon a unified tone or atmosphere throughout the story. If the very first sentence does not tend toward the preconceived effect or mood, he said, the first sentence is wasted. Throughout the story one mood is emphasized. It is like the dropping of water upon a rock, he explained. Eventually it will make an impression. How is the comic, ridiculous, or humorous tone supported and emphasized in this story? Give details about the characters, the scenes, the foolish arguments, and the like.

5. Are the characters so much "one-sided" (as Stella-Rondo said about Sister) or so near caricatures as to remove the story from literature that offers a criticism of life? Or do all of us have enough eccentricities that these lives hold the mirror up to our nature, as Hamlet said a drama should, and let us recognize our foibles?

6. What was the basic cause or causes of the enmity of these sisters? Who was at fault?

7. What "errors" of English grammar and usage serve best to define Sister's education?

THEME SUGGESTIONS

How We Come to Understand People in Real Life (in Fiction, in Drama)
Sister, a Character Sketch
A One-Sided Family
Siblings Are Mutually Antagonistic

4 | TOWN AND COUNTRY

FLORIDA, MISSOURI, AND THE QUARLES' FARM

Mark Twain

Mark Twain (Samuel Langhorne Clemens) (1835-1910) was born in Florida, Missouri, and spent his boyhood (1839-1853) in Hannibal. His life as a journeyman printer, Mississippi River pilot, prospector and newspaper reporter in Nevada and California, and his travels abroad became materials for his humorous and satirical writings. The Adventures of Huckleberry Finn *and* Life on the Mississippi *are considered his best works.*

[1] I was born the 30th of November, 1835, in the almost invisible village of Florida, Monroe County, Missouri. My parents removed to Missouri in the early 'thirties; I do not remember just when, for I was not born then and cared nothing for such things. It was a long journey in those days and must have been a rough and tiresome one. The village contained a hundred people and I increased the population by 1 per cent. It is more than many of the best men in history could have done for a town. It may not be modest in me to refer to this but it is true. There is no record of a person doing as much—not even Shakespeare. But I did it for Florida and it shows that I could have done it for any place—even London, I suppose.

[2] Recently some one in Missouri has sent me a picture of the house I was born in. Heretofore I have always stated that it was a palace but I shall be more guarded now.

[3] The village had two streets, each a couple of hundred yards long; the rest of the avenues mere lanes, with railfences and cornfields on either side. Both the streets and the lanes were paved with the same material—tough black mud in wet times, deep dust in dry.

[4] Most of the houses were of logs—all of them, indeed, except three or four; these latter were frame ones. There were none of brick, and none of stone. There was a log church, with a puncheon floor and slab benches. A puncheon floor is made of logs whose upper surfaces have been chipped flat with the adz. The cracks between the logs were not filled; there was no carpet; consequently, if you dropped anything smaller than a peach it was likely to go through. The church was perched upon short sections of logs, which elevated it two or three feet from the ground. Hogs slept under there, and whenever the dogs got after them during services the minister had to wait till the disturbance was over. In winter there was always a refreshing breeze up through the puncheon floor; in summer there were fleas enough for all.

[5] A slab bench is made of the outside cut of a saw-log, with the bark side down; it is supported on four sticks driven into auger holes at the ends; it has no back and no cushions. The church was twilighted with yellow tallow candles in tin sconces hung against the walls. Week days, the church was a schoolhouse.

[6] There were two stores in the village. My uncle, John A. Quarles, was proprietor of one of them. It was a very small establishment, with a few rolls of "bit" calicoes on half a dozen shelves; a few barrels of salt mackerel, coffee and New Orleans sugar behind the counter; stacks of brooms, shovels, axes, hoes, rakes and such things here and there; a lot of cheap hats, bonnets and tinware strung on strings and suspended from the walls; and at the other end of the room was another counter with bags of shot on it, a cheese or two and a keg of powder; in front of it a row of nail kegs and a few pigs of lead, and behind it a barrel or two of New Orleans molasses and native corn whisky on tap. If a boy bought five or ten cents' worth of anything he was entitled to half a handful of sugar from the barrel; if a woman bought a few yards of calico she was entitled to a spool of thread in addition to the usual gratis "trimmin's"; if a man bought a trifle he was at liberty to draw and swallow as big a drink of whisky as he wanted.

[7] Everything was cheap: apples, peaches, sweet potatoes, Irish potatoes and corn, ten cents a bushel; chickens, ten cents apiece; butter, six cents a pound; eggs, three cents a dozen; coffee and sugar, five cents a pound; whisky, ten cents a gallon. I do not know how prices are out

there in interior Missouri now but I know what they are here in Hart-
ford, Connecticut.[1] To wit: apples, three dollars a bushel; peaches, five
dollars; Irish potatoes (choice Bermudas), five dollars; chickens, a dollar to a dollar and a half apiece, according to weight; butter, forty-five
to sixty cents a pound; eggs, fifty to sixty cents a dozen; coffee, forty-five
cents a pound; native whisky, four or five dollars a gallon, I believe, but
I can only be certain concerning the sort which I use myself, which is
Scotch and costs ten dollars a gallon when you take two gallons—more
when you take less. . . .

[8] My uncle, John A. Quarles, was also a farmer, and his place was
in the country four miles from Florida. He had eight children and fifteen or twenty negroes and was also fortunate in other ways, particulary
in his character. I have not come across a better man than he was. I was
his guest for two or three months every year, from the fourth year after
we removed to Hannibal till I was eleven or twelve years old. I have
never consciously used him or his wife in a book but his farm has come
very handy to me in literature once or twice. In *Huck Finn* and in *Tom
Sawyer, Detective* I moved it down to Arkansas. It was all of six hundred
miles but it was no trouble; it was not a very large farm—five hundred
acres, perhaps—but I could have done it if it had been twice as large.
And as for the morality of it, I cared nothing for that; I would move a
state if the exigencies of literature required it.

[9] It was a heavenly place for a boy, that farm of my uncle John's.
The house was a double log one, with a spacious floor (roofed in) connecting it with the kitchen. In the summer the table was set in the middle of that shady and breezy floor, and the sumptuous meals—well it
makes me cry to think of them. Fried chicken, roast pig; wild and tame
turkeys, ducks and geese; venison just killed; squirrels, rabbits, pheasants,
partridges, prairie-chickens; biscuits, hot batter cakes, hot buckwheat
cakes, hot "wheat bread," hot rolls, hot corn pone; fresh corn boiled on
the ear, succotash, butter-beans, string-beans, tomatoes, peas, Irish potatoes, sweet potatoes; buttermilk, sweet milk, "clabber"; watermelons,
muskmelons, cantaloupes—all fresh from the garden; apple pie, peach
pie, pumpkin pie, apple dumplings, peach cobbler—I can't remember the
rest. . . .

[10] I can see the farm yet, with perfect clearness. I can see all its belongings, all its details; the family room of the house, with a "trundle"
bed in one corner and a spinning-wheel in another—a wheel whose rising
and falling wail, heard from a distance, was the mournfulest of all
sounds to me and made me homesick and low spirited and filled my atmosphere with the wandering spirits of the dead; the vast fireplace, piled
high on winter nights with flaming hickory logs from whose ends a

[1] Written in 1877.

sugary sap bubbled out but did not go to waste, for we scraped it off and ate it; the lazy cat spread out on the rough hearthstones; the drowsy dogs braced against the jambs and blinking; my aunt in one chimney corner, knitting; my uncle in the other, smoking his corn-cob pipe; the slick and carpetless oak floor faintly mirroring the dancing flame tongues and freckled with black indentations where fire coals had popped out and died a leisurely death; half a dozen children romping in the background twilight; "split"-bottomed chairs here and there, some with rockers; a cradle—out of service but waiting with confidence; in the early cold mornings a snuggle of children in shirts and chemises, occupying the hearthstone and procrastinating—they could not bear to leave that comfortable place and go out on the wind-swept floor space between the house and kitchen where the general tin basin stood, and wash.

[11] Along outside of the front fence ran the country road, dusty in the summertime and a good place for snakes—they liked to lie in it and sun themselves; when they were rattlesnakes or puff adders we killed them; when they were black snakes or racers or belonged to the fabled "hoop" breed we fled without shame; when they were "house snakes" or "garters" we carried them home and put them in Aunt Patsy's work basket for a surprise; for she was prejudiced against snakes, and always when she took the basket in her lap and they began to climb out of it it disordered her mind. She never could seem to get used to them; her opportunities went for nothing. And she was always cold toward bats, too, and could not bear them; and yet I think a bat is as friendly a bird as there is. My mother was Aunt Patsy's sister and had the same wild superstitions. A bat is beautifully soft and silky; I do not know any creature that is pleasanter to the touch or is more grateful for caressings, if offered in the right spirit. I know all about these coleoptera[1] because our great cave, three miles below Hannibal, was multitudinously stocked with them and often I brought them home to amuse my mother with. It was easy to manage if it was a school day because then I had ostensibly been to school and hadn't any bats. She was not a suspicious person but full of trust and confidence; and when I said, "There's something in my coat pocket for you," she would put her hand in. But she always took it out again, herself; I didn't have to tell her. It was remarkable the way she couldn't learn to like private bats. The more experience she had the more she could not change her views. . . .

[12] The country schoolhouse was three miles from my uncle's farm. It stood in a clearing in the woods and would hold about twenty-five boys and girls. We attended the school with more or less regularity once or twice a week, in summer, walking to it in the cool of the morning by the forest paths and back in the gloaming at the end of the day. All the

[1] Mark Twain meant chiroptera.

pupils brought their dinners in baskets—corn dodger, buttermilk and other good things—and sat in the shade of the trees at noon and ate them. It is the part of my education which I look back upon with the most satisfaction. My first visit to the school was when I was seven. A strapping girl of fifteen, in the customary sunbonnet and calico dress, asked me if I "used tobacco"—meaning did I chew it. I said no. It roused her scorn. She reported me to all the crowd and said:

[13] "Here is a boy seven years old who can't chaw tobacco." By the looks and comments which this produced I realized that I was a degraded object; I was cruelly ashamed of myself. I determined to reform. But I only made myself sick; I was not able to learn to chew tobacco. I learned to smoke fairly well but that did not conciliate anybody and I remained a poor thing and characterless. I longed to be respected but I never was able to rise. Children have but little charity for one another's defects.

[14] As I have said, I spent some part of every year at the farm until I was twelve or thirteen years old. The life which I led there with my cousins was full of charm, and so is the memory of it yet. I can call back the solemn twilight and mystery of the deep woods, the earthy smells, the faint odors of the wild flowers, the sheen of rain-washed foliage, the rattling clatter of drops when the wind shook the trees, the far-off hammering of woodpeckers and the muffled drumming of wood pheasants in the remoteness of the forest, the snapshot glimpses of disturbed wild creatures scurrying through the grass—I can call it all back and make it as real as it ever was, and as blessed. I can call back the prairie, and its loneliness and peace, and a vast hawk hanging motionless in the sky, with his wings spread wide and the blue of the vault showing through the fringe of their end feathers. I can see the woods in their autumn dress, the oaks purple, the hickories washed with gold, the maples and the sumachs luminous with crimson fires, and I can hear the rustle made by the fallen leaves as we plowed through them. I can see the blue clusters of wild grapes hanging among the foliage of the saplings, and I remember the taste of them and the smell. I know how the wild blackberries looked, and how they tasted, and the same with the pawpaws, the hazelnuts, and the persimmons; and I can feel the thumping rain, upon my head, of hickory nuts and walnuts when were were out in the frosty dawn to scramble for them with the pigs, and the gusts of wind loosed them and sent them down. I know the stain of blackberries, and how pretty it is, and I know the stain of walnut hulls, and how little it minds soap and water, also what grudged experience it had of either of them. I know the taste of maple sap, and when to gather it, and how to arrange the troughs and the delivery tubes, and how to boil down the juice, and how to hook the sugar after it is made, also how much better hooked sugar tastes than any that is honestly come by, let bigots say what they

will. I know how a prize watermelon looks when it is sunning its fat rotundity among pumpkin vines and "simblins"; I know how to tell when it is ripe without "plugging" it; I know how inviting it looks when it is cooling itself in a tub of water under the bed, waiting; I know how it looks when it lies on the table in the sheltered great floor space between house and kitchen, and the children gathered for the sacrifice and their mouths watering; I know the crackling sound it makes when the carving knife enters its end, and I can see the split fly along in front of the blade as the knife cleaves its way to the other end; I can see its halves fall apart and display the rich red meat and the black seeds, and the heart standing up, a luxury fit for the elect; I know how a boy looks behind a yard-long slice of that melon, and I know how he feels; for I have been there. I know the taste of the watermelon which has been honestly come by, and I know the taste of the watermelon which has been acquired by art. Both taste good, but the experienced know which tastes best. I know the look of green apples and peaches and pears on the trees, and I know how entertaining they are when they are inside of a person. I know how ripe ones look when they are piled in pyramids under the trees, and how pretty they are and how vivid their colors. I know how a frozen apple looks, in a barrel down cellar in the wintertime, and how hard it is to bite, and how the frost makes the teeth ache, and yet how good it is, notwithstanding. I know the disposition of elderly people to select the speckled apples for the children, and I once knew ways to beat the game. I know the look of an apple that is roasting and sizzling on a hearth on a winter's evening, and I know the comfort that comes of eating it hot, along with some sugar and a drench of cream. I know the delicate art and mystery of so cracking hickory nuts and walnuts on a flatiron with a hammer that the kernels will be delivered whole, and I know how the nuts, taken in conjunction with winter apples, cider, and doughnuts, make old people's old tales and old jokes sound fresh and crisp and enchanting, and juggle an evening away before you know what went with the time. I know the look of Uncle Dan'l's kitchen as it was on the privileged nights, when I was a child, and I can see the white and black children grouped on the hearth, with the firelight playing on their faces and the shadows flickering upon the walls, clear back toward the cavernous gloom of the rear, and I can hear Uncle Dan'l telling the immortal tales which Uncle Remus Harris was to gather into his books and charm the world with, by and by; and I can feel again the creepy joy which quivered through me when the time for the ghost story of the "Golden Arm" was reached—and the sense of regret, too, which came over me, for it was always the last story of the evening and there was nothing between it and the unwelcome bed.

[15] I can remember the bare wooden stairway in my uncle's house,

and the turn to the left above the landing, and the rafters and the slant-
ing roof over my bed, and the squares of moonlight on the floor, and the
white cold world of snow outside, seen through the curtainless window.
I can remember the howling of the wind and the quaking of the house
on stormy nights, and how snug and cozy one felt, under the blankets, listening; and how the powdery snow used to sift in, around the sashes, and
lie in little ridges on the floor and make the place look chilly in the morning and curb the wild desire to get up—in case there was any. I can remember how very dark that room was, in the dark of the moon, and how
packed it was with ghostly stillness when one woke up by accident away
in the night, and forgotten sins came flocking out of the secret chambers
of the memory and wanted a hearing; and how ill chosen the time seemed
for this kind of business; and how dismal was the hoo-hooing of the owl
and the wailing of the wolf, sent mourning by on the night wind.

[16] I remember the raging of the rain on that roof, summer nights,
and how pleasant it was to lie and listen to it, and enjoy the white splendor of the lightning and the majestic booming and crashing of the thunder. It was a very satisfactory room, and there was a lightning rod which
was reachable from the window, an adorable and skittish thing to climb
up and down, summer nights, when there were duties on hand of a sort
to make privacy desirable.

[17] I remember the 'coon and 'possum hunts, nights, with the negroes,
and the long marches through the black gloom of the woods, and the
excitement which fired everybody when the distant bay of an experienced dog announced that the game was treed; then the wild scramblings
and stumblings through briers and bushes and over roots to get to the
spot; then the lighting of a fire and the felling of the tree, the joyful
frenzy of the dogs and the negroes, and the weird picture it all made in
the red glare—I remember it all well, and the delight that everyone got
out of it, except the 'coon.

[18] I remember the pigeon seasons, when the birds would come in
millions and cover the trees and by their weight break down the branches.
They were clubbed to death with sticks; guns were not necessary and
were not used. I remember the squirrel hunts, and prairie-chicken hunts,
and wild-turkey hunts, and all that; and how we turned out, mornings,
while it was still dark, to go on these expeditions, and how chilly and
dismal it was, and how often I regretted that I was well enough to go.
A toot on a tin horn brought twice as many dogs as were needed, and in
their happiness they raced and scampered about, and knocked small people down, and made no end of unnecessary noise. At the word, they vanished away toward the woods, and we drifted silently after them in the
melancholy gloom. But presently the gray dawn stole over the world, the
birds piped up, then the sun rose and poured light and comfort all

around, everything was fresh and dewy and fragrant, and life was a boon again. After three hours of tramping we arrived back wholesomely tired, overladen with game, very hungry, and just in time for breakfast.

QUESTIONS AND COMMENT ON FORM AND CONTENT

1. How is Florida, Missouri, described?
2. How are the following defined?
   a. A puncheon floor
   b. A slab bench
3. Note how Twain builds up humor by telling in a very matter-of-fact manner about the hogs and the dogs, during church service. To what extent is the humor dependent on the choice of words?
4. What is the order of arrangement for the details of Quarles' store?
5. How is the punctuation and sentence structure handled in the second sentence of paragraph 10? Would a colon be more suitable today after "all the details"? What is the function of the semicolons used throughout the long sentence? What kinds of phrases are used instead of clauses?
6. From whose point of view are the bats and snakes described in paragraph 11? The frontier was noted for "practical jokes." Were the "surprises" for Aunt Patsy and his mother of this variety?
7. To what extent does his description of a snowy winter night under the rafters of the old house resemble a scence from Whittier's "Snow Bound"?
8. In paragraphs 14 to 18 why does Twain repeat the phrases "I can see . . . ," "I can feel . . . ," "I know how . . . ," "I can hear . . . ," and "I can remember"?
9. Which of the descriptions seems to be most vivid?
10. What kinds of humor do you find in Mark Twain's sketches? Exaggeration? The incongruous? Understatement? Irony?
11. Twain, who was also in great demand as a lecturer, found his writings (with slight alterations) suitable for stage purposes. His drawl and pauses are said to have added effectiveness. Read the following, as for the first time, observing the pauses.

> [my mother] was not a suspicious person but full of trust and confidence, and when I said, "There's something in my coat pocket for you, she would put her hand in. [pause] But she always took it out again, [pause] herself; [pause] It was remarkable the way she couldn't learn to like private bats. [pause] The more experience she had, the more she could not change her views.

THEME SUGGESTIONS

I Can Remember It All Now
Our Woods in Autumn (Spring, Winter, Summer)
Written or oral report: Twain's humor in one of his other writings such as *Life on the Mississippi* or *Innocents Abroad.*

HANNIBAL, MISSOURI

Mark Twain

In 1883 Mark Twain (1835-1910), in a reminiscent mood, drew upon his earlier exciting experiences to write Life on the Mississippi. *More exactly, the first twenty chapters, the best ones, were so written. The latter chapters came from revisiting the Mississippi. Our selection is from Chapter IV, "The Boy's Ambition," and first appeared in the* Atlantic Monthly *in 1875.*

Once a day a cheap, gaudy packet arrived upward from St. Louis, and another downward from Keokuk. Before these events, the day was glorious with expectancy; after they had transpired, the day was a dead and empty thing. Not only the boys, but the whole village, felt this. After all these years I can picture that old time to myself now, just as it was then: the white town drowsing in the sunshine of a summer's morning; the streets empty, or pretty nearly so; one or two clerks sitting in front of the Water Street stores, with their splint-bottomed chairs tilted back against the walls, chins on breasts, hats slouched over their faces, asleep—with shingle-shavings enough around to show what broke them down; a sow and a litter of pigs loafing along the sidewalk, doing a good business in watermelon rinds and seeds; two or three lonely little freight piles scattered about the "levee"; a pile of "skids" on the slope of the stone-paved wharf, and the fragrant town drunkard asleep in the shadow of them; two or three wood flats at the head of the wharf, but nobody to listen to the peaceful lapping of the wavelets against them; the great Mississippi, the majestic, the magnificent Mississippi, rolling its mile-wide tide along, shining in the sun; the dense forest away on the other side; the "point" above the town, and the "point" below, bounding the river-glimpse and turning it into a sort of sea, and withal a very still and brilliant and lonely one. Presently a film of dark smoke appears above one of those remote "points"; instantly a Negro drayman, famous for his quick eye and prodigious voice, lifts up the cry, "S-t-e-a-m-boat a-comin'!" and the scene changes! The town drunkard stirs, the clerks wake up, a furious clatter of drays follows, every house and store pours out a human contribution, and all in a twinkling the dead town is alive and moving. Drays, carts, men, boys, all go hurrying from many quarters to a common center, the wharf. Assembled there, the people fasten their eyes upon the coming boat as upon a wonder they are seeing for the first time. And the boat *is* rather a handsome sight, too. She is long and sharp and trim and pretty; she has two tall, fancy-topped chimneys, with a gilded device of some kind swung between them; a fanciful pilot-house, all glass and "ginger-bread," perched on top of the "texas" deck behind them; the paddle-boxes are gorgeous with a picture or with gilded rays above the boat's name; the boiler-deck, the hurricane-deck, and the texas deck are fenced and ornamented with clean white railings; there is a flag gallantly flying from the jack-staff; the furnace doors are open and the fires glaring bravely; the upper decks are black with passengers; the captain stands by the big bell, calm, imposing, the envy of all; great volumes of the blackest smoke are rolling and tumbling out of the chimneys—a hus-banded grandeur created with a bit of pitch-pine just before arriving at a town; the crew are grouped on the forecastle; the broad stage is run far out over the port bow, and an envied deck-hand stands picturesquely on the end of it with a coil of rope in his hand; the pent steam is scream-ing through the gauge-cocks; the captain lifts his hand, a bell rings, the wheels stop; then they turn back, churning the water to foam, and the steamer is at rest. Then such a scramble as there is to get aboard, and to get ashore, and to take in freight and to discharge freight, all at one and the same time; and such a yelling and cursing as the mates facilitate it all with! Ten minutes later the steamer is under way again, with no flag on the jack-staff and no black smoke issuing from the chimneys. After ten more minutes the town is dead again, and the town drunkard asleep by the skids once more.

QUESTIONS AND COMMENT ON FORM AND CONTENT

1. This long paragraph describes the effect on Hannibal of a single happen-ing, the arrival, the loading and unloading, and the departure of a steamboat. First, there is a picture of a sleepy river town "drowsing in the sunshine of a summer's morning," a scene which culminates in the view of "the great Mis-sissippi, the majestic, the magnificent Mississippi, rolling its mile-wide tide along, shining in the sun." Where does the sentence containing these phrases begin? How is this long sentence of over 200 words constructed? What substi-tutes for verbs? Does this type of sentence add to the nostalgic, drowsy scene?

2. Then the steamboat is announced and the mood changes. Is this change from a quiet, sleepy scene to a busy, noisy one accompanied by a basic change in sentence pattern? Explain. In both parts of the paragraph Twain accom-plishes concreteness without wordiness. How is this done? Look especially for words and phrases in apposition and in parallel structure.

3. If you were to break this long paragraph into two, three, or four para-graphs, where would you make the divisions? What would unify them?

THEME SUGGESTIONS

Try a similar contrasting scene in one or two paragraphs. Perhaps you could use your home town before and after the arrival of a circus, a carnival, a parade, or celebration of some kind. As the scene changes from a quiet to an exciting one, change the sentence patterns as Twain did. Distinguish between participles and verbs in your writing. (Note: If you use any fragments, your teacher may wish you to label them.)

SUBURBIA, OF THEE I SING

Phyllis McGinley

Phyllis McGinley (Mrs. Charles Hayden) (1905-   ) is noted for her light verse, children's books, and chatty, informal essays.

[1] Twenty miles east of New York City as the New Haven Railroad flies sets a village I shall call Spruce Manor. The Boston Post Road, there, for the length of two blocks, becomes Main Street, and on one side of that thundering thoroughfare are the grocery stores and the drugstores and the Village Spa where teen-agers gather of an afternoon to drink their Cokes and speak their curious confidences. There one finds the shoe repairers and the dry cleaners and the second-hand stores which sell "antiques" and the stationery stores which dispense comic books to ten-year-olds and greeting cards and lending library masterpieces to their mothers. On the opposite side stand the bank, the Fire House, the Public Library. The rest of this town of perhaps four or five thousand people lies to the south and is bounded largely by Long Island Sound, curving protectively on three borders. The movie theater (dedicated to the showing of second-run, single-feature pictures) and the grade schools lie north, beyond the Post Road, and that is a source of worry to Spruce Manorites. They are always a little uneasy about the children, crossing, perhaps, before the lights are safely green. However, two excellent policemen—Mr. Crowley and Mr. Lang—station themselves at the intersections four times a day, and so far there have been no accidents.

[2] Spruce Manor in the spring and summer and fall is a pretty town, full of gardens and old elms. (There are few spruces, but the village council is considering planting a few on the station plaza, out of sheer patriotism.) In the winter the houses reveal themselves as comfortable, well kept, architecturally insignificant. Then one can see the town for

what it is and has been since it left off being farm and woodland some sixty years ago—the epitome of Suburbia, not the country and certainly not the city. It is a commuter's town, the living center of a web which unrolls each morning as the men swing aboard the locals, and contracts again in the evening when they return. By day, with even the children pent in schools, it is a village of women. They trundle mobile baskets at the A & P, they sit under driers at the hairdressers, they sweep their porches and set out bulbs and stitch up slip covers. Only on week ends does it become heterogeneous and lively, the parking places difficult to find.

[3] Spruce Manor has no country club of its own, though devoted golfers have their choice of two or three not far away. It does have a small yacht club and a beach, which can be used by anyone who rents or owns a house here. The village supports a little park with playground equipment and a counselor, where children, unattended by parents, can spend summer days if they have no more pressing engagements.

[4] It is a town not wholly without traditions. Residents will point out the two-hundred-year-old Manor house, now a minor museum; and in the autumn they line the streets on a scheduled evening to watch the Volunteer Firemen parade. That is a fine occasion, with so many heads of households marching in their red blouses and white gloves, some with flaming helmets, some swinging lanterns, most of them genially out of step. There is a bigger parade on Memorial Day, with more marchers than watchers and with the Catholic priest, the rabbi, and the Protestant ministers each delivering a short prayer when the paraders gather near the War Memorial. On the whole, however, outside of contributing generously to the Community Chest, Manorites are not addicted to municipal get-togethers.

[5] No one is very poor here and not many families rich enough to be awesome. In fact, there is not much to distinguish Spruce Manor from any other of a thousand suburbs outside of New York City or San Francisco or Detroit or Chicago or even Stockholm, for that matter. Except for one thing. For some reason, Spruce Manor has become a sort of symbol to writers and reporters familiar only with its name or trivial aspects. It has become a symbol of all that is middle class in the worst sense, of settled-downness or rootlessness, according to what the writer is trying to prove; of smug and prosperous mediocrity or—even, in more lurid novels, of lechery at the country club and Sunday morning hangovers.

[6] To condemn Suburbia has long been a literary cliché, anyhow. I have yet to read a book in which the suburban life was pictured as the good life or the commuter as a sympathetic figure. He is nearly as much a stock character as the old stage Irishman: the man who "spends his

life riding to and from his wife," the eternal Babbitt who knows all about Buicks and nothing about Picasso, whose sanctuary is the club locker room, whose ideas spring ready-made from the illiberal newspapers. His wife plays politics at the P.T.A. and keeps up with the Joneses. Or—if the scene is more gilded and less respectable—the commuter is the high-powered advertising executive with a station wagon and an eye for the ladies, his wife a restless baggage given to too many cocktails in the afternoon.

[7] These clichés I challenge. I have lived in the country, I have lived in the city. I have lived in an average Middle Western small town. But for the best eleven years of my life I have lived in Suburbia and I like it. "Compromise!" cried our friends when we came here from an expensive, inconvenient, moderately fashionable tenement in Manhattan. It was the period in our lives when everyone was moving somewhere. Farther uptown, farther downtown, across town to Sutton Place, to a half-dozen rural acres in Connecticut or New Jersey or even Vermont. But no one in our rather rarefied little group was thinking of moving to the suburbs except us. They were aghast that we could find anything appealing in the thought of a middle-class house on a middle-class street in a middle-class village full of middle-class people. That we were tired of town and hoped for children, that we couldn't afford both a city apartment and a farm, they put down as feeble excuses. To this day they cannot understand us. You see, they read the books. They even write them.

[8] Compromise? Of course we compromise. But compromise, if not the spice of life, is its solidity. It is what makes nations great and marriages happy and Spruce Manor the pleasant place it is. As for its being middle-class, what is wrong with acknowledging one's roots? And how free we are! Free of the city's noise, of its ubiquitous doormen, of the soot on the windowsill and the radio in the next apartment. We have released ourselves from the seasonal hegira to the mountains or the seashore. We have only one address, one house to keep supplied with paring knives and blankets. We are free from the snows that block the countryman's roads in winter and his electricity which always goes off in a thunderstorm. I do not insist that we are typical. There is nothing really typical about any of our friends and neighbors here, and therein lies my point. The true suburbanite needs to conform less than anyone else; much less than the gentleman farmer with his remodeled salt-box or than the determined cliff dweller with his necessity for living at the right address. In Spruce Manor all addresses are right. And since we are fairly numerous here, we need not fall back on the people nearest us for total companionship. There is not here, as in a small city away from truly urban centers, some particular family whose codes must be ours. And we could not keep up with the Joneses even if we wanted to, for we

know many Joneses and they are all quite different people leading the most various lives.

[9] The Albert Joneses spend their weekends sailing, the Bertram Joneses cultivate their delphinium, the Clarence Joneses—Clarence being a handy man with a cello—are enthusiastic about amateur chamber music. The David Joneses dote on bridge, but neither of the Ernest Joneses understands it and they prefer staying home of an evening so that Ernest Jones can carve his witty caricatures out of pieces of old fruit wood. We admire each other's gardens, applaud each other's sailing records; we are too busy to compete. So long as our clapboards are painted and our hedges decently trimmed, we have fulfilled our community obligations. We can live as anonymously as in a city or we can call half the village by their first names.

[10] On our half-acre or three-quarters we can raise enough tomatoes for our salads and assassinate enough beetles to satisfy the gardening urge. Or we can buy our vegetables at the store and put the whole place to lawn without feeling that we are neglecting our property. We can have privacy and shade and the changing of the seasons and also the Joneses next door from whom to borrow a cup of sugar or a stepladder. Despite the novelists, the shadow of the country club rests lightly on us. Half of us wouldn't be found dead with a golf stick in our hands, and loathe Saturday dances. Few of us expect to be deliriously wealthy or world famous or divorced. What we do expect is to pay off the mortgage and send our healthy children to good colleges.

[11] For when I refer to life here, I think, of course, of living with children. Spruce Manor without children would be a paradox. The summer waters are full of them, gamboling like dolphins. The lanes are alive with them, the yards overflow with them, they possess the tennis courts and the skating pond and the vacant lots. Their roller skates wear down the asphalt, and their bicycles make necessary the twenty-five-mile speed limit. They converse interminably on the telephones and make rich the dentist and the pediatrician. Who claims that a child and a half is the American middle-class average? A nice medium Spruce Manor family runs to four or five, and we count proudly, but not with amazement, the many solid households running to six, seven, eight, nine, even twelve. Our houses here are big and not new, most of them, and there is a temptation to fill them up, let the décor fall where it may.

[12] Besides, Spruce Manor seems designed by providence and town planning for the happiness of children. Better designed than the city; better, I say defiantly, than the country. Country mothers must be constantly arranging and contriving for their children's leisure time. There is no neighbor child next door for playmate, no school within walking distance. The ponds are dangerous to young swimmers, the woods full

of poison ivy, the romantic dirt roads unsuitable for bicycles. An extra acre or two gives a fine sense of possession to an adult; it does not compensate children for the give-and-take of our village where there is always a contemporary to help swing the skipping rope or put on the catcher's mitt. Where in the country is the Friday evening dancing class or the Saturday morning movie (approved by the P.T.A)? It is the greatest fallacy of all time that children love the country as a year-around plan. Children would take a dusty corner of Washington Square, or a city sidewalk, even in preference to the lonely sermons in stones and books in running brooks which their contemporaries cannot share.

[13] As for the horrors of bringing up progeny in the city, for all its museums and other cultural advantages (so perfectly within reach of suburban families if they feel strongly about it), they were summed up for me one day last winter. The harried mother of one, speaking to me on the telephone just after Christmas, sighed and said, "It's been a really wonderful time for me, as vacations go. Barbara has had an engagement with a child in our apartment house every afternoon this week. I have had to take her almost nowhere." Barbara is eleven. For six of those eleven years, I realized her mother must have dreaded Christmas vacation, not to mention spring, as a time when Barbara had to be entertained. I thought thankfully of my own daughters whom I had scarcely seen since school closed, out with their skis and their sleds and their friends, sliding down the roped-off hill a block away, coming in hungrily for lunch and disappearing again, hearty, amused, and safe—at least as safe as any sled-borne child can be.

[14] Spruce Manor is not Eden, of course. Our taxes are higher than we like, and there is always the 8:11 in the morning to be caught and we sometimes resent the necessity of rushing from a theater to a train on a weekday evening. But the taxes pay for our really excellent schools and for our garbage collections (so that the pails of orange peels need not stand in the halls overnight as ours did in the city) and for our water supply, which does not give out every dry summer as it frequently does in the country. As for the theaters—they are twenty miles away and we don't get to them more than twice a month. But neither, I think, do many of our friends in town. The 8:11 is rather a pleasant train, too, say the husbands: it gets them to work in thirty-four minutes and they read the papers restfully on the way.

[15] "But the suburban mind!" cry our die-hard friends in Manhattan and Connecticut. "The suburban conversation! The monotony!" They imply that they and I must scintillate or we perish. Let me anatomize Spruce Manor, for them and for the others who envision Suburbia as a congregation of mindless housewives and amoral go-getters.

[16] From my window, now, on a June morning, I have a view. It con-

tains neither solitary hills nor dramatic skyscrapers. But I can see my roses in bloom, and my foxglove, and an arch of trees over the lane. I think comfortably of my friends whose houses line this and other streets rather like it. Not one of them is, so far as I know, doing any of the things that suburban ladies are popularly supposed to be doing. One of them, I happen to know, has gone bowling for her health and figure, but she has already tidied up her house and arranged to be home before the boys return from school. Some, undoubtedly, are ferociously busy in the garden. One lady is on her way to Ellis Island, bearing comfort and gifts to a Polish boy—a seventeen-year-old stowaway who did slave labor in Germany and was liberated by a cousin of hers during the war—who is being held for attempting to attain the land of which her cousin told him. The boy has been on the Island for three months. Twice a week she takes this tedious journey, meanwhile besieging courts and immigration authorities on his behalf. This lady has a large house, a part-time maid, and five children.

[17] My friend around the corner is finishing her third novel. She writes daily from nine-thirty until two. After that her son comes back from school and she plunges into maternity; at six she combs her pretty hair, refreshes her lipstick, and is charming to her doctor husband. The village dancing school is run by another neighbor, as it has been for twenty years. She has sent a number of ballerinas on to the theatrical world as well as having shepherded for many a successful season the white-gloved little boys and full-skirted little girls through their first social tasks.

[18] Some of the ladies are no doubt painting their kitchens or a nursery; one of them is painting the portrait, on assignment, of a very distinguished personage. Some of them are nurses' aides and Red Cross workers and supporters of good causes. But all find time to be friends with their families and to meet the 5:32 five nights a week. They read something besides the newest historical novel, Braque is not unidentifiable to most of them, and their conversation is for the most part as agreeable as the tables they set. The tireless bridge players, the gossips, the women bored by their husbands live perhaps in our suburb, too. Let them. Our orbits need not cross.

[19] And what of the husbands, industriously selling bonds or practicing law or editing magazines or looking through microscopes or managing offices in the city? Do they spend their evenings and their week ends in the gaudy bars of Fifty-second Street? Or are they the perennial householders, their lives a dreary round of taking down screens and mending drains? Well, screens they have always with them, and a man who is good around the house can spend happy hours with the plumbing even on a South Sea Island. Some of them cut their own lawns and some

of them try to break par and some of them sail their little boats all summer with their families for crew. Some of them are village trustees for nothing a year and some listen to symphonies and some think Milton Berle ought to be President. There is a scientist who plays wonderful bebop, and a corporation executive who has bought a big old house nearby and with his own hands is gradually tearing it apart and reshaping it nearer to his heart's desire. Some of them are passionate hedge-clippers and some read Plutarch for fun. But I do not know many—though there may be such—who either kiss their neighbors' wives behind doors or whose idea of sprightly talk is to tell you the plot of an old movie.

[20] It is June, now, as I have said. This afternoon my daughters will come home from school with a crowd of their peers at their heels. They will eat up the cookies and drink up the ginger ale and go down for a swim at the beach if the water is warm enough, that beach which is only three blocks away and open to all Spruce Manor. They will go unattended by me, since they have been swimming since they were four, and besides there are life guards and no big waves. (Even our piece of ocean is a compromise.) Presently it will be time for us to climb into our very old Studebaker—we are not car-proud in Spruce Manor—and meet the 5:32. That evening expedition is not vitally necessary, for a bus runs straight down our principal avenue from the station to the shore, and it meets all trains. But it is an event we enjoy. There is something delightfully ritualistic about the moment when the train pulls in and the men swing off, with the less sophisticated children running squealing to meet them. The women move over from the driver's seat, surrender the keys, and receive an absent-minded kiss. It is the sort of picture that wakes John Marquand screaming from his sleep. But, deluded people that we are, we do not realize how mediocre it all seems. We will eat our undistinguished meal, probably without even a cocktail to enliven it. We will drink our coffee at the table, not carry it into the living room; if a husband changes for dinner here it is into old and spotty trousers and more comfortable shoes. The children will then go through the regular childhood routine—complain about their homework, grumble about going to bed, and finally accomplish both ordeals. Perhaps later the Gerard Joneses will drop in. We will talk a great deal of unimportant chatter and compare notes on food prices; we will also discuss the headlines and disagree. (Some of us in the Manor are Republicans, some are Democrats, a few lean plainly leftward. There are probably anti-Semites and anti-Catholics and even anti-Americans. Most of us are merely anti-antis.) We will all have one highball and the Joneses will leave early. Tomorrow and tomorrow and tomorrow the pattern will be repeated. This is Suburbia.

[21] But I think that someday people will look back on our little intervals here, on our Spruce Manor way of life, as we now look back on the Currier and Ives kind of living, with nostalgia and respect. In a world of terrible extremes, it will stand out as the safe, important medium.

[22] Suburbia, of thee I sing!

QUESTIONS AND COMMENT ON FORM AND CONTENT

1. The first paragraph describes this imaginary and typical middle-class suburban town in a matter-of-fact way by listing the stores and public buildings on the two blocks of Main Street. What is the effect of giving the names of the "two excellent policemen"? Why is the word *antiques* put in quotation marks?

2. In paragraph 2 Miss McGinley says that by day it is a village of women. She might have said, "The women shop, get their hair done, plant, sweep, and sew." Instead, she says, "They trundle mobile baskets at the A & P, they sit under dryers at the hairdressers, they sweep their porches and set out bulbs and stitch up slip covers." What is the difference in effect? Can you find other examples where specific, concrete words were chosen rather than general words?

3. What attacks have been made on Suburbia? (What is the meaning of the word? Why does she capitalize it?)

4. With which paragraph do the answers to these charges begin? If we consider the attacks to be part two of the essay, the answer or refutation would be part three, the largest and most important part. What answers are given to each charge? How does the refutation here differ from that used in a formal argument? How does the author keep the interest while she "proves" that life in Suburbia is to be preferred—at least for families with children—to life in the city or country?

5. How does she treat the idea of "keeping up with the Joneses"?

6. To what extent is her picture of Suburbia realistic? To what extent is it idyllic or romantic? What seasons of the year get most emphasis? What does she mean by saying that life there is a sort of "Currier and Ives kind of living"? Is her title in keeping with her mood and intention? Where did the "of thee I sing" come from?

7. Comment on "We have only one address, one house to keep supplied with paring knives and blankets." Are these the only items needed for housekeeping?

8. What is the allusion in, "Tomorrow and tomorrow and tomorrow. . . ."?

VOCABULARY: WHAT DO THE ITALICIZED WORDS MEAN?

. . . the *epitome* of Suburbia (2)

. . . it becomes *heterogeneous* (2)

. . . of *smug* and prosperous *mediocrity* (5)

. . . the eternal *Babbitt* who knows all about Buicks and nothing about *Picasso* (6)

. . . rather *rarefied* little group (7)
. . . of its *ubiquitous* doormen (8)
. . . from the seasonal *hegira* (8)
. . . are enthusiastic about amateur *chamber music* (9)
Spruce Manor without children would be a *paradox* (11)
. . . let the *décor* fall where it may (11)
Let me *anatomize* Spruce Manor (15)
. . . who envision Suburbia as a congregation of mindless housewives and *amoral go-getters.* (15)
. . . on the *Currier and Ives* kind of living, with *nostalgia* (21)

THEME SUGGESTIONS

A Defense of Life in _____. Consider following Miss McGinley's scheme of presenting, first, a general view of life in the place chosen, but with enough of the concrete and specific to make it real, and second, the criticism made against this kind of environment, and, third, the reply or defense of this type of living.

(No) Suburbia for Me
In Defense of the Small Town (City) (Farm)

HERE IS NEW YORK

E. B. White

Elwyn Brooks White (1899-   ) is one of America's most skillful and perceptive essayists. Many of his best writings appeared in The New Yorker, *where he was associated with James Thurber, and in* Harper's Magazine, *where he conducted a department "One Man's Meat" from 1938 to 1943. Among his books are* Quo Vadimus?, The Second Tree from the Corner, One Man's Meat, *and* Stuart Little, *a children's book.*

[1] On any person who desires such queer prizes, New York will bestow the gift of loneliness and the gift of privacy. It is this largess that accounts for the presence within the city's walls of a considerable section of the population; for the residents of Manhattan are to a large extent strangers who have pulled up stakes somewhere and come to town, seeking sanctuary or fulfillment or some greater or lesser grail. The capacity to make such dubious gifts is a mysterious quality of New York. It can destroy an individual, or it can fulfill him, depending a

good deal on luck. No one should come to New York to live unless he is willing to be lucky.

[2] New York is the concentrate of art and commerce and sport and religion and entertainment and finance, bringing to a single compact arena the gladiator, the evangelist, the promoter, the actor, the trader and the merchant. It carries on its lapel the unexpungeable odor of the long past, so that no matter where you sit in New York you feel the vibrations of great times and tall deeds, of queer people and events and undertakings. I am sitting at the moment in a stifling hotel room in 90-degree heat, halfway down an air shaft, in midtown. No air moves in or out of the room, yet I am curiously affected by emanations from the immediate surroundings. I am twenty-two blocks from where Rudolph Valentino lay in state, eight blocks from where Nathan Hale was executed, five blocks from the publisher's office where Ernest Hemingway hit Max Eastman on the nose, four miles from where Walt Whitman sat sweating out editorials for the Booklyn *Eagle*, thirty-four blocks from the street Willa Cather lived in when she came to New York to write books about Nebraska, one block from where Marceline used to clown on the boards of the Hippodrome, thirty-six blocks from the spot where the historian Joe Gould kicked a radio to pieces in full view of the public, thirteen blocks from where Harry Thaw shot Stanford White, five blocks from where I used to usher at the Metropolitan Opera and only a hundred and twelve blocks from the spot where Clarence Day the Elder was washed of his sins in the Church of the Epiphany (I could continue this list indefinitely); and for that matter I am probably occupying the very room that any number of exalted and somewise memorable characters sat in, some of them on hot, breathless afternoons, lonely and private and full of their own sense of emanations from without.

[3] When I went down to lunch a few minutes ago I noticed that the man sitting next to me (about eighteen inches away along the wall) was Fred Stone. The eighteen inches were both the connection and the separation that New York provides for its inhabitants. My only connection with Fred Stone was that I saw him in *The Wizard of Oz* around the beginning of the century. But our waiter felt the same stimulus from being close to a man from Oz, and after Mr. Stone left the room the waiter told me that when he (the waiter) was a young man just arrived in this country and before he could understand a word of English, he had taken his girl for their first theater date to *The Wizard of Oz*. It was a wonderful show, the waiter recalled—a man of straw, a man of tin. Wonderful! (And still only eighteen inches away.) "Mr. Stone is a very hearty eater," said the waiter thoughtfully, content with his fragile participation in destiny, this link with Oz.

[4] New York blends the gift of privacy with the excitement of participation; and better than most dense communities it succeeds in insulating the individual (if he wants it, and almost everybody wants or needs it) against all enormous and violent and wonderful events that are taking place every minute. Since I have been sitting in this miasmic air shaft, a good many rather splashy events have occurred in town. A man shot and killed his wife in a fit of jealousy. It caused no stir outside his block and got only small mention in the papers. I did not attend. Since my arrival, the greatest air show ever staged in all the world took place in town. I didn't attend and neither did most of the eight million inhabitants, although they say there was quite a crowd. I didn't even hear any planes except a couple of westbound commercial airliners that habitually use this air shaft to fly over. The biggest ocean-going ships on the North Atlantic arrived and departed. I didn't notice them and neither did most other New Yorkers. I am told this is the greatest seaport in the world, with six hundred and fifty miles of water front, and ships calling here from many exotic lands, but the only boat I've happened to notice since my arrival was a small sloop tacking out of the East River night before last on the ebb tide when I was walking across the Brooklyn Bridge. I heard the *Queen Mary* blow one midnight, though, and the sound carried the whole history of departure and longing and loss. The Lions have been in convention. I've seen not one Lion. A friend of mine saw one and told me about him. (He was lame, and was wearing a bolero.) At the ballgrounds and horse parks the greatest sporting spectacles have been enacted. I saw no ballplayer, no race horse. The governor came to town. I heard the siren scream, but that was all there was to that—an eighteen-inch margin again. A man was killed by a falling cornice. I was not a party to the tragedy, and again the inches counted heavily.

[5] I mention these merely to show that New York is peculiarly constructed to absorb almost anything that comes along (whether a thousand-foot liner out of the East or a twenty-thousand-man convention out of the West) without inflicting the event on its inhabitants; so that every event is, in a sense, optional, and the inhabitant is in the happy position of being able to choose his spectacle and so conserve his soul. In most metropolises, small and large, the choice is often not with the individual at all. He is thrown to the Lions. The Lions are overwhelming; the event is unavoidable. A cornice falls, and it hits every citizen on the head, every last man in town. I sometimes think that the only event that hits every New Yorker on the head is the annual St. Patrick's Day parade, which is fairly penetrating—the Irish are a hard race to tune out, there are 500,000 of them in residence, and they have the police force right in the family.

[6] The quality in New York that insulates its inhabitants from life may simply weaken them as individuals. Perhaps it is healthier to live in a community where, when a cornice falls, you feel the blow; where, when the governor passes, you see at any rate his hat.

[7] I am not defending New York in this regard. Many of its settlers are probably here merely to escape, not face, reality. But whatever it means, it is a rather rare gift, and I believe it has a positive effect on the creative capacities of New Yorkers—for creation in in part merely the business of forgoing the great and small distractions.

[8] Although New York often imparts a feeling of great forlornness or forsakenness, it seldom seems dead or unresourceful; and you always feel that either by shifting your location ten blocks or by reducing your fortune by five dollars you can experience rejuvenation. Many people who have no real independence of spirit depend on the city's tremendous variety and sources of excitement for spiritual sustenance and mainte- nance of morale. In the country there are a few chances of sudden re- juvenation—a shift in weather, perhaps, or something arriving in the mail. But in New York the chances are endless. I think that although many persons are here from some excess of spirit (which caused them to break away from their small town), some too, are here from a de- ficiency of spirit, who find in New York a protection, or an easy substitu- tion.

[9] There are roughly three New Yorks. There is, first, the New York of the man or woman who was born here, who takes the city for granted and accepts its size and its turbulence as natural and inevitable. Second, there is the New York of the commuter—the city that is devoured by locusts each day and spat out each night. Third, there is the New York of the person who was born somewhere else and came to New York in quest of something. Of these three trembling cities the greatest is the last—the city of final destination, the city that is a goal. It is this third city that accounts for New York's high-strung disposition, its poetical deportment, its dedication to the arts, and its incomparable achieve- ments. Commuters give the city its tidal restlessness; natives give it solidity and continuity; but the settlers give it passion. And whether it is a farmer arriving from Italy to set up a small grocery store in a slum, or a young girl arriving from a small town in Mississippi to escape the indignity of being observed by her neighbors, or a boy arriving from the Corn Belt with a manuscript in his suitcase and a pain in his heart, it makes no difference: each embraces New York with the intense ex- citement of first love, each absorbs New York with the fresh eyes of an adventurer, each generates heat and light to dwarf the Consolidated Edison Company.

[10] The commuter is the queerest bird of all. The suburb he inhabits

has no essential vitality of its own and is a mere roost where he comes at day's end to go to sleep. Except in rare cases, the man who lives in Mamaroneck or Little Neck or Teaneck, and works in New York, discovers nothing much about the city except the time of arrival and departure of trains and buses, and the path to a quick lunch. He is desk-bound, and has never, idly roaming in the gloaming, stumbled suddenly on Belvedere Tower in the Park, seen the ramparts rise sheer from the water of the pond, and the boys along the shore fishing for minnows, girls stretched out negligently on the shelves of the rocks; he has never come suddenly on anything at all in New York as a loiterer, because he has had no time between trains. He has fished in Manhattan's wallet and dug out coins, but has never listened to Manhattan's breathing, never awakened to its morning, never dropped off to sleep in its night. About 400,000 men and women come charging onto the Island each week-day morning, out of the mouths of tubes and tunnels. Not many among them have ever spent a drowsy afternoon in the great rustling oaken silence of the reading room of the Public Library, with the book elevator (like an old water wheel) spewing out books onto the trays. They tend their furnaces in Westchester and in Jersey, but have never seen the furnaces of the Bowery, the fires that burn in oil drums on zero winter nights. They may work in the financial district downtown and never see the extravagant plantings of Rockefeller Center—the daffodils and grape hyacinths and birches and the flags trimmed to the wind on a fine morning in spring. Or they may work in a mid-town office and may let a whole year swing round without sighting Governor's Island from the sea wall. The commuter dies with tremendous mileage to his credit, but he is no rover. His entrances and exits are more devious than those in a prairie-dog village; and he calmly plays bridge while his train is buried in the mud at the bottom of the East River. The Long Island Rail Road alone carried forty million commuters last year; but many of them were the same fellow retracing his steps.

[11] The terrain of New York is such that a resident sometimes travels farther, in the end, than a commuter. Irving Berlin's journey from Cherry Street in the lower East Side to an apartment uptown was through an alley and was only three or four miles in length; but it was like going three times around the world.

[12] A poem compresses much in a small space and adds music, thus heightening its meaning. The city is like poetry: it compresses all life, all races and breeds, into a small island and adds music and the accompaniment of internal engines. The island of Manhattan is without any doubt the greatest human concentrate on earth, the poem whose magic is comprehensible to millions of permanent residents but whose full meaning will always remain elusive. At the feet of the tallest and

plushiest offices lie the crummiest slums. The genteel mysteries housed in the Riverside Church are only a few blocks from the voodoo charms of Harlem. The merchant princes, riding to Wall Street in their limousines down the East River Drive, pass within a few hundred yards of the gypsy kings; but the princes do not know they are passing kings, and the kings are not up yet anyway—they live a more leisurely life than the princes and get drunk more consistently.

[13] New York is nothing like Paris; it is nothing like London; and it is not Spokane multiplied by sixty, or Detroit multiplied by four. It is by all odds the loftiest of cities. It even managed to reach the highest point in the sky at the lowest moment of the depression. The Empire State Building shot twelve hundred and fifty feet into the air when it was madness to put out as much as six inches of new growth. (The building has a mooring mast that no dirigible has ever tied to; it employs a man to flush toilets in slack times; it has been hit by an airplane in a fog, struck countless times by lightning, and been jumped off of by so many unhappy people that pedestrians instinctively quicken step when passing Fifth Avenue and 34th Street.)

[14] Manhattan has been compelled to expand skyward because of the absence of any other direction in which to grow. This, more than any other thing, is responsible for its physical majesty. It is to the nation what the white church spire is to the village—the visible symbol of aspiration and faith, the white plume saying that the way is up. The summer traveler swings in over Hell Gate Bridge and from the window of his sleeping car as it glides above the pigeon lofts and back yards of Queens looks southwest to where the morning light first strikes the steel peaks of mid-town, and he sees its upward thrust unmistakeable: the great walls and towers rising, the smoke rising, the heat not yet rising, the hopes and ferments of so many awakening millions rising—this vigorous spear that presses heaven hard.

[15] It is a miracle that New York works at all. The whole thing is implausible. Every time the residents brush their teeth, millions of gallons of water must be drawn from the Catskill Mountains and the hills of Westchester. When a young man in Manhattan writes a letter to his girl in Brooklyn, the love message gets blown to her through a pneumatic tube—*pfft*—just like that. The subterranean system of telephone cables, power lines, steam pipes, gas mains and sewer pipes is reason enough to abandon the island to the gods and the weevils. Every time an incision is made in the pavement, the noisy surgeons expose ganglia that are tangled beyond belief. By rights New York should have destroyed itself long ago, from panic or fire or rioting or failure of some vital supply line in its circulatory system or from some deep labyrinthine short circuit. Long ago the city should have experienced an insoluble

traffic snarl at some impossible bottleneck. It should have perished of hunger when food lines failed for a few days. It should have been wiped out by a plague starting in its slums or carried in by ships' rats. It should have been overwhelmed by the sea that licks at it on every side. The workers in its myriad cells should have succumbed to nerves, from the fearful pall of smoke-fog that drifts over every few days from Jersey, blotting out all light at noon and leaving the high offices suspended, men groping and depressed, and the sense of world's end. It should have been touched in the head by the August heat and gone off its rocker.

[16] Mass hysteria is a terrible force, yet New Yorkers seem always to escape it by some tiny margin: they sit in stalled subways without claustrophobia, they extricate themselves from panic situations by some lucky wisecrack, they meet confusion and congestion with patience and grit—a sort of perpetual muddling through. Every facility is inadequate —the hospitals and schools and playgrounds are overcrowded, the express highways are feverish, the unimproved highways and bridges are bottlenecks; there is not enough air and not enough light, and there is usually either too much heat or too little. But the city makes up for its hazards and its deficiencies by supplying its citizens with massive doses of a supplementary vitamin—the sense of belonging to something unique, cosmopolitan, mighty and unparalleled.

[17] To an outlander a stay in New York can be and often is a series of small embarrassments and discomforts and disappointments: not understanding the waiter, not being able to distinguish between a sucker joint and a friendly saloon, riding the wrong subway, being slapped down by a bus driver for asking an innocent question, enduring sleepless nights when the street noises fill the bedroom. Tourists make for New York, particularly in summertime—they swarm all over the Statue of Liberty (where many a resident of the town has never set foot), they invade the Automat, visit radio studios, St. Patrick's Cathedral, and they window shop. Mostly they have a pretty good time. But sometimes in New York you run across the disillusioned—a young couple who are obviously visitors, newlyweds perhaps, for whom the bright dream has vanished. The place has been too much for them; they sit languishing in a cheap restaurant over a speechless meal.

[18] The oft-quoted thumbnail sketch of New York is, of course: "It's a wonderful place, but I'd hate to live there." I have an idea that people from villages and small towns, people accustomed to the convenience and the friendliness of neighborhood over-the-fence living, are unaware that life in New York follows the neighborhood pattern. The city is literally a composite of tens of thousands of tiny neighborhood units. There are, of course, the big districts and big units: Chelsea and Murray Hill and Gramercy (which are residential units), Harlem (a racial

unit), Greenwich Village (a unit dedicated to the arts and other matters), and there is Radio City (a commercial development), Peter Cooper Village (a housing unit), the Medical Center (a sickness unit) and many other sections each of which has some distinguishing characteristic. But the curious thing about New York is that each large geographical unit is composed of countless small neighborhoods. Each neighborhood is virtually self-sufficient. Usually it is no more than two or three blocks long and a couple of blocks wide. Each area is a city within a city within a city. Thus, no matter where you live in New York, you will find within a block or two a grocery store, a barbershop, a newsstand and shoeshine shack, an ice-coal-and-wood cellar (where you write your order on a pad outside as you walk by), a dry cleaner, a laundry, a delicatessen (beer and sandwiches delivered at any hour to your door), a flower shop, an undertaker's parlor, a movie house, a radio-repair shop, a stationer, a haberdasher, a tailor, a drugstore, a garage, a tearoom, a saloon, a hardware store, a liquor store, a shoe-repair shop. Every block or two, in most residential sections of New York, is a little main street. A man starts for work in the morning and before he has gone two hundred yards he has completed half a dozen missions: bought a paper, left a pair of shoes to be soled, picked up a pack of cigarettes, ordered a bottle of whiskey to be dispatched in the opposite direction against his home-coming, written a message to the unseen forces of the wood cellar, and notified the dry cleaner that a pair of trousers awaits call. Homeward bound eight hours later, he buys a bunch of pussy willows, a Mazda bulb, a drink, a shine—all between the corner where he steps off the bus and his apartment. So complete is each neighborhood, and so strong the sense of neighborhood, that many a New Yorker spends a lifetime within the confines of an area smaller than a country village. Let him walk two blocks from his corner and he is in a strange land and will feel uneasy till he gets back.

[19] Storekeepers are particularly conscious of neighborhood boundary lines. A woman friend of mine moved recently from one apartment to another, a distance of three blocks. When she turned up, the day after the move, at the same grocer's that she had patronized for years, the proprietor was in ecstasy—almost in tears—at seeing her. "I was afraid," he said, "now that you've moved away I wouldn't be seeing you any more." To him, *away* was three blocks, or about seven hundred and fifty feet.

[20] I am, at the moment of writing this, living not as a neighborhood man in New York but as a transient, or vagrant, in from the country for a few days. Summertime is a good time to re-examine New York and to receive again the gift of privacy, the jewel of loneliness. In summer the city contains (except for tourists) only die-hards and authentic char-

acters. No casual, spotty dwellers are around, only the real article. And the town has a somewhat relaxed air, and one can lie in a loincloth, gasping and remembering things. . . .

QUESTIONS AND COMMENT ON FORM AND CONTENT

1. What in White's first paragraph gets the reader's attention? Are the ideas expressed here in keeping with his main thesis about New York?

2. What is the stylistic effect in paragraph 2 of the use of *and* in "New York is the concentrate of art and commerce and sport and religion and entertainment and finance . . ."? Try using the ideas in an ordinary sentence. Is this variation of the ordinary series with commas worth using for certain effects? How does he end his sentence? How is the rest of paragraph 2 developed?

3. What are White's three New Yorks (or New Yorkers)? Which of the three is given most space and emphasis in paragraph 9? What do they contribute to the city?

4. In the ninth paragraph the commuters are locusts. In the tenth "the commuter is the queerest bird of all." What further use does White make of the *bird*, an expression that could be taken as rather outdated slang, but which is given new life here?

5. What details make each of the following outsiders individuals in paragraph 9: the farmer, the young girl, a boy? What do heat and light represent?

6. Show how in paragraph 10 and in two other selected paragraphs the author, through concrete details and specific instances, makes an experience seem real.

7. What is meant in paragraph 7 by "creation is in part merely the business of forgoing the great and small distractions."

8. How does White show that "Each neighborhood is virtually self-sufficient"? (paragraph 18)

9. Do you find any contrasts used effectively?

10. To what extent is the language informal? Quote some examples such as "they say there was quite a crowd," or "touched in the head . . . and gone off its rocker."

VOCABULARY: WHAT DO THE ITALICIZED WORDS MEAN?

It is this *largess* that accounts for [some of New York's population] (1)
. . . seeking *sanctuary* or *fulfillment* or some greater or lesser *grail* (1)
. . . sitting in this *miasmic* air shaft (4)
. . . ships calling from many *exotic* lands (4)
. . . you can experience *rejuvenation* (8)
. . . sit in stalled subways *unique, cosmopolitan,* mighty (16)
The city is *literally* a *composite* (18)

THEME SUGGESTIONS

After the manner of E. B. White present a scene from a city or town that you know quite well and that you think will interest your classmates. Do not neglect the concrete and even apparently insignificant details necessary to give life to a scene. Be careful to let your reader know the physical point of view— the place of your camera—and if it is a moving point of view, let him know that too. Give the scene a time of year, time of day, and, perhaps, day of the week. Can you involve several of the senses, not just sight alone? Do not over-work adjectives or clichés. Do not exaggerate or pretend to be impressed when you are not. Be honest with your reader.

CHICAGO

Carl Sandburg

"Chicago," by Carl Sandburg (1878-   ), appeared in Poetry, *a magazine sympathetic to the new poetry of the period, in 1914. The free verse and the colloquial and often crude language caused his poetry to be controversial at the time. Today, his poetry and his six-volume life of Abraham Lincoln are considered his notable literary accomplishments.*

> Hog Butcher for the World,
> Tool Maker, Stacker of Wheat,
> Player with Railroads and the Nation's Freight Handler;
> Stormy, husky, brawling,
> City of the Big Shoulders:
> They tell me you are wicked and I believe them, for I have seen your
>   painted women under the gas lamps luring the farm boys.
> And they tell me you are crooked and I answer: Yes, it is true I have
>   seen the gunman kill and go free to go and kill again.
> And they tell me you are brutal and my reply is: On the faces of women
>   and children I have seen the marks of wanton hunger.
> And having answered so I turn once more to those who sneer at this my
>   city, and I give them back the sneer and say to them:
> Come and show me another city with lifted head singing so proud to be
>   alive and coarse and strong and cunning.
> Flinging magnetic curses amid the toil of piling job on job, here is a tall
>   bold slugger set vivid against the little soft cities;

Fierce as a dog lapping for action, cunning as a savage pitted against
  the wilderness,
> Bareheaded,
> Shoveling,
> Wrecking,
> Planning,
> Building, breaking, rebuilding,

Under the smoke, dust all over his mouth, laughing with white teeth,
Under the terrible burden of destiny laughing as a young man laughs,
Laughing even as an ignorant fighter laughs who has never lost a battle,
Bragging and laughing that under his wrist is the pulse, and under his
  ribs the heart of the people,
> Laughing!

Laughing the stormy, husky, brawling laughter of Youth, half-naked,
  sweating, proud to be Hog Butcher, Tool Maker, Stacker of Wheat,
  Player with Railroads and Freight Handler to the Nation.

QUESTIONS AND COMMENT ON FORM AND CONTENT

1. Assuming that you know nothing of Chicago except what is pictured in
this poem, what would be your impression of the city? How does Sandburg get
this impression?

2. This poem like other good descriptions has a dominant tone or mood.
Which contributes most to this tone: the meaning of the words; the sound of
the words as used in phrases and clauses; the strong beat of the rhythm?

3. Although this is free verse, that is, verse without a definite type of foot
and number of feet in the line, do you find any pattern in the poem? See, for
example, the odd way it is printed on the page: five short lines (with many
capitals) followed by six long lines of approximately equal length. What about
the rest of the poem?

4. What does poetry, especially free verse, gain or lose by its comparative
freedom from ordinary syntax? Notice the use of modifying phrases.

5. Can we use some of Sandburg's own adjectives to apply to the tone of
this poem: loud, husky, brawling, fierce, stormy, brutal? Was his choice of
words here determined by the dominant mood that he wanted to give the
poem? Can you name another poem of his in which soft, gentle words are used?

THEME SUGGESTIONS

What is your dominant impression of a certain major American city such as
San Francisco, Pittsburgh, New Orleans, St. Louis, or Boston?

An Impressionistic Picture of _____

PART II

EMPHASIS ON IDEAS

Exposition and Argument

5 | GRAMMAR AND USAGE:
WHAT IS GOOD ENGLISH?

THE FUTURE OF GRAMMAR

Paul Roberts

Paul Roberts (1917-   ), Professor of English at San Jose State College, has written several textbooks in English in which he has applied the methods of linguistics to problems in grammar and usage.

[1] The last few decades have witnessed an amiable but spirited battle between linguistic scientists and defenders of traditional ways of teaching English. Linguists have been in revolt against two assumptions that underlie the tradition: (1) that there are absolute criteria—logical, analogical, etymological, or whatever—by which correctness can be measured; and (2) that there are universal, nonlinguistic concepts through which the linguistic categories of any language can be identified and defined. Ultimately this revolt will succeed; there need be no doubt of that. Provided only that our society retains the orientation it has had for the past several centuries, nothing can prevent the establishment in the school system of the views of linguistic science. Wherever, in our civilization, science and non-science conflict, it is non-science that gives way, as astrology gave way to astronomy and alchemy to chemistry. In the same way, linguistic science and structural analysis will triumph over traditional language teaching, although it may take a similarly long time. It is true that astrology does not now play the role that it did in 1350, but astrologers are still around.

Excerpted from *Inside the American College Dictionary*.

[2] Our purpose here is not to discuss when or whether the transition will take place but rather to suggest what its effects on English teaching are likely to be.

[3] Some effects there have been already, and not all of them are good. Linguists have long argued that correctness is altogether relative, having nothing to do with logic or the order of the universe, but depending on such variables as time, place, circumstance, age, sex. The language forms used, correctly, in addressing an umpire, may be incorrect in addressing a bishop. And vice versa. The sentence "We heard the sweetest little bird singing the dearest little song" is correct if you're a twelve-year-old girl but incorrect if you're a fifty-year-old bartender. In some circles, "Ain't you comin' back?" will get you blackballed; in others, "Shall you not return?" will get you tossed out on your ear.

[4] Logic has nothing to do with it. When they ask, "Is it correct?" linguists don't mean, "Is it logical?" They mean, "Would it be well received—at this time, in this place, in this social situation—from a person of this age and sex?" It doesn't matter whether or not, in algebra, two negatives make a positive. What matters is whether, in the language area being considered, it is customary to say, "We don't want no trouble," and, if so, whether it would be generally understood that the speaker wants trouble or doesn't.

[5] All this is old stuff. It is a principle now fully accepted by dictionaries, which don't tell us what to say but rather what we and our countrymen *do* say. It has also been accepted, to some degree, by most handbooks and by many teachers of English. But the implications for classroom procedure are still to be understood and faced.

[6] One thing that the idea of relativity of correctness does *not* mean is that it doesn't matter how we talk or write. Recently some educators have been disposed to tell us: "It isn't important *how* you say a thing; what is important is what you say." This is a pious thought, and it may be true in the sight of God, but it isn't true as the world goes and never will be. Possibly this notion is the linguists' responsibility, but it isn't the linguists' notion.

[7] Certainly it matters how you say a thing. Saying the right thing in the wrong way can get you fired, divorced, arrested, or expelled from the P.T.A. It's nice to be intelligible, but sometimes it is infinitely better to be unintelligible than incorrect. It makes a tremendous difference how you say a thing; it just doesn't always make the same difference. In fact, it probably never makes the same difference twice.

[8] This is what the growing heaps of linguistic information, like the *Linguistic Atlas* and the dialect dictionaries, are showing ever more clearly. We may suppose that any bit of speech, any word or phrase or

sentence, will, when uttered, be either correct or incorrect. But we cannot predict which without knowing all about the nonlinguistic environment in which the utterance occurs. The criteria of correctness are real enough, but they are staggeringly complex and constantly in motion, shifting subtly about us as we go from work to play, from night to morning, from anteroom to inner office, from Broadway to Cypress Street, from Peter to Paul. There is probably no American expression of which we can say, "This will always be correct." And none of which we can say, "This will always be wrong."

[9] So far we have tried to meet this difficulty with the concept of "levels of usage," dividing usage into several strata, usually three—standard, colloquial, vulgate. Now this concept has its uses where the intent is purely descriptive, as for example in a dictionary or a descriptive grammar. But as a device for instructing students in how to behave linguistically, it is using nets to catch the wind. The "levels of usage" concept has not led us, as some would say, to teach descriptively rather than prescriptively. It has simply led us to be prescriptive in a much more complicated way—and yet in a way not nearly complicated enough for the linguistic reality which our students face. If we must be prescriptive, it is more reasonable to select some single, more or less graspable area of usage—say the usage of the *Atlantic Monthly*—and make the student learn that and only that and bat his ears down when he departs from it.

[10] The alternative is to abandon the prescriptive idea altogether, to give up the notion of bringing the student to a foredetermined pattern of usage, and to seek other results entirely. We might aim not at conformity but at range, flexibility, adaptability. We might teach the student to observe his own language and the language of others and to describe them accurately. We might develop sensitivity for the nuances of speech and prose, an ear and an eye for the eternal subtle changes going on in them. We might train the student to use dictionaries as their makers intend them to be used—not as oracles but as collections of linguistic fact to be consulted in areas into which the user's experience does not reach and to be believed whenever they do not conflict with the user's own accurate observation.

[11] Experiments in this direction are already underway in many schools throughout the country. But it may be generations before the thing is done in the school system generally. Our teaching materials will need to be thoroughly revised, the curriculum in teacher-training institutions drastically modified. Most important, beliefs and attitudes as deep-seated as the belief of the Middle Ages in astrology will have to give way. But there is no reason to believe that the change will not take place

—in someone's lifetime—and that the change will not be generally for the better, resulting in a major improvement in the morale of English classes and in a general rise in the ability to speak and write fluently, intelligibly, gracefully, accurately, and even—in the best sense of the word—correctly.

QUESTIONS AND COMMENT ON FORM AND CONTENT

1. What, according to Paul Roberts, determines correctness in language?
2. Would he assert that the way of saying a thing is not important? What examples does he use for his answer?
3. Is the concept of three levels of usage (standard, colloquial, vulgate) of value? What are its limitations? What does he mean by "using nets to catch the wind"? (paragraph 9)
4. Is the teacher justified in emphasizing standard English rather than colloquial or sub-standard? Why? Of what practical advantage to you would a better acquantance with standard or formal English be? Do you need instruction in the use of the colloquial and vulgate?
5. In order to improve speaking and writing, what qualities of language, according to Roberts, need to be stressed?

VOCABULARY: WHAT DO THE ITALICIZED WORDS MEAN?

Linguists have been in revolt (1)
. . . there are *absolute criteria* (1)
. . . *logical, analogical, etymological* (1)
. . . *astrology* gave way to astronomy and *alchemy* to chemistry (2)
. . . will get you *blackballed* (3)
. . . to teach descriptively rather than *prescriptively* (9)

THEME SUGGESTIONS

Compare your use of language on formal occasions (as in applying for a position, meeting an important person, and the like) with that of such informal situations as a "bull session" with your roommate and close friends.

Report the actual usage on campus covering some of the items listed in an English handbook such as (Who) (Whom) were you with?, It is (I) (me), the double negative, the use of adjectives for adverbs, the use of slang, the use of *ain't,* and the like.

Write a theme based on the cowboy or hillbilly language as used on television. How realistic is it? To what extent is it used as a symbol to indicate lack of formal education?

BUT WHAT'S A DICTIONARY FOR?

Bergen Evans

Bergen Evans (1905-   ) is the author with Cornelia Evans of A Dictionary of Contemporary American Usage. *He is Professor of English at Northwestern University and leader in the nationally televised program* The Last Word.

[1] The storm of abuse in the popular press that greeted the appearance of *Webster's Third New International Dictionary* is a curious phenomenon. Never has a scholarly work of this stature been attacked with such unbridled fury and contempt. An article in the *Atlantic* viewed it as a "disappointment," a "shock," a "calamity," "a scandal and a disaster." The New York *Times,* in a special editorial, felt that the work would "accelerate the deterioration" of the language and sternly accused the editors of betraying a public trust. The *Journal* of the American Bar Association saw the publication as "deplorable," "a flagrant example of lexicographic irresponsibility," "a serious blow to the cause of good English." *Life* called it "a non-word deluge," "monstrous," "abominable," and "a cause for dismay." They doubted that "Lincoln could have modelled his Gettysburg Address" on it—a concept of how things get written that throws very little light on Lincoln but a great deal on *Life.*

[2] What underlies all this sound and fury? Is the claim of the G. & C. Merriam Company, probably the world's greatest dictionary maker, that the preparation of the work cost $3.5 million, that it required the efforts of three hundred scholars over a period of twenty-seven years, working on the largest collection of citations ever assembled in any language—is all this a fraud, a hoax?

[3] So monstrous a discrepancy in evaluation requires us to examine basic principles. Just what's a dictionary for? What does it propose to do? What does the common reader go to a dictionary to find? What has the purchaser of a dictionary a right to expect for his money?

[4] Before we look at basic principles, it is necessary to interpose two brief statements. The first of these is that a dictionary is concerned with words. Some dictionaries give various kinds of other useful information. Some have tables of weights and measures on the flyleaves. Some list historical events, and some, home remedies. And there's nothing wrong with their so doing. But the great increase in our vocabulary in the past three decades compels all dictionaries to make more efficient use of their

space. And if something must be eliminated, it is sensible to throw out these extraneous things and stick to words.

[5] Yet wild wails arose. The *Saturday Review* lamented that one can no longer find the goddess Astarte under a separate heading—though they point out that a genus of mollusks named after the goddess is included! They seemed to feel that out of sheer perversity the editors of the dictionary stooped to mollusks while ignoring goddesses and that, in some way, this typifies modern lexicography. Mr. Wilson Follett, folletizing (his mental processes demand some special designation) in the *Atlantic*, cried out in horror that one is not even able to learn from the Third International "that the Virgin was Mary the mother of Jesus"!

[6] The second brief statement is that there has been even more progress in the making of dictionaries in the past thirty years than there has been in the making of automobiles. The difference, for example, between the much-touted Second International (1934) and the much-clouted Third International (1961) is not like the difference between yearly models but like the difference between the horse and buggy and the automobile. Between the appearance of these two editions a whole new science related to the making of dictionaries, the science of descriptive linguistics, has come into being.

[7] Modern linguistics gets its charter from Leonard Bloomfield's *Language* (1933). Bloomfield, for thirteen years professor of Germanic philology at the University of Chicago and for nine years professor of linguistics at Yale, was one of those inseminating scholars who can't be relegated to any department and don't dream of accepting established categories and procedures just because they're established. He was as much an anthropologist as a linguist, and his concepts of language were shaped not by Strunk's *Elements of Style* but by his knowledge of Cree Indian dialects.

[8] The broad general findings of the new science are:

1. All languages are systems of human conventions, not systems of natural laws. The first—and essential—step in the study of any language is observing and setting down precisely what happens when native speakers speak it.

2. Each language is unique in its pronunciation, grammar, and vocabulary. It cannot be described in terms of logic or of some theoretical, ideal language. It cannot be described in terms of any other language, or even in terms of its own past.

3. All languages are dynamic rather than static, and hence a "rule" in any language can only be a statement of contemporary practice. Change is constant—and normal.

4. "Correctness" can rest only upon usage, for the simple reason that there is nothing else for it to rest on. And all usage is relative.

[9] From these propositions it follows that a dictionary is good only insofar as it is a comprehensive and accurate description of current usage. And to be comprehensive it must include some indication of social and regional associations.

[10] New dictionaries are needed because English has changed more in the past two generations than at any other time in its history. It has had to adapt to extraordinary cultural and technological changes, two world wars, unparalleled changes in transportation and communication, and unprecedented movements of populations.

[11] More subtly, but pervasively, it has changed under the influence of mass education and the growth of democracy. As written English is used by increasing millions and for more reasons than ever before, the language has become more utilitarian and more informal. Every publication in America today includes pages that would appear, to the purist of forty years ago, unbuttoned gibberish. Not that they are; they simply show that you can't hold the language of one generation up as a model for the next.

[12] It's not that you mustn't. You *can't*. For example, in the issue in which *Life* stated editorially that it would follow the Second International, there were over forty words, constructions, and meanings which are in the Third International but not in the Second. The issue of the New York *Times* which hailed the Second International as the authority to which it would adhere and the Third International as a scandal and a betrayal which it would reject used one hundred and fifty-three separate words, phrases, and constructions which are listed in the Third International but not in the Second and nineteen others which are condemned in the Second. Many of them are used many times, more than three hundred such uses in all. The Washington *Post*, in an editorial captioned "Keep Your Old Webster's," says in the first sentence, "don't throw it away," and in the second, "hang on to it." But the old Webster's labels *don't* "colloquial" and doesn't include "hang on to," in this sense, at all.

[13] In short, all of these publications are written in the language that the Third International describes, even the very editorials which scorn it. And this is no coincidence, because the Third International isn't setting up any new standards at all; it is simply describing what *Life*, the Washington *Post*, and the New York *Times* are doing. Much of the dictionary's material comes from these very publications, the *Times*, in particular, furnishing more of its illustrative quotations than any other newspaper.

[14] And the papers have no choice. No journal or periodical could sell a single issue today if it restricted itself to the American language of twenty-eight years ago. It couldn't discuss half the things we are interested in, and its style would seem stiff and cumbrous. If the editorials

were serious, the public—and the stockholders—have reason to be grateful that the writers on these publications are more literate than the editors.

[15] And so back to our questions: what's a dictionary for, and how, in 1962, can it best do what it ought to do? The demands are simple. The common reader turns to a dictionary for information about the spelling, pronunciation, meaning, and proper use of words. He wants to know what is current and respectable. But he wants—and has a right to—the truth, the full truth. And the full truth about any language, and especially about American English today, is that there are many areas in which certainty is impossible and simplification is misleading.

[16] Even in so settled a matter as spelling, a dictionary cannot always be absolute. *Theater* is correct, but so is *theatre*. And so are *traveled* and *travelled, plow* and *plough, catalog* and *catalogue,* and scores of other variants. The reader may want a single certainty. He may have taken an unyielding position in an argument, he may have wagered in support of his conviction and may demand that the dictionary "settle" the matter. But neither his vanity nor his purse is any concern of the dictionary's; it must record the facts. And the fact here is that there are many words in our language which may be spelled, with equal correctness, in either of two ways.

[17] So with pronunciation. A citizen listening to his radio might notice that James B. Conant, Bernard Baruch, and Dwight D. Eisenhower pronounce *economics* as ECKuhnomiks, while A. Whitney Griswold, Adlai Stevenson, and Herbert Hoover pronounce it EEKuhnomiks. He turns to the dictionary to see which of the two pronunciations is "right" and finds that they are both acceptable.

[18] Has he been betrayed? Has the dictionary abdicated its responsibility? Should it say that one *must* speak like the president of Harvard or like the president of Yale, like the thirty-first President of the United States or like the thirty-fourth? Surely it's none of its business to make a choice. Not because of the distinction of these particular speakers; lexicography, like God, is no respecter of persons. But because so widespread and conspicuous a use of two pronunciations among people of this elevation shows that there *are* two pronunciations. Their speaking establishes the fact which the dictionary must record.

[19] Among the "enormities" with which *Life* taxes the Third International is its listing of "the common mispronunciation" *heighth.* That it is labeled a "dialectal variant" seems, somehow, to compound the felony. But one hears the word so pronounced, and if one professes to give a full account of American English in the 1960s, one has to take some cognizance of it. All people do not possess *Life's* intuitive perception that the word is so "monstrous" that even to list it as a dialect variation is to merit

scorn. Among these, by the way, was John Milton, who, in one of the greatest passages in all literature, besought the Holy Spirit to raise him to the "highth" of his great argument. And even the *Oxford English Dictionary* is so benighted as to list it, in full boldface, right alongside of *height* as a variant that has been in the language since at least 1290.

[20] Now there are still, apparently, millions of Americans who retain, in this as in much else, some of the speech of Milton. This particular pronunciation seems to be receding, but the *American Dialect Dictionary* still records instances of it from almost every state on the Eastern seaboard and notes that it is heard from older people and "occasionally in educated speech," "common with good speakers," "general," "widespread."

[21] Under these circumstances, what is a dictionary to do? Since millions speak the word this way, the pronunciation can't be ignored. Since it has been in use as long as we have any record of English and since it has been used by the greatest writers, it can't be described as substandard or slang. But it is heard now only in certain localities. That makes it a dialectal pronunciation, and an honest dictionary will list it as such. What else can it do? Should it do?

[22] The average purchaser of a dictionary uses it most often, probably, to find out what a word "means." As a reader, he wants to know what an author intended to convey. As a speaker or writer, he wants to know what a word will convey to his auditors. And this, too, is complex, subtle, and forever changing.

[23] An illustration is furnished by an editorial in the Washington *Post* (January 17, 1962). After a ringing appeal to those who "love truth and accuracy" and the usual bombinations about "abdication of authority" and "barbarism," the editorial charges the Third International with "pretentious and obscure verbosity" and specifically instances its definition of "so simple an object as a door."

[24] The definition reads:

> a movable piece of firm material or a structure supported usu. along one side and swinging on pivots or hinges, sliding along a groove, rolling up and down, revolving as one of four leaves, or folding like an accordion by means of which an opening may be closed or kept open for passage into or out of a building, room, or other covered enclosure or a car, airplane, elevator, or other vehicle.

Then follows a series of special meanings, each particularly defined and, where necessary, illustrated by a quotation.

[25] Since, aside from roaring and admonishing the "gentlemen from Springfield" that "accuracy and brevity are virtues," the *Post*'s editorial

fails to explain what is wrong with the definition, we can only infer from "so simple" a thing that the writer takes the plain, downright, man-in-the-street attitude that a door is a door and any damn fool knows that.

[26] But if so, he has walked into one of lexicography's biggest booby traps: the belief that the obvious is easy to define. Whereas the opposite is true. Anyone can give a fair description of the strange, the new, or the unique. It's the commonplace, the habitual, that challenges definition, for its very commonness compels us to define it in uncommon terms. Dr. Johnson was ridiculed on just this score when his dictionary appeared in 1755. For two hundred years his definition of a network as "anything reticulated or decussated, at equal distances, with interstices between the intersections" has been good for a laugh. But in the merriment one thing is always overlooked: no one has yet come up with a better definition! Subsequent dictionaries defined it as a mesh and then defined a mesh as a network. That's simple, all right.

[27] Anyone who attempts sincerely to state what the word *door* means in the United States of America today can't take refuge in a log cabin. There has been an enormous proliferation of closing and demarking devices and structures in the past twenty years, and anyone who tries to thread his way through the many meanings now included under *door* may have to sacrifice brevity to accuracy and even have to employ words that a limited vocabulary may find obscure.

[28] Is the entrance to a tent a door, for instance? And what of the thing that seals the exit of an airplane? Is this a door? Or what of those sheets and jets of air that are now being used, in place of old-fashioned oak and hinges, to screen entrances and exits. Are they doors? And what of those accordion-like things that set off various sections of many modern apartments? The fine print in the lease takes it for granted that they are doors and that spaces demarked by them are rooms—and the rent is computed on the number of rooms.

[29] Was I gypped by the landlord when he called the folding contraption that shuts off my kitchen a door? I go to the Second International, which the editor of the *Post* urges me to use in preference to the Third International. Here I find that a door is

> The movable frame or barrier of boards, or other material, usually turning on hinges or pivots or sliding, by which an entranceway into a house or apartment is closed and opened; also, a similar part of a piece of furniture, as in a cabinet or bookcase.

This is only forty-six words, but though it includes the cellar door, it excludes the barn door and the accordion-like thing.

[30] So I go on to the Third International. I see at once that the new

definition is longer. But I'm looking for accuracy, and if I must sacrifice brevity to get it, then I must. And, sure enough, in the definition which raised the *Post*'s blood pressure, I find the words "folding like an accordion." The thing *is* a door, and my landlord is using the word in one of its currently accepted meanings.

[31] We don't turn to a work of reference merely for confirmation. We all have words in our vocabularies which we have misunderstood, and to come on the true meaning of one of these words is quite a shock. All our complacency and self-esteem rise to oppose the discovery. But eventually we must accept the humiliation and laugh it off as best we can.

[32] Some, often those who have set themselves up as authorities, stick to their error and charge the dictionary with being in a conspiracy against them. They are sure that their meaning is the only "right" one. And when the dictionary doesn't bear them out they complain about "permissive" attitudes instead of correcting their mistake.

[33] The New York *Times* and the *Saturday Review* both regarded as contemptibly "permissive" the fact that one meaning of one word was illustrated by a quotation from Polly Adler. But a rudimentary knowledge of the development of any language would have told them that the underworld has been a far more active force in shaping and enriching speech than all the synods that have ever convened. Their attitude is like that of the patriot who canceled his subscription to the *Dictionary of American Biography* when he discovered that the very first volume included Benedict Arnold!

[34] The ultimate of "permissiveness," singled out by almost every critic for special scorn, was the inclusion in the Third International of *finalize*. It was this, more than any other one thing, that was given as the reason for sticking to the good old Second International—that "peerless authority on American English," as the *Times* called it. But if it was such an authority, why didn't they look into it? They would have found *finalize* if they had.

[35] And why shouldn't it be there? It exists. It's been recorded for two generations. Millions employ it every day. Two Presidents of the United States—men of widely differing cultural backgrounds—have used it in formal statements. And so has the Secretary-General of the United Nations, a man of unusual linguistic attainments. It isn't permitting the word but omitting it that would break faith with the reader. Because it is exactly the sort of word we want information about.

[36] To list it as substandard would be to imply that it is used solely by the ignorant and the illiterate. But this would be a misrepresentation: President Kennedy and U Thant are highly educated men, and both are articulate and literate. It isn't even a freak form. On the contrary, it is a

classic example of a regular process of development in English, a process which has given us such thoroughly accepted words as *generalize, minimize, formalize,* and *verbalize.* Nor can it be dismissed on logical grounds or on the ground that it is a mere duplication of *complete.* It says something that *complete* doesn't say and says it in a way that is significant in the modern bureaucratic world: one usually *completes* something which he has initiated but *finalizes* the work of others.

[37] One is free to dislike the word. I don't like it. But the editor of a dictionary has to examine the evidence for a word's existence and seek it in context to get, as clearly and closely as he can, the exact meaning that it conveys to those who use it. And if it is widely used by well-educated, literate, reputable people, he must list it as a standard word. He is not compiling a volume of his own prejudices.

[38] An individual's use of his native tongue is the surest index to his position within his community. And those who turn to a dictionary expect from it some statement of the current status of a word or a grammatical construction. And it is with the failure to assume this function that modern lexicography has been most fiercely charged. The charge is based on a naïve assumption that simple labels can be attached in all instances. But they can't. Some words are standard in some constructions and not in others. There may be as many shades of status as of meaning, and modern lexicography instead of abdicating this function has fulfilled it to a degree utterly unknown to earlier dictionaries.

[39] Consider the word *fetch,* meaning to "go get and bring to." Until recently a standard word of full dignity ("Fetch me, I pray thee, a little water in a vessel"—I Kings 17:10), it has become slightly tainted. Perhaps the command latent in it is resented as undemocratic. Or maybe its use in training dogs to retrieve has made some people feel that it is an undignified word to apply to human beings. But, whatever the reason, there is a growing uncertainty about its status, and hence it is the sort of word that conscientious people look up in a dictionary.

[40] Will they find it labeled "good" or "bad"? Neither, of course, because either applied indiscriminately would be untrue. The Third International lists nineteen different meanings of the verb *to fetch.* Of these some are labeled "dialectal," some "chiefly dialectal," some "obsolete," one "chiefly Scottish," and two "not in formal use." The primary meaning— "to go after and bring back"—is not labeled and hence can be accepted as standard, accepted with the more assurance because the many shades of labeling show us that the word's status has been carefully considered.

[41] On grammatical questions the Third International tries to be equally exact and thorough. Sometimes a construction is listed without comment, meaning that in the opinion of the editors it is unquestionably

respectable. Sometimes a construction carries the comment "used by speakers and writers on all educational levels though disapproved by some grammarians." Or the comment may be "used in substandard speech and formerly also by reputable writers." Or "less often in standard than in substandard speech." Or simply "dial."

[42] And this very accurate reporting is based on evidence which is presented for our examination. One may feel that the evidence is inadequate or that the evaluation of it is erroneous. But surely, in the face of classification so much more elaborate and careful than any known heretofore, one cannot fly into a rage and insist that the dictionary is "out to destroy . . . every vestige of linguistic punctilio . . . every criterion for distinguishing between better usages and worse."

[43] Words, as we have said, are continually shifting their meanings and connotations and hence their status. A word which has dignity, say, in the vocabulary of an older person may go down in other people's estimation. Like *fetch*. The older speaker is not likely to be aware of this and will probably be inclined to ascribe the snickers of the young at his speech to that degeneration of manners which every generation has deplored in its juniors. But a word which is coming up in the scale—like *jazz*, say, or, more recently, *crap*—will strike his ear at once. We are much more aware of offenses given us than of those we give. And if he turns to a dictionary and finds the offending word listed as standard—or even listed, apparently—his response is likely to be an outburst of indignation.

[44] But the dictionary can neither snicker nor fulminate. It records. It will offend many, no doubt, to find the expression *wise up*, meaning to inform or to become informed, listed in the Third International with no restricting label. To my aging ears it still sounds like slang. But the evidence—quotations from the *Kiplinger Washington Letter* and the *Wall Street Journal*—convinces me that it is I who am out of step, lagging behind. If such publications have taken to using *wise up* in serious contexts, with no punctuational indication of irregularity, then it is obviously respectable. And finding it so listed and supported, I can only say that it's nice to be informed and sigh to realize that I am becoming an old fogy. But, of course, I don't have to use it (and I'll be damned if I will! "Let them smile, as I do now, At the old forsaken bough Where I cling").

[45] In part, the trouble is due to the fact that there is no standard for standard. Ideas of what is proper to use in serious, dignified speech and writing are changing—and with breathtaking rapidity. This is one of the major facts of contemporary American English. But it is no more the dictionary's business to oppose this process than to speed it up.

[46] Even in our standard speech some words are more dignified and some more informal than others, and dictionaries have tried to guide us

through these uncertainties by marking certain words and constructions as "colloquial," meaning "inappropriate in a formal situation." But this distinction, in the opinion of most scholars, has done more harm than good. It has created the notion that these particular words are inferior, when actually they might be the best possible words in an informal statement. And so—to the rage of many reviewers—the Third International has dropped this label. Not all labels, as angrily charged, but only this one out of a score. And the doing so may have been an error, but it certainly didn't constitute "betrayal" or "abandoning of all distinctions." It was intended to end a certain confusion.

[47] In all the finer shades of meaning, of which the status of a word is only one, the user is on his own, whether he likes it or not. Despite *Life's* artless assumption about the Gettysburg Address, nothing worth writing is written *from* a dictionary. The dictionary, rather, comes along afterwards and describes what *has been* written.

[48] Words in themselves are not dignified, or silly, or wise, or malicious. But they can be used in dignified, silly, wise, or malicious ways by dignified, silly, wise, or malicious people. *Egghead,* for example, is a perfectly legitimate word, as legitimate as *highbrow* or *long-haired.* But there is something very wrong and very undignified, by civilized standards, in a belligerent dislike for intelligence and education. *Yak* is an amusing word for persistent chatter. Anyone could say, "We were just yakking over a cup of coffee," with no harm to his dignity. But to call a Supreme Court decision *yakking* is to be vulgarly insulting and so, undignified. Again, there's nothing wrong with *confab* when it's appropriate. But when the work of a great research project, employing hundreds of distinguished scholars over several decades and involving the honor of one of the greatest publishing houses in the world, is described as *confabbing* (as the New York *Times* editorially described the preparation of the Third International), the use of this particular word asserts that lexicographers had merely sat around and talked idly. And the statement becomes undignified—if not, indeed, slanderous.

[49] The lack of dignity in such statements is not in the words, nor in the dictionaries that list them, but in the hostility that deliberately seeks this tone of expression. And in expressing itself the hostility frequently shows that those who are expressing it don't know how to use a dictionary. Most of the reviewers seem unable to read the Third International and unwilling to read the Second.

[50] The *American Bar Association Journal,* for instance, in a typical outburst ("a deplorable abdication of responsibility"), picked out for special scorn the inclusion in the Third International of the word *irregardless.* "As far as the New Webster's is concerned," said the *Journal,*

"this meaningless verbal bastard is just as legitimate as any other word in the dictionary." Thirty seconds spent in examining the book they were so roundly condemning would have shown them that in it *irregardless* is labeled "nonstand."—which means "nonstandard," which means "not conforming to the usage generally characteristic of educated native speakers of the language." Is that "just as legitimate as any other word in the dictionary"?

[51] The most disturbing fact of all is that the editors of a dozen of the most influential publications in America today are under the impression that *authoritative* must mean *authoritarian*. Even the "permissive" Third International doesn't recognize this identification—editors' attitudes being not yet, fortunately, those of the American people. But the Fourth International may have to.

[52] The new dictionary may have many faults. Nothing that tries to meet an ever-changing situation over a terrain as vast as contemporary English can hope to be free of them. And much in it is open to honest, and informed, disagreement. There can be linguistic objection to the eradication of proper names. The removal of guides to pronunciation from the foot of every page may not have been worth the valuable space it saved. The new method of defining words of many meanings has disadvantages as well as advantages. And of the half million or more definitions, hundreds, possibly thousands, may seem inadequate or imprecise. To some (of whom I am one) the omission of the label "colloquial" will seem meritorious; to others it will seem a loss.

[53] But one thing is certain: anyone who solemnly announces in the year 1962 that he will be guided in matters of English usage by a dictionary published in 1934 is talking ignorant and pretentious nonsense.

QUESTIONS AND COMMENT ON FORM AND CONTENT

1. Bergen Evans begins his article by citing the "storm of abuse that appeared in the popular press upon the appearance of *Webster's Third New International Dictionary*. Yet, he notes, the publishers claim that the work cost $3.5 million and the work of 300 scholars over a period of 27 years. Can the reader tell from the title and the adjectives used which side of the debate the author will take? If so, cite some words.

2. Next he gives some principles of modern linguistics. What are these principles? How do they help to justify his point of view?

3. Much of the criticism has been that the new dictionary has been too permissive, that there has been an abdication of authority. What is Evans' answer?

4. One of his most telling devices in argument is known as "turning the tables." How is this method of refutation used in paragraphs 12 and 13?

5. What is said about *finalize* (paragraph 34), *fetch* (paragraph 39), *wise up* (paragraph 44), *colloquial* as a usage label (paragraph 46 to the end of paragraph 52), *irregardless* (paragraph 50)?

6. What does he mean by saying (paragraph 48), "Words in themselves are not dignified, or silly, or wise, or malicious"?

7. What difference is there between *authoritative* and *authoritarian*?

8. What is the style or tone used by the author?

VOCABULARY: WHAT DO THE ITALICIZED WORDS MEAN?

. . . example of *lexicographic* irresponsibility (1)

. . . throw out these *extraneous* things (4)

. . . out of *sheer perversity* the editors . . . *stooped* (5)

. . . one of those *inseminating* scholars who can't be *relegated* to any department (7)

. . . more *subtly*, but *pervasively*, it has changed (11)

. . . the language has become more *utilitarian* (11)

. . . pages that would appear, to the *purist* of forty years ago, *unbuttoned gibberish* (11)

. . . its style would seem stiff and *cumbrous* (14)

. . . writers are more *literate* than the editors (14)

Has the dictionary *abdicated* its responsibility? (18)

That it is labeled a *"dialectal variant"* seems . . . to *compound* the *felony* (19)

. . . even the OXFORD ENGLISH DICTIONARY is so *benighted* (19)

. . . charges the Third International with *"pretentious* and *obscure verbosity* (23)

. . . an enormous *proliferation* of closing and *demarking* devices (27)

But the dictionary can neither *snicker* nor *fulminate* (44)

THEME SUGGESTIONS

What Is Good English?

What's a Dictionary For?

In a paragraph define some everyday object such as a percolator, a teakettle, a screwdriver, a hammer, or a pair of scissors.

Oral or written report: Wilson Follett, "Sabotage in Springfield," *Atlantic Monthly*, January, 1962.

THE LEXICOGRAPHER'S EASY CHAIR

James Sledd

James Sledd (1914-   ), Professor of English at Northwestern University, is the author of A Short Introduction to English Grammar, 1959. *In the review, part of which is reprinted below, the author points out to the critics of* Webster's Third *that lexicographers have for two hundred years agreed that they are historians and not lawgivers. He then discusses some problems in usage.*

[1] Some criticism of the dictionary's treatment of usage has been . . . frivolous. An excellent bad example appeared in *Life,* whose editors compressed a remarkable amount of confusion into a single sentence when they attacked "Editor Gove" for "saying that if a word is misused often enough, it becomes acceptable." Though one can argue how much use and by what speakers is enough, consistency would force *Life's* editors into silence. Their sacred kye are scrawnier than Pharaoh's seven kine, and it is shocking that the influence of such a magazine should force learning to debate with ignorance.

[2] Yet so loud a stridulation of critics cannot simply be ignored. There is a real question whether the *Third International,* though justly called "the most comprehensive guide to usage currently available," has recorded usage as precisely as it might have done. Were the editors right to abandon "the status label *colloquial*"? Have they adequately reported not only what people say and write but also those opinions concerning speech and writing which properly enter into their own definitions of *standard* and of *Standard English?* Those are legitimate questions to ask of a dictionary "prepared with a constant regard for the needs of the high school and college student" and of the general reader. However diffidently and respectfully, a reviewer must give the best answers that he can.

[3] Several reasons have been offered, by various authorities, for the abandonment of the label *colloquial.* Those reasons are not all alike. It is one thing to say that we cannot know "whether a word out of context is colloquial or not" (Gove), that lexicographers cannot distinguish the "many different degrees of standard usage" by status labels but can only suggest them by quotations (Gove), or that "the bases for discrimination are often too subtle for exact and understandable verbal statement" (Ives); it is quite another thing to argue against marking words *colloquial* be-

Reprinted with the permission of the National Council of Teachers of English and James Sledd. The review originally appeared in *College English,* May, 1962.

cause many readers have wrongly concluded that a word so marked is somehow bad (Ives). In a matter to which the editors must have given their best thought, the variety itself of these justifications and the failure to order them in any coherent and inclusive statement is somewhat puzzling; and the impertinent might be tempted to inquire how 200,000 quotations will enable the inexpert reader to do what 10,000,000 quotations did not make possible for the expert lexicographer or how a dictionary can be made at all if nothing can go into it which the ignorant might misinterpret. One reason for the widespread misinterpretation of the policy adopted is surely that the underlying theory has not been clearly explained.

[4] And that is not all. The very defenses of the new policy appear sometimes to refute the contention that finer discriminations are not possible than those in *Webster's Third*. When the newspapers attack the dictionary for listing words like *double-dome* and *finalize* as standard, defenders reply by citing other slangy or colloquial or much reprobated terms from the columns of those same newspapers. What is the force of the attack or the defense unless the intelligent layman can draw precisely that distinction between "the formal and informal speech and writing of the educated" which the *Third International* refuses to draw for him? If he lacked that ability, both attackers and defenders would be wasting their citations.

[5] Much can be said, of course, about the confusion of styles in modern writing. Perhaps distinctions among styles are now indeed less clear and stable than they were in a less troubled age; perhaps the clumsier writers do ignore the existing distinctions while the sophisticated use them to play sophisticated tunes; perhaps the scrupulously objective lexicographer cannot establish those distinctions from his quotation slips alone. For all that, distinctions do exist. They exist in good writing, and they exist in the linguistic consciousness of the educated. Dr. Gove's definers prove they exist when they give *egghead* as a synonym for *double-dome* but then define *egghead* in impeccably formal terms as "one with intellectual interests or pretensions" or as "a highly educated person." Such opposition between theory and practice strikes even a timid and generally admiring reviewer as rather odd, as though some notion of scientific objectivity should require the scientist to deny that he knows what he knows because he may not know how he knows it.

[6] In the absence, then, of convincing argument to the contrary, a simple reader is left with the uneasy feeling that the abandonment of "colloq." was a mistake which the introduction of more quotations does not quite rectify and that as a teacher he must now provide foreigners and inexperienced students both with some general principles of linguis-

tic choice and with specific instruction in instances where the new dictionary does not discriminate finely enough among stylistic variants. The dictionary leaves unlabeled many expressions which this teacher would not allow a beginning writer to use in serious exposition or argument except for clearly intended and rather special effects: (*to be caught*) *with one's pants down, dollarwise, stylewise* (*s.v. -wise*), (*to give one*) *the bird, dog* "something inferior of its kind," *to enthuse, to level* "deal frankly," *schmaltz, chintzy, the catbird seat, to roll* "rob," *to send* "delight," *shindig, shook-up, square* "an unsophisticated person," *squirrelly, to goof,* and the like. Enforcing such modest niceties will now be more difficult; for classroom lawyers and irate parents will be able to cite the dictionary which the teacher has taught Johnny how to read but which has collapsed the distinction between formal and informal Standard English. Similar difficulties could occur with various mild obscenities, such as *pissed off* and *pisspoor,* which should be marked not only as slang but with some one of the warning labels that the dictionary attaches to the almost quite adequately recorded four-letter words; and the label *slang* itself might well be more freely used with the various synonyms for *drunk—stewed, stinko, stoned, tight, tanked, sozzled, potted, pie-eyed, feeling no pain, blind, looped, squiffed, boiled, fried, high,* etc. Odzooks!

[7] The convenience of a classroom teacher, however, is a rather petty criterion by which to judge a great dictionary, and the tiny handful of evidence here alleged must not be taken as justifying the shrill lament that *Webster's Third* is "a scandal and a disaster." The wake has been distinctly premature. Both the dictionary and the language it records are likely to survive the keening critics, whose exaggerations are something of a stumbling block themselves. The mere extent of the information in a dictionary unabridged should fix in a reviewer's mind the salutary knowledge that as no one man can make such a book, so no one man can judge it; but the popular reviews of the *Third International* have merely skimmed its surface and have said little of its technical features or substantial accomplishments.

QUESTIONS AND COMMENT ON FORM AND CONTENT

1. What are sacred cows (archaic *kye, kine*)?
2. What is meant by *colloquial?*
3. Why did the *Third International* omit *colloquial* as a label for usage?
4. What objection does Sledd have to this omission? Would the inclusion of the label *colloquial* and the more frequent use of the label *slang* be helpful to you? If you can, give an example from your own experience.

VOCABULARY: WHAT DO THE ITALICIZED WORDS MEAN?

. . . so loud a *stridulation* of critics (2)
However *diffidently* and respectfully, a reviewer must give the best answers that he can. (2)
　. . . whether a word out of *context* is colloquial (3)
　. . . slangy or colloquial or much *reprobated* terms (4)
　. . . the *scrupulously objective lexicographer* (5)
The *wake* has been distinctly premature. (7)
　. . . likely to survice the *keening* critics (7)
　. . . the *salutary* knowledge (7)

THEME SUGGESTIONS

The choice of the word with the right degree of formality or informality for a given occasion is often as difficult as the choice of appropriate clothes. Write a theme illustrating how the language appropriate for one occasion would not be suitable for a quite different situation. For example, you could illustrate the language used in a letter to a former high school classmate and a letter to the principal of the high school or to a possible employer. What varieties do you hear on television? Look up such words as *colloquial, slang, euphemism, cant, jargon* in a dictionary or, better still, in *A Dictionary of Modern English Usage* (1965) by H. W. Fowler, revised and edited by Sir Ernest Gowers, or in *A Dictionary of Contemporary American Usage* (1957) by Bergen Evans and Cornelia Evans.
　What is Slang?
　Varieties of American English

THE RIGHT WORD TO WRITE

Granville Hicks

Granville Hicks (1901-　　　) is a lecturer and writer. He is the author of The Great Tradition—an Interpretation of American Literature *and many other books. This article first appeared in the* Saturday Review, *July 17, 1965.*

[1] Theodore Bernstein, assistant managing editor of the *New York Times* and well known to the staff of that newspaper as an authority on English usage, made an impression on a wider audience a few years ago

Reprinted by permission of the author and of the *Saturday Review.*

with *Watch Your Language* and its sequel, *More Language That Needs Watching*, both based on a bulletin written for circulation among writers and editors of the *Times*. Now he has published *The Careful Writer: A Modern Guide to English Usage* (Atheneum, $7.95), a useful reference work and a book that has given me a good deal of pleasure.

[2] The word to notice in the title is "writer," for this is a book about written, not spoken, language. As one who has spent most of his life in small towns, associating with people who know nothing about grammar or usage, I have been impressed by the clarity, vividness, and power with which semiliterate people can express themselves. Bernstein knows this, and he also knows that today even the most careful writers will, as a rule, relax when they are talking informally. But he believes that there are standards which should be preserved in written English.

[3] The controversy over the third edition of *Webster's New International Dictionary* and the writings of the structural linguists have made many of us a little touchy about this question of standards. Bernstein is quite specific about the formation of his standards. They are based on: (1) "the practices of reputable writers, past and present"; (2) "the observations and discoveries of linguistic scholars"; (3) "the predilections of teachers of English"; (4) "observation of what makes for clarity, precision, and logical presentation"; (5) "personal preferences of the author"; (6) experience as an editor of the *Times*.

[4] The fourth point seems to me the important one. Some changes in usage don't diminish the effectiveness of the language, but others do. I couldn't bring myself to use "like" for "as" in speech, let alone in writing; but if "like" wins out, as it seems bound to do, the damage will not be great. If, however, "infer" comes to be accepted as meaning what "imply" means, we have lost a valuable word. (Maybe I dreamt it, but I believe I have seen "infer" misused in the *Times*.)

[5] Bernstein discusses a dozen pairs of words about which confusion exists: disinterested, uninterested; incredible, incredulous; nauseous, nauseated; oral, verbal; tortuous, torturous; turbid, turgid; venal, venial; deprecate, depreciate; hail, hale; flaunt, flout; gantlet, gauntlet. When distinctions are clearly stated, as he states them, anyone can see why they are worth preserving.

[6] On the other hand he is more lenient than Miss Thistlebottom, his imaginary teacher of grammar a generation ago. His discussion of "contact" is a good example of the way his mind works. After saying that "contact" as a verb is useful to businessmen, he suggests that a practiced writer can do very well without it. He concludes: "The verb will undoubtedly push its way into standard usage sometime. Do you think you can wait?" He is sensible on split infinitives, prepositions at the end of

sentences, and "shall" and "will." Many people will be relieved to know that they *graduated* from college; it is not necessary for them to say that they *were* graduated.

[7] There are excellent discussions of more general topics. Bernstein, who likes puns, talks about "ad-diction," giving many examples of ways in which advertising men are doing their best to debase the language. (They are given much assistance, he points out, by the editors of *Time* Magazine and the writers of headlines, although, as a newspaperman, he has sympathy for the latter.) In less than twenty pages he provides as handy a summary of rules of punctuation as you can find, and in ten pages he tells the careful writer all he is likely to need to know about rhetorical figures and faults. It's a useful book.

[8] Bernstein writes: "The area of highly formal writing has shrunk considerably; it is now confined to such things as state papers, articles in learned publications, commencement addresses (and by no means all of those), legal documents, court decisions, and prefaces to dictionaries." As he goes on to say, colloquialisms—he prefers to call them "casualisms" —have become increasingly common in serious writing of many kinds. But he might have gone further: the skillful use of colloquialisms is an important element in some of the most effective writing in our time. He says, "There are, of course, gradations of casualisms: *falsies* is low and unacceptable in most contexts." But I can think of a number of contexts in which the word would be extremely convenient if not indispensable.

[9] Perhaps, however, Bernstein is right in suggesting that the careful writer ought not to take chances. Last fall, in reviewing Roy Newquist's *Counterpoint,* I wrote, "He begins with a brief but usually fulsome introduction of the author to be interviewed." I received two letters, one indignant and the other condescending, asking me if I didn't know that "fulsome" means "offensive, disgusting." I replied by quoting from the *Oxford Universal Dictionary*: "7. of language, style, behavior, etc.; Offensive to good taste; *esp.* from excess or want of measure." That is just what I meant. If I had been able to consult Bernstein, however, this is what I would have found: "It does not mean full, copious, or bounteous. . . . It means overfull and offensive because of insincerity; repulsive, odious. It most often appears—and appears incorrectly, of course—in the phrase 'fulsome praise'." I think that praise often is fulsome according to his definition, but I know that if I used that phrase I'd get into trouble.

[10] As we all, including Bernstein, know, Shakespeare wasn't a careful writer in Bernstein's sense of the term; he mixed metaphors all over the place, and played hob with rules of grammar. Many other of our eminent creative writers have been as lawless. But most of us are not great creative writers, and Bernstein is our man. If we are going to go

against the rules, we ought at least to know what we are doing, and he can tell us.

[11] Ever since it was published in 1926, I have been both instructed and entertained by H. W. Fowler's *Modern English Usage*,[1] for no lexicographer since Dr. Johnson has written with such cantankerous charm. As for Bergen and Cornelia Evans's *Dictionary of Contemporary Usage*, it seems to me more useful than Bernstein in some ways and less useful in others. I am glad that I have both, together with Fowler.

QUESTIONS AND COMMENT ON FORM AND CONTENT

1. In his book review Granville Hicks points out that Theodore Bernstein's *The Careful Writer: A Modern Guide to English Usage* "is a book about written, not spoken, language." Why does the reviewer think this fact worthy of mention?

2. On what are Bernstein's six standards of usage based? Which one or ones do you consider most important and which one or ones least important? Which one does Hicks think most important?

3. What is Bernstein's advice to writers, including those on the New York *Times*, about using *contact* in "I'll *contact* you later"? What is mean by being "sensible on split infinitives, prepositions at the end of sentences, and *shall* and *will*"? (Consult dictionaries and handbooks.)

4. In addition to dictionaries, what three books on usage does Hicks recommend?

5. Why might one expect the managing editor of a highly respected metropolitan newspaper to be more conservative in usage than Bergen Evans, a college teacher of the English language?

6. Does this book review cover what readers would want to know about a book on usage? In general, what does the review tell besides the name of the publisher, the name of the author, and the price of the book?

7. What are the topic sentences for paragraphs 3, 4, 5, 6, 7, 8, and 9? How are these paragraphs developed? Why does Hicks put the last sentence of paragraph 4 in parentheses?

VOCABULARY: WHAT DO THE ITALICIZED WORDS MEAN?

. . . the *predilections* of teachers of English (3)

If . . . *infer* comes to be accepted as meaning what *imply* means (4)

. . . pairs of words about which confusion exists: *disinterested, uninterested; incredible, incredulous.* . . . (See also the other pairs of words in paragraph 5.)

. . . has written with such *cantankerous* charm (10)

[1] The second edition, 1965, has been revised and edited by Sir Ernest Gowers.

THEME SUGGESTIONS

Write a book, movie, or play review, giving such details and opinions as you think a reader would want. Do not tell the story of a novel or movie or play. Coleridge suggested that a criticism should answer three questions: What was the writer trying to do? Did he do it? Was it worth doing? The last question, in particular, calls for some evaluation or comparison.

6 | SOME PRINCIPLES
OF WRITTEN STYLE

PLEASANT AGONY

John Mason Brown

John Mason Brown (1900-   ) is an essayist, lecturer, and drama critic. For many years he was columnist for the Saturday Review, *where this essay appeared. It was also included in a volume* Still Seeing Things *(1950).*

[1] For several years now, mine has been the privilege, hence the pleasant agony, of filling a page each week, or almost every week, in the *Saturday Review of Literature.* I say pleasant agony because I know of no other words with which to describe what writing is to me.

[2] I claim no singularity in this. There may be, there must be, writers to whom writing comes as effortlessly as breathing. There may even be (though I doubt it) writers whose happiness is complete while they are actually writing. But most of us who live by putting words together are not so fortunate. We are tortured while we write and would be tortured were we not allowed to do so. Although when we are done we feel "delivered," as Sainte-Beuve put it, this delirium of delivery is not accomplished without labor pains for which medicine has, as yet, provided no soothing drugs. If all attempts to coerce words into doing what we would have them do are at best painful pleasures, the pains and pleasures of summoning the right words to meet a weekly deadline are of a special kind.

Reprinted with the permission of the author and the *Saturday Review.*

[3] A cook faced with getting dinner when lunch is over knows something of the routine, if not all the anguishes, of a columnist. No mortals, however, have appetites as insatiable as a column's. A column is an omnivorous beast. Its hunger is never appeased. Feed it, and almost at once it demands to be fed again.

[4] Though he used a different image to express this same idea, even Shaw, seemingly the most easeful of writers, knew this. When he abandoned the job of drama critic on London's *Saturday Review*, he protested against the weekly deadlines which had confronted him for nearly four years. He likened himself to a man fighting a windmill. "I have hardly time," wrote he, "to stagger to my feet from the knockdown blow of one sail, when the next strikes me down."

[5] His successor in the same job on that same fortunate magazine shared an identical dislike of deadlines. For twelve years, Max Beerbohm admitted in his valedictory article, Thursdays had been for him the least pleasant day of the week. Why Thursday? Because that was the day, the latest possible one, he set aside each week to get his writing done. On every Wednesday, therefore, he would be engulfed by "a certain sense of oppression, of misgiving, even of dread." It was only on Friday, when once the danger was passed, that the sun would shine again. Then he would move on dancing feet.

[6] I quote my betters to console myself by the reminder that they, too, knew the pangs of weekly columnizing. Yet the consolation I seek is denied me when I discover, for example, that it took Beerbohm one, and only one, short day of pain to turn out the delectable copy which he could write. Shaw, I am certain, was also a one-day man. I wish I were. I wish even more ardently that I could claim any of the merits which glorify their reviews for what it takes me two, three, or sometimes five days of ceaseless sweating to produce as fodder for my columns.

[7] Beerbohm ascribed his disrelish for the act of writing to "the acute literary conscience" with which he had been cursed. It was this conscience, he maintained, which kept his pen from ever running away with him. I know what he means. Unblessed with any of his gifts, I am nonetheless cursed with something of his conscience. Beerbohm insisted that "to seem to write with ease and delight is one of the duties which a writer owes to his readers." If he worked hard at his sentences, it was because Beerbohm hoped they would read easily. In other words, he was in complete agreement with Sheridan's "easy writing's vile hard reading." One statement of Beerbohm's I could truthfully apply to my own efforts for the *SRL*. It runs, "I may often have failed, in my articles here, to disguise labor. But the effort to disguise it has always been loyally made."

[8] There is a passage in *The Goncourt Journals* which has haunted me since I read it. Envy has kept it green for me, and wonder (or is it dis-

belief?) has kept it alive. I have in mind Gautier's boast that he never thought about what he was going to write. "I take up my pen," he explained, "and write. I am a man of letters and am presumed to know my job. . . . I throw my sentences into the air and I can be sure that they will come down on their feet, like cats. . . . Look here: here's my script: not a word blotted."

[9] When I think of the one-legged kittens that land on my pages; when I remember the false starts, illegible scribblings, unfinished sentences, discarded drafts, changed constructions, and altered words which mark my beginnings, my continuings, and my endings, I blush with shame and, like the voyagers in Dante's realm, abandon all hope.

[10] In these journalistic days the first word that pops into an author's mind is held to be the acceptable, if not the best, word. We are supposed to smile because Wordsworth, at a day's end, was wearied from his quest for the exact word. But where Wordsworth the man may win a smile, Wordsworth the writer, fatiguing himself by doing what is a writer's duty, is far from laughable. The *mot juste* is not just any word. Even if it eludes its pursuer, the search for it seems to me to remain among the obligations of authorship. Indeed, the true hope of anyone who loves the language and respects it is to stumble upon, not the correct word or phrase, but the word or phrase which is so right that it seems inevitable.

[11] The word and the phrase are not the only hurdles—and joys— of authorship. The sentence and the paragraph, by means of which points are made, thoughts communicated, emotions transferred, pictures painted, personalities caught, rhythms established, and cadences varied, offer other challenges and should supply their own sources of delight and pride. When so much hurried writing is done for hurried reading, I find it comforting to have Shaw, a veritable geyser with words and ideas, admit in his *Sixteen Self Sketches* how depleting he found his labors as a weekly feuilletonist for ten years. Why? Because, says he, of "taking all the pains I was capable of to get to the bottom of every sentence I wrote."

[12] One of the modern world's luckier occurrences was what happened at Harrow when a boy named Winston Churchill was being "menaced with Education." Three times, he tells us in *A Roving Commission*, his backwardness as a classical scholar forced him to remain in the same form and hence repeat the same elementary course in English. "Thus," writes he (and who can question him?), "I got into my bones the essential structure of the ordinary British sentence—which is a noble thing. . . . Naturally I am biased in favor of boys learning English. I would make them all learn English: and then I would let the clever ones learn Latin as an honor, and Greek as a treat. But the only thing I would whip them for would be for not knowing English. I would whip them hard for that." One trembles to think how many of us whose profession is writing

would be flogged today if lapses in English, or American, were whippable offenses.

[13] Later on in that same grand book, Churchill has his more precise say on the subtleties, intricacies, and possibilities of the writer's craft. It is his opinion, and one worth heeding, that, "just as the sentence contains one idea in all its fulness, so the paragraph should embrace a distinct episode; and as sentences should follow one another in harmonious sequence, so the paragraphs must fit on to one another like the automatic couplings of railway carriages."

[14] I quote Churchill and these others belonging to the peerage of prose writers because, for any author with a memory, one of the disheartening and humbling aspects of writing is the recollection, as his own pen moves, of how those whom he admires have faced and solved identical problems. This recollection of what has been done, this sensing of what could and should be done, this awareness of what one hopes to do regardless of whether one can or cannot do it—these are parts of that literary conscience, mentioned by Beerbohm, which keeps a writer's pen from running away with him. I know they are factors in retarding my own pen (meaning my typewriter, pencil, or dictation) even on those happy days when a subject seems to write itself, when sentences come easily, and one paragraph gives way to another.

[15] Style is a strange and mysterious thing. Some contemporary writers appear to get along without it and to want to do so, and most of us rightly disparage it when it shows the effort that has gone into it. Few of us, for example, can read Pater today without being irritated and put off by the labyrinthian intricacies of his sentences. His style, once held to be a model, remains a model, although as we see it it is one to be avoided rather than followed. Pater could not bring himself to say a simple thing simply. His orchestration is so elaborate that the melody of his thought is lost.

[16] Hazlitt comes closer to present-day tastes. More than being the enemy of the gaudy and "Occult" schools of writing, Hazlitt was not only a champion but at his best a matchless practitioner of "The Familiar Style." Although he had the art to make a long sentence seem short, he knew the value of short sentences. "I hate anything," wrote he, "that occupies more space than it is worth. I hate to see a load of band-boxes go along the street, and I hate to see a parcel of big words without any meaning in them."

[17] The perpetual challenge of writing, the challenge presented by each new sentence is to say exactly what one wants to say exactly as one wants to say it. This is where the anguish of composition mixes with the delights. This is where, too, style, as I see it, comes into the picture. Style

is merely the means, chosen or instinctive (doubtless both), by which a writer has his precise and personal say.

[18] Certainly, style is not affectation. Conscious though it may be, when self-conscious it is an obstruction. Its purpose, to my way of thinking, is to give the reader pleasure by sparing him the work which the writer is duty-bound to have done for him. Writers, notwithstanding their hopes or ambitions, may or may not be artists. But there is no excuse for their not being artisans. Although in the final and spiritual sense the style is the man, it is more than that. It is the writing man *in print*. It is, so to speak, his written voice and, if it is truly his voice, even in print it should be his and his alone. The closer it comes to the illusion of speech, perhaps the better. Yet the closeness of the written word to the spoken can, and in fact should, never be more than an illusion. For the point of the written word is planning, as surely as the charm of the spoken word can be its lack of planning.

[19] Without shame I confess that, regardless of how unsatisfactory the results may be, I have labored when writing my weekly pieces to lighten the labor of those who may read them. That I have failed again and again I know to my own chagrin, but I can honestly say I have tried. I not only rewrite; I often rewrite and rewrite again. I do this though I am well aware that the result is sentences and paragraphs which do not bear rereading. I rewrite partly in longhand, partly by dictation, occasionally sitting down, sometimes walking, but most often snaking my way across the floor on my stomach. My desk, a migratory one, is the small piece of beaverboard I push before me. On it are sheets of typewriter paper darkened with hieroglyphics which must be deciphered immediately to be read at all.

[20] Endeavoring to square my writing with my writing conscience, and having to live with the difference between what I would like to have done and am able to do, is one of the reasons why writing is to me an agony, however pleasant.

QUESTIONS AND COMMENT ON FORM AND CONTENT

1. The contradictory words "pleasant agony" can be called an oxymoron. What is an oxymoron? Compare the word *moron*.

2. Other figures used by Brown to describe the ordeal of writing a weekly column are "delirium of delivery," "labor pains," and feeding an "omnivorous beast." What figures were used by George Bernard Shaw and by Max Beerbohm to indicate the trials of a columnist? Can you suggest a still different figure that describes your theme-writing tasks? Can you suggest a figure to substitute for Brown's "one-legged kittens that land on my pages"?

3. Draw up some rules that can be deduced from Brown's advice on writing. Which seem to you most important?

4. What is the author's definition of style or good style? What is his objection to the writing of Walter Pater, a Victorian essayist and critic? To what did Churchill attribute his skill as a writer of English?

5. For Brown, what does conscience have to do with writing? Describe his way of writing. Should the reader be made aware of the hard work that goes into good writing? What is meant by "easy writing's vile hard reading"?

6. How does a good written style compare with a spoken one?

7. Brown approves of Churchill's statement that the "paragraphs must fit on to one another like the automatic couplings of railway carriages." Are Brown's paragraphs coupled in this essay?

VOCABULARY: WHAT DO THE ITALICIZED WORDS MEAN?

. . . appetites as *insatiable* as a column's (3)
A column is an *omnivorous* beast. (3)
Its hunger is never *appeased*. (3)
. . . admitted in his *valedictory* article (5)
Envy has kept it *green* for me (8)
The *mot juste* is not just any word. (10)
. . . belonging to the *peerage* of prose writers (14)
. . . most of us rightly *disparage* it (15)
. . . *put off* by the *labyrinthian* intricacies of his sentences (15)
. . . no excuse for their not being *artisans* (18)
. . . paper darkened with *hieroglyphics* (19)

THEME SUGGESTIONS

The Pleasant Agony of Theme Writing
The Delirium of Delivery in Theme Writing
On Writing and Rewriting

THE CLICHÉ EXPERT REVEALS HIMSELF IN HIS TRUE COLORS

Frank Sullivan

Frank Sullivan (1892-   ) is the author of several volumes of humorous sketches.

Q: Mr. Arbuthnot, would you mind telling us today how you happened to become a cliché expert? Was it easy?

A: Easy! Don't make me laugh, Mr. Crouse. It was an uphill climb. A cliché novitiate is no bed of roses, and if anyone ever tells you it is, do you know how I want you to take his statement?

Q: How?

A: With a grain of salt. I shall tell you about my career, since you insist, and as a special treat, I shall describe it to you entirely in terms of the seesaw cliché.

Q: The seesaw cliché?

A: You'll see what I mean. Before I made my mark as a cliché expert, I had my ups and downs. Sometimes, when everything was at sixes and sevens, it almost seemed as though my dearest ambitions were going to rack and ruin. I had moments when I was almost tempted to believe that everything was a snare and a delusion. Even my own flesh and blood discouraged me, in spite of the fact that I was their pride and joy . . . You aren't listening, Mr. Crouse.

Q: Yes I am. I just closed my eyes because the light hurt. You were saying that your own kith and kin discouraged you.

A: I didn't say kith and kin, but it doesn't matter. For a considerable period of time it was nip and tuck whether I would sink or swim. If I had not been hale and hearty, and well equipped for a rough-and-tumble struggle, I wouldn't have come through. But I kept at it, hammer and tongs. I gave 'em tit for tat . . . Mr. Crouse, you *are* asleep.

Q: No, I'm not, Mr. Arbuthnot. You were saying you went after your goal hard and fast.

A: I did. I eschewed wine, woman, and song—

Q: Ah, but wine, woman, and song is not a seesaw cliché, Mr. Arbuthnot.

A: Yes it is, too. Woman is standing in the middle, balancing. I worked morning, noon, and night, and kept to the straight and narrow. The consequence was that in the due course of time—

Q: And tide?

A: Please! In the due course of time things began to come my way by fits and starts, and a little later by leaps and bounds. Now, I'm fine and dandy.

Q: High, wide, and handsome, eh?

A: I wish I had said that, Mr. Crouse.

Q: You—

A: Will, Oscar. Had you there, Mr. Crouse, didn't I, ha ha! When I started I was free, white, and twenty-one. Now I'm fat, fair, and forty, and I venture to predict that no man, without regard to race, creed, or color, is a better master of the cliché than your servant—your *humble* servant—Magnus Arbuthnot. So much for my life story in terms of the seesaw cliché.

Q: It certainly is an interesting story, Mr. Arbuthnot—by and large.

A: Well, in all due modesty, I suppose it is, although sometimes, to tell you the truth, I think there is neither rhyme nor reason to it.

Q: Where were you born, Mr. Arbuthnot?

A: In the altogether.

Q: I see. How?

A: On the impulse of the moment.

Q: And when?

A: In the nick of time.

Q: It is agreeable to find a man so frank about himself, Mr. Arbuthnot.

A: Why not? You asked me a question. You know what kind of question it was?

Q: Impertinent?

A: Oh, my dear man, no.

Q: Personal?

A: Civil. You asked me a civil question. I answered you by telling you the truth. I gave it to you, if I may be permitted to say so, straight from the shoulder. I revealed myself to you in my—

Q: True colors?

A: Ah, someone told you. Rather, someone *went* and told you.

Q: Were you ever in love, Mr. Arbuthnot, or am I out of order in asking that?

A: Not at all. I have had my romances.

Q: How nice.

A: Ah, you wouldn't say so if you knew what kind of romances they were.

Q: What kind were they?

A: Blighted romances, all of 'em. I kept trying to combine single blessedness with wedded bliss. It didn't work. I had a sweetheart in every port, and I worshipped the ground they walked on, each and every one of them. This ground amounts to a matter of 18,467 acres, as of my latest blighted romance.

Q: Hm! You must have been quite a pedestrian.

A: Well, those are the figures when the tide was out; only 16,468 acres at the neap. I was land-poor at the end. And you take the advice of a sadder—

Q: And a wiser man.

A: That's what I was going to say. And never trust the weaker sex, or you'll have an awakening. You seem to be so smart, interrupting me all the while, maybe you can tell me what kind of awakening.

Q: Awakening? Awakening? I'm afraid you have me.

A: Rude awakening.

Q: Oh, of course. Now, I don't think your story would be complete, Mr. Arbuthnot, without some statement from you regarding your material circumstances. Are you well-to-do, or are you—

A: Hard pressed for cash? No, I'm solvent. I'm well paid.

Q: You mean you get a handsome salary?

A: I prefer to call it a princely stipend. You know what kind of coin I'm paid in?

Q: No. What?

A: Coin of the realm. Not that I give a hoot for money. You know how I refer to money?

Q: As the root of all evil?

A: No, but you have a talking point there. I call it lucre—filthy lucre.

Q: On the whole, you seem to have a pretty good time, Mr. Arbuthnot.

A: Oh, I'm not complaining. I'm as snug as a bug in a rug. I'm clear as crystal—when I'm not dull as dishwater. I'm cool as a cucumber, quick as a flash, fresh as a daisy, pleased as Punch, good as my word, regular as clockwork, and I suppose at the end of my declining years, when I'm gathered to my ancestors, I'll be dead as a doornail.

Q: *Eh bien! C'est la vie!*

A: *Mais oui, mon vieux.* I manage. I'm the glass of fashion and the mold of form. I have a finger in every pie, all except this finger. I use it for pointing with scorn. When I go in for malice, it is always malice aforethought. My nods are significant. My offers are standing. I am at cross-purposes and in dire straits. My motives are ulterior, my circles are vicious, my retainers are faithful, and my hopefuls are young. My suspicions are sneaking, my glee is fiendish, my stories are likely. I am drunk.

Q: Drunk?

A: Yes, with power. You know where?

Q: Where?

A: Behind the throne. I am emotional. My mercies are tender, and when I cry, I cry quits. I am lost in thought and up in arms. I am a square shooter with my trusty revolver. My courage is vaunted and my shame is crying, but I don't care—a rap. I have been in the depths of despair, when a watery grave in the briny deep seemed attractive. Eventually I want to marry and settle down, but the woman I marry must be clever.

Q: Clever?

A: With the needle.

Q: Well, I'd certainly call you a man who has led a full life, Mr. Arbuthnot, and a likable chap, too.

A: Yes, I'm a peach of a fellow. I'm a diamond in the rough, all wool and a yard wide. I'm too funny for words and too full for utterance. I'm a gay dog, and I like to trip the light fantastic and burn the candle at both ends with motley throngs of boon companions. I may be foolish but my folly is at least sheer.

Q: I think you certainly have run—

A: I certainly have. The entire gamut of human emotions. I know the facts of life. I'm afraid I've got to go now, Mr. Crouse. I'm due back at my abode. Do you know what kind of abode I live in?

Q: Humble, Mr. Arbuthnot?

A: Certainly not. Palatial! Goodbye, my little periwinkle!

QUESTIONS AND COMMENT ON FORM AND CONTENT

1. What is a cliché? What is its greatest weakness?

2. Frank Sullivan says in the fourth paragraph that he is going to tell about his career "entirely in terms of the seesaw cliché." What kind of cliché is this? He uses it frequently in the first fourth of the essay concluding its main use with "So much for . . . the seesaw cliché." How does he try to include "wine, woman, and song" in this classification?

3. What other types of clichés are there? Make your own informal or incomplete classification.

4. What is the greatest weakness of a cliché? Why, in general, should a cliché be avoided or at least questioned in our writing?

5. What, on the other hand, can be said for the occasional use of a cliché? Do some clichés communicate effectively and economically?

VOCABULARY: WHAT DO THE ITALICIZED WORDS MEAN?

. . . your own *kith* and *kin* discouraged you
I gave 'em *tit* for *tat*
I *eschewed* wine, woman, and song
I prefer to call it a *princely stipend*.
I call it *lucre*—filthy lucre.

THEME SUGGESTIONS

Tell about an imaginary or real adventure, using as many clichés as you can. Underline the clichés. Rewrite the theme, eliminating the clichés.

Do the same with a sports story, life in a fraternity house, life of a commuter, or some other topic of your choice.

SOCIOLOGICAL HABIT PATTERNS IN LINGUISTIC TRANSMOGRIFICATION

Malcolm Cowley

Malcolm Cowley (1898-   ) is an American critic, poet, and essayist. He is the author of Exile's Return, *1934, 1951, which describes the so-called "lost generation."*

[1] I have a friend who started as a poet and then decided to take a postgraduate degree in sociology. For his doctoral dissertation he combined his two interests by writing on the social psychology of poets. He had visited poets by the dozen, asking each of them a graded series of questions, and his conclusions from the interviews were modest and useful, though reported in what seemed to me a barbarous jargon. After reading the dissertation I wrote and scolded him. "You have such a fine sense of the poet's craft," I said, "that you shouldn't have allowed the sociologists to seduce you into writing their professional slang—or at least that's my judgmental response to your role selection."

[2] My friend didn't write to defend himself; he waited until we met again. Then, dropping his voice, he said: "I knew my dissertation was badly written, but I had to get my degree. If I had written it in English, Professor Blank"—he mentioned a rather distinguished name—"would have rejected it. He would have said it was merely belletristic."

[3] From that time I began to study the verbal folkways of the sociologists. I read what they call "the literature." A few sociologists write the best English they are capable of writing, and I suspect that they are the best men in the field. There is no mystery about them. If they go wrong, their mistakes can be seen and corrected. Others, however—and a vast majority—write in a language that has to be learned almost like Esperanto. It has a private vocabulary which, in addition to strictly sociological terms, includes new words for the commonest actions, feelings, and circumstances. It has the beginnings of a new grammar and syntax, much inferior to English grammar in force and precision. So far as it has an effect on standard English, the effect is largely pernicious.

[4] Sometimes it misleads the sociologists themselves, by making them think they are profoundly scientific at points where they are merely being verbose. I can illustrate by trying a simple exercise in translation, that is, by expressing an idea first in English and then seeing what it looks like in the language of sociology.

Reprinted by permission of Malcolm Cowley and of *The Reporter,* where it first appeared on September 20, 1956.

[5] An example that comes to hand is the central idea of an article by Norman E. Green, printed in the February, 1956, issue of the *American Sociological Review*. In English his argument might read as follows:

[6] "Rich people live in big houses set farther apart than those of poor people. By looking at an aerial photograph of an American city, we can distinguish the richer from the poorer neighborhoods."

[7] I won't have to labor over a sociological expression of the same idea, because Mr. Green has saved me the trouble. Here is part of his contribution to comparative linguistics. "In effect, it was hypothesized," he says—a sociologist must never say "I assumed," much less "I guessed" —"that certain physical data categories including housing types and densities, land use characteristics, and ecological location"—not just "location," mind you, but "ecological location," which is almost equivalent to locational location—"constitute a scalable content area. This could be called a continuum of residential desirability. Likewise, it was hypothesized that several social data categories, describing the same census tracts, and referring generally to the social stratification system of the city, would also be scalable. This scale could be called a continuum of socio-economic status. Thirdly, it was hypothesized that there would be a high positive correlation between the scale types on each continuum."

[8] Here, after ninety-four words, Mr. Green is stating, or concealing, an assumption with which most laymen would have started, that rich people live in good neighborhoods. He is now almost ready for his deduction, or snapper:

[9] "This relationship would define linkages between the social and physical structure of the city. It would also provide a precise definition of the commonalities among several spatial distributions. By the same token, the correlation between the residential desirability scale and the continuum of socio-economic status would provide an estimate of the predictive value of aerial photographic data relative to the social ecology of the city."

[10] Mr. Green has used 160 words—counting "socio-economic" as only one—to express an idea that a layman would have stated in thirty-three. As a matter of fact, he has used many more than 160 words, since the whole article is an elaboration of this one thesis. Whatever may be the virtues of the sociological style—or Socspeak, as George Orwell might have called it—it is not specifically designed to save ink and paper. Let us briefly examine some of its other characteristics.

[11] A layman's first impression of sociological prose, as compared with English prose, is that it contains a very large proportion of abstract words, most of them built on Greek or Latin roots. Often—as in the example just quoted—they are used to inflate or transmogrify a meaning

that could be clearly expressed in shorter words surviving from King Alfred's time.

[12] These Old English or Anglo-Saxon words are in number less than one-tenth of the entries in the largest dictionaries. But they are the names of everyday objects, attributes, and actions, and they are also the pronouns, the auxiliary verbs, and most of the prepositions and conjunctions, so that they form the grammatical structure of the language. The result is that most novelists use six Anglo-Saxon words for every one derived from French, Latin, or Greek, and that is probably close to the percentage that would be found in spoken English.

[13] For comparison or contrast, I counted derivations in the passage quoted from the *American Sociological Review,* which is a typical example of "the literature." No less than 49 percent of Mr. Green's prose consists of words from foreign or classical languages. By this standard of measurement, his article is more abstruse than most textbooks of advanced chemistry and higher mathematics, which are said to contain only 40 percent of such words.

[14] In addition to being abstruse, the language of the sociologists is also rich in neologisms. Apparently they like nothing better than inventing a word, deforming a word, or using a technical word in a strange context. Among their favorite nouns are "ambit," "extensity" (for "extent"), "scapegoating," "socializee," "ethnicity," "directionality," "cathexis," "affect" (for "feeling"), "maturation" (for both "maturing" and "maturity"), and "commonalities" (for "points in common"). Among their favorite adjectives are "processual," "prestigeful," and "insightful"— which last is insightful to murder—and perhaps their favorite adverb is "minimally," which seems to mean "in some measure." Their maximal pleasure seems to lie in making new combinations of nouns and adjectives and nouns used as adjectives, until the reader feels that he is picking his way through a field of huge boulders, lost among "universalistic-specific achievement patterns" and "complementary role-expectation-sanction systems," as he struggles vainly toward "ego-integrative action orientation," guided only by "orientation to improvement of the gratification-deprivation balance of the actor"—which last is Professor Talcott Parson's rather involved way of saying "the pleasure principle."

[15] But Professor Parsons, head of the Sociology Department at Harvard, is not the only delinquent recidivist, convicted time and again of corrupting the language. Among sociologists in general there is a criminal fondness for using complicated terms when there are simple ones available. A child says "Do it again," a teacher says "Repeat the exercise," but the sociologist says "It was determined to replicate the investigation." Instead of saying two things are alike or similar, as a layman would do, the sociologist describes them as being either isomor-

phic or homologous. Instead of saying that they are different he calls them allotropic. Every form of leadership or influence is called a hegemony.

[16] A sociologist never cuts anything in half or divides it in two like a layman. Instead he dichotomizes it, bifurcates it, subjects it to a process of binary fission, or restructures it in a dyadic conformation—around polar foci.

[17] So far I have been dealing with the vocabulary of sociologists, but their private language has a grammar too, and one that should be the subject of intensive research by the staff of a very well-endowed foundation. I have space to mention only a few of its more striking features.

[18] The first of these is the preponderance of nouns over all the other parts of speech. Nouns are used in hyphenated pairs or dyads, and sometimes in triads, tetrads, and pentads. Nouns are used as adjectives without change of form, and they are often used as verbs, with or without the suffix "ize." The sociological language is gritty with nouns, like sanded sugar.

[19] On the other hand, it is poor in pronouns. The singular pronoun of the first person has entirely disappeared, except in case histories, for the sociologist never comes forward as "I." Sometimes he refers to himself as "the author" or "the investigator," or as "many sociologists," or even as "the best sociologists," when he is advancing a debatable opinion. On rare occasions he calls himself "we," like Queen Elizabeth speaking from the throne, but he usually avoids any personal form and writes as if he were a force of nature.

[20] The second-personal pronoun has also disappeared, for the sociologist pretends to be speaking not to living persons but merely for the record. Masculine and feminine pronouns of the third person are used with parsimony, and most sociologists prefer to say "the subject," or "X——," or "the interviewee," where a layman would use the simple "he" or "she." As for the neuter pronoun of the third person, it survives chiefly as the impersonal subject of a passive verb. "It was hypothesized," we read, or "It was found to be the case." Found by *whom?*

[21] The neglect and debasement of the verb is another striking feature of "the literature." The sociologist likes to reduce a transitive verb to an intransitive, so that he speaks of people's adapting, adjusting, transferring, relating, and identifying, with no more of a grammatical object than if they were coming or going. He seldom uses transitive verbs of action, like "break," "injure," "help," and "adore." Instead he uses verbs of relation, verbs which imply that one series of nouns and adjectives, used as the compound subject of a sentence, is larger or smaller than, series of nouns and adjectives.

[22] Considering this degradation of the verb, I have wondered how dominant over, subordinate to, causative, or resultant from another

one of Julius Caesar's boasts could be translated into Socspeak. What Caesar wrote was *"Veni, vidi, vici"*—only three words, all of them verbs. The English translation is in six words: "I came, I saw, I conquered," and three of the words are first-personal pronouns, which the sociologist is taught to avoid. I suspect that he would have to write: "Upon the advent of the investigator, his hegemony became minimally coextensive with the areal unit rendered visible by his successive displacements in space."

[23] The whole sad situation leads me to dream of a vast allegorical painting called "The Triumph of the Nouns." It would depict a chariot of victory drawn by the other conquered parts of speech—the adverbs and adjectives still robust, if yoked and harnessed; the prepositions bloated and pale; the conjunctions tortured; the pronouns reduced to sexless skeletons; the verbs dichotomized and feebly tottering—while behind them, arrogant, overfed, roseate, spilling over the triumphal car, would be the company of nouns in Roman togas and Greek chitons, adorned with laurel branches and flowering hegemonies.

QUESTIONS AND COMMENT ON FORM AND CONTENT

1. One characteristic of jargon or "professional slang" as Malcolm Cowley labels it, is to use nouns as adjectives quite freely. What word in the title, used ordinarily as a noun is used here as an adjective? Is the word *transmogrification* in your collegiate dictionary? If so, is there any indication of its usage?

2. Is the author being satiric when he says at the end of paragraph 1, "at least that's my judgmental response to your role selection"? Can you rewrite it in plain English?

3. Every profession or occupation has its special vocabulary, sometimes referred to (especially when used for purposes of showmanship or from habit) as jargon or cant. What justification is there for use of highly technical language? When should it be avoided as much as possible?

4. What is the point made about the use of words built on Greek or Latin roots as compared with those of the native Old-English stock?

5. The author's criticism of the writing of some prominent sociologists goes deeper than the mere use of an unnecessary technical term. What, specifically, does he charge them with? Do his examples justify the charge?

6. From what Cowley says about bad writing what suggestions would he likely make for good writing?

VOCABULARY: WHAT DO THE ITALICIZED WORDS MEAN?

. . . it was merely *belletristic* (2)
. . . the effect is largely *pernicious* (3)
. . . merely being *verbose* (4)

In effect it was *hypothesized* (7)
. . . there would be a high *positive correlation* (7)
. . . article is more *abstruse* than most textbooks (13)
. . . the language of the sociologists is also rich in *neologisms* (14)
. . . is not the only *delinquent recidivist* (15)
. . . pronouns of the third person are used with *parsimony* (20)
. . . reduce a *transitive* verb to an *intransitive* (21)

THEME SUGGESTIONS

Rewrite a passage from a famous speech or essay into the jargon of some profession. Example: Lincoln's Gettysburg Address
Write a speech using the argot of a certain business or profession.
Characteristics of a Good Style

LUCIDITY, SIMPLICITY, EUPHONY

W. Somerset Maugham

W. Somerset Maugham (1874-1965) was born in Paris, but received his education in England and Germany. Of Human Bondage *is usually considered his best novel. He was a prolific writer of essays, novels, short stories, autobiographies, and plays—almost forty volumes in all, including* The Summing Up *(1938), from which our selection is taken.*

[1] I discovered my limitations and it seemed to me that the only sensible thing was to aim at what excellence I could within them. I knew that I had no lyrical quality. I had a small vocabulary and no efforts that I could make to enlarge it much availed me. I had little gift of metaphor; the original and striking simile seldom occurred to me. Poetic flights and the great imaginative sweep were beyond my powers. I could admire them in others as I could admire their far-fetched tropes and the unusual but suggestive language in which they clothed their thoughts, but my own invention never presented me with such embellishments; and I was tired of trying to do what did not come easily to me. On the other hand, I had an acute power of observation and it seemed to me that I could see a great many things that other people missed. I could put down in clear terms what I saw. I had a logical sense, and if no great feeling for the richness and strangeness of words, at all events a lively

appreciation of their sound. I knew that I should never write as well as I could wish, but I thought with pains I could arrive at writing as well as my natural defects allowed. On taking thought it seemed to me that I must aim at lucidity, simplicity and euphony. I have put these three qualities in the order of the importance I assigned to them.

[2] I have never had much patience with the writers who claim from the reader an effort to understand their meaning. You have only to go to the great philosophers to see that it is possible to express with lucidity the most subtle reflections. You may find it difficult to understand the thought of Hume, and if you have no philosophical training its implications will doubtless escape you; but no one with any education at all can fail to understand exactly what the meaning of each sentence is. Few people have written English with more grace than Berkeley. There are two sorts of obscurity that you find in writers. One is due to negligence and the other to wilfulness. People often write obscurely because they have never taken the trouble to learn to write clearly. This sort of obscurity you find too often in modern philosophers, in men of science, and even in literary critics. Here it is indeed strange. You would have thought that men who passed their lives in the study of the great masters of literature would be sufficiently sensitive to the beauty of language to write if not beautifully at least with perspicuity. Yet you will find in their works sentence after sentence that you must read twice to discover the sense. Often you can only guess at it, for the writers have evidently not said what they intended.

[3] Another cause of obscurity is that the writer is himself not quite sure of his meaning. He has a vague impression of what he wants to say, but has not, either from lack of mental power or from laziness, exactly formulated it in his mind and it is natural enough that he should not find a precise expression for a confused idea. This is due largely to the fact that many writers think, not before, but as they write. The pen originates the thought. The disadvantage of this, and indeed it is a danger against which the author must be always on his guard, is that there is a sort of magic in the written word. The idea acquires substance by taking on a visible nature, and then stands in the way of its own clarification. But this sort of obscurity merges very easily into the wilful. Some writers who do not think clearly are inclined to suppose that their thoughts have a significance greater than at first sight appears. It is flattering to believe that they are too profound to be expressed so clearly that all who run may read, and very naturally it does not occur to such writers that the fault is with their own minds which have not the faculty of precise reflection. Here again the magic of the written word obtains. It is very easy to persuade oneself that a phrase that one does not quite under-

stand may mean a great deal more than one realizes. From this there is only a little way to go to fall into the habit of setting down one's impressions in all their original vagueness. Fools can always be found to discover a hidden sense in them. There is another form of wilful obscurity that masquerades as aristocratic exclusiveness. The author wraps his meaning in mystery so that the vulgar shall not participate in it. His soul is a secret garden into which the elect may penetrate only after overcoming a number of perilous obstacles. But this kind of obscurity is not only pretentious; it is short-sighted. For time plays it an odd trick. If the sense is meagre time reduces it to a meaningless verbiage that no one thinks of reading. This is the fate that has befallen the lucubrations of those French writers who were seduced by the example of Guillaume Apollinaire. But occasionally it throws a sharp cold light on what had seemed profound and thus discloses the fact that these contortions of language disguised very commonplace notions. There are few of Mallarmé's poems now that are not clear; one cannot fail to notice that his thought singularly lacked originality. Some of his phrases were beautiful; the materials of his verse were the poetic platitudes of his day.

[4] Simplicity is not such an obvious merit as lucidity. I have aimed at it because I have no gift for richness. Within limits I admire richness in others, though I find it difficult to digest in quantity. I can read one page of Ruskin with delight, but twenty only with weariness. The rolling period, the stately epithet, the noun rich in poetic associations, the subordinate clauses that give the sentence weight and magnificence, the grandeur like that of wave following wave in the open sea; there is no doubt that in all this there is something inspiring. Words thus strung together fall on the ear like music. The appeal is sensuous rather than intellectual, and the beauty of the sound leads you easily to conclude that you need not bother about the meaning. But words are tyrannical things, they exist for their meanings, and if you will not pay attention to these, you cannot pay attention at all. Your mind wanders. This kind of writing demands a subject that will suit it. It is surely out of place to write in the grand style of inconsiderable things. No one wrote in this manner with greater success than Sir Thomas Browne, but even he did not always escape this pitfall. In the last chapter of *Hydriotaphia* the matter, which is the destiny of man, wonderfully fits the baroque splendour of the language, and here the Norwich doctor produced a piece of prose that has never been surpassed in our literature; but when he describes the finding of his urns in the same splendid manner the effect (at least to my taste) is less happy. When a modern writer is grandiloquent to tell you whether or no a little trollop shall hop into bed with a commonplace young man you are right to be disgusted.

[5] But if richness need gifts with which everyone is not endowed, simplicity by no means comes by nature. To achieve it needs rigid discipline. So far as I know ours is the only language in which it has been found necessary to give a name to the piece of prose which is described as the purple patch; it would not have been necessary to do so unless it were characteristic. It was not always so. Nothing could be more racy, straightforward and alive than the prose of Shakespeare; but it must be remembered that this was dialogue written to be spoken. We do not know how he would have written if like Corneille he had composed prefaces to his plays. It may be they would have been as euphuistic as the letters of Queen Elizabeth. But earlier prose, the prose of Sir Thomas More, for instance, is neither ponderous, flowery, nor oratorical. It smacks of the English soil. To my mind King James's Bible has been a very harmful influence on English prose. I am not so stupid as to deny its great beauty. It is majestical. But the Bible is an oriental book. Its alien imagery has nothing to do with us. Those hyperboles, those luscious metaphors, are foreign to our genius. I cannot but think that not the least of the misfortunes that the Secession from Rome brought upon the spiritual life of our country is that this work for so long a period became the daily, and with many the only, reading of our people. Those rhythms, that powerful vocabulary, that grandiloquence, became part and parcel of the national sensibility. The plain, honest English speech was overwhelmed with ornament. Blunt Englishmen twisted their tongues to speak like Hebrew prophets. There was evidently something in the English temper to which this was congenial, perhaps a native lack of precision in thought, perhaps a naïve delight in fine words for their own sake, an innate eccentricity and love of embroidery, I do not know; but the fact remains that ever since, English prose has had to struggle against the tendency to luxuriate. When from time to time the spirit of the language has reasserted itself, as it did with Dryden and the writers of Queen Anne, it was only to be submerged once more by the pomposities of Gibbon and Dr. Johnson. When English prose recovered simplicity with Hazlitt, the Shelley of the letters and Charles Lamb at his best, it lost it again with De Quincey, Carlyle, Meredith and Walter Pater. It is obvious that the grand style is more striking than the plain. Indeed many people think that a style that does not attract notice is not style, They will admire Walter Pater's, but will read an essay by Matthew Arnold without giving a moment's attention to the elegance, distinction and sobriety with which he set down what he had to say.

[6] The dictum that the style is the man is well known. It is one of those aphorisms that say too much to mean a great deal. Where is the man in Goethe, in his birdlike lyrics or in his clumsy prose? And Hazlitt? But I suppose that if a man has a confused mind he will write in a con-

fused way, if his temper is capricious his prose will be fantastical, and if he has a quick, darting intelligence that is reminded by the matter in hand of a hundred things he will, unless he has great self-control, load his pages with metaphor and simile. There is a great difference between the magniloquence of the Jacobean writers, who were intoxicated with the new wealth that had lately been brought into the language, and the turgidity of Gibbon and Dr. Johnson, who were the victims of bad theories. I can read every word that Dr. Johnson wrote with delight, for he had good sense, charm and wit. No one could have written better if he had not wilfully set himself to write in the grand style. He knew good English when he saw it. No critic has praised Dryden's prose more aptly. He said of him that he appeared to have no art other than that of expressing with clearness what he thought with vigour. And one of his Lives he finished with the words: "Whoever wishes to attain an English style, familiar but not coarse, and elegant but not ostentatious, must give his days and nights to the volumes of Addison." But when he himself sat down to write it was with a very different aim. He mistook the orotund for the dignified. He had not the good breeding to see that simplicity and naturalness are the truest marks of distinction.

[7] For to write good prose is an affair of good manners. It is, unlike verse, a civil art. Poetry is baroque. Baroque is tragic, massive and mystical. I cannot but feel that the prose writers of the baroque period, the authors of King James's Bible, Sir Thomas Browne, Glanville, were poets who had lost their way. Prose is a rococo art. It needs taste rather than power, decorum rather than inspiration and vigour rather than grandeur. Form for the poet is the bit and the bridle without which (unless you are an acrobat) you cannot ride your horse; but for the writer of prose it is the chassis without which your car does not exist. It is not an accident that the best prose was written when rococo with its elegance and moderation, at its birth attained its greatest excellence. For rococo was evolved when baroque had become declamatory and the world, tired of the stupendous, asked for restraint. It was the natural expression of persons who valued a civilized life. Humour, tolerance and horse sense made the great tragic issues that had preoccupied the first half of the seventeenth century seem excessive. The world was a more comfortable place to live in and perhaps for the first time in centuries the cultivated classes could sit back and enjoy their leisure. It has been said that good prose should resemble the conversation of a well-bred man. Conversation is only possible when men's minds are free from pressing anxieties. Their lives must be reasonably secure and they must have no grave concern about their souls. They must attach importance to the refinements of civilization. They must value courtesy, they must pay attention to their persons (and have we not also been told that good prose should

be like the clothes of a well-dressed man, appropriate but unobtrusive?), they must fear to bore, they must be neither flippant nor solemn, but always apt; and they must look upon "enthusiasm" with a critical glance. This is a soil very suitable for prose. It is not to be wondered at that it gave a fitting opportunity for the appearance of the best writer of prose that our modern world has seen, Voltaire. The writers of English, perhaps owing to the poetic nature of the language, have seldom reached the excellence that seems to have come so naturally to him. It is in so far as they have approached the ease, sobriety and precision of the great French masters that they are admirable.

[8] Whether you ascribe importance to euphony, the last of the three characteristics that I mentioned, must depend on the sensitiveness of your ear. A great many readers, and many admirable writers, are devoid of this quality. Poets as we know have always made a great use of alliteration. They are persuaded that the repetition of a sound gives an effect of beauty. I do not think it does so in prose. It seems to me that in prose alliteration should be used only for a special reason; when used by accident it falls on the ear very disagreeably. But its accidental use is so common that one can only suppose that the sound of it is not universally offensive. Many writers without distress will put two rhyming words together, join a monstrous long adjective to a monstrous long noun, or between the end of one word and the beginning of another have a conjunction of consonants that almost breaks your jaw. These are trivial and obvious instances. I mention them only to prove that if careful writers can do such things it is only because they have no ear. Words have weight, sound and appearance; it is only by considering these that you can write a sentence that is good to look at and good to listen to.

[9] I have read many books on English prose, but have found it hard to profit by them; for the most part they are vague, unduly theoretical, and often scolding. But you cannot say this of Fowler's *Dictionary of Modern English Usage*. It is a valuable work. I do not think anyone writes so well that he cannot learn much from it. It is lively reading. Fowler liked simplicity, straightforwardness and common sense. He had no patience with pretentiousness. He had a sound feeling that idiom was the backbone of a language and he was all for the racy phrase. He was no slavish admirer of logic and was willing enough to give usage right of way through the exact demesnes of grammar. English grammar is very difficult and few writers have avoided making mistakes in it. So heedful a writer as Henry James, for instance, on occasion wrote so ungrammatically that a schoolmaster, finding such errors in a schoolboy's essay, would be justly indignant. It is necessary to know grammar, and it is better to write grammatically than not, but it is well to remember

that grammar is common speech formulated. Usage is the only test. I would prefer a phrase that was easy and unaffected to a phrase that was grammatical. One of the differences between French and English is that in French you can be grammatical with complete naturalness, but in English not invariably. It is a difficulty in writing English that the sound of the living voice dominates the look of the printed word. I have given the matter of style a great deal of thought and have taken great pains. I have written few pages that I feel I could not improve and far too many that I have left with dissatisfaction because, try as I would, I could do no better. I cannot say of myself what Johnson said of Pope: "He never passed a fault unamended by indifference, nor quitted it by despair." I do not write as I want to; I write as I can.

[10] But Fowler had no ear. He did not see that simplicity may sometimes make concessions to euphony. I do not think a far-fetched, an archaic or even an affected word is out of place when it sounds better than the blunt, obvious one or when it gives a sentence a better balance. But, I hasten to add, though I think you may without misgiving make this concession to pleasant sound, I think you should make none to what may obscure your meaning. Anything is better than not to write clearly. There is nothing to be said against lucidity, and against simplicity only the possibility of dryness. This is a risk that is well worth taking when you reflect how much better it is to be bald than to wear a curly wig. But there is in euphony a danger that must be considered. It is very likely to be monotonous. When George Moore began to write, his style was poor; it gave you the impression that he wrote on wrapping paper with a blunt pencil. But he developed gradually a very musical English. He learnt to write sentences that fall away on the ear with a misty languor and it delighted him so much that he could never have enough of it. He did not escape monotony. It is like the sound of water lapping a shingly beach, so soothing that you presently cease to be sensible of it. It is so mellifluous that you hanker for some harshness, for an abrupt dissonance, that will interrupt the silky concord. I do not know how one can guard against this. I suppose the best chance is to have a more lively faculty of boredom than one's readers so that one is wearied before they are. One must always be on the watch for mannerisms and when certain cadences come too easily to the pen ask oneself whether they have not become mechanical. It is very hard to discover the exact point where the idiom one has formed to express oneself has lost its tang. As Dr. Johnson said: "He that has once studiously formed a style, rarely writes afterwards with complete ease." Admirably as I think Matthew Arnold's style was suited to his particular purposes, I must admit that his mannerisms are often irritating. His style was an instrument that he had forged

once for all; it was not like the human hand capable of performing a variety of actions.

[11] If you could write lucidly, simply, euphoniously and yet with liveliness you would write perfectly: you would write like Voltaire. And yet we know how fatal the pursuit of liveliness may be: it may result in the tiresome acrobatics of Meredith. Macaulay and Carlyle were in their different ways arresting; but at the heavy cost of naturalness. Their flashy effects distract the mind. They destroy their persuasiveness; you would not believe a man was very intent on ploughing a furrow if he carried a hoop with him and jumped through it at every other step. A good style should show no sign of effort. What is written should seem a happy accident. I think no one in France now writes more admirably than Colette, and such is the ease of her expression that you cannot bring yourself to believe that she takes any trouble over it. I am told that there are pianists who have a natural technique so that they can play in a manner that most executants can achieve only as the result of unremitting toil, and I am willing to believe that there are writers who are equally fortunate. Among them I was much inclined to place Colette. I asked her. I was exceedingly surprised to hear that she wrote everything over and over again. She told me that she would often spend a whole morning working upon a single page. But it does not matter how one gets the effect of ease. For my part, if I get it at all, it is only by strenuous effort. Nature seldom provides me with the word, the turn of phrase, that is appropriate without being far-fetched or commonplace.

QUESTIONS AND COMMENT ON FORM AND CONTENT

1. The earlier part of Maugham's article (not reprinted here) gives instances in which others have criticized his writing. Our selection starts with his conclusions: ". . . I must aim at lucidity, simplicity and euphony." Do these qualities form the outline of what he has to say? If so, in what order are they taken up? Does he inform the reader as he moves from point to point?

2. Instead of writing about lucidity in paragraph 2, he writes about its opposite—obscurity. One cause of obscurity is covered in paragraph 2. What is it? The other, wilfulness, is discussed in paragraph 3. What does he mean by *wilfulness?*

3. What is paragraph 4 about?

4. Where does the part on euphony begin?

5. What does the combining form *eu–* at the beginning of a word signify? What does *phon-* or *phono-* mean? Name other English words using these combining forms.

6. What does Maugham mean by saying that even clarity and euphony can be used excessively?

7. In the end, Maugham suggests a fourth quality. What is it?

8. Does Maugham's own writing have these four qualities? Which does he consider most important?

9. He confesses to certain weaknesses in his writing. What are they?

10. Do you find many figures of speech in his writing? What does he say about richness in style?

11. What distinction does he make between poetry and prose? In your opinion, is there an absolute dividing line?

12. What does he say about the styles of John Ruskin, Sir Thomas Browne, the King James Bible, Dr. Johnson, Voltaire, Addison, and Fowler?

13. When grammar and usage clash, which does he think should take precedence? Why? Do you agree?

VOCABULARY: WHAT DO THE ITALICIZED WORDS MEAN?

. . . to write if not beautifully at least with *perspicuity* (2)

. . . a *naive* delight in fine words, . . . an *innate eccentricity* (5)

The *dictum* that the style is the man . . . is one of those *aphorisms* (6)

There is a great difference between the *magniloquence* of the Jacobean writers . . . and the *turgidity* of Gibbon and Dr. Johnson (6)

For *rococo* was evolved when *baroque* had become declamatory (7)

THEME SUGGESTIONS

Write a précis (condensation, summary) of this essay. Make it about one-tenth as long as the original. Include the main points. In general, omit lengthy illustrations. Use your own words wherever possible and your own sentence structure. Do not quote. Observe the four principles of style suggested by Maugham.

My Main Trouble Is Saying What I Mean

My Themes Lack ———

7 | SCIENCE AND SCIENTIFIC THINKING

THE METHOD OF SCIENTIFIC INVESTIGATION

Thomas Henry Huxley

Thomas Henry Huxley (1825-1895), biologist and professor of natural history, became noted for his vigorous defense of the Darwinian theory of evolution. He believed that our knowledge of natural laws and of the universe is a vital part of a liberal education. The essay that follows was originally part of an address to workingmen.

[1] The method of scientific investigation is nothing but the expression of the necessary mode of working of the human mind. It is simply the mode at which all phenomena are reasoned about, rendered precise and exact. There is no more difference, but there is just the same kind of difference, between the mental operations of a man of science and those of an ordinary person, as there is between the operations and methods of a baker or of a butcher weighing out his goods in common scales, and the operation of a chemist in performing a difficult and complex analysis by means of his balance and finely graduated weights. It is not that the action of the scales in the one case, and the balance in the other, differ in the principles of their construction or manner of working; but the beam of one is set on an infinitely finer axis than the other, and of course turns by the addition of a much smaller weight.

[2] You will understand this better, perhaps, if I give you some familiar example. You have all heard it repeated, I dare say, that men of science work by means of induction and deduction, and that by the help of

these operations, they, in a sort of sense, wring from Nature certain other things, which are called natural laws, and causes, and that out of these, by some cunning skill of their own, they build up hypotheses and theories. And it is imagined by many that the operations of the common mind can be by no means compared with these processes, and that they have to be acquired by a sort of special apprenticeship to the craft. To hear all these large words, you would think that the mind of a man of science must be constituted differently from that of his fellow men; but if you will not be frightened by terms, you will discover that you are quite wrong, and that all these terrible apparatus are being used by yourselves every day and every hour of your lives.

[3] There is a well-known incident in one of Molière's plays, where the author makes the hero express unbounded delight on being told that he had been talking prose during the whole of his life. In the same way, I trust that you will take comfort, and be delighted with yourselves, on the discovery that you have been acting on the principles of inductive and deductive philosophy during the same period. Probably there is not one here who has not in the course of the day had occasion to set in motion a complex train of reasoning, of the very same kind, though differing of course in degree, as that which a scientific man goes through in tracing the causes of natural phenomena.

[4] A very trivial circumstance will serve to exemplify this. Suppose you go into a fruiterer's shop, wanting an apple—you take up one, and, on biting it, you find it is sour; you look at it, and see that it is hard and green. You take up another one, and that too is hard, green, and sour. The shopman offers you a third; but, before biting it, you examine it, and find that it is hard and green, and you immediately say that you will not have it, as it must be sour, like those that you have already tried.

[5] Nothing can be more simple than that, you think; but if you will take the trouble to analyze and trace out into its logical elements what has been done by the mind, you will be greatly surprised. In the first place, you have performed the operation of induction. You found that, in two experiences, hardness and greenness in apples went together with sourness. It was so in the first case, and it was confirmed by the second. True, it is a very small basis, but still it is enough to make an induction from; you generalize the facts, and you expect to find sourness in apples where you get hardness and greenness. You found upon that a general law, that all hard and green apples are sour; and that, so far as it goes, is a perfect induction. Well, having got your natural law in this way, when you are offered another apple which you find is hard and green, you say, "All hard and green apples are sour; this apple is hard and green, therefore this apple is sour." That train of reasoning is what logicians call a syllogism, and has all its various parts and terms—its

major premise, its minor premise, and its conclusion. And, by the help
of further reasoning, which, if drawn out, would have to be exhibited
in two or three other syllogisms, you arrive at your final determination,
"I will not have that apple." So that, you see, you have, in the first place,
established a law by induction, and upon that you have founded a deduction, and reasoned out the special conclusion of the particular case.
Well now, suppose, having got your law, that at some time afterwards,
you are discussing the qualities of apples with a friend: you will say to
him, "It is a very curious thing, but I find that all hard and green apples
are sour!" Your friend says to you, "But how do you know that?" You
at once reply, "Oh, because I have tried them over and over again, and
have always found them to be so." Well, if we were talking science instead of common sense, we should call that an experimental verification.
And, if still opposed, you go further, and say, "I have heard from the
people in Somersetshire and Devonshire, where a large number of apples are grown, that they have observed the same thing. It is also
found to be the case in Normandy, and in North America. In short, I
find it to be the universal experience of mankind wherever attention has
been directed to the subject." Whereupon, your friend, unless he is a
very unreasonable man, agrees with you, and is convinced that you
are quite right in the conclusion you have drawn. He believes, although
perhaps he does not know he believes it, that the more extensive verifications are—that the more frequently experiments have been made, and
the results of the same kind arrived at—that the more varied the conditions under which the same results are attained, the more certain is the
ultimate conclusion, and he disputes the question no further. He sees
that the experiment has been tried under all sorts of conditions, as to
time, place, and people, with the same result; and he says with you,
therefore, that the law you have laid down must be a good one, and he
must believe it.

[6] In science we do the same thing; the philosopher exercises precisely the same faculties, though in a much more delicate manner. In
scientific inquiry it becomes a matter of duty to expose a supposed law
to every possible kind of verification, and to take care, moreover, that
this is done intentionally, and not left to a mere accident, as in the case
of the apples. And in science, as in common life, our confidence in a
law is in exact proportion to the absence of variation in the result of
our experimental verifications. For instance, if you let go your grasp of
an article you may have in your hand, it will immediately fall to the
ground. That is a very common verification of one of the best established
laws of nature—that of gravitation. The method by which men of science
establish the existence of that law is exactly the same as that by which
we have established the trivial proposition about the sourness of hard

and green apples. But we believe it in such an extensive, thorough, and unhesitating manner because the universal experience of mankind verifies it, and we can verify it ourselves at any time; and that is the strongest possible foundation on which any natural law can rest.

[7] So much, then, by way of proof that the method of establishing laws in science is exactly the same as that pursued in common life. Let us now turn to another matter (though really it is but another phase of the same question), and that is the method by which, from the relations of certain phenomena, we prove that some stand in the position of causes towards the others.

[8] I want to put the case clearly before you, and I will therefore show you what I mean by another familiar example. I will suppose that one of you, on coming down in the morning to the parlor of your house, finds that a teapot and some spoons which had been left in the room on the previous evening are gone—the window is open, and you observe the mark of a dirty hand on the window frame, and perhaps, in addition to that, you notice the impress of a hobnailed shoe on the gravel outside. All these phenomena have struck your attention instantly, and before two seconds have passed you say, "Oh, somebody has broken open the window, entered the room, and run off with the spoons and the teapot!" That speech is out of your mouth in a moment. And you will probably add, "I know there has; I am quite sure of it!" You mean to say exactly what you know; but in reality you are giving expression to what is, in all essential particulars, an hypothesis. You do not *know* it at all; it is nothing but an hypothesis rapidly framed in your own mind. And it is an hypothesis founded on a long train of inductions and deductions.

[9] What are those inductions and deductions, and how have you got at this hypothesis? You have observed, in the first place, that the window is open; but by a train of reasoning involving many inductions and deductions, you have probably arrived long before at the general law —and a very good one it is—that windows do not open of themselves; and you therefore conclude that something has opened the window. A second general law that you have arrived at in the same way is that teapots and spoons do not go out of a window spontaneously, and you are satisfied that, as they are not now where you left them, they have been removed. In the third place, you look at the marks on the window sill, and the shoe-marks outside, and you say that in all previous experience the former kind of mark has never been produced by anything else but the hand of human being; and the same experience shows that no other animal but man at present wears shoes with hobnails in them such as would produce the marks in the gravel. I do not know, even if we could discover any of those "missing links" that are talked about, that they would help us to any other conclusion! At any rate the law

which states our present experience is strong enough for my present purpose. You next reach the conclusion that as these kinds of marks have not been left by any other animals than men, or are liable to be formed in any other way than by a man's hand and shoe, the marks in question have been formed by a man in that way. You have, further, a general law, founded on observation and experience, and that, too, is, I am sorry to say, a very universal and unimpeachable one—that some men are thieves; and you assume at once from all these premises—and that is what constitutes your hypothesis—that the man who made the marks outside and on the window sill, opened the window, got into the room, and stole your teapot and spoons. You have now arrived at a *vera causa;* you have assumed a cause which, it is plain, is competent to produce all the phenomena you have observed. You can explain all these phenomena only by the hypothesis of a thief. But that is a hypothetical conclusion, of the justice of which you have no absolute proof at all; it is only rendered highly probable by a series of inductive and deductive reasonings.

[10] I suppose your first action, assuming that you are a man of ordinary common sense, and that you have established this hypothesis to your own satisfaction, will very likely be to go off for the police, and set them on the track of the burglar, with the view to the recovery of your property. But just as you are starting with this object, some person comes in, and on learning what you are about, says, "My good friend, you are going on a great deal too fast. How do you know that the man who really made the marks took the spoons? It might have been a monkey that took them, and the man may have merely looked in afterwards." You would probably reply, "Well, that is all very well, but you see it is contrary to all experience of the way teapots and spoons are abstracted; so that, at any rate, your hypothesis is less probable than mine." While you are talking the thing over in this way, another friend arrives, one of that good kind of people that I was talking of a little while ago. And he might say, "Oh, my dear sir, you are certainly going on a great deal too fast. You are most presumptuous. You admit that all these occurrences took place when you were fast asleep, at a time when you could not possibly have known anything about what was taking place. How do you know that the laws of Nature are not suspended during the night? It may be that there has been some kind of supernatural interference in this case." In point of fact, he declares that your hypothesis is one of which you cannot at all demonstrate the truth, and that you are by no means sure that the laws of Nature are the same when you are asleep as when you are awake.

[11] Well, now, you cannot at the moment answer that kind of reasoning. You feel that your worthy friend has you somewhat at a disadvantage. You will feel perfectly convinced in your own mind, however,

that you are quite right, and you say to him, "My good friend, I can only be guided by the natural probabilities of the case, and if you will be kind enough to stand aside and permit me to pass, I will go and fetch the police." Well, we will suppose that your journey is successful, and that by good luck you meet with a policeman; that eventually the burglar is found with your property on his person, and the marks correspond to his hand and to his boots. Probably any jury would consider those facts a very good experimental verification of your hypothesis, touching the cause of the abnormal phenomena observed in your parlor, and would act accordingly.

[12] Now, in this suppositious case, I have taken phenomena of a very common kind, in order that you might see what are the different steps in an ordinary process of reasoning, if you will only take the trouble to analyze it carefully. All the operations I have described, you will see, are involved in the mind of any man of sense in leading him to a conclusion as to the course he should take in order to make good a robbery and punish the offender. I say that you are led, in that case, to your conclusion by exactly the same train of reasoning as that which a man of science pursues when he is endeavoring to discover the origin and laws of the most occult phenomena. The process is, and always must be, the same; and precisely the same mode of reasoning was employed by Newton and Laplace in their endeavors to discover and define the causes of the movements of the heavenly bodies, as you, with your own common sense, would employ to detect a burglar. The only difference is that the nature of the inquiry being more abstruse, every step has to be most carefully watched, so that there may not be a single crack or flaw in your hypothesis. A flaw or crack in many of the hypotheses of daily life may be of little or no moment as affecting the general correctness of the conclusions at which we may arrive; but, in a scientific inquiry, a fallacy, great or small, is always of importance, and is sure to be in the long run constantly productive of mischievous, if not fatal, results.

[13] Do not allow yourselves to be misled by the common notion that an hypothesis is untrustworthy simply because it is an hypothesis. It is often urged, in respect to some scientific conclusion, that, after all, it is only an hypothesis. But what more have we to guide us in nine-tenths of the most important affairs of daily life than hypotheses, and often very ill-based ones? So that in science, where the evidence of an hypothesis is subjected to the most rigid examination, we may rightly pursue the same course. You may have hypotheses and hypotheses. A man may say, if he likes, that the moon is made of green cheese: that is an hypothesis. But another man, who has devoted a great deal of time and attention to the subject, and availed himself of the most powerful telescopes and the results of the observations of others, declares that in his

opinion it is probably composed of materials very similar to those of which our own earth is made up: and that is also only an hypothesis. But I need not tell you that there is an enormous difference in the value of the two hypotheses. That one which is based on sound scientific knowledge is sure to have a corresponding value; and that which is a mere hasty random guess is likely to have but little value. Every great step in our progress in discovering causes has been made in exactly the same way as that which I have detailed to you. A person observing the occurrence of certain facts and phenomena asks, naturally enough, what process, what kind of operation known to occur in Nature applied to the particular case, will unravel and explain the mystery? Hence you have the scientific hypothesis; and its value will be proportionate to the care and completeness with which its basis had been tested and verified. It is in these matters as in the commonest affairs of practical life: the guess of the fool will be folly, while the guess of the wise man will contain wisdom. In all cases, you see that the value of the result depends on the patience and faithfulness with which the investigator applies to his hypothesis every possible kind of verification.

QUESTIONS AND COMMENT ON FORM AND CONTENT

1. After assuring the audience that the methods of science are very much like those of our everyday actions in life, Huxley gives us a simple example of how we act and reason in a fruit store. Is our procedure there inductive or deductive or both? What is the difference between induction and deduction? Does the etymology of the two words help us to understand the meaning?

2. What is a syllogism? What is meant by major premise, minor premise, and conclusion?

3. Why does Huxley emphasize the great care and caution used by scientists in coming to a conclusion? Can this be related to his general purpose in lecturing—to give people confidence in the findings of scientists—especially those concerned with evolution? To what extent does a generalization depend upon the number of instances observed?

4. With paragraph 8 Huxley begins "another familiar example." How does this example differ from the first one? What "laws" are cited to support the conclusion? What is the meaning of *law* as Huxley uses it here?

5. Why does he raise the question in paragraph 10 about the temporary suspension of "the laws of Nature"? Could this, also, be related to the arguments of those who opposed Huxley and Darwin?

6. What is an hypothesis? What is the difference between the two hypotheses concerning the composition of the moon? (See paragraph 13.)

7. Is there anything in the diction and sentence structure to indicate that this was a lecture rather than a written article?

8. The first sentence in paragraph 7 is a fragment (incomplete sentence).

Structurally, what does it lack? Are fragments frequently used for purposes of summary or transition? What is the function of the parentheses in paragraph 7? What is the purpose of each mark of punctuation in the sentence in paragraph 9 that begins, "You have, further, . . ."?

VOCABULARY: WHAT DO THE ITALICIZED WORDS MEAN?

. . . an *experimental verification* (5)
. . . a *general* law, . . . a very *universal* and *unimpeachable* one (9)
. . . arrived at a *vera causa* (9)
. . . you are most *presumptuous* (10)
. . . the inquiry being more *abstruse* (12)

THEME SUGGESTIONS

On Sound and Hasty Generalizations
Some Deductive Arguments Against (some type of government, morals, education, etc.)
Deductions in Detective Stories
Are Superstitions Logical?
A False Hypothesis

GALILEO

Bertrand Russell

Bertrand Russell (1882-   ) is an English mathematician and philosopher. Among his books are The Principles of Mathematics, Marriage and Morals, *and* The Conquest of Happiness. *He received the Nobel Prize in literature in 1953.*

[1] Scientific method, although in its more refined forms it may seem complicated, is in essence remarkably simple. It consists in observing such facts as will enable the observer to discover general laws governing facts of the kind in question. The two stages, first of observation, and second of inference to a law, are both essential, and each is susceptible of almost indefinite refinement; but in essence the first man who said "fire burns" was employing scientific method, at any rate if he had allowed himself to be burnt several times. This man had already passed through the two stages of observation and generalization. He had not, however,

From Chapter I of Bertrand Russell's *The Scientific Outlook*. Reprinted by permission of George Allen & Unwin, Ltd., London. Copyright 1931 by Bertrand Russell.

what scientific technique demands—a careful choice of significant facts on the one hand, and, on the other hand, various means of arriving at laws otherwise than by mere generalization. The man who says "unsupported bodies in air fall" has merely generalized, and is liable to be refuted by balloons, butterflies, and aeroplanes; whereas the man who understands the theory of falling bodies knows also why certain exceptional bodies do not fall.

[2] Scientific method, simple as it is in essence, has been acquired only with great difficulty, and is still employed only by a minority, who themselves confine its employment to a minority of the questions upon which they have opinions. If you number among your acquaintances some eminent man of science, accustomed to the minutest quantitative precision in his experiments and the most abstruse skill in his inference from them, you will be able to make him the subject of a little experiment which is likely to be by no means unilluminating. If you tackle him on party politics, theology, income tax, house-agents, the bumptiousness of the working-classes and other topics of a like nature, you are pretty sure, before long, to provoke an explosion, and to hear him expressing wholly untested opinions with a dogmatism which he would never display in regard to the well-founded results of his laboratory experiments.

[3] As this illustration shows, the scientific attitude is in some degree unnatural to man; the majority of our opinions are wish fulfilments like dreams in the Freudian theory. The mind of the most rational among us may be compared to a stormy ocean of passionate convictions based upon desire, upon which float perilously a few tiny boats carrying a cargo of scientifically tested beliefs. Nor is this to be altogether deplored: life has to be lived, and there is no time to test rationally all the beliefs by which our conduct is regulated. Without a certain wholesome rashness, no one could long survive. Scientific method, therefore, must, in its very nature, be confined to the more solemn and official of our opinions. A medical man who gives advice on diet should give it after full consideration of all that science has to say on the matter, but the man who follows his advice cannot stop to verify it, and is obliged to rely, therefore, not upon science, but upon his belief that his medical adviser is scientific. A community impregnated with science is one in which the recognized experts have arrived at their opinions by scientific methods, but it is impossible for the ordinary citizen to repeat the work of the experts for himself. There is, in the modern world, a great body of well-attested knowledge on all kinds of subjects which the ordinary man accepts on authority without any need for hesitation; but as soon as any strong passion intervenes to warp the expert's judgment he becomes unreliable, whatever scientific equipment he may possess. The views of medical men on pregnancy, child-birth, and lactation were until fairly recently impregnated

with sadism. It requires, for example, more evidence to persuade them that anaesthetics may be used in child-birth than it would have required to persuade them of the opposite. Anyone who desires an hour's amusement may be advised to look up the tergiversations of eminent craniologists in their attempts to prove from brain measurements that women are stupider than men.[1]

[4] It is not, however, the lapses of scientific men that concern us when we are trying to describe scientific method. A scientific opinion is one which there is some reason to believe true; an unscientific opinion is one which is held for some reason other than its probable truth. Our age is distinguished from all ages before the seventeenth century by the fact that some of our opinions are scientific in the above sense. I except the bare matters of fact, since generality in a greater or less degree is an essential characteristic of science, and since men (with the exception of a few mystics) have never been able wholly to deny the obvious facts of their everyday existence.

[5] The Greeks, eminent as they were in almost every department of human activity, did surprisingly little for the creation of science. The great intellectual achievement of the Greeks was geometry, which they believed to be an *a priori* study proceeding from self-evident premises, and not requiring experimental verification. The Greek genius was deductive rather than inductive, and was therefore at home in mathematics. In the ages that followed, Greek mathematics was nearly forgotten, while other products of the Greek passion for deducation survived and flourished, notably theology and law. The Greeks observed the world as poets rather than as men of science, partly, I think, because all manual activity was ungentlemanly, so that any study which required experiment seemed a little vulgar. Perhaps it would be fanciful to connect with this prejudice the fact that the department in which the Greeks were most scientific was astronomy, which deals with bodies that only can be seen and not touched.

[6] However that may be, it is certainly remarkable how much the Greeks discovered in astronomy. They early decided that the earth is round, and some of them arrived at the Copernican theory that it is the earth's rotation, and not the revolution of the heavens, that causes the apparent diurnal motion of the sun and stars. Archimedes, writing to King Gelon of Syracuse, says: "Aristarchus of Samos brought out a book consisting of some hypotheses of which the premises lead to the conclusion that the universe is many times greater than that now so called. His hypotheses are that the fixed stars and the sun remain unmoved, that the earth revolves about the sun in the circumference of a circle, the sun lying in the centre of the orbit." Thus the Greeks discovered not only

[1] See Havelock Ellis, *Man and Woman,* 6th edition, p. 119ff.

the diurnal rotation of the earth, but also its annual revolution about the sun. It was the discovery that a Greek had held this opinion which gave Copernicus courage to revive it. In the days of the Renaissance, when Copernicus lived, it was held that any opinion which had been entertained by an ancient might be true, but an opinion which no ancient had entertained could not deserve respect. I doubt whether Copernicus would ever have become a Copernican but for Aristarchus, whose opinion had been forgotten until the revival of classical learning.

[7] The Greeks also discovered perfectly valid methods of measuring the circumference of the earth. Eratosthenes the Geographer estimated it at 250,000 stadia (about 24,662 miles), which is by no means far from the truth.

[8] The most scientific of the Greeks was Archimedes (287-212 B.C.). Like Leonardo da Vinci in a later period, he recommended himself to a prince on the ground of his skill in the arts of war, and like Leonardo he was granted permission to add to human knowledge on condition that he subtracted from human life. His activities in this respect were, however, more distinguished than those of Leonardo, since he invented the most amazing mechanical contrivances for defending the city of Syracuse against the Romans, and was finally killed by a Roman soldier when that city was captured. He is said to have been so absorbed in a mathematical problem that he did not notice the Romans coming. Plutarch is very apologetic on the subject of the mechanical inventions of Archimedes, which he feels to have been hardly worthy of a gentleman; but he considers him excusable on the ground that he was helping his cousin the king at a time of dire peril.

[9] Archimedes showed great genius in mathematics and extraordinary skill in the invention of mechanical contrivances, but his contributions to science, remarkable as they are, still display the deductive attitude of the Greeks, which made the experimental method scarcely possible for them. His work on Statics is famous, and justly so, but it proceeds from axioms like Euclid's geometry, and the axioms are supposed to be self-evident, not the result of experiment. His book *On Floating Bodies* is the one which according to tradition resulted from the problem of King Hiero's crown, which was suspected of being not made of pure gold. This problem, as everyone knows, Archimedes is supposed to have solved while in his bath. At any rate, the method which he proposes in his book for such cases is a perfectly valid one, and although the book proceeds from postulates by a method of deduction, one cannot but suppose that he arrived at the postulates experimentally. This is, perhaps, the most nearly scientific (in the modern sense) of the works of Archimedes. Soon after his time, however, such feeling as the Greeks had had for the scientific investigation of natural phenomena decayed, and though pure mathemat-

ics continued to flourish down to the capture of Alexandria by the Mohammedans, there were hardly any further advances in natural science, and the best that had been done, such as theory of Aristarchus, was forgotten.

[10] The Arabs were more experimental than the Greeks, especially in chemistry. They hoped to transmute base metals into gold, to discover the philosopher's stone, and to concoct the elixir of life. Partly on this account chemical investigations were viewed with favour. Throughout the Dark Ages it was mainly by the Arabs that the tradition of civilization was carried on, and it was largely from them that Christians such as Roger Bacon acquired whatever scientific knowledge the later Middle Ages possessed. The Arabs, however, had a defect which was the opposite of that of the Greeks: they sought detached facts rather than general principles, and had not the power of inferring general laws from the facts which they discovered.

[11] In Europe, when the scholastic system first began to give way before the Renaissance, there came to be, for a time, a dislike of all generalizations and all systems. Montaigne illustrates this tendency. He likes queer facts particularly if they disprove something. He has no desire to make his opinions systematic and coherent. Rabelais also, with his motto: "Fais ce que voudras," is as adverse from intellectual as from other fetters. The Renaissance rejoiced in the recovered liberty of speculation, and was not anxious to lose this liberty even in the interests of truth. Of the typical figures of the Renaissance by far the most scientific was Leonardo, whose note-books are fascinating and contain many brilliant anticipations of later discoveries, but he brought almost nothing to fruition, and remained without effect upon his scientific successors.

[12] Scientific method, as we understand it, comes into the world full-fledged with Galileo (1564-1642), and, to a somewhat lesser degree, in his contemporary, Kepler (1571-1630). Kepler is known to fame through his three laws: he first discovered that the planets move round the sun in ellipses, not in circles. To the modern mind there is nothing astonishing in the fact that the earth's orbit is an ellipse, but to minds trained on antiquity anything except a circle, or some complication of circles, seemed almost incredible for a heavenly body. To the Greeks the planets were divine, and must therefore move in perfect curves. Circles and epicycles did not offend their aesthetic susceptibilities, but a crooked, skew orbit such as the earth's actually is would have shocked them deeply. Unprejudiced observation without regard to aesthetic prejudices required therefore, at that time, a rare intensity of scientific ardour. It was Kepler and Galileo who established the fact that the earth and the other planets go round the sun. This had been asserted by Copernicus, and, as we have seen, by certain Greeks, but they had not succeeded in giving proofs.

Copernicus, indeed, had no serious arguments to advance in favour of his view. It would be doing Kepler more than justice to suggest that in adopting the Copernican hypothesis he was acting on purely scientific motives. It appears that, at any rate in youth, he was addicted to sun-worship, and thought the centre of the universe the only place worthy of so great a deity. None but scientific motives, however, could have led him to the discovery that the planetary orbits are ellipses and not circles.

[13] He, and still more Galileo, possessed the scientific method in its completeness. While much more is known than was known in their day, nothing essential has been added to method. They proceeded from observation of particular facts to the establishment of exact quantitative laws, by means of which future particular facts could be predicted. They shocked their contemporaries profoundly, partly because their conclusions were inherently shocking to the beliefs of that age, but partly also because the belief in authority had enabled learned men to confine their researches to libraries, and the professors were pained at the suggestion that it might be necessary to look at the world in order to know what it is like.

[14] Galileo, it must be confessed, was something of a *gamin*. When still very young he became Professor of Mathematics at Pisa, but as the salary was only fifteen cents a day, he does not seem to have thought that a very dignified bearing could be expected of him. He began by writing a treatise against the wearing of cap and gown in the University, which may perhaps have been popular with undergraduates, but was viewed with grave disfavour by his fellow-professors. He would amuse himself by arranging occasions which would make his colleagues look silly. They asserted, for example, on the basis of Aristotle's *Physics,* that a body weighing ten pounds would fall through a given distance in one-tenth of the time that would be taken by a body weighing one pound. So he went up to the top of the Leaning Tower of Pisa one morning with a ten-pound shot, and just as the professors were proceeding with leisurely dignity to their respective lecture-rooms in the presence of their pupils, he attracted their attention and dropped the two weights from the top of the tower to their feet. The two weights arrived practically simultaneously. The professors, however, maintained that their eyes must have deceived them, since it was impossible that Aristotle could be in error.

[15] On another occasion he was even more rash. Giovanni de' Medici, who was the Governor of Leghorn, invented a dredging machine of which he was very proud. Galileo pointed out that whatever else it might do it would not dredge, which proved to be a fact. This caused Giovanni to become an ardent Aristotelian.

[16] Galileo became unpopular and was hissed at his lectures—a fate

which has at times also befallen Einstein in Berlin. Then he made a tele-
scope and invited the professors to look through it at Jupiter's moons.
They refused on the ground that Aristotle had not mentioned these satel-
lites, and therefore anybody who thought he saw them must be mistaken.

[17] The experiment from the Leaning Tower of Pisa illustrated Galileo's first important piece of work, namely, the establishment of the Law
of Falling Bodies, according to which all bodies fall at the same rate in
a vacuum and at the end of a given time have a velocity proportional to
the time in which they have been falling, and have traversed a distance
proportional to the square of that time. Aristotle had maintained otherwise but neither he nor any of his successors throughout nearly two
thousand years had taken the trouble to find out whether what he said
was true. The idea of doing so was a novelty, and Galileo's disrespect
for authority was considered abominable. He had, of course, many
friends, men to whom the spectacle of intelligence was delightful in
itself. Few such men, however, held academic posts, and university opinion was bitterly hostile to his discoveries.

[18] As everyone knows, he came in conflict with the Inquisition at
the end of his life for maintaining that the earth goes round the sun. He
had had a previous minor encounter from which he had emerged without great damage, but in the year of 1632 he published a book of dia-
logues on the Copernican and Ptolemaic systems, in which he had the
temerity to place some remarks that had been made by the Pope into the
mouth of a character named Simplicius. The Pope had hitherto been
friendly to him, but at this point became furious. Galileo was living at
Florence on terms of friendship with the Grand Duke, but the Inquisition
sent for him to come to Rome to be tried, and threatened the Grand
Duke with pains and penalties if he continued to shelter Galileo. Galileo
was at this time seventy years old, very ill, and going blind; he sent a
medical certificate to the effect that he was not fit to travel, so the Inquisition sent a doctor of their own with orders that as soon as he was
well enough he should be brought in chains. Upon hearing that this
order was on its way, he set out voluntarily. By means of threats he was
induced to make submission. . . .

[19] The formula of abjuration, which, as a consequence of this sentence, Galileo was compelled to pronounce, was as follows:

> I, Galileo Galilei, son of the late Vincenzio Galilei of Florence, aged
> seventy years, being brought personally to judgment, and kneeling before
> you, Most Eminent and Most Reverend Lords Cardinals, General Inquisi-
> tors of the Universal Christian Republic against heretical depravity, hav-
> ing before my eyes the Holy Gospels which I touch with my own hands,
> swear that I have always believed, and, with the help of God, will in fu-
> ture believe, every article which the Holy Catholic and Apostolic Church

of Rome holds, teaches, and preaches. But because I have been enjoined, by this Holy Office, altogether to abandon the false opinion which maintains that the sun is the centre and immovable, and forbidden to hold, defend, or teach, the said false doctrine in any manner; and because, after it had been signified to me that the said doctrine is repugnant to the Holy Scripture, I have written and printed a book, in which I treat of the same condemned doctrine, and adduce reasons with great force in support of the same, without giving any solution, and therefore have been judged grievously suspected of heresy; that is to say, that I held and believed that the sun is the centre of the world and immovable, and that the earth is not the centre and movable, I am willing to remove from the minds of your Eminences, and of every Catholic Christian, this vehement suspicion rightly entertained towards me, therefore, with a sincere heart and unfeigned faith, I abjure, cure, and detest the said errors and heresies, and generally every other error and sect contrary to the said Holy Church; and I swear that I will never more in future say, or assert anything, verbally or in writing, which may give rise to a similar suspicion of me; but that if I shall know any heretic, or anyone suspected of heresy, I will denounce him to this Holy Office, or to the Inquisitor and Ordinary of the place in which I may be. I swear, moreover, and promise that I will fulfil and observe fully all the penances which have been or shall be laid on me by this Holy Office. But if it shall happen that I violate any of my said promises, oaths, and protestations (which God avert!), I subject myself to all the pains and punishments which have been decreed and promulgated by the sacred canons and other general and particular constitutions against delinquents of this description. So, may God help me, and His Holy Gospels, which I touch with my own hands, I, the above-named Galileo Galilei, have abjured, sworn, promised, and bound myself as above; and, in witness thereof, with my own hand have subscribed this present writing of my abjuration, which I have recited word for word.

At Rome, in the Convent of Minerva, June 22, 1633, I Galileo Galilei, have adjured as above with my own hand.[2]

It is not true that after reciting this abjuration, he muttered: *"Eppur si muove."* It was the world that said this—not Galileo.

[20] The conflict between Galileo and the Inquisition is not merely the conflict between free thought and bigotry or between science and religion; it is a conflict between the spirit of induction and the spirit of deduction. Those who believe in deduction as the method of arriving at knowledge are compelled to find their premises somewhere, usually in a sacred book. Deduction from inspired books is the method of arriving at truth employed by jurists, Christians, Mohammedans, and Communists. Since deduction as a means of obtaining knowledge collapses when doubt

---

[2] From *Galileo, His Life and Work,* by J. J. Fahie, 1903, p. 313ff.

is thrown upon its premises, those who believe in deduction must necessarily be bitter against men who question the authority of the sacred books. Galileo questioned both Aristotle and the Scriptures, and thereby destroyed the whole edifice of mediaeval knowledge. His predecessors had known how the world was created, what was man's destiny, the deepest mysteries of metaphysics, and the hidden principles governing the behaviour of bodies. Throughout the moral and material universe nothing was mysterious to them, nothing hidden, nothing incapable of exposition in orderly syllogisms. Compared with all this wealth, what was left to the followers of Galileo?—a law of falling bodies, the theory of the pendulum, and Kepler's ellipses. Can it be wondered at that the learned cried out at such a destruction of their hard-won wealth? As the rising sun scatters the multitude of stars, so Galileo's few proved truths banished the scintillating firmament of mediaeval certainties.

[21] Socrates had said that he was wiser than his contemporaries because he alone knew that he knew nothing. This was a rhetorical device. Galileo could have said with truth that he knew something, but knew he knew little, while his Aristotelian contemporaries knew nothing, but thought they knew much. Knowledge, as opposed to fantasies of wish-fulfilment, is difficult to come by. A little contact with real knowledge makes fantasies less acceptable. As a mater of fact, knowledge is even harder to come by than Galileo supposed, and much that he believed was only approximate; but in the process of acquiring knowledge at once secure and general, Galileo took the first great step. He is, therefore, the father of modern times. Whatever we may like or dislike about the age in which we live, its increase of population, its improvement in health, its trains, motor-cars, radio, politics, and advertisements of soap—all emanate from Galileo. If the Inquisition could have caught him young, we might not now be enjoying the blessings of air-warfare and poisoned gas, nor, on the other hand, the diminution of poverty and disease which is characteristic of our age.

[22] It is customary amongst a certain school of sociologists to minimize the importance of intelligence, and to attribute all great events to large impersonal causes. I believe this to be an entire delusion. I believe that if a hundred of the men of the seventeenth century had been killed in infancy, the modern world would not exist. And of these hundred, Galileo is the chief.

QUESTIONS AND COMMENT ON FORM AND CONTENT

1. How does Bertrand Russell define *scientific method?* What distinction does he make between scientific opinion and unscientific opinion?

2. On what kinds of questions are scientists likely to have unscientific opinions? What is illustrated or proved from the examples of medical men? (See paragraph 3.)

3. What are the several meanings of *a priori*? Which meaning is the author using in paragraph 5? What is meant by the assertion that the Greek genius was deductive rather than inductive?

4. What kinds of chemical experiments did the Arabs carry out? Which of two steps of an induction did they neglect?

5. Why was Kepler's discovery that the earth's orbit is an ellipse (not a circle) discredited? Why did the professors refuse to look at what Galileo said was Jupiter's moons and refuse to believe their eyes when two different weights fell from the tower at Pisa simultaneously?

6. During the Inquisition Galileo was forced to recant opinions that differed from those of the Church. What does Russell mean by saying that the conflict is not merely "between free thought and bigotry or between science and religion; it is a conflict between the spirit of induction and the spirit of deduction"?

7. Why were many religious people disturbed by the assertion that the earth revolved about the sun? What later scientific hypotheses or proofs caused similar disturbance? Does man, in general, dislike to have his opinions disproved? Why or why not?

8. If the Inquisition had caught Galileo young, according to Russell, what would be the probable effect on us? How would we be different today if one hundred important men of the Seventeenth Century had been killed in infancy? Is history, as Carlyle said, largely the elongated shadow of great men? Without great men and women in each generation would we revert to savagery?

9. Is the title "Galileo" an accurate indication of the contents of this essay? Where does the part on Galileo begin? Is the first half of the essay mere introduction? Or did Russell choose a title that would attract readers? If his title is not an accurate one, what could be substituted if logic were the only consideration?

10. In what order, in general, is the article developed?

11. Does the satire found here and there throughout the article (see, for example, paragraphs 20 and 21) add to its effectiveness? Point out specific examples.

VOCABULARY: WHAT DO THE ITALICIZED WORDS MEAN?

. . . opinions were *impregnated* with *sadism* (3)
. . . the *tergiversations* of *eminent craniologists* (3)
. . . self-evident *premises,* and not requiring experimental *verification* (5)
The Arabs . . . hoped to . . . discover the *philosopher's stone* and to *concoct the elixir* of life (10)
Galileo . . . was something of a *gamin* (14)

. . . he had the *temerity* (18)
. . . deepest mysteries of *metaphysics* (20)
. . . *exposition* in orderly *syllogisms* (20)

THEME SUGGESTIONS

What Kind of Government (Education, etc.) Is Best?
Knowledge or Wish Fulfillment?
A Deductive Argument
The Limits of Deduction (Induction)

LOGIC AND LOGICAL FALLACIES

Robert Gorham Davis

Robert Gorham Davis (1908-   ) is Professor of English at Colum-
bia University. This essay was written for freshman English students at
Harvard.

UNDEFINED TERMS

[1] The first requirement for logical discourse is knowing what the
words you use actually mean. Words are not like paper money or counters
in a game. Except for technical terms in some of the sciences, they do not
have a fixed face value. Their meanings are fluid and changing, influenced
by many considerations of context and reference, circumstance and association. This is just as true of common words such as *fast* as it is of
literary terms such as *romantic*. Moreover, if there is to be communication, words must have approximately the same meaning for the reader
that they have for the writer. A speech in an unknown language means
nothing to the hearer. When an adult speaks to a small child or an expert to a layman, communications may be seriously limited by lack of
a mature vocabulary or ignorance of technical terms. Many arguments
are meaningless because the speakers are using important words in quite
different senses.

[2] Because we learn most words—or guess at them—from the contexts in which we first encounter them, our sense of them is often
incomplete or wrong. Readers sometimes visualize the Assyrian who
comes down like the wolf on the fold as an enormous man dressed in

cohorts (some kind of fancy armor, possibly) gleaming in purple and gold. "A rift in the lute" suggests vaguely a cracked mandolin. Failure to ascertain the literal meaning of figurative language is a frequent reason for mixed metaphors. We are surprised to find that the "devil" in "the devil to pay" and "the devil and the deep blue sea" is not Old Nick, but part of a ship. Unless terms mean the same thing to both writer and reader, proper understanding is impossible.

ABSTRACTIONS

[3] The most serious logical difficulties occur with abstract terms. An abstraction is a word which stands for a quality found in a number of different objects or events from which it has been "abstracted" or taken away. We may, for instance, talk of the "whiteness" of paper or cotton or snow without considering qualities of cold or inflammability or usefulness which these materials happen also to possess. Usually, however, our minds carry over other qualities by association. See, for instance, the chapter called "The Whiteness of the Whale" in *Moby-Dick*.

[4] In much theoretic discussion the process of abstraction is carried so far that although vague associations and connotations persist, the original objects or events from which the qualities have been abstracted are lost sight of completely. Instead of thinking of words like *sincerity* and *Americanism* as symbols standing for qualities that have to be abstracted with great care from examples and test cases, we come to think of them as real things in themselves. We assume that Americanism is Americanism just as a bicycle is a bicycle, and that everyone knows what it means. We forget that before the question "Is Arthur Godfrey sincere?" can mean anything, we have to agree on the criteria of sincerity.

[5] When we try to define such words and find examples, we discover that almost no one agrees on their meaning. The word *church* may refer to anything from a building on the corner of Spring Street to the whole tradition of institutionalized Christianity. *Germany* may mean a geographical section of Europe, a people, a governing group, a cultural tradition, or a military power. Abstractions such as *freedom, courage, race, beauty, truth, justice, nature, honor, humanism, democracy* should never be used in a theme unless their meaning is defined or indicated clearly by the context. Freedom for whom? To do what? Under what circumstances? Abstract terms have merely emotional value unless they are strictly defined by asking questions of this kind. The study of a word such as *nature* in a good unabridged dictionary will show that even the dictionary, indispensable though it is, cannot determine for us the sense in which a word is being used in any given instance. Once the student understands

the importance of definition, he will no longer be betrayed into fruitless arguments over such questions as whether free verse is "poetry" or whether you can change "human nature."

NAME-CALLING

[6] It is a common unfairness in controversy to place what the writer dislikes or opposes in a generally odious category. The humanist dismisses what he dislikes by calling it *romantic;* the liberal, by calling it *fascist;* the conservative, by calling it *communistic.* These terms tell the reader nothing. What is *piety* to some will be *bigotry* to others. *Non-Catholics* would rather be called *Protestants* than *heretics.* What is *right-thinking* except a designation for those who agree with the writer? Social security measures become *creeping socialism:* industrial organizations, *forces of reaction;* investigation into communism, *witch hunts;* prison reform, *coddling;* progressive education, *fads and frills.* Such terms are intended to block thought by an appeal to prejudice and associative habits. Three steps are necessary before such epithets have real meaning. First, they must be defined; second, it must be shown that the object to which they are applied actually possesses these qualities; third, it must be shown that the possession of such qualities in this particular situation is necessarily undesirable. Unless a person is alert and critical both in choosing and in interpreting words, he may be alienated from ideas with which he would be in sympathy if he had not been frightened by a mere name.

GENERALIZATION

[7] Similar to the abuse of abstract terms and epithets is the habit of presenting personal opinions in the guise of universal laws. The student often seems to feel that the broader the terms in which he states an opinion, the more effective he will be. Ordinarily the reverse is true. An enthusiasm for Thomas Wolfe should lead to a specific critical analysis of Wolfe's novels that will enable the writer to explain his enthusiasm to others; it should not be turned into the argument that Wolfe is "the greatest American novelist," particularly if the writer's knowledge of American novelists is somewhat limited. The same questions of *who* and *when* and *why* and under what *circumstances* which are used to check abstract terms should be applied to generalizations. Consider how contradictory proverbial wisdom is when detached from particular circumstances. "Look before you leap," but "he who hesitates is lost."

[8] Superlatives and the words *right* and *wrong, true* and *untrue,*

never and *always* must be used with caution in matters of opinion. When a student says flatly that X is true, he often is really saying that he or his family or the author of a book he has just been reading, persons of certain tastes and background and experience, *think* that X is true. If his statement is based not on logic and examination of evidence, but merely reproduces other people's opinions, it can have little value or relevance unless these people are identified and their reasons for thinking so explained. Because many freshmen are taking survey courses in which they read a single work by an author or see an historical event through the eyes of a single historian whose bias they may not be able to measure, they must guard against this error.

SAMPLING

[9] Assertions of a general nature are frequently open to question because they are based on insufficient evidence. Some persons are quite ready, after meeting one Armenian or reading one medieval romance, to generalize about Armenians and medieval romances. One ought, of course, to examine objectively as many examples as possible before making a generalization, but the number is far less important than the representativeness of the example chosen. The Literary Digest Presidential Poll, sent to hundreds of thousands of people selected from telephone directories, was far less accurate than the Gallup Poll which questioned far fewer voters, but selected them carefully and proportionately from all different social groups. The "typical" college student, as portrayed by moving pictures and cartoons, is very different from the "average" college student as determined statistically. We cannot let uncontrolled experience do our sampling for us; instances and examples which impress themselves upon our minds do so usually because they are exceptional. In propaganda and arguments extreme cases are customarily treated as if they were characteristic.

[10] If one is permitted to select some examples and ignore others, it is possible to find convincing evidence for almost any theory, no matter how fantastic. The fact that the mind tends naturally to remember those instances which confirm its opinions imposes a duty upon the writer, unless he wishes to encourage prejudice and superstition, to look carefully for exceptions to all generalizations which he is tempted to make. We forget the premonitions which are not followed by disaster and the times when our hunches failed to select the winner in a race. Patent medicine advertisements print the letters of those who survived their cure, and not of those who died during it. All Americans did not gamble on the stock exchange in the twenties, or become Marxists in the thirties,

and all Vermonters are not thin-lipped and shrewd. Of course the search
for negative examples can be carried too far. Outside of mathematics of
the laboratory, few generalizations can be made airtight, and most are
not intended to be. But quibbling is so easy that resort to it is very common, and the knowledge that people can and will quibble over generalizations is another reason for making assertions as limited and explicitly
conditional as possible.

FALSE ANALOGY

[11] Illustration, comparison, analogy are most valuable in making an
essay clear and interesting. It must not be supposed, however, that they
prove anything or have much argumentative weight. The rule that what
is true of one thing in one set of circumstances is not necessarily true of
another thing in another set of circumstances seems almost too obvious
to need stating. Yet constantly nations and businesses are discussed as
if they were human beings with human habits and feelings; human bodies are discussed as if they were machines; the universe, as if it were
a clock. It is assumed that what held true for seventeenth century New
England or the thirteen Atlantic colonies also holds true for an industrial
nation of 160,000,000 people. Carlyle dismissed the arguments for representative democracy by saying that if a captain had to take a vote among
his crew every time he wanted to do something, he would never get
around Cape Horn. This analogy calmly ignores the distinction between
the lawmaking and the executive branches of constitutional democracies.
Moreover, voters may be considered much more like the stockholders of
a merchant line than its hired sailors. Such arguments introduce assumptions in a metaphorical guise in which they are not readily detected or
easily criticized. In place of analysis they attempt to identify their position with some familiar symbol which will evoke a predictable, emotional
response in the reader. The revival during the 1932 presidential campaign of Lincoln's remark, "Don't swap horses in the middle of the
stream," was not merely a picturesque way of saying keep Hoover in the
White House. It made a number of assumptions about the nature of de-
pressions and the function of government. This propagandist technique
can be seen most clearly in political cartoons.

DEGREE

[12] Often differences in degree are more important than differences
in kind. By legal and social standards there is more difference between
an habitual drunkard and a man who drinks temperately, than between

a temperate drinker and a total abstainer. In fact, differences of degree produce what are regarded as differences of kind. At known temperatures ice turns to water and water boils. At an indeterminate point affection becomes love and a man who needs a shave becomes a man with a beard. The fact that no men or systems are perfect makes rejoinders and counter-accusations very easy if differences in degree are ignored. Newspapers in totalitarian states, answering American accusations of brutality and suppression, refer to lynchings and gangsterism here. Before a disinterested judge could evaluate these mutual accusations, he would have to settle the question of the degree to which violent suppression and lynching are respectively prevalent in the countries under consideration. On the other hand, differences in degree may be merely apparent. Lincoln Steffens pointed out that newspapers can create a "crime wave" any time they wish, simply by emphasizing all the minor assaults and thefts commonly ignored or given an inch or two on a back page. The great reported increases in insanity may be due to the fact that in a more urban and institutionalized society cases of insanity more frequently come to the attention of authorities and hence are recorded in statistics.

CAUSATION

[13] The most common way of deciding that one thing causes another thing is the simple principle: *post hoc, ergo propter hoc*, "After this, therefore because of this." Rome fell after the introduction of Christianity; therefore Christianity was responsible for the fall of Rome. Such reasoning illustrates another kind of faulty generalization. But even if one could find ten cases in which a nation "fell" after the introduction of Christianity, it still would not be at all certain that Christianity caused the fall. Day, it has frequently been pointed out, follows night in every observable instance, and yet night cannot be called the cause of day. Usually a combination of causes produces a result. Sitting in a draught may cause a cold, but only given a certain physical condition in the person sitting there. In such instances one may distinguish between necessary and sufficient conditions. Air is a necessary condition for the maintenance of plant life, but air alone is not sufficient to produce plant life. And often different causes at different times may produce the same result. This relation is known as plurality of causes. If, after sitting in a stuffy theatre on Monday, and then again after eating in a stuffy restaurant on Thursday, a man suffered from headaches, he might say, generalizing, that bad air gave him headaches. But actually the headache on Monday may be been caused by eyestrain and on Thursday by indigestion. To isolate the causative factor it is necessary that all other condi-

tions be precisely the same. Such isolation is possible, except in very simple instances, only in the laboratory or with scientific methods. If a picture falls from the wall every time a truck passes, we can quite certainly say that the truck's passing is the proximate or immediate cause. But with anything as complex and conditional as a nation's economy or human character, the determination of cause is not easy or certain. A psychiatrist often sees a patient for an hour daily for a year or more before he feels that he understands his neurosis.

[14] Ordinarily when we speak of cause we mean the proximate or immediate cause. The plants were killed by frost; we had indigestion from eating lobster salad. But any single cause is one in an unbroken series. When a man is murdered, is his death caused by the loss of blood from the wound, or by the firing of the pistol, or by the malice aforethought of the murderer? Was the World War "caused" by the assassination at Sarajevo? Were the Navigation Acts or the ideas of John Locke more important in "causing" the American Revolution? A complete statement of cause would comprise the sum total of the conditions which preceded an event, conditions stretching back indefinitely into the past. Historical events are so interrelated that the isolation of a causative sequence is dependent chiefly on the particular preoccupations of the historian. An economic determinist can "explain" history entirely in terms of economic development; an idealist, entirely in terms of the development of ideas.

SYLLOGISTIC REASONING

[15] The formal syllogism of the type,

All men are mortal
John is a man
Therefore John is mortal,

is not so highly regarded today as in some earlier periods. It merely fixes an individual as a member of a class, and then assumes that the individual has the given characteristics of the class. Once we have decided who John is, and what "man" and "mortal" mean, and have canvassed all men, including John, to make sure that they are mortal, the conclusion naturally follows. It can be seen that the chief difficulties arise in trying to establish acceptable premises. Faults in the premises are known as "material" fallacies, and are usually more serious than the "formal" fallacies, which are logical defects in drawing a conclusion from the premises. But although directly syllogistic reasoning is not much practiced, buried syllogism can be found in all argument, and it is often a useful clarification to outline your own or another writer's essay in syllogistic form. The two most frequent defects in the syllogism itself are the undistributed and the ambiguous middle. The middle term is the one that appears in each of the premises and not in the conclusion. In the syllogism,

.All good citizens vote
John votes
Therefore John is a good citizen,

the middle term is not "good citizens," but "votes." Even though it were true that all good citizens vote, nothing prevents bad citizens from voting also, and John may be one of the bad citizens. To distribute the middle term "votes" one might say (but only if that is what one meant),

All voters are good citizens
John is a voter
Therefore John is a good citizen.

[16] The ambiguous middle term is even more common. It represents a problem in definition, while the undistributed middle is a problem in generalization. All acts which benefit others are virtuous, losing money at poker benefits others, therefore losing at poker is a virtuous act. Here the middle term "act which benefits others" is obviously used very loosely and ambiguously.

NON-SEQUITUR

[17] This phrase, meaning "it does not follow," is used to characterize the kind of humor found in pictures in which the Marx Brothers used to perform. It is an amusing illogicality because it usually expresses, beneath its apparent incongruity, an imaginative, associative, or personal truth. "My ancestors came over on the *Mayflower*; therefore I am naturally opposed to labor unions." It is not logically necessary that those whose ancestors came over on the *Mayflower* should be opposed to unions; but it may happen to be true as a personal fact in a given case. It is usually a strong personal conviction which keeps people from realizing that their arguments are non-sequiturs, that they do not follow the given premises with logical necessity. Contemporary psychologists have effectively shown us that there is often such a wide difference between the true and the purported reasons for an attitude that, in rationalizing our behavior, we are often quite unconscious of the motives that actually influence us. A fanatical antivivisectionist, for instance, may have tem-

peramental impulses toward cruelty which he is suppressing and compensating for by a reasoned opposition to any kind of permitted suffering. We may expect, then, to come upon many conclusions which are psychologically interesting in themselves but have nothing to do with the given premises.

IGNORATIO ELENCHI

[18] This means, in idiomatic English, "arguing off the point," or ignoring the question at issue. A man trying to show that monarchy is the best form of government for the British Empire may devote most of his attention to the charm of Elizabeth II and the affection her people feel for her. In ordinary conversational argument it is almost impossible for disputants to keep to the point. Constantly turning up are tempting side-issues through which one can discomfit an opponent or force him to irrelevant admissions that seem to weaken his case.

BEGGING THE QUESTION; ARGUING IN A CIRCLE

[19] The first of these terms means to assume in the premises what you are pretending to prove in the course of your argument. The function of logic is to demonstrate that because one thing or group of things is true, another must be true as a consequence. But in begging the question you simply say in varying language that what is assumed to be true is assumed to be true. An argument which asserts that we shall enjoy immortality because we have souls which are immaterial and indestructible establishes nothing, because the idea of immortality is already contained in the assumption about the soul. It is the premise which needs to be demonstrated, not the conclusion. Arguing in a circle is another form of this fallacy. It proves the premise by the conclusion and the conclusion by the premise. The conscience forbids an act because it is wrong; the act is wrong because the conscience forbids it.

ARGUMENTS AD HOMINEM AND AD POPULUM

[20] It is very difficult for men to be persuaded by reason when their interest or prestige is at stake. If one wishes to preach the significance of physiognomy, it is well to choose a hearer with a high forehead and a determined jaw. The arguments in favor of repealing the protective tariff on corn or wheat in England were more readily entertained by

manufacturers than by landowners. The cotton manufacturers in New England who were doing a profitable trade with the South were the last to be moved by descriptions of the evils of slavery. Because interest and desire are so deeply seated in human nature, arguments are frequently mingled with attempts to appeal to emotion, arouse fear, play upon pride, attack the characters of proponents of an opposite view, show that their practice is inconsistent with their principles; all matters which have, strictly speaking, nothing to do with the truth or falsity, the general desirability or undesirability, of some particular measure. If men are desperate enough they will listen to arguments proper only to an insane asylum but which seem to promise them relief.

[21] After reading these suggestions, which are largely negative, the student may feel that any original assertion he can make will probably contain one or several logical faults. This assumption is not true. Even if it were, we know from reading newspapers and magazines that worldly fame is not dimmed by the constant and, one suspects, conscious practice of illogicality. But generalizations are not made only by charlatans and sophists. Intelligent and scrupulous writers also have a great many fresh and provocative observations and conclusions to express and are expressing them influentially. What is intelligence but the ability to see the connection between things, to discern causes, to relate the particular to the general, to define and discriminate and compare? Any man who thinks and feels and observes closely will not want for something to express.

[22] And in his expression a proponent will find that a due regard for logic does not limit but rather increases the force of his argument. When statements are not trite, they are usually controversial. Men arrive at truth dialectically; error is weeded out in the course of discusson, argument, attack, and counterattack. Not only can a writer who understands logic show the weakenesses of arguments he disagrees with, but also, by anticipating the kind of attack likely to be made on his own ideas, he can so arrange them, properly modified with qualifications and exceptions, that the anticipated attack is made much less effective. Thus, fortunately, we do not have to depend on the spirit of fairness and love of truth to lead men to logic; it has the strong support of argumentative necessity and of the universal desire to make ideas prevail.

QUESTIONS AND COMMENT ON FORM AND CONTENT

1. What is logic? What are logical fallacies?
2. Has your present vocabulary been learned mostly by context or by dictionary definition? Why is it especially important in argument that we under-

stand the meaning of the words used by the speaker or writer? Explain why abstract words, in particular, are likely to need exact definition. Use as examples words from Mr. Davis's list in paragraph 5.

3. Why is name-calling to be closely associated with definition? If someone should call your plan to reform city government "a radical scheme," what could you logically ask him to establish?

4. What do people mean by calling a statement "a hasty generalization"? How are the sections called "generalization" and "sampling" related? What precautions should one take in making generalizations? Do "exceptions prove the rule"? (Look up the word *prove* as used here.)

5. Give an argument by analogy for or against each of the following propositions:

a. That special dormitory rules for women should be abolished.

b. That cigarette advertising should be prohibited by Federal law.

What is the most important single test for an argument by analogy? What other tests seem to you valuable?

6. What does Mr. Davis mean by saying that "Often differences in degree are more important than differences in kind"?

7. If we did not know the reason for it, why would we still assume some causal connection between thunder and lightning? Thomas Carlyle said that Aesop's fly, sitting on the axle of the chariot, has been much laughed at for exclaiming, "What a dust do I raise!" Wherein is the fly's assumption different from ours on the relationship of thunder and lightning? Why has it been difficult to establish a causal relationship between certain diseases and cigarette smoking? Would a controlled experiment be the best way to discover if there is causal connection between two phenomena? If an experiment is not feasible, how might careful observation and sampling give reasonably satisfactory evidence in most cases?

8. Instead of using complete syllogisms, we usually omit the major premise or general law. What is assumed in the following statements? Do you agree with the assumptions?

a. *Huckleberry Finn* is not a great novel because its characters are crude and illiterate.

b. The poll tax is a fair one because under it every voter pays an equal tax.

c. We know that Governor X is a friend of labor, because as a boy he labored in the coal mines.

d. Since it is generally admitted that final examinations are not always a fair test of a student's knowledge, they should be abolished.

9. What do the last four logical fallacies (paragraphs 17-20) have in common? Which one do we sometimes refer to in politics as a red herring drawn across the trail? What do paragraphs 21 and 22 accomplish?

10. Select one of the paragraphs. What is its topic sentence? How is it developed? Note the conciseness of Mr. Davis's explanation and the orderly presentation of ideas.

VOCABULARY: WHAT DO THE ITALICIZED WORDS MEAN?

. . . the *devil* and the deep blue sea (2)
. . . the *devil* to pay (2)
. . . the process of *abstraction* (4)
. . . abuse of *abstract* terms and *epithets* (7)
Such arguments introduce *assumptions* in a *metaphorical guise* (11)
When we speak of cause we mean the *proximate* or immediate cause (14)
. . . men arrive at truth *dialectically* (22)

THEME SUGGESTIONS

Fallacies in Some Letters to the Editor
Write a letter such as you might write to a college or city paper advocating some change in university affairs.
Write a letter replying to one which appeared in a college or city newspaper.

GETTING AT THE TRUTH

Marchette Chute

Marchette Chute (1909-   ) is the author of Ben Jonson of Westminster, *a biography. She has also written other books about Shakespeare and the Elizabethan period of English literature, including* Shakespeare of London *(1949) and* Introduction to Shakespeare *(1957).*

[1] This is a rather presumptuous title for a biographer to use, since truth is a very large word. In the sense that it means the reality about a human being it is probably impossible for a biographer to achieve. In the sense that it means a reasonable presentation of all the available facts it is more nearly possible, but even this limited goal is harder to reach than it appears to be. A biographer needs to be both humble and cautious when he remembers the nature of the material he is working with, for a historical fact is rather like the flamingo that Alice in Wonderland tried to use as a croquet mallet. As soon as she got its neck nicely straightened out and was ready to hit the ball, it would turn and look at her with a puzzled expression, and any biographer knows that what is called a "fact" has a way of doing the same.

[2] Here is a small example. When I was writing my forthcoming biography, *Ben Jonson of Westminister,* I wanted to give a paragraph or two to Sir Philip Sidney, who had a great influence on Jonson. No one thinks of Sidney without thinking of chivalry, and to underline the point I intended to use a story that Sir Fulke Greville told of him. Sidney died of gangrene, from a musket shot that shattered his thigh, and Greville says that Sidney failed to put on his leg armor while preparing for battle because the marshal of the camp was not wearing leg armor and Sidney was unwilling to do anything that would give him a special advantage.

[3] The story is so characteristic both of Sidney himself and of the misplaced high-mindedness of late Renaissance chivalry that I wanted to use it, and since Sir Fulke Greville was one of Sidney's closest friends the information seemed to be reliable enough. But it is always well to check each piece of information as thoroughly as possible and so I consulted another account of Sidney written by a contemporary, this time a doctor who knew the family fairly well. The doctor, Thomas Moffet, mentioned the episode but he said that Sidney left off his leg armor because he was in a hurry.

[4] The information was beginning to twist in my hand and could no longer be trusted. So I consulted still another contemporary who had mentioned the episode, to see which of the two he agreed with. This was Sir John Smythe, a military expert who brought out his book a few years after Sidney's death. Sir John was an old-fashioned conservative who advocated the use of heavy armor even on horseback, and he deplored the current craze for leaving off leg protection, "the imitating of which . . . cost that noble and worthy gentleman Sir Philip Sidney his life."

[5] So here I was with three entirely different reasons why Sidney left off his leg armor, all advanced by careful writers who were contemporaries of his. The flamingo had a legitimate reason for looking around with a puzzled expression.

[6] The only thing to do in a case like this is to examine the point of view of the three men who are supplying the conflicting evidence. Sir Fulke Greville was trying to prove a thesis: that his beloved friend had an extremely chivalric nature. Sir John Smythe also was trying to prove a thesis: that the advocates of light arming followed a theory that could lead to disaster. Only the doctor, Thomas Moffet, was not trying to prove a thesis. He was not using his own explanation to reinforce some point he wanted to make. He did not want anything except to set down on paper what he believed to be the facts; and since we do not have Sidney's own explanation of why he did not put on leg armor, the chances are that Dr. Moffet is the safest man to trust.

[7] For Moffet was without desire. Nothing can so quickly blur and distort the facts as desire—the wish to use the facts for some purpose of your own—and nothing can so surely destroy the truth. As soon as the witness wants to prove something he is no longer impartial and his evidence is no longer to be trusted.

[8] The only safe way to study contemporary testimony is to bear constantly in mind this possibility of prejudice and to put almost as much attention on the writer himself as on what he has written. For instance, Sir Anthony Weldon's description of the Court of King James is lively enough and often used as source material; but a note from the publisher admits that the pamphlet was issued as a warning to anyone who wished to "side with this bloody house" of Stuart. The publisher, at any rate, did not consider Weldon an impartial witness. At about the same time Arthur Wilson published his history of Great Britain, which contained an irresistibly vivid account of the agonized death of the Countess of Somerset. Wilson sounds reasonably impartial; but his patron was the Earl of Essex, who had good reason to hate that particular countess, and there is evidence that he invented the whole scene to gratify his patron.

[9] Sometimes a writer will contradict what he has already written, and in that case the only thing to do is to investigate what has changed his point of view. For instance, in 1608 Captain John Smith issued a description of his capture by Powhatan, and he made it clear that the Indian chief had treated him with unwavering courtesy and hospitality. In 1624 the story was repeated in Smith's *General History of Virginia*, but the writer's circumstances had changed. Smith needed money, "having a prince's mind imprisoned in a poor man's purse," and he wanted the book to be profitable. Powhatan's daughter, the princess Pocahontas, had recently been in the news, for her visit to England had aroused a great deal of interest among the sort of people that Smith hoped would buy his book. So Smith supplied a new version of the story, in which the once-hospitable Powhatan would have permitted the hero's brains to be dashed out if Pocahontas had not saved his life. It was the second story that achieved fame, and of course it may have been true. But it is impossible to trust it because the desire of the writer is so obviously involved; as Smith said in his prospectus, he needed money and hoped that the book would give "satisfaction."

[10] It might seem that there was an easy way for a biographer to avoid the use of this kind of prejudiced testimony. All he has to do is to construct his biography from evidence that cannot be tampered with —from parish records, legal documents, bills, accounts, court records, and so on. Out of these solid gray blocks of impersonal evidence it should surely be possible to construct a road that will lead straight to

the truth and that will never bend itself to the misleading curve of personal desire.

[11] This might be so if the only problem involved were the reliability of the material. But there is another kind of desire that is much more subtle, much more pervasive, and much more dangerous than the occasional distortions of fact that contemporary writers may have permitted themselves to make; and this kind of desire can destroy the truth of a biography even if every individual fact in it is as solid and as uncompromising as rock. Even if the road is built of the best and most reliable materials it can still curve away from the truth because of this other desire that threatens it: the desire of the biographer himself.

[12] A biographer is not a court record or a legal document. He is a human being, writing about another human being, and his own temperament, his own point of view, and his own frame of reference are unconsciously imposed upon the man he is writing about. Even if the biographer is free from Captain Smith's temptation—the need for making money—and wants to write nothing but the literal truth, he is still handicapped by the fact that there is no such thing as a completely objective human being.

[13] An illustration of what can happen if the point of view is sufficiently strong is the curious conclusion that the nineteenth-century biographers reached about William Shakespeare. Shakespeare joined a company of London actors in 1594, was listed as an actor in 1598 and 1603, and was still listed as one of the "men actors" in the company in 1609. Shortly before he joined this company Shakespeare dedicated two narrative poems to the Earl of Southampton, and several years after Shakespeare died his collected plays were dedicated to the Earl of Pembroke. This was his only relationship with either of the two noblemen, and there is nothing to connect him with them during the fifteen years in which he belonged to the same acting company and during which he wrote nearly all his plays.

[14] But here the desire of the biographers entered in. They had been reared in the strict code of nineteenth-century gentility and they accepted two ideas without question. One was that there are few things more important than an English lord; the other was that there are few things less important than a mere actor. They already knew the undeniable fact that Shakespeare was one of the greatest men who ever lived; and while they could not go quite so far as to claim him as an actual member of the nobility, it was clear to them that he must have been the treasured friend of both the Earl of Southampton and the Earl of Pembroke and that he must have written his plays either while basking in their exalted company or while he was roaming the green countryside

by the waters of the river Avon. (It is another basic conviction of the English gentleman that there is nothing so inspiring as nature.) The notion that Shakespeare had spent all these years as the working member of a company of London actors was so abhorrent that it was never seriously considered. It could not be so; therefore it was not.

[15] These biographers did their work well. When New South Wales built its beautiful memorial library to Shakespeare, it was the coat of arms of the Earl of Southampton that alternated with that of royalty in dignified splendor over the bookshelves. Shakespeare had been recreated in the image of desire, and desire will always ignore whatever is not revelant to its purpose. Because the English gentlemen did not like Shakespeare's background it was explained away as though it had never existed, and Shakespeare ceased to be an actor because so lowly a trade was not suited to so great a man.

[16] All this is not to say that a biography should be lacking in a point of view. If it does not have a point of view it will be nothing more than a kind of expanded article for an encyclopedia—a string of facts arranged in chronological order with no claim to being a real biography at all. A biography must have a point of view and it must have a frame of reference. But it should be a point of view and a frame of reference implicit in the material itself and not imposed upon it.

[17] It might seem that the ideal biographical system, if it could be achieved, would be to go through the years of research without feeling any kind of emotion. The biographer would be a kind of fact-finding machine and then suddenly, after his years of research, a kind of total vision would fall upon him and he would transcribe it in his best and most persuasive English for a waiting public. But research is fortunately not done by machinery, nor are visions likely to descend in that helpful manner. They are the product not only of many facts but also of much thinking, and it is only when the biographer begins to get emotional in his thinking that he ought to beware.

[18] It is easy enough to make good resolutions in advance, but a biographer cannot altogether control his sense of excitement when the climax of his years of research draws near and he begins to see the pieces fall into place. Almost without his volition, A, B, and D, fit together and start to form a pattern, and it is almost impossible for the biographer not to start searching for C. Something turns up that looks remarkably like C, and with a little trimming of the edges and the ignoring of one very slight discrepancy it will fill the place allotted for C magnificently.

[19] It is at this point that the biographer ought to take a deep breath and sit on his hands until he has had time to calm down. He has no real, fundamental reason to believe that his discovery is C, except for the fact

that he wants it to be. He is like a man looking for a missing piece in a difficult jigsaw puzzle, who has found one so nearly the right shape that he cannot resist the desire to jam it into place.

[20] If the biographer had refused to be tempted by his supposed discovery of C and had gone on with his research, he might have found not only the connecting, illuminating fact he needed but much more besides. He is not going to look for it now. Desire has blocked the way. And by so much his biography will fall short of what might have been the truth.

[21] It would not be accurate to say that a biographer should be wholly lacking in desire. Curiosity is a form of desire. So is the final wish to get the material down on paper in a form that will be fair to the reader's interest and worthy of the subject. But a subconscious desire to push the facts around is one of the most dangerous things a biographer can encounter, and all the more dangerous because it is so difficult to know when he is encountering it.

[22] The reason Alice had so much trouble with her flamingo is that the average flamingo does not wish to be used as a croquet mallet. It has other purposes in view. The same thing is true of a fact, which can be just as self-willed as a flamingo and has its own kind of stubborn integrity. To try to force a series of facts into a previously desired arrangement is a form of misuse to which no self-respecting fact will willingly submit itself. The best and only way to treat it is to leave it alone and be willing to follow where it leads, rather than to press your own wishes upon it.

[23] To put the whole thing into a single sentence: you will never succeed in getting at the truth if you think you know, ahead of time, what the truth ought to be.

QUESTIONS AND COMMENT ON FORM AND CONTENT

1. Which of her two definitions of truth does Miss Chute find most useful?
2. What kind of testimony was Miss Chute seeking? Why didn't she go to an encyclopedia instead of to Greville, Moffet, and Smythe for her facts? Why did she eventually prefer the testimony of Dr. Moffet to the others? What qualifications would you look for in a person who is to testify as to fact? Would you add any other qualifications if the person is to give an opinion judgment?
3. What is the point about the flamingo that Alice in Wonderland tried to use as a croquet mallet? What reasons could be given for using this fanciful incident at both the beginning and ending of the essay? In what other way does the first paragraph serve as an introduction to the essay? Is the thesis specifically stated?

4. Consider paragraphs 22 and 23 as the conclusion to the essay. What is covered in these paragraphs? Are they effective?

5. Why does the author tend to question the truth of Captain John Smith's 1624 version of the romantic Pocahontas story?

6. How did the desires of certain nineteenth-century biographers lead them to draw what Miss Chute considers false conclusions about Shakespeare as actor and courtier?

7. In the figure of speech in paragraph 10, why does the author use the word *gray* to describe the "blocks of impersonal evidence"? The biographers using these blocks may have a temptation similar to that of the man looking for a missing piece in a jigsaw puzzle. What is this temptation? Must the biographer, then, be without purpose or desire to present a rounded picture?

8. Describe the writing style of Miss Chute. In your answer consider choice of words, economy in the use of words, figurative and concrete language, the coherence of sentences, the variety of sentence structure, and the transitional devices.

VOCABULARY: WHAT DO THE ITALICIZED WORDS MEAN?

. . . *presumptuous* title . . . to use (1)
. . . misplaced *high-mindedness* of late Renaissance chivalry (3)
. . . trying to prove a *thesis* (6)
Smith . . . hoped that the book would give *"satisfaction."* (9)
. . . *basking* in the *exalted* company (14)
. . . a *frame of reference implicit* in the material itself and not *imposed* upon it. (16)
. . . almost without his *volition* (18)
. . . with . . . the ignoring of one very slight *discrepancy* (18)

THEME SUGGESTIONS

To Tell the Truth
Kinds of Evidence
On Evaluating Evidence
Opinion or Expert Testimony
Circumstantial Evidence
On Evaluating Character
Reports of Eye Witnesses
Primary and Secondary Sources in Research
Biography (Autobiography) and Truth
On Using Statistics

OF STUDIES

Sir Francis Bacon

Francis Bacon (1561-1626) was one of the last to undertake the impossible task of surveying all knowledge and reorganizing it for the benefit of mankind. In his own words, "I have taken all knowledge to be my province." The language of his scientific writing was Latin, which he believed to be the permanent language. His essays, however, were written in English. They are noted for their concentrated and aphoristic worldly wisdom and need to be read slowly and thoughtfully—"chewed and digested," as he put it. Sentences from "Of Studies" are frequently quoted.

Studies serve for delight, for ornament, and for ability. Their chief use for delight is in privateness and retiring; for ornament, is in discourse; and for ability, is in the judgment and disposition of business. For expert men can execute and perhaps judge of particulars, one by one; but the general counsels, and the plots and marshalling of affairs, come best from those that are learned. To spend too much time in studies is sloth; to use them too much for ornament is affectation; to make judgment wholly by their rules is the humor[1] of a scholar. They perfect nature, and are perfected by experience; for natural abilities are like natural plants, that need pruning by study; and studies themselves do give forth directions

[1] whim

too much at large, except they be bounded in by experience. Crafty men[2] condemn studies; simple[3] men admire them; and wise men use them; for they teach not their own use; but that is a wisdom without them and above them, won by observation. Read not to contradict and confute; nor to believe and take for granted; nor to find talk and discourse; but to weigh and consider. Some books are to be tasted, others to be swallowed, and some few to be chewed and digested: that is, some books are to be read only in parts; others to be read, but not curiously;[4] and some few to be read wholly, and with diligence and attention. Some books also may be read by deputy, and extracts made of them by others; but that would be only in the less important arguments, and the meaner sort of books; also distilled books are like common distilled waters, flashy things. Reading maketh a full man; conference a ready man; and writing an exact man. And therefore, if a man write little, he had need have a great memory; if he confer little, he had need have a present wit; and if he read little, he need have much cunning, to seem to know that he doth not. Histories make men wise; poets witty,[5] the mathematics subtile; natural philosophy deep; moral grave; logic and rhetoric able to contend. *Abeunt studia in mores.*[6] Nay, there is no stond [7] or impediment in the wit, but may be wrought out[8] by fit studies: like as diseases of the body may have appropriate exercises. Bowling is good for the stone and reins;[9] shooting for the lungs and breast; gentle walking for the stomach; riding for the head; and the like. So if a man's wit be wandering, let him study the mathematics; for in demonstrations, if his wit be called away never so little, he must begin again: if his wit be not apt to distinguish or find differences, let him study the schoolmen;[10] for they are *cymini sectores.*[11] If he be not apt to beat over matters, and to call one thing to prove and illustrate another, let him study the lawyers' cases: so every defect of the mind may have a special receipt.

[2] skilled in handicrafts
[3] ignorant
[4] diligently
[5] fanciful
[6] "Studies have an influence upon the manners of those that are conversant in them."
[7] stoppage
[8] removed
[9] kidneys
[10] medieval philosophers
[11] "splitters of hairs"

QUESTIONS AND COMMENT ON FORM AND CONTENT

1. Bacon starts his essay by telling in the first two sentences the purposes of studies. The language used by Bacon is that of about the time of Shakespeare and the King James Bible. Explain his meaning in modern words. Perhaps if Bacon were writing today he would give examples or illustrations of this first point.

2. His second point begins with "To spend too much time. . . ." and ends with "bounded in by experience." This section could be called "How to Use Studies." This point, like the other points of the highly condensed essay would be ordinarily developed by detailed explanations, illustrations, and the like. Could they also be paragraphed separately?

3. What title could you give to the sentence beginning with "Crafty men . . . ? Would carpenters, bricklayers, repairmen, and the like take a similar attitude to "crafty" men of Bacon's day?

4. Similarly, give titles to the sections beginning with "Read not to contradict. . . . ," "Reading maketh a full man. . . . ," and "Histories make men wise. . . ."

5. What, according to Bacon, should be one's attitude toward a given piece of reading?

6. Is there any advice in the essay that would no longer be acceptable today?

7. Note the figures of speech in such sentences as "Some books are to be tasted. . . ." What is the advantage of a figure of speech?

VOCABULARY: WHAT DO THE ITALICIZED WORDS MEAN?

. . . *expert* men can *execute*
. . . the *humor* of a scholar
. . . the *meaner* sort of books
So every defect of the mind may have a special *receipt*.

THEME SUGGESTIONS

How to Read a Book
On Reading Improvement
The World of Books
The Wise Use of Studies

FOUR KINDS OF STUDENTS

Thomas Fuller

Thomas Fuller (1608-1661), clergyman and one of the best-loved writers of his day, is noted for his wit. Our selection is taken from a part of his "character writing" in which he describes the good schoolmaster in the volume The Holy State. *Our concern is with the good schoolmaster's analysis of students.*

[1] He studieth his scholars' natures as carefully as they their books, and ranks their dispositions into several forms. And though it may seem difficult for him in a great school to descend to all particulars, yet experienced schoolmasters may quickly make a grammar of boys' natures, and reduce them all, saving some few exceptions, to these general rules:

[2] Those that are ingenious and industrious. The conjunction of two such planets in a youth presages much good unto him. To such a lad a frown may be a whipping, and a whipping a death; yea, where their master whips them once, shame whips them all the week after. Such natures he useth with all gentleness.

[3] Those that are ingenious and idle. These think, with the hare in the fable, that running with snails (so they count the rest of their schoolfellows) they shall come soon enough to the post, though sleeping a good while before their starting. Oh, a good rod would finely take them napping!

[4] Those that are dull and diligent. Wines, the stronger they be, the more lees they have when they are new. Many boys are muddy-headed till they be clarified with age, and such afterwards prove the best. Bristol diamonds are both bright and squared and pointed by nature, and yet are soft and worthless; whereas, orient ones in India are rough and rugged naturally. Hard, rugged, and dull natures of youth acquit themselves afterwards the jewels of the country, and therefore their dullness at first is to be borne with, if they be diligent. That schoolmaster deserves to be beaten himself who beats nature in a boy for a fault. And I question whether all the whipping in the world can make their parts, which are naturally sluggish, rise one minute before the hour nature hath appointed.

[5] Those that are invincibly dull, and negligent also. Correction may reform the latter, not amend the former. All the whetting in the world can never set a razor's edge on that which hath no steel in it. Such boys he consigneth over to other professions. Shipwrights and boatmakers will

choose those crooked pieces of timber which other carpenters refuse. Those may make excellent merchants and mechanics who will not serve for scholars.

QUESTIONS AND COMMENT ON FORM AND CONTENT

1. Instead of starting with the best students and ending with the worst, Thomas Fuller could have used the reverse order. Do you see any advantage in his arrangement? Is it more interesting? Or was it to make his point on the cruelty of some schoolmasters of his day?

2. Note the parallel topics used at the beginning of paragraphs 2, 3, 4, and 5. Should the word *industrious* be substituted for diligent in paragraph 4 in order to make it parallel with paragraph 2?

3. From what science is the second sentence in paragraph 2 taken?

4. What is the reference in paragraph 3 to the hare and the snails?

5. Explain the meaning and application of the following:

   a. Wines, the stronger they be, the more lees they have when they are new." (paragraph 4)

   b. "All the whetting in the world can never set a razor's edge on that which hath no steel in it." (paragraph 5)

   c. "Shipwrights and boatmakers will choose those crooked pieces of timber which other carpenters refuse." (paragraph 5)

6. Which type of student, according to Fuller, would be definitely harmed by whipping? Why?

VOCABULARY: WHAT DO THE ITALICIZED WORDS MEAN?

Those that are *ingenious* [Compare *ingenuous.*] (2)
Those that are *invincibly* dull (5)

THEME SUGGESTIONS

Using first names only or fictitious names, select one of your former high school classmates for each of Fuller's classifications. Include yourself if you wish. Describe each of them in some detail.

IN THE LABORATORY WITH AGASSIZ

Samuel H. Scudder

Samuel H. Scudder (1837-1911), American author and entomologist, was the founder of American insect paleontology and an authority on butterflies.

[1] It was more than fifteen years ago that I entered the laboratory of Professor Agassiz, and told him I had enrolled my name in the Scientific School as a student of natural history. He asked me a few questions about my object in coming, my antecedents generally, the mode in which I afterwards proposed to use the knowledge I might acquire, and, finally, whether I wished to study any special branch. To the latter I replied that, while I wished to be well grounded in all departments of zoology, I purposed to devote myself specially to insects.

[2] "When do you wish to begin?" he asked.

[3] "Now," I replied.

[4] This seemed to please him, and with an energetic "Very well!" he reached from a shelf a huge jar of specimens in yellow alcohol.

[5] "Take this fish," said he, "and look at it; we call it a haemulon; by and by I will ask what you have seen."

[6] With that he left me, but in a moment returned with explicit instructions as to the care of the object entrusted to me.

[7] "No man is fit to be a naturalist," said he, "who does not know how to take care of specimens."

[8] I was to keep the fish before me in a tin tray, and occasionally moisten the surface with alcohol from the jar, always taking care to replace the stopper tightly. Those were not the days of ground-glass stoppers and elegantly shaped exhibition jars; all the old students will recall the huge neckless glass bottles with their leaky, wax-smeared corks, half eaten by insects, and begrimed with cellar dust. Entomology was a cleaner science than ichthyology, but the example of the Professor, who had unhesitatingly plunged to the bottom of the jar to produce the fish, was infectious; and though this alcohol had a "very ancient and fishlike smell," I really dared not show any aversion within these sacred precincts, and treated the alcohol as though it were pure water. Still I was conscious of a passing feeling of disappointment, for gazing at a fish did not commend itself to an ardent entomologist. My friends at home, too, were annoyed when they discovered that no amount of eau-de-Cologne would drown the perfume which haunted me like a shadow.

[9] In ten minutes I had seen all that could be seen in that fish, and started in search of the Professor—who had, however, left the Museum; and when I returned, after lingering over some of the odd animals stored in the upper apartment, my specimen was dry all over. I dashed the fluid over the fish as if to resuscitate the beast from a fainting-fit, and looked with anxiety for a return of the normal sloppy appearance. This little excitement over, nothing was to be done but to return to a steadfast gaze at my mute companion. Half an hour passed—an hour—another hour; the fish began to look loathsome. I turned it over and around; looked it in the face—ghastly; from behind, beneath, above,

sideways, at a three-quarters' view—just as ghastly. I was in despair; at an early hour I concluded that lunch was necessary; so, with infinite relief, the fish was carefully replaced in the jar, and for an hour I was free.

[10] On my return, I learned that Professor Agassiz had been at the Museum, but had gone, and would not return for several hours. My fellow-students were too busy to be disturbed by continued conversation. Slowly I drew forth that hideous fish, and with a feeling of desperation again looked at it. I might not use a magnifying glass; instruments of all kinds were interdicted. My two hands, my two eyes, and the fish: it seemed a most limited field. I pushed my finger down its throat to feel how sharp the teeth were. I began to count the scales in the different rows, until I was convinced that that was nonsense. At last a happy thought struck me—I would draw the fish; and now with surprise I began to discover new features in the creature. Just then the Professor returned.

[11] "That is right," said he; "a pencil is one of the best of eyes. I am am glad to notice, too, that you keep your specimen wet, and your bottle corked."

[12] With these encouraging words, he added:

[13] "Well, what is it like?"

[14] He listened attentively to my brief rehearsal of the structure of parts whose names were still unknown to me: the fringed gill-arches and movable operculum; the pores of the head, fleshy lips and lidless eyes; the lateral line, the spinous fins and forked tail; the compressed and arched body. When I had finished, he waited as if expecting more, and then, with an air of disappointment:

[15] "You have not looked very carefully; why," he continued more earnestly, "you haven't even seen one of the most conspicuous features of the animal, which is as plainly before your eyes as the fish itself; look again, look again!" and he left me to my misery.

[16] I was piqued; I was mortified. Still more of that wretched fish! But now I set myself to my task with a will, and discovered one new thing after another, until I saw how just the Professor's criticism had been. The afternoon passed quickly; and when, toward its close, the Professor inquired:

[17] "Do you see it yet?"

[18] "No," I replied, "I am certain I do not, but I see how little I saw before."

[19] "That is next best," said he, earnestly, "but I won't hear you now; put away your fish and go home; perhaps you will be ready with a better answer in the morning. I will examine you before you look at the fish."

[20] This was disconcerting. Not only must I think of my fish all night, studying, without the object before me, what this unknown but most visible feature might be; but also, without reviewing my discoveries, I must give an exact account of them the next day. I had a bad memory; so I walked home by Charles River in a distracted state, with my two perplexities.

[21] The cordial greeting from the Professor the next morning was reassuring; here was a man who seemed to be quite as anxious as I that I should see for myself what he saw.

[22] "Do you perhaps mean," I asked, "that the fish has symmetrical sides with paired organs?"

[23] His thoroughly pleased "Of course! of course!" repaid the wakeful hours of the previous night. After he had discoursed most happily and enthusiastically—as he always did—upon the importance of this point, I ventured to ask what I should do next.

[24] "Oh, look at your fish!" he said, and left me again to my own devices. In a little more than an hour he returned, and heard my new catalogue.

[25] "That is good, that is good!" he repeated; "but that is not all; go on"; and so for three long days he placed that fish before my eyes, forbidding me to look at anything else, or to use any artificial aid. "Look, look, look," was his repeated injunction.

[26] This was the best entomological lesson I ever had—a lesson whose influence has extended to the details of every subsequent study; a legacy the Professor has left to me, as he has left it to many others, of inestimable value, which we could not buy, with which we cannot part.

[27] A year afterward, some of us were amusing ourselves with chalking outlandish beasts on the Museum blackboard. We drew prancing starfishes; frogs in mortal combat; hydra-headed worms; stately crawfishes, standing on their tails, bearing aloft umbrellas; and grotesque fishes with gaping mouths and staring eyes. The Professor came in shortly after, and was amused as any at our experiments. He looked at the fishes.

[28] "Haemulons, every one of them," he said; "Mr. ——— drew them."

[29] True; and to this day, if I attempt a fish, I can draw nothing but haemulons.

[30] The fourth day a second fish of the same group was placed beside the first, and I was bidden to point out the resemblances and differences between the two; another and another followed, until the entire family lay before me, and a whole legion of jars covered the table and surrounding shelves; the odor had become a pleasant perfume; and even now, the sight of an old, six-inch, worm-eaten cork brings memories.

[31] The whole group of haemulons was thus brought in review; and, whether engaged upon the dissection of the internal organs, the preparation and examination of the bony framework, or the description of the various parts, Agassiz's training in the method of observing facts and their orderly arrangement was ever accompanied by the urgent exhortation not to be content with them.

[32] "Facts are stupid things," he would say, "until brought into connection with some general law."

[33] At the end of eight months, it was almost with reluctance that I left these friends and turned to insects; but what I had gained by this outside experience has been of greater value than years of later investigation in my favorite groups.

QUESTIONS AND COMMENT ON FORM AND CONTENT

1. The arrangement of this essay is chronological. What is the advantage of this order? What type of writing usually uses it? What is the value to the reader of the bits of dialogue?

2. After ten minutes Scudder thought that he "had seen all that could be seen in that fish. . . ." How much longer did he have to look?

3. At the end of the first day the professor inquired whether Scudder had seen it.

"No," I replied, "I am certain I do not, but I see how little I saw before."

"That is next best," said he earnestly. . . .

What did the professor mean?

4. In paragraph 26 Scudder speaks very highly of the educational value of this experience. Just what was it he considered of so much value? Would it have been better if Agassiz had first lectured on the fish and given Scudder an outline of what he would be expected to see in order to pass the examination?

5. Explain the statement, "Facts are stupid things," he would say, "until brought into connection with some general law." (paragraph 32)

6. How is *ae* in *haemulon* pronounced?

VOCABULARY: WHAT DO THE ITALICIZED WORDS MEAN?

He asked me a few questions about . . . my *antecedents* (1)

. . . *explicit* instructions (6)

Entomology was a cleaner science than *ichthyology* (8)

I really dared not show any *aversion* (8)

. . . instruments of all kinds were *interdicted* (10)

I was *piqued;* I was *mortified.* (16)
This was *disconcerting* (20)
. . . the fish has *symmetrical* sides (22)

THEME SUGGESTIONS

My Most Valuable Lesson in Science (or in some other subject)
Teaching Versus Telling
A Great Teacher
A Poor Teacher: a Contrast
How I Learned My Lesson
The Teacher Is Only a Guide
Education Is Essentially Self-Education

HOW TO MARK A BOOK

Mortimer J. Adler

Mortimer J. Adler (1902-   ), Director of the Institute for Philosophical Research, has written many articles on reading and on the ideas in great books.

[1] You know you have to "read between the lines" to get the most out of anything. I want to persuade you to do something equally important in the course of your reading. I want to persuade you to "write between the lines." Unless you do, you are not likely to do the most efficient kind of reading.

[2] I contend, quite bluntly, that marking up a book is not an act of mutilation but of love.

[3] You shouldn't mark up a book which isn't yours. Librarians (or your friends) who lend you books expect you to keep them clean, and you should. If you decide that I am right about the usefulness of marking books, you will have to buy them. Most of the world's great books are available today, in reprint editions, at less than a dollar.

[4] There are two ways in which one can own a book. The first is the property right you establish by paying for it, just as you pay for clothes and furniture. But this act of purchase is only the prelude to possession. Full ownership comes only when you have made it a part of yourself, and the best way to make yourself a part of it is by writing in it. An il-

Reprinted by permission of the author and of the *Saturday Review*.

lustration may make the point clear. You buy a beefsteak and transfer it from the butcher's icebox to your own. But you do not own the beefsteak in the most important sense until you consume it and get it into your bloodstream. I am arguing that books, too, must be absorbed in your bloodstream to do you any good.

[5] Confusion about what it means to *own* a book leads people to a false reverence for paper, binding, and type—a respect for the physical thing—the craft of the printer rather than the genius of the author. They forget that it is possible for a man to acquire the idea, to possess the beauty, which a great book contains, without staking his claim by pasting his bookplate inside the cover. Having a fine library doesn't prove that its owner has a mind enriched by books; it proves nothing more than that he, his father, or his wife, was rich enough to buy them.

[6] There are three kinds of book owners. The first has all the standard sets and best-sellers—unread, untouched. (This deluded individual owns woodpulp and ink, not books.) The second has a great many books—a few of them read through, most of them dipped into, but all of them as clean and shiny as the day they were bought. (This person would probably like to make books his own, but is restrained by a false respect for their physical appearance.) The third has a few books or many—every one of them dog-eared and dilapidated, shaken and loosened by continual use, marked and scribbled in from front to back. (This man owns books.)

[7] Is it false respect, you may ask, to preserve intact and unblemished a beautifully printed book, an elegantly bound edition? Of course not. I'd no more scribble all over a first edition of *Paradise Lost* than I'd give my baby a set of crayons and an original Rembrandt! I wouldn't mark up a painting or a statue. Its soul, so to speak, is inseparable from its body. And the beauty of a rare edition or of a richly manufactured volume is like that of a painting or a statue.

[8] But the soul of a book *can* be separated from its body. A book is more like the score of a piece of music than it is like a painting. No great musician confuses a symphony with the printed sheets of music. Arturo Toscanini reveres Brahms, but Toscanini's score of the C-minor Symphony is so thoroughly marked up that no one but the maestro himself can read it. The reason why a great conductor makes notations on his musical scores—marks them up again and again each time he returns to study them—is the reason why you should mark your books. If your respect for magnificent binding or typography gets in the way, buy yourself a cheap edition and pay your respects to the author.

[9] Why is marking up a book indispensable to reading it? First, it keeps you awake. (And I don't mean merely conscious; I mean wide awake.) In the second place, reading, if it is active, is thinking, and thinking tends to express itself in words, spoken or written. The marked

book is usually the thought-through book. Finally, writing helps you remember the thoughts you had, or the thoughts the author expressed. Let me develop these three points.

[10] If reading is to accomplish anything more than passing time, it must be active. You can't let your eyes glide across the lines of a book and come up with an understanding of what you have read. Now an ordinary piece of light fiction, like, say, *Gone with the Wind,* doesn't require the most active kind of reading. The books you read for pleasure can be read in a state of relaxation, and nothing is lost. But a great book, rich in ideas and beauty, a book that raises and tries to answer great fundamental questions, demands the most active reading of which you are capable. You don't absorb the ideas of John Dewey the way you absorb the crooning of Mr. Vallee. You have to reach for them. That you cannot do while you're asleep.

[11] If, when you've finished reading a book, the pages are filled with your notes, you know that you read actively. The most famous *active* reader of great books I know is President Hutchins, of the University of Chicago. He also has the hardest schedule of business activities of any man I know. He invariably reads with a pencil, and sometimes, when he picks up a book and pencil in the evening, he finds himself, instead of making intelligent notes, drawing what he calls "caviar factories" on the margins. When that happens, he puts the book down. He knows he's too tired to read, and he's just wasting time.

[12] But, you may ask, why is writing necessary? Well, the physical act of writing, with your own hand, brings words and sentences more sharply before your mind and preserves them better in your memory. To set down your reaction to important words and sentences you have read, and the questions they have raised in your mind, is to preserve those reactions and sharpen those questions.

[13] Even if you wrote on a scratch pad, and threw the paper away when you had finished writing, your grasp of the book would be surer. But you don't have to throw the paper away. The margins (top and bottom, as well as side), the end-papers, the very space between the lines, are all available. They aren't sacred. And, best of all, your marks and notes become an integral part of the book and stay there forever. You can pick up the book the following week or year, and there are all your points of agreement, disagreement, doubt, and inquiry. It's like resuming an interrupted conversation with the advantage of being able to pick up where you left off.

[14] And that is exactly what reading a book should be: a conversation between you and the author. Presumably he knows more about the subject than you do; naturally, you'll have the proper humility as you approach him. But don't let anybody tell you that a reader is supposed to

be solely on the receiving end. Understanding is a two-way operation; learning doesn't consist in being an empty receptacle. The learner has to question himself and question the teacher. He even has to argue with the teacher, once he understands what the teacher is saying. And marking a book is literally an expression of your differences, or agreements of opinion, with the author.

[15] There are all kinds of devices for marking a book intelligently and fruitfully. Here's the way I do it:

[16] 1. *Underlining:* of major points, of important or forceful statements.

[17] 2. *Vertical lines at the margin:* to emphasize a statement already underlined.

[18] 3. *Star, asterisk, or other doo-dad at the margin:* to be used sparingly, to emphasize the ten or twenty most important statements in the book. (You may want to fold the bottom corner of each page on which you use such marks. It won't hurt the sturdy paper on which most modern books are printed, and you will be able to take the book off the shelf at any time and, by opening it at the folded-corner page, refresh your recollection of the book.)

[19] 4. *Numbers in the margin:* to indicate the sequence of points the author makes in developing a single argument.

[20] 5. *Numbers of other pages in the margin:* to indicate where else in the book the author made points relevant to the point marked; to tie up the ideas in a book, which, though they may be separated by many pages, belong together.

[21] 6. *Circling of key words or phrases.*

[22] 7. *Writing in the margin, or at the top or bottom of the page, for the sake of:* recording questions (and perhaps answers) which a passage raised in your mind; reducing a complicated discussion to a simple statement; recording the sequence of major points right through the book. I use the end-papers at the back of the book to make a personal index of the author's points in the order of their appearance.

[23] The front end-papers are, to me, the most important. Some people reserve them for a fancy bookplate. I reserve them for fancy thinking. After I have finished reading the book and making my personal index on the back end-papers, I turn to the front and try to outline the book, not page by page, or point by point (I've already done that at the back), but as an integrated structure, with a basic unity and an order of parts. This outline is, to me, the measure of my understanding of the work.

[24] If you're a die-hard anti-book-marker, you may object that the margins, the space between the lines, and the end-papers don't give you room enough. All right. How about using a scratch pad slightly

smaller than the page-size of the book—so that the edges of the sheets won't protude? Make your index, outlines, and even your notes on the pad, and then insert these sheets permanently inside the front and back covers of the book.

[25] Or, you may say that this business of marking books is going to slow up your reading. It probably will. That's one of the reasons for doing it. Most of us have been taken in by the notion that speed of reading is a measure of our intelligence. There is no such thing as the right speed for intelligent reading. Some things should be read quickly and effortlessly, and some should be read slowly and even laboriously. The sign of intelligence in reading is the ability to read different things differently according to their worth. In the case of good books, the point is not to see how many of them you can get through, but rather how many can get through you—how many you can make your own. A few friends are better than a thousand acquaintances. If this be your aim, as it should be, you will not be impatient if it takes more time and effort to read a great book than it does a newspaper.

[26] You may have one final objection to marking books. You can't lend them to your friends because nobody else can read them without being distracted by your notes. Furthermore, you won't want to lend them because a marked copy is a kind of intellectual diary, and lending it is almost like giving your mind away.

[27] If your friend wishes to read your Plutarch's *Lives,* Shakespeare, or *The Federalist Papers,* tell him gently but firmly to buy a copy. You will lend him your car or your coat—but your books are as much a part of you as your head or your heart.

QUESTIONS AND COMMENT ON FORM AND CONTENT

1. This is an exposition of a process. From the very first sentence you will notice a personal, intimate, I-to-you tone. Read several paragraphs aloud observing the style. The second short paragraph composed of only one sentence answers an objection many would have to this "act of mutilation." The third paragraph points out the obvious and manages to get in a plug for the ownership of great books, one of Mr. Adler's vital interests. Can you account for the short paragraphs? Did the place of publication have anything to do with it? Examine a copy of the *Saturday Review.*

2. How does he define ownership when applied to books? Describe the three kinds of owners.

3. What are some of the specific reasons for marking a book? This may be considered as part two of the article.

4. The third part of the article begins with paragraph 15. What title would

you give it? Which of the seven devices mentioned do you use? Which are most useful?

5. We hear much today about increasing our speed in reading. Does this article contradict that advice? Did Bacon ("Of Studies") also know about the proper speed for reading? Explain.

6. In the final four paragraphs Mr. Adler tries to clinch the argument by answering questions of the "die-hard anti-book-marker." Note how he uses objections to score points. How does he "turn the tables" in connection with the objecton that "marking books is going to slow up your reading"?

VOCABULARY: WHAT DO THE ITALICIZED WORDS MEAN?

. . . every one of [the books] *dog-eared* and *dilapidated* (6)
Star, *asterisk,* or other *doo-dad* (18)
. . . as an *integrated* structure (23)

THEME SUGGESTIONS

How I Mark a Book
Book Marking and Note Taking
On Talking Back to Authors
Reading Is a Two-Way Street
On Book Lending
Book Borrowers and Book Keepers
Reading Textbooks

WHAT EVERY YALE FRESHMAN SHOULD KNOW

Edmund S. Morgan

Edmund S. Morgan (1916-   ) is the author of many articles and books on American history. He has been on the faculty of Yale University since 1955. This talk was given to freshmen. It also appeared in the Saturday Review, *January 23, 1960 issue.*

[1] The world does not much like curiosity. The world says that curiosity killed the cat. The world dismisses curiosity by calling it idle, or *mere* idle, curiosity—even though curious persons are seldom idle. Parents do their best to extinguish curiosity in their children, because it makes life difficult to be faced every day with a string of unanswerable

Used by permission of the author and of the *Saturday Review.*

questions about what makes fire hot or why grass grows, or to have to halt junior's investigations before they end in explosion and sudden death. Children whose curiosity survives parental discipline and who manage to grow up before they blow up are invited to join the Yale faculty. Within the university they go on asking their questions and trying to find the answers. In the eyes of a scholar, that is mainly what a university is for. It is a place where the world's hostility can be defied.

[2] Some of the questions that scholars ask seem to the world to be scarcely worth asking, let alone answering. They ask about the behavior of protons, the dating of a Roman coin, the structure of a poem. They ask questions too minute and specialized for you and me to understand without years of explanation.

[3] If the world inquires of one of them why he wants to know the answer to a particular question, he may say, especially if he is a scientist, that the answer will in some obscure way make possible a new machine or weapon or gadget. He talks that way because he knows that the world understands and respects utility and that it does not understand much else. But to his colleagues and to you he will probably not speak this language. You are now part of the university, and he will expect you to understand that he wants to know the answer simply because he does not know it, the way a mountain climber wants to climb a mountain simply because it is there.

[4] Similarly a historian, when asked by outsiders why he studies history, may come out with a line of talk that he has learned to repeat on such occasions, something about knowledge of the past making it possible to understand the present and mold the future. I am sure you have all heard it at one time or another. But if you really want to know why a historian studies the past, the answer is much simpler: he wants to know about it because it is there. Something happened, and he would like to know about it.

[5] All this does not mean that the answers which scholars find to their questions have no consequences. They may have enormous consequences; they may completely alter the character of human life. But the consequences seldom form the reason for asking questions or pursuing the answers. It is true that scholars can be put to work answering questions for the sake of the consequences, as thousands are working now, for example, in search of a cure for cancer. But this is not the primary function of the scholar. For the scholar the consequences are usually incidental to the satisfaction of curiosity. Even for the medical scholar, the desire to stamp out a dreaded disease may be a less powerful motive than the desire to find out about the nature of living matter. Similarly Einstein did not wish to create an atomic bomb or to harness atomic energy. He simply wanted to find out about energy and matter.

[6] I said that curiosity was a dangerous quality. It is dangerous not only because of incidental effects like the atomic bomb but also because it is really nothing more or less than a desire for truth. For some reason this phrase sounds less dangerous than curiosity. In fact, the desire for truth sounds rather respectable. Since so many respectable people assure us that they had found the truth, it does not sound like a dangerous thing to look for. But it is. The search for it has again and again overturned institutions and beliefs of long standing, in science, in religion, and in politics. It is easy enough today that these past revolutions brought great benefits to mankind. It was less easy to see the benefits while the revolutions were taking place, especially if you happened to be quite satisfied with the way things were before. Similarly it is not always easy today to see that the satisfaction of a scholar's curiosity is worth the disruption of society that may result from it. The search for truth is, and always has been, a subversive activity. And scholars have learned that they cannot engage in it without an occasional fight.

[7] You may therefore find them rather belligerent toward any threat to the free pursuit of curiosity. They are wary of committing themselves to institutions or beliefs that might impose limitations on them or deliver ready-made answers to their questions. You will find them suspicious of loyalty oaths, religious creeds, or affiliations with political parties. In particular they will try to preserve their university as a sanctuary within whose walls *any* question can be asked.

[8] This wariness of commitment can sometimes degenerate into a scholarly vice, a vice that paralyzes curiosity instead of preserving it. A scholar at his worst sometimes seems to be simply a man who cannot make up his mind. Every classroom from here to Melbourne has echoed with the feeble phrases of academic indecision: "There are two schools of thought on this question, and the truth probably lies halfway between them." When you hear this sentence repeated, or when you are tempted to repeat it yourself, remember that the truth may lie between two extremes, but it assuredly does not lie halfway between right and wrong. Don't short-circuit your curiosity by assuming you have found the answer when you have only made a tidy list of possible answers.

[9] Dedication to curiosity should not end in indecision. It should, in fact, mean willingness to follow the mind into difficult decisions.

[10] A second quality that makes a scholar has no apparent relation to the first and yet is inseparably connected to it. It is a compulsion to communicate. A scholar is driven by a force as strong as his curiosity, that compels him to tell the world the things he has learned. He cannot rest with learning something: he has to tell about it. Scholarship begins in curiosity, but it ends in communication. And though scholars may in

a university take refuge from the world, they also acknowledge responsibility to the world, the responsibility to communicate freely and fully everything that they discover within the walls of their sanctuary. The search for truth needs no justification, and when a man thinks he has found any part of it, he cannot and ought not to be silent. The world may sometimes not care to listen, but the scholar must keep telling it until he has succeeded in communicating.

[11] Now, there are only two methods of communication for scholars, writing and speaking. The scholar publishes his discoveries in books and articles and he teaches them in the classroom. Sometimes one or the other method will satisfy him, but most of us feel the need for both. The scholar who merely writes books falls into the habit of speaking only to the experts. If he works at his subject long enough, he reaches the position where there is no one else quite expert enough to understand him, and he winds up writing to himself. On the other hand, if he writes not at all, he may become so enamored of his own voice that he ceases to be a scholar and becomes a mere showman.

[12] Communication is not merely the desire and the responsibility of the scholar; it is his discipline, the proving ground where he tests his findings against criticism. Without communication his pursuit of truth withers into eccentricity. He necessarily spends much of his time alone, in the library or the laboratory, looking for the answers to his questions. But he needs to be rubbing constantly against other minds. He needs to be tested, probed, and pushed around. He needs to be made to explain himself. Only when he has expressed himself, only when he has communicated his thoughts, can he be sure that he is thinking clearly.

[13] The scholar, in other words, needs company to keep him making sense. And in particular he needs the company of fresh minds, to whom he must explain things from the beginning. He needs people who will challenge him at every step, who will take nothing for granted. He needs, in short, you.

[14] You may have various purposes in coming here, and you may fulfill them: you may play football or tennis or the trombone; you may sing in the glee club, act in plays, and act up on college weekends. But what the faculty expects of you is four years of scholarship, and they will be satisfied with nothing less. For four years we expect you to join us in the pursuit of truth, and we will demand of you the same things we demand of ourselves: curiosity and communication.

[15] Curiosity, of course, is not something you get simply by wishing for it. But it is surprisingly contagious. The curiosity we expect is more than a passing interest. We will not be satisfied by your ability to ask an occasional bright question, nor yet by your assimilation of a lot

of predigested information. The accumulation of information is a necessary part of scholarship, and unfortunately the part most likely to be tested on examinations, especially those wretched ones called "objective examinations" where the truth is always supposed to lie in an answer space A, B, C, D, or E, but never apparently in X, Y, or Z. But the curiosity we expect of you cannot be satisfied by passing examinations or by memorizing other people's answers to other people's questions. We do not wish to put you through a mere course of mental gymnastics. We want you to be content with nothing less than the whole truth about the subject that interests you. Which means that we want you to be forever discontent with how little you know about it and with how little we know about it. We want you to back us into corners, show us up, make us confess we don't know. Does this sound formidable? It is not. We may tell you what we know with great assurance, but push us and you will find the gaps.

[16] Follow your own minds into the gaps. Follow your minds where curiosity takes them. You will not get the whole truth, not about protons, not about the structure of a poem, not even about a Roman coin. Nobody does. But if you learn anything, it ought to change your minds, and hopefully it will change ours too. It will be a sign that we have both wasted four years if you leave here thinking pretty much the same way that you do now or if you leave us thinking the same way *we* do now.

[17] We expect of you, then, that you will be curious for the truth. We also expect that you communicate whatever truth you find, and that you do it both in speech and in writing. Many people suppose that they know something if they can stammer out an approximation of what they mean in speech. They are mistaken. It is extremely unlikely that you have thought clearly if you cannot express yourself clearly, especially in writing. Writing is more than an instrument of communication. It is an instrument of thought. You should have acquired some competence in its use by now. I suspect from past experience that you have not. But even if you have, you have a great deal more to learn about it. And if you do not know much more about it four years from now, it will again be a sign that we have failed in part of our job of making you communicate clearly.

[18] Communication is a two-way process, and a university is a community of scholars, where questions are asked and the answers communicated, your answers to us, ours to you. For the next four years we will be engaged as scholars together in this community. After the four years are over, most of you will leave Yale, but if our community is a successful one, if we really do communicate with each other, I believe that you will continue to be in some sense scholars, asking new questions, looking for new answers, and communicating them to the world.

QUESTIONS AND COMMENT ON FORM AND CONTENT

1. Discuss the effectiveness of the introductory paragraph. How does Mr. Morgan define *curiosity?* Why do the world and parents try to extinguish it?

2. Does research need to have a practical aim—such as curing cancer?

3. Mr. Morgan says, "The search for Truth is, and always has been, a subversive activity." What does he mean by *subversive?* Is he, therefore, opposed to the search for truth? Explain his position.

4. The essay is organized around two main ideas. What are they? Where does discussion of the second one begin?

5. Why, according to Mr. Morgan, is it necessary for the scholar to communicate in both writing and speaking?

6. Comment on the following: "It is extremely unlikely that you have thought clearly if you cannot express yourself clearly, especially in writing. Writing is more than an instrument of communication. It is an instrument of thought." Someone is reported to have said, "How do I know what I mean until I have said it?" Is this related to Morgan's thought?

7. Select several paragraphs at random and notice the variety of sentence patterns. Do you find any parallelism or balanced sentences?

8. Thomas Hardy in a poem "Lausanne" pretends to quote another historian, Gibbon, long dead, as asking whether it is still true that

> Truth like a bastard comes into the world
> Never without ill-fame to him who gave her birth.

Can you recall instances from history where the discoverer of truth was persecuted?

VOCABULARY: WHAT DO THE ITALICIZED WORDS MEAN?

. . . dangerous because of *incidental* effects (6)

. . . *wariness* of *commitment* can sometimes degenerate into a scholarly vice (8)

. . . become so *enamored* of his own voice (11)

THEME SUGGESTIONS

Various Kinds of Curiosity
I Want to Know Why
Curiosity and Communication
Other Purposes of College
Why I Came to College

THE UNFADING BEAUTY: A WELL-FILLED MIND

John Ciardi

John Ciardi (1916-   ), poet, editor, and former college teacher, has been poetry editor of the Saturday Review *since 1956. He has published several volumes of poetry and has translated Dante's* Inferno. *"The Unfading Beauty: A Well-Filled Mind" was given as a commencement address at Wells College.*

[1] Anatole France once observed of his countrymen that they raised their daughters in convents and then married them to pirates. Most of today's college girls will find themselves married not long after graduation, and whether or not they later think of their college days as having been passed in a convent, few of them will find themselves married to anything quite as dramatic as a real pirate, or quite as revolting as a late-nineteenth-century French pirate of finance. The present-day standard model husband is more likely to come out as a serious suburban gardener who flies his week-end flag from the patio of a split-level, and who does his daily cruising in a car pool or on the 7:45 local in the morning and on the 4:40 in the afternoon. The girls are headed for a well-advertised and basically well-padded way of life, but the gist of Anatole France's observation may still apply: it may still be that what the girls do in school is no real preparation for what they will be doing after graduation.

[2] What a liberal arts college is supposed to do in theory is certainly clear enough and can be summarized in the single phrase: "To see life steadily and see it whole." The college exists to teach some sense of the dimensions of a meaningful life. Were our college infallibly fulfilling that purpose, there would be nothing to say to college girls, today's or yesterday's, except to congratulate, to admire them, and to envy them happily.

[3] World as it is, however, being in college is no occasion for unreserved congratulation. Hundreds of bachelor's degrees are being conferred annually by American colleges, and not one of them serves as any real evidence in itself that a reasonably adequate education has taken place, or that the holder of the degree has some viable sense of the whole dimension of the life that starts next.

[4] True, it is still possible for an able and willing student to get something like an education in almost any college in the land, but the fact

seems to be that no college any longer insists upon it. The educational insistence of a college is defined by its minimum standards, and the minimum standards of American colleges are everywhere too low. Even Harvard, proud as it is of its scholarly tradition, will grant a Bachelor's degree on a four-year scholastic average of three C's and a D. "Three C's and a D and keep your name out of the papers," the rule runs: practical sounding, certainly, but a bit smaller in scale than "To see life steadily and see it whole."

[5] The colleges, for their part, can educate only up to the level permitted by society, and our society has been reluctant as a general thing to support "egghead institutions" that think Aristotle is more important than a well-rounded social life that somehow develops a quality called "leadership," a quality that seems to be best developed by doing exactly the same thing everyone else does.

[6] I do not know by what confusion of the national mores we are so insistent on this idea of leadership, but I have received hundreds of application forms in the last year or two, and there is hardly a one that does not contain a dotted line labeled "Leadership?" Certainly as things are, no man need be an intellectual explorer to do well in American business. The chances are, in fact, that he will go further on a little common sense and a lot of social manner than he will on an enthusiasm for Chaucer. No salesman who has made the mistake of acquiring a Phi Beta Kappa key can afford to make the mistake of wearing it when he goes to call on a customer.

[7] Nor is it likely that the affable young man with his destiny in an attaché-case is going to scour the *summa cum laude* list when he starts looking for a wife. He wants her pretty, easy to get along with, a good mixer, a good dancer, and without any freakishly high-brow ideas. Besides, there really isn't room for more than a small decorative bookcase in the rumpus-room of a split-level—not once you have put in the bar, the TV set, the TV chairs, and the card table.

[8] The girls all know this very well, and to the extent that they know it, they have before them no such transition as Anatole France saw from the convent to the pirate's bed. They know the adverstised standard and most of them will slip into it eagerly and without a hitch. The chance they must take, however, is that the dreary gist of that advertised standard will eventually trap them into dullness. A few years ago one of our largest corporations prepared for distribution in the Ivy League colleges a pamphlet advising the boys how to behave as undergraduates if they wanted a corporation career after graduation. One sentence from that pamphlet could not be improved as a summary of the necessary intellectual tone. "Personal opinions," it read, "can cause a lot of trouble." The student editor of the Princeton newspaper assaulted the pamphlet and

especially that sentence as a desecration of the free mind, and the corporation sent down as trouble-shooters the man who had written the pamphlet and a vice-president in charge of public relations. As I have the story, the pamphlet writer could not see what there was to argue. Personal opinions *can* cause a lot of trouble; everyone knows that. The vice-president, on the other hand, granted the student's point and the pamphlet was withdrawn and later rewritten. Victory for the free mind, perhaps, but there still remains one speculation: did the vice-president really see that a great principle was involved, or was he simply acting as a good public-relations man soothing a possibly troublesome crackpot?

[9] Wherever the speculation comes out, the girls are reasonably well aware of what is required of a successful corporate wife, and while they have enough public-relations sense on their own to get along with the fuddy-duddy faculty, they are certainly not going to ruin their chances by getting themselves reputations as bookworm intellectuals.

[10] So it happens that our colleges are divided into two cultural groups whose values tend to meet only in the most tangential ways. The faculty group is made up of men and women not particularly distinguished as smooth dancers but, rather, dedicated to books; so dedicated, in fact, that they are willing to live on academic salaries in return for the freedom of having their reading interfered with by students, most of whom are only taking the course because they have to. The student group does share the same campus with the faculty group, but tends to center around the jukebox in the snack bar rather than around the library. Professor Jones is eager to explain the Greek aorist and to show its connection with the Latin ablative absolute, but what the girls really want out of Greek Week is a good date for the dance. Let the faculty praise great minds; the girls are there to get married, most of them as per the advertised standard.

[11] And were that advertised standard a sufficient and a lasting truth, the colleges would be more than justified in becoming finishing schools of the minor social graces. And may the graces flourish: the least thing the world needs is ungainly and ungracious women. The trouble with the advertised standard is that it simply is not true enough. It does to lounge in; it cannot do to live by. Its plot starts well, but the later chapters have an alarming tendency to fall to pieces.

[12] It is those later chapters the girls generally fail to foresee, and it is that failure that still gives point to Anatole France's observation. For it may well be argued that we are raising our daughters in some sort of illusory heaven and then turning them loose to be mortal. Americans have always tended to be a bit surprised at their own deaths; it all seems so unprogressive. It almost seems that the Constitution, or at least General Motors, should have taken care of that.

[13] But why should the girls be thinking of mortality? They have better things to foresee, glorious things. They see the excitement of the wedding, of the honeymoon, of setting up housekeeping, of the children arriving, and of the busy happy years of raising a family. It seems a paradise, and it is. It seems an eternity, and it is not. But who needs Plato among the nursery babble? As Yeats put it, beginning with what might very reasonably be taken as a reference to the faculty:

> That is no country for old men. The young
> In one another's arms, birds in the trees
> —Those dying generations—at their song,
> The salmon-falls, the mackerel crowded seas,
> Fish, flesh, or fowl, commend all summer long
> Whatever is begotten, born, or dies.
> Caught in that sensual music, all neglect
> Monuments of unageing intellect.

[14] The faculty has no place in paradise. Their monuments of unaging intellect are meaningless to those caught up in that sensual music. The monuments have point only in the silence that follows the music.

[15] And that silence comes. By the time today's college girl has reached thirty-five and forty, having spent fifteen or twenty years busily and happily rearing a family that has needed her, she will find that the children have grown free. There will come a morning after the last of them has moved out to his own life. She will get up at 7:30 for a strangely silent breakfast with her husband who eight years ago was promoted from the 7:45 local to the 8:50. She would like to talk to him, but through her busy years she will have lost touch with his business affairs. And he, doggedly working away at his thrombosis, has his own thoughts to think.

[16] By 8:30 he will have left, and there is the day stretching ahead. Dawdle as she will, the breakfast dishes are in the dishwasher by 9:00. The cleaning woman will be in tomorrow to do the house, which is immaculate anyhow. And the ironing woman will be in the day after to do the clothes. She could write that letter to Mary, but 10:00 o'clock is still a long way off. And 11:00. And is lunch worth bothering with just for herself? Well, maybe a really fancy dinner. But that is hours ahead and the push-button oven will do most of that anyhow. And what is there to do? Today, tomorrow, and the next day? What will there ever be to do?

[17] She will have entered the First Loneliness. Statistically, too, she will have entered the circle of possible widowhood. The years that follow are those in which her husband is more and more likely to achieve the final thrombosis of his success. American women outlive their husbands by an average of six years. Six years is perhaps not an alarming figure, but to begin with it is a bit higher among the wives of professional

men. And if the average for all is six years, it must follow that the average for half will be more nearly twelve, and that for a quarter of them it will be more nearly twenty-four. May it be later rather than sooner, but there can be no doubt that the unadvertised years also lie ahead.

[18] And what will today's college girls take into those long, well-padded, and lonely years? There is touring, of course. And there is bridge. And there is TV. And there are community projects, and gardening, and gay little shopping trips with the other girls. But is it enough? Ernest Hemingway once said to Marlene Dietrich, "Daughter, never confuse motion with action." Our better suburbs—and by this time most of the girls will have graduated from the split-level to the custom-built house—are full of little organizations devoted to making motions for the girls to go through. But there still remains that force at the core of the unstultified psyche that cries for a more meaningful and more human thing to do, that cries for action rather than motion.

[19] Many such women make sudden awkward gestures of turning to the arts again. They used to play the piano rather well. Or they used to write for the college magazine. Now that they no longer have the P.T.A. on their hands, why not start again?

[20] Many of them turn to poetry; and because a poet is easily taken as some sort of summonable clergyman, many have sent their poems to me, as if I had no more to do than to spend a day reading and criticizing them. At that, one would somehow make the time if the poems were not so hopeless. For invariably it is too late. There is that about an art form that will not survive being held in abeyance for a decade or two. They should have had enough devotion to have kept it alive. If only in a stolen hour of the day. If only at the expense of sleep. It can be done. As Salvador Dali once declared: "One always has time to do what he really wants to do." One may have to pay a price for it, but one does pay the price for his true hungers. It is not easy, but to quote Yeats once again:

> To be born woman is to know,
> Though it's not taught to us at school,
> That we must labor to be beautiful.

No, it is not easy. It is something better than easy: it is joyous. It is as Frost put it, "The pleasure of taking pains." That gracious lady, distinguished biographer, and my good friend, Catherine Drinker Bowen, raised her family and managed her household for years while turning out a series of meticulously researched biographies, stealing one piece of every day at whatever cost, putting herself through the routine busyness of her day on the excitement of anticipating that hour at her own particular work. She had, in fact, had two books selected by the Book of the Month Club before she dared label her income-tax form "author" rather than "housewife."

[21] A human being is finally defined by what he does with his attention. It is difficult to keep one's attention in order; difficult and demanding. How much easier it is to let one's mind into a lawn chair of the advertised life and to tune it there to Hollywood scenarios, or to let it drift into what Aldous Huxley called "the endless idiot gibberish of the reverie." It is easier to be inane; but the price is boredom, emptiness, and finally the inability to communicate meaningfully with any human being. How many mothers are there in America today who have begotten sons of their own body and pain and are now unable to speak to them except in the stereotype of "Mom" and "Dicky-boy," rather than as human being to human being, open to both joys and distresses but bound together by a love that includes understanding. It was a better thing than stereotypes that Adam and Eve began, and whoever allows that better thing to be lessened in himself lessens the possibility of the race.

[22] It is what one does with his attention that defines him, and because art is the best ordering we have of human attention, there can be no truly meaningful life without the dimension of art. The arts—and I take them to include religion, philosophy, and history at those points where they are least dogmatic and most speculative—teach us not only ideas but the very dimension of possibility in idea. There is a resonance in a great line of poetry without which the mind cannot truly tune itself. Listen to your own mind. Think the best thing you know. Then measure it against such a line as Wallace Stevens' "The major abstraction is the idea of man." Who can permit himself to think that what was in his mind before he read that line was as good as what was in his mind as he read it? Or listen to John Donne: "And now goodmorrow to our waking souls/Which watch not one another out of fear." Those lines may take a bit of mental focusing, but what a concept of love they speak! Whatever mental effort they require is indistinguishable from joy, and what the effort leaves behind it is a better human being.

[23] Art is the resonance of inseeing joy, but that resonance is only the beginning. Every work of art is a piece of life one may have for the taking. It is not a thing said about an experience, it is the experience itself, not only re-enacted but given form, and therefore, value. Art is the best memory of the race. Art stores up in everlasting form the most meaningful experiences of the most perceptive minds of the past, and because there is such a thing as vicarious experience any man is free to relive those experiences, which is to say, he is free to take those lives into his life. May heaven defend those people who live no lives but their own.

Imagine being only Susie Jones when one could also be Penelope, and Cleopatra, and Ophelia, and Madame DuBarry, and Emma Bovary, and Anna Karenina. And may heaven defend the man married to the woman who has not tried all those other necessary lives into herself. Nothing will defend monogamy sooner than a wife who—this side of schizophrenia, to be sure—contains her pluralities. "Age cannot wither her, nor custom stale/Her infinite variety."

[24] And that finally is what any good book is about. A good book offers the reader a life he has no time for on the clock-as-it-ticks, and a world he may enter *as if* in actual fact. A great book is distinguished from a good book only by the size of the life and the world it offers, but no novel or book of poems is worth the reading unless it has that basic fact of experience to offer.

[25] Art cannot fend loss and loneliness from any life. Loss and loneliness will fall as they must, and for many people they will fall inevitably. But let the meaningful woman look at the statistical probability of that loss and loneliness that lies before her, and let her ask what she will take into those years. Can a mind with Mozart in it ever be as lost as a mind with nothing in it? If girls now in college, just out of college, or even several years away from it do no more than set themselves a twenty-year program of reading meaningfully and carrying alive in their minds one passage a day from the English poets, can they fail to see that they will be more valuable to their families as mothers, and more valuable to themselves as widows?

[26] One of Hemingway's characters in "Winner Take Nothing" is told that so-and-so is a coward and he answers, "He didn't invent it." The line is underplayed but a great understanding and a great mercy shines through it. One could do worse than to store a bit of that understanding and mercy for himself. So stored, one may learn in time that whatever happens to him is not his own invention. He may learn to see then that there is such a thing as the experience of the race on this planet, and learning that he will learn that one who takes that experience into himself has joined himself to the ever-uncertain but ever-hopeful and sometimes continuum of man-and-woman born of man-and-woman.

[27] It is that one must say to today's college girls. That they are beautiful, and ignorant, and illusory. And that only as they learn to shape their attention to the long memory we call the humanities, can they be beautiful after the bloom is off, and understandingly compassionate as time furrows them, and real to the lives they labor to make shapely.

QUESTIONS AND COMMENT ON FORM AND CONTENT

1. Does the title indicate the central idea of the address? What does Anatole France's statement about French girls have to do with the theme idea?

2. How, in general, does society influence the kind of education colleges offer? Should it do so?

3. Why are "egghead institutions" and "leadership" put in quotation marks?

4. How does Mr. Ciardi contrast the phrase "To see life steadily and see it whole" with the aims of American colleges?

5. To what extent does a college education fit women for early married life? For later married life and possible widowhood?

6. What does the author say about a consistent study of the arts as a defense against boredom?

7. Since this "essay" was prepared and delivered as a commencement address, read some of the paragraphs aloud and comment on its style. Does a speech tend to differ in sentence structure and diction from an essay or article?

8. Mr. Ciardi presents a problem and then gives at least a partial solution. What is the problem? What is the partial solution? Can you think of other modern areas of life where the problem-solution pattern would be useful? What makes this kind of pattern educationally or psychologically valuable?

9. Elsewhere Mr. Ciardi has said that a poet is a person who believes in metaphors. Do you find him using figurative language in this address?

VOCABULARY: WHAT DO THE ITALICIZED WORDS MEAN?

Were our colleges *infallibly* fulfilling that purpose (2)

. . . holder of the degree has some *viable* sense . . . of life (3)

. . . reluctant . . . to support *"egghead institutions"* (5)

. . . the national *mores* (6)

. . . acquiring a *Phi Beta Kappa key* (6)

. . . assaulted . . . that sentence as a *desecration* of the free mind (8)

. . . a possibly troublesome *crackpot* (8)

. . . the *fuddy-duddy* faculty (9)

. . . in the most *tangential* ways (10)

And may the *graces* flourish (11)

. . . core of the *unstultified psyche* (18)

. . . nothing will defend *monogamy* sooner than a wife who—this side of *schizophrenia* . . . contains her *pluralities*. (23)

THEME SUGGESTIONS

Take one of Mr. Ciardi's memorable statements, such as one of those given below, and write a paragraph, developing it with your own thoughts, explanations, and experiences. Place the quoted sentence at the beginning of the paragraph as your topic sentence.

"A human being is finally defined by what he does with his attention."

"Can a mind with Mozart in it ever be as lost as a mind with nothing in it?"

"Every work of art is a piece of life one may have for the taking."

"Personal opinion can cause a lot of trouble."

"May heaven defend those people who live no lives but their own."

Education for Living

A Liberal Education

Coeducation: a Mixed Blessing

Education and the Arts

9 | CRABBED AGE AND YOUTH

OF YOUTH AND AGE

Sir Francis Bacon

This essay of Sir Francis Bacon (1561-1626) like the one in Chapter 8 is aphoristic and needs to be chewed most carefully for proper digestion.

[1] A man that is young in years may be old in hours if he have lost no time. But that happenth rarely. Generally youth is like the first cogitations, not so wise as the second. For there is a youth in thoughts as well as in ages. And yet the invention of young men is more lively than that of old; and imaginations stream into their minds better and, as it were, more divinely. Natures that have much heat, and great and violent desires and perturbations, are not ripe for action till they have passed the meridian of their years, as it was with Julius Caesar and Septimius Severus, of the latter of whom it is said, *Juventutem egit erroribus, imo furoribus, plenam.*[1] And yet he was the ablest emperor almost of all the list. But reposed natures may do well in youth, as it is seen in Augustus Caesar, Cosmos, Duke of Florence, Gaston de Foix, and others. On the other side, heat and vivacity in age is an excellent composition for business. Young men are fitter to invent than to judge, fitter for execution than for counsel, and fitter for new projects than for settled business. For the experience of age, in things that fall within the compass of it, directeth

---

[1] *Juventutem . . . plenam.* He spent his youth in errors and even in mad acts.

them; but in new things, abuseth them. The errors of young men are the ruin of business; but the errors of aged men amount but to this, that more might have been done, or sooner.

[2] Young men, in the conduct and manage of actions, embrace more than they can hold; stir more than they can quiet; fly to the end, without consideration of the means and degrees; pursue some few principles, which they have chanced upon, absurdly; care not to innovate,[2] which draws unknown inconveniences; use extreme remedies at first; and, that which doubleth all errors, will not acknowledge or retract them, like an unready horse, that will neither stop nor turn. Men of age object too much, consult too long, adventure too little, repent too soon, and seldom drive business home to the full period, but content themselves with a mediocrity of success. Certainly it is good to compound employments of both, for that will be good for the present, because the virtues of either age may correct the defects of both; and good for succession, that young men may be learners, while men in age are actors; and, lastly, good for extern[3] accidents, because authority followeth old men, and favor and popularity youth. But for the moral part perhaps youth will have the preeminence, as age hath for the politic. A certain rabbin[4] upon the text, "Your young men shall see visions, and your old men shall dream dreams," inferreth that young men are admitted nearer to God than old, because vision is a clearer revelation than a dream. And certainly the more a man drinketh of the world the more it intoxicateth; and age doth profit rather in the powers of understanding than in the virtues of the will and affections. There be some have an over-early ripeness in their years, which fadeth betimes; these are, first, such as have brittle wits, the edge whereof is soon turned—such as was Hermogenes, the rhetorician, whose books are exceeding subtle, who afterwards waxed stupid. A second sort is of those that have some natural dispositions, which have better grace in youth than in age, such as is a fluent and luxuriant speech, which becomes youth well, but not age; so Tully saith of Hortensius, *Idem manebat, neque idem decebat!* [5] The third is of such as take too high a strain at the first, and are magnanimous more than tract of years can uphold, as was Scipio Africanus, of whom Livy saith in effect, *Ultima primis cedebant.*[6]

[2] *care not to innovate,* are not cautious
[3] *extern,* external
[4] *rabbin,* rabbi
[5] *Idem . . . decebat,* He continued the same when it was no longer suitable.
[6] *Ultima primis cedebant.* His last deeds fell below the first ones.

QUESTIONS AND COMMENT ON FORM AND CONTENT

1. What is the meaning of "A man that is young in years may be old in hours, if he have lost no time"? Why does Bacon use "if he *have*" rather than "if he *has*"?

2. Why would it be advisable, according to Bacon, to employ both old and young?

3. What, according to Bacon, are the virtues and weaknesses of (1) youth and (2) age?

VOCABULARY: WHAT DO THE ITALICIZED WORDS MEAN?

Generally youth is like the first *cogitations* (1)
. . . passed the *meridian* of their years (1)
. . . *reposed* natures may do well in youth (1)
. . . fitter for *execution* than council (1)
. . . content themselves with a *mediocrity* of success (2)
. . . it is good to *compound* employments (2)
. . . the *rhetorician*, whose books are exceeding subtle (2)
. . . who afterward *waxed* stupid (2)

THEME SUGGESTIONS

In a short theme tell how a committee composed of undergraduate students and older faculty members will probably disagree on a specific campus problem or program.

An elderly father brings his college-age son into the family business venture. Name the business and discuss possible disagreements.

Crabbed Age and Youth

Irresponsible Youth and Age

WAR OF THE GENERATIONS

Louis E. Reik

Louis E. Reik (1906-　　　), psychiatrist in the University Health Service at Princeton University, is the author of various papers on the mental health of students. This article appeared in the Nation, *May 16, 1959.*

Reprinted by permission of the *Nation.*

[1] By the time a student reaches college age, he should be well launched on a good, brisk war of independence. His object is to express to his satisfaction the ferment of energy with which sometimes he is all but bursting. He no longer endows his elders with the godlike authority they had for him in the days of his helpless childhood. In fact, now that he has learned that even his parents are not so wealthy, wise and infallible as he had previously imagined them to be, he enters a phase when he exaggerates their shortcomings. Not infrequently, he feels constrained to apologize for them to his friends, or to express a blend of rebellious attitudes ranging from condescension to open hostility. At the point where cold war threatens to give way to a hot one in the home, he packs up and goes off to college, often to the immense relief of all concerned.

[2] In its physical aspect, a college campus seems one of the most peaceful and beautiful places in the world. But behind this idyllic façade, the student continues to wage his war for independence. He has achieved a truce, if not a victory, in his struggle to free himself from those powerful despots in the home who had only to assert their wishes to establish them as family law. But at the university he is confronted with some of the same demands for unquestioning obedience to the seemingly arbitrary dictates of his elders and presumably his betters. It is true that at first he is ready to have more tolerance for these elders than for his parents, but the role of submissive neophyte in which he is cast, with its demands for subordinating private inclinations to an unrelenting succession of assignments, requirements and examinations inevitably stirs up the urge to revolt to a more or less intense degree. But while this urge is probably common to students everywhere, it remains for the most part covert and unnoticed, except in occasional times of riot. Students, obviously, have too much to lose to run the risk of open rebellion during their college days. Actually, there seems to be a clear and startling analogy between the educational customs of civilized people and the primitive initiation rites for adolescents practiced the world over from ancient times. The modern student, like his primitive brother, is faced with the necessity of submitting to an ordeal at the hands of his elders as the price he must pay for the privileges of adulthood. It is debatable which ordeal is worse—the student's with its prolonged psychological torments, or the primitive boy's with its relatively fleeting physical hardships. In any event, the student's initiation into the world of civilized men cannot be assumed, even under the most auspicious circumstances, to be an entirely painless affair, or to proceed without provoking conflict, hidden or expressed.

[3] Both at home and in the university, there are confusing elements that prevent the average student from achieving independence, or even from recognizing clearly that this may be desirable. After all, it is unde-

niable that parents and teachers ostensibly have his own best interests at heart, so that filial duty and gratitude demand that he give up his own inclinations when they clash with theirs. Moreover, he is confronted with the additional difficulty of discriminating between what his elders in their wisdom unselfishly advocate for him and what they mistakenly imagine is best because it would be best for themselves. Henry Fielding observed long ago of this tendency of the older generation to confuse their children's identity with their own, thus making both parties completely miserable in the process: "Though it is almost universal in parents, [it] hath always appeared to me to be the most unaccountable of all the absurdities which ever entered into the brain of that strange prodigious creature man." Bernard Shaw, in one of his prefaces, went even further, presuming not only to find the cause of the absurdity but also to prescribe for its cure: "If adults will frankly give up their claim to know better than children what the purposes of the Life Force are, and treat the child as an experiment like themselves, and possibly a more successful one, and at the same time relinquish their monstrous parental claims to personal private property in children, the rest may be left to common sense." Just recently, the veteran child psychoanalyst, Gerald H. J. Pearson, in his monograph *Adolescence and the Conflict of Generations*, after convincingly tracing some of the hidden psychological origins of the conflict, concluded that since its main roots on both sides are so deeply anchored in a tangle of emotional attitudes of which self-love is by no means the least important, he has small hope that either parents or adolescents could profit much from a generalized intellectual explanation of the affairs of the heart—which nevertheless he proceeded to give in his book.

[4] These emotional affairs of the heart have such a distinct and primitive logic of their own that psychiatrists long before Freud have steadfastly and repeatedly observed that a man may be brilliantly endowed from the intellectual viewpoint and simultaneously an irresponsible child where his emotions are concerned. Or he may be the reverse: a genius when it comes to the affairs of the heart, but an intellectual moron as measured by his IQ. In this connection, it is worth remembering that following the introduction of Binet's intelligence test in the early years of this century, situations in ordinary school and social life that before seemed baffling because someone was involved whose feeble-mindedness remained unrecognized, became clear and susceptible to control when approached with the new knowledge. Undoubtedly, some day we shall also have better indices of emotional development, a kind of EQ, which will enable teachers and parents to take a more calm and realistic attitude towards problems posed by students that now seem inexplicable or of deliberate malevolent intent.

[5] Meanwhile, we have outgrown old superstitions in the ruling power of witches, devils, planets and charms, but have still to discard the notions that emotional attitudes and motives are readily controlled by the intelligence, or that they depend only on external circumstances, or that they are utterly mysterious beyond comprehension. On the contrary, medical psychology, particularly during the last half-century, has been accumulating an impressive mass of clinical data, drawn from normal as well as abnormal subjects, that demonstrates something of the peculiar evolution and logic of the emotional life.

[6] In college practice, for example, the psychiatrist has many opportunities for observing that a student's attitude towards his father seems to determine his attitude towards college authorities. A student who has been strongly attached to, and simultaneously overwhelmed by, the father is apt to view the college teacher as the embodiment of the wisdom of the ages. His war for intellectual independence does not go well because the more he admires his mentors the more he is inclined to be uncritically influenced by them and to belittle himself. Educators are familiar with students of this type, who are variously called "perfectionists," "over-achievers" or "over-conscientious." The more they belittle themselves, the less capable they become of achieving self-assurance and spontaneous, original work. Their energies, instead, are used up in curbing natural impulse and in preoccupation with superficial detail.

[7] One such student, for example, felt compelled to memorize the dates of withdrawal and return on the librarian's card in a book of assigned reading, to say nothing of a staggering mass of excerpts he had copied down. The psychiatrist sees this as a kind of self-defeating compromise, in which there has been no whole-hearted acceptance of either the self or the father. Its object, essentially, is to keep the peace and to win rewards and esteem from parents and teachers for a kind of mechanical compliance characteristic of the rote-learning of childhood days, rather than to achieve satisfying growth and true self-expressions. Deficient self-esteem and an exaggerated estimate of authority make such students slaves to duty and routine, a slavery which the world too frequently applauds, but which nevertheless defeats the aims of liberal education and provides fertile soil for private misery and neurotic symptoms, such as fatigue, insomnia, incapacitating tension, and sometimes despair.

[8] Likewise, it is frequently observed that students who have been inclined to defy and underestimate the father are similarly inclined to belittle authority in general. In extreme form, their behavior is variously regarded as immature, abnormal, delinquent or even criminal, depending on how badly the community feels its interests have been violated and how it assesses the responsibility of the offender. As long ago as 1910, the psychiatrist Stewart Paton (who incidentally was the first to advocate

a mental-health program for college students) is said to have been astonished when he first began his work at Princeton University to discover "students who had pronounced suicidal, homicidal impulses, sex perverts, those who stole, cheated, were exceedingly egotistical, aggressive and showed other signs of serious maladjustment." He saw no point in making "every attempt . . . to induce all, the unfit as well as the fit, to pass through the educational mill" which, he noted, is in sharp contrast to the more realistic policy in schools and colleges of preventing those with weak hearts or lungs from taking part in strenuous athletic pursuits. Since then, colleges have gradually been paying more attention to the need for earlier recognition and more intelligent treatment of students with serious emotional disturbances.

[9] When it comes to the less serious problems posed by rebellious but essentially healthy students, any good educator knows that the rebel is only confirmed in his defiance when he sees himself vindictively or scornfully treated with little, if any, concern as an individual, in spite of the professed brotherly love for him of the Christian community. The late psychoanalyst Fritz Wittels rightly pointed out the enormous difference in the effect on the culprit when punishment is administered by those who care for him, as by a father in childhood who wants to continue to love the naughty child, or by those in institutions or state who neither care for him nor are interested in his welfare. The wise father and the good teacher intuitively know that lasting repentance and ultimate self-discipline are not products of terror and force alone.

[10] The student's war for independence does not, however, always display the more obvious forms of submission and rebellion described above. The majority of students seem to oscillate somewhere between these extremes, being on the whole perhaps more rebellious than submissive. Those who read standard histories of university life, where, as Rashdall observed, "the life of the virtuous student has no annals," are not surprised to find that they have been a rebellious lot from the beginning. Haskins in his informative *The Rise of the Universities* records that in 1317 the students at Bologna not only brought the townsmen to terms by threatening to go elsewhere, but also laid down strict regulations governing the teaching of their professors, who were subject to fines for absences and other controlling maneuvers. We also learn that in medieval Paris students went about armed with sword and knives, attacking citizens, abusing women and slashing off one another's fingers. Elsewhere, it is said that prior to the present century, outbreaks of violence against college officials and property were more extensive and frequent than they are today in American colleges, and were seemingly worst at the most puritanical colleges. On the other hand, it is well known that there have been periods when students submitted to a much more rigorous academic

discipline than at present, at least in a physical sense. From the stand-point of the psychological relationship today between the older and younger generations, it would be an anomaly if in these more democratic times either generation were to revert to the attempts at physical domi-nation of the feudal past. But he who looks will find that the conflict goes on in other less obvious ways. It has, so to speak, been driven under-ground.

[11] For instance, a student complains of a perplexing inability to con-centrate on academic material, yet emphasizes that he would like ulti-mately to follow his father's career in teaching; meanwhile, he feels tense and miserable *except* when engaged in extracurricular activities. Another has had extensive medical investigations, with entirely negative results, of his complaint of recurring digestive upset, which, on inquiry, is found to be associated particularly with times of stress and examination. A third, while professing to want to remain in the university from which his father graduated, is in danger of dismissal because he cuts classes from oversleeping, which he says he can neither correct nor understand.

[12] Examples like these could be multiplied. But a recital of their bare outlines does not adequately convey the rich and subtle interplay of defensive and offensive maneuver that goes on. Often conflict is not os-tensibly with authority at all, but with what we now recognize as its inner representative and ally, the conscience. The college psychiatrist en-counters many instances where such inner warfare leads to apparently senseless dilemmas or pointless activities. These can only be understood when viewed in terms of the struggle within, reflecting in part a desire to yield to temptation and in part the scruples about it. Students can, of course, justify themselves with compelling logic and eloquence, recalling Shaw's observation that excellent reasons can be found "for every con-ceivable course of conduct, from dynamiting and vivisection to martyr-dom." I share the feeling with colleagues that a university would be a dead and dusty place if all students were models of conformity. But I can also sympathize with the professor who once said that a university would be a wonderful place if there were no undergraduates in it.

QUESTIONS AND COMMENT ON FORM AND CONTENT

1. Does Louis Reik approve of the student who wages a war of inde-pendence?

2. What similarity exists between the "educational customs of civilized people and the primitive initiation rites for adolescents practiced the world over from ancient times"? In the author's opinion, which is the worse ordeal? Is the educational ordeal a necessary one?

3. Do you agree that a student's attitude toward his father usually determines what his attitude will be toward his college teachers and the college administration?

4. What is the penalty paid by the student who tries only to win grades, awards, and esteem?

5. What serious mistake of parents is described in paragraph 3?

6. How should the noncomformist be handled? What difference does it make in the attitude of the culprit if he is punished by those who love him or by those who do not?

7. In which of the twelve paragraphs has the author placed the topic sentence at the beginning of the paragraph? Are there any paragraphs in which several sentences could be combined to form the topic sentence? Would a single topic sentence express the thoughts of paragraphs 4 and 5? Of paragraphs 11 and 12? What is the function of the last sentence of paragraph 10?

8. What transitional words or phrases are used to link paragraphs 5, 6, 7, and 8 with the paragraph that precedes each? What transitional words are used in paragraph 11 to assist the reader?

VOCABULARY: WHAT DO THE ITALICIZED WORDS MEAN?

. . . behind the *idyllic façade* (2)
. . . role of submissive *neophyte* (2)
. . . most *auspicious* circumstances (2)
. . . teachers *ostensibly* have . . . [the student's] own best interests at heart (3)
. . . *relinquish* their *monstrous* parental claims (3)
. . . deliberate *malevolent* intent (4)
. . . admire his *mentors* (6)
. . . fertile soil for private misery and *neurotic* symptoms (7)
. . . suicidal, *homicidal* impulses (8)
. . . sees himself *vindictively* or scornfully treated (9)
. . . father and the good teacher *intuitively* know (9)
. . . students seem to *oscillate* (10)
. . . the most *puritanical* colleges (10)
. . . it would be an *anomaly* (10)
. . . from dynamiting and *vivisection* to *martyrdom* (12)

THEME SUGGESTIONS

My War of Independence
Young Radicals
Kicking over the Traces
Silent Rebellion
Father (Mother) And I

THE KITCHEN

Alfred Kazin

Alfred Kazin (1915-   ) was reared in New York City and attended the City College of New York and Columbia University. He is noted as a literary critic and college lecturer. The selection "The Kitchen" is from his autobiography Walker in the City.

[1] In Brownsville tenements the kitchen is always the largest room and the center of the household. As a child I felt that we lived in a kitchen to which four other rooms were annexed. My mother, a "home" dressmaker, had her workshop in the kitchen. She told me once that she had begun dressmaking in Poland at thirteen; as far back as I can remember, she was always making dresses for the local women. She had an innate sense of design, a quick eye for all the subtleties in the latest fashions, even when she despised them, and great boldness. For three or four dollars she would study the fashion magazines with a customer, go with the customer to the remnants store on Belmont Avenue to pick out the material, argue the owner down—all remnants stores, for some reason, were supposed to be shady, as if the owners dealt in stolen goods—and then for days would patiently fit and baste and sew and fit again. Our apartment was always full of women in their housedresses sitting around the kitchen table waiting for a fitting. My little bedroom next to the kitchen was the fitting room. The sewing machine, an old nut-brown Singer with golden scrolls painted along the black arm and engraved along the two tiers of little drawers massed with needles and thread on each side of the treadle, stood next to the window and the great coal-black stove which up to my last year in college was our main source of heat. By December the two outer bedrooms were closed off, and used to chill bottles of milk and cream, cold borscht and jellied calves' feet.

[2] The kitchen held our lives together. My mother worked in it all day long, we ate in it almost all meals except the Passover *seder*, I did my homework and first writing at the kitchen table, and in winter I often had a bed made up for me on three kitchen chairs near the stove. On the wall just over the table hung a long horizontal mirror that sloped to a ship's prow at each end and was lined in cherry wood. It took up the whole wall, and drew every object in the kitchen to itself. The walls were a fiercely stippled whitewash, so often rewhitened by my father in slack seasons that the paint looked as if it had been squeezed and

cracked into the walls. A large electric bulb hung down the center of the kitchen at the end of a chain that had been hooked into the ceiling; the old gas ring and key still jutted out of the wall like antlers. In the corner next to the toilet was the sink at which we washed, and the square tub in which my mother did our clothes. Above it, tacked to the shelf on which were pleasantly ranged square, blue-bordered white sugar and spice jars, hung calendars from the Public National Bank on Pitkin Avenue and the Minsker Progressive Branch of the Workman's Circle; receipts for the payment of insurance premiums, and household bills on a spindle; two little boxes engraved with Hebrew letters. One of these was for the poor, the other to buy back the Land of Israel. Each spring a bearded little man would suddenly appear in our kitchen, salute us with a hurried Hebrew blessing, empty the boxes (sometimes with a sidelong look of disdain if they were not full), hurriedly bless us again for remembering our less fortunate Jewish brothers and sisters, and so take his departure until the next spring, after vainly trying to persuade my mother to take still another box. We did occasionally remember to drop coins in the boxes, but this was usually only on the dreaded morning of "midterms" and final examinations, because my mother thought it would bring me luck. She was extremely superstitious, but embarrassed about it, and always laughed at herself whenever, on the morning of an examination, she counseled me to leave the house on my right foot. "I know it's silly," her smile seemed to say, "but what harm can it do? It may calm God down."

[3] The kitchen gave a special character to our lives: my mother's character. All my memories of that kitchen are dominated by the nearness of my mother sitting all day long at her sewing machine, by the clacking of the treadle against the linoleum floor, by the patient twist of her right shoulder as she automatically pushed at the wheel with one hand or lifted the foot to free the needle where it had got stuck in a thick piece of material. The kitchen was her life. Year by year, as I began to take in her fantastic capacity for labor and her anxious zeal, I realized it was ourselves she kept stitched together. I can never remember a time when she was not working. She worked because the law of her life was work, work and anxiety; she worked because she would have found life meaningless without work. She read almost no English; she could read the Yiddish paper, but never felt she had time to. We were always talking of a time when I would teach her how to read, but somehow there was never time. When I awoke in the morning she was already at her machine, or in the great morning crowd of housewives at the grocery getting fresh rolls for breakfast. When I returned from school she was at her machine, or conferring over *McCall's* with some neighborhood woman who had come in pointing hopefully to an illustration—"Mrs. Kazin! Mrs.

Kazin! Make me a dress like it shows here in the picture!" When my father came home from work she had somehow mysteriously interrupted herself to make supper for us, and the dishes cleared and washed, was back at her machine. When I went to bed at night, often she was still there, pounding away at the treadle, hunched over the wheel, her hands steering a piece of gauze under the needle with a finesse that always contrasted sharply with her swollen hands and broken nails. Her left hand had been pierced through when as a girl she had worked in the infamous Triangle Shirtwaist Factory on the East Side. A needle had gone straight through the palm, severing a large vein. They had sewn it up for her so clumsily that a tuft of flesh always lay folded over the palm.

[4] The kitchen was the great machine that set our lives running; it whirred down a little only on Saturdays and holy days. From my mother's kitchen I gained my first picture of life as a white, overheated, starkly lit workshop redolent with Jewish cooking, crowded with women in housedresses, strewn with fashion magazines, patterns, dress material, spools of thread—and at whose center, so lashed to her machine that bolts of energy seemed to dance out of her hands and feet as she worked, my mother stamped the treadle hard against the floor, hard, hard, and silently, grimly at war, beat out the first rhythm of the world for me.

[5] Every sound from the street roared and trembled at our windows— a mother feeding her child on the doorstep, the screech of the trolley cars on Rockaway Avenue, the eternal smash of a handball against the wall of our house, the clatter of *"der Italyéner's"* cart packed with watermelons, the sing-song of the old-clothes men walking Chester Street, the cries *"Árbes! Árbes! Kinder! Kinder! Heyse gute árbes!"* All day long people streamed into our apartment as a matter of course—"customers," upstairs neighbors, downstairs neighbors, women who would stop in for a half-hour's talk, salesmen, relatives, insurance agents. Usually they came in without ringing the bell—everyone knew my mother was always at home. I would hear the front door opening, the wind whistling through our front hall, and then some familiar face would appear in our kitchen with the same bland, matter-of-fact inquiring look: no need to stand on ceremony: my mother and her kitchen were available to everyone all day long.

[6] At night the kitchen contracted around the blaze of light on the cloth, the patterns, the ironing board where the iron had burned a black border around the tear in the muslin cover; the finished dresses looked so frilly as they jostled on their wire hangers after all the work my mother had put into them. And then I would get that strangely ominous smell of tension from the dress fabrics and the burn in the cover of the ironing

board—as if each piece of cloth and paper crushed with light under the naked bulb might suddenly go up in flames. Whenever I pass some small tailoring shop still lit up at night and see the owner hunched over his steam press; whenever in some poorer neighborhood of the city I see through a window some small crowded kitchen naked under the harsh light glittering in the ceiling, I still smell that fiery breath, that warning of imminent fire. I was always holding my breath. What I must have felt most about ourselves, I see now, was that we ourselves were like kindling —that all the hard-pressed pieces of ourselves and all the hard-used objects in that kitchen were like so many slivers of wood that might go up in flames if we came too near the white-blazing filaments in that naked bulb. Our tension itself was fire, we ourselves were forever burning—to live, to get down the foreboding in our souls, to make good.

[7] Twice a year, on the anniversaries of her parents' deaths, my mother placed on top of the ice-box an ordinary kitchen glass packed with wax, the *yortsayt*, and lit the candle in it. Sitting at the kitchen table over my homework, I would look across the threshold to that mourning-glass, and sense that for my mother the distance from our kitchen to *der heym*, from life to death, was only a flame's length away. Poor as we were, it was not poverty that drove my mother so hard; it was loneliness—some endless bitter brooding over all those left behind, dead or dying or soon to die; a loneliness locked up in her kitchen that dwelt every day on the hazardousness of life and the nearness of death, but still kept struggling in the lock, trying to get us through by endless labor.

[8] With us, life started up again only on the last shore. There seemed to be no middle ground between despair and the fury of our ambition. Whenever my mother spoke of her hopes for us, it was with such unbelievingness that the likes of us would ever come to anything, such abashed hope and readiness for pain, that I finally came to see in the flame burning on top of the ice-box death itself burning away the bones of poor Jews, burning out in us everything but courage, the blind resolution to live. In the light of that mourning-candle, there were ranged around me how many dead and dying—how many eras of pain, of exile, of dispersion, of cringing before the powers of this world!

[9] It was always at dusk that my mother's loneliness came home most to me. Painfully alert to every shift in the light at her window, she would suddenly confess her fatigue by removing her pince-nez, and then wearily pushing aside the great mound of fabrics on her machine, would stare at the street as if to warm herself in the last of the sun. "How sad it is!" I once heard her say. "It grips me! It grips me!" Twilight was the bottommost part of the day, the chillest and loneliest time for her. Always so near to her moods, I knew she was fighting some deep inner dread, strug-

gling against the returning tide of darkness along the streets that invariably assailed her heart with the same foreboding—Where? Where now? Where is the day taking us now?

[10] Yet one good look at the street would revive her. I see her now, perched against the windowsill, with her face against the glass, her eyes almost asleep in enjoyment, just as she starts up with the guilty cry— "What foolishness is this in me!"—and goes to the stove to prepare supper for us: a moment, only a moment, watching the evening crowd of women gathering at the grocery store for fresh bread and milk. But between my mother's pent-up face at the window and the winter sun dying in the fabrics—"Alfred, see how beautiful!"—she has drawn for me one single line of sentience.

QUESTIONS AND COMMENT ON FORM AND CONTENT

1. Why is this essay called "The Kitchen" rather than "Mother"? The first sentence of each of the first four paragraphs helps to answer this question. Are these sentences also topic sentences of the paragraphs?

2. Since the mother appears only in the kitchen, does this fact give added focus (unity) to the writing?

3. Paragraph 2 could be divided into two paragraphs. If so divided, what would be the topic of the second part? What is the topic sentence of the paragraph as it stands? Which version do you prefer?

4. Paragraph 2 shows the mother as slightly superstitious. What other characteristics does she have?

5. The naked light bulb, the candle on the ice-box on the anniversaries of the deaths of the mother's parents, and the burn on the ironing board cover become symbols of life. Show how Kazin relates these to the life of his family and ancestors. Is there something of fear represented? Ambition? (See paragraphs 6 to 9.)

6. What is the effect of the last paragraph? What in particular causes the mother's change of mood from the preceding paragraph?

7. Why are the father and Alfred Kazin himself scarcely mentioned in the essay?

8. What words are used to indicate the street sounds in paragraph 4?

9. What is the effect of the repetition of *work* (*worked, working*) in the following passage?

> I can never remember a time when she was not *working*. She *worked* because the law of her life was *work*, work and anxiety; she *worked* because she would have found life meaningless without *work*.

THEME SUGGESTIONS

Write a character sketch of a person as he is carrying on either his regular occupation or his hobby. (This could be your father or your mother or a relative, if you wish.)

OLD JUNIOR'S PROGRESS—
FROM PREP SCHOOL TO SEVERANCE PAY

William S. White

William S. White (1907-   ) is a newspaper and magazine writer and is the author of The Story of the United States Senate, 1957. *He received the Pulitzer Prize in Letters in 1955. This essay appeared in* Harper's Magazine, *July, 1961.*

[1] While our graduates are still atingle from the unearned and usually nonsensical tributes paid to them by middle-aged commencement speakers, this might be a good time to tell off the younger generation, male.

[2] In kindly and avuncular summary, I find them (on the whole) a distressingly poor lot—moderately displeasing at the best and positive stinkers at the worst. If I were a newspaper city editor, I would not willingly hire any fellow under thirty without a searching investigation. If I were an adviser to the Peace Corps, I should be most suspicious of those fresh-faced lads who wish to go off to Kenya awash with brotherhood.

[3] And if I were a trustee of an institution of higher learning I would try, against all the odds, to put some guts into its faculty, and a couple of additional courses into its curriculum. One of these would be instruction in manners. Another would be some drill in what used to be common appreciation for one's elders—not *because* they are elders, but because they are now being forced to bear an unconscionable load of work and responsibility. Only the wealth is being shared by the youngsters; the burden remains exclusively the privilege of the grownups.

[4] Let's face it, the kids are running hog-wild. Much had gone into the development of this correspondent's tired, fed-up malice in this matter. For a starter, here is an episode which illustrates with pristine clarity some of the things that are wrong with American youth, male.

[5] Recently I received a letter from a "Mr." So-and-so who briskly demanded my aid—and time—on a project for his course in journalism. (Unhappily, the most unpleasing qualities in the younger generation seem to be most prevalent among boys and girls taking either journalism or political science.) My correspondent required me to answer twenty questions which he had posed to help prepare himself for his chosen career as a magazine writer.

[6] No man, not even one so churlish as I, would rightly grumble if some of his queries were impossible to reply to—as for example: *"How*

long does it take to get to the top?" But, I submit, the mushiest old pater-familias would find his temperature rising as this letter went on.

[7] For as I read, it began to be borne in upon me that an extraordinarily high percentage of the questions dealt, not with writing or reporting techniques or other points of professional interest, but rather with matters which one might reasonably suppose could be left to chance and merit and to a considerably later point in the life of my correspondent.

[8] "*What is the average salary of a magazine reporter? And at the beginning?*

[9] "*What are the sick benefits and unemployment benefits in this profession?*

[10] "*What is the retirement age?*

[11] "*Is this profession under Social Security?*"

[12] As my aging eyes fell upon this row of querulous queries—hardly full of that gallantry, that ardent spirit of youth-on-the-march—my mind went a bit blank. I looked again at the accompanying letter in the belief that those eyes had tricked me and that I had received a communication from a man of sixty-five whose arteries were beginning to harden and whose spirit was reaching out for the prospect of rest.

[13] But no; there it was. The letter was from a boy in the sophomore year of high school.

[14] Now, I do not argue that this is the common approach to life of today's younger male generation. But I do say that it is far more nearly common than ordinary logic would suppose. I base this bleak judgment not upon subjective reason, but on actual evidence accumulated over the years. As a syndicated newpaper columnist, as well as a columnist for *Harper's,* I get a great deal of mail, and a good proportion of it is from the young. I am, moreover, more than usually exposed to communications from students of journalism and political science.

[15] You may take my word for it that these inquiries are almost invariably innocent of any graciousness of tone. I often have the feeling that I am to consider myself fortunate to have been addressed in the first place; that I should not shilly-shally about replying; and that my uninhibited correspondent would not think of uttering anything warmer than a sour treble-grunt of thanks. He would never be caught dead saying "Sir."

[16] Many a time I have been commanded by an aspirant for one degree or another to put aside my trifling personal tasks and, in effect, to write his thesis for him. One young person offering me this opportunity had been assigned to do a paper in connection with the Senate. He observed to me, in passing, that while he understood I had written a book about the Senate, he did not propose to read it: I would understand, of

course, that he was busy. Moreover he already knew he would not agree with the book, anyhow.

[17] Nearly all of us know fathers and mothers who are trying desperately to cope with this sort of oaf: He is in his twenties, at an age when we used to think in this country (as most people in Europe still think) that a chap was a man if he was ever going to be. But this fellow remains obdurately a most repellent little boy. Though long since eligible to shave and vote, he must be cosseted endlessly by his driven parents. Except for him and his boyish demands, they would by now be materially solvent and spiritually able to enjoy those small rewards of travel and relaxation which they have well earned.

[18] This fellow is a common type. He spent his years in prep school or high school mooning about in that drippy way which we wrongly tend to associate with the girls of his age. (In plain truth, the girls are a different and a happier breed altogether. They have far more gumption than the males, more manners and perspective, more common sense and self-discipline. If, as many people think, we Americans have long been living under a matriarchy, one thing is sure: the present younger generation of the American male will not redress the balance. It well may be that within ten or fifteen years the present dominance of the female in adult society will be seen in retrospect as relatively a golden age of manhood.)

[19] But to return to my male type-figure. Having some time ago emerged from prep or high school in incorrupted ignorance, he has since put in years of a dreary aimlessness. Somehow or another, the military had him for a while: a "trainee," reluctant at the beginning and untrained, in every sense, at the end. When this Sad Sack period of ambiguous service had wound to its dull close, the military had returned him, with relief, to his parents—who persisted in being doting parents, there being not much else to do.

[20] They went about frantically trying to get him into some college. He had, of course, held out for Yale or Harvard or Princeton, or some other institution high in cost and standards. His marks did not remotely qualify him for such a school; nor did his true interest, or what the educators call his "motivation." Actually he had pitched his desire upon an Ivy League college (one cannot say his "ambition," for ambition is one of the many things which he has not got) because he thought this would be a smart place to go to, where he could drive about in his convertible with the top down.

[21] Now this sort of "motivation" would not be vastly amiss—in a boy. But remember that this hardy adolescent is past twenty-one. And if all goes well he might conceivably be in a position to shift for himself by the time he is, say, thirty-three.

[22] When the inevitable happens and all the big colleges say No, he is shipped off to some cow college which will open its doors to all who can read (plus a lot who can't). Then the rather pathetic little plot begins to thicken. For Old Junior suddenly decides that he must be married, perhaps because the television ads showing domestic bliss among the cleaning fluids and car-washing materials have put him into a strongly romantic frame of mind.

[23] "Daddy"—this will remain Old Junior's term for his father long after Old Junior himself has fathered several entrants to the family line— is quietly apoplectic. Mother (and, ultimate horror, she in many cases is still "Mommy" to Old Junior) is aghast. They have been driven to the wall, emotionally and financially, by providing simply for Old Junior himself. Now they must somehow find the money—and the moral strength— to launch his wedding, complete to the flowers. Of course, they ought to call in their son and say:

[24] "Now look here, Old Junior, enough is enough, and in this instance there has been too much already. We wish you well as our child —though, frankly, we could wish, too, that you had not insisted on remaining a child so very long. But this is how it is, Old Junior. Regretfully we must tell you to go to hell. If there is any more college for you, you will pay for it. If there is to be a marriage for you, you will pay for that, too. If you intend to found a family you will be responsible for and pay for that family, too. Old Junior, this is where you get off the gravy train; or, to be more exact, this is where you descend from the lollipop express. Why don't you go ahead now and just get a job in a filling station?"

[25] But Daddy and Mommy will not take this Spartan course. Instead, Daddy will grit his teeth (which should have been looked after long ago but were not because Old Junior was, at the time, in the Army and required a weekly check to supplement his military earnings). He will go out and add a mortgage to the two or three he is already carrying. Mommy will again pass up the coat she thought she might be able at last to buy, and she will tear up the folders about Bermuda.

[26] So they will usher Old Junior into the wedded state with wistful fanfare—and their troubles will begin to multiply. The apartment they had found for Old Junior and Mrs. Old Junior (and one must pity this hapless girl) will very shortly be too small or otherwise not suitable. A bigger apartment—and a bigger remittance to Old Junior—will then follow.

[27] Whatever Daddy and Mommy do, however, to make Old Junior comfortable in his academic pursuits, it will turn out to have been too little. Old Junior's growing family will interfere with his intellectual life, and the kindly college of his non-choice will begin to murmur that even *its* standards Old Junior is failing to meet. He will switch from a major

in one of the arcane subjects like history to a major in, say, the management of hotel barber shops.

[28] But however Old Junior twists and turns and works and works at his studies (sometimes two or three whole hours a week), he will increasingly need help. The Dean will join Daddy and Mommy in his line of support; and other hands will be enlisted. At length, these hands will include those of a Marriage Counselor, summoned to help Straighten Out Old Junior—although Old Junior, characteristically, will think that this lady has come into the menage to Straighten Out the deplorable maladjustments of *Mrs.* Old Junior.

[29] Mrs. Old Junior by this time will begin to wonder whether it is all worthwhile. And sometimes, right in front of Old Junior, she will exchange wordless glances of quiet meaning with Old Junior's Daddy and Mommy. So it will all wind up, of course, in divorce. Mrs. Old Junior will go to work, but she will not be able—because she has had no training—to take care alone of the three or four children magnanimously left in her care by Old Junior. Daddy and Mommy will come forward again—and again.

[30] Old Junior himself will move into the fraternity house, an enigmatic elderly figure of domestic tragedy to the sophomores there in residence; but still a Little Boy to himself. He will now complete his intellectual training. And when the time comes for the preparation of his thesis upon the Management of Certain Types of Barber Shops, he will bestir himself mightily and find the name and address of some suitable professional adviser. His eye will fall upon some unfortunate Master Barber; and he will then briskly privilege this citizen with orders to put down his shears, lock his shop doors, and "help" Old Junior to write the thesis which will establish his *bona fides,* vindicate his long search for knowledge, and declare him at last to be a Man. And poor Old Junior will say to himself—just as he is telephoning Daddy to be sure to make him an appointment with those who employ masters in the art of the management of barber shops—that it has been a long hard way up but that now, by God, he has made it at last.

[31] Daddy and Mommy, too, can now feel some sense of qualified relaxation—until the day, that is, when Old Junior's employer incontinently and ungenerously hurls him out upon the public streets. His ears will be full of the boss's maledictions but his pocket will be soothed by the boss's check for severance pay and a booklet on how to apply for unemployment compensation.

QUESTIONS AND COMMENT ON FORM AND CONTENT

1. As in a short story, a poem, a play, or a novel, the mood of this article is set from the very beginning. Why does the author use the word *old* in connection with *junior*? What is the mood suggested by the following expressions?
    a. "still atingle"
    b. "tell off the younger generation, male"
    c. "kindly and avuncular summary"
    d. "kids are running hog-wild"
    e. "this correspondent's tired, fed-up malice"

2. Why does William White mix colloquial and slang expressions with formal or learned words?

3. What disturbs the author about the high school letter?

4. How would you describe Old Junior? What are White's most serious charges against him? Does this essay tend to prove that the present college generation of men is irresponsible?

5. Who is responsible for Old Junior's attitude?

VOCABULARY: WHAT DO THE ITALICIZED WORDS MEAN?

. . . row of *querulous queries* (2)
. . . I should not *shilly-shally* (15)
. . . this sort of *oaf* (17)
. . . this fellow remains *obdurately* a most *repellent* little boy (17)
. . . he must be *cosseted* . . . by his parents (17)
. . . will not *redress* the balances (18)
. . . switch from a major in one of the *arcane* subjects like history (27)
. . . an *enigmatic* elderly figure (30)
. . . employer *incontinently* . . . hurls him out (31)
. . . the boss's *maledictions* (31)

THEME SUGGESTIONS

I Know an Old Junior
The Problem of Mrs. Old Junior
Old Juniors: Whose Responsibility?
College Marriages and Parents
Courtesy
In Defense of Old Junior
The Use and Abuse of Satire

TEEN-AGE HEROES:
MIRRORS OF MUDDLED YOUTH

Thomas B. Morgan

Formerly an editor of Look *and of* Esquire, *Thomas Bryce Morgan
(1926-   ) has written scores of magazine articles, including many
on theatre. His film script of* Albert Schweitzer *won the Academy Award.
He is also the author of* Self-Creations *(1965), a novel.*

[1] Eighteen million American teen-agers growing older in a world
they didn't make—a world overpopulated and underfed, overorganized
and yet disorganized, impersonal and self-indulgent, machine-tooled,
purposeless, yet filled with unrealized possibility and in danger of coming to an apocalyptic end—have settled a new world of their own. They
have established a colony Out There in Teen-Land, a kind of pseudo-
adult world. It is not a young world, if youth means daring and imagination, idealism and individualism, skepticism and iconoclasm. But it does
have such a definite identity and appearance that one can visit it as a
tourist, with camera, dictionary, and sick pills. (A nice place to visit,
yes; but no place to live.) Because they have to live at home, go to
school, belong to clubs, shop for supplies, and appear in court, the teen-
agers' colony is attached to the American mainland and carries on foreign
relations with it. The hearts and minds of teen-agers, though, are usually
in Teen-Land: they are totally aware of themselves as Teen-Agers, something their parents never were when they were younger. They feel and
are made to feel (no doubt by articles such as this) that they are a race
apart, a minority in an alien land. Thus, they cling with fierce pride to a
private set of folkways that seem mysterious and confounding in the
extreme to outsiders. These folkways create pressures to conform and
inhibit the individual as insistently as those in the adult world, but they
give the teen-ager an illusion of choice. Paralleling the adult world,
Teen-Land is built on insecurity and its greatest concern is for safety.
The cost of safety is uniqueness of personality and the measure of it is
membership in the herd.

[2] To understand this complex, young world, one should get to know
the heroes of teen-agers. Here is what prompted this inquiry: the assumption that heroes directly and indirectly reveal much about the
hero-worshipers' values and that the heroes of teen-agers would con-

tribute some understanding of those who idolize them in an era in which communication between generations has all but broken down.

[3] This assumption isn't made because all teen-age heroes have special knowledge. Today, a young man is elected to heroship by teen-age girls who buy phonograph records without regard for his insights. The hero, after a short wait, is then accepted by teen-age boys, who buy him uncritically, perhaps to please the girls. The boys don't have feminine heroines of their own. There are girl singers who are popular with teen-agers, but none receive the adulation that the girls lavish on the males. It seems that teen-age girls, maturing faster than boys, have no interest in worshiping a member of their own sex. They are prepared to accept a male symbol long before the boys have extricated themselves from Mother. It has even been suggested that boys do not care for girl singers because the female voice reminds them of Mom and, worse, Discipline. As it works out, then, both sexes accept the choice of heroes made by one sex, and the weaker sex at that.

[4] What makes the heroes themselves, in the flesh, a potential source of information about teen-agers is that they are, of course, more than mere show-business characters. Most of them are teen-agers and only one is out of his twenties. They not only perform; they also reflect those whom they are performing for and are approved by. They are part of Teen-Land as well as symbols of it. Some are virtually overnight sensations and none are so far from a time when they were nobodies that they cannot remember their own experiences as members of the teen world on the far side of the footlights.

[5] Recently, some of these heroes were tarnished by the payola scandals. But in the outcry over payola, the essential nature of the idols themselves was ignored. The superficial crookedness of individuals in the record business was excoriated, leaving untouched something deeper—the irresponsibility of many who profoundly affect teen-age life.

[6] One recent night, a nineteen-year-old boy named Frankie Avalon, a rock-and-roll ballad singer physically reminiscent of Frank Sinatra, was seen doing his turn at the Steel Pier Music Hall on the boardwalk at Atlantic City. When he stepped on the stage, about two hundred well-fed, well-enough-dressed girls in the first six rows and in the side balconies shrieked in the typically violent and mechanical way we have all come to know and love. The sound was a cross between an explosive high-school cheer and the mating call of the red squirrel. A number of the screamers were not looking at their hero, but at each other, to make sure that they were being seen screaming—that is, belonging. In general, the Frankie Avalon fans were seated screamers, not the old dance-in-the-aisle kind of the naïve Sinatra days, which had merely been a kind of premonition of things to come. A few, however, left their seats to run up

the aisle and take flashbulb pictures of Avalon, screaming a little as they went. Back of the forward wall of noise, row upon row of teen-agers applauded conventionally. This may have been because they were less enthusiastic, but more than likely they did not scream because they were outside the bright glow of the footlights. If the management had turned up the house lights, they might have achieved a more perfect pandemonium.

[7] But perfect or not, by enabling post-pubescent girls to express themselves within the damp warmth and safety of the crowd, a modern teen-age hero, such as Avalon, fulfills his function and collects his money. The expression takes many forms. In New Haven, Connecticut, girls in summer frocks pulled the shoes off Avalon's feet in an attempt to drag him from the stage, into the audience. In Buffalo, New York, a wild herd of little women trampled him and sprained his back, while in Milwaukee twenty-one girls fainted during one show. When Avalon sang *Boy Without a Girl* on a television show, the camera panned on girls sobbing in the audience. After that, wherever he appeared in person, girls who had seen him on TV sobbed while he sang this song. Avalon's merchandising business keeps the idolatry percolating at long distance: among his wares for young women are Avalon shirts, sweaters, bracelets, buttons and authentic locks of hair. The latter are collected when Avalon goes to the barbershop—which reminds one of that old boast of the hog business: "We use everything but the squeal."

[8] Now the stimulus for all this is 5 feet 7 inches tall and weighs less than 135 pounds. On stage at the Steel Pier Music Hall, his hair was wavy, his face sweet-to-babyish, eyes sad, skin sallow under make-up, and mouth uncertain. His clothes were a careful combination of show-biz elegance and Pat Boone purity: silk suits and white buck shoes. By nature or design, his manner was gentle, a little frightened, and awesomely humble.

[9] This humility, which is characteristic of many teen-age heroes (Fabian, Ricky Nelson, and the like), was a response to the felt need of the audience to identify with one who was celestial and yet not far out of reach. Since the aspirations of many teen-agers seem to be at the lowest level in the history of America, too much self was taboo and anyone too far away (or out) would be ignored. The cardinal principle of the successful hero would be that humbleness creates an indispensable aura of accessibility.

[10] Avalon first sang *Pretty-eyed Baby*, the words of which were totally unintelligible, followed by *De De Dinah*, his first recorded hit song, which was also unintelligible. He sang with a microphone, but his voice was almost inaudible. He did a little soft shoe, which must have been intended to tell those who couldn't hear that the music was playing.

Avalon was drowned out not only by the repeated squealings of the audience down front, but also by the orchestra itself, which played loud and hard, driving the backbeat. The trumpet was loud, in part deliberately and in part due to the fact that the trumpet player had cotton stuffed in his ears against the waves of sound from the teen-agers. The drummer accented every second and fourth beat, which is the standard rock-and-roll accent. He kicked the bass drum like the pit man in a burlesque house. Indeed, Avalon's performance contained echoes of burlesque. His least suggestive movements produced ear-splitting cries for more, such as when he merely kicked the toe of a shoe out toward the audience. While this may not seem erotic in cold type, the girls who saw it sighed mightily.

[11] The sum of his performance was very young, very immature, and even tender (all said at the risk of sounding old), because Avalon had so little audible singing ability and his audience needed to believe otherwise. Moreover, though they screamed like baby banshees, the girls were making believe they were adults. They struck poses which seemed to represent their idea of *adult* poses: in a moment of sudden restraint, some would sit back, place an index finger along a check, tighten their eyes, and listen critically. Like opera-goers, they whispered knowingly between numbers. When Avalon's half-hour was over, they wore expressions of adultlike sophistication on their faces: cool, satisfied, almost blasé.

[12] At the stage door, still another crowd of girls gathered to wait for Avalon, held back by a chain. They might have been the same two hundred girls who had had the choice seats in the Music Hall. They milled about the door impatiently. A uniformed guard taunted them ("He ain't never coming out, girls!") while stealing looks through a small window into the hall that led to Avalon's backstage dressing room. When Avalon appeared in the hall, the guard unhooked the chain and demanded that the girls form two lines so that the star and his entourage could pass through to a waiting auto. Instead, the girls surged forward, breathlessly. Nonchalant at first, the guard swung the chain at them, rippling it softly. Then he cracked it hard across the front rank at chest level. The girls, who had been about to crush Avalon, fell back. Avalon walked behind a phalanx made up of his guitar player, the Steel Pier press agent, and three other men. "Touch me, Frankie!" girls shouted. "Over here, man. Just look at me!" Looking neither right nor left, Avalon escaped into the back seat of the waiting car. The entourage piled in after him. Female hands, heads, and torsos surged in at the windows and jammed open the front door. Two well-aimed, shoving blows from the driver cleared the front door, the windows were rolled up, and the car drove off with its precious cargo. The girls waved, disappointed but not

angry. They had enjoyed the melee, the mob violence of which was the other side of the group sex rites that had taken place inside.

[13] Ten minutes later, safe in a restaurant, Frankie Avalon said: "I think it's great to be a teen-ager."

[14] Avalon had no more to say, really, than this one line. Yet even that underlined the modern, crowd-cultured teen-ager's deep and novel sense of belonging to a special group. Avalon was as unaware of his function as a hero of that special group as he had once been of his own potentialities. (He had started in show business as a trumpet player.) He was their outlet for vicarious sex and real violence, those primitive means of self-expression to which one turns when prouder means—ambition, creativity, ability, the sheer desire to change the world—have been denied, devalued, or have failed. Avalon did not know it and, not knowing, felt no sense of responsibility for it.

[15] While Avalon was in New Jersey, six teen-age heroes were in Hollywood pursuing their various commitments to television, movies, and night clubs. Ricky Nelson was taping "The Adventures of Ozzie and Harriet" with his mother and father. Edd "Kookie" Byrnes was acting in "77 Sunset Strip," a filmed weekly TV show. Pat Boone and Dick Clark (the non-singer of the group) were making movies and, simultaneously, Clark was producing some of his TV programs for tape. Fabian was working in a movie called *Hound Dog Man* and Bobby Darin had an adult-world night-club date. One could see them individually in the surroundings of their trade.

[16] Ricky Nelson was rather well protected by his father and the family press agent in a barren office across from the "Ozzie and Harriet" TV-show sound stage. When they let him in edgewise, it was apparent that he was at least partly conscious of the nuances of his appeal to teen-agers. His commodity is sincere sex. He was most aware of the need for sincerity. It seemed crucial to him that no one should get the idea that he was different—"I'm just another teen-ager," he said—or that he was anything but sincere. Like most teen-agers, his sentences were larded with the phrase "you know," partially from habit, but also, it seemed, to impress one with his complete frankness and desire to be understood.

[17] In 1957, when he was sixteen, Ricky studied guitar for a while, then walked on the stage of Hamilton High School in Los Angeles for his first public appearance as a prospective solo performer. He did not swing his hips or otherwise attempt to excite the audience. Yet, the screaming began before he sang a note, the girls got out of hand, and the members of the football team had to help him escape. Thus the hero was born, as all teen-age heroes are born, in the presence and at the pleasure of screaming young women. Six of his records have since sold

over one million copies each, representing a cool net of $40,000 each. His personal appearances have been smashing, thanks in some degree to the careful organization of 10,000 fan clubs all over the country. His income last year was estimated to be $400,000. To earn it, Ricky selected each hit song by himself from hundreds of demonstration records submitted by publishers and song writers. He knew exactly what he wanted:

[18] "The record should not be too complicated," Ricky said. "If it's not, you know, sincere, it's not too good. In a song, I hate to hear lingo, you know, about hop and bop. I like a song that tells a story without meaningless words, you know, like 'dig that crazy chick.' Now you listen to *Lonesome Town*. It should be a simple song like that, you know? *Lonesome Town* is about this fictitious town called Lonesome Town, you know, where you can forget this girl. I mean lots of times you get jilted and feel like the end of the world's come. So, it's from what I feel sincerely, I decide to do a song. Now, you asked me about teen-age values. I feel my values are pretty good. I mean, I like anything I feel is sincere."

[19] Edd "Kookie" Byrnes touches a different chord out of necessity. He is perhaps the only teen-age hero who achieved his exalted position by playing a role—that of "Kookie," the jive-talking parking-lot attendant of "77 Sunset Strip"—and maintains it by continuing to be what he isn't. In public, his speech sounds like a tape-recording made at the bar in Birdland. The rest of the time he talks like a conventional twenty-six-year-old. Seen at lunch and between scenes at Warner's, there was nothing about him that suggested the character of "Kookie" except the long brown hair and routine good looks. To teen-agers, however, he is "Kookie" whose long suit is a devilish narcissism. His trade-mark is a comb which he is endlessly passing through his locks. Teen-agers might be expected to frown on such self-conceit, but "Kookie" manages to convey the impression that he is just kidding. If teen-agers were really in revolt against the adult world instead of merely huddled together in their own adultified colony, Byrnes's "Kookie" probably would not be a strong-enough character to appeal to them. As it is, he is a symbol of a small rebellion. He says that the "77 Sunset Strip" adventure that won the teen-agers for "Kookie" involved an incident in which he was falsely blamed for an auto accident. "They think I did it," "Kookie" said, "because I'm young." The line could have been the title of a rock-and-roll golden record. Inevitably, as his fame grew, Byrnes turned to the teen-age record market. After a dozen or more attempts to record his first tune on key, the A & R man sent him home and pasted together a master out of pieces from each of the tapes. The result was *Kookie, Lend Me Your Comb*, which sold 2,000,-000 single records, a monument to the taste and perception of our teens.

[20] Fabian, like "Kookie," became a teen-age hero in spite of the fact

that he was no bundle of singing talent. "Maybe I would have never made it if I could sing," Fabian has said. His appeal is similar to Ricky Nelson's, but also he elicits motherly sympathy from the girls because he is so obviously awkward and inept. It is now one of the hoary legends of Teen-Land that Fabian was discovered sitting on a doorstep in South Philadelphia by Bob Marcucci, a former waiter who is himself not yet thirty. With his partner, Peter De Angelis, Marcucci had discovered and then promoted Frankie Avalon to stardom. Having developed the magic touch, he searched for and found Fabian two years ago. Fabian was fourteen, had never sung a note in anger, and thought that the $6 a week he was earning in a drugstore was fair money. When last seen, he was getting $35,000 for acting (not badly, by Hollywood standards) in Fox's *Hound Dog Man.*

[21] Sitting just behind the camera in one of those canvas chairs, Marcucci was watching every move his gold mine made. Marcucci is a short, swarthy man who reminds one of a nervous assistant director at a boy's camp. He has the ability to analyze precisely the demands of the teen-age public and to know what to do about it. He has found a career in exporting talent to Teen-Land. First, he selects promising raw material. Then he molds it. He indoctrinates it for three months. Then he takes it to live TV shows so that it can see what the business is like. Then he lets it make a few test records. Since it cannot sing too well without an orchestra and the electronic facilities (echo chambers, bass and treble modulators, tape splicers and the works) of a recording studio, he teaches it to pantomime while its records play over the loud-speaker during its first public appearance before an audience of two hundred. He dresses it, first in sweaters and white bucks, then in open-Belafonte shirts and big belt buckles. He coifs it by modifying the duck-tail and getting more of the Ricky Nelson bob. He postures it, taking advantage of good shoulders, which should bunch forward, and narrow hips, which should always be off-keel. He takes it on the road, shows it to disc jockeys, and advertises it in trade papers. He decides (brilliantly) to use only its first name instead of its last. He interests Dick Clark in it, and after one shot on TV, it breaks up an audience of 24,000 in Albany, New York. It sells 300,000 copies of a record called *I'm a Man,* then 750,000 of *Turn Me Loose.* It records *Tiger:*

> . . . You kept my heart jump-ing like a kan-ga-roo
> I'm float-ing like an on-ion in a bowl of stew . . .
> Come right now, 'cause I'm on the prowl
> Like a ti-ger oo-oo-oo, like a ti-ger." [1]

[1] *Tiger,* by Ollie Jones. Copyright © 1959 by Roosevelt Music Co., Inc.

[22] After these lyrics (tiger is the word you *hear*), it is known not only as Fabian, but as Tiger, too. It is a hero.

[23] In Fabian, Marcucci consciously or unconsciously produced a caricature that combined the sure-fire qualities of Ricky with those of his own Frankie Avalon. The mood in Teen-Land permits even such an obvious construction to become a hero. What Marcucci could not have planned, however, was the fact that Fabian's inability to sing would really be an asset. Marcucci tried to teach him; he went through four singing teachers trying. Fortunately, all efforts failed. Here was the ultimate in humbleness and teen-audience identification. Nobody in the audience could sing either, so that made the inept sex-pot, Fabian, seem all the more accessible. Mediocrity fell in love with its own image.

[24] Bobby Darin has what Fabian doesn't have and vice versa. Instead of half-closed eyes, a build and a hairdresser, Darin has the most low-down, mature, masculine voice of all the teen-age heroes. During the past year, his records have sold more than 5,000,000 copies (*Splish Splash, Mack the Knife,* which got the Grammy award etc.). Found at a Sunset Strip night club, Darin (without teen-agers) demonstrated that the humbleness required by them does not become him; he fairly bursts with self-confidence before an adult audience. He is about twenty-four, short, average-looking, and honest with himself. "I know I'm not a pretty boy," he said. "I feel a little out of place in front of teen-agers because even though they buy my records they don't have that fervor for me when they see me. It's a physical thing with them. I don't put them down for it, but I don't think I'm one of them." He said he would sing anything teen-agers wanted to hear—à la Avalon, the sense of responsibility was missing. "It's bad the way the papers have screwed them up. The kids have got the idea now that they all have to band together and act like teen-agers. They have phony heroes and no individuality. They don't know who's leading them. I feel for them, but I'm *not* going to lead them, Charlie. You call the roll of commercial guys, put me first."

[25] Pat Boone would save the teen-ager from himself if he could. His book, *'Twixt Twelve and Twenty,* was a tender try in that direction and he has said, "I hope that fellows like me and Ricky and Elvis aren't distracting kids from the real things in life and from becoming people instead of just fans." Boone has been around longer as a teen-age hero than anyone except Elvis Presley. He was a married man with a baby and a second (with two more in the future) on the way before he became a popular idol. He was deeply religious. Thus, he was absolutely safe and pure, too. This combination was immensely appealing to many teen-age girls. His records sold 20,000,000 at last count, second only to Elvis. On the movie set, *Journey to the Center of the Earth,* a wholesome Jules Verne tale, Boone seemed made for Victorian costumery. He does not

have conventional good looks, but rather a strong, open boy's face which suggests ball games and picnics. He does not simmer like the members of the Presley-Nelson-Fabian-Byrnes syndrome. In his time, though, he has had his share of screaming and fainting and clothes-grabbing by teen fans. "I can't believe it's bad or abnormal," he said. "It's fun and a form of recreation and a release of tension."

[26] Dick Clark has defended the teen-agers' *status quo* even more stoutly than Pat Boone. He has virtually become a go-between in the two worlds. To the teen-ager, he is an adult who likes them, a big brother who watches out for them, and an authority who sanctions both their idols and their folkways. For the adult world, he is an emissary from Teen-Land not many years out of the age group himself (he's thirty, looks twenty), a young man whose taste and judgment are respected (after all, indecent lyrics are banned from his programs); and a celebrity who approves of their children. With all this going for him, it's no wonder that Clark is one of the hot properties in show business. He has six TV shows a week on ABC, many magazine-writing assignments, and a fat contract with Columbia Pictures. (Until recently, when he was advised to withdraw, he had a music-publishing and record-pressing business.)

[27] Television is Clark's first love. Both *American Bandstand* and the Saturday *Dick Clark Show* are major outlets for teen-age heroes and their music. The shows are so popular that Clark is probably the most powerful personality-and-song plugger in the teen field. Such power implies responsibility, so Clark is due his share of credit for conditions that prevail in Teen-Land. Last summer, after watching two Saturday shows from the wings (Clark tapes his summer Saturday shows mid-week), one could be sure Clark would never have one of those "There, that'll hold the little bastards!" episodes in his career. He is a careful man and, besides, he believes in teen-agers "the way they are." All of his TV programs devote many minutes to camera views of teen-agers.

[28] Clark's magazine-writing career is based on a column in *This Week Magazine,* but his "talks to teen-agers" have also appeared in *Seventeen, Look,* and others. He is the teen-agers' Norman Vincent Peale. His position is reassuring: the way teens live is pretty much okay. Nothing downs his optimism. Typically, he sums up his advice with, "Keep at it and I know you'll be successful"; or, "I think you will be surprised at how soon there will be nothing to worry about." Once, however, in a conversation, he said:

[29] "I don't think teen-agers are doing anything today that adults don't do also. They have all the same problems that adults have nowadays—money problems, success problems, appearance problems. They are appreciated as a group as never before and they want to be looked on as adults. They're worldly, so much more worldly than we were.

They're practically adults. They're sophisticated at a very early age. Take the day Sal Mineo was leaving my studio. He got in his car and a teen-age girl threw herself under the front wheels. 'Run over me, Sal!' she cried. That was dreadful, yes; but a week later in Atlantic City, a forty-year-old woman in a mink coat threw herself in front of Frank Sinatra's car and cried, 'Run over me, Frankie!' That's what I mean. There's no difference between teen-agers and adults."

[30] Clark apparently meant this as a justification for himself as well as the teen-agers who idolize him. In any case, it was an accurate description of juvenile adults and adultified teen-agers.

[31] What Clark and the others suggest in symbol and sentiment is that millions of teen-agers have taken refuge in a pseudo-world that is spoiled and banal and hypererotic and in headlong flight from reality and easily fooled and commercialized and exploited and fatuous. Such a world may be satisfactory for adults, but somehow one has greater expectations from youth.

[32] Every world has means of expressing itself—a culture. Our 18,-000,000 teen-agers (exceptions duly noted) spend $10,000,000,000 to support theirs. They have publications written in their own language (Teen-glish?) which keep them abreast of their times. *Dig, Ingenue, Seventeen, 16, Teen,* etc., instruct them in custom, ritual, propriety, sex mores, and proper-think; their goal is to inculcate group values. One magazine not long ago defined "What is a Square?" for its readers, who were told, among other things, that a square is one who refuses to go with a group to a movie he has already seen. Then there are motion pictures, television shows, and radio programs, which provide a kind of cultural game of ring-around-the-rosie. The teens influence the adults who provide the entertainments which in turn influence the teens and so on, and on. After sex and violence, the main theme of these entertainments is a kind of dead-pan morality which would be funny if it did not border on madness. Thus, the producer of *I Was a Teenage Frankenstein* defended himself against an attack on his very popular picture by pointing out that none of the young villains and monsters in the movie drank or smoked. And in the basic boy-meets-girl film, scripts are adjusted to make sure that a curious kind of justice, appealing to teen-agers, triumphs. In a teen picture, after the boy gets the girl pregnant, he's got to get stabbed. Watching rock-and-roll programs, citizens of Teen-Land may learn the newest folk dances while they follow the fashions of the times. Hearing the disc jockeys on radio, too, teen-agers can absorb their culture. They are infused with meaningful backbeat rhythms and simultaneously absorb the philosophies of the modern jocks, which are a mixture of Beat, Babbitt and Payola. Beyond these visual and aural items of acculturation, there is the automobile. What the frontier was to

our pioneers, what Miami is to our modern adult culture, the auto is to the teen—the means of getting away.

[33] Finally, away out on the fringe of Teen-Land, heroin takes some teen-agers where they cannot get by car.

[34] The primary focus of the teen culture, however, is the teen-age hero who, like heroes of all cultures, represents the final expression of those values by which it lives. The seven aforementioned heroes are the Apollos and Zeuses of Teen-Land. A few years ago, the movies supplied most of the heroes for adolescent Americans. Marlon Brando and James Dean were two, but the former's receding hairline and the latter's death disconnected them from the young. Chances are they would have faded anyway, because rock-and-roll was bigger than both of them. Now, except for Dick Clark, every first-class teen-age hero is a recording star. No athlete, politician, businessman, or intellectual is accorded comparable esteem, nor could he be, given the teen-agers' demand for safety. The ideal athlete is admired for courage, the politician for principles, the businessman for enterprise, and the intellectual for devotion to hard truths —all represent values that tend to separate the individual from the crowd, that expose him, and that lead him into an uncertain and dangerous future. Teen-agers make virtues of conformity, mediocrity and sincerity. It is a simple matter of survival: there's safety in the crowd. They can express themselves through their safe-sex heroes, each one of whom represents his own brand of sex—rebellious sex, sincere sex, clean sex, low-down sex, motherly sex, cool sex—at no risk. It's perfect: it's sex, but it's safe. Without leaving the warmth and security of the crowd, you can say what you want to say to the world.

[35] You can have your cake without being eaten.

[36] It is not easy to know precisely what the teen-agers want to say through their heroes. The means of expression is primordial; the words are often indistinguishable from straight static. In that they are designed (often willfully) to hold a mirror up to the nature of teen life, they offer perhaps our most significant clue.

[37] Two of the most successful people in the teen-age song business are Jerry Leiber and Mike Stoller, a words-and-music team which seems to know precisely what it is that teen-agers want to say. Their rock-and-roll songs have sold over 30,000,000 records: *Hound Dog* sold more than 5,000,000 records; *Black Denim Trousers,* a supposed spoof of motorcycle bums which was taken seriously by them, sold more than 2,000,000 records; *Love Me, Loving You, Searching, Don't* and *Jailhouse Rock* also sold more than 2,000,000; *King Creole, Charley Brown, Yakety Yak, Along Came Jones* and *Poison Ivy* sold more than 1,000,000. After eight years of song-writing (each is now but twenty-six years old) Leiber and Stoller have sold four times as many records as Jerome Kern sold in his lifetime.

[38] It did them no harm that Elvis Presley (still in the Army as this is written) performed several of their songs. Along Tin Pan Alley, it is still generally assumed that Presley, the king of the teen-age heroes, could sell one million records of himself singing Clementine Paddleford's recipe for boiled beef to the tune of *Juanita*. He is expected to resume the throne upon his discharge this spring.

[39] Leiber and Stoller had the good fortune to begin writing songs for teen-age heroes in the early Fifties when Negro music known as "rhythm and blues" was being discovered by white teen-agers. About 1953, this music was taken over for the commercial teen market although it had been played for years on Negro radio stations and had been sung down South as a form of the blues since the Civil War. At the same time, "country music" with its strong influence from both the Baptist church and white folk music was discovered. The two themes, one earthy, the other moralistic, both plaintive, came together and were revised downward to the teen-age level; they became "rock-and-roll." The rock-and-roll fad spread like a pox, carried first by independent record companies with singing groups, and then by Elvis Presley, with his country guitar and Gypsy Rose Lee hips. In Presley's larynx, songs that had arisen out of realistic needs for a job, a woman, or a drink were replaced by teen-age needs and expressions that were only dimly related to the sources of the new music. "Cold pouring down rain blues" became "They don't understand us because we're teen-agers rock."

[40] Presley was followed by a horde of imitators. The surprise was that they were almost as successful as he was. Always before, a segment of youth had zeroed in on a single personality—a Vallee or a Sinatra—and had disdained copies of the real thing. Elvis, however, was more than a personality; he was the leader of a movement which provided a hero for every boy and girl, and finally resulted in the identification of teen-agers as a race apart. Leiber and Stoller wrote on the head of a drum.

"Anger and protest, self-pity and adulation, these are the things the teen-age heroes sing about," Jerry Leiber says.

[41] Repeating the same salty, nasty phrase again and again, such a song as *Hound Dog* is a pure expression of hostility while *Don't* is equally pure self-pity. What teen-agers seem to want to say is, "I'm mad at the world, at authority, at the way things are," and "I can't do anything about it, so pity poor me." Both would be perfectly legitimate statements, loaded with potentialities, if that was what teen-agers actually meant.

[42] "Basically," Leiber says, "these songs are a means of escape from reality. We write the lyrics deliberately vague. The songs aren't addressed to anybody real, but to dream characters. The songs are egocentric and dreamy. Lots of basic blues ideas wouldn't work as rock-and-roll ideas

because the blues are too real, too earthy. You have to make them dream-like and very moral. That's why you're rarely going to hear even a plain *happy* rock-and-roll song, because happiness is a real emotion."

[43] We have, therefore, not only rebels without causes, we have a generation with nothing to say. All that seems real about teen-age self-expression through the safe-sex heroes is their dedication to unreality, to songs of watered-down, self-pitying blues-that-aren't-blues, and to aimless hostility.

[44] One can hope that in some area of life, teen-agers are giving as much passionate attention to the real business of youth—which is growing up as well as older—as they are giving to their heroes. But if Dick Clark is right, that there is no difference between the generations as he sees them, growing up may be as outmoded as the 78 r.p.m. phonograph record. There may be nothing to grow up to. Yet a comparison must be made. The adult world has an existence apart from its obvious responsibility for what has happened in Teen-Land. There are adults and there are teen-agers. Even on the teen-agers' terms, if a choice had to be made, one would a hell of a lot rather have his woman run over by Frank Sinatra.

QUESTIONS AND COMMENT ON FORM AND CONTENT

1. What is the meaning of *mirrors* in the title? Can youth be judged by its heroes? Can adults be similarly judged?

2. Teen-Land suggests an unreality like Disneyland. Is the rest of the essay consistent with this view? Why should one bring a camera, dictionary, and sick pills? Why does the author say, "It is not a young world . . ."? Is this his principal criticism of it? Does he come back to this criticism at the end of the article? What qualities does he expect of youth?

3. The topic sentence of paragraph 2 is also the topic of the main section of the essay—"One should get to know the heroes of teen-agers." What is accomplished in paragraph 1?

4. Do boys or girls have the most effect on the type of music adults can hear on television and radio? (See paragraph 3.)

5. What is the author's point in paragraph 5 about payola and irresponsibility?

6. How does Mr. Morgan account for the more sensational effects produced by teen-age heroes?

7. Which of the heroes hold up the clearest, most revealing mirrors?

8. How do the writers of rock-and-roll songs (See paragraph 42) describe their songs?

9. If youth is really muddled in its values, who is responsible? Is it important what songs a nation sings?

VOCABULARY: WHAT DO THE ITALICIZED WORDS MEAN?

. . . coming to an *apocalyptic* end (1)
. . . a kind of *pseudo-adult* world (1)
. . . if youth means daring and imagination, *idealism,* and *individualism, skepticism* and *iconoclasm* (1)
. . . tarnished by the *payola* scandals (5)
The *superficial* crookedness . . . was *excoriated* (5)
. . . a more perfect *pandemonium* (6)
. . . humbleness creates an *indispensable aura* of *accessibility* (9)
. . . cool, satisfied, almost *blasé* (11)
. . . a devilish *narcissism* (19)
Teen-agers make virtues of *conformity, mediocrity,* and sincerity (34)

THEME SUGGESTIONS

A Rock-and-Roll Hero
I (Don't) Want My Children To Be Squares
Creative Youth
A Teen-Age Rock-and-Roll Audience
A Defense of Youth
Whose Responsibility?
Exploitation of Youth

LETTERS TO HIS SON

Lord Chesterfield

Philip Stanhope, Lord Chesterfield (1694-1773), the influential leader in the House of Lords who gave us the adjective Chesterfieldian, *is perhaps best remembered for his 413 letters written to his illegitimate son, for whom he had great social and political ambitions. Although the letters were not intended for publication, they are models of clarity in organization, sentence structure, and diction. Moreover, they possess an informality that largely conceals the care and effort that must have gone into their composition.*

The three letters reproduced here were written when the boy was nine, fifteen, and sixteen, respectively. If, in places, we feel that the letters are not adapted to a young boy's understanding, we must remember that the boy kept them and, no doubt, later reread them.

Spa, July 25, n.s. 1741

[1] Dear Boy: I have often told you in my former letters (and it is most certainly true) that the strictest and most scrupulous honor and

virtue can alone make you esteemed and valued by mankind; that parts and learning can alone make you admired and celebrated by them; but that the possession of lesser talents was most absolutely necessary towards making you liked, beloved, and sought after in private life. Of these lesser talents, good breeding is the principal and most necessary one, not only as it is very important in itself; but as it adds great luster to the more solid advantages both of the heart and the mind.

[2] I have often touched upon good breeding to you before; so that this letter shall be upon the next necessary qualification to it, which is a genteel, easy manner and carriage, wholly free from those odd tricks, ill habits, and awkwardnesses, which even very many worthy and sensible people have in their behavior. However trifling a genteel manner may sound, it is of very great consequence towards pleasing in private life, especially the women; which, one time or other, you will think worth pleasing; and I have known many a man, from his awkwardness, give people such a dislike of him at first, that all his merit could not get the better of it afterwards. Whereas a genteel manner prepossesses people in your favor, bends them towards you, and makes them wish to like you.

[3] Awkwardness can proceed but from two causes: either from not having kept good company, or from not having attended to it. As for your keeping good company, I will take care of that; do you take care to observe their ways and manners, and to form your own upon them. Attention is absolutely necessary for this, as indeed it is for everything else; and a man without attention is not fit to live in the world. When an awkward fellow first comes into a room, it is highly probable that his sword gets between his legs, and throws him down, or makes him stumble at least; when he has recovered this accident, he goes and places himself in the very place of the whole room where he should not; there he soon lets his hat fall down; and, taking it up again, throws down his cane; in recovering his cane, his hat falls a second time; so that he is a quarter of an hour before he is in order again. If he drinks tea or coffee, he certainly scalds his mouth, and lets either the cup or the saucer fall, and spills the tea or coffee in his breeches. At dinner, his awkwardness distinguishes itself particularly, as he has more to do; there he holds his knife, fork, and spoon differently from other people; eats with his knife to the great danger of his mouth, picks his teeth with his fork, and puts his spoon, which has been in his throat twenty times, into the dishes again. If he is to carve, he can never hit the joint; but, in his vain efforts to cut through the bone, scatters the sauce in everybody's face. He generally daubs himself with soup and grease, though his napkin is commonly stuck through a button-hole, and tickles his chin. When he drinks he infallibly coughs in his glass, and besprinkles the company. Besides all this, he has strange tricks and gestures; such as snuffing up his nose, mak-

ing faces, putting his fingers in his nose, or blowing it and looking afterwards in his handkerchief, so as to make the company sick. His hands
are troublesome to him when he has not something in them, and he does
not know where to put them; but they are in perpetual motion between
his bosom and his breeches; he does not wear his clothes, and, in short,
does nothing like other people. All this, I own, is not in any degree criminal; but it is highly disagreeable and ridiculous in company, and ought
most carefully to be avoided by whoever desires to please.

[4] From this account of what you should not do, you may easily judge
what you should do; and a due attention to the manners of people of
fashion, and who have seen the world, will make it habitual and familiar
to you.

[5] There is, likewise, an awkwardness of expression and words, most
carefully to be avoided; such as false English, bad pronunciation, old
sayings, and common proverbs; which are so many proofs of having kept
bad and low company. For example; if, instead of saying that tastes are
different, and that every man has his own peculiar one, you should let
off a proverb, and say, That what is one man's meat is another man's poison; or else, Everyone as they like, as the good man said when he kissed
his cow; everybody would be persuaded that you had never kept company with anybody above footmen and housemaids.

[6] Attention will do all this; and without attention nothing is to be
done. Want of attention, which is really want of thought, is either folly
or madness. You should not only have attention to everything, but a
quickness of attention, so as to observe, at once, all the people in the
room; their motions, their looks, and their words; and yet without staring at them, and seeming to be an observer. This quick and unobserved
observation is of infinite advantage in life, and is to be acquired with
care; and, on the contrary, what is called absence, which is a thought-
lessness, and want of attention about what is doing, makes a man so
like either a fool or a madman, that, for my part, I see no real difference.
A fool never has thought; a madman has lost it; and an absent man is,
for the time, without it.

[7] Adieu! Direct your next to me, *chez Monsieur Chabert, Banquier,
à Paris;* and take care that I find the improvements I expect at my return.

QUESTIONS AND COMMENT ON FORM AND CONTENT

1. How does the first paragraph in the 1741 letter connect this letter with
previous letters? Are honor and virtue ends in themselves for Chesterfield or
principally means to other ends? Or is he adapting his appeals to the boy?

2. How does the second paragraph announce the theme of this letter? What
is meant by *breeding*? What is meant by *genteel* and *carriage*?

3. What does the writer mean by *attention*? How does he develop his definition of it? What type of words can frequently be defined in this manner?

4. How does Chesterfield bring faulty English and clichés into this letter without violating unity? In other words, what joins paragraph 5 to paragraph 4?

5. In what respect is a person who fails to give attention to what he is doing like a fool or a madman?

THEME SUGGESTIONS

Define *honor, temperance, patriot* or some other abstract word by telling what it is not. Note how Chesterfield defines the opposite of *attention* in paragraphs 3, 4, 5, and 6.

London, October 9, o.s. 1747.

[1] Dear Boy: People of your age have, commonly, an unguarded frankness about them; which makes them the easy prey and bubbles of the artful and the experienced; they look upon every knave or fool, who tells them that he is their friend, to be really so; and pay that profession of simulated friendship with an indiscreet and unbounded confidence, always to their loss, often to their ruin. Beware, therefore, now that you are coming into the world, of these proffered friendships. Receive them with great civility, but with great incredulity too; and pay them with compliments, but not with confidence. Do not let your vanity and self-love make you suppose that people become your friends at first sight, or even upon a short acquaintance. Real friendship is a slow grower, and never thrives unless ingrafted upon a stock of known and reciprocal merit.

[2] There is another kind of nominal friendship among young people, which is warm for the time, but, by good luck, of short duration. This friendship is hastily produced, by their being accidentally thrown together, and pursuing the course of riot and debauchery. A fine friendship, truly, and well cemented by drunkenness and lewdness. It should rather be called a conspiracy against morals and good manners, and be punished as such by the civil magistrate. However, they have the impudence and folly to call this confederacy a friendship. They lend one another money, for bad purposes; they engage in quarrels, offensive and defensive, for their accomplices; they tell one another all they know, and often more too, when, of a sudden, some accident disperses them, and they think no more of each other, unless it be to betray and laugh at their imprudent confidence. Remember to make a great difference between companions and friends; for a very complaisant and agreeable companion may, and often does, prove a very improper and a very dangerous friend.

[3] People will, in a great degree, and not without reason, form their

opinion of you upon that which they have of your friends; and there is a Spanish proverb which says very justly, "Tell me whom you live with, and I will tell you who you are." One may fairly suppose that a man who makes a knave or a fool his friend has something very bad to do or to conceal. But, at the same time that you carefully decline the friendship of knaves and fools, if it can be called friendship, there is no occasion to make either of them your enemies, wantonly and unprovoked; for they are numerous bodies, and I would rather choose a secure neutrality, than alliance, or war, with either of them. You may be a declared enemy to their vices and follies, without being marked out by them as a personal one. Their enmity is the next dangerous thing to their friendship. Have a real reserve with almost everybody, and have a seeming reserve with almost nobody; for it is very disagreeable to seem reserved, and very dangerous not to be so. Few people find the true medium; many are ridiculously mysterious and reserved upon trifles, and many imprudently communicative of all they know.

[4] The next thing to the choice of your friends is the choice of your company. Endeavor, as much as you can, to keep company with people above you. There you rise, as much as you sink with people below you; for (as I have mentioned before) you are whatever the company you keep is. Do not mistake, when I say company above you, and think that I mean with regard to their birth; that is the least consideration; but I mean with regard to their merit, and the light in which the world considers them.

[5] There are two sorts of good company: one, which is called the *beau monde,* and consists of people who have the lead in courts and in the gay part of life; the other consists of those who are distinguished by some peculiar merit, or who excel in some particular and valuable art or science. For my own part, I used to think myself in company as much above me, when I was with Mr. Addison and Mr. Pope, as if I had been with all the princes in Europe.

[6] You may possibly ask me whether a man has it always in his power to get into the best company? And how? I say, Yes, he has, by deserving it; provided he is but in circumstances which enable him to appear upon the footing of a gentleman. Merit and good breeding will make their way everywhere. Knowledge will introduce him, and good breeding will endear him, to the best companies; for, as I have often told you, politeness and good breeding are absolutely necessary to adorn any or all good qualities or talents. Without them no knowledge, no perfection whatsoever, is seen in its best light. The scholar, without good breeding, is a pedant; the philosopher, a cynic; the soldier, a brute; and every man disagreeable.

[7] I long to hear, from my several correspondents at Leipsig, of your

arrival there, and what impression you make on them at first; for I have Arguses, with a hundred eyes each, who will watch you narrowly, and relate to me faithfully. My accounts will certainly be true; it depends upon you, entirely, of what kind they shall be. Adieu!

QUESTIONS AND COMMENT ON FORM AND CONTENT

1. Would you modify in any way Chesterfield's advice on how to deal with new or proffered friendships: "pay them with compliments but not with confidence"?

2. What distinction does he make between companions and friends? Should one make enemies, according to Chesterfield, of knaves and fools? What is his real concept of the value of friendship? Do you agree?

3. Do you approve of his having "Arguses, with a hundred eyes each, who will watch you narrowly, and relate to me faithfully"? What are Arguses? (Comparison could be made with Polonius, who sends a spy to observe his son Laertes. *Hamlet,* Act II, Scene i.)

4. Choose or write the topic sentence of each of these seven paragraphs. What title could be used for the entire letter? What forms the link or transition between paragraphs 1 and 2? Between paragraphs 3 and 4? Could paragraphs 4 and 5 have been combined? What key words remind the reader of the close connection of paragraphs 4, 5, and 6?

5. Are your letters as carefully planned as Chesterfield's? Does he retain an informal tone despite his formal plan? (Reread paragraph 6.) Clarity is a characteristic of the prose of Chesterfield as well as of the eighteenth century in general. How does he attain clarity?

THEME SUGGESTIONS

Write a letter to a younger brother or sister giving advice on how to get the best out of college.

London, September 5 o.s. 1748.

[1] Dear Boy: As women are a considerable, or at least a pretty numerous part of company; and as their suffrages go a great way towards establishing a man's character in the fashionable part of the world (which is of great importance to the fortune and figure he proposes to make in it), it is necessary to please them. I will, therefore, upon this subject let you into certain *arcana,* that will be very useful for you to know, but which you must, with the utmost care, conceal; and never seem to know.

[2] Women, then, are only children of a larger growth; they have an entertaining tattle, and sometimes wit; but for solid reasoning, good sense, I never knew in my life one that had it, or who reasoned or acted

consequentially for four and twenty hours together. Some little passion or humor always breaks in upon their best resolutions. Their beauty neglected or controverted, their age increased or their supposed understandings depreciated, instantly kindles their little passions, and overturns any system of consequential conduct, that in their most reasonable moments they might have been capable of forming. A man of sense only trifles with them, plays with them, humors and flatters them, as he does with a sprightly, forward child; but he neither consults them about, nor trusts them with, serious matters; though he often makes them believe that he does both; which is the thing in the world that they are proud of; for they love mightily to be dabbling in business (which, by the way, they always spoil); and being justly distrustful, that men in general look upon them in a trifling light, they almost adore that man who talks more seriously to them, and who seems to consult and trust them; I say, who seems; for weak men really do, but wise ones only seem to do it. No flattery is either too high or too low for them. They will greedily swallow the highest, and gratefully accept of the lowest; and you may safely flatter any woman, from her understanding down to the exquisite taste of her fan.

[3] Women who are either indisputably beautiful, or indisputably ugly, are best flattered upon the score of their understandings; but those who are in a state of mediocrity are best flattered upon their beauty, or at least their graces; for every woman, who is not absolutely ugly, thinks herself handsome; but not hearing often that she is so, is the more grateful, and the more obliged to the few who tell her so; whereas a decided and conscious beauty looks upon every tribute paid to her beauty only as her due; but wants to shine, and to be considered on the side of her understanding; and a woman who is ugly enough to know that she is so, knows that she has nothing left for it but her understanding, which is consequently (and probably in more senses than one) her weak side. But these are secrets, which you must keep inviolably, if you would not, like Orpheus, be torn to pieces by the whole sex; on the contrary, a man who thinks of living in the great world must be gallant, polite, and attentive to please the women. They have, from the weakness of men, more or less influence in all courts; they absolutely stamp every man's character in the *beau monde,* and make it either current, or cry it down, and stop it in payments. It is, therefore, absolutely necessary to manage, please, and flatter them, and never to discover the least mark of contempt, which is what they never forgive; but in this they are not singular, for it is the same with men; who will much sooner forgive an injustice than an insult. Every man is not ambitious, or covetous, or passionate; but every man has pride enough in his composition to feel and resent the least slight and contempt. Remember, therefore, most carefully to conceal your con-

tempt, however just, wherever you would not make an implacable enemy. Men are much more unwilling to have their weaknesses and imperfections known, than their crimes, and if you hint to a man that you think him silly, ignorant, or even ill-bred or awkward, he will hate you more and longer, than if you tell him, plainly, that you think him a rogue. Never yield to that temptation, which to most young men is very strong, of exposing other people's weaknesses and infirmities, for the sake either of diverting the company, or showing your own superiority. You may get the laugh on your side by it for the present; but you will make enemies by it forever; and even those who laugh with you then, will, upon reflection, fear, and consequently hate you; besides that, it is ill-natured, and a good heart desires rather to conceal than expose other people's weaknesses or misfortunes. If you have wit, use it to please, and not to hurt; you may shine, like the sun in the temperate zones, without scorching. Here it is wished for; under the Line it is dreaded.

[4] These are some of the hints which my long experience in the great world enables me to give you; and which, if you attend to them, may prove useful to you, in your journey through it. I wish it may be a prosperous one, at least; I am sure that it must be your own fault if it is not.

[5] Make my compliments to Mr. Harte, who, I am very sorry to hear, is not well. I hope by this time he is recovered. Adieu!

QUESTIONS AND COMMENT ON FORM AND CONTENT

1. To what extent does the reason Chesterfield gives for pleasing women show his goals in life? What seems to be his main ambition for his son?

2. The second paragraph begins, "Women are only children of a larger growth." Dryden (*All for Love, Act IV, Scene i*) had said, "Men are but children of a larger growth." To what extent does Chesterfield's advice apply only to women? In which paragraph are men included?

3. Are the ideas expressed in this letter consistent with those in the other letters read?

4. What particular kind of flattery does he recommend as most effective?

5. What is the reference to Orpheus?

VOCABULARY: WHAT DO THE ITALICIZED WORDS MEAN?

. . . their *suffrages* go a great way toward establishing a man's character (1)

I will . . . let you into certain *arcana* (1)

They absolutely *stamp* every man's character in the *beau monde* (3)

. . . under the *Line* it is dreaded (3)

THEME SUGGESTIONS

On Flattery
Equal Education: Its Effect on the Status of Women
Women in Business Today
The Good (Bad) Qualities of Chesterfield's Advice
Women (Men) Are Children

PAUL'S CASE

Willa Cather

Willa Cather (1876-1947) was brought up in the Nebraska prairie country, which she wrote about in the novels O Pioneers, The Song of the Lark, *and* My Antonia. *She also wrote other novels and several volumes of short stories incluing* Youth and the Bright Medusa, *from which our selection is taken.*

She taught English for a time in Pittsburgh, the scene of "Paul's Case." She did not want her style of writing to distract the reader. She said, "I'd like the writing to be so lost in the object that it doesn't exist for the reader."

[1] It was Paul's afternoon to appear before the faculty of the Pittsburgh High School to account for his various misdemeanors. He had been suspended a week ago, and his father had called at the Principal's office and confessed his perplexity about his son. Paul entered the faculty room suave and smiling. His clothes were a trifle outgrown, and the tan velvet on the collar of his open overcoat was frayed and worn; but for all that there was something of the dandy about him, and he wore an opal pin in his neatly knotted black four-in-hand, and a red carnation in his buttonhole. This latter adornment the faculty somehow felt was not properly significant of the contrite spirit befitting a boy under the ban of suspension.

[2] Paul was tall for his age and very thin, with high, cramped shoulders and a narrow chest. His eyes were remarkable for a certain hysterical brilliancy, and he continually used them in a conscious, theatrical sort of way, peculiarly offensive in a boy. The pupils were abnormally large, as though he were addicted to belladonna, but there was a glassy glitter about them which that drug does not produce.

[3] When questioned by the Principal as to why he was there, Paul stated, politely enough, that he wanted to come back to school. This was a lie, but Paul was quite accustomed to lying; found it, indeed, indispensable for overcoming friction. His teachers were asked to state their respective charges against him, which they did with such a rancour and aggrievedness as evinced that this was not a usual case. Disorder and impertinence were among the offenses named, yet each of his instructors felt that it was scarcely possible to put into words the real cause of the trouble, which lay in a sort of hysterically defiant manner of the boy's; in the contempt which they all knew he felt for them, and which he seemingly made not the least effort to conceal. Once, when he had been making a synopsis of a paragraph at the blackboard, his English teacher had stepped to his side and attempted to guide his hand. Paul had started back with a shudder and thrust his hands violently behind him. The astonished woman could scarcely have been more hurt and embarrassed had he struck at her. The insult was so involuntary and definitely personal as to be unforgettable. In one way and another, he had made all his teachers, men and women alike, conscious of the same feeling of physical aversion. In one class he habitually sat with his hand shading his eyes; in another he always looked out of the window during the recitation; in another he made a running commentary on the lecture, with humorous intent.

[4] His teachers felt this afternoon that his whole attitude was symbolized by his shrug and his flippantly red carnation flower, and they fell upon him without mercy, his English teacher leading the pack. He stood through it smiling, his pale lips parted over his white teeth. (His lips were continually twitching, and he had a habit of raising his eyebrows that was contemptuous and irritating to the last degree.) Older boys than Paul had broken down and shed tears under that ordeal, but his set smile did not once desert him, and his only sign of discomfort was the nervous trembling of the fingers that toyed with the buttons of his overcoat, and an occasional jerking of the other hand which held his hat. Paul was always smiling, always glancing about him, seeming to feel that people might be watching him and trying to detect something. This conscious expression, since it was as far as possible from boyish mirthfulness, was usually attributed to insolence or "smartness."

[5] As the inquisition proceeded, one of his instructors repeated an impertinent remark of the boy's, and the Principal asked him whether he thought that a courteous speech to make to a woman. Paul shrugged his shoulders slightly and his eyebrows twitched.

[6] "I don't know," he replied. "I didn't mean to be polite or impolite, either. I guess it's a sort of way I have of saying things regardless."

[7] The Principal asked him whether he didn't think that a way it

would be well to get rid of. Paul grinned and said he guessed so. When he was told that he could go, he bowed gracefully and went out. His bow was like a repetition of the scandalous red carnation.

[8] His teachers were in despair, and his drawing master voiced the feeling of them all when he declared there was something about the boy which none of them understood. He added: "I don't really believe that smile of his comes altogether from insolence; there's something sort of haunted about it. The boy is not strong, for one thing. There is something wrong about the fellow."

[9] The drawing master had come to realize that, in looking at Paul, one saw only his white teeth and the forced animation of his eyes. One warm afternoon the boy had gone to sleep at his drawing-board, and his master had noted with amazement what a white, blue-veined face it was; drawn and wrinkled like an old man's about the eyes, the lips twitching even in his sleep.

[10] His teachers left the building dissatisfied and unhappy; humiliated to have felt so vindictive toward a mere boy, to have uttered this feeling in cutting terms, and to have set each other on, as it were, in the the gruesome game of intemperate reproach. One of them remembered having seen a miserable street cat set at bay by a ring of tormentors.

[11] As for Paul, he ran down the hill whistling the Soldiers' Chorus from *Faust,* looking wildly behind him now and then to see whether some of his teachers were not there to witness his light-heartedness. As it was now late in the afternoon and Paul was on duty that evening as usher at Carnegie Hall, he decided that he would not go home to supper.

[12] When he reached the concert hall the doors were not yet open. It was chilly outside, and he decided to go up into the picture gallery— always deserted at this hour—where there were some of Raffelli's gay studies of Paris streets and an airy blue Venetian scene or two that always exhilarated him. He was delighted to find no one in the gallery but the old guard, who sat in the corner, a newspaper on his knee, a black patch over one eye and the other closed. Paul possessed himself of the place and walked confidently up and down, whistling under his breath. After a while he sat down before a blue Rico and lost himself. When he bethought him to look at his watch, it was after seven o'clock, and he rose with a start and ran downstairs, making a face at Augustus Caesar, peering out from the cast-room, and an evil gesture at the Venus of Milo as he passed her on the stairway.

[13] When Paul reached the ushers' dressing-room half a dozen boys were there already, and he began excitedly to tumble into his uniform. It was one of the few that at all approached fitting, and Paul thought it very becoming—though he knew the tight, straight coat accentuated his narrow chest, about which he was exceedingly sensitive. He was always ex-

cited while he dressed, twanging all over to the tuning of the strings and the preliminary flourishes of the horns in the music-room; but tonight he seemed quite beside himself, and he teased and plagued the boys until, telling him that he was crazy, they put him down on the floor and sat on him.

[14] Somewhat calmed by his suppression, Paul dashed out to the front of the house to seat the early comers. He was a model usher. Gracious and smiling he ran up and down the aisles. Nothing was too much trouble for him; he carried messages and brought programs as though it were his greatest pleasure in life, and all the people in his section thought him a charming boy, feeling that he remembered and admired them. As the house filled, he grew more and more vivacious and animated, and the color came to his cheeks and lips. It was very much as though this were a great reception and Paul were the host. Just as the musicians came out to take their places, his English teacher arrived with checks for the seats which a prominent manufacturer had taken for the season. She betrayed some embarrassment when she handed Paul the tickets, and a *hauteur* which subsequently made her feel very foolish. Paul was startled for a moment, and had the feeling of wanting to put her out; what business had she here among all these fine people and gay colors? He looked her over and decided that she was not appropriately dressed and must be a fool to sit downstairs in such togs. The tickets had probably been sent her out of kindness, he reflected, as he put down a seat for her, and she had about as much right to sit there as he had.

[15] When the symphony began Paul sank into one of the rear seats with a long sigh of relief, and lost himself as he had done before the Rico. It was not that symphonies, as such, meant anything in particular to Paul, but the first sigh of the instruments seemed to free some hilarious spirit within him; something that struggled there like the Genius in the bottle found by the Arab fisherman. He felt a sudden zest of life; the lights danced before his eyes and the concert hall blazed into unimaginable splendor. When the soprano soloist came on, Paul forgot even the nastiness of his teacher's being there, and gave himself up to the peculiar intoxication such personages always had for him. The soloist chanced to be a German woman, by no means in her first youth, and the mother of many children; but she wore a satin gown and a tiara, and she had that indefinable air of achievement, that world-shine upon her, which always blinded Paul to any possible defects.

[16] After a concert was over, Paul was often irritable and wretched until he got to sleep—and tonight he was even more than usually restless. He had the feeling of not being able to let down; of its being impossible to give up this delicious excitement which was the only thing that could be called living at all. During the last number he withdrew and, after

hastily changing his clothes in the dressing-room, slipped out to the side door where the singer's carriage stood. Here he began pacing rapidly up and down the walk, waiting to see her come out.

[17]Over yonder the Schenley, in its vacant stretch, loomed big and square through the fine rain, the windows of its twelve stories glowing like those of a lighted cardboard house under a Christmas tree. All the actors and singers of any importance stayed there when they were in the city, and a number of the big manufacturers of the place lived there in the winter. Paul had often hung about the hotel, watching the people go in and out, longing to enter and leave school-masters and dull care behind him forever.

[18] At last the singer came out, accompanied by the conductor, who helped her into her carriage and closed the door with a cordial *"Auf Wiedersehen"*—which set Paul to wondering whether she were not an old sweetheart of his. Paul followed the carriage over to the hotel, walking so rapidly as not to be far from the entrance when the singer alighted and disappeared behind the swinging glass doors which were opened by a Negro in a tall hat and a long coat. In the moment that the door was ajar, it seemed to Paul that he, too, entered. He seemed to feel himself go after her up the steps, into the warm, lighted building, into an exotic, a tropical world of shiny, glistening surfaces and basking ease. He reflected upon the mysterious dishes that were brought into the dining-room, the green bottles in buckets of ice, as he had seen them in the supper party pictures of the Sunday supplement. A quick gust of wind brought the rain down with sudden vehemence, and Paul was startled to find that he was still outside in the slush of the gravel driveway; that his boots were letting in the water and his scanty overcoat was clinging wet about him; that the lights in front of the concert hall were out, and that the rain was driving in sheets between him and the orange glow of the windows above him. There it was, what he wanted—tangibly before him like the fairy world of a Christmas pantomime; as the rain beat in his face, Paul wondered whether he were destined always to shiver in the black night outside, looking up at it.

[19] He turned and walked reluctantly toward the car tracks. The end had to come sometime; his father in his night-clothes at the top of the stairs, explanations that did not explain, hastily improvised fictions that were forever tripping him up, his upstairs room and its horrible yellow wall-paper, the creaking bureau with the greasy plush collar-box, and over his painted wooden bed the pictures of George Washington and John Calvin, and the framed motto, "Feed my Lambs," which had been worked in red worsted by his mother, whom Paul could not remember.

[20] Half an hour later Paul alighted from the Negley Avenue car and went slowly down one of the side streets off the main thoroughfare. It

was a highly respectable street, where all the houses were exactly alike, and where business men of moderate means begot and reared large families of children, all of whom went to Sabbath-school and learned the shorter catechism, and were interested in arithmetic; all of whom were as exactly alike as their homes, and of a piece with the monotony in which they lived. Paul never went up Cordelia Street without a shudder of loathing. His home was next the house of the Cumberland minister. He approached it tonight with the nerveless sense of defeat, the hopeless feeling of sinking back forever into ugliness and commonness, that he had always had when he came home. The moment he turned into Cordelia Street, he felt the waters close above his head. After each of these orgies of living, he experienced all the physical depression which follows a debauch; the loathing of respectable beds, of common food, of a house permeated by kitchen odors; a shuddering repulsion for the flavorless, colorless mass of everyday existence; a morbid desire for cool things and soft lights and fresh flowers.

[21] The nearer he approached the house, the more absolutely unequal Paul felt to the sight of it all; his ugly sleeping chamber; the cold bathroom with the grimy zinc tub, the cracked mirror, the dripping spigots; his father, at the top of the stairs, his hairy legs sticking out from his nightshirt, his feet thrust into carpet slippers. He was so much later than usual that there would certainly be inquiries and reproaches. Paul stopped short before the door. He felt that he could not be accosted by his father tonight; that he could not toss again on that miserable bed. He would not go in. He would tell his father that he had no carfare, and it was raining so hard he had gone home with one of the boys and stayed all night.

[22] Meanwhile, he was wet and cold. He went around to the back of the house and tried one of the basement windows, found it open, raised it cautiously, and scrambled down the cellar wall to the floor. There he stood, holding his breath, terrified by the noise he had made; but the floor above him was silent, and there was no creak on the stairs. He found a soap-box, and carried it over to the soft ring of light that streamed from the furnace door, and sat down. He was horribly afraid of rats, so he did not try to sleep, but sat looking distrustfully at the dark, still terrified lest he might have awakened his father. In such reactions, after one of the experiences which made days and nights out of the dreary blanks of the calendar, when his senses were deadened, Paul's head was always singularly clear. Suppose his father had heard him getting in at the window and had come down and shot him for a burglar? Then, again, suppose his father had come down, pistol in hand, and he had cried out in time to save himself, and his father had been horrified to think how nearly he had killed him? Then, again, suppose a day should come when his father would remember that night, and wish there had been no warn-

ing cry to stay his hand? With this last supposition Paul entertained himself until daybreak.

[23] The following Sunday was fine; the sodden November chill was broken by the last flash of autumnal summer. In the morning Paul had to go to church and Sabbath-school, as always. On seasonable Sunday afternoons the burghers of Cordelia Street usually sat out on their front "stoops," and talked to their neighbors on the next stoop, or called to those across the street in neighborly fashion. The men sat placidly on gay cushions placed upon the steps that led down to the sidewalk, while the women, in their Sunday "waists," sat in rockers on the cramped porches, pretending to be greatly at their ease. The children played in the streets; there were so many of them that the place resembled the rec- reation grounds of a kindergarten. The men on the steps—all in their shirt sleeves, their vests unbuttoned—sat with their legs well apart, their stomachs comfortably protruding, and talked of the prices of things, or told anecdotes of the sagacity of their various chiefs and overlords. They occasionally looked over the multitude of squabbling children, listened affectionately to their high-pitched, nasal voices, smiling to see their own proclivities reproduced in their offspring, and interspersed their legends of the iron kings with remarks about their sons' progress at school, their grades in arithmetic, and the amounts they had saved in their toy banks.

[24] On this last Sunday of November, Paul sat all the afternoon on the lowest step of his "stoop," staring into the street, while his sisters, in their rockers, were talking to the minister's daughters next door about how many shirtwaists they had made in the last week, and how many waffles some one had eaten at the last church supper. When the weather was warm, and his father was in a particularly jovial frame of mind, the girls made lemonade, which was always brought out in a red-glass pitcher, ornamented with forget-me-nots in blue enamel. This the girls thought very fine, and the neighbors joked about the suspicious color of the pitcher.

[25] Today Paul's father, on the top step, was talking to a young man who shifted a restless baby from knee to knee. He happened to be the young man who was daily held up to Paul as a model, and after whom it was his father's dearest hope that he would pattern. This young man was of a ruddy complexion, with a compressed, red mouth, and faded, near-sighted eyes, over which he wore thick spectacles, with gold bows that curved about his ears. He was clerk to one of the magnates of a great steel corporation, and was looked upon in Cordelia Street as a young man with a future. There was a story that, some five years ago— he was now barely twenty-six—he had been a trifle "dissipated," but in order to curb his appetites and save the loss of time and strength that a sowing of wild oats might have entailed, he had taken his chief's advice,

oft reiterated to his employés, and at twenty-one had married the first woman whom he could persuade to share his fortunes. She happened to be an angular school-mistress, much older than he, who also wore thick glasses, and who had now borne him four children, all near-sighted, like herself.

[26] The young man was relating how his chief, now cruising in the Mediterranean, kept in touch with all the details of the business, arranging his office hours on his yacht just as though he were at home, and "knocking off work enough to keep two stenographers busy." His father told, in turn, the plan his corporation was considering, of putting in an electric railway plant at Cairo. Paul snapped his teeth; he had an awful apprehension that they might spoil it all before he got there. Yet he rather liked to hear these legends of the iron kings, that were told and retold on Sundays and holidays; these stories of palaces in Venice, yachts on the Mediterranean, and high play at Monte Carlo appealed to his fancy, and he was interested in the triumphs of cash boys who had become famous, though he had no mind for the cash-boy stage.

[27] After supper was over, and he had helped to dry the dishes, Paul nervously asked his father whether he could go to George's to get some help in his geometry, and still more nervously asked for carfare. This latter request he had to repeat, as his father, on principle, did not like to hear requests for money, whether much or little. He asked Paul whether he could not go to some boy who lived nearer, and told him that he ought not to leave his school work until Sunday; but he gave him the dime. He was not a poor man, but he had a worthy ambition to come up in the world. His only reason for allowing Paul to usher was that he thought a boy ought to be earning a little.

[28] Paul bounded upstairs, scrubbed the greasy odor of the dishwater from his hands with the ill-smelling soap he hated, and then shook over his fingers a few drops of violet water from the bottle he kept hidden in his drawer. He left the house with his geometry conspicuously under his arm, and the moment he got out of Cordelia Street and boarded a downtown car, he shook off the lethargy of two deadening days, and began to live again.

[29] The leading juvenile of the permanent stock company which played at one of the downtown theatres was an acquaintance of Paul's, and the boy had been invited to drop in at the Sunday-night rehearsals whenever he could. For more than a year Paul had spent every available moment loitering about Charley Edwards's dressing-room. He had won a place among Edwards's following not only because the young actor, who could not afford to employ a dresser, often found him useful, but because he recognized in Paul something akin to what churchmen term "vocation."

[30] It was at the theatre and at Carnegie Hall that Paul really lived; the rest was but a sleep and a forgetting. This was Paul's fairy tale, and it had for him all the allurement of a secret love. The moment he inhaled the gassy, painty, dusty odor behind the scenes, he breathed like a prisoner set free, and felt within him the possibility of doing or saying splendid, brilliant things. The moment the cracked orchestra beat out the overture from *Martha*, or jerked at the serenade from *Rigoletto*, all stupid and ugly things slid from him, and his senses were deliciously, yet delicately fired.

[31] Perhaps it was because, in Paul's world, the natural nearly always wore the guise of ugliness, that a certain element of artificiality seemed to him necessary in beauty. Perhaps it was because his experience of life elsewhere was so full of Sabbath-school picnics, petty economies, wholesome advice as to how to succeed in life, and the unescapable odors of cooking, that he found this existence so alluring, these smartly-clad men and women so attractive, that he was so moved by these starry apple orchards that bloomed perennially under the limelight.

[32] It would be difficult to put it strongly enough how convincingly the stage entrance of that theatre was for Paul the actual portal of Romance. Certainly none of the company ever suspected it, least of all Charley Edwards. It was very like the old stories that used to float about London of fabulously rich Jews, who had subterranean halls, with palms, and fountains, and soft lamps and richly appareled women who never saw the disenchanting light of London day. So, in the midst of that smoke-palled city, enamored of figures and grimy toil, Paul had his secret temple, his wishing-carpet, his bit of blue-and-white Mediterranean shore bathed in perpetual sunshine.

[33] Several of Paul's teachers had a theory that his imagination had been perverted by garish fiction; but the truth was, he scarcely ever read at all. The books at home were not such as would either tempt or corrupt a youthful mind, and as for reading the novels that some of his friends urged upon him—well, he got what he wanted much more quickly from music, from an orchestra to a barrel organ. He needed only the spark, the indescribable thrill that made his imagination master of his senses, and he could make plots and pictures enough of his own. It was equally true that he was not stage-struck—not, at any rate, in the usual acceptation of that expression. He had no desire to become an actor, any more than he had to become a musician. He felt no necessity to do any of these things; what he wanted was to see, to be in the atmosphere, float on the wave of it, to be carried out, blue league after blue league, away from everything.

[34] After a night behind the scenes, Paul found his schoolroom more

than ever repulsive; the hard floors and naked walls; the prosy men who never wore frock coats, or violets in their button-holes; the women with their dull gowns, shrill voices, and pitiful seriousness about prepositions that govern the dative. He could not bear to have the other pupils think, for a moment, that he took these people seriously; he must convey to them that he considered it all trivial, and was there only by way of a joke, anyway. He had autograph pictures of all the members of the stock company which he showed his classmates, telling them the most incredible stories of his familiarity with these people, of his acquaintance with the soloists who came to Carnegie Hall, his suppers with them and the flowers he sent them. When these stories lost their effect, and his audience grew listless, he would bid all the boys goodbye, announcing that he was going to travel for a while; going to Naples, to California, to Egypt. Then, next Monday, he would slip back, conscious and nervously smiling; his sister was ill, and he would have to defer his voyage until spring.

[35] Matters went steadily worse with Paul at school. In the itch to let his instructors know how heartily he despised them, and how thoroughly he was appreciated elsewhere, he mentioned once or twice that he had no time to fool with theorems; adding—with a twitch of the eyebrows and a touch of that nervous bravado which so perplexed them— that he was helping the people down at the stock company; they were old friends of his.

[36] The upshot of the matter was, that the Principal went to Paul's father, and Paul was taken out of school and put to work. The manager at Carnegie Hall was told to get another usher in his stead; the doorkeeper at the theatre was warned not to admit him to the house; and Charley Edwards remorsefully promised the boy's father not to see him again.

[37] The members of the stock company were vastly amused when some of Paul's stories reached them—especially the women. They were hard-working women, most of them supporting indolent husbands or brothers, and they laughed rather bitterly at having stirred the boy to such fervid and florid inventions. They agreed with the faculty and with his father, that Paul's was a bad case.

[38] The eastbound train was plowing through a January snowstorm; the dull dawn was beginning to show gray when the engine whistled a mile out of Newark. Paul started up from the seat where he had lain curled in uneasy slumber, rubbed the breath-misted window glass with his hand, and peered out. The snow was whirling in curling eddies above the white bottom lands, and the drifts lay already deep in the fields and along the fences, while here and there the long dead grass and dried

weed stalks protruded black above it. Lights shone from the scattered houses, and a gang of laborers who stood beside the track waved their lanterns.

[39] Paul had slept very little, and he felt grimy and uncomfortable. He had made the all-night journey in a day coach because he was afraid if he took a Pullman he might be seen by some Pittsburgh business man who had noticed him in Denny & Carson's office. When the whistle woke him, he clutched quickly at his breast pocket, glancing about him with an uncertain smile. But the little, clay-bespattered Italians were still sleeping, the slatternly women across the aisle were in open-mouthed oblivion, and even the crumby, crying babies were for the nonce stilled. Paul settled back to struggle with his impatience as best he could.

[40] When he arrived at the Jersey City Station, he hurried through his breakfast, manifestly ill at ease and keeping a sharp eye about him. After he reached the Twenty-third Street Station, he consulted a cabman, and had himself driven to a men's furnishing establishment which was just opening for the day. He spent upward of two hours there, buying with endless reconsidering and great care. His new street suit he put on in the fitting-room; the frock coat and dress clothes he had bundled into the cab with his new shirts. Then he drove to a hatter's and a shoe house. His next errand was at Tiffany's, where he selected silver-mounted brushes and a scarf-pin. He would not wait to have his silver marked, he said. Lastly, he stopped at a trunk shop on Broadway, and had his purchases packed into various traveling bags.

[41] It was a little after one o'clock when he drove up to the Waldorf, and, after settling with the cabman, went into the office. He registered from Washington; said his mother and father had been abroad, and that he had come down to await the arrival of their steamer. He told his story plausibly and had no trouble, since he offered to pay for them in advance, in engaging his rooms: a sleeping-room, sitting-room and bath.

[42] Not once, but a hundred times Paul had planned this entry into New York. He had gone over every detail of it with Charley Edwards, and in his scrap book at home there were pages of description about New York hotels, cut from the Sunday papers.

[43] When he was shown to his sitting-room on the eighth floor, he saw at a glance that everything was as it should be; there was but one detail in his mental picture that the place did not realize, so he rang for the bell boy and sent him down for flowers. He moved about nervously until the boy returned, putting away his new linen and fingering it delightedly as he did so. When the flowers came, he put them hastily into water, and then tumbled into a hot bath. Presently he came out of his white bathroom, resplendent in his new silk underwear, and playing with the tassels of his red robe. The snow was whirling so fiercely outside

his windows that he could scarcely see across the street; but within, the air was deliciously soft and fragrant. He put the violets and jonquils on the tabouret beside the couch, and threw himself down with a long sigh, covering himself with a Roman blanket. He was thoroughly tired; he had been in such haste, he had stood up to such a strain, covered so much ground in the last twenty-four hours, that he wanted to think how it had all come about. Lulled by the sound of the wind, the warm air, and the cool fragrance of the flowers, he sank into deep, drowsy retrospection.

[44] It had been wonderfully simple; when they had shut him out of the theatre and concert hall, when they had taken away his bone, the whole thing was virtually determined. The rest was a mere matter of opportunity. The only thing that at all surprised him was his own courage —for he realized well enough that he had always been tormented by fear, a sort of apprehensive dread that, of late years, as the meshes of the lies he had told closed about him, had been pulling the muscles of his body tighter and tighter. Until now, he could not remember a time when he had not been dreading something. Even when he was a little boy, it was always there—behind him, or before, or on either side. There had always been the shadowed corner, the dark place into which he dared not look, but from which something seemed always to be watching him —and Paul had done things that were not pretty to watch, he knew.

[45] But now he had a curious sense of relief, as though he had at last thrown down the gauntlet to the thing in the corner.

[46] Yet it was but a day since he had been sulking in the traces; but yesterday afternoon that he had been sent to the bank with Denny & Carson's deposit as usual—but this time he was instructed to leave the book to be balanced. There was above two thousand dollars in checks, and nearly a thousand in the bank notes which he had taken from the book and quietly transferred to his pocket. At the bank he had made out a new deposit slip. His nerves had been steady enough to permit of his returning to the office, where he had finished his work and asked for a full day's holiday tomorrow, Saturday, giving a perfectly reasonable pretext. The bank book, he knew, would not be returned before Monday or Tuesday, and his father would be out of town for the next week. From the time he slipped the bank notes into his pocket until he boarded the night train for New York, he had not known a moment's hesitation.

[47] How astonishingly easy it had all been; here he was, the thing done; and this time there would be no awakening, no figure at the top of the stairs. He watched the snowflakes whirling by his window until he fell asleep.

[48] When he awoke, it was four o'clock in the afternoon. He bounded up with a start; one of his precious days gone already! He spent nearly an hour in dressing, watching every stage of his toilet carefully in the

mirror. Everything was quite perfect; he was exactly the kind of boy he had always wanted to be.

[49] When he went downstairs, Paul took a carriage and drove up Fifth Avenue toward the Park. The snow had somewhat abated; carriages and tradesmen's wagons were hurrying soundlessly to and fro in the winter twilight; boys in woolen mufflers were shoveling off the doorsteps; the avenue stages made fine spots of color against the white street. Here and there on the corners were stands, with whole flower gardens blooming behind glass windows, against which the snowflakes stuck and melted; violets, roses, carnations, lilies of the valley—somehow vastly more lovely and alluring that they blossomed thus unnaturally in the snow. The Park itself was a wonderful stage winter piece.

[50] When he returned, the pause of the twilight had ceased, and the tune of the streets had changed. The snow was falling faster, lights streamed from the hotels that reared their many stories fearlessly up into the storm, defying the raging Atlantic winds. A long, black stream of carriages poured down the avenue, intersected here and there by other streams, tending horizontally. There were a score of cabs about the entrance of his hotel, and his driver had to wait. Boys in livery were running in and out of the awning stretched across the sidewalk, up and down the red velvet carpet laid from the door to the street. Above, about, within it all, was the rumble and roar, the hurry and toss of thousands of human beings as hot for pleasure as himself, and on every side of him towered the glaring affirmation of the omnipotence of wealth.

[51] The boy set his teeth and drew his shoulders together in a spasm of realization; the plot of all dramas, the text of all romances, the nerve-stuff of all sensations was whirling about him like the snowflakes. He burnt like a faggot in a tempest.

[52] When Paul came down to dinner, the music of the orchestra floated up the elevator shaft to greet him. As he stepped into the thronged corridor, he sank back into one of the chairs against the wall to get his breath. The lights, the chatter, the perfumes, the bewildering medley of color—he had, for a moment, the feeling of not being able to stand it. But only for a moment; these were his own people, he told himself. He went slowly about the corridors, through the writing-rooms, smoking-rooms, reception-rooms as though he were exploring the chambers of an enchanted palace, built and peopled for him alone.

[53] When he reached the dining-room he sat down at a table near a window. The flowers, the white linen, the many-colored wine glasses, the gay toilettes of the women, the low popping of corks, the undulating repetitions of the *Blue Danube* from the orchestra, all flooded Paul's dream with bewildering radiance. When the roseate tinge of his champagne was added—that cold, precious bubbling stuff that creamed and

foamed in his glass—Paul wondered that there were honest men in the world at all. This was what all the world was fighting for, he reflected; this was what all the struggle was about. He doubted the reality of his past. Had he ever known a place called Cordelia Street, a place where fagged-looking business men boarded the early car? Mere rivets in a machine they seemed to Paul—sickening men, with combings of children's hair always hanging to their coats, and the smell of cooking in their clothes. Cordelia Street—ah, that belonged to another time and country! Had he not always been thus, had he not sat here night after night, from as far back as he could remember, looking pensively over just such shimmering textures, and slowly twirling the stem of a glass like this one between his thumb and middle finger? He rather thought he had.

[54] He was not in the least abashed or lonely. He had no especial desire to meet or to know any of these people; all he demanded was the right to look on and conjecture, to watch the pageant. The mere stage properties were all he contended for. Nor was he lonely later in the evening, in his loge at the Opera. He was entirely rid of his nervous misgivings, of his forced aggressiveness, of the imperative desire to show himself different from his surroundings. He felt now that his surroundings explained him. Nobody questioned his purple; he had only to wear it passively. He had only to glance down at his dress coat to reassure himself that here it would be impossible for any one to humiliate him.

[55] He found it hard to leave his beautiful sitting-room to go to bed that night, and sat long watching the raging storm from his turret window. When he went to sleep, it was with the lights turned on in his bedroom; partly because of his old timidity, and partly so that, if he should wake in the night, there would be no wretched moment of doubt, no horrible suspicion of yellow wallpaper, or of Washington and Calvin above his bed.

[56] On Sunday morning the city was practically snowbound. Paul breakfasted late, and in the afternoon he fell in with a wild San Francisco boy, a freshman at Yale, who said he had run down for a "little flyer" over Sunday. The young man offered to show Paul the night side of the town, and the two boys went off together after dinner, not returning to the hotel until seven o'clock the next morning. They had started out in the confiding warmth of a champagne friendship, but their parting in the elevator was singularly cool. The freshman pulled himself together to make his train, and Paul went to bed. He awoke at two o'clock in the afternoon, very thirsty and dizzy, and rang for ice-water, coffee, and the Pittsburgh papers.

[57] On the part of the hotel management, Paul excited no suspicion. There was this to be said for him, that he wore his spoils with dignity

and in no way made himself conspicuous. His chief greediness lay in his ears and eyes, and his excesses were not offensive ones. His dearest pleasures were the gray winter twilights in his sitting-room; his quiet enjoyment of his flowers, his clothes, his wide divan, his cigarette and his sense of power. He could not remember a time when he had felt so at peace with himself. The mere release from the necessity of petty lying, lying every day and every day, restored his self-respect. He had never lied for pleasure, even at school; but to make himself noticed and admired, to assert his difference from other Cordelia Street boys; and he felt a good deal more manly, more honest, even, now that he had no need for boastful pretensions, now that he could, as his actor friends used to say, "dress the part." It was characteristic that remorse did not occur to him. His golden days went by without a shadow, and he made each as perfect as he could.

[58] On the eighth day after his arrival in New York, he found the whole affair exploited in the Pittsburgh papers, exploited with a wealth of detail which indicated that local news of a sensational nature was at a low ebb. The firm of Denny & Carson announced that the boy's father had refunded the full amount of his theft, and that they had no intention of prosecuting. The Cumberland minister had been interviewed, and expressed his hope of yet reclaiming the motherless lad, and Paul's Sabbath-school teacher declared that she would spare no effort to that end. The rumor had reached Pittsburgh that the boy had been seen in a New York hotel, and his father had gone East to find him and bring him home.

[59] Paul had just come in to dress for dinner; he sank into a chair, weak in the knees, and clasped his head in his hands. It was to be worse than jail, even; the tepid waters of Cordelia Street were to close over him finally and forever. The gray monotony stretched before him in hopeless, unrelieved years; Sabbath-school, Young People's Meeting, the yellow-papered room, the damp dish-towels; it all rushed back upon him with sickening vividness. He had the old feeling that the orchestra had suddenly stopped, the sinking sensation that the play was over. The sweat broke out on his face, and he sprang to his feet, looked about him with his white, conscious smile, and winked at himself in the mirror. With something of the childish belief in miracles with which he had so often gone to class, all his lessons unlearned, Paul dressed and dashed whistling down the corridor to the elevator.

[60] He had no sooner entered the dining-room and caught the measure of the music, than his remembrance was lightened by his old elastic power of claiming the moment, mounting with it, and finding it all-sufficient. The glare and glitter about him, the mere scenic accessories had again, and for the last time, their old potency. He would show himself that he was game, he would finish the thing splendidly. He doubted,

more than ever, the existence of Cordelia Street, and for the first time he drank his wine recklessly. Was he not, after all, one of these fortunate beings? Was he not still himself, and in his own place? He drummed a nervous accompaniment to the music and looked about him, telling himself over and over that it had paid.

[61] He reflected drowsily, to the swell of the violin and the chill sweetness of his wine, that he might have done it more wisely. He might have caught an outbound steamer and been well out of their clutches before now. But the other side of the world had seemed too far away and too uncertain then; he could not have waited for it; his need had been too sharp. If he had to choose over again, he would do the same thing tomorrow. He looked affectionately about the dining-room, now gilded with a soft mist. Ah, it had paid indeed!

[62] Paul was awakened next morning by a painful throbbing in his head and feet. He had thrown himself across the bed without undressing, and had slept with his shoes on. His limbs and hands were lead-heavy, and his tongue and throat were parched. There came upon him of those fateful attacks of clear-headedness that never occurred except when he was physically exhausted and his nerves hung loose. He lay still and closed his eyes and let the tide of his realities wash over him.

[63] His father was in New York; "stopping at some joint or other," he told himself. The memory of successive summers on the front stoop fell upon him like a weight of black water. He had not a hundred dollars left; and he knew now, more than ever, that money was everything, the wall that stood between all he loathed and all he wanted. The thing was winding itself up; he had thought of that on his first glorious day in New York, and had even provided a way to snap the thread. It lay on his dressing-table now; he had got it out last night when he came blindly up from dinner—but the shiny metal hurt his eyes, and he disliked the look of it, anyway.

[64] He rose and moved about with a painful effort, succumbing now and again to attacks of nausea. It was the old depression exaggerated; all the world had become Cordelia Street. Yet somehow he was not afraid of anything, was absolutely calm; perhaps because he had looked into the dark corner at last, and knew. It was bad enough, what he saw there; but somehow not so bad as his long fear of it had been. He saw everything clearly now. He had a feeling that he had made the best of it, that he had lived the sort of life he was meant to live, and for half an hour he sat staring at the revolver. But he told himself that was not the way, so he went downstairs and took a cab to the ferry.

[65] When Paul arrived at Newark, he got off the train and took another cab, directing the driver to follow the Pennsylvania tracks out of the town. The snow lay heavy on the roadways and had drifted

deep in the open fields. Only here and there the dead grass or dried weed stalks projected, singularly black, above it. Once well into the country, Paul dismissed the carriage and walked, floundering along the tracks, his mind a medley of irrelevant things. He seemed to hold in his brain an actual picture of everything he had seen that morning. He remembered every feature of both his drivers, the toothless old woman from whom he had bought the red flowers in his coat, the agent from whom he had got his ticket, and all of his fellow-passengers on the ferry. His mind, unable to cope with vital matters near at hand, worked feverishly and deftly at sorting and grouping these images. They made for him a part of the ugliness of the world, of the ache in his head, and the bitter burning on his tongue. He stooped and put a handful of snow into his mouth as he walked, but that, too, seemed hot. When he reached a little hillside, where the tracks ran through a cut some twenty feet below him, he stopped and sat down.

[66] The carnations in his coat were drooping with the cold, he noticed; all their red glory over. It occurred to him that all the flowers he had seen in the show windows that first night must have gone the same way, long before this. It was only one splendid breath they had, in spite of their brave mockery at the winter outside the glass. It was a losing game in the end, it seemed, this revolt against the homilies by which the world is run. Paul took one of the blossoms carefully from his coat and scooped a little hole in the snow, where he covered it up. Then he dozed a while, from his weak condition, seeming insensible to the cold.

[67] The sound of an approaching train woke him, and he started to his feet, remembering only his resolution, and afraid lest he should be too late. He stood watching the approaching locomotive, his teeth chattering, his lips drawn away from them in a frightened smile; once or twice he glanced nervously sidewise, as though he were being watched. When the right moment came, he jumped. As he fell, the folly of his haste occurred to him with merciless clearness, the vastness of what he had left undone. There flashed through his brain, clearer than ever before, the blue of Adriatic water, the yellow of Algerian sands.

[68] He felt something strike his chest—his body was being thrown swiftly through the air, on and on, immeasurably far and fast, while his limbs gently relaxed. Then, because the picture-making mechanism was crushed, the disturbing visions flashed into black, and Paul dropped back into the immense design of things.

QUESTIONS AND COMMENT ON FORM AND CONTENT

1. What does the word *case* in the title suggest?

2. Like most modern short stories this one begins with an unsatisfactory situation—unsatisfactory to Paul and to all who dealt with him, especially to his teachers and his father. The first paragraph explains the situation (the *who, why, where, when,* sometimes called the "exposition") and gives his general appearance, the impression he would make on us. What items in this paragraph and the one that follows reveal character or personality?

3. Perhaps because this is a "case study," dialogue and detailed reproduction of scenes are used sparingly. Why did the teachers become petty and prejudiced?

4. How does each scene that follows, including the main ones in New York, help us to understand Paul? What caused Paul's rebellion and tragedy? One way of portraying a person is to show his effect on others. How did Paul affect others?

5. Could he have been helped by a sympathetic father, mother, or teacher? Should he have been encouraged to become a musician, an actor, or what?

6. Discuss the symbolism of the red carnation. How does Willa Cather use snow for mood and symbol?

7. Is the figure of speech in the final sentence effective? (This was written before television was familiar.)

VOCABULARY: WHAT DO THE ITALICIZED WORDS MEAN?

Paul entered the faculty room *suave* and smiling. (1)
. . . with such *rancour* and *aggrievedness* as *evinced* (3)
. . . feeling of physical *aversion* (3)
As the *inquisition* proceeded (5)
. . . grew more and more *vivacious* and *animated* (14)
She *betrayed* some embarrassment . . . and a *hauteur* (14)
. . . into an *exotic,* a tropical world (18)
. . . see their own *proclivities* reproduced (23)
. . . crying babies were for the *nonce* stilled (39)
. . . *manifestly* ill at ease (40)
. . . *glaring affirmation* of the *omnipotence* of wealth (50)
. . . not in the least *abashed* or lonely (54)
. . . the *homilies* by which the world is run (66)

THEME SUGGESTIONS

I Knew a Paul (or Mary) in High School
A High School Dropout
The Idols of Cordelia Street
Paul's View of Cordelia Street

A FATHER TO HIS SON

Carl Sandburg

Carl Sandburg (1878-   ) uses free verse in his poetry. See also comments in Chapters 2 and 4.

A father sees his son nearing manhood.
What shall he tell that son?
"Life is hard; be steel; be a rock."
And this might stand him for the storms
and serve him for humdrum and monotony
and guide him amid sudden betrayals
and tighten him for slack moments.
"Life is a soft loam; be gentle; go easy."
And this too might serve him.
Brutes have been gentled where lashes failed.
The growth of a frail flower in a path up
has sometimes shattered and split a rock.
A tough will counts. So does desire.
So does a rich soft wanting.
Without rich wanting nothing arrives.
Tell him too much money has killed men
and left them dead years before burial:
the quest of lucre beyond a few easy needs
has twisted good enough men
sometimes into dry thwarted worms.
Tell him time as a stuff can be wasted.
Tell him to be a fool every so often
and to have no shame over having been a fool
yet learning something out of every folly
hoping to repeat none of the cheap follies
thus arriving at intimate understanding
of a world numbering many fools.
Tell him to be alone often and get at himself
and above all tell himself no lies about himself
whatever the white lies and protective fronts
he may use amongst other people.
Tell him solitude is creative if he is strong

and the final decisions are made in silent rooms.
Tell him to be different from other people
if it comes natural and easy being different.
Let him have lazy days seeking his deeper motives.
Let him seek deep for where he is a born natural.
    Then he may understand Shakespeare
    and the Wright brothers, Pasteur, Pavlov,
    Michael Faraday and free imaginations
bringing changes into a world resenting change.
    He will be lonely enough
    to have time for the work
    he knows as his own.

QUESTIONS AND COMMENT ON FORM AND CONTENT

1. Can you list Sandburg's advice under the title "Sandburg's Ten Commandments"? Are there more or fewer than ten? Are some contradictory?
2. Can you resolve any seeming contradictions?
3. Are some of the qualities given added importance by space (number of lines) or position (at the beginning or end)?

THEME SUGGESTIONS

My Father's (Mother's) Advice to His (Her) Son (Daughter): An Imaginary Letter
Report: Polonius' Advice to Laertes (*Hamlet*, Act I, Scene iii)

A PRAYER FOR MY DAUGHTER

William Butler Yeats

William Butler Yeats (1865-1939) was one of the great poets of modern times. An active participant in the revival of the Irish theatre, he not only wrote plays for it but led in directing them. He received the Nobel Prize for his poetic plays in 1923. He was also a senator of the Irish Free State.

In this poem, Yeats is depressed because of civil strife in Ireland. He

feels still worse times are coming. With this feeling and a storm as a back-
ground he prays for his infant daughter.

Once more the storm is howling, and half hid
Under this cradle-hood and coverlid
My child sleeps on. There is no obstacle
But Gregory's wood and one bare hill
Whereby the haystack- and roof-levelling wind,
Bred on the Atlantic, can be stayed;
And for an hour I have walked and prayed
Because of the great gloom that is in my mind.

I have walked and prayed for this young child an hour
And heard the sea-wind scream upon the tower,
And under the arches of the bridge, and scream
In the elms above the flooded stream;
Imagining in excited reverie
That the future years had come,
Dancing to a frenzied drum,
Out of the murderous innocence of the sea.

May she be granted beauty and yet not
Beauty to make a stranger's eye distraught,
Or hers before a looking-glass, for such,
Being made beautiful overmuch,
Consider beauty a sufficient end,
Lose natural kindness and maybe
The heart-revealing intimacy
That chooses right, and never find a friend.

Helen[1] being chosen found life flat and dull
And later had much trouble from a fool,
While that great Queen,[2] that rose out of the spray,
Being fatherless could have her way
Yet chose a bandy-leggèd smith for man.
It's certain that fine women eat
A crazy salad with their meat
Whereby the Horn of Plenty is undone.

In courtesy I'd have her chiefly learned;

[1] Helen of Troy.
[2] Aphrodite, goddess of beauty who chose a lame blacksmith for a husband.

Hearts are not had as a gift but hearts are earned
By those that are not entirely beautiful;
Yet many, that have played the fool
For beauty's very self, has charm made wise,
And many a poor man that has roved,
Loved and thought himself beloved,
From a glad kindness cannot take his eyes.

May she become a flourishing hidden tree
That all her thoughts may like the linnet be,
And have no business but dispensing round
Their magnanimities of sound,
Nor but in merriment begin a chase,
Nor but in merriment a quarrel.
O may she live like some green laurel
Rooted in one dear perpetual place.

My mind, because the minds that I have loved,
The sort of beauty that I have approved,
Prosper but little, has dried up of late,
Yet knows that to be choked with hate
May well be of all evil chances chief.
If there's no hatred in a mind
Assault and battery of the wind
Can never tear the linnet from the leaf.

An intellectual hatred is the worst,
So let her think opinions are accursed.
Have I not seen the loveliest woman born[3]
Out of the mouth of Plenty's horn,
Because of her opinionated mind
Barter that horn and every good
By quiet natures understood
For an old bellows full of angry wind?

Considering that, all hatred driven hence,
The soul recovers radical innocence
And learns at last that it is self-delighting,
Self-appeasing, self-affrighting,
And that its own sweet will is Heaven's will;

[3] A reference to Maud Gonne, a political agitator, whom Yeats wooed unsuccessfully.

She can, though every face should scowl
And every windy quarter howl
Or every bellows burst, be happy still.

And may her bridegroom bring her to a house
Where all's accustomed, ceremonious;
For arrogance and hatred are the wares
Peddled in the thoroughfares.
How but in custom and in ceremony
Are innocence and beauty born?
Ceremony's a name for the rich horn,
And custom for the spreading laurel tree.

QUESTIONS AND COMMENT ON FORM AND CONTENT

1. What kind of person does Yeats want his daughter to become?

2. What especially does he want her to avoid?

3. What is another name for the rich horn or the horn of Plenty? What could it mean in the poem?

4. How did Yeats's experience with Maud Gonne apparently affect the choice of words, the figures of speech, the background of storm, and the prayer in general?

5. What is the rhyming scheme? Are the rhymes all exact? Are the lines all iambic pentameter? To what extent does the sentence structure differ from that of prose? If it had been written as prose, would you have identified it as poetry?

THEME SUGGESTIONS

A Prayer for My Daughter
A Prayer for My Son
A Prayer for My Son's Father

10 | COLLEGE LIFE

CAMPUS MARRIAGES—FOR BETTER OR FOR WORSE

James H. S. Bossard and Eleanor Stoker Boll

James H. S. Bossard (1888-1960), sociologist, was director of the William T. Carter Foundation for Child Development at the University of Pennsylvania.
Eleanor Stoker Boll (1888-   ), specialist in family relations, has also been associated with the William T. Carter Foundation for Child Development. She is Director, Educational Service Bureau, University of Pennsylvania.

[1] Until the late Nineteen Forties, the elders of higher education held firmly to the belief that marriage and education could never mix. Then the returning veterans of World War II arrived on college campuses. Some of them brought wives with them; some acquired wives after they came. Being married—a state hitherto reserved for administration or faculty members—was eagerly accepted by the college population, and an age-old academic tradition was shattered almost overnight.

[2] In 1957, according to the latest report by the Census Bureau, 29 percent of male college students and 10 percent of female students were married and living with their spouses. If students in the professional schools, 20 to 34 years of age, are included, the percentages are even

higher—41 percent of all male students and almost 18 percent of female students being married.

[3] "However, both men and women college students," the report continues, "were more likely to be attending on a part-time basis if they were married." Of part-time male students, 65 percent were married; of part-time female students, 27 percent were married. Of students attending full time, 17 percent of the men and 4 percent of the women were married.

[4] All this means that campus marriages are here to stay, and that the practice is not confined to an exceptional minority. Considering that our college population totaled three and a half million persons in 1957–58, we are concerned here with a revolution in both marriage and collegiate patterns of living.

[5] Obviously, this youthful revolution on the campus raises a number of important questions. First, how do campus marriages affect scholastic performance and participation in campus activities? Second, how do such marriages turn out as marriages? Do they tend to be brief interludes, a sort of practice experience to qualify for the later finals, or are they substantially like marriages off campus? Third, how will the total experience involved in these marriages affect the subsequent attitudes and philosophies of those concerned?

[6] Attempting to answer questions like these is not easy. One of the difficulties is the fact that campus marriages, like marriages in general, do not conform to one pattern about which broad generalizations can be made. There are a number of different types. Chief among them are marriages in which:

[7] (1) Both spouses are students. Bob and Alice were freshmen when they met. They married during the summer before their junior year. There is no question of their not finishing college. They live on campus in a rooming house, with familial duties minimized. Almost always, when both are students, they are subsidized by their families, either wholly or in part; rarely can two students marry and support themselves.

[8] (2) The husband is the student. Chet and Bea met at a fraternity house party. He still had a year and a half of undergraduate work to do. Bea, who had gone to secretarial school after graduation from high school, had a position in a bank that paid her $85 a week. Since Chet had a partial tuition scholarship, Bea decided they could marry with her footing the bills.

[9] (3) The wife is the student. Ed and Doris waited to marry until Ed had graduated and could support them—that was during Christmas vacation of Doris's junior year. Ed gave Doris, who had been a straight-A

student her first two years, every encouragement. He helped her with her school work and pinch-hit in the kitchen when she had examinations.

[10] (4) The couple has children. A baby creates special problems in any campus marriage. For the wife supporting her husband, pregnancy is little short of disaster. For the student wife supported by her husband, a baby means conflict between the roles of mother and student, both of which are demanding.

[11] These are the four major patterns in campus marriages, and each offers a different possibility in its effect on those involved and in the final outcome.

[12] *How do campus marriages affect scholastic performance and participation in campus activities?* Reports from several large universities agree that both men's and women's grades improve with engagement and after marriage. Several explanations are given for this. One sees it as the result of a "settling down" after the preoccupations with dating and other activities of the chase. The need of men students to get that degree in order to support families is sobering.

[13] Again, if both the bride and bridegroom are students, they may share a common interest in their studies, may aid each other, or even find an incentive in competing with each other. True, the last may lead to other problems, but at least there is a salutary effect upon grades.

[14] In the division of our own university in which the largest number of women is enrolled, no married woman has ever been dropped for scholastic deficiency. Withdrawals for other reasons occur, to be sure. Chief among these are pregnancy and financial difficulties, the two often appearing simultaneously. Later on, the new mother may return, and often does, to complete the requirements for her degree.

[15] But marriage seems to lessen participation in campus activities. Most of the married students find that running a home, nurturing a marriage and studying combine to make a sufficiently full schedule. Also, many seem to feel that marriage has given them a maturity beyond that of their single friends who are still interested in dating and "being in on things."

[16] This withdrawal seems to be less true of married male students. Here, often, the student activity may be related to future plans or aspirations, as in the case of the athlete who plans to commercialize on his ability after graduation, or the star debater who is planning to go to law school. However, administrators report that even among the men promising campus leaders tend to become less active after marriage; if they become fathers, too, then they are little more than commuters to classes.

[17] *How do campus marriages turn out as marriages?* Our information on this point, gathered from our own and several other universities, shows a variety of outcomes. There were Julia and Jack, who eloped when they were juniors, and made every effort to keep the marriage a secret, especially from their parents. But Jack's parents found out, were angered, and withdrew their financial support. Julia's parents did not, and continued their generous allowance to her. Jack got a job, working seven hours a day.

[18] For the rest of their university life, the going was tough. But they stuck to it, grimly, both graduating. Since then, both have been working, and have lived modestly. It has been a long and hard pull, but they are coming through.

[19] The case of Liz was quite different. Never a stable person, she married on impulse, possibly to keep up with three other girls in her sorority who did the same. "Isn't it exciting!" she said.

[20] But it wasn't for long. Liz was divorced a year later, dropped out of college, and now goes with a boy whom she introduces as "My Number Two." Liz' case illustrates one of the ways in which, through the contagion of imitation, campus marriages affect other students.

[21] In-laws present one of the frequent and serious difficulties in campus marriages. Some parents, seeing other people's children marry, or worried at the lack of popularity of their own, may encourage such marriages. Other parents may not be too pleased by campus marriages, but continue financial support. But apparently many of these parents feel privileged, because of their financial aid, to interfere.

[22] In one case, for example, the boy's parents financed the marriage —on the strict stipulation that there should be no children. Another mother cooperated financially until there was a baby; she especially disliked being called "Grandma." Then there was Paul's mother, who encouraged him to marry while at college because "the right kind of girl would help Paul find himself." When Paul didn't find himself, "she" was not the right kind of girl—"Paul really should try again." Such interference by in-laws not only complicates the marriages of their own children; the knowledge of it tends to spread among single students, and for them it is not a promising preview of marriage.

[23] Other in-laws act as shock-absorbers, preventing campus marriages from bouncing off the road. Many students admit they could not have continued with school or with marriage, without the unfailing help of parents.

[24] One lad who was supporting himself, wife and baby by various campus jobs was asked how he was making out. His reply was, "Just about to the last cent, and just squeaking through my courses. We three are all healthy, but I think I would be so worried about emergencies that

I couldn't continue except for one thing. Our parents are with us 100 percent. So far, we have not had to ask for financial help. We don't want to; but if we have to, we know we can count on our families."

[25] Though married students appreciate the problems that having children brings, reports from a number of universities indicate a relative lack of success of campus-wed couples in controlling the activities of the stork. One study, made on a Michigan university campus and based on interviews with couples who had one or more children, showed that one-third had sought to avoid pregnancy. And, of course, there were those who, for religious and other reasons, could not conscientiously harmonize their attitudes toward birth control with the need for postponing the coming of the children.

[26] *How will the total experience involved in these marriages affect the subsequent attitudes and philosophies of those concerned?* Only the more superficial students of human situations are content with the observance of immediate results. This is particularly true of such a long-time relationship as that of marriage, where the ultimate effects differ so often and so markedly from the immediate ones. What, then, are some of the more long-range consequences of campus marriages already discernible?

[27] First, there are the possible effects upon the children. Present-day child behavior experts make a great distinction between the wanted and the unwanted child, noting that children sense very, very early in life what the true attitude of the parents, and particularly of the mother, may be. What is already quite clear is that many children born of campus marriages are not wanted, at least not at the time of their arrival.

[28] Next, there are the more remote consequences for the wives in these marriages. Various patterns already emerge. There is, for one, the wife who sacrifices her own educational ambitions for those of her husband. Many couples make this decision thinking that it will be the most profitable in the long run, and that the wife can complete her college work several years later. But getting back later on is usually done in the face of many difficulties. If, for any of a number of reasons, the wife does not get back, she is apt to repent, and resent, her sacrifice.

[29] One of the most common practices in campus marriages is for the wife to work full time to support the family while the husband continues his education. The wife doing this is commonly spoken of as working for her P.H.T. degree, meaning Putting Hubby Through. This arrangement obtains even more frequently when the husband is taking advanced or professional training.

[30] Such an arrangement has already proved its dangers, and in a variety of ways. We have found cases where the working wife loses her-

self in a dead-end job, which, while it enables the couple to make ends meet financially and permits the husband to develop his educational program and forge ahead in his intellectual development, offers no such opportunities for the wife. Several years later, there is a considerable educational gap between husband and wife which bodes ill for their marriage.

[31] In other instances, the difficulties grow out of the wife's anxieties, as in the case of Lanny and Isabel. Lanny is a sophomore at the university. Isabel took an office job after graduating from high school. Lanny comes home full of stories about the day's work at the university. He makes reference to coeds in his class, and occasionally speaks about some particular one as being well-dressed, or making good grades, or sitting beside him in class.

[32] Isabel, never having been to college, must imagine these situations. Soon she begins to wonder. How about these girls? She has seen some of them. She envies them, too. And her Lanny is with them every day, and will be for two more years.

[33] Then one day, there is a flare-up about some trivial matter. All her pent-up fears and anxieties explode. Harsh words are said, some of which are not forgotten, and remain to fester. After two years, Lanny thinks that his wife is a jealous and unreasonable shrew; Isabel thinks that Lanny is a philanderer and not appreciative of what she has done for him.

[34] Edith was a campus wife who came to show signs of another kind. She graduated two years ahead of Ralph, whom she married as soon as she obtained a job. Ralph continued his studies, largely on her earnings. Her advancement at work was rapid, and soon she began to "feel her oats," as a friend put it.

[35] When Ralph remarked about the number of times she had to work at night, Edith answered with remarks about who was "pulling most of the oar." Ralph began visiting his widowed mother, who sympathized with him in a way that confirmed his suspicions. Ralph's running home to mother led Edith to downgrade her husband still further. Basically, Edith is a go-getter and finds it hard to respect a man who isn't "cutting a man's figure."

[36] William, another campus husband, is keenly aware of his failure to play a husband's traditional role. He is known to the personnel officer of his college, to a psychiatrist, and to an old friend as one who has strong feelings of apprehension about going to school on his wife's earnings. He comes from a family with strong masculine traditions, and with a keen sense of the importance of a college education. William has the constant feeling that he is unworthy as a man, "letting a woman support me." At times he hates himself; at other times, he hates his wife Ann for having gotten him into "this situation."

[37] Although Ann gives every indication of being satisfied with their arrangement, William remains a prey to doubts and misgivings, to the point where they interfere with his studies.

[38] And then there is Lester. Lester told of an organized group on his campus—young men on the prowl for girls from moneyed families or girls with good jobs who can subsidize a quite receptive husband in his collegiate search for culture and the higher values. Since Lester told of this, he has "made it."

[39] In the light of the foregoing, are campus marriages good or bad? On the basis of our own studies as family sociologists, we consider such marriages not only undesirable but highly risky. There are the harmful early effects on children who are usually unlooked-for and unwanted. There is the financial insecurity for most, with all the strains and stresses it brings. And there are the dangerous consequences to the persons themselves, whether they be the working wife who drops below her husband's educational level or the husband unable to adjust emotionally to being supported by his wife.

[40] Mostly, campus marriages fly in the face of human experience. Maturity and economic preparation are requisites for lasting success in marriage, and life on the campus of dear old Siwash delays the attainment of both. The Talmud's statement that "a man should first build a house, then plant a vineyard, and then marry" is timeless in its application. "First thrive, then wive," wrote Benjamin Franklin—advice as modern in its truth as in its brevity.

[41] Granted there are cases of campus marriages between serious, intelligent and well-balanced young people who have managed to overcome their problems and who are maturing together in their common, and changing, interests. But these are the exceptions. Moreover, in most cases the time is yet too soon to say with certainty. Marital success is not measured in terms of a year or a decade; it is "for keeps."

[42] Campus marriages, like so many of the youthful marriages of today, seem as far from meeting the requirements for successful marriage as rock 'n' roll is from Beethoven's Fifth.

QUESTIONS AND COMMENT ON FORM AND CONTENT

1. The authors of this article might have started by saying, as they say later, "We consider . . . [campus] marriages not only undesirable but highly risky." What effect would this introductory statement have on a college student who was looking for some logical, authoritative support for his marriage plans? Would he read it with an open mind or would he feel that the authors are prejudiced against campus marriages?

2. What is the actual approach? Do the writers start with opinion or fact?

3. More specifically, what items are covered in each of the first ten short paragraphs?

4. What is the function of paragraph 11?

5. Paragraphs 12, 17, and 26 begin with questions. What is the value of the question-answer pattern? Why were italics used? Is there any other device used to set off these sections?

6. Where does the conclusion start? Is it set off in any way?

7. What, in general, are some of the mechanical devices writers use to help the reader?

8. To what extent is the conclusion (set forth in paragraph 39, sentence 2) based on assumed principles or axioms, a deductive process?

9. Earlier in the essay, other generalizations were based on facts or statistics, an inductive process. See, for example, paragraphs 12 to 16 inclusive. Are the facts or examples sufficient in number? Are they typical? Can anything be proved by a single instance or example, as in paragraphs 17 and 18 or in 19 and 20? Is such an example satisfactory if our own experience would support its truth? If so, then the example does no more than remind us of our experiences.

10. In this article there is little use of figurative language. What is the effect of the simile used in the final sentence of the essay? Does it carry weight as logical argument?

THEME SUGGESTIONS

Campus Marriages Can Succeed
Campus Marriages Are Hazardous for the Husband (Wife)
Why College Boys (Girls) Marry
The Advantages (Disadvantages) of Early (Campus) Marriages
Parents Should (Not) Help
I Am a Campus (Bride) (Groom)

COURTSHIP THROUGH THE AGES

James Thurber

James Thurber (1894-1961) was born in Columbus and graduated from the Ohio State University. He is best remembered as a humorous essayist, cartoonist, and playwright. Many of his essays and cartoons were done for the New Yorker.

[1] Surely nothing in the astonishing scheme of life can have nonplussed Nature so much as the fact that none of the females of any of the species she created really cared very much for the male, as such. For the past ten million years Nature has been busily inventing ways to make the male attractive to the female, but the whole business of courtship, from the marine annelids up to man, still lumbers heavily along, like a complicated musical comedy. I have been reading the sad and absorbing story in Volume 6 (Cole to Dama) of the *Encyclopaedia Britannica*. In this volume you can learn all about cricket, cotton, costume designing, crocodiles, crown jewels, and Coleridge, but none of these subjects is so interesting as the Courtship of Animals, which recounts the sorrowful lengths to which all males must go to arouse the interest of a lady.

[2] We all know, I think, that Nature gave man whiskers and a mustache with the quaint idea in mind that these would prove attractive to the female. We all know that, far from attracting her, whiskers and mustaches only made her nervous and gloomy, so that man had to go in for somersaults, tilting with lances, and performing feats of parlor magic to win her attention; he also had to bring her candy, flowers and the fur of animals. It is common knowledge that in spite of all these "love displays" the male is constantly being turned down, insulted, or thrown out of the house. It is rather comforting, then, to discover that the peacock, for all his gorgeous plumage, does not have a particularly easy time in courtship; none of the males in the world do. The first peahen, it turned out, was only faintly stirred by her suitor's beautiful train. She would often go quietly to sleep while he was whisking it around. The *Britannica* tells us that the peacock actually had to learn a certain little trick to wake her up and revive her interest: he had to learn to vibrate his quills so as to make a rustling sound. In ancient times man himself, observing the ways of the peacock, probably tried vibrating his whiskers to make a rustling sound; if so, it didn't get him anywhere. He had to go in for something else; so, among other things, he went in for gifts. It is not unlikely that he got this idea from certain flies and birds who were making no headway at all with rustling sounds.

[3] One of the flies of the family Empidae, who had tried everything, finally hit on something pretty special. He contrived to make a glistening transparent balloon which was even larger than himself. Into this he would put sweetmeats and tidbits and he would carry the whole envelope through the air to the lady of his choice. This amused her for a time, but she finally got bored with it. She demanded silly little colorful presents, something that you couldn't eat but that would look nice around the house. So the male Empis had to go around gathering flower petals and pieces of bright paper to put into his balloon. On a courtship flight a male Empis cuts quite a figure now, but he can hardly be said to be

happy. He never knows how soon the female will demand heavier presents, such as Roman coins and gold collar buttons. It seems probable that one day the courtship of the Empidae will fall down, as man's occasionally does, of its own weight.

[4] The bowerbird is another creature that spends so much time courting the female that he never gets any work done. If all the male bowerbirds became nervous wrecks within the next ten or fifteen years, it would not surprise me. The female bowerbird insists that a playground be built for her with a specially constructed bower at the entrance. This bower is much more elaborate than an ordinary nest and is harder to build; it costs a lot more, too. The female will not come to the playground until the male has filled it up with a great many gifts: silvery leaves, red leaves, rose petals, shells, beads, berries, bones, dice, buttons, cigar bands, Christmas seals, and the Lord knows what else. When the female finally condescends to visit the playground, she is in a coy and silly mood and has to be chased in and out of the bower and up and down the playground before she will quit giggling and stand still long enough even to shake hands. The male bird is, of course, pretty well done in before the chase starts, because he has worn himself out hunting for eye glass lenses and begonia blossoms. I imagine that many a bowerbird, after chasing a female for two or three hours, says the hell with it and goes home to bed. Next day, of course, he telephones someone else and the same trying ritual is gone through with again. A male bowerbird is as exhausted as a nightclub habitué before he is out of his twenties.

[5] The male fiddler crab has a somewhat easier time, but it can hardly be said that he is sitting pretty. He has one enormously large and powerful claw, usually brilliantly colored, and you might suppose that all he had to do was reach out and grab some passing cutie. The very earliest fiddler crabs may have tried this, but, if so, they got slapped for their pains. A female fiddler crab will not tolerate any cave-man stuff; she never has and she doesn't intend to start now. To attract a female, a fiddler crab has to stand on tiptoe and brandish his claw in the air. If any female in the neighborhood is interested—and you'd be surprised how many are not—she comes over and engages him in light badinage, for which he is not in the mood. As many as a hundred females may pass the time of day with him and go on about their business. By nightfall of an average courting day, a fiddler crab who has been standing on tiptoe for eight or ten hours waving a heavy claw in the air is in pretty sad shape. As in the case of the males of all species, however, he gets out of bed next morning, dashes some water on his face, and tries again.

[6] The next time you encounter a male web-spinning spider, stop and reflect that he is too busy worrying about his love life to have any desire to bite you. Male web-spinning spiders have a tougher life than any other

males in the animal kingdom. This is because the female web-spinning spiders have very poor eyesight. If a male lands on a female's web, she kills him before he has time to lay down his cane and gloves, mistaking him for a fly or a bumblebee who has stumbled into her trap. Before the species figured out what to do about this, millions of males were murdered by ladies they called on. It is the nature of spiders to perform a little dance in front of the female, but before a male spinner could get near enough for the female to see who he was and what he was up to, she would lash out at him with a flatiron or a pair of garden shears. One night, nobody knows when, a very bright male spinner lay awake worrying about calling on a lady who had been killing suitors right and left. It came to him that this business of dancing as a love display wasn't getting anybody anywhere except the grave. He decided to go in for web-twitching, or strand-vibrating. The next day he tried it on one of the nearsighted girls. Instead of dropping in on her suddenly, he stayed outside the web and began monkeying with one of its strands. He twitched it up and down and in and out with such a lilting rhythm that the female was charmed. The serenade worked beautifully; the female let him live. The *Britannica*'s spider-watchers, however, report that this system is not always successful. Once in a while, even now, a female will fire three bullets into a suitor or run him through with a kitchen knife. She keeps threatening him from the moment he strikes the first low notes on the outside strings, but usually by the time he has got up to the high notes played around the center of the web, he is going to town and she spares his life.

[7] Even the butterfly, as handsome a fellow as he is, can't always win a mate merely by fluttering around and showing off. Many butterflies have to have scent scales on their wings. Hepialus carries a powder puff in a perfumed pouch. He throws perfume at the ladies when they pass. The male tree cricket, Oecanthus, goes Hepialus one better by carrying a tiny bottle of wine with him and giving drinks to such doxies as he has designs on. One of the male snails throws darts to entertain the girls. So it goes, through the long list of animals, from the bristle worm and his rudimentary dance steps to man and his gift of diamonds and sapphires. The golden-eye drake raises a jet of water with his feet as he flies over a lake; Hepialus has his powder puff, Oecanthus his wine bottle, man his etchings. It is a bright and melancholy story, the age-old desire of the male for the female, the age-old desire of the female to be amused and entertained. Of all the creatures on earth, the only males who could be figured as putting any irony into their courtship are the grebes and certain other diving birds. Every now and then a courting grebe slips quietly down to the bottom of a lake and then, with a mighty "Whoosh!", pops out suddenly a few feet from his girl friend, splashing water all

over her. She seems to be persuaded that this is a purely loving display, but I like to think that the grebe always has a faint hope of drowning her or scaring her to death.

[8] I will close this investigation into the mournful burdens of the male with the *Britannica's* story about a certain Argus pheasant. It appears that the Argus displays himself in front of a female who stands perfectly still without moving a feather. (If you saw "June Moon" some years ago and remember the scene in which the songwriter sang "Montana Moon" to his grim and motionless wife, you have some idea what the female Argus probably thinks of her mate's display.) The male Argus the *Britannica* tells about was confined in a cage with a female of another species, a female who kept moving around, emptying ash-trays and fussing with lampshades all the time the male was showing off his talents. Finally, in disgust, he stalked away and began displaying in front of his water trough. He reminds me of a certain male (Homo sapiens) of my acquaintance who one night after dinner asked his wife to put down her detective magazine so that he could read her a poem of which he was very fond. She sat quietly enough until he was well into the middle of the thing, intoning with great ardor and intensity. Then suddenly there came a sharp, disconcerting *slap!* It turned out that all during the male's display, the female had been intent on a circling mosquito and had finally trapped it between the palms of her hands. The male in this case did not stalk away and display in front of a water trough; he went over to Tim's and had a flock of drinks and recited the poem to the fellas. I am sure they all told bitter stories of their own about how their displays had been interrupted by females. I am also sure that they all ended up singing "Honey, Honey, Bless Your Heart."

QUESTIONS AND COMMENT ON FORM AND CONTENT

1. The introductory paragraph not only announces the theme, that of courtship, but also sets the mood. What kind of person does Thurber pretend to be in this essay? The capitalization of *Nature* is a bit old-fashioned, as is the assumption that "nature has been busily inventing ways to make the male attractive to the female. . . ." Note, too, that "Nature is nonplussed," that the "whole business of courtship from the marine annelids up to man, still lumbers heavily along like a complicated musical comedy."

Consider also the pretense to scholarship and the irrelevant fact that articles may also be found about "cricket, cotton, crocodiles. . . ." Does this fictional *I* remain constant throughout the essay?

2. Which paragraphs deal largely and directly with man? Which deal with the lower animals? Which paragraphs deal with only one creature?

3. Can you show specifically that the real Thurber was concerned or

amused throughout the essay principally with man's courtship? Is the article a sort of extended analogy?

4. Describe and illustrate Thurber's type of humor. To what extent is the humor dependent on a whimsical point of view? Give examples. Is the choice of the right word necessary for this slant? Illustrate. Is there any exaggeration, slapstick comedy, or understatement used?

5. Would a change in the final paragraph to a serious tone to discuss the implications of courtship and marriage have been desirable? Explain your answer.

VOCABULARY: WHAT DO THE ITALICIZED WORDS MEAN?

. . . nothing . . . can have *nonplussed* Nature so much (1)
. . . courtship . . . still *lumbers* heavily along (1)
. . . with the *quaint* idea in mind (2)
. . . as exhausted as a night-club *habitué* (4)
. . . his *rudimentary* dance steps (7)

THEME SUGGESTIONS

Much Great Humor Reveals Truth
Thurber's Type(s) of Humor
The Trouble with Man (Woman) Is⸻
Campus Courtships
Courtship as Revealed by Current Hit Tunes

THE MAN JONES

Frances Gray Patton

Frances Gray Patton (1906-   ) is best known for her novel Good Morning, Miss Dove *and for her short stories.*

[1] James Manigault Jones (who kept quiet about his middle name and was known to his college acquaintances as Jim or, when they were feeling high-flown and literary, as Eternity) paid a visit to Wendell Dormitory during the short interval between his lunch and his two-o'clock zoology-lab period. He carried a bunch of jonquils bought from a street-corner peddler—a poor, crop-legged man with hard-leather pads on his kneecaps—and as he entered the building he felt suddenly furtive, partly

Reprinted by permission of Dodd, Mead & Company from *A Piece of Luck* by Frances Gray Patton (originally published in *The New Yorker*). Copyright © 1955 by Frances Gray Patton.

because he thought he must look foolish clutching those "flowers that bloom in the spring, trala" and partly because he suspected he was out of bounds. He hesitated in the vestibule, of half a mind to toss the jonquils in the trash can and retreat before anybody saw him. But he rose above the timid impulse. He started for the stairs, trying not to notice how his footsteps echoed in the empty corridor.

[2] Early that morning, Jim and the rest of the boys had cleared out of Wendell, the main freshman dormitory at Amity College; in their wake, a crew of charwomen had arrived to make Wendell fit to receive a host of delicate visitors—the girls who were coming to the prom. The women had worked with a furious thoroughness that suggested contempt for the gross habits of the dormitory's regular inmates, scrubbing and polishing as if the place were far dirtier than it actually was. Now, in the purged, anomalous atmosphere, Jim had a fleeting illusion of being somewhere else. All this—the odors of soap and wax and furniture oil, the drone of a vacuum sweeper, and the rhythmic slipslap of a wet mop on the stairs —was like spring-cleaning week at home. He caught himself listening for his mother to call, "Is that you, Mannie boy? Will you take the kitchen screens in the back yard and squirt the hose on them before you settle down?" He frowned. He was too easily reminded of home, he thought, and it was abnormal to see a resemblance between anything here at Amity—this suave Eastern college, this "civilized oasis"—and Apex City, Georgia.

[3] He picked his way up the stairs, walking on his toes to avoid tracking the still damp marble. On the first landing, he saw a stringy woman lift a pail of water and begin toiling toward the second floor.

[4] "Here. Let me have that," Jim said. He snatched the bucket from the woman's hand and ran lightly up the half flight. "This where you want it, Ma'am?" (He could have kicked himself for letting that "Ma'am" slip out.)

[5] The woman nodded. "That was real nice of you," she said. "They's not many students as thoughtful as that. Thank you." Her sallow, equine face grew soft with the expression of maternal approval that older women, to Jim's discomfiture, were likely to bestow upon him. "Thank you, *sir!*"

[6] "You bet," said Jim.

[7] "A bokay for your lady?"

[8] "These?" Jim said. "Oh, they're just something I bought from a cripple"—he was miserably certain that the scrubwoman knew he had bought them because he'd remembered how his mother put fresh flowers in the guest room—"and now I've got to do something with 'em."

[9] "That was a Christian act," the woman said. "And they'll make your room look like a home away from home."

[10] "I figured they'd brighten it up," Jim said. "It's pretty austere, you

know." He yearned to get away—to make sure the room was all right, to indulge in lonely fantasies about the marvellous girl who was soon to occupy it—but he didn't know how to. It seemed rude to leave while the woman wanted to talk.

[11] "The little things in life make the big difference," she said. "You tell your mama for me she raised a true Southern gentleman."

[12] Jim felt himself blush, and knew that his heightened color gave him a heightened bloom of youth and innocence. He was a long-legged boy, with curly brown hair and pink cheeks. He looked like some mother's darling—which, indeed, he was—but, with a smile he hoped was a leer, he said, "She'll be surprised to hear *that!*"

[13] "She prob'ly knows," the woman said. "I guess there ain't much a mother's heart don't know about her son." She plunged her mop into her pail, swished it, and plopped it down with a wet, slimy sound. "You don't happen to be Jones, do you? Room 202?"

[14] "The man in person," said Jim.

[15] "A special delivery come for you. I slipped it under your door."

[16] "A special delivery? For *me?*" Jim's bowels constricted. The letter, he was agonizingly sure, could be from no one but Barbara. From Barbara, breaking her date for the dance. And it seemed to him that he wasn't really surprised—that all week he had known such a letter was bound to come.

[17] "I hope you ain't stood up," the woman said, leaning on her mop and regarding Jim with mournful eyes. "With the bokay and all, that would be a crime."

[18] Her sympathy was a mirror. In it Jim saw reflected the image of what he feared was his true self. Not an Amity man—cool, civilized, capable of taking such things as freshman proms and the vagaries of girls with cynical undismay—but a skinny kid from the Bible Belt. A nice Sunday-school boy with yellow flowers in his fist. A boy who addressed a scrubwoman as "Ma'am" and blubbered into her bucket when somebody "went and hurt his Southern pride." In that drowning moment of self-realization, all that sustained Jim was the conviction, recently acquired from converse with a junior who was majoring in psychology, that self-realization, per se, was good. To view oneself objectively, ruthlessly—it was only thus that one gained insight into one's motivations and detached them from false values formed in infancy or even *in utero*. But to become aware of one's own hideous ignominy was one thing, to show it to a woman with a mop was another.

[19] Jim cocked his left eyebrow—a muscular discipline that he practiced constantly. "There are plenty more fish in the sea," he said. His remark lacked urbanity, he knew—it was a disgruntled boast that one heard frequently in the Owl Drugstore in Apex City—but it had to

serve. With a magnificent try at nonchalance, he sauntered down the long, quiet hall to Room 202.

[20] Jim had met Barbara a week before, when he attended a dance at Hannah Benson, a small but reputedly sophisticated college for women. He had attended the function, with heavy misgivings, on the bid of a girl named Earline Fitch—a girl who had grown up next door to him and who had beaten him out by a slim academic margin for the position of high-school valedictorian. He had nothing against Earline—he was even fond of her, in an old-time's-sake sort of way—but he did not care to establish a public connection with her here in the East.

[21] Earline was a big, bouncy, uncomplicated girl who poked you in the ribs to make sure you got the point of her jokes. She had a passion for food, and a passion, very like in character, for what she called ideas. "I can't get the McCarthy problem off my chest," she would declare, her carrying voice soaring above the sound of the juke box at the Owl. "I can't bear to think he honestly represents the deep-down spiritual calibre of the average American." At a moonlight picnic, when the other couples had wandered off into the shade of the pine woods, she would remain sitting in full lunar glare beside Jim (somehow, he was usually paired off with Earline) and would say, less softly than the whippoorwills, "Now take salvation through faith—here's my slant on it. . . ." Her strong white teeth would glisten just as they did when they were about to seize upon a king-sized hamburger, succulent with chopped pickle and mustard. Worse still, she called Jim—and would always call him—by the humiliating abbreviation of his middle name. She called him Mannie.

[22] Jim's immediate impulse had been to decline the invitation with emphasis. In the end, however, he had decided to accept it for two cogent, if disparate, reasons. First, he had wished not to embarrass his mother, who was a close friend of Mrs. Fitch's; second, he was aware that at Amity, where Earline's qualities were mercifully unknown, it wouldn't sound bad to say he had a date up to Benson. So he had gone to the dance, frozen-faced and wary, and there he had met the girl whom he'd always known he was fated to meet someday. (Jim, for all his determination to treat himself ruthlessly, nursed no morbid doubts as to Fate's tender preoccupation with his felicity.) He had assumed that the meeting would occur at some distant point in time when, as a key man in the diplomatic service, a novelist on safari in Africa, or, perhaps, a psychiatrist long since beyond astonishment, he would be more than equal to it. Certainly he had never considered Earline Fitch as a probable instrument of destiny. But Fate moved in her own sweet way!

[23] The visit to Benson had not begun auspiciously. The train had

run late, and Jim had procured his supper from a vender. (A sorry meal it had been, consisting of a carton of milk and a dry sandwich; its sole virtue, Jim had thought morosely, was that it saved him from having to watch Earline eat.) Arriving, hungry and pessimistic, he'd had just time to change his clothes in the village's one dinky hotel before joining Earline at her dormitory.

[24] "Mannie Jones! You're a sight for sore eyes!" Earline cried, bursting into the reception room almost immediately after he had sat down to wait for her. She had on a ballooning sky-blue taffeta dress (the one in which she had delivered the valedictory), and it made her appear larger than life and crude-colored, like the blonde on the Holsum Bakery calendar in the Joneses' kitchen. Showing her teeth, she advanced across the carpet. Jim stepped back and bumped into a floor lamp.

[25] "That's right! Break up the furniture!" Earline exclaimed, catching the lamp before it toppled. She grasped Jim's hand and ground its bones together. "Gee! Seeing you makes me feel like I'm back in good old Apex City!"

[26] Jim retrieved his hand. "You're looking fit," he said.

[27] "I keep fit," Earline said. "I'm on the house hockey team and I never skip my daily dozens at the gym. Notice my tummy." She slapped it. "Flat as a board. *Mens sana in corpore sano!*"

[28] "Good going," said Jim.

[29] "Listen, Mannie," Earline said. "I'm sick about tonight. This is an old-fashioned card dance, and I gave four numbers to Jane Sadler, one of the keenest girls in our class. She's here on a Religious Ed. scholarship, like me."

[30] "She is?" said Jim.

[31] "You and Jane would have hit it off like ham and eggs. I told her how you were an Eagle Scout and how you'd won the Kiwanis medal for your oration on crime prevention, and she was wild to meet you. But this morning she woke up all broken out!"

[32] "Too bad," said Jim.

[33] "Well, not too bad, one way you look at it," Earline said knowledgeably. "It's German measles, and, of course, it's good to get that over with before you get pregnant."

[34] "I guess it is," Jim agreed quickly. Hoping to forestall a detailed lecture upon obstetrical hazards, he added gallantly, "Anyhow, it gives me four more dances with you."

[35] "Well, no, it doesn't," Earline said. "I'd already promised those four to some other folks for their dates. So I got Jane's roommate, Barbara Davis, to pinch-hit."

[36] "Much wrong with Barbara?"

[37] "Not much," Earline said. "But she's not your type. Not very

eager, you know. She wasn't even planning to come tonight. Said she preferred dances on men's campuses, where she had no responsibility! Though I must admit she was nice about filling in for Jane."

[38] Jim's spirits, though scarcely bleeding for the loss of the eager Jane, were depressed by this juggling of partners. It was typical of the confusion—the absence of savoir-faire—that he had expected from Earline.

[39] "Shall we shove off?" Earline said. "On with the dance, let joy be unrefined!" She jabbed her elbow into Jim' ribs. "Huh, Mannie?"

[40] Jim made no attempt to smile. "Where do I call a cab?" he inquired. Earline hooted. "What kind of gold-digger do you take me for? A walk in the nippy air will tune up our blood pressure."

[41] Before long, fox-trotting with Earline in the crowded ballroom, Jim understood why she had wanted a preliminary workout. Earline was a person in whom physical exercise excited the instinct for competition.

[42] "I believe you're winded," she said to Jim when the orchestra had stopped playing. "Relax!"

[43] "Shall we sit the next one out?" Jim asked.

[44] "Oh, the next belongs to Barbara," she told him. "Here she is, Johnny-on-the-spot, to claim you now." She grabbed Jim by the arm and spun him around. "Barbara Davis. Mannie Jones."

[45] Barbara was a slightly built girl, five feet three or so in height, with quiet, regular features, a pale complexion, and very soft, shiny brown hair, which hung just clear of her shoulders. In broad day, with his faculties collected, Jim would have thought her pretty; in the dim light of festivity, dizzy from Earline's whirls and gallops, he saw her as the pure, incarnate principle of beauty. She stood so still. She was so undemanding. Her lips were curved in a half smile, amiable but aloof. Everything about her—her fragile white shoulders, the hollow at the base of her clavicle, the way she tilted her head, and even her dress, which was made of some foamy black stuff with pink shimmering through it—seemed serene and poised, and veiled in the filmy mystery of dream. She was, in brief, notably unlike Earline Fitch.

[46] Barbara did not struggle for supremacy in the dance. Leaning on Jim's chest ("Light as a leaf on the wind," he thought), she seemed to float with him to the time of the music. She did not chatter, but by dint of direct questioning Jim learned something about her. She was from New York—"the city, not the suburbs." (Jim sneered with disdain at commuters' families, skulking in New Jersey.) She would like to live in Paris someday—or maybe Rome or Vienna. She guessed she was a gypsy at heart. (Jim decided definitely on foreign diplomacy instead of medicine.) She had never been to Amity (her tone implied familiarity with

Yale, Princeton, Dartmouth, and the Service Academies), but she understood it was steeped in tradition. A civilized oasis, she said.

[47] "Would you come down to my class prom next Friday?" Jim asked. He was shocked by the temerity of his question, blurted out bluntly, with no civilized prelude.

[48] Barbara said why, yes, she'd love to come if he really meant it. "Only," she added, "you'll have to tell me your name. I can't very well call you what Earline did when she introduced us!" She began to laugh, noiselessly but uncontrollably, so that she was obliged, for a moment, to hide her face against his waistcoat.

[49] "What did she call me?" asked Jim with death in his heart.

[50] "She called you 'the man Jones'!" Barbara told him. She choked, and began to laugh again. "That's what she said—'Barbara Davis. The man Jones'!"

[51] "Is that what she said? I never listen to poor Earline," said Jim. "My name's Jim."

[52] "I like Jim," Barbara said. "It's a virile name. Last summer, I saw this revival of an old movie called 'Lord Jim.' It was a scream in parts—you know how those old movies are—but Ronald Colman was wonderful. I knew you reminded me of somebody."

[53] And now, Jim thought as he approached Room 202, Barbara wasn't coming! Well, why should she? Why should a girl with the Ivy League at her feet climb on the smelly local train they called the Hedge-hopper and ride for three hours, stopping at every wide place in the road, to attend a freshman dance with a boy from the upcountry of Georgia. It was out of sheer kindness—the reluctance to give pain—that she'd agreed to come in the first place. (He had read somewhere that beautiful women were invariably kind, frequently to their undoing!) Her letter would be kind, too. It would say that she had a cold, or a quiz to study for, or maybe that her family wanted her home for some special party at the Stork Club or "21."

[54] He was not angry with Barbara. She was remote from human anger, like a classic myth. He was angry, and disgusted, with himself. He recalled several rich phrases in which he had described the girl's charms to his friends, and several optimistic hints as to the favorable light in which she regarded him. He remembered the government bond that his uncle had sent him on his eighteenth birthday, which he'd cashed to defray the expenses of the weekend; the new white dinner coat hanging in his locker at the gym; the orchid, selected and paid for, at the florist's; the table for two reserved at the Stromboli Tavern and the tip he'd added to the cover charge as tacit insurance against the management's querying

his age when he ordered drinks. The thought of all that elaborate preparation for what should have been, to a young man of reasonable sang-froid, a routine occasion was mortifying to Jim. Like the charwoman's pity, it flayed him. It put his sentiment for Barbara into a mawkish category, along with his uncomfortable memories of the time he had stayed after school and cleaned the blackboards in order to be alone with a buxom teacher named Miss Myrtle Stubbs. (He had picked jonquils for Miss Myrtle—early February ones that bloomed in the sheltered corner of the dining-room ell—and his mother had fitted a lace-paper doily around their stems to make them look like a valentine.) Jim winced. He opened his door.

[55] The letter lay on a strip of bare floor between sill and rug. Against the dark wood, the white envelope looked as bleak as an old, bleached bone. But as Jim, sweating, forced himself to stoop for it, he saw that it could scarcely contain a message of doom. It was postmarked Apex City and addressed, in the sloping, Palmer-method hand of his mother, to Mr. J. Manigault Jones!

[56] Relief did not come to Jim by degrees, as it comes to timeworn people who must absorb it gradually into veins long torpid with chronic anxiety. It hit him full force, flooding him with a lovely, sanguine warmth. (He had a nebulous vision of Barbara. She sat, leaning toward him, at a small table illumined by a single candle. Something glittered, like a spangle of stars, in her hair. As she gazed languorously at him above a crystal cocktail glass, the orchid he'd sent her rose and fell on her breast. He saw himself, in his white coat, guiding her through an intricate maze of dancers; over the shoulders of their commonplace partners his jealous classmates eyed him with respect.) He tossed the letter, unopened, upon the dresser. Humming a few bars from "Some Enchanted Evening," he went into the adjoining bathroom, where he arranged the jonquils in his toothbrush glass.

[57] He returned to the bedroom. He set the flowers upon the night table beside *War and Peace,* a volume of poems by Ogden Nash, and the current issue of *Holiday*—an assortment that spelled, he felt, a catholic and unimpeachable taste in literature. He stood back and surveyed the room. It was a single room, narrow and utilitarian. Without the Varga girls that he'd removed from the walls, lest they strike Barbara as a display of naïveté, it had, Jim fancied, a monkish aspect. But it was clean. Its bed was smoothly made. Its general effect could be called civilized.

[58] Jim tried to imagine how that room—that celibate cell—would look after the dance. He conjured up a vague, intoxicating impression of diaphanous garments flung over a chair and of a girl's gently curving form swelling the covers on the bed. The girl's face was indistinct, but her

hair made a shadowy mist on the pillow, and one shoulder—bare except for a wisp of black lace—was visible above the blanket. "Are you warm enough?" Jim whispered.

[59] The scene changed. Years had passed. Jim sat in a closed compartment on a train that sped through the wine country of France. He was hard and lean. His eyes were shrewd. In his briefcase reposed the record—in code, of course—of an investigation that would point the way to international peace for a generation. His papers were complete save for one scrap of information. One missing link. And he would get that. He always got what he wanted.

[60] Or did he? Had he? He was a lonely man.

[61] The door of the compartment opened. A cold thrill shot along Jim's nerves, but his hand remained so steady that the long ash on the end of his cigar was undisturbed. Silently as a shadow, a woman entered the compartment. She was veiled, and wrapped in exotic furs. She tossed a fine linen handkerchief upon Jim's knee. Its monogram, Jim saw at a glance, provided the clue; it was the missing link.

[62] "Do you not know me?" the woman asked. She spoke with the faint foreign accent of the expatriate, but the timbre of her voice was familiar. It took Jim back, back, back. Dance music. Spring. A handful of simple golden flowers. He laid down his cigar. He rose and lifted the veil that hid the face of his visitor. It was a face that showed the ravages of passion and danger, but its bones had stayed beautiful. Its lips were curved in the old half smile. "Well, Lord Jim," said Barbara. She closed the door. She snapped off the light. "We are no longer children, Lord Jim!"

[63] The clock in the tower of Amity College Library struck the half hour. "Whew!" Jim said. He moved to the looking glass above the dresser, half expecting to find his own face marked by the ravages of life. Observing that it was still round and sleek, he sucked in his cheeks to encourage in himself a lean-jawed look. Then, with a start of alarm, he saw his mother's neglected letter. Why had she sent it special delivery? Was something wrong at home?

[64] He ripped open the envelope and drew out a folded sheet of paper, inscribed closely on both sides. A five-dollar bill—an old soft bill that wouldn't crackle and advertise its presence—lay in the fold. "Gosh!" Jim said, with the feeling of unworthiness that his mother's small attentions always gave him. He pictured her fingers as they'd smoothed the bill and as, immediately afterward, they'd seized a pencil to jot down "$5" under "Miscellaneous" in a black leather account book. He read her letter.

[65] "Dear Mannie," she began. Jim stiffened. He had told his mother,

as tactfully as he could, that he deplored being called Mannie—that it sounded babyish, like "Sonny" or "Bud"—but she had never been willing to see his point. It was short for a distinguished name, she had argued. His Manigault ancestor had been a Huguenot, a man who had sacrificed advantage to principle. It was a name to revere. Take it easy, Jim advised himself. She's too old to learn new tricks. She means well. She sent you five dollars. He began again:

[66] Dear Mannie:

This is just a line to let you know I'm thinking of you on the eve of your first big college dance and that I'll be with you in spirit, enjoying the sound of revelry by night. Earline wrote her mother that you'd asked a mighty pretty Benson girl to be your partner. Naturally, I'm a trifle disappointed that you didn't ask Earline [Jim groaned], because I've always liked the way your wholesome friendship with her expressed itself in work as well as play. You were pals on the debating platform as well as in the swimming pool. And then it *would* have been polite after she made the first move. I'm afraid the Fitches may be wounded. [To hell with the Fitches, thought Jim.] Earline doesn't think this girl—Barbara, isn't she? —is quite your intellectual or spiritual equal, but then Earline can't judge for you.

[67] ["You're damn right she can't!" said Jim out loud], and I know you could never be ensnared by mere physical appeal. I'm thankful we discussed the mating instinct long ago [I merely asked the girl to a *dance*, Jim thought indignantly], and I'll always cherish the recollection of the clear-eyed way you looked at me after we had everything straight and said, "Biology is as neat as algebra, isn't it?" I hope you'll never forget that, either.

[68] Would that I could, thought Jim. The "frank discussion" to which his mother referred had taken place three years before, when he was only fifteen, but every wretched word of it haunted his memory. He had been setting out for a Hi-Y hay ride—Earline Fitch was his date—when his mother had urged him to sit down and have "an intimate little chat" with her. He recalled the scene objectively now—a plump, earnest woman in a Boston rocker, and a blob of a boy, *himself,* sitting pigeon-toed on the edge of a Victorian love seat—but not so objectively that he failed to recover a sense of being trapped. His hands, resting on his knees, had seemed limp and heavy and grossly oversized; his mother, in her determination not to whisper, had spoken more loudly than usual. She had begun by asking Jim if he had noticed that his voice was changing and if he recognized that change as Nature's way of telling him he was growing into manhood. She had gone on to say, in a booming voice, that she'd heard that some boys and girls, being uninstructed and confused by their budding instincts, didn't always conduct themselves sensibly in

a truck full of hay—with the chaperon, no doubt, sitting up front with the driver. She wished Mannie to be forewarned, so that if the proximity of Earline's young body should give him a queer sensation, he would know what it was. He mustn't be frightened, though. The desire to mate was a healthy, holy thing, so long as it was controlled.

[69] Glassy-eyed with chagrin, Jim had known that he had to say something—and something in his mother's vein—before he could escape. With the algebraic analogy he had bought his freedom. He was morally certain that his fatuous remark had been widely quoted in PTA circles; also, it had effectively nipped Jim's incipient interest in higher mathematics.

> [70] Forgive me for clucking [the letter continued]. I know you're a man now and I want you to make your own independent decisions. Maybe you can ask Earline another time. I hope the enclosure will ease the strain on your allowance. With love always,
>
> Mamma

[71] Jim put the bill into his wallet. It would take more than five dollars, he reflected wryly, to ease his strain. Amity wasn't like Apex City, where a girl was satisfied with a drive-in movie and a bag of popcorn. But he'd eke out. He'd heard some of the fellows say you could sell your blood to the hospital for fifty bucks a quart.

[72] The library clock struck the third quarter. Jim went into the bathroom. He tore his mother's letter into fine fragments and flushed it down the toilet.

[73] Jauntily, he walked along the hall, descended the gleaming stairs, and left the building. The cleaning woman, in a brown hat and coat, was leaving, too.

[74] "You look like your news warn't so bad," she said.

[75] "Everything's rosy," said Jim. "Just a spot of dough from home."

[76] At the moment, he meant what he said. But as he loped down the path that led to the Zoology Building, Jim realized that the true substance of the letter had not gone down the drain. It stayed in his consciousness and smirked at him. Its moralistic baby talk—such expressions as "wholesome friendship" and "mere physical appeal"—reduced the daring of the imagination to childish grandiosity. He would never, he was now persuaded, seem distinguished to a girl like Barbara Davis. He would never smoke an expensive cigar as he was borne through the wine country of France, or do anything beyond the ordinary. He would finish college (possibly with a B average), serve his time in the Army, and go back to Apex City and sell real estate. He would marry a local girl.

(But *not* Earline!) He would lead, like other men, a life "of quiet desperation."

[77] Yet only a short time before, the future had been his particular peach. And his mother had put a blight on it!

[78] Jim's parents had been middle-aged when he was born. His father had died shortly thereafter, leaving his son's upbringing to his widow. He could not have left it in more consecrated hands. Mrs. Jones was a wonderful mother. (All Apex City said so, and until recently Jim had not dreamed that anyone would question the consensus.) Self-reliance, she had claimed, was her desire for her son, and she had consistently refused to weaken that quality by acts of overprotection. Other toddlers, when they skinned their knees, were gathered to maternal bosoms, there to howl against cosmic injustice; all little Jim got from Mrs. Jones was a cheerful "Upsy-daisy" and a stinging dab of iodine. Later, when problems of personal conduct arose, Jim was refused the support of hard-and-fast rules. On such matters as church attendance, playing marbles for keeps, and reading comic books, Jim was told to think things out and be guided by his conscience. (That his conscience generally led him down paths that Mrs. Jones approved had seemed a happy accident.) When he began, now and then, to take the car out at night, his mother never sat up for him. Turning in to the driveway after a Scout meeting or a school party, Jim often saw her lighted bedroom window go dark; next morning she would say, "I slept like a log, Mannie. I didn't hear you come in."

[79] The transparent lie had always touched Jim, but when, in a nostalgic, confidential mood, he had related it to his friend the psychology major, he had regretted doing so.

[80] "Why did she wish to deceive you?" the psychology major asked.

[81] "To keep me from knowing she worried," Jim replied, surprised by his friend's obtuseness. "To make me independent."

[82] "Not to render your chains invisible? Not to deprive you of the incentive to rebel?" the psychology major suggested.

[83] "Ahhh, baloney!" Jim retorted. "I was just a kid! Naturally, she worried."

[84] "If it was natural, why was she ashamed?"

[85] "She wasn't ashamed," said Jim.

[86] "No. Your insight tells you that much," the other student said, slowly and significantly. "She wasn't ashamed, but she was making goddam sure *you'd* be ashamed if you ever stayed out late—tomcatting in the red clay hills of Georgia."

[87] "For Christ's sake!" Jim scoffed, hoping the oath did not sound as unaccustomed as it was. "I told you I was just a kid."

[88] "Well, unless you want to remain a kid, you'd better get wise.

You're in danger. You'd better make your break while there's time. Ruthlessly."

[89] "You don't know my mother," Jim told him. "If she wanted me chained, why did she help me leave home? Why did she send me to college"—he checked himself; he had been about to say "up North," the way they did in Apex City—"in the East?"

[90] "Any number of reasons. Guilt. Prestige." The psychology major shrugged. Then he whistled, as if in pain. "But, boy, the light going off in the upstairs window—that was practically Machiavellian!"

[91] Jim had laughed. The notion of his innocent mother employing a fine Italian hand had been plain funny.

[92] Now, beneath the budding elms of Amity, Jim was not inclined to mirth. His friend had not exaggerated. He *was* in danger. "'Ah want y'all to make y'all's own independent decisions,'" he muttered between his teeth, with a contemptuous distortion of his mother's Southern accent and diction. "'Maybe y'all kin ask Uhline another time!'" He knew he had to act.

[93] He cut across the sprouting turf of the quadrangle and went to the post office, where he bought a stamped airmail envelope. Then he went to the college snack bar. He bought a milk shake, took it to an empty booth, sat down, and opened his loose-leaf notebook. He furrowed his brow. (Anyone seeing him would think him too deeply absorbed in scholarship to brook interruption.) After a while, when his anger had crystallized into sentences, he took his fountain pen (a Lifetime Sheaffer that his mother had given him when he won the Kiwanis medal) and started writing.

[94] My dear Mother [he wrote, making his letters dark and vertical]: Thank you for the enclosure. Your generosity was unnecessary but not unappreciated. The big dance, as you put it, does not seem overwhelming to me. I expect, however, that it will prove diverting. Miss Davis, who is to be my guest, is from a prominent family in New York City—not the suburbs. She is not intimate with Earline Fitch nor does she care to be. She would be amazed to know that she had been discussed by Mrs. Fitch. I shall have to ask you not to bandy the names of my friends around the neighborhood. Who I take to a dance is absolutely none of the Fitches' business. It is the business of nobody but myself and the other party involved. After mature consideration, I trust you will see that at my age any other state of affairs would lack valid reality.

[95] In the future please address your letters to James M. Jones. Here in the East pedigrees are taken for granted and unusual middle names are not impressive.

Aff'y,

Jim

[96] Jim lit a cigarette. He pictured his mother reading his communication. She looked older than she had at Christmas, and lonelier, like a patient woman on a Mother's Day card. Her face wore a blank, puzzled expression.

[97] I'd better soften it, Jim thought. He added a postscript: "I must be cruel in order to be kind."

[98] But the quotation, apt as it was, didn't seem to help much. It would not console his mother; it would only persuade her that her son had gone crazy. Why, she was liable to get right into her car—the old green Chevrolet that Jim had learned to drive in—and come straight to Amity. He could see her driving down the main street, sitting very straight and wearing the fierce, dedicated expression that she always wore in the face of illness. "Could any of you gentlemen direct me to Wen*dell?*" she would call out to a group of students on the sidewalk. "I'm looking for Mannie Jones."

[99] Jim tore the sheet from his notebook, crumpled it into a ball, placed it in his ash tray, and struck a match to it. He would have to do the thing over again a different way, he thought, as he watched the little conflagration flare and die out. He must say exactly what he'd said, but in his mother's native language.

[100] This time, Jim wrote slowly. Now and again, he paused, trying out phrases in his mind and often shuddering as he set them down on paper. Short though his letter was, its composition consumed the better part of two hours.

> [101] Dear Mama [he wrote]: Pardon this notebook paper. I'm in the snack bar guzzling a malted to rebuild my tissues after a day of intellectual (?) labor. It was swell of you to send me the fiver and I can really use it! The prom is going to be terrific. We've got Buzz King's orchestra—Buzz used to play trombone with Guy Lombardo—and at intermission we'll have strawberry punch and homemade cookies served by the wives of the profs on the Freshman Advisory Council. My date is an awfully nice girl, a real slick chick, named Barbara Davis. She's from New York. The city, not the suburbs. She's a better dancer than Earline. She lets me lead.
> [102] And now I have to say something I reckon most mother's couldn't take. But you and I have always been frank so I know you won't be hurt; It's this, Mama. Please stop being inquisitive about my date-life. You see, I've reached a stage in my development where I need to achieve emotional independence. Even if I make mistakes. Do you remember how it was when I first started driving the car? Other guys came home and found their families sitting up for them, ready to put them through the third degree. But you never did. Gee, I felt proud when I found the house dark and you asleep. I knew you trusted me. Well, that's what I can use now, Mama. Not questions. Not advice. Just *Trust* that's too big for words.

[103] Jim read over what he had written. It was ghastly. It reminded him of articles concerning the problems of adolescence that appeared in the women's magazines, which his mother read and often left (by design, perhaps?) in the bathroom. It was no less priggish—and infinitely less polished—than what he said before the Hi-Y hay ride. But, as he had been obliged to escape then, so he was obliged now. His mother would understand this letter. What was more, she would respect it. She would let him alone.

[104] "Your loving son," Jim wrote. He sighed. He might as well go whole hog. "Manigault," he signed himself. Sadly, with the air of a poet forced to speak the vernacular of the masses, he folded the sheet of paper and put it into the stamped envelope, which he addressed and slid in his inside coat pocket.

[105] A freshman stopped at the booth. "Missed you in lab," he said.

[106] "I wasn't in the mood," said Jim.

[107] "Hell, neither was I, but with this shindig tonight I couldn't afford a makeup. Sometimes I wonder if women are worth it."

[108] "My ma sent me a little extra dough," said Jim.

[109] The boy looked impressed. "My people have hearts of stone," he said. "Your girl come yet? Mine was due on the bus an hour ago but I guess she's wending her own sweet way to Wendell. She's my brother-in-law's kid sister."

[110] "Mine's coming on the four-twenty," Jim said. "The Hedgehopper." As he spoke, he realized that, with the lab period over, it must be close to four. He rose, stretched, and feigned a yawn. "I'd better get along over to the depot."

[111] Jim arrived at the station a few minutes before the train was due. In the waiting room, two of his classmates sat, half reclining, on the wooden bench. Their eyes were closed; their legs looking boneless and bored, were thrust far into the public passageway. Jim considered taking a place beside them, but an unwelcome twinge of honesty deterred him. The fashionable ennui that to most of his friends (so he thought) was as natural as skin would never be more than a thin, protective glaze on him. It was safe to assume that neither of those boys had just written home begging his mother to trust him!

[112] Jim went out onto the open-air-platform and paced up and down. A switch engine was backing and filling on the track. The fireman lifted a hand in salute to Jim; Jim lifted a hand to the fireman, as he'd done a hundred times, waiting at the grade crossing in the center of Apex City. He was glad that only a baggage porter observed his small-town gesture.

[113] In the distance, a diesel engine grunted.

[114] "There she blows," the porter said.

[115] "On time, for a change," Jim said with an air of indifference.

[116] A bell clanged. The Hedgehopper, a comical little train composed of a converted steam engine and a short string of antiquated coaches, charged into the station and shook itself to a stop.

[117] The two boys emerged from the waiting room. "Pawing the earth, Jones?" one of them said.

[118] "That's right," said Jim. Panic chilled him. Suppose she hadn't come. But there she was, alighting from the last coach!

[119] She wore a tan coat, and a long plaid scarf hung around her neck. She looked much younger than she had at Benson. She gave the curious impression, which Jim took as spurious, of being scared. But her hair was the same. Her hair and the way she stood—stiller than most girls, with her chin raised a little.

[120] Jim hurried to her. "Hello, Barbara," he said. He had meant to say something cleverer than that.

[121] "Hello, Jim," said Barbara. Her voice sounded relieved. She smiled in a broad, shy, delighted way that made her face look plump. "Lord Jim!"

[122] "Were you afraid you wouldn't know me?"

[123] "That you wouldn't know *me!*"

[124] "Never fear," Jim said. "This your bag?"

[125] "Yes," Barbara said. "Only—listen, Jim. It's utterly ridic, but I promised my mother I'd mail her this the second I got here." She handed Jim a postcard upon which the single word "Safe" was written in a dark, vertical, sarcastic-looking hand. "I can't imagine what dire thing she thought could happen to me on the Hedgehopper!"

[126] "I guess people in cities get the habit of being cautious," Jim said. "Just wait where you are."

[127] He sprinted to the railway post box. He dropped Barbara's card through the slot and was about to follow it with his own letter when he was pierced by a shaft of sweet and humorous tenderness for his mother. The manifestations of her nervous love that had sickened and seemed to threaten him earlier were now clothed in natural dignity. They were universal foibles, common to all parents—even to those who chose to dwell in the heart of a metropolis. He stuffed the letter back in his pocket.

[128] He was filled with a heady and perfectly wonderful sense of buoyancy. The evening lay ahead, bright with orchids, with candle flame at the Stromboli, and with the agreeable envy of friends. Beyond the evening, the world—his peach—hung suspended from a golden bough, ripening, ready to drop at the proper moment into the palm of his outstretched hand.

QUESTIONS AND COMMENT ON FORM AND CONTENT

1. Until the reader is well along in the story he expects the main focus or interest to be the week-end party. Instead, he finds a quite different theme or conflict. What is it?

2. How do each of the following relate to the main theme?
   a. The fears of Jim
   b. The scene with the charwoman
   c. The letter from his mother
   d. Jim's Walter-Mitty-like daydreaming
   e. Earline Fitch
   f. Jim's letters to his mother
   g. The psychology major
   h. The arrival of Barbara and the mailing of her card to her mother
   i. Jim's stuffing his letter back in his pocket

3. What kind of letter will Jim write to his mother? Will he sign it as "Jim" or "Manny"?

4. How are the major characters, including Jim, presented to the reader?

5. Who tells the story? What would be the effect if Jim told it?

6. Why does Miss Patton have the charwoman speak in ungrammatical, sub-standard English, including clichés?

7. What kind of language does the psychology major use?

8. How do you account for the rather ponderous language in certain scenes, as, for example, in the second half of paragraph 18?

9. To what extent does a writer of fiction, including television scripts, indicate the level of education or intelligence of the characters by the level of language put into their mouths? Give examples. Compare Shaw's *Pygmalion* (the musical *My Fair Lady*).

10. Draw up three or four rules on the technique of paragraphing dialogue. When is the description of action included in the paragraph with the quotation? What is the position of the period, the comma, and the question mark when used with quotation marks? How do you account for the single quotation marks in paragraphs 50 and 52?

11. Is the ending satisfactory? What would be the effect on the unity of the story if the story continued to include the party and, perhaps, the engagement of Jim and Barbara? Can you name any prominent short stories that are essentially love stories? Is the love theme as effective in a short story as in a novel?

VOCABULARY: WHAT DO THE ITALICIZED WORDS MEAN?

. . . he felt suddenly *furtive* (1)
. . . in their *wake*, a crew of charwomen had arrived (2)
Now, in the *purged, anomalous* atmosphere (2)

. . . this *suave* Eastern college (2)

Her sallow *equine* face (5)

It's pretty *austere,* you know (10)

. . . with a smile he hoped was a *leer* (12)

. . . talking such things as the *vagaries* of girls with cynic undismay (18)

But to become aware of one's own hideous *ignominy* (18)

. . . conviction . . . that *self-realization, per se,* was good (18)

His remark lacked *urbanity* (19)

With a magnificent try at *nonchalance,* he *sauntered* down . . . the hall (19)

. . . a small but reputedly *sophisticated* college for women (20)

. . . he had decided to accept the invitation for two *cogent,* if *disparate,* reasons (22)

The visit to Benson had not begun *auspiciously* (23)

Earline said, . . . *"mens sana in corpore sano!"* (27)

. . . the absence of *savoir-faire*—that he had expected from Earline (38)

He was shocked by the *temerity* of his question (47)

. . . to a young man of reasonable *sang-froid* (54)

It put his sentiment for Barbara into a *mawkish category* (54)

. . . a *buxom* teacher named Miss Myrtle Stubbs (54)

. . . veins long *torpid* with chronic anxiety (56)

. . . a *catholic* and *unimpeachable* taste in literature (57)

It was a single room, narrow and *utilitarian* (57)

. . . lest they [the pictures] strike Barbara as a display of *naïveté* (57)

She was veiled, and wrapped in *exotic* furs. (61)

He was morally certain that his *fatuous* remark had been . . . widely quoted (69)

. . . he reflected *wryly* (71)

. . . the light going off in the upstairs window—that was practically *Machiavellian* (90)

. . . the fashionable *ennui* (111)

THEME SUGGESTIONS

Foolish Fears

Growing Pains

Insecurity

The Sophisticated Pose

The Battle for Freedom from Parents

A Declaration of Independence

I Know the Man Jones (a Barbara) (an Earline)

COLLEGE ATHLETICS: THEIR PRESSURE ON HIGH SCHOOLS

Eugene Youngert

Eugene Youngert (1908-   ) has been superintendent-principal of high schools in Illinois, has taught in several universities, and has been associated with Dr. James Bryant Conant in his studies of American public education.

[1] A university professor was talking to some people from a town in the Middle West. He said with asperity, "Your high school does not prepare its students for college work." Then, he used as an example in proof of his statement a boy who had gone to the university from that high school and been flunked out for poor academic work. But the professor did not put the blame where it belonged—namely on his own university.

[2] What were the facts in the case? In a high school graduating class of 157, the boy in question was number 155, third from the bottom of the class. In high school, the lad had neither intention nor desire to go to college. He had no business to go to college. He had not taken a college preparatory course. He could not get a college entrance recommendation from his high school. But he was a superb athlete, and that meant that he was desirable to many colleges. He was "worked on" by representatives from several universities, and the one lucky enough to get him was the professor's university.

[3] However, in his freshman year it became clear that the boy was not up to university football. Therefore he was dropped from the freshman squad. The athletic officers demonstrated that they had no further use for him, so he was flunked out of college, and soon after that the professor was using the boy as illustration for his statement that "your high school does not prepare its students for college work."

[4] This incident is taken from an official report of a committee of one of our regional associations that accredits colleges and secondary schools. Now, let me relate a case told to me in a letter that I have just received from the principal of a high school in the Eastern part of our country. I shall tell the story directly from the letter, but omitting names of colleges and calling the boy Sonny.

[5] "Until Sonny came along, our quiet little school was virtually unknown to the majority of collegiate institutions. However, thanks to this lad, we became the crossroads meeting place for college admissions officers and coaches.

[6] "Sonny was a lad whose I.Q. remained a steadfast 92-95, and we never considered him of college caliber. But what an athlete he was! It was a shame to see the devices a host of coaches and some admissions officers used to try to buy this boy. College people came, literally, from all over the country to get Sonny for dear old Alma Mater. There were free round trips to visit campuses, with parties thrown in for atmosphere. Appropriately enough, the representatives of one university interviewed Sonny in a famous New York night club.

[7] "Sonny finally went to a university where he received a full 'free ride' scholarship, plus the following perquisites: private tutors to keep him passing in his courses, a campus job for his father and a low-rent apartment for the family, and spending money for Sonny. But Sonny lost interest in trying to study even the diluted program he was asked to follow, and early in the second year he left college and joined the army.

[8] "The sad part of this tale is that we had to work like the dickens to get highly qualified, intelligent boys into the very colleges and universities that were vying with one another for our Sonny and his 92-95 I.Q."

[9] If these cases were exceptions there would be little point in telling them here. But they are not, as the evidence on my desk bears out. Nor were the colleges that sought the boys only those known popularly as "athletic mills." In fact, among them were some that are distinguished for academic excellence. The recruiting letters of athletic departments of some of the universities would be good models for the admissions offices of those same universities. I wish that admissions officers would as assiduously seek information about academic ability as athletic officers seek information about athletic ability. I have before me some recruiting letters turned over to me by the boys who received them. The information requested about athletic prowess is fascinating, as is also the extent to which the recruiting goes: "List names and addresses of football players whom [sic] you feel would make good university prospects"; "Name the most outstanding linemen and backs against whom you played last fall." Incidentally, the boys who received these letters had not asked for them.

[10] There are two major ways in which high schools are hurt by the athletic pressure in colleges and universities. First there are the recruiting and scholarship procedures, and secondly the practices of professionalized athletics that are carried into high schools by coaches who have used professional tactics in college.

[11] A young boy in his senior year in high school received twenty-six scholarship offers to play football in colleges and universities. One of the offers, which I saw, was a telegram so funny as to be laughable, and yet so honest in its commercial appeal as to be highly interesting: "Accept no offers until you see ours." This telegram was from a university that year in and year out fields one of the formidable football machines

of our country. Think what that kind of recruitment can do to a seven-teen-year-old's sense of values, especially when the offers are followed by persistent visits from college representatives, who avidly seek the boy's favor through financial lures far greater than those offered to the aca-demically talented students in the class.

[12] Here is a quotation from a letter to a high school principal. "We should like to have the boy come to our campus for a weekend and get the feel of our athletic facilities. If you will bring him to us, we will invite you and your wife, your athletic director and his wife, and the boy's mother and father to spend the weekend here as our guests. We shall provide first-class transportation and campus hospitality." A seventeen-year-old would have to have his feet pretty firmly planted not to have his common sense warped by that kind of talk.

[13] Is an institution interested in a boy's sense of values when it en-gages in this sort of recruiting activity? Or, isn't the interest in what the boy can do for the institution and for those who are seeking his services? I remember a basketball coach from a college whose basketball team is always one of the pacesetters. He was out on his annual talent search and had stopped in at the school I long served as principal to ask whether the athletics department had any prospects to suggest. In fun, one of our men asked whether he would like the name of a strong football star, to which he replied, "Well, look, after all, I've got my own job to pro-tect." There is about as casual a definition of exploitation as we could hope to see!

[14] I do not mean that coaches do not have strong feelings of affec-tion for the boys who make their teams. Quite to the contrary, I know that they often do have those feelings. But in the recruiting activity I see nothing but exploitation. Furthermore, I believe that that is what a college faculty would call it had it the courage to make an independent study of athletic recruitment, beginning with the machinery for uncover-ing prospects and proceeding to the recruitment letters, interviews, and the pressure that eventually bring the boys to the campus and its teams.

[15] It has been my privilege to talk with a large number of men broadly experienced in college athletics administration. Without excep-tion they have said that recruitment and its scholarship bait are by all odds the major problem in college athletics practice. All that one needs to do is follow the disciplining procedure of the NCAA to realize that this expert judgment of the serious nature of the recruitment problem is correct. In the face of this fact, it is hard to understand how college faculties—the most powerful single force in a college—can ignore athletic recruiting and scholarships as though they were not their problems but only the president's. Certainly, they are the faculty's problems, since all admissions must go through the admissions office and since the admissions

office is responsible to the faculty for those whom it submits for instruction and whom it recommends for scholarship aid because of ability to perform at a level worthy of scholarship aid.

[16] College recruitment of athletes is hurtful to the high schools because of its effect both on the athletes and on the student body. I have spoken about what the bidding for boys must do to their sense of values. I could write at some length of what athletic scholarships cause high school athletes to do when they know they must get the attention of the talent scouts. But I want here to include a word about the cynicism that infects the students as a whole when they see favoritism and free ride scholarships bestowed on boys whose classroom work has been mediocre. Under such circumstances, high school students cannot be blamed if they think that we are shedding crocodile tears today in our wailing about the lack of intellectual vigor in our secondary schools.

[17] The argument commonly advanced in defense of free ride athletic scholarships is that modern football is so complex a game, and must be so perfectly learned in order to meet normal competition, that players have no time in which to earn any of the money needed to cover their college expenses. This argument assumes that players and their families have no means of their own and that it is *good practice* that a college recreational game be so professionalized as to need all of an athlete's spare time and even some that he might well be giving to his classes (presumably his principal reason for being in college). So generally accepted is this notion that college athletics should be on a professional level that a wag has said, "No self-respecting college coach or alumnus, and not many college presidents, would be satisfied with a college football team that played like a bunch of amateurs."

[18] It is this professionalization of college athletics, and the elimination of the amateur spirit from the college game, that brings me to the second way in which I believe that intercollegiate athletics are having a harmful influence upon high schools and high school sport. What I am thinking of now is the infusion of the "pro" attitude and spirit into high school athletics, and the shady practices that such infusion carries in its wake—practices that are shady from the point of view of the amateur's sportsmanship code. To quite an extent, high school coaches are the product of professionalized college sport, and they tend to coach as they were coached. Here, I do not write disparagingly of coaches as men. I have known a lot of them, and with few exceptions they are fine men personally. But I agree with what G. W. (Sec) Taylor said of them when he made his presidential address to the Football Writers Association: "Coaches have their job to do, and for the most part they do those jobs exactly the way that is expected of them by the president, the

faculty, and the public. They are simply caught in the whirlpool of pressure athletics and are helpless to do anything about it until the college presidents and faculties give them some help." In this quotation, Mr. Taylor explained the situation, but he did not condone it.

[19] Very few remember the sportsmanship code: "Honorable victory; respect for a worthy opponent; no personal or team advantage, and no disadvantage to the opponents, through dishonorable and unfair means." Ideally, this should be the heart of the athletics program in college and school. It is the reflection of the purpose of an educational institution— of the integrity upon which the entire program of a college or school must rest if society is to be served well. It is the greatest lesson that college and school athletics can teach. But the code is breaking down, first on the college level, and then, by the example of the colleges, on the high school level. When victory is demanded at any price, the means to victory, whether honorable or dishonorable, sportsmanlike or unsportsmanlike, becomes a matter of relative indifference.

[20] A well-known college basketball coach was lecturing to high school basketball coaches. Among other things, he told how his team defeated one of the highest-rated teams of the year. He said that his real obstacle was the star forward on the opposing team and that the route to victory lay in tempting that man into the fouls necessary to cause his ejection from the game. And he taught it as sound game tactics that although it took deliberate fouling by four successive players, they tricked their victim into the necessary fouls, got rid of him, and then won the game. Now, I suspect that that could be called a species of respect for a worthy opponent, but I doubt that it is the kind of respect envisaged in the code. Furthermore, it conflicts pretty directly with the clause that forbids "dishonorable and unfair means." It is the kind of bad practice that under the pro spirit is transmuted into "smart ball," and I submit that it has no place in college or high school sport.

[21] Another illustration of bad practice is the injury feigned in order to get another time-out period to give more time for the one additional play that may win the game or at least stave off defeat. After one well-remembered college game in which that device was used, cries of "smart football" were legion, although some angered sports writers called it dirty ball. We in the high schools do not want this kind of play in our games, or anything in the spirit of "win at any price, by any means," even though our elders by example portray it as sensible play. But it is hard to resist the pressure of intercollegiate sport, which we sometimes have to do if we are to convince new coaches that we actually want our high school teams coached to revere the sportsmanship code.

[22] A third bad practice is one that some of us in high schools call "the exalted spotter." Some years ago, a professional football league

coach placed an assistant on top of the stands to telephone reports to the bench on the formations of the opponent and how to outmaneuver them. Were I in the professional league, I'd do the same thing, for I would have to win games in order to attract a heavy gate. Many college coaches who needed to draw heavy gates quickly adopted the exalted spotter technique. Apparently, they have little respect for the ability of quarterbacks to assess the field and call the plays; or perhaps the pressure is so great that they dare not release to an underling the pivotal responsibility of calling plays. But now the exalted spotter has entered the high school lists, and in high school and college the game is taken away from the players and directed by the tactician on the bench. Thus a boy is denied one of the main benefits of athletics: the opportunity, on his own, to think fast and independently and to make decisions as the game develops on the field.

[23] These three examples, out of many, are not isolated instances of pro college practices that are hurting high school athletics; they are illustrations of a *spirit* that is inimical to the sportsmanship code. Particularly objectionable is the insistence that every team must win all of its games, and that the coach who cannot achieve that result should be fired. Bad team practices are bound to result from such an impossible condition.

[24] "Caught in the whirlpool of pressure athletics," as Mr. Taylor expressed it, coaches have done what they might have been expected to do. Asked to win or leave, they have demanded more money, both to compensate for strain and to serve as insurance between hirings and firings. Furthermore, they have gone out to find or buy players with whom to win. The strange thing is that some bad athletic policies have become so respectable with use that the subsidization of college athletes, to such an extent as almost to constitute their *employment* as athletes, is often defended as the bedrock prerequisite of amateur sport!

[25] Is there any hope in the college athletics situation? Yes, there is a lot of hope, if the one force capable of doing something about the situation will stop ignoring it and actively insist upon its correction. That force is the college faculty. The athletics situation is primarily a faculty situation. As I said earlier, it is agreed that recruitment and subsidization constitute the major problems in college athletics, and these eventually are matters for the admissions office. Here is where the faculty comes in, for it is to the faculty that the admissions office is responsible for those whom it recommends, both for instruction and for scholarship aid. The NCAA and some athletic conferences are doing what they can, but they face two hard facts: 1) some colleges do not want reform, and will cheat;

2) bad practices have been frozen into conference codes. The real cure must take place in the individual college.

[26] What can the faculty do? It can do what it should have done long ago. It can adopt a resolution, the enforcement of which it can demand and, if necessary, police. The resolution would say about six things. There should be no substandard admissions. All scholarships should be granted on the one basis of apparent ability to do college work on the scholarship level recommended by the faculty. Scholarship amounts should be based on need. Job opportunities should be genuine jobs, and pay should be regulated according to the accepted local scale. There should be no snap courses designed to favor any particular group of students. All students should be evaluated on the same general basis: their course work in classes. Of course, the resolution can say whatever else needs to be said to cure the local situation. If a college faculty really means business, administrative officers will think hard before they will deny a resolution of the faculty. But the catch is that the faculty must mean business.

[27] In my experience, athletes in general are an intelligent group of boys. They would not and they should not be discriminated against under the recommended resolution. On their merit as students, they would win their fair share of scholarships and other financial help. I know that college athletics, if they were fairly and firmly handled, would become highly respected as a student activity. They would no longer be an enterprise run for financial profit, public relations, protection of vested interests, and as a sop for the alumni.

QUESTIONS AND COMMENT ON FORM AND CONTENT

1. How shall I begin? How can I get the attention of the reader and his interest and confidence in what I have to say? Mr. Youngert gets attention by means of some case histories of high school students who were weak scholastically but who were given special opportunities because of their athletic abilities. But what can be proved by a few case histories? Do we have the word of Mr. Youngert that they are not unusual?

2. What is the author's main proposition or thesis? Express it in the form of a resolution (Resolved that. . . .) such as used in debates or in the form of a question. Word it in such a way that the author would take the affirmative side.

3. What is the standing of the following italicized expressions as indicated by your collegiate dictionary? When the expression is given without comment or note, it may be considered as in standard usage. (If convenient, compare the usage of the expressions as given in *Webster's Seventh Collegiate Dictionary* with another collegiate dictionary. The *Seventh Collegiate Dictionary*

is based on *Webster's Third New International Dictionary.* See Bergen Evans's article in Chapter 5.

    a. *flunked out* for poor academic work (1)

    b. he was *worked on* by representatives (2)

    c. he was not *up to* university football (3)

    d. thanks to this *lad* (5)

    e. we had to work *like the dickens* (8)

4. The author says that high schools are harmed in two ways by the professionalization of college athletics. What are they? In which paragraph does he let the reader know that he has moved from the first point to the second?

5. What is the argument given for the financial support of athletes? What does Mr. Youngert say this argument assumes?

6. What specific violations of the sportsmanship code are cited? Are these, in his opinion, isolated instances? As evidence for his argument, does it matter whether they are typical?

7. Where does the last section begin? Is the author specific in his suggestions for solutions to the problems raised? Is it usually necessary that a writer or speaker provide solutions to evils that he has exposed? Cite examples *pro* and *con.*

VOCABULARY: WHAT DO THE ITALICIZED WORDS MEAN?

He said with *asperity* (1)

. . . *assiduously* seek information (9)

List names . . . of players whom [*sic*] you feel will make. . . . (9)

. . . who *avidly* seek the boy's favor (11)

. . . we are shedding *crocodile tears* (16)

THEME SUGGESTIONS

Spectator Sports

High School Athlete: A Case History

The Awarding of College Scholarships

Are College Athletics Too Commercialized?

GIVE THE GAMES BACK TO THE STUDENTS

Henry Steele Commager

Henry Steele Commager (1902-   ), an eminent American historian, is co-author of The Growth of the American Republic *(1931-1942). The article that follows was published in the* New York Times Magazine, *April 16, 1941.*

[1] Almost every year the public is startled by revelations of some new scandal in college athletics—the bribery of basketball players, the open purchase of football players, the flagrant violation of rules by the college authorities themselves.

[2] It is regrettable that these scandals should excite so much attention, for, by dramatizing the ostentatious immoralities of college athletics, they tend to distract attention from the more permanent and pervasive immoralities.

[3] Indignation at the more overt manifestations of corruption is thus a kind of moral catharsis; having expressed it, we then can contemplate with apathy the conditions which almost inevitably produce the corruption.

[4] Thirty years ago a report of the Carnegie Foundation on College Athletics concluded as follows:

[5] The paid coach, the special training tables, the costly sweaters and extensive journeys in special Pullman cars, the recruiting from high schools, the demoralizing publicity showered on players, the devotion of an undue proportion of time to training, the devices for putting a desirable athlete, but a weak scholar, across the hurdles of the examinations, these ought to stop and the intramural sports be brought back to a stage in which they can be enjoyed by a large number of students and where they do not involve an expenditure of time and money wholly at variance with any ideal of honest study.

[6] "These ought to stop!" Instead, they have become all but universally accepted and legalized—nay, the malpractices themselves have become respectable, and we can look back upon our old view of them with a certain nostalgia.

[7] For today's malpractices are more extreme and more widespread. Worse yet, they have percolated down to the high school and they have corrupted large segments of our society.

[8] For almost half a century now, educators have talked hopefully about de-emphasizing college athletics. And every year the emphasis has grown greater, not weaker.

[9] The problem is not one of overemphasis. It is not even one of emphasis. The problem is the enterprise itself—intercollegiate athletics.

[10] If we are going to solve that problem, we must begin by restating principles so elementary and so obvious that they should not have to be stated at all:

[11] The function of colleges and universities is to advance education.

[12] Whatever contributes to education is legitimate. Whatever does not contribute to education is illegitimate.

[13] The only justification, therefore, for games, sports, athletics, is that these do in some way contribute to education.

[14] By education we mean nothing narrow. Clearly, it involves physical and moral as well as intellectual well-being. But these are by-products of education. There are a number of institutions that have responsibility for the physical and moral well-being of the young, but the schools and colleges are the only institutions that have primary responsibility for their intellectual well-being.

[15] Does our current system of intercollegiate or interschool athletics contribute either to the central function of education, or to its by-products?

[16] Clearly, it does not. As now organized and directed in most colleges and in a good many, if not most, high schools as well, athletics contribute nothing whatsoever to education. They simply distract the time, the energy and the attention of the whole community from the main business of education—and from its legitimate by-products.

[17] Our system of athletics does not contribute to the physical fitness of the young. On the contrary, it concentrates on physical training for a mere handful of students—whom it often harms by overtraining—and reduces the great majority of students to the role of passive spectators, or television viewers. Even the facilities provided for physical training are often monopolized by the "teams," to the detriment of most of the student body.

[18] It does not contribute to sportsmanship—which was one of its original purposes. On the contrary, the tremendous emphasis on winning the game has largely destroyed sportsmanship and has corrupted both players and spectators.

[19] It does not contribute to initiative, independence, alertness and other desirable qualities. Instead, by centering authority in paid coaches whose primary interest is winning games, it has gone far to destroy initiative and independence on the part of the players.

[20] No impartial student of college and high-school athletics today can doubt that, on balance, these sports—far from making any contribution—actually do immense and irreparable harm. It is not only physical training and sports that are corrupted by the current malpractices; it is the whole educational enterprise. And since the whole community is involved in the educational enterprise, it is the whole community.

[21] Educational institutions themselves are corrupted. They publicly confirm that their athletic functions are more important than their academic, and acquiesce in malpractices that they would not tolerate in any other branch of their activities.

[22] Colleges that spend more money on athletics than on the library,

that excite more interest in basketball than in music, that cater to the demand for "winning teams" rather than for sportsmanship are faithless to their moral and intellectual obligations.

[23] The community itself is corrupted by being bribed with athletic spectacles to support educational programs which should be supported on their merits.

[24] Perhaps worst of all, the boys and girls of the country are corrupted: here is the real corruption of the innocent. Almost every newspaper, every weekly magazine, every television network makes clear to them that what is most important in education is athletics, and what is most important in athletics is winning.

[25] No newspaper ever celebrates the scholarly achievements of local students in its biggest headlines. Why, then, should we expect the young to believe us when we tell them, on ceremonial occasions, that it is the scholarly achievements that are important? Alumni demand a winning team, and so does the community. Not long ago, a North Carolina coach was quoted as asking, "How can I be proud of a losing team?" Can we, then, expect young people to take us seriously when we tell them that it is the game that counts—not the victory?

[26] What is the explanation of this deep and pervasive corruption of games and sports? What has happened to us?

[27] What has happened is that we have taken games away from the students, to whom they belong, and given them to adults, to whom they do not belong.

[28] We now require of high school and college boys—and, sometimes, girls—that they provide entertainment for the community and bring money to local shopkeepers and restaurants and other business men. (Recently a New York official said of an Army-Syracuse game that "the restaurants reported business to be fabulous . . . the Transit Authority reported 28,000 extra riders that day . . . immensely increased hotel business.") They are expected to provide copy for the local newspapers, for magazines, and for TV and radio.

[29] We do not permit children to work in shops or factories for our profit. Why should they be expected to make money for business interests in the community?

[30] We do not permit our daughters to put on performances in burlesque shows or night clubs for our entertainment. Why should we require our sons to put on gladiatorial spectacles in stadia for our entertainment?

[31] We do not expect the young to pay school taxes, or to support the chemistry department of a university. Why should we expect them to earn money for the athletic programs of the local high school, or to support the athletic departments of our colleges and universities?

[32] The problem is deep and pervasive, but fortunately not complex. The solution is drastic, but fortunately not difficult; all that is needed is the will to apply it. The solution is threefold:

First, give games back to the students.
Second, eliminate all outside pressures to win games.
Third, take the dollar sign entirely out of school and college athletics.

[33] First: Let students manage their own games, as they do at English universities. Let them play their games for the fun of it, not to entertain adults, or make money for the community or win glory for old Pugwash.

[34] An end to games as spectacles. An end to bands in uniforms and drum majorettes and well-trained cheering sections, all of them artificial and all giving a fantastically exaggerated importance to the games. An end to the recruiting of players by coaches or alumni, to coaches who play the games from the side lines and, for that matter, to formal coaching. If there must be coaches, let them depart on the day of the game and permit the players to play their own games. After all, professors do not help the students pass examinations!

[35] Second: Eliminate all outside pressures. Alumni letters about the football team should go into the waste basket, where they belong. An end to pressure from coaches; their jobs should not depend on victories. An end to pressure from newspapers; let them report professional games, and leave students alone to play as well or as badly as they please. An end to pressure from public relations offices of colleges; let them report academic activities or go out of business. An end to pressure from townspeople; they can get their entertainment, find emotional safety valves and get rid of their vicarious sadism elsewhere.

[36] Third: Eliminate money—all the way. No more paid coaches. Let students do their own coaching, or let school teams draw on "old boys," or get such aid as they need from members of the teaching staff who are primarily and legitimately teachers. After all, paid coaches are both new and singular in history: they did not exist until this century, and they do not now exist in England or Europe.

[37] An end to all athletic subsidies, direct and indirect; to athletic "scholarships," a contradiction in terms. No student should be encouraged, in high school, to subordinate studies to athletic prowess. No student should be admitted to college on any grounds but those of academic competence; no student should be allowed to stay in college unless he is intellectually competent.

[38] An end to separate athletic budgets; to admission charges for games; to the expectation that football or basketball will somehow "pay for" other parts of physical training. Games should be as much a normal

part of school or college as music or drama or the college newspaper, and should no more expect to be self-sustaining.

[39] An end to the building or maintenance of costly stadia. Let us make drastic reductions in expenditures for athletic equipment, for uniforms, for other superfluities. No more travel expenditures for spring training camps, for fall training camps, for airplane junkets to the other end of the country. Let schools play their neighbors in the same town or —at an extreme—in the same state.

[40] Adopt these policies and nine-tenths of the evils that plague intercollegiate athletics would evaporate overnight.

[41] Of course, if they *were* adopted, the games would deteriorate— as spectacles. Those who want to see brilliant performances in football or basketball can then go to professional games, as even now they go to professional rather than to college baseball games.

[42] Let the fans—the subway alumni of Notre Dame or the vicarious old grads of Michigan—organize city or state football and basketball teams, just as the English have city or county soccer teams.

[43] Naturally, student interest in organized athletics will decline; it should. Sensible students already know that if they are going to get on with their education—if they are going to get into a law school or a medical school—they have no time for organized athletics.

[44] European universities have managed to survive for centuries without the benefit of "teams," and doubtless American colleges and universities can learn to do so.

[45] Of course, there will be a falling-off in enthusiasm for old Siwash among certain kinds of alumni. Perhaps, in time, colleges can produce alumni whose interest is in intellectual rather than in athletic programs. In any event, there seems to be a pretty close correlation between high-powered athletics and low-powered finances. It is a sardonic commentary on the current scene that public pressure for winning teams rarely finds expression in lavish gifts or in generous appropriations. Institutions such as M.I.T. and Amherst, at any rate, seem to manage pretty well without the exploitation of athletics, and institutions such as Ohio State, which has yielded to pressure for winning teams, are treated with niggardliness by an ungrateful legislature.

[46] These are negative consequences which we may anticipate from the elimination of money and of pressures from college athletics and the return of games to the students. The positive consequences which we may confidently anticipate are exhilarating.

[47] This simple program will restore integrity to athletics, making clear once more the blurred distinction between the amateur and the professional. And it will enormously improve programs for physical ed-

ucation for the young people in schools and colleges, an improvement desperately needed.

[48] It will release the energies of educators and students for the primary job of education. The colleges will be freed from improper pressures and influences and permitted to do what they are best equipped to do and what they have a moral responsibility to do: educate the young.

QUESTIONS AND COMMENT ON FORM AND CONTENT

1. Since this article appeared in a magazine which is a part of a newspaper, the newspaper style of paragraphing is used. In this style, adopted mainly because of the narrow columns, the paragraphs are quite short, frequently a single sentence. Could the first two or three paragraphs be combined into one paragraph and still have the unity and coherence we have come to expect of expository, argumentative, and descriptive paragraphs? What would be its topic sentence?

2. Why does the author begin with scandals? What is his point about them? Explain, in particular, the third paragraph. Can you apply the same principle to the public attitude toward other evils in American life? Does the word *scapegoat* apply to this tendency?

3. As a historian, the author traces athletics over the preceding thirty years. What does he find objectionable? Are conditions, in his opinion, improving?

4. Having listed the malpractices, Mr. Commager says that in order to correct them we must reconsider the purpose of education. Why did he find it necessary to define such a common term as *education?* What phase of education does he consider the main responsibility of the college or university?

5. This type of argument is deductive.

Major premise: Whatever does not contribute to education is illegitimate.

Minor premise: X (see paragraphs 15 to 25) does not contribute to education.

Conclusion: Therefore, X is illegitimate.

If you agree with the statement in the major premise, including his definition of *education,* and if you agree with the statement about the item in the minor premise, then you must, logically, accept the conclusion. Specifically, what are the practices that do not contribute, according to the author, to education?

6. In paragraphs 11 to 14 there are five consecutive sentences using the word *education.* Is this repetition desirable? In paragraphs 15 to 20 the word *contribute* is repeated many times. Does this repetition (along with parallel structure) help the reader to follow the argument?

7. To support his argument that athletics are requiring too much of high school and college boys, the author uses several analogies based on (1) the treatment of children, (2) daughters, and (3) the young in general. What is an analogy? Are these analogies apt and effective as argument? Are the cases

compared basically similar? Or are they dissimilar in essential matters? Do they, at least, show a point of view clearly?

8. In paragraphs 34 to 39 Mr. Commager uses one or more fragments (incomplete sentences) in each paragraph. What is a fragment or incomplete sentence? Are fragments effective as used here? Does the use of parallel sentence structure add to their effectiveness?

9. Three solutions are outlined in paragraph 32. Which of the paragraphs that follow paragraph 32 develop the first point? The second point? The third point?

10. What are the two kinds of consequences?

11. Compare the literal analogies used in paragraphs 41, 44, and 45 with the figurative analogy in paragraph 51.

12. Compare the solutions of Commager and Youngert (preceding selection) to the athletic problem.

VOCABULARY: WHAT DO THE ITALICIZED WORDS MEAN?

. . . the *flagrant* violations of rules (1)

. . . *dramatizing* the *ostentatious* immoralities of college athletics (2)

. . . the more *overt* manifestations of corruption is thus a kind of moral *catharsis* (3)

. . . can contemplate with *apathy* (3)

. . . *intramural* sports (5)

. . . look back with . . . *nostalgia* (6)

. . . immense and *irreparable* harm (20)

. . . *acquiesce* in *malpractices* (21)

An end to all athletic *subsidies* (37)

. . . airplane *junkets* to the other end of the country (39)

It is a *sardonic* commentary (45)

THEME SUGGESTIONS

Football and Education
Athletic Scholarships Are Necessary (Unnecessary)
Intercollegiate versus Intramural Sports
A Sound Health Education and Recreation Program
College Spirit and Football (Basketball, etc.)
Athletic Scandals
Scapegoats

11 | MASS COMMUNICATION

THE AD AND THE ID

Vance Packard

Vance Packard (1914-   ) has been a reporter, editor, lecturer, and author of books. Perhaps his best known books are The Hidden Persuaders *and* The Status Seekers.

[1] The early nineteen fifties witnessed the beginnings of a revolution in American advertising: Madison Avenue became conscious of the *unconscious*. Evidence had piled up that the responses of consumers to the questions of market researchers were frequently unreliable—in other words, that people often don't want what they say they want. Some years ago, for instance, a great automobile company committed one of the costliest blunders in automobile history through reliance on the old-style "nose counting" methods. Direct consumer surveys indicated that people wanted a sensible car in tune with the times—without frills, maneuverable and easy to park. A glance at today's cars—elongated, fish-finned and in riotous technicolor—shows how misleading were the results of the survey. Errors of this sort convinced manufacturers and advertisers that they must take into account the irrationality of consumer behavior—that they must carry their surveys into the submerged areas of the human mind. The result is a strange and rather exotic phenomenon entirely new to the market place—the use of a kind of mass psychoanalysis to guide

campaigns of persuasion. The ad is being tailored to meet the needs of the id.

[2] The so-called "depth approach" to selling problems is known as motivational research, or simply M.R. Social scientists by the hundreds have been recruited for this massive exploration of the consumer's psyche, and hundreds of millions of dollars are being spent on it. Two-thirds of the nation's leading advertising agencies have been using the depth approach (along with the more conventional methods), and one major agency resorts to it for every single product it handles, to detect possible hidden appeals and resistances.

[3] A number of factors have contributed to the rapid growth of motivational research. By the mid-nineteen fifties, American producers were achieving a fabulous output. This meant that we must be persuaded to buy more and more to keep the wheels of the economy turning. As the president of National Sales Executives exclaimed: "Capitalism is dead —consumerism is king!" Another formidable obstacle that faced the merchandisers in our advanced technology was the increasing similarity of competing products. While it might still be possible for people of discrimination to distinguish between brands of cigarettes, whiskey, detergent, and so on, it became increasingly difficult to teach them to do so on any rational basis. Still, loyalty to a particular brand had to be created, and it was done in many instances by "building a personality" —playful, conservative or showy—into the brand. In this way, Procter and Gamble's image makers have projected a living personification for each of their brands of soap (Ivory is mother and daughter on a sort of pedestal of purity; Camay a glamorous woman), and a Chicago chain of food stores decided that the image which would give it the edge over its competitors should have "the traits we like in our friends"—generosity, cleanliness, etc.

[4] What the depth researchers are looking for, of course, are the hidden *whys* of our behavior—why many people are intimidated by banks, why men are drawn into showrooms by convertibles but emerge with sedans, why women go into a trance-like state at the supermarket and why junior likes noisy cereal. The principal tools of M.R. are the techniques of psychiatry—interviews "in depth" (but without the couch, which might make the consumer guinea pig wary); Rorschach (ink blot) tests; stress tests, in which the rate at which you blink your eyes is recorded by hidden cameras; lie detectors; word association tests; and finally the group interview, which, surprisingly, has the effect of breaking down inhibitions. (One candid statement prompts another and presently a roomful of people are freely discussing laxatives, deodorants, weight reducers and athlete's foot.)

[5] The efforts of the persuaders to probe our everyday habits for

hidden meanings are often fascinating purely for the revelations—some amusing, some rather appalling—which they offer us about ourselves. The average American likes to think of himself as a rugged individualist and, above all, a thoughtful, hardheaded consumer of the products of American enterprise. But in the findings of the motivational researchers, we are apt to emerge as comic actors in a genial if twitchy Thurberian world—bundles of daydreams, secret yearnings and curious emotional quirks.

[6] In learning to sell to our subconscious, the persuaders soon discovered unsuspected areas of tension and guilt. Self-indulgent and easy-does-it products are a significant sector of the total American market, yet Americans, it seems, have in them a larger streak of Puritanism than is generally recognized. For instance, the hidden attitude of women toward labor-saving devices is decidedly surprising. Working wives can accept them, but the full-time housewife is liable to feel that they threaten her importance and creativity. The research director of an ad agency sadly explained the situation as follows: "If you tell the housewife that by using your washing machine, drier or dishwasher she can be free to play bridge, you're dead!—the housewife today already feels guilty about the fact that she is not working as hard as her mother. Instead, you should emphasize that appliances free her to have more time with her children." Makers of ready-mixes and foods with "built in maid service" ran into the same sort of problem. In the early days, the packages promised to take over all the work, but wives were not grateful for this boon. A leading motivational analyst, James Vicary, has stated the reason. Cake-making, he finds, is steeped in creative symbolism for women—it is, in fact, "a traditional acting out of the birth of a child." This feeling shows up in our folklore in such jokes as the one which says that brides whose cakes fall obviously can't produce a baby yet. (A Chicago analyst has noted that gardening, too, is a symbolic "pregnancy activity" and thus is particularly popular with women past the child-bearing age who need creative outlets.)

[7] Subconscious tensions about food also rose to plague the makers of Jello a few years ago. Jello had become known to millions of households as a quick dessert, simple and shirt-sleeved in character. Then the ad-men, trying to make it more captivating, started showing it in beautiful, layered, lavishly decorated concoctions. The ads were not a success, and the Institute for Motivational Research was able to tell why. Many women, looking at these feats of fussy preparation, wondered if they could duplicate them, and often concluded that if they had to go to all that work, they would much rather make their own dessert without someone standing over their shoulder telling them how to do it. The Jello people, alerted, went back to showing simple mounds of the stuff,

and added to their attraction largely by such simple devices as fairy-tale drawings.

[8] The whole area of food, in fact, would seem to be booby-trapped with hidden problems for women. Mr. Vicary noticed, for instance, that young wives in particular tended to avoid the smaller, clerk-manned grocery stores in favor of the supermarket. He was able to isolate the explanation: newly married women are more ignorant about food than older women and are afraid the clerk will find them out. A Midwestern grocery chain found that this state of fearfulness centered around butcher clerks in particular. Faced with a discussion of cuts of meat, where their lack of knowledge is often profound, many women feel anxiety. After "depth-probing" the situation, the chain began training its butchers to exhibit extraordinary patience and garrulity with younger women, and the strategy has paid off by turning the chain into a haven for innocents.

[9] Supermarkets, on the other hand, are so tension-free as to make many women fall into a state bordering on hypnotic trance. Anxious to trace the reasons for the enormous rise in so-called impulse buying in American supermarkets (today seven out of ten purchases in super-markets are made on impulse—the shopping list of old is becoming obso-lete), Mr. James Vicary made a remarkable test. He had assumed that some special psychology must be at work to put women in an impulsive state when they got into supermarkets, possibly the tension of confront-ing so many products and having to make rapid decisions. Since our blink rate is one rough index of our inner tension, Mr. Vicary installed hidden cameras to record the blink rate of women shoppers. Normally, we blink about thirty-two times a minute, and he expected to see the rate go up as the ladies faced their decisions. Nothing of the sort occurred. The rate went down, down, down to a subnormal fourteen blinks a minute for the average woman—a condition of hypnoidal trance. Many of the women collided with boxes or passed the whirring cameras with-out noticing them. But when they approached the checkout counters with their loaded carts, their blink rate would start rising back toward normal; and when they heard the bell of the cash register, the rate shot up to the abnormal figure of forty-five a minute, a symptom of acute anxiety. Mr. Vicary's explanation of the trance: the woman feels herself a queen in a fairyland filled with lovely, accessible objects, unimaginable in former years and all whispering "buy me, buy me."

[10] The calorie consciousness which swept the country, beginning a few years ago, created other psychological troubles for foodmakers. A number of brewing companies, who had thought to capitalize on the phenomenon, tried to outdo one another in plugging low-caloried beer, and for a time sales did go up. But M.R. hoisted warning flags. Dr. Ernest Dichter, head of the Institute for Motivational Research, warned

that calorie consciousness is a sort of psychological penance. People
go on diets because they are trying to punish themselves for past indul-
gence. Hence, low-calorie diets are not supposed to be pleasant. What
the brewers were conveying in effect, was that real beer must be fattening
and that low-calorie beer was somehow denatured. "Thus," said the
Institute, "when a beer advertises itself as low in calories, the consumer
reacts by feeling the beer has a poor taste." Perhaps this cautionary note
was responsible for one brewer's recent clarion call: "Made by people
who like beer for people who drink beer, and plenty of it!"

[11] Another product which found its market temporarily constricted
because of too much harping on calories was Ry-Krisp, which ran advertisements containing calorie tables and showing very slim people nib-
bling the wafers. Motivational analysts found that Ry-Krisp had developed for itself a self-punishment image as a food that was "good" for
people—an image which drove away people not in a self-punishing
mood. Corrective action was taken: in advertisements, Ry-Krisp began
appearing with tempting foods and was described as delicious and fes-
tive. This more permissive approach nearly doubled sales in test areas.

[12] Even in travel we have hidden anxieties which marketers find
it profitable to take into account. A number of years ago, an airline became
disturbed by the fact that so many passengers flew only when pressed
for time, and it hired a conventional research firm to find out why. The
simple answer came back that they didn't fly because they were afraid
of being killed, but an intensive advertising campaign emphasizing safety
yielded disappointing results. At last Dr. Dichter was called in. His answer, based on picture tests which encouraged potential travelers to imagine themselves involved in airline crashes, was different and astonishing. What the traveler feared was not death but a sort of posthumous
embarrassment. The husband pictured his wife receiving the news and
saying, "The damned fool, he should have gone by train." The obvious
answer was to convince wives of the common sense of flying, which would
bring their husbands home faster from business trips, and to get them
in the air (to get their feet wet, as it were) with tempting family flying
plans.

[13] Still other subconscious fears, and not always the obvious ones,
relate to money. Motivational studies have proved, for example, that it
is not guilt about owing money which makes people hesitate to approach the bank for a loan. The fear is of the bank itself, which is seen
as an angry father-figure who will disapprove of our untidy financial
affairs. Many people would rather go to a loan company, in spite of the
higher interest rate, simply because the moral tone associated with it
is lower; in fact, there is a complete shift in moral dominance in which
the borrower becomes a righteous fellow, temporarily forced into low

company, and the higher cost of the loan is a small price to pay for such a changed view of ourselves. It is worth noting that a good many banks today are trying to mellow the stern image of themselves by removing the bars on teller windows, making wider use of glass fronts and staging folksy little exhibits which depict them—at worst—as rather crusty but charming old gentlemen in Scotch hats.

[14] It will surprise nobody to learn that sex plays an enormously important part in selling. But how it works *is* frequently surprising. Sex images have, of course, long been cherished by ad-makers, but in the depth approach sex takes on some extraordinary ramifications and subtleties. A classic example is the study of automobiles made by Dr. Dichter which became known as "Mistress Versus Wife"—a study responsible for the invention of the most successful new car style introduced to the American market for several years. Dealers had long been aware that a convertible in the window drew the male customer into the showroom. They also knew that he usually ended by choosing a four-door sedan. The convertible, said Dr. Dichter, had associations of youth and adventure—it was symbolic of the mistress. But the sedan was the girl one married because she would make a good wife and mother. How could an automobile symbolically combine the appeals of mistress and wife? The answer was the celebrated hardtop, which Dr. Dichter's organization takes full credit for inspiring.

[15] A company advertising a home permanent wave ran into another sexual problem, which was solved by M.R. They had thought it would be a brilliant idea to picture a mother and daughter with identical hairdos captioned: "A Double Header Hit with Dad." Wives, interviewed at the conscious level, said they didn't object at all to the implied idea of competition for the husband-father's admiration, but the company was still apprehensive—rightly, as it turned out. Depth interviews revealed that women would indeed deeply resent the "hit with dad" theme, and it was hastily dropped.

[16] As for the American male, he stands in equal need of sexual reassurance, particularly as women continue to invade the traditional strongholds. The fact that cigar makers have been enjoying their greatest prosperity in twenty years has been credited by many to the man-at-bay, and at least one ad agency disagrees with the efforts of the Cigar Institute of America to draw women into the picture. This agency, puzzled by the failure of a campaign which had pictured a smiling woman offering cigars to a group of men, ordered a depth survey to uncover the reason. The conclusion was that men enjoy cigars precisely because they are objectionable to women; nor is the man sincere who politely asks if the ladies mind his lighting up. As the head of the agency put it: "He knows . . . he is going to stink up the room."

[17] Motivational analysis has even discovered certain products to be sexually "maladjusted," and it is responsible for several spectacular cases of planned transvestitism. When the cancer scare drove millions of men to try filter tips, the makers of Marlboro cigarettes decided to cash in by changing the sex of a cigarette originally designed for women. The ads began to show a series of rugged males, engaged in virile occupations and all of them, by an extraordinary coincidence, tattooed. The tattoo motif puzzled a good many people, since the tattoo is a common phenomenon among delinquents in reformatories. Marlboro, however, decided it was exactly what was needed to give its men a virile and "interesting past" look—the same look arrived at, by other means, in the one-eyed man in the Hathaway shirt.

[18] When Lloyd Warner published his book, *Social Class in America*, in 1948, it created a respectful stir in academic circles; but in later years it was to create an even greater one among merchandisers. Like David Riesman in his classic, *The Lonely Crowd*, or Russell Lynes, whose famous dissection of high-, middle- and low-brows charted the social significance of such items as tossed salad and rye whiskey, Warner defined social classes less in terms of wealth and power than criteria of status, and merchandisers have begun to give considerable thought to his conclusions. Burleigh Gardener, for example, founder of the M.R. firm of Social Research, Inc., has taken Warner's concepts as his guiding thesis. Social Research has put a class label on many sorts of house-furnishings: the solid color carpet, it appears, is upper class; the "knickknack" shelf lower class; Venetian blinds are upper middle class.

[19] Chicago's Color Research Institute (a psychoanalytically minded group) ran into some of the intricacies of class structure when it was asked to design two candy boxes, one intended to sell to lower class buyers at $1.95, the other to an upper class clientele at $3.50. The Institute's researches led it to a curious recommendation: the box for the cheaper candy would be in vermilion metal tied with a bright blue ribbon, and it would have to cost fifty cents; the box for the expensive candy could be made of pale pink pasteboard at a cost of no more than nine cents. The reason? Candy-giving is an important rite in the lower class, and the girl is likely to treasure the box, whereas the upper class girl will ignore the box (the candy is what counts) and will probably throw it away.

[20] Many advertising men have filled the air above their Madison Avenue rookeries with arguments over the validity and potency of M.R. And the researchers themselves have added to the confusion by disagreeing with each other's methods and results. Of more concern, however, to the average citizen are the possibilities for mass manipulation opened up by motivational research. Disturbing examples of such manipula-

tion have, unfortunately, appeared in politics, industrial relations (a California engineering school boasts that its graduates are "custom-built men") and even in the church, where ministers are being advised how they can more effectively control their congregations. The manipulative approach to politics is not, of course, new—Machiavelli was perfectly familiar with it. But the manipulation of the people by a tyrant is an infinitely simpler problem than that of dealing with the citizens of a free society, who can spurn your solicitations if they want to. Now, however, mass persuasion in this kind of situation has been greatly reinforced by the techniques of the symbol manipulators, who have drawn on Pavlov and his conditioned reflexes, Freud and his father images, Riesman and his concept of modern American voters as spectator-consumers of politics. In the 1956 election, both parties tried to "merchandise" their candidates by commercial marketing methods, using on billboards slogans of scientifically tested appeal, hammering out key messages until the public was saturation-bombed, and grooming their candidates to look "sincere" in front of the TV camera. As one advertising man put it: "I think of a man in a voting booth who hesitates between the two levers as if he were pausing between competing tubes of tooth paste in a drugstore. The brand that has made the highest penetration in his brain will win his choice."

[21] What are the implications of all this persuasion in terms of morality? The social scientists and psychiatrists have a workable rationale for explaining their co-operation with, say, the merchandisers. They are broadening the world's knowledge of human behavior; and knowledge, as Alfred Whitehead has said, keeps no better than fish. But there remains the disturbing fact by scientifically catering to the irrational, the persuaders are working toward a progressively less rational society. We may wonder if, in a few decades when it becomes technically feasible, we will be ripe for biocontrol, a brand new science for controlling mental processes, emotional reactions and sense perceptions by bioelectrical signals. Already, rats with full bellies have been made to feel ravenously hungry, and to feel fear when they had nothing to be afraid of. As one electronic engineer has said: "The ultimate achievement of biocontrol may be the control of man himself. . . . The controlled subjects would never be permitted to think as individuals. A few months after birth, a surgeon would equip each child with a socket mounted under the scalp and electrodes reaching selected areas of brain tissue. . . . The child's sensory perceptions and muscular activity could either be modified or completely controlled by bioelectric signals radiating from state-controlled transmitters." He added that the electrodes would cause no discomfort.

[22] I'm sure the persuaders of 1957 would be appalled by such a

prospect. Most of them are likeable, earnest men who just want to control us a little bit, to maneuver us into buying something that we may actually need. But when you start manipulating people, where exactly do you stop?

QUESTIONS AND COMMENT ON FORM AND CONTENT

1. What is the meaning of the title?

2. What does Mr. Packard mean by saying "people often don't want what they say they want"?

3. Do the people answering questionnaires intentionally give the wrong answers or do they not know or admit to themselves what they really want in cars, homes, jewelry, clothing, entertainment, and the like?

4. What is meant by the depth of approach or motivational research? What are some of the tools of the researcher in M.R.? What was discovered about selling each of the following: labor-saving devices; supermarket products; low-calorie products; cigarettes and cigars; convertibles, sedans, and hardtops; packaged candy; loans from a bank?

5. Who was Machiavelli?

6. How does the author describe the average American buyer? (See paragraph 5.) Do you agree with his description? Do you buy some products mainly on impulse? Do you feel that, in general, you have been manipulated by the advertisers?

7. The first sentence of a paragraph is frequently a topic sentence. It is also frequently transitional, carrying the reader smoothly from the preceding topic to the new one being developed. Can you find examples of both ideas in the paragraphs here?

VOCABULARY: WHAT DO THE ITALICIZED WORDS MEAN?

. . . a strange and rather *exotic* phenomenon (1)
. . . *massive* exploration of the consumer's *psyche* (2)
. . . patience and *garrulity* with younger women (8)
. . . cases of planned *transvestitism* (17)

THEME SUGGESTIONS

The Necessity of Advertising
Advertising: An Economic Waste
Appeals in TV Advertising
Truth in Advertising
Magazine Advertising

Logic in Advertising
Appeals Used in Selling Automobiles (Detergents, Cigarettes, Perfumes, etc.)
I Bought a White Elephant
Extravagant Buying Is Depleting Our Natural Resources

A CUB REPORTER BECOMES DISILLUSIONED

Eric Sevareid

Eric Sevareid (1912-   ) is an author, broadcaster, and news analyst. Some of his scripts have been published in Not So Wild a Dream *(1946),* In One Ear *(1952), and* Small Sounds in the Night *(1956).*

[1] If a young man goes directly from secondary school to the university, and completes the study of his profession in theory and principle before entering his first office, everything is quite different. The faces, the titles, the very arrangement of the desks and departments he sees as a functional pattern. He has his mind on the end product of the concern; he knows how and why his product came about in modern society; he knows its present status in terms of history, and he no doubt understands the relationship of himself and his work to the times in which he lives. It must be a great advantage to begin that way, but it also means missing a brief period of complete enchantment. The old Minneapolis *Journal,* no longer extant, was an imposing and venerable institution in that northwest country, identified with the permanent structures of the landscape—the original buildings of Fort Snelling, the first dam on the upper Mississippi, the first roadbed laid by Jim Hill, the Empire Builder. It spoke with authority in the land, if not with wisdom, and it was an interconnecting cog in the social machinery of a widely scattered civilization. I was unaware that its directors were in, hand and glove, with the potentates of railroad, timber, and milling who for a very long time dictated, as if by kingly right, the political and economic affairs of this civilization. I was unaware that the men who wrote its pages *were* aware, bitterly so, of the paper's true function. To me at eighteen it was that most remarkable, most fascinating of all human institutions, a daily newspaper, peopled with those glamorous, incomparable men known as reporters and editors, actually there, alive, touchable, knowable. The ceremony of the "ghost walking" with the pay envelopes on Saturday afternoon was merely one of the more delightful moments of the week, a necessary bit of the engrossing ritual that preceded the ceremony of

drinking beer down below at the "Greasy Spoon." The pay check of course was not really essential, these superhuman creatures being above anything so prosaic as the need for food, but was merely a kind of token and badge to signify that one Belonged. There was a positive sensual pleasure when one hurried from below-zero weather, so early it was scarcely light, into the warmth and smells of the city room where the telegraph editor was already waiting for the first yellow strips from the press association machines, into the warmer, noisier, greasier composing room upstairs where the limp, moist galley proofs of overset matter were piled and waiting for distribution below. The movement and noise built up with every hour, with the ordered cacophony of improvised symphony to the thundering finale by the great presses below the street, followed by the quiet aftermath of triumph when I would stagger into the city room with fifty fresh, pungent copies in my arms for the relaxing virtuosi who waited there, feet upon their instruments, gifted fingers lighting cigarettes.

[2] This was my entry into the world of private enterprise in which most Americans pass their earthly existence. Surely, this was the best of all possible systems of life, where one simply chose the thing he most wanted to do, and, because he loved it, worked as hard as he could, and, because he worked hard, steadily rose from position to position, until he had "arrived," when the world would hold no more secrets or problems, and life gracefully leveled out on a plane of confidence, security, and happiness. I was convinced of the truth of this when after only six weeks as a copy runner I was made a reporter, with a desk of my own, admission to the Saturday night poker game around the copy desk, and fifteen dollars a week. Up to that time I had never made an enemy, never known anyone to feel that I was a threat to him, nor felt that anyone else was a threat to me. When I broke the news that I was to become a reporter, to a rewrite man I worshipped, I received the first shock and hurt and began to learn. I expected warm congratulations and perhaps admiring predictions of future greatness. Instead, the Godlike journalist looked at me coldly and said: "For Christ's sake. The bastards." It was some time before I realized that experienced reporters, family men who required more than fifteen dollars a week, were being rebuffed each day in their search for employment.

[3] My one regular chore on the paper, the inescapable heritage of the newest and rawest cub, was to spend each Friday as "religious editor," which meant putting together a page of copy with a summed-up story of Sunday's events, followed by several columns of "church notices" in six-point type. It meant interviewing a few visiting clerics of distinction, who never turned down the request. One of these was Billy Sunday, the evangelist, then in his last days. In his case, no questions were needed. He

bounded about the hotel room, now peering intently out the window with one foot on the sill, now grasping the dressing table firmly in both hands while lecturing his reflection in the mirror. I never opened my mouth after introducing myself and scarcely remembered a word of what he said. Suddenly he ceased talking and darted out of the room, whereupon "Ma" Sunday unhooked a half-dozen typewritten sheets from a loose-leaf folder and handed them to me. This was the interview, all prepared, his emphasis marked by capitalized words and phrases in red ink with many exclamation marks. When I first took over this task on the paper I mentioned it one day to a Protestant pastor I happened to know rather well. He clasped his hands together, cast a brief glance upwards, and said: "Thank God for that! I have been grieving over the lack of publicity for our little church." He gripped my shoulder in a brotherly manner and said: "I hope this will be the answer to my prayers." I was quickly to learn that of all the citizens who rang the newspaper or came to the lobby seeking publicity, the men of the church were the most demanding and insatiable. I was frequently embroiled in controversy with pastors who would demand why I had not run the photographs of themselves which they had just sent in, whereas Pastor X had had *his* picture in the paper twice in the last three months. The rabbis were equally desirous, but generally more clever about it, while the important Catholic priests simply let their assistants handle the publicity question and rarely entered the negotiations in person. I learned that the newspaper was frightened of the preachers. The city desk could tell a vaudeville press agent to go to hell when his demands overreached the decent limit, but nobody ever spoke anything but soft words to the press agent of a church. I could see why nobody else wanted my task, but no doubt it was good training in basic diplomacy.

[4] I was firmly convinced that a newspaper reporter "saw life" as did no one else in current society. (He sees no more of life than the iceman does, but he is compelled to note down and comment and thus acquires some habit of observation, if not reflection. That's all the difference there is.) I wanted to observe "human nature" and for some reason did not believe preachers exhibited any manifestations of human nature. So I seized any other kind of assignment anybody else was too lazy or too wise to want: interviews with the drinkers of canned heat who lived, and often died, in the caves and shacks along the riverbed, with movie stars of more majestic condescension than any bishop. Once I dressed as a waiter and served Katharine Hepburn her breakfast in bed after she had kept the reporters waiting in bitter cold for two hours at the station, then refused to see them. I have a vivid memory of knocking at apartment doors in the dead of night, to inform a young wife that her husband had just been killed in an accident or a police shooting, and did she have a

photograph of him? Usually she turned white and ran to grab up the baby from its crib. These experiences left me limp and shaking. But somehow these wretched people—if they were poor, with poor people's belief that the newspapers were powerful things with unquestioned rights—would find a photograph, would, between sobs, answer my questions. It was a surprise to find that the rich did not react the same way. When I went to ask questions of the wife of a manufacturer who had killed a man in disgraceful circumstances, she waited until I had spoken, then coolly requested me to leave the premises before she called the police. I spent three weeks in police headquarters, in Washington Avenue saloons, in the parlors of innumerable citizens, trying to solve the celebrated local mystery of the missing baby, stolen from the bed of its fifteen-year-old "unwed mother" in the city hospital. I worked morning, noon, and night, uncovered various bits of evidence, and finally located a youthful suspect who the police were convinced was the kidnapper, but whom they were unable to convict. I had always had the normal citizen's respect for the police, but during this experience discovered to my surprise that we reporters were frequently hours and days ahead of them unraveling the mystery.

[5] One became, at that age, aware of social structure but not of social forces. One knew that certain individuals represented certain levels of the structure, in the city and inside the office, but one was scarcely aware that these individuals themselves were pushed and pulled by invisible pressures of a class allegiance, in society and business. It took me a long time to understand that the publisher had far more in common with, far more loyalty to, the bankers or grain merchants with whom he lunched at the Minneapolis Club than to the editors and reporters who worked with him to produce the paper. I began work with an idealistic view of the newspaper as the mounted knight of society, pure in heart, its strength as the strength of ten, owing no favor, fearing no man. I did not know that, while many great organs had begun that way (a few retained their integrity) with rugged, incorruptible founders, they had been handed down to sons and grandsons who were less interested in the true social function of the institution than its money-making capacities which secured their position in the luxury class to which they, unlike their fathers and grandfathers, were born. You learned. You learned by listening to the servile voices of the women who wrote the society pages as they asked the great ladies of Lowry Hill to be so very kind as to give them the names of their reception guests. You learned by discovering that if you became involved in controversy with an important businessman about the handling of a given story, you were always wrong and the businessman was always right. You learned by finding that if a picture were published of a Negro, however distinguished, and one of

the great ladies, who happened to be from Georgia, telephoned to pro-test that she was offended, profuse apologies would be offered the sen-sitive creature.

[6] With this general discovery of the structure of community life came the simultaneous discovery that nearly all men, working in a large Amer-ican concern, did their daily work under the tyranny of fear. It varied in intensity from man to man, from prosperity to depression, but it was always there. The reporters were afraid of the city editor, the assistant city editor was afraid of the city editor, and the city editor, worried about his job, was afraid of his assistant. All were afraid of the managing editor, who in turn was afraid of the publisher. None of them wanted to feel that way, few were really "after" another's position, but each understood the pressures on the other which might at any moment cause the latter in self-protection to bear down upon the former. I might have learned all this much earlier, as most boys do from their fathers, who come home at night and relate to their wives at dinner the latest move in their "office politics." But my father had been an independent operator most of his life, and even when he did join a large establishment his sense of per-sonal dignity and honor forbade him to discuss his superiors or inferiors, even with his family. And so I had begun working life in the simple faith that one's rise or fall was a matter solely of one's own capacities.

[7] There was a charming old man who lived like an office hermit in a musty room in the interior labyrinths of the *Journal*. He was a scholar of some distinction, in love with the history of the northwest country, and he wrote graceful essays and homilies for the Sunday edition. I was charmed by his style and occasionally would take my portable lunch and bottle of milk at noon to eat with him. I assumed that with his literary attainments he was an important and respected person in the establish-ment. Once I stayed longer than usual; we were both spellbound with his own fascinating account of a vanished village. He looked suddenly at his watch. He became extremely agitated, grabbed up his copy in trem-bling fingers, and said: "Excuse me, excuse me. The editors. They will be very rough with me. I am very late." His bent figure shuffled rapidly from the room. He had spent his life on that newspaper.

[8] The financial editor worked at a desk directly behind my own. One night when I was working exceptionally late, he came in slightly unsteady from drinking. He emptied into a suitcase the contents of his locker, a few books, a batch of clippings, a pair of golf shoes. I asked in surprise if he was leaving. He said: "I've been on this paper eighteen years, son. I've just been fired by a guy I used to teach where to put commas." He staggered out, leaving me with a sick, hollow feeling in the pit of my stomach and a dark light dawning in my head. Innocence departed. Life, it seemed, was a relentless, never-ending battle; one never "arrived"; loy-

alty, achievement, could be forgotten in a moment; a single man's whim could ruin one. I began to take stock of the situation and discovered that the men who got to the top, no matter how long they stayed there, were nearly all men who had studied in universities, who knew something besides the routine of their own desks. It was fear as much as anything else that drove me to college, purely personal ambition as much as curiosity about the world I lived in and what had made it the way I found it to be.

QUESTIONS AND COMMENT ON FORM AND CONTENT

1. What is a cub reporter?

2. The first few sentences show by inference some values that should go with a college education. What are they?

3. A new paragraph could have been started with sentence 5, "The old Minneapolis *Journal.* . . ." What, then, would be the unifying topic of each? As it stands, it is a paragraph developed by contrast. What is contrasted? Notice the extended metaphor or analogy of the last sentence of paragraph 1. With whom are the newspaper personnel compared?

4. How is Eric Sevareid rudely awakened from his dream? (See paragraph 2.) Why did the rewrite man act this way?

5. What did Sevareid learn from his work as religious editor?

6. What comparison is made between the newspaper editor and the iceman?

7. What did the cub reporter gradually learn about social forces? (See paragraph 5.)

8. How is paragraph 6 developed? How are paragraphs 7 and 8 related to paragraph 6? Could all three have been combined into one long paragraph? What idea would tie them together?

9. What drove the author to college? The reasons are given in the final sentence. In what respect does the article end as it began?

10. To what extent is the arrangement of ideas in the article based on time order? Where does the time or narrative order seem to be discarded for an expository order in which an idea or point of view is explained?

VOCABULARY: WHAT DO THE ITALICIZED WORDS MEAN?

. . . no longer *extant* (1)
. . . an imposing and *venerable* institution (1)
. . . its directors were in, *hand in glove,* with the *potentates* of railroad (1)
. . . a necessary bit of *engrossing ritual* (1)
. . . with the *ordered cacophony* of *improvised* symphony (1)
. . . to the thundering *finale* of the great presses (1)

. . . for the relaxing *virtuosi* (1)
. . . most demanding and *insatiable* (3)
. . . wrote graceful essays and *homilies* (7)

THEME SUGGESTIONS

Have you, like Mr. Sevareid, had some work experience that has led you to some conclusions about employer-employee relationship or about the relation of an industry to a community? You might begin with some narrative paragraphs and end with some well-supported conclusions.
My First Job
The Boss Fired Me
A Summer in the Steel Mill (Supermarket, Fields, Drugstore, etc.)

THE GIGANTIC TASK AHEAD

Robert M. Hutchins

Robert M. Hutchins (1899-   ) is President of the Fund for the Republic and former Chancellor of the University of Chicago.

[1] We judge an activity in terms of its purpose. The purpose of commercial television is to sell goods. In these terms it is a great success. Why complain?

[2] In the debate in the House of Lords on television last June, Lord James of Rusholme said that if we aim to sell soap flakes and cereals as efficiently as possible we shall avoid anything that can lead to a genuinely independent and critical attitude on the part of the viewer and we shall pander to the intellectual idleness, the cupidity and the love of escape that exist in all people.

[3] Lord James went on to say that since the sale of detergents was not a proper aim for this immensely powerful new medium, the proposed third channel in England should go to the BBC, which, with all its faults, "does quite consciously seek to raise rather than to lower standards."

[4] In an article in the magazine *Mass Media*, the late Shelby Gordon, a writer for television, summarized the American situation by saying, "As long as public morals continue to corrupt television, it will continue to corrupt our kids."

[5] Mr. Gordon saw no remedy except through a public revolt. His diagnosis and prescription were: "The public is getting just what it de-

serves. If the economic threats of a handful of people can convince three networks of the folly of ideas, 170,000,000 people ought to be able to reverse the trend. The profit motive is very compelling, and there should be no difficulty in getting the networks and the advertisers to do something about Westerns, crime and brutality on television if the public really has strong convictions about it."

[6] What Mr. Gordon proposed is impossible because it is self-contradictory. Mr. Gordon and Lord James made the same assumption about people: most of them are idle, greedy, bored and frustrated most of the time. If you want to be sure of selling most people something all of the time, you have to move the idle, the greedy, and the bored and frustrated. The fact that no human being is idle, greedy, bored, and frustrated all of the time, that some are less so less often than others and that all human beings have the capacity to be lifted up as well as degraded, must be disregarded by a medium committed to selling the greatest possible quantities of goods to the largest possible of buyers.

[7] Mr. Gordon was altogether too lighthearted with his quip about 170,000,000 people reversing the trend. It is precisely the problem of a large, industrial, bureaucratic society that the mysterious, remote, irresponsible, unchosen few can and do render it impossible for the people to make their wishes known, still less to get them acted on. A justifiable sense of futility overcomes us all when we try to do anything about anything, from government to education to political parties to labor unions to corporations to television. I wish Mr. Gordon had seriously pictured to himself what it would take by way of effort, organization, money and time to effect through the agitation of 170,000,000 a drastic alteration in the standards of a medium committed to selling the largest number of people the greatest quantities of goods all of the time.

[8] I am for an independent, continuing agency to appraise the performance of the media of mass communication. I have been since the Commission on the Freedom of the Press recommended it thirteen years ago. I believe that in time such a group, spending much effort and money, would be influential in modifying, if not reversing, the trend. It could at least remind us that we are being corrupted; it could point out periodically the rate and extent of the corruption; and its prestige might be such that advertisers and broadcasters might exercise greater restraint in their appeal to our worse nature. But I am under no illusions about the difficulties of this task or about the extent of the improvement that can be expected within the framework of a system aimed at selling the most goods to the most people. For fundamental improvement, alternatives to that system must be devised, alternatives that have different purposes and that will be judged by different standards.

[9] Alternative purposes involve alternative financing and control:

a. Magazines are mass media. They sell goods. But the object of their owners is not to sell goods, but to sell their magazines. Hence it does not occur to them that the advertisers should determine the contents of their magazines, still less write them.

b. Apart from television, the sellers of entertainment sell it to those who want to pay for it. In the case of these commercial operations, the taste of the public is controlling. The test of a successful commercial motion picture is not whether it sells millions of pads that wipe off perspiration, but whether millions of people want to see it.

c. The experience of the Book-of-the-Month Club, to take only a single example, in one realm after another suggests that an historic role and a profitable future await the entrepreneur who will offer "culture" on television to those who are willing to pay for it. The mass sellers are not interested in this field. They can find no place for the modest experiments of *Omnibus,* or even for the tepid middlebrowism of *The Voice of Firestone.* They should not object to "cultural" subscription television.

d. The "educational" stations are few and underfinanced. Philanthropic foundations should recognize that if these stations are to succeed, their managers cannot spend all their time coping with one financial crisis after another. These stations should at once obtain permission from the FCC to charge for their services.

e. Serious consideration should be given to a public network, financed by the Government, that would "consciously seek to raise rather than to lower standards." Even in this country it ought to be possible to devise means of protecting such a public corporation from abuse by politicians. The Tennessee Valley Authority, for all its troubles, has been quite successful. We have got to get over our undemocratic fear of our Government. This might be a good time and place to begin.

QUESTIONS AND COMMENT ON FORM AND CONTENT

1. What does the first sentence mean? Does it mean we approve of any activity if it succeeds in attaining its goal? Can you think of exceptions? Is television an exception? What is its goal according to Hutchins?

2. A member of the British House of Lords is reported to have said that if we aim to sell soap flakes and cereals as efficiently as possible we must avoid certain attitudes and include others. What are these attitudes? Do you agree with his argument?

3. Mr. Hutchins uses a familiar form of argument—that of presenting first the evils or weaknesses of a system and then a remedy or partial remedy. What is Mr. Gordon's remedy? What does Mr. Hutchins mean by saying Mr. Gordon's proposal is self-contradictory?

4. Do you agree with Mr. Gordon's and Lord James's assumption about peo-

ple? To debate about these adjectives applied to people, would you have to define them?

5. What changes does Mr. Hutchins suggest to improve television programs? Why does he put the word *educational* in quotation marks? What important difference does he see between commercial television and such other mass media as magazines and commercial moving pictures? What is the point about the Book-of-the-Month Club?

VOCABULARY: WHAT DO THE ITALICIZED WORDS MEAN?

. . . we shall *pander* to the intellectual idleness and *cupidity* and love of *escape* (2)

A justifiable sense of *futility* overcomes us (7)

. . . agency to *appraise* the performance (8)

. . . the *media* of *mass communication* (8)

. . . an *historic role* and a profitable future await the *entrepreneur* who will offer *"culture"* on television (9 c)

Philanthropic foundations should [help] (9 d)

THEME SUGGESTIONS

Television Is Getting Better (Getting Worse) (Unchanging)
Television's Greatest Weakness (Strength)
Children's Programs
Westerns
Violence on Television
Movies on Television
We Pause for Station Identification
The Case for Subscription Television
The Growth of Non-Commercial Television
Reading and Television
TV as a Babysitter
Parental Control of Television Watching
TV: Its Power to Elevate or Degrade

TELEVISION: THE LION THAT SQUEAKS

Arnold J. Toynbee

Arnold Toynbee (1889-   ), an English historian, completed in 1954 his monumental 10-volume A Study of History *and in 1956* An Historian's Approach to Religion. *He believes that the progress or decline of a civilization depends upon the way it meets the problems of its times.*

[1] Television is not the only one of our marvellous modern means of communication that is being largely wasted on frivolities. The same sad tale is told by the headlines and advertisements in the evening newspapers—and not only in the evening ones—all over the world.

[2] There is a contrast here, and a misfit, that is striking and painful: On the one hand a technology that is a *chef-d'oeuvre* of intellectual creative power and ingenuity; on the other hand a prostitution of this product of mature human genius to serve childish tastes.

[3] A pessimist, looking into the future, might predict that this really shocking combination of incongruous means and ends will condition mankind into becoming a race of technician-morons—creatures that will be lower than our prehuman ancestors in terms of truly human values.

[4] What causes this disconcerting trend? Can it be arrested, reversed?

[5] One thing, for certain, is *not* the cause. It is not the inventors' fault that their inventions are being so deplorably misused. The apparatus with which our inventive geniuses have endowed us is neutral. It could be used, just as easily and effectively, for the highest purposes as it is being used for the lowest purposes today. It is, in fact, happily, being used already, though, so far, only on a relatively small scale, in education. If this potent new instrument is being so largely misused at present, the fault lies not with the human inventors of these mechanical genies; it lies with their human users.

[6] Which set of users is chiefly to blame? The viewers of television or the commercial purveyors of it, who stand between the viewers and the inventors? They share the blame, I should say. If the viewers were to stop viewing such inferior stuff, then sheer commercial self-interest would push the purveyors into giving their customers something better.

[7] Conversely, if the purveyors did give the customers something better, they would be educating the public to raise the standard of its demand.

[8] In so far as the viewers' present abysmally low standard is low by the viewers' own choice, and not because this standard has been imposed on them by the purveyors, what is it that accounts for the viewers' childishness? I think there are several causes on which one can put one's finger.

[9] One cause of present-day childishness in grown-up people is the change in the character of the work by which an ever-increasing proportion of the world's population has come to be earning its living since the beginning of the Industrial Revolution. The mechanization of the world's work has been lightening mankind's physical labor, but tnis at the price

of imposing on the factory worker a psychological curse from which the pre-industrial farmer was free. This curse is the curse of boredom.

[10] The farmer's work on an unmechanized farm of the traditional kind is laborious. He must work from dawn to dark, year in and year out; his cows, sheep, and fowls require as constant attention as human infants.

[11] But, by the same token, a farmer's life is never dull. A human mother does not easily get bored with her gruelling job of bringing up her children, and the farmer does not get bored—in the sense of time on his hands—with his livestock and crops.

[12] On the other hand, how can the factory worker's life *not* be dull? The "means of production" that he is tending are machines processing "raw materials"—a poor exchange, in psychological terms, for his farmer-grandfather's fields and pastures and crops and cows. The factory worker's relation to the machinery is impersonal.

[13] If the wheels are to be made to pay, they must be kept turning 24 hours in the day, so the machine-tender works on a shift; the machine is not his own, in the sense in which the farmer's cow and crop are his.

[14] The factory is not only kept in operation all round the clock, it is insulated from the elements. A thermostat automatically keeps it at whatever temperature the technician chooses; and rain and hail can batter on the factory roof without any effect on the work that is going on under the roof's shelter. The control of the environment inside the factory walls makes the output regular and predictable, but it consequently makes the job of producing the output dull.

[15] The factory worker will be able to hand over to the next shift, and to leave the building, the moment his stint of work is completed. He may come out physically fresh; but he is likely to find himself psychologically jaded. What he craves for, in his off-time, is recreation; and, of course, he is tempted to choose the kind of recreation that makes the lowest spiritual demand on him.

[16] The middle-class office worker is also making the same choice, without having the same excuse. In his case, perhaps, the cause is not so much boredom as it is anxiety. His higher education has made him more acutely aware of problems—political, social, moral, and spiritual—that are baffling him. His flight from these cares to soap-box opera is a case of escapism.

[17] Moreover, the incentives to seek frivolous distractions are growing in strength. The problems that create anxiety become more menacing, and daily work becomes more boring as automation's pace accelerates.

[18] Working hours are continually becoming shorter and leisure hours correspondingly longer; and here we have a second cause of the public's present choice of forms of recreation that are frivolous and childish.

[19] For the mass of mankind—for everyone except a tiny privileged minority—leisure was, till within living memory, a blessing, or curse, of which they had had hardly any experience. Abundant leisure has now suddenly descended on them while they are still psychologically unprepared for coping with it.

[20] This social revolution (it amounts to that) has been sudden because the pace of technological advance has become so fast. People are still unprepared for it because the pace of psychological change has always been slower than the pace of technological change—and the pace of psychological change cannot be speeded up, to match, by any ingenious mechanical inventions.

[21] In the fable, the tortoise won its race against the hare—but turn the live hare into an electric hare, and what chance is left to the tortoise for keeping pace with that?

[22] When human beings are given leisure, they misuse it unless and until they have educated themselves to do better than that. I have mentioned the tiny privileged minority that enjoyed a monopoly of leisure in the pre-mechanical age. By the eighteenth century, this minority had already had about five thousand years for learning how to use its leisure for social, cultural and spiritual purposes.

LEISURE WASTED ON FRIVOLITY

[23] But what is that privileged 18th-Century minority's record? It flattered itself that it was an élite. Yet, for one Voltaire, Franklin, Rousseau, Jefferson, or Wesley, there were thousands who misspent their leisure on hunting, gambling and philandering.

[24] The frivolities on which the majority is now largely wasting its recently acquired leisure have, on the whole, less vice in them than the leisured eighteenth-century minority's frivolous pursuits had. That, however, is a small mercy to be thankful for. The misspending of leisure, even on comparatively innocent frivolities, will lead to social, cultural and moral regression if it continues unchecked.

[25] In our attitude towards this evil, we cannot afford to be indulgent or complacent. We have to get the viewer of television to raise his sights. How far does this depend on him, and how far does it depend on the policy of the commercial organization that purveys to him those silly programs to which the viewer is now giving an appallingly high proportion of his viewing time?

[26] Here, I am afraid, we are caught in a vicious circle. The purveyor of television, like other tradesmen, is primarily concerned to sell his wares as profitably for himself as he can; and this consideration governs

his policy. Shall he try to raise his viewers' standards by giving them programs that will be rather higher than the level of their average present demand as estimated by the purveying firm's customer-research department?

[27] The purveyor shrinks from venturing on this public-spirited experiment. He shrinks because he fears that, if he did raise the standard even one inch above the average level of demand, there might be a mass flight from television.

[28] The purveyor therefore allows himself a margin of safety. He sets the level of his wares below the average level of demand, not above it, and this poor-spirited policy gives him greater freedom of play; for his researchers tell him that he can depress the level of his wares at least twelve inches below the average level of demand before his low-brow customers will give up television in disgust because they are finding it too banal to please even them.

[29] Can this vicious circle be broken? No doubt there is some hope to be found in the spread of higher education. In this sphere, television is already beginning to be used for constructive purposes. But it is only in our time that higher education has become accessible to the majority, and the first generation of children who receive it have to come to it without the help of any cultural background in their homes. It is only in the second or third generation that the effects of higher education in school and college begin to become cumulative by creating a fund of culture in the home to give the high school and university student's education an initial boost and a perpetual encouragement.

[30] Will this hoped-for effect of the spread of higher education be enough to produce an improvement in the quality of the average demand of television viewers? We are relying here on education in the formal sense, and this may be capable of producing a change for the better in taste.

CHANGE OF HEART NEEDED

[31] But will just educating the head be enough? The head cannot run far in advance of the heart; and, for bringing about a change of heart, something more than an improvement in formal education is required. A spiritual revolution is needed; and here, I think, we are touching the heart of the matter. We are putting our finger on what is wrong, not just with present-day television, but with present-day Western life. In present-day Ethiopia there is no commercial television yet, but for centuries there have been viewers there. What they come to view—sometimes walk-

ing many miles over the mountains—is the pictures of the Bible story on the walls of their churches.

[32] Our own medieval ancestors, too, were viewers of that kind. In our time, we have lost the lofty vision and the serious purpose with which our forefathers used to be inspired by their ancestral religions. This inspiration has now been lost by many people who still attend church and temple and mosque. How is this vital inspiration to be regained? The future of television, and of everything else, will depend on our answer.

QUESTIONS AND COMMENT ON FORM AND CONTENT

1. Mr. Toynbee points out that one of the chief products of intellectual creative power and ingenuity, namely television, is used today mainly to serve childish tastes. What two groups, according to his argument, are at fault? What can each group do to improve the situation?

2. To what extent are the viewers' tastes affected by their occupations? Why?

3. Is any immediate or future solution offered? What does the point about Ethiopia and our medieval ancestors prove?

4. What does Toynbee mean by the vicious circle? For what reason might the purveyor aim considerably below the public taste?

5. As a historian, Mr. Toynbee compares our use of leisure time with that of earlier periods. What is his point? Would he agree with Oswald Spengler, German historian, that our whole Western culture is in decline and will decline further?

6. If you disagree with any of Mr. Toynbee's arguments, what evidence would you need to convince you of their truth? How would you attack his arguments? Is it difficult for us to prove anything about taste to one who disagrees essentially with our standards or values? Must we, then, abandon all attempts to improve taste?

7. What is the connotation of the title?

VOCABULARY: WHAT DO THE ITALICIZED WORDS MEAN?

. . . a *technology* that is a *chef-d'oeuvre* of . . . ingenuity (2)
. . . the commercial *purveyors* (6)
. . . *abysmally* low standard (8)
. . . find himself psychologically *jaded* (15)
. . . cultural and moral *regression* (24)
. . . caught in a *vicious circle* (26)
. . . too *banal* to please (28)

THEME SUGGESTIONS

A Farmer's Life Is Not Boring
TV As Escape from Boredom
The Lowest Common Denominator
Leisure Time: A Blessing or a Curse?

REFLECTIONS ON MASS CULTURE

Ernest van den Haag

Ernest van den Haag (1914-   ) was born in The Hague, Holland, and was educated in Naples, Florence, and the United States. He is the author of several books and more than forty articles which appeared in general-interest magazines and journals of sociology.

[1] By and large, people seriously concerned with mass culture fall into three groups. There is first a nucleus of artists and literary men, supported by a few theoreticians. They feel isolated, alienated, submerged and pushed aside by mass culture; their hopes are dim and they detest it. The literati and the theoreticians are opposed by another group—the practical men, who have decided it is their duty to work for the mass media in spite of the opulent salaries pressed on them. Sedulously aided by academic fellow travellers, they resolutely defend popular culture and their own *sacrificium intellectus.*

[2] The third and largest group stays squarely in the middle, although for motley reasons. Most sociologists are located here; they have been taught that to be anywhere else, particularly when cultural matters are involved, is unscientific. Besides, many of them lack the trained sensibility that would discriminate between, say, English prose and their own writing. Liberal philosophers, on the other hand, have investigated the impossibilities of justifying value judgments for so long that they regard anyone criticizing mass culture for moral or aesthetic reasons as bold but naïve. There is no evidence, they seem to say, for practically any view; hence, let's close our eyes and discuss methodology.

[3] With all that, liberal philosophers seem to stress, somewhat unilaterally, the lack of evidence for negative views of mass culture. Perhaps they feel uneasy with rejections of mass culture because of political fears—misplaced ones, in my opinion. They seem unable to free them-

Reprinted by permission of Ernest van den Haag. This article first appeared in the *American Scholar*, Spring, 1960.

selves from the suspicion that a rejection of mass culture implies a rejection of the masses (although the contrary is no less logical) and is, therefore, antidemocratic. However, this is a *non sequitur*. One might think little of the cultural capacity of the masses but not therefore of their political capacity.[1] But even if one thinks little of their political competence, one might still feel that there is no reason why they should not suffer, benefit and possibly learn from its use (and no more is needed to argue for democracy). Finally, although one might be somewhat pessimistic about the masses, one might be even more so about the political capacity of restricted groups. At any rate, neither mass culture nor objections to it seem to promote specific political views: fascists and communists, as often as liberals, favor mass culture, although they occasionally borrow some phrases from its opponents.

[4] Historians, who of all men might be expected to discern the uniqueness of mass culture, seldom do. When they pay heed to mass culture as a historical phenomenon, they seem to take the wrong cue. Thus, Stuart Hughes recently observed, in a perceptive paper, that "our students yawn over the classics" because they have "very little to do with their own lives." He implies that we might as well forget about the classics. This seems odd. Students have always yawned over the classics—only, in times past, teachers were not so sensitive to their own popularity rating nor so eager to entertain their students as to be willing to drop the classics. They dropped some yawning students instead and kept the interested ones. An immature mind cannot understand the classics; and it matures, in part, by learning to understand them—or, at least, to know them so that they be understood later. Students brought up in an age of rapid technological change may be convinced that literature, like machinery, is subject to obsolescence—a conviction some teachers share or dare not oppose enough to crack the shell. Perhaps this is what makes the classics seem irrelevant.

[5] Yet the classics, if truly classic, cannot be irrelevant, for they deal with subjects relevant to the universal human predicament in ways to be re-experienced perennially. Of course, it is possible that we have become irrelevant to the classics: if our lives have lost all meaning, then no literature worthy of that name can be meaningful to us. For it is the possible meaning of human life that classic literature explores; and we cannot be interested without any experience of meaning and style in our own lives. If we have no such experience, then entertainment bereft of meaning—diversion from boredom, time killing, mass culture—is all that remains. In this case, the relevant must become irrelevant, and only what

---

[1] Conversely, I have not found cultivated people to be politically very sagacious. (I'd prefer to entrust my political destiny to farmers or workers rather than to professors as a group.)

is irrelevant to begin with can be absorbed. But I'm not yet willing to give up altogether. Under favorable conditions, the study of literature helps us see the possibilities of man's career on earth.

[6] While some are ready to yield to those bored by high culture, others are convinced that the mass media can serve, indeed do serve, to bring high culture to the masses, and that in doing so they justify their existence or, at least, render an important service. Popular magazines may have authors such as Norman Vincent Peale, the argument goes, but don't they also publish an occasional uncensored article by Bertrand Russell? They do. However, a piece by a major philosopher does not make a philosophical magazine out of *Look*—it may make a popular journalist out of the philosopher. In the stream of, at best, diverting banalities, the worth-while piece tends to disappear without impact. It may seduce a Russell to lower his standards and write more such pieces, becoming less worthwhile and more acceptable in the process. It won't lure *Look* readers into the *Principia Mathematica*. Mass culture can be decorated with high culture pieces without being otherwise changed.

[7] Note further that Russell's opinions are not offered to *Look* readers because of their intrinsic merit; they are offered because they are *his* opinions. Russell is by now a public figure, which means that he can be published without being taken seriously. Had I written the same words, I could not have broken into *Look*, precisely because people might have taken the utterance seriously instead of gobbling it up with the rest of the fare, while captivated by the utterer's fame.

[8] Not everybody defends the mass media as vehicles that bring elements of high culture to the masses. Some depict the culture of the masses, articulated by the mass media in their normal offerings, as superior to high culture to begin with. Thus, one of mass culture's most faithful admirers, Mr. Gilbert Seldes, recently explained that he thinks more highly of Charlie Chaplin than of Marcel Proust because the former has brought more happiness to more people than the latter. Now happiness is hard to measure, and I am not sure that it makes sense to compare the feeling of a person reading Proust to that of another seeing Chaplin. We my grant, however, that more persons have been amused and diverted by Chaplin than by Proust. Still more people are made happy or are diverted by whiskey, apple pie, penicillin, Marilyn Monroe or, perhaps, by a movie that Mr. Seldes and I might agree is thoroughly bad. In short, making people happy is a criterion only if that is what one sets out to do—and I doubt that this was Proust's purpose or the purpose of any serious writer. Surely more persons enjoy Rodgers and Hammerstein than Bach—more enjoy Liberace than Glenn Gould. By definition, popular culture is enjoyed by more people than high culture. Mr.

Seldes' view would sanction the elimination of art in favor of entertainment—high-class entertainment, at best.

[9] And this is precisely what I am afraid of. Mass culture demands entertainment and so extravagantly rewards those who provide it with money, prestige and power that serious artists become isolated—and tempted. To be sure, such tendencies have always existed; but now they prevail. The strength of the offerings of mass culture, compared with those of art, has risen immensely, and the dividing line has been blurred.

[10] The chances for the values of mass culture to be internalized in childhood also have greatly increased, so that what I have described as temptation is not felt to be such, but, on the contrary, as the due reward for well-directed, talented efforts. The view held by Mr. Seldes in all innocence is widely accepted by less articulate persons. It is a very basic American view, a naïvely pragmatic and philanthropic view that refuses to recognize what cannot be tangibly measured in terms at once hedonistic and altruistic.[2] The measurement for art thus becomes the number of people made happy—and as soon as this becomes the end of art, art ends.

[11] The answer to those who oppose pessimistic views on mass culture lies here. They argue that there is no evidence that the masses are culturally worse off. (I suspect they are far from well off, but comparisons are nearly impossible.) As far as the elite is concerned, they ask what prevents it from being as creative as ever? Why can't it coexist with mass culture? Haven't there always been several coexisting levels of culture? Can't we have a pluralistic society?

[12] This reasonable argument overlooks the historically most distinctive and important characteristic of mass culture: the dominant power of the mass of consumers over production, public opinion and prestige. The elite in the past was sufficiently isolated and protected from the masses (which, properly speaking, did not exist as such) to be able to cultivate its own garden. And the mass market (hardly in existence) had nothing much to offer. Further, power, income and prestige distribution being what they were, the masses had no desire to impinge on the culture of the elite; on the contrary, they made room for it. At any rate, if they had a wish to participate or encroach, they had no way of making their demands felt and of articulating them. (Even political revolutions,

[2] When the Puritan American heritage collided with the more hedonistic attitudes of later immigrants, an interesting fusion resulted. Pleasure, the Puritans implied, is bad; sacrifice, good. The immigrants wanted to pursue happiness. The resulting attitude is: the pleasure sacrificed and given to others is all right, as is the happiness shared and given. What is bad becomes good if it is not enjoyed by oneself but produced for others.

before Hitler, were led and inspired by members of the elite.) But this has changed. We all now cultivate cash crops in market gardens. Mass culture is manufactured according to the demands of the mass market. No *independent* elite culture is left, for mass culture is far too pervasive to permit it. Cultivated individuals and islands of high culture remain, of course. But they are interstitial and on the defensive even when admired and respected; indeed, then more than ever, for they easily may be "taken up" and typecast. The intellect when alive is not part of our social structure, nor does it have its own domicile.

[13] A convinced egalitarian may ask, So what? No more elite, no more high culture; but the great majority of people—who never belonged— have what they wish. To be sure, most people never were, are not now, and are unlikely ever to be interested in high culture. Yet, it does not follow that high culture is unimportant. Its importance cannot be measured by the number of people to whom it is important. Political issues may be decided by majority vote (or, at least, by letting the majority choose who is to decide them). This is surely not a good way, but nevertheless, I think, the best available.

[14] However, the analogy between political issues and cultural issues (or, for that matter, moral ones) is inappropriate. Political issues, by whatever means they are decided, require collective action. Taxes cannot be levied only on those who feel they benefit proportionately from a pattern of public expenditure, or on individuals who are willing to vote for them. With art and literature it is otherwise, or it was. They could be cultivated by intellectual elites, without mass participation. This is becoming less possible every day. Mass culture threatens to decide cultural issues by a sort of universal suffrage. This is a threat to culture, not an occasion for rejoicing. For once cultural issues are regarded as indivisible, the majority view will prevail—and the majority prefers entertainment to art. Yet, unlike properly political matters, cultural ones do not require collective action, but rather that the mass of people and the law do not interfere. Culture cannot be created by political actions, although it can be destroyed by them. (The support of social groups is required, of course, but not that of society—or the masses—except inasmuch as it makes the existence of the social groups possible.) There would never have been any serious art, philosophy or literature if a majority vote had decided whether a given work was to be created and presented.

[15] Yet, even if these things are important only to a few people, they are the best and most important people, the saving remnant. Actually, these things and these people are important even to those who ignorantly sneer at them. Such feelings as love; such experiences as wit, beauty or moral obligation; or styles of congress, housing and living—all, however

degenerate they may become, are brought into existence and elaborated by artists and intellectuals. Without them, life is formless. With them, there is, at least, a paradigm. The most common of human experiences and the most trite still depend on artists and intellectuals to become fully conscious and articulate. Even the silliest entertainer and his public are part of, or are parasites of, a long line of creators of cultural expression—artists, philosophers, writers, composers, et cetera. For as Bernard Berenson suggested, "Popular art is always a derivation from professional individual art." Just as the technician depends on pure scientists he may never have heard of, so civilized nations in general depend on the creators of cultural expression—intellectuals and artists. The relation of the cultural elite to the masses may be compared to the relation of the saints and the cloistered to the faithful at large. Or, the cultural elite may be compared to the playwrights and the actors on stage, whose words, actions, costumes and settings are of significance to the spectators across the footlights, even though they are but spectators.

[16] Although few people become outstanding mathematicians, scholars and artists, or understand what these are doing, society must permit those who cultivate such activities their separate existence or cease to be civilized. And the loss and degeneration of civilization injures everyone—the living and the unborn generations for whom we should hold in trust their rightful heritage. It is not enough, either, to permit some individual specialists to go their way. We need an intellectual and artistic elite (joined, of course, by merit) supported by a necessarily restricted and therefore discriminating public, both with reasonably continuous traditions. If this elite is not allowed autonomy and self-cultivation, if instead it is induced to follow mass tastes and to cater to them, there can be no cultural creation. We may parasitically ring a few changes on the culture of the past; we may find ways to entertain ourselves; but we won't have a style and an experience of our own.

[17] I should not object to cultural pluralism—to mass culture coexisting with high culture—if it were possible. (Folk culture is long dead—although many people don't know a zombie when they see one.) A universally shared high culture is, of course, absurd and self-contradictory. This may sound snobbish, but I didn't make the world; I'm merely describing it. Talents as well as intelligence and sensitivity to various values are differentially distributed. We are lucky if 1 or 2 percent of the population can be creative in any sense and 15 to 20 percent can cultivate some sensibility. The remainder benefits indirectly.

[18] The trouble with mass culture is that in various direct and indirect ways it tends to make the existence of high culture impossible. In our eagerness to open opportunity to everybody, we have greatly diminished the prizes available to anybody. Good wine is hard to cultivate

when it is habitually diluted and we are brought up to be indiscriminate. We might do well to abandon the sterile and injurious attempts to "improve" mass culture, for its main effect is to debase high culture by "bringing it to the masses." What we must do is to bring some gifted people—not masses—to transmit high culture independently of the culture of mass society. My own view is pessimistic. I should like nothing better than to be proved wrong.

QUESTIONS AND COMMENT ON FORM AND CONTENT

1. Who are the three groups seriously concerned with mass culture? How do their views differ? With which group would you associate Ernest van den Haag?

2. What mistakes, according to the author, do historians (as represented by Stuart Hughes) make about teaching the classics?

3. What reasons are given for thinking the classics are not irrelevant? Under favorable conditions what can the study of great literature do for us? (See paragraph 5.)

4. What reason is given for believing that high culture cannot be presented through mass media? Do you agree? What is the point about Norman Vincent Peale and Bertrand Russell?

5. Why does Mr. Gilbert Seldes think more highly of Charlie Chaplin than of Marcel Proust? What analogies are used to refute Mr. Seldes? Are they sound? Why does our author say that acceptance of the view expressed by Mr. Seldes would mark the end of art?

6. What is the point about political issues and cultural (or moral) issues? (See paragraph 14.)

7. Is popular art as parasitic as Bernard Berenson suggested? (See paragraph 15.)

8. Specifically, what is van den Haag's objection to or fear of mass culture?

9. Are his words sufficiently clear without definition? Are *high culture* and *mass culture* absolute or only relative terms? Does your answer seriously affect the argument?

10. What is the topic sentence of paragraph 8? How is it developed? What transitional words are used to link paragraph 8 to paragraph 7?

11. How do you account for a rather learned diction and tone in this article?

VOCABULARY: WHAT DO THE ITALICIZED WORDS MEAN?

They feel isolated, *alienated, submerged* (1)

The *literati* and the *theoreticians* are opposed by . . . the practical men (1)

Sedulously aided by *academic fellow travellers,* they *resolutely* defend popular culture and their own *sacrificium intellectus* (1)

. . . for moral or *aesthetic* reasons (2)

However, this is *non sequitur* (3)

 . . . in the stream of, at best, *diverting banalities* (6)

 . . . because of their *intrinsic* merit (7)

 . . . less *articulate* persons (10)

 . . . in terms at once *hedonistic* and *altruistic* (10)

 . . . no independent *elite* culture is left (12)

A convinced *egalitarian* may ask (13)

 . . . many people don't know a *zombie* when they see one (17)

THEME SUGGESTIONS

A theme could be based on one of the statements of the author or on one of the statements of other people quoted. You could agree or disagree with the opinion as long as you presented sufficiently valid reasons for your point of view.

My Own View of Mass Culture Is Optimistic (Pessimistic)

Why a Classic Is a Classic

WHATEVER HOPE WE HAVE

Maxwell Anderson

Maxwell Anderson (1888-1959) is best remembered for such plays as Winterset, Both Your Houses, *and* Elizabeth the Queen. *Some of his plays were written in poetry. In his* Prelude to Poetry in the Theatre *he said, "It is incumbent on the dramatist to be a poet, and incumbent on the poet to be prophet, dreamer and interpreter of the racial dream."*

[1] There is always something slightly embarrassing about the public statements of writers and artists, for they should be able to say whatever they have to say in their work, and let it go at that. Moreover, the writer or artist who brings a message of any importance to his generation will find it impossible to reduce that message to a bald statement, or even a clearly scientific statement, because the things an artist has to communicate can be said only in symbols, in the symbols of his art. The work of art is a hieroglyph, and the artist's endeavor is to set forth his vision of the world in a series of picture writings which convey meanings beyond the scope of direct statement. There is reason for believing that there is no other way of communicating new concepts save the artist's way of illuminating new pathways in the mind. Even the mathematician leaves

the solid plane of the multiplication table and treads precariously among symbols when he advances toward ideas previously unattained.

[2] It may be that I am trying, at this moment, to reduce to plain statement an intuitive faith of my own which cannot be justified by logic and which may lose, even for me, some of its iridescence when examined under a strong light by many searching eyes. For though the question I meant to take up was only the utility of prizes for artistic excellence, I can find no approach to that question save through a definition of the artist's faith as I see it, and no definition of that faith without an examination of the artist's place in his universe, his relation to the national culture and the dependence of a nation on its culture for coherence and enduring significance.

[3] Let me begin then, quite simply and honestly, even naïvely, with a picture of the earth as I see it. The human race, some two billion strong, finds itself embarked on a curious voyage among the stars, riding a planet which must have set out from somewhere, and must be going somewhere, but which was cut adrift so long ago that its origin is a matter of speculation and its future beyond prophecy. Our planet is of limited area, and our race is divided into rival nations and cultures that grow and press on one another, fighting for space and the products of the ground.

[4] We are ruled by men like ourselves, men of limited intelligence, with no foreknowledge of what is to come, and hampered by the constant necessity of maintaining themselves in power by placating our immediate selfish demands. There have been men among us from time to time who had more wisdom than the majority, and who laid down precepts for the conduct of a man's brief life. Some of them claimed inspiration from beyond our earth, from spirits or forces which we cannot apprehend with our five senses. Some of them speak of gods that govern our destinies, but no one of them has had proof of his inspiration or of the existence of a god. Nevertheless, there have been wise men among them, and we have taken their precepts to heart and taken their gods and their inspiration for granted.

[5] Each man and woman among us, with a short and harried life to live, must decide for himself what attitude he will take toward what they have said, and toward the shifting patterns of government, justice, religion, business, morals and personal conduct. We are hampered as well as helped in these decisions by every prejudice of ancestry and race, but no man's life is ready-made for him. Whether he chooses to conform or not to conform, every man's religion is his own, every man's politics is his own, every man's vice or virtue is his own, for he alone makes decisions for himself. Every other freedom in this world is restricted, but the

individual mind is free according to its strength and desire. The mind has no master save the master it chooses.

[6] Yet it must make its choices, now as always, without sufficient knowledge and without sufficient wisdom, without certainty of our origin, without certainty of what undiscovered forces lie beyond known scientific data, without certainty of the meaning of life, if it has a meaning, and without an inkling of our racial destiny. In matters of daily and yearly living, we have a few, often fallible, rules of thumb to guide us, but on all larger questions the darkness and silence about us is complete.

[7] Or almost complete. Complete save for an occasional prophetic voice, an occasional gleam of scientific light, an occasional extraordinary action which may make us doubt that we are utterly alone and completely futile in this incomprehensible journey among the constellations. From the beginning of our story men have insisted that they had a destiny to fulfill—that they were part of a gigantic scheme which was understood somewhere, though they themselves might never understand it.

[8] There are no proofs of this. There are only indications—in the idealism of children and young men, in the sayings of such teachers as Christ and Buddha, in the vision of the world we glimpse in the hieroglyphics of the masters of the great arts and in the discoveries of pure science, itself an art, as it pushes away the veils of fact to reveal new powers, new laws, new mysteries, new goals for the eternal dream. The dream of the race is that it may make itself better and wiser than it is, and every great philosopher or artist who has ever appeared among us has turned his face away from what man is toward whatever seems to him most godlike that man may become.

[9] Whether the steps proposed are immediate or distant, whether he speaks in the simple parables of the New Testament or the complex musical symbols of Bach and Beethoven, the message is always to the effect that men are not essentially as they are but as they imagine and as they wish to be. The geologists and anthropologists, working hand in hand, tracing our ancestry to a humble little animal with a rudimentary forebrain which grew with use and need, reinforce the constant faith of prophet and artist. We need more intelligence and more sensitivity if ever an animal needed anything. Without them we are caught in a trap of selfish interest, international butchery, and a creed of survival that periodically sacrifices the best to the worst, and the only way out that I can see is a race with a better brain and superior inner control. The artist's faith is simply a faith in the human race and its gradual acquisition of wisdom.

[10] Now it is always possible that he is mistaken or deluded in what he believes about his race, but I myself accept his creed as my own. I

make my spiritual code out of my limited knowledge of great music, great poetry and great plastic and graphic arts, including with these, not above them, such wisdom as the Sermon on the Mount and the last chapter of Ecclesiastes. The test of a man's inspiration for me is not whether he spoke from a temple or the stage of a theatre, from a martyr's fire or a garden in Hampstead. The test of a message is its continuing effect on the minds of men over a period of generations.

[11] The world we live in is given meaning and dignity, is made an endurable habitation, by the great spirits who have preceded us and set down their records of nobility or torture or defeat in blazons and symbols which we can understand. I accept these not only as prophecy, but as direct motivation toward some far goal of racial aspiration. He who meditates with Plato, or finds himself shaken by Lear's "five-fold never" over Cordelia, or climbs the steep and tragic stairway of symphonic music, is certain to be better, both intellectually and morally, for the experience.

[12] The nobler a man's interests the better citizen he is. And if you ask me to define nobility, I can answer only by opposites, that it is not buying and selling, or betting on the races. It might be symbolized by such a figure as a farmer boy in Western Pennsylvania plowing corn through a long afternoon and saying over and over to himself certain musical passages out of Marlowe's "Doctor Faustus." He might plow his corn none too well, he might be full of what we used to call original sin, but he carries in his brain a catalytic agent the presence of which fosters ripening and growth. It may be an impetus that will advance him or his sons an infinitesimal step along the interminable ascent.

[13] The ascent, if we do climb, is so slow, so gradual, so broken, that we can see little or no evidence of it between the age of Homer and our own time. The evidence we have consists in a few mountain peaks of achievement, the age of Pericles, the centuries of Dante and Michelangelo, the reign of Elizabeth in England, the century and a half of music in Germany, peaks and highlands from which the masters seem to have looked forward into the distance far beyond our plodding progress. Between these heights lie long valleys of mediocrity and desolation, and artistically, at least, we appear to be miles beneath the upper levels traversed behind us. It must be our hope as a nation, that either in pure art or in pure science we may arrive at our own peak of achievement, and earn a place in human history by making one more climb above the clouds.

[14] The individual, the nation and the race are all involved together in this effort. Even in our disillusioned era, when fixed stars of belief fall from our sky like a rain of meteors, we find that men cling to what central verities they can rescue or manufacture, because without a core

of belief neither man nor nation has courage to go on. This is no figure of speech, no sanctimonious adjuration—it is a practical, demonstrable fact which all men realize as they add to their years. We must have a personal, a national and a racial faith, or we are dry bones in a death valley, waiting for the word that will bring us life.

[15] Mere rationalism is mere death. Mere scientific advance without purpose is an advance toward the waterless mirage and the cosmic scavengers. The doctrine of Machiavelli is a fatal disease to the citizen of the State. The national conscience is the sum of personal conscience; the national culture, the sum of personal culture—and the lack of conscience is an invitation to destruction; the lack of culture, an assurance that we shall not even be remembered.

[16] No doubt I shall be accused of talking a cloudy philosophy, of mixed metaphors and fantasy, but unless I misread my history, the artist has usually been wiser even about immediate aims than the materialist or the enthusiast for sweeping political reform. The artist is aware that man is not perfect, but that he seeks perfection. The materialist sees that men are not perfect, and erects his philosophy on their desire for selfish advantage. He fails quickly, always, because men refuse to live by bread alone.

[17] The utopian sees that men seek perfection and sets out to achieve it or legislate it for them. He fails because he cannot build an unselfish state out of selfish citizens, and he who asks the impossible gets nothing. The concepts of truth and justice are variables approaching an imaginary limit which we shall never see; nevertheless, those who have lost their belief in truth and justice and no longer try for them are traitors to the race, traitors to themselves, advocates of the dust.

[18] To my mind a love of truth and justice is bound up in men with a belief in their destiny; and the belief in their destiny is of one piece with national and international culture. The glimpse of the godlike in man occasionally vouchsafed in a work of art or prophecy is the vital spark in a world that would otherwise stand stock still or slip backward down the grade, devoid of motive power.

[19] For national growth and unity the artist's vision is the essential lodestone without which there is no coherence. A nation is not a nation until it has a culture which deserves and receives affection and reverence from the people themselves. Our culture in this country has been largely borrowed or sectional or local; what we need now to draw us together and make us a nation is a flowering of the national arts, a flowering of the old forms in this new soil, a renaissance of our own.

[20] How much the gardeners may contribute to the making of such a new garden we can only guess, for genius is not readily producible, cannot be forced or anticipated, cannot be bred from known varieties. It is

our hope that it can be encouraged, and the prizes that are given for excellence in the theatre, in music and in painting do seem to have a kind of effectiveness. A prize is more effective than mere monetary success, for it confers leadership, lends a sense of direction and imparts a dignity to the attempt which is not bestowed by popular acclaim or ready sales.

[21] Let us remember always that no award is final, and that current opinion is subject to the veto of next year, next decade and next century. Sophocles did not win first place in the annual competition with his "Oedipus Tyrannus," though it seems to us now the best of the Greek tragedies. We can only judge honestly for ourselves, give what encouragement we can to what seems to us the best in our generation, and hope that some of the work produced by our contemporaries will grow and not disintegrate with the passing of time.

[22] Looking ahead, myself, I still have no more than a hope that our nation will some time take as great a place in the cultural history of the world as has been taken by Greece or Italy or England. So far we have, perhaps, hardly justified even the hope. But let us do what we can to encourage our nascent arts, for if we are to be remembered as more than a mass of people who lived and fought wars and died, it is for our arts that we will be remembered. The captains and the kings depart; the great fortunes wither, leaving no trace; the multitudes blow away like locusts, the records and barriers go down. The rulers, too, are forgotten unless they have had the forethought to surround themselves with singers and makers, poets and artificers in things of the mind.

[23] This is not immortality, of course. So far as I know there is no immortality. But the arts make the longest reach toward permanence, create the most enduring monuments, project the farthest, widest, deepest influence of which human prescience and effort are capable. The Greek religion is gone, but Aeschylus remains. Catholicism shrinks back toward the Papal State, but the best of medieval art perishes only where its pigments were perishable. The Lutheranism of Bach retains little content for us, but his music is indispensable. And there is only one condition that makes possible a Bach, an Aeschylus or a Michelangelo—it is a national interest in and enthusiasm for the art he practices.

[24] The supreme artist is only the apex of a pyramid; the pyramid itself must be built of artists and art lovers, apprentices and craftsmen so deeply imbued with a love for the art they follow or practice that it has become for them a means of communication with whatever has been found highest and most admirable in the human spirit. To the young people of this country I wish to say, if you now hesitate on the threshold of your maturity, wondering what rewards you should seek, wondering

perhaps whether there are any rewards beyond the opportunity to feed and sleep and breed, turn to the art which has moved you most readily, take what part in it you can, as participant, spectator, secret practitioner or hanger-on and waiter at the door. Make your living any way you can, but neglect no sacrifice at your chosen altar.

[25] It may break your heart, it may drive you half mad, it may betray you into unrealizable ambitions or blind you to mercantile opportunities with its wandering fires. But it will fill your heart before it breaks it; it will make you a person in your own right; it will open the temple doors to you and enable you to walk with those who have come nearest among men to what men may sometimes be. If the time arrives when our young men and women lose their extravagant faith in the dollar and turn to the arts, we may then become a great nation, nurturing great artists of our own, proud of our own culture and unified by that culture into a civilization worthy of our unique place on this rich and lucky continent between its protecting seas.

QUESTIONS AND COMMENT ON FORM AND CONTENT

1. What does Maxwell Anderson mean by saying "the things an artist has to communicate can be said only in symbols, in the symbols of his art"? In what other ways in paragraph 1 does he express a similar thought?

2. What guidance does he say we have for the hard decisions we have to make?

3. What do the parables of the New Testament have in common with the complex musical symbols of Bach and Beethoven?

4. Explain what he may mean by saying that we need more intelligence and more sensitivity to avoid being caught in a trap of selfish interest.

5. What do the Sermon on the Mount and the last chapter of Ecclesiastes have in common?

6. How does Anderson define *nobility?*

7. Has art made great advances since Homer?

8. What does the figure of dry bones in a death valley suggest?

9. Why does the author think that the artist has been wiser than the materialist?

10. What national conditions are necessary for "a Bach, an Aeschylus or a Michelangelo"?

11. What are Anderson's final hopes for the young men and women growing up in America? What dissappointments and what rewards will there be?

12. The last sentence in paragraph 2 ends the introduction and suggests three phases of the subject to be discussed. Where does each phase begin and end? Paragraphs 24 and 25 can be considered as the conclusion.

13. What poetic or rhetorical devices aid in creating the elevated tone in

paragraphs 24 and 25? Could this part be considered the peroration? See the etymology of *peroration*.

VOCABULARY: WHAT DO THE ITALICIZED WORDS MEAN?

The work of art is a *hieroglyph* (1)
. . . may lose . . . some of its *iridescence* (2)
. . . carries in his brain a *catalytic* agent (12)
This is no . . . *sanctimonious adjuration* (14)
The *doctrine* of *Machiavelli* is a fatal disease (15)
. . . encourage our *nascent* arts (22)

THEME SUGGESTIONS

The Need for Intelligence Today
The Need for Sensitivity Today
The Arts As Leisure Time Hobbies
Opening the Temple Doors of Art

From *THE FIGURE A POEM MAKES*

Robert Frost

Robert Frost (1874-1963) has been called by the English poet Robert Graves "the first American who could be honestly reckoned a master poet by world standards." Frost's prose reflects much of the imaginative quality to be found in his poetry. Disarmingly simple and informal in manner, the prose, like the poetry, succeeds in concealing an unexpected depth of thought and flash of insight.

Frost believed that good poetry and good prose should spring from the rhythms and tones of spoken language. While he admired the sonorous bookish language often used by great writers of the past, he preferred to keep close to the natural spoken language of everyday life. In poetry he avoided free verse, which was very popular in the period of his early writing. He said it was too much like playing tennis with the net down. He also avoided the monotony of a too-regular meter—often called dog- gerel. He liked, as he said, to break the irregular rhythm and accent of

spoken language across the regular accent of meter. It reminded him of
the regular beat of waves breaking irregularly on the beach.

[1] It should be of the pleasure of a poem itself to tell how it can
[have both wildness and a fulfilled subject]. The figure a poem makes.
It begins in delight and ends in wisdom. The figure is the same as for love.
No one can really hold that the ecstasy should be static and stand still
in one place. It begins in delight, it inclines to the impulse, it assumes
direction with the first line laid down, it runs a course of lucky events,
and ends in a clarification of life—not necessarily a great clarification,
such as sects and cults are founded on, but in a momentary stay against
confusion. It has denouement. It has an outcome that though unforseen
was predestined from the first image of the original mood—and indeed
from the very mood. It is but a trick poem and no poem at all if the
best of it was thought of first and saved for the last. It finds its own name
as it goes and discovers the best waiting for it in some final phrase at
once wise and sad—the happy-sad blend of the drinking song.

[2] No tears in the writer, no tears in the reader. No surprise for the
writer, no surprise for the reader. For me the initial delight is in the
surprise of remembering something I didn't know I knew. I am in a
place, in a situation, as if I had materialized from cloud or risen out of
the ground. There is a glad recognition of the long lost and the rest
follows. Step by step the wonder of unexpected supply keeps growing.
The impressions most useful to my purpose seem always those I was
unaware of and so made no note of at the time when taken, and the conclusion is come to that like giants we are always hurling experience ahead
of us to pave the future with against the day when we may want to
strike a line of purpose across it for somewhere. The line will have the
more charm for not being mechanically straight. We enjoy the straight
crookedness of a good walking stick. Modern instruments of precision
are being used to make things crooked as if by eye and hand in the old
days.

QUESTIONS AND COMMENT ON FORM AND CONTENT

1. These two paragraphs selected from a longer article or speech on poetry
raises the question common to all the arts: how much wildness or formlessness
is desirable in art? How can we have both freedom and pattern? Frost's answer comes in the form of an exposition of how a poem is written. How, according to Frost, is it written? How does this tend to give it form (unity,
point) without formalism?

2. What does Frost mean by saying that a poem "begins in delight and ends
in wisdom" and that "the figure is the same for love"? Does a poem, then, re-

veal a truth? a moral? What is a "momentary stay against confusion"? What would make a poem, in his opinion, merely a trick poem?

3. Does Frost's prose also have something of the same appeal because of its unpredictableness? Does the fact that it is charged with feeling cause it to deviate from strictly logical form and to adopt something of the pattern, form, or repetition of poetry? What is the point about "the straight crookedness of a good walking stick"?

VOCABULARY: WHAT DO THE ITALICIZED WORDS MEAN?

It has *denouement* (1)

. . . an outcome that though unforeseen was *predestined* (1)

THEME SUGGESTIONS

My Favorite Poet (Poem)
Rhythm in Speech and Poetry
My Favorite Art
Free Verse
Free Form in Art

THE CREATIVE PROCESS IN MUSIC

Aaron Copland

Aaron Copland (1900-   ), American composer and music critic, has composed symphonies, sonatas, and opera. He is the author of What to Listen for in Music *(1939, 1957).*

[1] Most people want to know how things are made. They frankly admit, however, that they feel completely at sea when it comes to understanding how a piece of music is made. Where a composer begins, how he manages to keep going—in fact, how and where he learns his trade—all are shrouded in impenetrable darkness. The composer, in short, is a man of mystery to most people, and the composer's workshop an unapproachable ivory tower.

[2] One of the first things most people want to hear discussed in relation to composing is the question of inspiration. They find it difficult to believe that composers are not as preoccupied with that question as

they had supposed. The layman always finds it hard to realize how natural it is for the composer to compose. He has a tendency to put himself into the position of the composer and to visualize the problems involved, including that of inspiration, from the perspective of the layman. He forgets that composing to a composer is like fulfilling a natural function. It is like eating or sleeping. It is something that the composer happens to have been born to do; and, because of that, it loses the character of a special virtue in the composer's eyes.

[3] The composer, therefore, confronted with the question of inspiration, does not say to himself: "Do I feel inspired?" He says to himself: "Do I feel like composing today?" And if he feels like composing, he does. It is more or less like saying to himself: "Do I feel sleepy?" If you feel sleepy, you go to sleep. If you don't feel sleepy, you stay up. If the composer doesn't feel like composing, he doesn't compose. It's as simple as that.

[4] Of course, after you have finished composing, you hope that everyone, including yourself, will recognize the thing you have written as having been inspired. But that is really an idea tacked on at the end.

[5] Someone once asked me, in a public forum, whether I waited for inspiration. My answer was: "Every day!" But that does not, by any means, imply a passive waiting around for the divine afflatus. That is exactly what separates the professional from the dilettante. The professional composer can sit down day after day and turn out some kind of music. On some days it will undoubtedly be better than others; but the primary fact is the ability to compose. Inspiration is often a by-product.

[6] The second question that most people find intriguing is generally worded thus: "Do you or don't you write your music at the piano?" A current idea exists that there is something shameful about writing a piece of music at the piano. Along with that goes a mental picture of Beethoven composing out in the fields. Think about it a moment and you will realize that writing away from the piano nowadays is not nearly so simple a matter as it was in Mozart or Beethoven's day. For one thing, harmony is so much more complex than it was then. Few composers are capable of writing down entire compositions without at least a passing reference to the piano. In fact, Stravinsky in his *Autobiography* has even gone so far as to say that it is a bad thing to write music away from the piano because the composer should always be in contact with *la matière sonore*. That's a violent taking of the opposite side. But, in the end, the way in which a composer writes is a personal matter. The method is unimportant. It is the result that counts.

[7] The really important question is: "What does the composer start with; where does he begin?" The answer to that is, Every composer be-

gins with a musical idea—a *musical* idea, you understand, not a mental, literary, or extra-musical idea. Suddenly a theme comes to him. (Theme is used as synonymous with musical idea.) The composer starts with his theme; and the theme is a gift from Heaven. He doesn't know where it comes from—has no control over it. It comes almost like automatic writing. That's why he keeps a book very often and writes themes down whenever they come. He collects musical ideas. You can't do anything about that element of composing.

[8] The idea itself may come in various forms. It may come as a melody—just a one-line simple melody which you might hum to yourself. Or it may come to the composer as a melody with an accompaniment. At times he may not even hear a melody; he may simply conceive an accompanimental figure to which a melody will probably be added later. Or, on the other hand, the theme may take the form of a purely rhythmic idea. He hears a particular kind of drumbeat, and that will be enough to start him off. Over it he will soon begin hearing an accompaniment and melody. The original conception, however, was a mere rhythm. Or, a different type of composer may possibly begin with a contrapuntal web of two or three melodies which are heard at the same instant. That, however, is a less usual species of thematic inspiration.

[9] All these are different ways in which the musical idea may present itself to the composer.

[10] Now, the composer has the idea. He has a number of them in his book, and he examines them in more or less the way that you, the listener, would examine them if you looked at them. He wants to know what he has. He examines the musical line for its purely formal beauty. He likes to see the way it rises and falls, as if it were a drawn line instead of a musical one. He may even try to retouch it, just as you might in drawing a line, so that the rise and fall of the melodic contour might be improved.

[11] But he also wants to know the emotional significance of his theme. If all music has expressive value, then the composer must become conscious of the expressive values of his theme. He may be unable to put it into so many words, but he feels it! He instinctly knows whether he has a gay or a sad theme, a noble or diabolic one. Sometimes he may be mystified himself as to its exact quality. But sooner or later he will probably instinctively decide what the emotional nature of his theme is, because that's the thing he is about to work with.

[12] Always remember that a theme is, after all, only a succession of notes. Merely by changing the dynamics, that is, by playing it loudly and bravely or softly and timidly, one can transform the emotional feeling of the very same succession of notes. By a change of harmony a new

poignancy may be given the theme; or by a different rhythmic treatment the same notes may result in a war dance instead of a lullaby. Every composer keeps in mind the possible metamorphoses of his succession of notes. First he tries to find its essential nature, and then he tries to find what might be done with it—how that essential nature may momentarily be changed.

[13] As a matter of fact, the experience of most composers has been that the more complete a theme is the less possibility there is of seeing it in various aspects. If the theme itself, in its original form, is long enough and complete enough, the composer may have difficulty in seeing it in any other way. It already exists in its definitive form. That is why great music can be written on themes that in themselves are insignificant. One might very well say that the less complete, the less important, the theme the more likely it is to be open to new connotations. Some of Bach's greatest organ fugues are constructed on themes that are comparatively uninteresting in themselves.

[14] The current notion that all music is beautiful according to whether the theme is beautiful or not doesn't hold true in many cases. Certainly the composer does not judge his theme by that criterion alone.

[15] Having looked at his thematic material, the composer must now decide what sound medium will best fit it. Is it a theme that belongs in a symphony, or does it seem more intimate in character and therefore better fitted for a string quartet? Is it a lyrical theme that would be used to best advantage in a song; or had it better be saved, because of its dramatic quality, for operatic treatment? A composer sometimes has a work half finished before he understands the medium for which it is best fitted.

[16] Thus far I have been presupposing an abstract composer before an abstract theme. But actually I can see three different types of composers in musical history, each of whom conceives music in a somewhat different fashion.

[17] The type that has fired public imagination most is that of the spontaneously inspired composer—the Franz Schubert type, in other words. All composers are inspired of course, but this type is more spontaneously inspired. Music simply wells out of him. He can't get it down on paper fast enough. You can almost always tell this type of composer by his prolific output. In certain months, Schubert wrote a song a day. Hugo Wolf did the same.

[18] In a sense, men of this kind begin not so much with a musical theme as with a completed composition. They invariably work best in the shorter forms. It is much easier to improvise a song than it is to improvise a symphony. It isn't easy to be inspired in that spontaneous

way for long periods at a stretch. Even Schubert was more successful in handling the shorter forms of music. The spontaneously inspired man is only one type of composer, with his own limitations.

[19] Beethoven symbolizes the second type—the constructive type, one might call it. This type exemplifies my theory of the creative process in music better than any other, because in this case the composer really does begin with a musical theme. In Beethoven's case there is no doubt about it, for we have the notebooks in which he put the themes down. We can see from his notebooks how he worked over his themes—how he would not let them be until they were as perfect as he could make them. Beethoven was not a spontaneously inspired composer in the Schubert sense at all. He was the type that begins with a theme; makes it a germinal idea; and upon that constructs a musical work, day after day, in painstaking fashion. Most composers since Beethoven's day belong to this second type.

[20] The third type of creator I can only call, for lack of a better name, the traditionalist type. Men like Palestrina and Bach belong in this category. They both exemplify the kind of composer who is born in a particular period of musical history, when a certain musical style is about to reach its fullest development. It is a question at such a time of creating music in a well-known and accepted style and doing it in a way that is better than anyone has done it before you.

[21] Beethoven and Schubert started from a different premise. They both had serious pretensions to originality! After all, Schubert practically created the song form singlehanded; and the whole face of music changed after Beethoven lived. But Bach and Palestrina simply improved on what had gone before them.

[22] The traditionalist type of composer begins with a pattern rather than with a theme. The creative act with Palestrina is not the thematic conception so much as the personal treatment of a well-established pattern. And even Bach, who conceived forty-eight of the most varied and inspired themes in his *Well-Tempered Clavichord,* knew in advance the general formal mold that they were to fill. It goes without saying that we are not living in a traditionalist period nowadays.

[23] One might add, for the sake of completeness, a fourth type of composer—the pioneer type: men like Gesualdo in the seventeenth century, Moussorgsky and Berlioz in the nineteenth, Debussy and Edgar Varese in the twentieth. It is difficult to summarize the composing methods of so variegated a group. One can safely say that their approach to composition is the opposite of the traditionalist type. They clearly oppose conventional solutions of musical problems. In many ways, their attitude is experimental—they seek to add new harmonies, new sonorities, new

formal principles. The pioneer type was the characteristic one at the turn of the seventeenth century and also at the beginning of the twentieth century, but it is much less evident today.[1]

[24] But let's return to our theoretical composer. We have him with his idea—his musical idea—with some conception of its expressive nature, with a sense of what can be done with it, and with a preconceived notion of what medium is best fitted for it. Still he hasn't a piece. A musical idea is not the same as a piece of music. It only induces a piece of music. The composer knows very well that something else is needed in order to create the finished composition.

[25] He tries, first of all, to find other ideas that seem to go with the original one. They may be ideas of a similar character, or they may be contrasting ones. These additional ideas will probably not be so important as the one that came first—usually they play a subsidiary role. Yet they definitely seem necessary in order to complete the first one. Still that's not enough! Some way must be found for getting from one idea to the next, and it is generally achieved through use of so-called bridge material.

[26] There are also two other important ways in which the composer can add to his original material. One is the elongation process. Often the composer finds that a particular theme needs elongating so that its character may be more clearly defined. Wagner was a master at elongation. I referred to the other way when I visualized the composer's examining the possible metamorphoses of his theme. That is the much written-about development of his material, which is a very important part of his job.

[27] All these things are necessary for the creation of a full-sized piece —the germinal idea, the addition of other lesser ideas, the elongation of the ideas, the bridge material for the connection of the ideas, and their full development.

[28] Now comes the most difficult task of all—the welding together of all that material so that it makes a coherent whole. In the finished product, everything must be in its place. The listener must be able to find his way around in the piece. There should be no possible chance of his confusing the principal theme with the bridge material, or vice versa. The composition must have a beginning, a middle, and an end; and it is up to the composer to see to it that the listener always has some sense of where he is in relation to beginning, middle, and end. Moreover, the whole thing should be managed artfully so that none can say where the soldering began—where the composer's spontaneous invention left off and the hard work began.

[29] Of course, I do not mean to suggest that in putting his materials

---

[1] Recent experiments with electronically produced music, however, point to a new species of scientifically trained composer as the pioneer type of our time.

together the composer necessarily begins from scratch. On the contrary, every well-trained composer has, as his stock in trade, certain normal structural molds on which to lean for the basic framework of his compositions. These formal molds I speak of have all been gradually evolved over hundreds of years as the combined efforts of numberless composers seeking a way to ensure the coherence of their compositions. . . .

[30] But whatever the form the composer chooses to adopt, there is always one great desideratum: The form must have what in my student days we used to call *la grande ligne* (the long line). It is difficult adequately to explain the meaning of that phrase to the layman. To be properly understood in relation to a piece of music, it must be felt. In mere words, it simply means that every good piece of music must give us a sense of flow—a sense of continuity from first note to last. Every elementary music student knows the principle, but to put it into practice has challenged the greatest minds in music! A great symphony is a man-made Mississippi down which we irresistibly flow from the instant of our leave-taking to a long foreseen destination. Music must always flow, for that is part of its very essence, but the creation of that continuity and flow—that long line—constitutes the be-all and end-all of every composer's existence.

QUESTIONS AND COMMENT ON FORM AND CONTENT

1. Given an opportunity, an audience that is curious about a process, a device, an organization and the like, will ask questions. These questions (real or imaginary) provide the speaker or writer with an outline or plan of presentation admirably adapted to the audience. What questions would be asked, and in what order would they be asked about the given subject? Aaron Copland draws upon his experiences with audiences to know what questions they would ask about how a piece of music is made. What are the three questions he is most frequently asked? Which one does he consider most important?

2. What is his answer to the questions about inspiration? What is the difference, in his opinion, between the professional and the dilettante? Does the modern composer do his writing at the piano?

3. What is meant by *theme* or *musical idea*? (How does this compare with the theme or thesis of a piece of writing?) In what forms may the musical idea or theme come to the composer? (See paragraph 8.)

4. How does the composer test the emotional significance of his theme?

5. What is the next step? (See paragraph 15.)

6. What is accomplished by paragraph 16?

7. How does the author characterize the three major types of composers? Why does he add a fourth type, almost as an afterthought?

8. What is accomplished in paragraph 24? In paragraph 27?

9. What is meant by the *long line*? Is the figure used in the last paragraph

effective? From what famous speech is the expression "be-all and end-all" drawn?

10. If you were dividing this essay into three or four parts, what name would you give to each part?

11. What ideas from Mr. Copland's explanation of "how a piece of music is made" can be applied to how a composition is written or how a poem is made? (For the latter compare Frost's "The Figure a Poem Makes," in the preceding selection.)

12. How, in general, does Mr. Copland make a difficult technical subject readable? Do you feel that he is writing specifically for you? Is he careful to define technical terms? As you read, how does he let you know where you have been, where you are, and where you are going? In what other ways does he keep the tone informal and personal?

VOCABULARY: WHAT DO THE ITALICIZED WORDS MEAN?

. . . the composer's workshop [is] an unapproachable *ivory tower* (1)
. . . passive waiting around for the *divine afflatus* (5)
. . . separates the professional from the *dilettante* (5)
. . . theme is used as *synonymous* with musical idea (7)
. . . changing the *dynamics* (12)
By a change of *harmony* a new *poignancy* may be given (12)
. . . the possible *metamorphosis* of his succession of notes (12)
It already exists in its *definitive* form (13)
. . . always one great *desideratum:* The form must have . . . *la grande ligne* (the *long line*) (30)

THEME SUGGESTIONS

The Creative Process in Fiction (Poetry) (the Essay) (Art) (Science)
Inspiration and Perspiration
The Professional versus the Amateur
Franz Schubert: Composer of Songs
What to Listen for in Music
What to See in a Poem (a Picture) (a Novel)

MODERN ARCHITECTURE: THE CARDBOARD HOUSE

Frank Lloyd Wright

Frank Lloyd Wright (1869-1959) was one of America's most original architects. He lectured widely and wrote in support of his concept of

Reprinted by the permission of the publisher, Horizon Press, from *The Future of Architecture* by Frank Lloyd Wright. Copyright 1953.

modern architecture. An Autobiography—Frank Lloyd Wright (*1932, revised 1943*) *tells his story.*

[1] Let us take for text on this, our fourth afternoon, the greatest of all references to simplicity, the inspired admonition: "*Consider the lilies of the field—they toil not, neither do they spin, yet verily I say unto thee —Solomon in all his glory was not arrayed like one of these.*" An inspired saying—attributed to an humble Architect in ancient times, called Carpenter, who gave up Architecture nearly two thousand years ago to go to work upon its Source.

[2] And if the text should seem to you too far away from our subject this afternoon—

"The Cardboard House"

—consider that for that very reason the text has been chosen. The cardboard house needs an antidote. The antidote is far more important than the house. As antidote—and as practical example, too, of the working out of an ideal of organic simplicity that has taken place here on American soil, step by step, under conditions that are your own—could I do better than to take apart for your benefit the buildings I have tried to build, to show you how they were, long ago, dedicated to the Ideal of Organic Simplicity? It seems to me that while another might do better than that, I certainly could not—for that is, truest and best, what I know about the Subject. What a man *does, that* he has.

[3] When, "in the cause of Architecture," in 1893, I first began to build the houses, sometimes referred to by the thoughtless as "The New School of the Middle West" (some advertiser's slogan comes along to label everything in this our busy woman's country), the only way to simplify the awful building in vogue at the time was to conceive a finer entity—a better building—and get it built. The buildings standing then were all tall and all tight. Chimneys were lean and taller still, sooty fingers threatening the sky. And beside them, sticking up by way of dormers through the cruelly sharp, saw-tooth roofs, were the attics for "help" to swelter in. Dormers were elaborate devices, cunning little buildings complete in themselves, stuck to the main roof slopes to let "help" poke heads out of the attic for air.

[4] Invariably the damp sticky clay of the prairie was dug out for a basement under the whole house, and the rubblestone walls of this dank basement always stuck up above the ground a foot or more and blinked, with half-windows. So the universal "cellar" showed itself as a bank of some kind of masonry running around the whole house, for the house to sit up on—like a chair. The lean, upper house-walls of the usual two floors above this stone or brick basement were wood, set on top of this

masonry-chair, clapboarded and painted, or else shingled and stained, preferably shingled and mixed, up and down, all together with mouldings crosswise. These overdressed wood house-walls had, cut in them—or cut out of them, to be precise—big holes for the big cat and little holes for the little cat to get in and out or for ulterior purposes of light and air. The house-walls were be-corniced or bracketed up at the top into the tall, purposely profusely complicated roof, dormers plus. The whole roof, as well as the roof as a whole, was scalloped and ridged and tipped and swanked and gabled to madness before they would allow it to be either shingled or slated. The whole exterior was be-deviled—that is to say, mixed to puzzle-pieces, with corner boards, panel-boards, window-frames, corner-blocks, plinth-blocks, rosettes, fantails, ingenious and jigger work in general. This was the only way they seemed to have, then, of "putting on style." The scroll-saw and turning-lathe were at the moment the honest means of this fashionable mongering by the wood-butcher and to this entirely "moral" end. Unless the householder of the period were poor indeed, usually an ingenious corner-tower on his house eventuated into a candle-snuffer dome, a spire, an inverted rutabaga or radish or onion or—what is your favorite vegetable? Always elaborate bay-windows and fancy porches played "ring around a rosy" on this "imaginative" corner feature. And all this the building of the period could do equally well in brick or stone. It was an impartial society. All material looked pretty much alike in that day.

[5] Simplicity was as far from all this scrap-pile as the pandemonium of the barn-yard is far from music. But it was easy for the Architect. All he had to do was to call: "Boy, take down No. 37, and put a bay-window on it for the lady!"

[6] So—the first thing to do was to get rid of the attic and, therefore, of the dormer and of the useless "heights" below it. And next, get rid of the unwholesome basement, entirely—yes, absolutely—in any house built on the prairie. Instead of lean, brick chimneys, bristling up from steep roofs to hint at "judgment" everywhere, I could see necessity for one only, a broad generous one, or at most, for two, these kept low down on gently sloping roofs or perhaps flat roofs. The big fireplace below, inside, became now a place for a real fire, justified the great size of this chimney outside. A real fireplace at that time was extraordinary. There were then "mantels" instead. A mantel was a marble frame for a few coals, or a piece of wooden furniture with tiles stuck in it and a "grate," the whole set slam up against the wall. The "mantel" was an insult to comfort, but the *integral* fireplace became an important part of the building itself in the houses I was allowed to build out there on the prairie. It refreshed me to see the fire burning deep in the masonry of the house itself.

[7] Taking a human being for my scale, I brought the whole house down in height to fit a normal man; believing in no other scale, I broadened the mass out, all I possibly could, as I brought it down into spaciousness. It has been said that were I three inches taller (I am 5 feet 8½ inches tall), all my houses would have been quite different in proportion. Perhaps.

[8] House-walls were now to be started at the ground on a cement or stone water-table that looked like a low platform under the building, which it usually was, but the house-walls were stopped at the second story window-sill level, to let the rooms above come through in a continuous window-series, under the broad eaves of a gently sloping, overhanging roof. This made enclosing screens out of the lower walls as well as light screens out of the second story walls. Here was true *enclosure of interior space*. A new sense of building, it seems.

[9] The climate, being what it was, a matter of violent extremes of heat and cold, damp and dry, dark and bright, I gave broad protecting roof-shelter to the whole, getting back to the original purpose of the "Cornice." The undersides of the roof projections were flat and light in color to create a glow of reflected light that made the upper rooms not dark, but delightful. The overhangs had double value, shelter and preservation for the walls of the house as well as diffusion of reflected light for the upper story, through the "light screens" that took the place of the walls and were the windows.

[10] At this time, a house to me was obvious primarily as interior space under fine shelter. I liked the sense of *shelter*. I liked the sense of shelter in the "look of the building." I achieved it, I believe. I then went after the variegated bands of material in the old walls to eliminate odds and ends in favor of one material and a single surface from grade to eaves, or grade to second story sill-cope, treated as simple enclosing screens,—or else made a plain screen band around the second story above the window-sills, turned up over on to the ceiling beneath the eaves. This screen band was of the same material as the under side of the eaves themselves, or what architects call the "soffit." The planes of the building parallel to the ground were all stressed, to grip the whole to earth. Sometimes it was possible to make the enclosing wall below this upper band of the second story, from the second story window-sill clear down to the ground, a heavy "wainscot" of fine masonry material resting on the cement or stone platform laid on the foundation. I liked that wainscot to be of masonry material when my clients felt they could afford it.

[11] As a matter of form, too, I liked to see the projecting base, or water-table, set out over the foundation walls themselves—as a substantial preparation for the building. This was managed by setting the studs

of the walls to the inside of the foundation walls, instead of to the out-side. All door and window tops were now brought into line with each other with only comfortable head-clearance for the average human being. Eliminating the sufferers from the "attic" enabled the roofs to lie low. The house began to associate with the ground and become natural to its prairie site. And would the young man in architecture ever believe that this was all "new" then? Not only new, but destructive heresy—or ridic-ulous eccentricity. So New that what little prospect I had of ever earning a livelihood by making houses was nearly wrecked. At first, "they" called the houses "dress-reform" houses, because Society was just then excited about that particular "reform." This simplification looked like some kind of "reform" to them. Oh, they called them all sorts of names that cannot be repeated, but "they" never found a better term for the work unless it was "Horizontal Gothic," "Temperance Architecture" (with a sneer), etc., etc. I don't know how I escaped the accusation of another "Renais-sance."

[12] What I have just described was all on the *outside* of the house and was there chiefly because of what had happened *inside*. Dwellings of that period were "cut-up," advisedly and completely, with the grim de-termination that should go with any cutting process. The "interiors" con-sisted of boxes beside or inside other boxes, called *rooms*. All boxes in-side a complicated boxing. Each domestic "function" was properly box to box. I could see little sense in this inhibition, this cellular sequestra-tion that implied ancestors familiar with the cells of penal institutions, except for the privacy of bed-rooms on the upper floor. They were per-haps all right as "sleeping boxes." So I declared the whole lower floor as one room, cutting off the kitchen as a laboratory, putting servants' sleeping and living quarters next to it, semi-detached, on the ground floor, screening various portions in the big room, for certain domestic purposes —like dining or reading, or receiving a formal caller. There were no plans like these in existence at the time and my clients were pushed toward these ideas as helpful to a solution of the vexed servant-problem. Scores of doors disappeared and no end of partition. They liked it, both clients and servants. The house became more free as "space" and more livable, too. Interior spaciousness began to dawn.

[13] Having got what windows and doors that were left lined up and lowered to convenient human height, the ceilings of the rooms, too, could be brought over on to the walls, by way of the horizontal, broad bands of plaster on the walls above the windows, the plaster colored the same as the room ceilings. This would bring the ceiling-surface down to the very window tops. The ceilings thus expanded, by extending them down-ward as the wall band above the windows, gave a generous overhead to even small rooms. The sense of the whole was broadened and made

plastic, too, by this expedient. The enclosing walls and ceilings were thus made to flow together.

[14] Here entered the important element of Plasticity—indispensable to successful use of the Machine, for true expression of Modernity. The outswinging windows were fought for because the casement window associated the house with out-of-doors—gave free openings, outward. In other words the so-called "casement" was simple and more human. In use and effect, more natural. If it had not existed I should have invented it. It was not used at that time in America, so I lost many clients because I insisted upon it when they wanted the "guillotine" or "double-hung" window then in use. The Guillotine was not simple nor human. It was only expedient. I used it once in the Winslow House—my first house— and rejected it thereafter—forever. Nor at that time did I entirely eliminate the wooden trim. I did make it "plastic," that is, light and continuously flowing instead of the heavy "cut and butt" of the usual carpenter work. No longer did the "trim," so-called, look like carpenter work. The machine could do it perfectly well as I laid it out. It was all after "quiet." This plastic trim, too, with its running "back-hand" enabled poor workmanship to be concealed. It was necessary with the field resources at hand at that time to conceal much. Machinery versus the union had already demoralized the workmen. The Machine resources were so little understood that extensive drawings had to be made merely to show the "mill-man" what to leave off. But the "trim" finally became only a single, flat, narrow, horizontal wood-band running around the room, one at the top of the windows and doors and another next to the floors, both connected with narrow, vertical, thin wood-bands that were used to divide the wall-surfaces of the whole room smoothly and flatly into folded color planes. The trim merely completed the window and door openings in this same plastic sense. When the interior had thus become wholly plastic, instead of structural, a New element, as I have said, had entered Architecture. Strangely enough an element that had not existed in Architectural History before. Not alone in the trim, but in numerous ways too tedious to describe in words, this revolutionary sense of the plastic whole, an instinct with me at first, began to work more and more intelligently and have fascinating, unforeseen consequences. Here was something that began to organize itself. When several houses had been finished and compared with the house of the period, there was very little of that house left standing. Nearly every one had stood the house of the period as long as he could stand it, judging by appreciation of the change. Now all this probably tedious description is intended to indicate directly in bare outline how thus early there *was* an ideal of organic simplicity put to work, with historical consequences, here in your own country. The main motives and indications were (and I enjoyed them all):

First—To reduce the number of necessary parts of the house and the separate rooms to a minimum, and make all come together as enclosed space—so divided that light, air and vista permeated the whole with a sense of unity.

Second—To associate the building as a whole with its site by extension and emphasis of the planes parallel to the ground, but keeping the floors off the best part of the site, thus leaving that better part for use in connection with the life of the house. Extended level planes were found useful in this connection.

Third—To eliminate the room as a box and the house as another by making all walls enclosing screens—the ceilings and floors and enclosing screens to flow into each other as one large enclosure of space, with minor subdivisions only. Make all house proportions more liberally human, with less wasted space in structure, and structure more appropriate to material, and so the whole more livable. *Liberal* is the best word. Extended straight lines or streamlines were useful in this.

Fourth—To get the unwholesome basement up out of the ground, entirely above it, as a low pedestal for the living-portion of the home, making the foundation itself visible as a low masonary platform, on which the building should stand.

Fifth—To harmonize all necessary openings to "outside" or to "inside" with good human proportions and make them occur naturally—singly or as a series in the scheme of the whole building. Usually they appeared as "light-screens" instead of walls, because all the "Architecture" of the house was chiefly the way these openings came in such walls as were grouped about the rooms as enclosing screens. The *room* as such was now the essential architectural expression, and there were to be no holes cut in the walls as holes are cut in a box, because this was not in keeping with the ideal of "plastic." Cutting holes was violent.

Sixth—To eliminate combinations of different materials in favor of monomaterial so far as possible; to use no ornament that did not come out of the nature of materials to make the whole building clearer and more expressive as a place to live in, and give the conception of the building appropriate revealing emphasis. Geometrical or straight lines were natural to the machinery at work in the building trades then, so the interiors took on this character naturally.

Seventh—To incorporate all heating, lighting, plumbing so that these systems became constituent parts of the building itself. These service features became architectural and in this attempt the ideal of an organic architecture was at work.

Eighth—To incorporate as organic Architecture—so far as possible—furnishings, making them all one with the building and designing them in simple terms for machine work. Again straight lines and rectilinear forms.

Ninth—Eliminate the Decorator. He was all curves and all efflorescence, if not all "period."

[15] This was all rational enough so far as the thought of an organic architecture went. The particular forms this thought took in the feeling of it all could only be personal. There was nothing whatever at this time to help make them what they were. All seemed to be the most natural thing in the world and grew up out of the circumstances of the moment. Whatever they may be worth in the long run is all they are worth.

[16] Now *simplicity* being the point in question in this early constructive effort, organic simplicity I soon found to be a matter of true coordination. And Beauty I soon felt to be a matter of the sympathy with which such coordination was affected. Plainness was not necessarily simplicity. Crude furniture of the Roycroft-Stickley-Mission Style, which came along later, was offensively plain, plain as a barn door—but never was simple in any true sense. Nor, I found, were merely machine-made things in themselves simple. To think "in simple," is to deal in simples, and that means with an eye single to the altogether. This, I believe, is the secret of simplicity. Perhaps we may truly regard nothing at all as simple in itself. I believe that no one thing in itself is ever so, but must achieve simplicity (as an Artist should use the term) as a perfectly realized part of some organic whole. Only as a feature or any part becomes an harmonious element in the harmonious whole does it arrive at the estate of simplicity. Any wild flower is truly simple, but double the same wild flower by cultivation, it ceases to be so. The *scheme* of the original is no longer clear. Clarity of design and perfect significance both are first essentials of the spontaneously born simplicity of the lilies of the field who neither toil nor spin, as contrasted with Solomon who had "toiled and spun"—that is to say, no doubt had put on himself and had put on his temple, properly "composed," everything in the category of good things but the cook-stove.

[17] Five lines where three are enough is stupidity. Nine pounds where three are sufficient is stupidity. But to eliminate expressive words that intensify or vivify meaning in speaking or writing is not simplicity; nor is similar elimination in Architecture simplicity—it, too, may be stupidity. In Architecture, expressive changes of surface, emphasis of line and especially textures of material, may go to make facts eloquent, forms more significant. Elimination, therefore, may be just as meaningless as elaboration, perhaps more often so. I offer any fool, for an example.

[18] To know what to leave out and what to put in, just where and just how—Ah, *that* is to have been educated in the knowledge of simplicity.

[19] As for Objects of Art in the house even in that early day they were the "bête noir" of the new simplicity. If well chosen, well enough in the house, but only if each was properly digested by the whole. Antique or modern sculpture, paintings, pottery, might become objectives in the Architectural scheme and I accepted them, aimed at them, and assimilated them. Such things may take their places as elements in the design of any house. They are then precious things, gracious and good to live with. But it is difficult to do this well. Better, if it may be done, to design all features together. At that time, too, I tried to make my clients see that furniture and furnishings, not built in as integral features of the building, should be designed as attributes of whatever furniture was built in and should be seen as minor parts of the building itself, even if detached or kept aside to be employed on occasion. But when the building itself was finished, the old furniture the clients already possessed went in with them to await the time when the interior might be completed. Very few of the houses were, therefore, anything but painful to me after the clients moved in and, helplessly, dragged the horrors of the old order along after them.

[20] But I soon found it difficult, anyway, to make some of the furniture in the "abstract"; that is, to design it as architecture and make it "human" at the same time—fit for human use. I have been black and blue in some spot, somewhere, almost all my life from too intimate contacts with my own furniture. Human beings must group, sit or recline —confound them—and they must dine, but dining is much easier to manage and always was a great artistic opportunity. Arrangements for the informality of sitting comfortably, singly or in groups, where it is desirable or natural to sit, and still to belong in disarray to the scheme as a whole—that is a matter difficult to accomplish. But it can be done now, and should be done, because only those attributes of human comfort and convenience, made to belong in this digested or integrated sense to the architecture of the home as a whole, should be there at all, in Modern Architecture. For that matter about four-fifths of the contents of nearly every home could be given away with good effect to that home. But the things given away might go on to poison some other home. So why not at once destroy undesirable things . . . make an end of them?

[21] Here then, in foregoing outline, is the gist of America's contribution to Modern American Architecture as it was already under way in 1893. But the gospel of elimination is one never preached enough. No matter how much preached, Simplicity is a spiritual ideal seldom organ-

ically reached. Nevertheless, by assuming the virtue by imitation—or by increasing structural make-shifts to get superficial simplicity—the effects may cultivate a taste that will demand the reality in course of time, but it may also destroy all hope of the real thing.

[22] Standing here, with the perspective of long persistent effort in the direction of an organic Architecture in view, I can again assure you out of this initial experience that Repose is the reward of true simplicity and that organic simplicity is sure of Repose. Repose is the highest quality in the Art of Architecture, next to integrity, and a reward for integrity. Simplicity may well be held to the fore as a spiritual ideal, but when actually achieved, as in the "lilies of the field," it is something that comes of itself, something spontaneously born out of the nature of the doing whatever it is that is to be done. Simplicity, too, is a reward for fine feeling and straight thinking in working a principle, well in hand, to a consistent end. Solomon knew nothing about it, for he was only wise. And this, I think, is what Jesus meant by the text we have chosen for this discourse—"Consider the lilies of the field," as contrasted, for beauty, with Solomon.

[23] Now, a chair *is* a machine to sit in.

[24] A home *is* a machine to live in.

[25] The human body *is* a machine to be worked by will.

[26] A tree *is* a machine to bear fruit.

[27] A plant *is* a machine to bear flowers and seeds.

[28] And, as I've admitted before somewhere, a heart *is* a suction-pump. Does that idea thrill you?

[29] Trite as it is, it may be as well to think it over because the *least* any of these things may be, *is* just that. All of them are that before they are anything else. And to violate that mechanical requirement in any of them is to finish before anything of higher purpose can happen. To ignore the fact is either sentimentality or the prevalent insanity. Let us acknowledge in this respect, that this matter of mechanics is just as true of the work of Art as it is true of anything else. But, were we to stop with that trite acknowledgment, we should only be living in a low, rudimentary sense. This skeleton rudiment accepted, *understood,* is the first condition of any fruit or flower we may hope to get from ourselves. Let us continue to call this flower and fruit of ourselves, even in this Machine Age, Art. Some Architects, as we may see, now consciously acknowledge this "Machine" rudiment. Some will eventually get to it by circuitous mental labor. Some *are* the thing itself without question and already in need of "treatment." But "Americans" (I prefer to be more specific and say "Usonians") have been educated "blind" to the higher human uses of it all—while actually in sight of this higher human use all the while.

[30] Therefore, now let the declaration that "all is machinery" stand

nobly forth for what it is worth. But why not more profoundly declare that "Form follows Function" and let it go at that? Saying, "Form follows Function," is not only deeper, it is clearer, and it goes further in a more comprehensive way to say the thing to be said, because the implication of this saying includes the heart of the whole matter. It may be that Function follows Form, as, or if, you prefer, but it is easier thinking with the first proposition just as it is easier to stand on your feet and nod your head than it would be to stand on your head and nod your feet. Let us not forget that Simplicity of the Universe is very different from the Simplicity of a Machine.

[31] New significance in Architecture implies new materials qualifying form and textures, requires fresh feeling, which will eventually qualify both as "ornament." But "Decoration" must be sent on its way or now be given the meaning that it has lost, if it is to stay. Since "Decoration" became acknowledged as such, and ambitiously set up for itself as Decoration, it has been a make-shift, in the light of this ideal of Organic Architecture. Any House Decoration, as such, is an architectural make-shift, however well it may be done, unless the decoration, so-called, is part of the Architect's design in both concept and execution.

[32] Since Architecture in the old sense died and Decoration has had to shift for itself more and more, all so-called Decoration has become *ornamental,* therefore no longer *integral.* There can be no true simplicity in either Architecture or Decoration under any such condition. Let Decoation, therefore, die for Architecture, and the Decorator become an Architect, but not an "Interior Architect."

[33] Ornament can never be applied to Architecture any more than Architecture should ever be applied to Decoration. All ornament, if not developed within the nature of Architecture and as organic part of such expression, vitiates the whole fabric no matter how clever or beautiful it may be as something in itself.

[34] Yes—for a century or more Decoration has been setting up for itself, and in our prosperous country has come pretty near to doing very well, thank you. I think we may say that it is pretty much all we have now to show as Domestic Architecture still goes with us at the present time. But we may as well face it. The Interior Decorator thrives with us because we have no Architecture. Any Decorator is the natural enemy of organic simplicity in Architecture. He, persuasive Doctor-of-Appearances that he *must* be when he becomes Architectural substitute, will give you an imitation of anything, even an imitation of imitative simplicity. Just at the moment, May, 1930, he is expert in this imitation. France, the born Decorator, is now engaged with "Madame," owing to the good fortune of the French market, in selling us this ready-made or made-to-order simplicity. Yes, Imitation Simplicity is the latest addition

to imported "stock." The Decorators of America are now equipped to furnish *especially* this. Observe. And how very charming the suggestions conveyed by these imitations sometimes are!

[35] Would you have again the general principles of the spiritual-ideal of organic simplicity at work in our Culture? If so, then let us reiterate: First, Simplicity is Constitutional Order. And it is worthy of note in this connection that 9 times 9 equals 81 is just as simple as 2 plus 2 equals 4. Nor is the obvious more simple necessarily than the occult. The obvious is obvious simply because it falls within our special horizon, is therefore easier for us to *see;* that is all. Yet all simplicity near or far has a countenance, a visage, that is characteristic. But this countenance is visible only to those who can grasp the whole and enjoy the significance of the minor part, as such, in relation to the whole when in flower. This is for the critics.

[36] This characteristic visage may be simulated—the real complication glossed over, the internal conflict hidden by surface and belied by mass. The internal complication may be and usually is increased to create the semblance of and get credit for—simplicity. This is the Simplicity-lie usually achieved by most of the "surface and mass" architects. This is for the young architect.

[37] Truly ordered simplicity in the hands of the great artist may flower into a bewildering profusion, exquisitely exuberant, and render all more clear than ever. Good William Blake says exuberance is *beauty,* meaning that it is so in this very sense. This is for the Modern Artist with the Machine in his hands. False Simplicity—Simplicity as an affectation, that is Simplicity constructed as a Decorator's outside put upon a complicated, wasteful engineer's or carpenter's "Structure," outside or inside—is not good enough Simplicity. It cannot be simple at all. But that is what passes for Simplicity, now that startling Simplicity-effects are becoming the *fashion.* That kind of Simplicity is *violent.* This is for "Art and Decoration."

[38] Soon we shall want Simplicity inviolate. There is one way to get that Simplicity. My guess is, there is *only* one way to get it. And that way is, on principle, by way of *Construction* developed as Architecture. That is for us, one and all.

QUESTIONS AND COMMENT ON FORM AND CONTENT

1. Consider the quotation at the beginning of this essay. Is it suitable and does it promote his point of view? What other uses may a quotation at the beginning of an article have? Who was the Architect called Carpenter of nearly two thousand years ago?

2. Wright begins with what is sometimes called the "present evils" of a situation, in this instance with the faults houses had when he began to build them in 1893. What were these faults? What does "The Cardboard House" mean?

3. The second part tells how these faults can be remedied. Where does this part begin? What remedies does he have for the outside of the house? How does he define a house?

4. Where does he start to suggest improvements for the interior of houses? What are these changes? Why does he change the windows? Why does he call the double-hung window the guillotine?

5. At the end of paragraph 14 he summarizes the major changes and gives some motives for them. What does he mean by "organic architecture"? He also speaks in paragraph 2 and elsewhere of "Organic Simplicity." What is this? How are simplicity in architecture and in writing and speaking compared? (See paragraph 17.)

6. What is meant by "repose"? How is it related to integrity and organic simplicity? Why is Solomon again referred to? (See paragraph 22.)

7. What does Wright have to say about the use of furniture and art objects in modern architecture? What criticism does he have of the interior decorator? How is this criticism connected with his theme or thesis? Is decoration, in his opinion, ornamental or integral?

8. What is his attitude toward machinery? What does he mean by the "machine"? Is it related to "integrity" and "Form follows Function"? What does he think about "Function follows Form"?

9. From the last four paragraphs of the essay, can you select several sentences that summarize Wright's "general principles of the spiritual ideal of organic simplicity"?

10. How do you account for the unusual use of capitals for such words as *Simplicity, Machine, Organic Architecture, Construction, Decorator,* and the like?

11. What adjectives would you use to describe the style and mood of paragraphs 3, 4, and 5?

VOCABULARY: WHAT DO THE ITALICIZED WORDS MEAN?

The cardboard house needs an *antidote* (2)

I could see little sense in this *inhibition* this *cellular sequestration* that implied ancestors familiar with the cells of *penal* institutions (12)

. . . in favor of *monomaterial* as far as possible (14)

As for Objects of Art . . . they were the *"bête noir"* of the new *simplicity* (19)

But "Americans" (I prefer to . . . say *"Usonians"*) have been educated "blind" (29)

Nor is the obvious more simple necessarily than the *occult* (35)

. . . simplicity may *flower* into a bewildering *profusion, exquisitely exuberant* (37)

THEME SUGGESTIONS

It's Pretty but Is It Art?
The Functional in Architecture (Painting) (Sculpture) (Ceramics)
Thoreau, Emerson, and Simplicity
Whitman's Organic Poetry
Form Follows Function
No Wright House for Me
Wright Is Wrong

TERENCE, THIS IS STUPID STUFF

A. E. Housman

A great classical scholar, A. E. Housman (1859-1936) was Professor of Latin at University College, London, and, later, at Cambridge. In 1896 at the age of thirty-seven he published his best known volume, A Shropshire Lad. *In 1922 he said, "I can not longer expect to be revisited by the continuous excitement under which . . . I wrote the greater part of my other book, nor indeed could I well sustain it if it came." His* Collected Poems *were published in 1940. In the poem that follows, note the characteristic simplicity and lack of undue ornament. The dialogue form adds to the informality.*

> "Terence, this is stupid stuff:
> You eat your victuals fast enough;
> There can't be much amiss, 'tis clear,
> To see the rate you drink your beer.
> But oh, good Lord, the verse you make,
> It gives a chap the belly-ache.
> The cow, the old cow, she is dead;
> It sleeps well the horned head:
> We poor lads, 'tis our turn now
> To hear such tunes as killed the cow.
> Pretty friendship 'tis to rhyme
> Your friends to death before their time

Moping melancholy mad:
Come, pipe a tune to dance to, lad."

Why, if 'tis dancing you would be,
There's brisker pipes than poetry.
Say, for what were hop-yards meant,
Or why was Burton built on Trent?
Oh many a peer of England brews
Livelier liquor than the Muse,
And malt does more than Milton can
To justify God's ways to man.
Ale, man, ale's the stuff to drink
For fellows whom it hurts to think:
Look into the pewter pot
To see the world as the world's not.
And faith, 'tis pleasant till 'tis past:
The mischief is that 'twill not last.
Oh I have been to Ludlow fair
And left my necktie God knows where,
And carried half-way home, or near,
Pints and quarts of Ludlow beer:
Then the world seemed none so bad,
And I myself a sterling lad;
And down in lovely muck I've lain,
Happy till I woke again.
Then I saw the morning sky:
Heigho, the tale was all a lie;
The world, it was the old world yet,
I was I, my things were wet,
And nothing now remained to do
But begin the game anew.

Therefore, since the world has still
Much good, but much less good than ill,
And while the sun and moon endure
Luck's a chance, but trouble's sure,
I'd face it as a wise man would,
And train for ill and not for good.
'Tis true, the stuff I bring for sale
Is not so brisk a brew as ale:
Out of a stem that scored the hand
I wrung it in a weary land.
But take it: if the smack is sour,

'Tis better for the embittered hour;
It should do good for heart and head
When your soul is in my soul's stead;
And I will friend you if I may,
In the dark and cloudy day.

There was a king reigned in the East:
There, when kings will sit to feast,
They get their fill before they think
With poisoned meat and poisoned drink.
He gathered all that springs to birth
From the many-venomed earth;
First a little, thence to more,
He sampled all her killing store;
And easy, smiling, seasoned sound,
Sate the king when healths went round.
They put arsenic in his meat
And stared aghast to watch him eat;
They poured strychnine in his cup
And shook to see him drink it up:
They shook, they stared as white's their shirt:
Them it was their poison hurt.
—I tell the tale that I heard told.
Mithridates, he died old.

QUESTIONS AND COMMENT ON FORM AND CONTENT

1. Notice that someone is addressing Terence, Housman's name for himself, in the first 14 lines. What complaint is being made about Housman's poetry? Have you heard similar complaints about serious music and poetry?

2. What is Housman's answer? Hops, malt, Burton, and Trent have reference to beer, malt, and breweries. In the introduction to *Paradise Lost* Milton says his purpose is to "justify the ways of God to men." Does Housman prove his point that "malt does more than Milton can/To justify God's ways to man"? What are its limitations for "fellows whom it hurts to think"?

3. What is the poet's conclusion in the third stanza?

4. In the last section, a story is told about King Mithridates. What is the point of the story? What connection has it with the rest of the poem? Which lines of the poem best summarize the theme of the poem?

5. In addition to a rather regular rhythm and meter, what other devices add to the effect of the poem? How much of the language is to be taken as figurative rather than literal? Does prose similarly use rhythmical language? Does it use figurative language as freely as poetry?

6. In prose one might introduce the illustration in the final section by saying, "Pliny in his *Natural History* tells a story that illustrates the point I have been making." How does Housman introduce it in poetry? Is the poetic method more dramatic? Are the connections in most poetry less obvious, more dependent upon association than logic?

7. Give the equivalent in abstract or generalized words of the italicized words:

    a. But take it: if the *smack* is sour . . .
    b. It should do good for *heart* and *head* . . .
    c. In the *dark* and *cloudy day.*

THEME SUGGESTIONS

Irony in *A Shropshire Lad*
Pessimism in *A Shropshire Lad*
Art as Escape
Realism in Art
Training for Adversity

SHOOTING AN ELEPHANT

George Orwell

George Orwell, pen name of Eric Blair (1903-1950), was born in India, attended schools in England, and served for five years (1922-1927) in the Indian Imperial Police. He became a sharp critic of British Imperialism —the "Conscience of his generation." His most widely known works are Animal Farm *and* 1984, *both satires on totalitarian society.*

[1] In Moulmein, in Lower Burma, I was hated by large numbers of people—the only time in my life that I have been important enough for this to happen to me. I was sub-divisional police officer of the town, and in an aimless, petty kind of way anti-European feeling was very bitter. No one had the guts to raise a riot, but if a European woman went through the bazaars alone somebody would probably spit betel juice over her dress. As a police officer I was an obvious target and was baited whenever it seemed safe to do so. When a nimble Burman tripped me up on the football field and the referee (another Burman) looked the other way, the crowd yelled with hideous laughter. This happened more than once. In the end the sneering yellow faces of young men that met me everywhere, the insults hooted after me when I was at a safe distance, got badly on my nerves. The young Buddhist priests were

the worst of all. There were several thousands of them in the town and none of them seemed to have anything to do except stand on street corners and jeer at Europeans.

[2] All this was perplexing and upsetting. For at that time I had already made up my mind that imperialism was an evil thing and the sooner I chucked up my job and got out of it the better. Theoretically —and secretly, of course—I was all for the Burmese and all against their oppressors, the British. As for the job I was doing, I hated it more bitterly than I can perhaps make clear. In a job like that you see the dirty work of Empire at close quarters. The wretched prisoners huddling in the stinking cages of the lock-ups, the grey, cowed faces of the long-term convicts, the scarred buttocks of the men who had been flogged with bamboos—all these oppressed me with an intolerable sense of guilt. But I could get nothing into perspective. I was young and ill-educated and I had had to think out my problems in the utter silence that is imposed on every Englishman in the East. I did not even know that the British Empire is dying, still less did I know that it is a great deal better than the younger empires that are going to supplant it. All I knew was that I was stuck between my hatred of the empire I served and my rage against the evil-spirited little beasts who tried to make my job impossible. With one part of my mind I thought of the British Raj as an unbreakable tyranny, as something clamped down, in *saecula saeculorum*, upon the will of prostrate peoples; with another part I thought that the greatest joy in the world would be to drive a bayonet into a Buddhist priest's guts. Feelings like these are the normal by-products of imperialism; ask any Anglo-Indian official, if you can catch him off duty.

[3] One day something happened which in a round-about way was enlightening. It was a tiny incident in itself, but it gave me a better glimpse than I had had before of the real nature of imperialism—the real motives for which despotic governments act. Early one morning the sub-inspector at a police station the other end of the town rang me up on the 'phone and said that an elephant was ravaging the bazaar. Would I please come and do something about it? I did not know what I could do, but I wanted to see what was happening and I got on to a pony and started out. I took my rifle, an old .44 Winchester and much too small to kill an elephant, but I thought the noise might be useful in *terrorem*. Various Burmans stopped me on the way and told me about the elephant's doings. It was not, of course, a wild elephant, but a tame one which had gone "must." It had been chained up, as tame elephants always are when their attack of "must" is due, but on the previous night it had broken its chain and escaped. Its mahout, the only person who could manage it when it was in that state, had set out

in pursuit, but had taken the wrong direction and was now twelve hours'
journey away, and in the morning the elephant had suddenly reappeared
in the town. The Burmese population had no weapons and were quite
helpless against it. It had already destroyed somebody's bamboo hut;
killed a cow and raided some fruit-stalls and devoured the stock; also it
had met the municipal rubbish van, and, when the driver jumped out and
took to his heels, had turned the van over and inflicted violences upon it.

[4] The Burmese sub-inspector and some Indian constables were
waiting for me in the quarter where the elephant had been seen. It was
a very poor quarter, a labyrinth of squalid bamboo huts, thatched with
palm-leaf, winding all over a steep hillside. I remember that it was
a cloudy, stuffy morning at the beginning of the rains. We began questioning the people as to where the elephant had gone, and, as usual,
failed to get any definite information. That is invariably the case in
the East; a story always sounds clear enough at a distance, but the
nearer you get to the scene of events the vaguer it becomes. Some of
the people said that the elephant had gone in one direction, some said
that he had gone in another, some professed not even to have heard
of any elephant. I had almost made up my mind that the whole story
was a pack of lies, when we heard yells a little distance away. There
was a loud, scandalized cry of "Go away, child! Go away this instant!"
and an old woman with a switch in her hand came round the corner of
a hut, violently shooing away a crowd of naked children. Some more
women followed, clicking their tongues and exclaiming; evidently there
was something that the children ought not to have seen. I rounded the
hut and saw a man's dead body sprawling in the mud. He was an Indian,
a black Dravidian coolie, almost naked, and he could not have been
dead many minutes. The people said that the elephant had come suddenly upon him round the corner of the hut, caught him with its trunk,
put its foot on his back and ground him into the earth. This was the
rainy season and the ground was soft, and his face had scored a trench
a foot deep and a couple of yards long. He was lying on his belly with
arms crucified and head sharply twisted to one side. His face was coated
with mud, the eyes wide open, the teeth bared and grinning with an
expression of unendurable agony. (Never tell me, by the way, that
the dead look peaceful. Most of the corpses I have seen looked devilish.)
The friction of the great beast's foot had stripped the skin from his
back as neatly as one skins a rabbit. As soon as I saw the dead man I sent
an orderly to a friend's house nearby to borrow an elephant rifle. I had
already sent back the pony, not wanting it to go mad with fright and
throw me if it smelled the elephant.

[5] The orderly came back in a few minutes with a rifle and five cartridges, and meanwhile some Burmans had arrived and told us that the

elephant was in the paddy fields below, only a few hundred yards away. As I started forward practically the whole population of the quarter flocked out of the houses and followed me. They had seen the rifle and were all shouting excitedly that I was going to shoot the elephant. They had not shown much interest in the elephant when he was merely ravaging their homes, but it was different now that he was going to be shot. It was a bit of fun to them, as it would be to an English crowd; besides they wanted the meat. It made me vaguely uneasy. I had no intention of shooting the elephant—I had merely sent for the rifle to defend myself if necessary—and it is always unnerving to have a crowd following you. I marched down the hill, looking and feeling a fool, with the rifle over my shoulder and an ever-growing army of people jostling at my heels. At the bottom, when you got away from the huts, there was a metalled road and beyond that a miry waste of paddy fields a thousand yards across, not yet ploughed but soggy from the first rains and dotted with coarse grass. The elephant was standing eight yards from the road, his left side towards us. He took not the slightest notice of the crowd's approach. He was tearing up bunches of grass, beating them against his knees to clean them and stuffing them into his mouth.

[6] I had halted on the road. As soon as I saw the elephant I knew with perfect certainty that I ought not to shoot him. It is a serious matter to shoot a working elephant—it is comparable to destroying a huge and costly piece of machinery—and obviously one ought not to do it if it can possibly be avoided. And at that distance, peacefully eating, the elephant looked no more dangerous than a cow. I thought then and I think now that his attack of "must" was already passing off; in which case he would merely wander harmlessly about until the mahout came back and caught him. Moreover, I did not in the least want to shoot him. I decided that I would watch him for a little while to make sure that he did not turn savage again, and then go home.

[7] But at that moment I glanced round at the crowd that had followed me. It was an immense crowd, two thousand at the least and growing every minute. It blocked the road for a long distance on either side. I looked at the sea of yellow faces above the garish clothes—faces all happy and excited over this bit of fun, all certain that the elephant was going to be shot. They were watching me as they would watch a conjurer about to perform a trick. They did not like me, but with the magical rifle in my hands I was momentarily worth watching. And suddenly I realized that I should have to shoot the elephant after all. The people expected it of me and I had got to do it; I could feel their two thousand wills pressing me forward, irresistibly. And it was at this moment, as I stood there with the rifle in my hands, that I first grasped the hollowness, the futility of the white man's dominion in the East. Here was I, the

white man with his gun, standing in front of the unarmed native crowd —seemingly the leading actor of the piece; but in reality I was only an absurd puppet pushed to and fro by the will of those yellow faces behind. I perceived in this moment that when the white man turns tyrant it is his own freedom that he destroys. He becomes a sort of hollow, posing dummy, the conventionalized figure of a sahib. For it is the condition of his rule that he shall spend his life in trying to impress the "natives," and so in every crisis he has got to do what the "natives" expect of him. He wears a mask, and his face grows to fit it. I had got to shoot the elephant. I had committed myself to doing it when I sent for the rifle. A sahib has got to act like a sahib; he has got to appear resolute, to know his own mind and do definite things. To come all that way, rifle in hand, with two thousand people marching at my heels, and then to trail feebly away, having done nothing—no, that was impossible. The crowd would laugh at me. And my whole life, every white man's life in the East, was one long struggle not to be laughed at.

[8] But I did not want to shoot the elephant. I watched him beating his bunch of grass against his knees, with that preoccupied grandmotherly air that elephants have. It seemed to me that it would be murder to shoot him. At that age I was not squeamish about killing animals, but I had never shot an elephant and never wanted to. (Somehow it always seems worse to kill a *large* animal.) Besides, there was the beast's owner to be considered. Alive, the elephant was worth at least a hundred pounds; dead, he would only be worth the value of his tusks, five pounds, possibly. But I had got to act quickly. I turned to some experienced-looking Burmans who had been there when we arrived, and asked them how the elephant had been behaving. They all said the same thing: he took no notice of you if you left him alone, but he might charge if you went too close to him.

[9] It was perfectly clear to me what I ought to do. I ought to walk up to within, say, twenty-five yards of the elephant and test his behavior. If he charged I could shoot, if he took no notice of me it would be safe to leave him until the mahout came back. But also I knew that I was going to do no such thing. I was a poor shot with a rifle and the ground was soft mud into which one would sink at every step. If the elephant charged and I missed him, I should have about as much chance as a toad under a steam-roller. But even then I was not thinking particularly of my own skin, only of the watchful yellow faces behind. For at that moment, with the crowd watching me, I was not afraid in the ordinary sense, as I would have been if I had been alone. A white man mustn't be frightened in front of "natives"; and so, in general, he isn't frightened. The sole thought in my mind was that if anything went wrong those two thousand Burmans would see me pursued, caught, trampled on and reduced

to a grinning corpse like that Indian up the hill. And if that happened
it was quite probable that some of them would laugh. That would never
do. There was only one alternative. I shoved the cartridges into the magazine and lay down on the road to get a better aim.

[10] The crowd grew very still, and a deep, low, happy sigh, as of people who see the theatre curtain go up at last, breathed from innumerable
throats. They were going to have their bit of fun after all. The rifle was
a beautiful German thing with cross-hair sights. I did not then know
that in shooting an elephant one would shoot to cut an imaginary bar
running from ear-hole to ear-hole. I ought, therefore, as the elephant was
sideways on, to have aimed straight at his ear-hole; actually I aimed
several inches in front of this, thinking the brain would be further forward.

[11] When I pulled the trigger I did not hear the bang or feel the
kick—one never does when a shot goes home—but I heard the devilish
roar of glee that went up from the crowd. In that instant, in too short
a time, one would have thought, even for the bullet to get there, a mysterious, terrible change had come over the elephant. He neither stirred
nor fell, but every line of his body had altered. He looked suddenly
stricken, shrunken, immensely old, as though the frightful impact of the
bullet had paralyzed him without knocking him down. At last, after what
seemed a long time—it might have been five seconds, I dare say—he
sagged flabbily to his knees. His mouth slobbered. An enormous senility
seemed to have settled upon him. One could have imagined him thousands of years old. I fired again into the same spot. At the second shot he
did not collapse but climbed with desperate slowness to his feet and
stood weakly upright, with legs sagging and head drooping. I fired a
third time. That was the shot that did for him. You could see the agony
of it jolt his whole body and knock the last remnant of strength from
his legs. But in falling he seemed for a moment to rise, for as his hind
legs collapsed beneath him he seemed to tower upwards like a huge
rock toppling, his trunk reaching skywards like a tree. He trumpeted, for
the first and only time. And then down he came, his belly towards me,
with a crash that seemed to shake the ground even where I lay.

[12] I got up. The Burmans were already racing past me across the
mud. It was obvious that the elephant would never rise again, but he
was not dead. He was breathing very rhythmically with long rattling
gasps, his great mound of a side painfully rising and falling. His mouth
was wide open—I could see far down into the caverns of pale pink throat.
I waited a long time for him to die, but his breathing did not weaken.
Finally I fired my two remaining shots into the spot where I thought his
heart must be. The thick blood welled out of him like red velvet, but
still he did not die. His body did not even jerk when the shots hit

him, the tortured breathing continued without a pause. He was dying, very slowly and in great agony, but in some world remote from me where not even a bullet could damage him further. I felt that I had got to put an end to that dreadful noise. It seemed dreadful to see the great beast lying there, powerless to move and yet powerless to die, and not even to be able to finish him. I sent back for my small rifle and poured shot after shot into his heart and down his throat. They seemed to make no impression. The tortured gasps continued as steadily as the ticking of a clock.

[13] In the end I could not stand it any longer and went away. I heard later that it took him half an hour to die. Burmans were bringing dahs and baskets even before I left, and I was told they had stripped his body almost to the bones by the afternoon.

[14] Afterwards, of course, there were endless discussions about the shooting of the elephant. The owner was furious, but he was only an Indian and could do nothing. Besides, legally I had done the right thing, for a mad elephant has to be killed, like a mad dog, if its owner fails to control it. Among the Europeans opinion was divided. The older men said I was right, the younger men said it was a damn shame to shoot an elephant for killing a coolie, because an elephant was worth more than any damn Coringhee coolie. And afterwards I was very glad that the coolie had been killed; it put me legally in the right and it gave me a sufficient pretext for shooting the elephant. I often wondered whether any of the others grasped that I had done it solely to avoid looking a fool.

QUESTIONS AND COMMENT ON FORM AND CONTENT

1. Is this a short story or an essay? What does Orwell call it in the book title?

2. Is it mainly about shooting an elephant or is the shooting only an illustration of something else?

3. How did imperialism affect the natives of Burma? How, in turn, was Orwell affected? How did he feel about the Burmese—especially the young Burmese priests?

4. What are some conflicts in Orwell's feelings?

5. What does the episode of the elephant show him about the effect of the white man's dominion in the East?

6. Orwell passes over, apparently without feeling, the killing of the Coringhee coolie, yet is so moved by the death throes of an elephant that he can stand it no longer. Is the attitude toward the coolie (see also the last paragraph) a part of the imperialist pose? Or is it, as he says, because he "could get nothing in perspective. I was young and ill-educated."?

7. Like a short story, "Shooting an Elephant" begins with an unsatisfactory

situation between Orwell and the natives. The elephant episode brings it to a head—with considerable clarification of the situation. Suspense follows, as in a short story, with Orwell debating with himself whether to kill the elephant or to await a better outcome. Orwell uses this period of suspense to glean all he can learn (and teach) from the situation. Is he really a hero to this audience of 2,000 Burmese? If not, what is he? How does he describe himself? What is he most afraid of? What happens to man when he turns tyrant? Explain "He wears a mask, and his face grows to fit it."

8. Consider the repetition of *got* in paragraph 7. Is it effective? What usage label, if any, does your dictionary use with *got* (see also *get*) when *got* indicates necessity, as in "I had *got* to shoot the elephant"? What dictionary did you use? Do dictionaries always agree on the degree of informality of words?

9. How would you compare the two vivid, realistic descriptions—the one in the second half of paragraph 4 and the other in paragraphs 11, 12, and 13? What senses are appealed to? What figurative language is used?

10. What is striking and effective about the final paragraph?

VOCABULARY: WHAT DO THE ITALICIZED WORDS MEAN?

I could get nothing into *perspective* (2)
. . . a *labyrinth* of *squalid* bamboo huts (4)
An enormous *senility* seemed to have settled upon him. (11)
. . . blood *welled* out of him like red velvet (12)
. . . sufficient *pretext* for shooting the elephant (14)

THEME SUGGESTIONS

The Effect of Tyranny on the Tyrant
The Effect of Tyranny on the Victims
Living up to Great Expectations
The Face Grows to Fit the Mask
On Being Laughed At
Poker Faces
Hostile Faces
Mixed Feelings

AREOPAGITICA

John Milton

John Milton (1608-1674) was not only one of the world's greatest poets but also a prolific and vigorously imaginative writer on controversial religious and political questions. Areopagitica *takes its name from the hill of Ares (Mars) in Athens. The essay remains one of the most powerful arguments for freedom of the press.*

Milton was educated at Christ's College, Cambridge, and served the Puritan Commonwealth as Latin Secretary. Among his great poems are Paradise Lost (1667), Paradise Regained (1671), "Lycidas," and many lyrics and sonnets.

[1] I deny not but that it is of greatest concernment in the church and commonwealth, to have a vigilant eye how books demean themselves as well as men; and thereafter to confine, imprison, and do sharpest justice on them as malefactors: for books are not absolutely dead things, but do contain a potency of life in them to be as active as that soul was whose progeny they are; nay, they do preserve as in a vial the purest efficacy and extraction of that living intellect that bred them. I know they are as lively, and as vigorously productive, as those fabulous dragon's teeth;[1] and being sown up and down, may chance to spring up armed men.

[2] And yet, on the other hand, unless wariness be used, as good almost kill a man as kill a good book: who kills a man kills a reasonable creature, God's image; but he who destroys a good book, kills reason itself, kills the image of God, as it were, in the eye. Many a man lives a burden to the earth; but a good book is the precious life-blood of a master-spirit, embalmed and treasured up on purpose to a life beyond life. 'Tis true, no age can restore a life, whereof, perhaps, there is no great loss; and revolutions of ages do not oft recover the loss of a rejected truth, for the want of which whole nations fare the worse. We should be wary therefore what persecution we raise against the living labors of public men, how we spill that seasoned life of man, preserved and stored up in books; since we see a kind of homicide may be thus committed, sometimes a martyrdom; and if it extend to the whole impression, a kind of massacre, whereof the execution ends not in the slaying of an elemental life, but strikes at that ethereal and fifth essence,[2] the breath of reason itself; slays an immortality rather than a life. . . .

[3] Good and evil we know in the field of this world grow up together almost inseparably; and the knowledge of good is so involved and interwoven with the knowledge of evil, and in so many cunning resemblances hardly to be discerned, that those confused seeds which were imposed upon Psyche[3] as an incessant labor to cull out and sort asunder, were not

[1] Ovid, *Metamorphoses*, III, 95-126. The fabulous teeth which, when sown, produced a crop of armed men who destroyed each other.

[2] The ethereal quintessence, or fifth element, an imperishable substance identified with the spirit.

[3] Psyche was given the impossible task of separating various seeds. The ants helped her.

more intermixed. It was from out the rind of one apple tasted that the knowledge of good and evil, as two twins cleaving together, leaped forth into the world. And perhaps this is that doom which Adam fell into of knowing good and evil, that is to say, of knowing good by evil.

[4] As therefore the state of man now is, what wisdom can there be to choose, what continence to forbear, without the knowledge of evil? He that can apprehend and consider vice with all her baits and seeming pleasures, and yet abstain, and yet distinguish, and yet prefer that which is truly better, he is the true wayfaring Christian. I cannot praise a fugitive and cloistered virtue, unexercised and unbreathed, that never sallies out and sees her adversary, but slinks out of the race, where that immortal garland is to be run for, not without dust and heat. Assuredly we bring not innocence into the world, we bring impurity much rather: that which purifies us is trial, and trial is by what is contrary. That virtue therefore which is but a youngling in the contemplation of evil, and knows not the utmost that vice promises to her followers, and rejects it, is but a blank virtue, not a pure; her whiteness is but an excremental whiteness; which was the reason why our sage and serious poet Spenser[4] (whom I dare be known to think a better teacher than Scotus or Aquinas), describing true temperance under the person of Guion, brings him in with his palmer through the cave of Mammon and the bower of earthly bliss, that he might see and know, and yet abstain.

[5] Since therefore the knowledge and survey of vice is in this world so necessary to the constituting of human virtue, and the scanning of error to the confirmation of truth, how can we more safely and with less danger scout into the regions of sin and falsity than by reading all manner of tractates, and hearing all manner of reason? And this is the benefit which may be had of books promiscuously read.

QUESTIONS AND COMMENT ON FORM AND CONTENT

1. Milton concedes that church and state need to keep an eye on books, just at they do on men, because books may also be real malefactors. What is the allusion to the sowing of dragon's teeth?

2. Yet "unless wariness be used, as good almost kill a man as kill a good book." How does Milton, by use of varied but harmonious figures of speech, bring this thought home to us? Does he not, in his analogies, suggest that in many respects "killing" a book causes a more serious loss to mankind than killing a man? Could the thought be expressed as vigorously without the use of metaphors?

3. Paragraph 3 is a good illustration of Milton's intermixing of the abstract and literal and the figurative. He could have said "Good and evil are inter-

[4] See Spenser's *Faerie Queene*, II, viii.

mixed." Instead, his highly imaginative mind sees the two growing as in a field, where the weeds become mixed with the wheat. He adds the allusion to Psyche's task of separating seeds. Finally, he is not satisfied to make a simple allusion to Adam and Eve. He gives us a picture: "It was from out the rind of one apple tasted that the knowledge of good and evil, as two twins cleaving together, leaped forth into the world." The "two twins" expression is, of course, redundant and therefore frowned upon today. But like the double negative, it carries emphasis, and Milton wanted, above all, to flash before us the picture of this ill-fated pair.

4. Paragraph 4 has been justly praised for its vigor, rhythm, and picture making as well as for the argument presented. What is the argument? How does Milton make us see the picture? Where could he have used capitals to indicate personification?

5. Obscenity and pornography are today banned from the mails. Can these words be accurately defined? Should there be any censorship of books, magazines, moving pictures, television, newspapers? If so, who should do it? Do you feel that you need someone to protect your viewing and reading? Do children need special protection?

VOCABULARY: WHAT DO THE ITALICIZED WORDS MEAN?

. . . how books *demean* themselves (1)
. . . justice on them as *malefactors* (1)
. . . whose *progeny* they are (1)
What wisdom can there be to choose, what *continence* to forbear (4)
I cannot praise a *fugitive* and *cloistered* virtue (4)
. . . *sallies* out and sees her *adversary* (4)
. . . with his *palmer* through the cave of *Mammon* and the *bower* of earthly bliss (4)
. . . reading all manner of *tractates* (5)
. . . of books *promiscuously* read (5)

THEME SUGGESTIONS

A Fugitive Virtue
On Censorship of Books (Movies) (Television)
Milton's Prose Style
Freedom of Speech
Freedom of the Press

EXTREMISM IN AMERICAN POLITICS

Arthur M. Schlesinger

Arthur M. Schlesinger (1888-1965) was noted as an historian, especially of social history, and as a defender of civil rights. Among his books are The Rise of the City, Paths to the Present, The American as Reformer, *and* The Rise of Modern America. *The article reprinted here, written shortly before his death, is the last he wrote.*

[1] The Presidential campaign of 1964 introduced the word "extremism" into our political vocabulary as a synonym for ultraconservatism, but the phenomenon itself is anything but new. Throughout our history it has lurked under the surface of public life, finding an escape hatch at more or less definite intervals. Psychologically the outbreaks have also borne striking resemblances, even though the professed objectives have shifted as occasion required. For these reasons a consideration of the leading examples should contribute to a better understanding of this recurring aspect of American politics.

[2] Nearly a century and a half ago, in 1826, the abduction and presumed murder of one William Morgan of Batavia in western New York set off a wave of popular hysteria that became a force in state and national affairs. Morgan, a bricklayer, was a Mason who had written a book exposing the order's secrets, and widespread report instantly attributed his disappearance to retaliation on the part of vengeful members. When four persons were found guilty just of the kidnaping and got off with light sentences, suspicion of the fraternity's covert control of the courts, and probably also of all other departments of the government, hardened into certainty. Incidentally, the most diligent search failed to yield any trace of "the martyr's" body. The mystery remains to this day.

[3] From New York the excitement spread to New England and the Middle Atlantic states as well as inland to Ohio and Indiana. Antimasonic newspapers and magazines sprang up to fan the flames. Traveling lecturers denounced the "hydra-headed monster." Churches expelled Masonic preachers and laymen. Many lodges disbanded; in New York State alone their number dropped from 600 in 1826 to 50 in 1834. The Antimasons successfully ran candidates in local and state elections; several legislatures banned extrajudicial oaths; and Rhode Island and Pennsylvania required all secret societies henceforth to reveal their proceedings in annual reports.

[4] In the national arena, politicians like Thurlow Weed and William

Reprinted by permission of Mrs. Arthur M. Schlesinger and the *Saturday Review*.

H. Seward in New York and Thaddeus Stevens in Pennsylvania, seeking to oust President Jackson and the Democratic party from power in 1832, seized on the furor to consolidate a nationwide opposition. In doing so, however, they injected other issues and wrenched the movement so far from its original purpose that William Wirt, the Antimasonic nominee, failed to condemn the order in his letter of acceptance. Though both Jackson and Henry Clay, the National Republican candidate, were active or former Masons, Wirt received only Vermont's seven electoral votes, while his rivals won 219 and 49 respectively.

[5] The party then soon flickered out. The reason, according to a committee of the Pennsylvania legislature, was that "It envies the possessors of office. It is ignorant. It absurdly denounces as a mysterious institution full of guilt and blood a society of which . . . ten or fifteen thousand of our most useful, intelligent, and eminent citizens of all parties are members." Probably more decisive was the fact that questions of crucial national importance such as the tariff and the United States Bank had arisen to give the voters something more tangible to worry about.

[6] Already events were setting the stage for a new exhibition of frenzy. Oddly enough, these alarmists saw no danger in mystic brotherhoods and in due course donned the cloak of secrecy themselves. Their fear arose from the large inflow of Irish and Germans into the United States in the 1830s and 1840s, with the Irish in particular arousing wide hostility. As Catholics they seemed to menace America's traditional Protestantism, and as a copious supply of cheap labor they jeopardized the living standards of native workers. Rumors also coursed far and fast of "Romish" plots to subvert the public schools and even the republic itself.

[7] The popular reaction was swift and tempestuous. In 1834 a mob burned down a convent school in Charlestown, Massachusetts, and later years saw rioting, often attended with bloodshed as well as incendiarism, in New York, Philadelphia, Detroit, Louisville, and elsewhere. Anti-Catholic lecturers and periodicals flourished. In 1836 a pretended ex-nun, Maria Monk, published the *Awful Disclosures* of imagined immorality and infanticide in a convent, which sold 300,000 copies before the Civil War. Even Samuel F. B. Morse, the portraitist and inventor of the telegraph, took up arms against Rome with his *Foreign Conspiracy against the Liberties of the United States* (1834) and later tracts.

[8] In the ensuing decade the nativists formed secret fraternal organizations to further the cause, such as the Order of United Americans, the Junior Order of United American Mechanics, and the Order of the Star-Spangled Banner. The last band, established in 1849 and the most militant of the lot, in turn set afoot the American or Know-Nothing party. The Know Nothings, popularly so dubbed because they denied to inquirers knowledge of the party's existence, demanded the exclusion of all

foreign-born from office ("Americans must rule America"), a twenty-one-year naturalization period for voting, and the rigid separation of church and state. Aided by the nationwide consternation over the revival of the slavery controversy by the Kansas-Nebraska Act in 1854, and conducting no public campaign, they carried Massachusetts, Pennsylvania, and Delaware in the fall elections, also sent seventy-some supporters to Congress, and a year later captured five more states.

[9] Exhilarated by these successes, the Know Nothings in 1856 nominated a national standard-bearer, the Whig ex-President Millard Fillmore, thereby bringing the historic Whig party to an end. By now, however, feeling throughout the country had reached such a pitch over the sectional question that the Know Nothings themselves could no longer ignore it, and it opened serious rifts in their convention. Although Fillmore mustered nearly a quarter of all the popular votes, they were so scattered as to win only Maryland's eight electoral ones. Another fledgling party, the Republican, founded expressly to curb the expansion of slavery, obtained a much larger popular support and the 114 electoral votes of eleven states. Though it, too, lost to the Democrats, it could look confidently to the future. The Know Nothings shortly passed into oblivion.

[10] How potent a force they might have become had the sectional issue not intruded no one can say. Yet, as the Antimasonic movement showed and later evidence confirmed, such conflagrations in America have always quickly burned themselves out. While the Know-Nothing convulsion was still at its height, the politically observant Horace Greeley declared it would "vanish as suddenly as it appeared." And the Indiana Congressman George W. Julian, writing after the fact, undoubtedy expressed the sober second thought of the electorate in terming it "a horrid conspiracy against decency, the rights of man, and the principle of human brotherhood."

[11] The next great outbreak of fear and hate occurred after the Civil War, this time in the conquered South. The remaking of race relations by Congress in the measures known as Reconstruction had distorted the section's traditional pattern of life beyond recognition. The slaves were now not only free but were voters and officeholders helping run the reconstituted state governments to the exclusion of the old master class. For ingrained believers in white supremacy this reversed the natural order of things and meant the region's "Africanization."

[12] With no relief to be expected from a Northern-controlled Congress or at the polls, the aroused whites formed clandestine societies of resistance. The Ku Klux Klan, the best known, started in 1866 at the little town of Pulaski in southern Tennessee as a social club of returned Confederate veterans who for fun rode about the countryside after dark, masked and clad in white on white-sheeted horses. But when the weird

proceedings were seen to excite the superstitious dread of Negroes, the members, taking advantage of the fact, visited insubordinate blacks and their white allies at dead of night to warn them to desist or decamp. The Pulaski example gave birth to imitators in other parts of Tennessee and in other Southern states, and in April 1867 a secret gathering at Nashville combined the units or "dens" under the name of the Invisible Empire of the South, with officers bearing awesome titles.

[13] As time went on, violence became the chief reliance. Victims might now be beaten, maimed, or murdered. Criminal bands, too, adopted the eerie disguise for purposes of loot or private vengeance. In Louisiana alone, federal records show that 1,885 persons suffered injury or death during the 1868 Presidential election year. The situation was already well out of hand when in January 1869 the "Grand Wizard" of the order decreed its dissolution. This action, however, only worsened conditions, for many of the dens refused to comply and the departure of the more responsible members gave the lawless elements full rein. Besides, scores of similar organizations had meanwhile sprung up, notably the Knights of the White Camelia, which, independently of the Klan, operated in the region from Texas to the Carolinas under the nominal control of a supreme council in New Orleans. The total number involved in these underground activities has been estimated at 550,000, though obviously the exact figure can never be known.

[14] No other American extremist movement, before or since, has so brazenly defied the federal authority. Accordingly this has been the only instance (prior to the sporadic resistance to the school-desegregation decision of 1954 and the later civil rights acts) to bring down the might of the national government. In 1870 and 1871 Congress in successive laws empowered President Grant to end the societies with armed force if necessary and to appoint supervisors when required to assure Negroes full voting rights in federal elections. Soon hundreds of accused were arrested, United States troops reappeared in the South, and for a time the writ of habeas corpus was suspended in nine South Carolina counties. Consequently "Ku Kluxing" virtually ceased early in 1872. By then, however, the resourceful whites had learned they could frighten Negroes away from the polls by the mere threat of maltreatment. Later on, of course, when the South recovered full control of its affairs, they secured the same end by intricate election laws and the falsifying of returns.

[15] The flare-up of intolerance to follow originated in the Midwest, being the handiwork of an anti-Catholic secret society, the American Protective Association. Founded in 1887 by one Henry F. Bowers, a lawyer of Clinton, Iowa, the APA reflected not only the ancient Protestant hostility to Catholicism but also, more directly, rural dislike of the rap-

idly growing cities, where the bulk of the Catholics resided, as well as urban resentment of the economic competition due to the mounting immigration from the papist countries of Southern and Eastern Europe. Every initiate swore to oppose "the diabolical work of the Roman Catholic Church" and, specifically, to hire or vote for none of its communicants or condone their appointment as teachers in the public schools.

[16] As the membership spread east and west through the land, the principal features of the earlier Know-Nothing agitation were reproduced and expanded. "Escaped nuns" and "ex-priests" recited their shocking tales. Anti-Catholic weeklies and pamphlets whipped up passion. Forged documents, including an alleged encyclical commanding the faithful to "exterminate all heretics" on a given day in 1893, exposed Rome's designs against democratic Protestant America. A whispering campaign reported the collecting of arms in Catholic church basements. Mob violence likewise erupted, a Boston collision in 1895 causing the death of one man and the injury of many others. As a dismayed contemporary said of the APA, "In the name of freedom it stabs freedom in the dark; in the name of Christianity . . . it uses the weapons of the devil."

[17] The members as a rule operated within the fold of the Republican party, since Irish Catholics comprised a mainstay of the Democrats. Assisted by self-styled patriotic societies with similar aims, the APA helped win many city and a number of state elections, contributed to William McKinley's victory in his race for governor of Ohio in 1893, and claimed 100 supporters in Congress the following year. At its peak in late 1894 it probably numbered 100,000 persons, with the greatest concentration in the Middle West. By the 1896 Presidential campaign, however, the bitter strife of the major parties over free silver and Bryanism obliterated the "Catholic menace" from the voters' minds, and the order disappeared from view.

[18] The first outburst of zealotry in the present century was a throwback to both the Ku Klux Klan and the American Protective Association. Indeed, the new organization appropriated the name and methods of the Reconstruction body besides being itself Southern-born. Established in 1915 at Atlanta by William J. Simmons, an erstwhile itinerant preacher, it pledged its members to eliminate from political life all but white native-born Protestants. "By some scheme of Providence," Simmons declared, "the Negro was created a serf." Georgia already had a record of leading the Union in the number of its colored lynchings.

[19] Because of the distracting effects of World War I, however, the resuscitated Klan made little headway until peace returned. Then alarm over the prospective deluging of the country by impoverished and perhaps revolutionary comers from devastated Europe caused it to extend

rapidly through the South and Midwest, with strong outposts elsewhere as well; and in course of doing so it added animosity toward Jews to the older hatred of Negroes, Catholics, and immigrants. The anti-Semitism, long dormant but never before an overt issue, rested avowedly on a set of fraudulent documents of obscure Russian origin, *The Protocols of the Elders of Zion.* These allegedly unveiled a plot to assert Jewish predominance of the entire globe. As regards the United States, a contributor in the Klan organ, *The Searchlight,* offered to prove that Jews were already engaged in inciting the Afro-Americans to a race war. He indeed avowed he had "never met a disloyal American who failed to be either foreign-born or a Semitic." Men so thinking turned a deaf ear when the *Oklahoma Leader* rebuked this "new sort of Christianity that would flog Christ for being a Jew and a foreigner."

[20] The night-riding Klansmen in ghostly attire, dotting the landscape as they went with fiery crosses, employed threats, beatings, arson, and murder against their victims, white and colored, and these unfortunates in due course came to include upholders even of such causes as the League of Nations, evolution, and birth control. In 1922 the organization entered politics, dominating for a time the states of Ohio, Indiana, Oklahoma, Arkansas, Texas, California, and Oregon with spokesmen in Congress. It wielded enough influence in the 1924 Democratic convention to deny the Presidential nomination to Alfred E. Smith, the Catholic governor of New York. A year later 40,000 Klansmen paraded down Washington's Pennsylvania Avenue. At its zenith the membership supposedly embraced between four and five million.

[21] As in past instances of the kind, however, popular revulsion to brute force and lawlessness set in, hastened by revelations of financial and other misdoings of the leaders. In Indiana the scandals sent a "Grand Dragon," a Congressman, the mayor of Indianapolis, and various lesser officials to prison. Even before this, legislation in New York, Michigan, Minnesota, Iowa, Texas, and some other states had banned masked brotherhoods. Further evidence of the decline appeared in the Democratic nomination of Al Smith in 1928 and the same year saw the United States Supreme Court, in a case appealed from New York, denounce the Klan for "conduct inimical to personal rights and welfare" in taking the law secretly into its hands.

[22] Of greener memory is the scaremongering associated with the term McCarthyism. This affair, different from its predecessors, was largely the work of one man operating from an important position in the federal government under the protection of Congressional immunity. As in the other episodes particular circumstances facilitated his success. The public, only recently recovered from the shock of World War II, faced with dread new perils to peace from the postwar aggressions of the Soviet Un-

ion on neighboring states, its acquisition of the atom bomb, and disclosures of several instances of Communist infiltration of the United States
Government. On top of all these, America's springing to arms to save
Korea from Communism brought the danger vividly home to every segment of the population.

[23] Senator Joseph R. McCarthy of Wisconsin, hitherto an inconspicu-
ous figure, seized the opportunity to exploit the anxieties apparently in
a compulsive desire to win national prominence. Starting in 1950 he
recklessly accused federal officials, high and low, of connivance with
Russia. He charged that the State Department was knowingly harboring
scores of card-carrying Communists. As chairman of a Senate committee
he further assailed in public hearings persons of unblemished probity in
the military and foreign services, wrecking their reputations and ruining
their careers. When General Eisenhower ran for President in 1952, even
that popular hero omitted from a speech a tribute to George C. Marshall
out of deference to the Wisconsin Senator who had branded the army
chief of staff in World War II and later Secretary of State as a party to
a "conspiracy, the world-wide web of which had been spun in Moscow."

[24] Through the nation at large as well as in Congress, McCarthy, in
the troubled state of the popular mind, rallied an impassioned following
regardless of party. Though many people privately denounced his methods, only the bravest dared speak out lest they, too, be pilloried for disloyalty. In due time, however, the public grew tired of the cries of "Wolf!
Wolf!" when not one of McCarthy's accusations produced a court conviction. Violations of the constitutional rights of citizens came to loom
larger than unsupported allegations of treason. The United States Senate
itself administered the final blow when in December 1954 it adopted a
resolution condemning McCarthy by the overwhelming vote of sixty-
seven to twenty-two.

[25] What did this series of extremist movements have in common?
Their basic kinship lay in the purpose to deny to fellow citizens sacrosanct
constitutional safeguards, whether freedom of religion, speech, and association, due process of law, the right of suffrage, or other guarantees.
It is easy therefore to regard the upsurges as un-American. But, had they
really been so, they would not all have been indigenous in origin and
gathered the strength they did. The truth is that they reveal an aspect of
the national character we tend to forget: the presence of impulses and
forces which, though usually latent, are never dead and spring into life
when conditions prove favorable.

[26] Moreover, those affected, however credulous they may seem in
retrospect, were by and large well-meaning persons believing earnestly

that they were fighting dragons that threatened catastrophe to themselves and the country. This gave many of them a dedicated sense of participating for the first time in decisions of vital public concern. As soon, however, as the cause demonstrated vote-getting promise, politicians cannily used it to advance their personal fortunes. Only two of the movements, however, generated national parties, and neither outlasted the single campaign. The rest bored from within one or the other or both of the established organizations.

[27] The goals they sought naturally varied according to the special circumstances, but these were always unmistakably set forth, since people are more easily aroused when offered cure-alls for their worries. Xenophobia and Negrophobia received the highest priority. Ironically enough, the initial provocation, Antimasonry, made so transitory an impress that the later insurgencies commonly themselves assumed the form of oath-bound orders.

[28] Emotion was the mainspring of all of them. "Grand Wizard" Simmons of the second Ku Klux Klan undoubtedly spoke for the lot in saying, "The Klan does not believe that the fact that it is emotional and instinctive, rather than coldly intellectual, is a weakness. All action comes from emotion, rather than from ratiocination." With this conviction the leaders freely resorted to misrepresentation, distortion, and the Big Lie; and their overwrought followers responded by persecuting persons who offered opposition. Bodily harm and arson or, in the case of the McCarthy paroxysm, character assassination constituted their notion of serving the public good instead of the slow and (to them) highly suspect workings of the law.

[29] These repressive movements occurred with a certain regularity, as though a people noted for hard common sense in day-to-day doings had to break loose from time to time when dealing with public matters. About twenty years separated the crests of the four waves in the last century, and thirty years in the two of the present one, thus suggesting that the intervals are growing longer. Despite these differences, however, the outcome was in every case the same, for each upon reaching its peak speedily declined, as if the public, surprised at itself, suddenly recovered its balance. Only once did federal legislation enter in as a factor. The United States is an undoctrinaire country, jealous for the rights and liberties of the individual; and if the testimony of history counts for anything, no movement built on prejudice is ever likely to gain more than a temporary hold.

[30] Against this background the extremism of the Goldwater candidacy should be viewed. Superficially it surpassed all its forerunners by

capturing the national convention of one of the two great parties and dictating its nominees and platform. The dramatic victory, however, resulted from the failure of the moderate or progressive Republicans to unite their strength against a determined and well-organized minority. The tail wagged the dog. When Goldwater declared in his acceptance speech, "Extremism in the defense of liberty is no vice. Moderation in the pursuit of justice is no virtue," one of his unsuccessful rivals expressed the general sentiment of the party in sternly rejoining, "To extol extremism—whether 'in defense of liberty' or 'in pursuit of justice'—is dangerous, irresponsible, and frightening." The weeks that followed the convention saw massive Republican defections.

[31] From the start, then, the new leaders lacked the broad base of party support from which they had expected to operate. Beyond this they confronted a difficulty which a knowledge of the earlier agitations could have helped them solve. They did not define with clarity the enemy they were fighting and thus denied their followers an effective recruiting cry. Goldwater, on the one hand, pleaded nostalgically for a return to simpler government and greater state autonomy and, on the other, demanded an aggressive foreign policy—two positions hard to reconcile. In addition, his appeal was confused by the vigorous backing of the John Birch Society and of the White Citizens Councils and scattered reincarnations of the Ku Klux Klan in the South. These groups, the first McCarthyistic and the others racist, advocated measures which Goldwater himself neither explicitly avowed nor disclaimed.

[32] Finally, the Goldwater endeavor proved ill-timed. If these upheavals partake of a roughly cyclical character, as the evidence suggests, even a more ably conceived campaign could not have got very far in 1964, since not twenty or thirty years but only ten had elapsed since the previous eruption. As it was, Goldwater went down to disastrous defeat, winning only his home state of Arizona and five others in the South. Although these latter had usually been Democratic politically, they saw in his issue of states' rights a means of suppressing the Negroes' human rights. A polling organization, moreover, reported that three out of every four of the relatively few Republican votes he received nationally stemmed from party loyalty, not confidence in the man or his program.

[33] The uniform failure of this procession of extremist movements, even when well managed, to make more than a fleeting impression in the past augurs that they will not fare better in the future. Efforts to intimidate or manhandle fellow Americans because of their personal or social views, or to achieve the same end through repressive legislation, can never hope to win the lasting favor of a people dedicated historically to the principles of fair play and the equal protection of the law.

QUESTIONS AND COMMENT ON FORM AND CONTENT

1. What is accomplished by the introductory paragraph? What is extremism?

2. According to the author, what were the four extremist movements in the nineteenth century? Why did each one arise? Why did each one fail after a limited period? Is sufficient evidence given to prove that each is "extremist"?

3. What were the two extremist movements of the twentieth century? What did each hope to accomplish? Why did each fail after a short time?

4. What do these six movements have in common? Did Schlesinger believe that a well-organized extremist movement could succeed in America? Why or why not?

5. Such movements occurred about every twenty years in the nineteenth century and every thirty years in the twentieth century. Does this increased span indicate progress in the wisdom of the American people? If this inductive reasoning (simple generalization) is too hasty, would the generalization carry more weight if we added some deductive arguments supporting it? For example, we could mention the spread of education in the United States or the better means of communication. What supporting deductions are suggested by Schlesinger in paragraph 29?

6. From paragraph 21 draw up a general statement, axiom, or major premise from which a conclusion denouncing the Ku Klux Klan could be constructed. Use the full form of a syllogism: major premise, minor premise, and conclusion.

7. Why are such phrases as the *"Catholic menace"* (paragraph 17) and *"escaped nuns"* and *"ex-priests"* (paragraph 16) put into quotation marks?

8. Do you agree with the statement in paragraph 28, "All action comes from emotion rather than from ratiocination"? What part should logic (reason) play in argument as compared with feelings or emotion?

9. What kind of evidence was used to support these extremist positions? What kind of emotional appeals were used?

VOCABULARY: WHAT DO THE ITALICIZED WORDS MEAN?

. . . the *professed* objectives have shifted (1)

. . . attributed his disappearance to *retaliation* . . . of *vengeful* members (2)

. . . fraternity's *covert* control of the courts (2)

. . . denounced the *hydra-headed* monster (3)

. . . legislatures banned *extrajudicial* oaths (3)

. . . questions of *crucial* national importance (5)

. . . bloodshed as well as *incendiarism* (7)

. . . immorality and *infanticide* (7)

The Know Nothings shortly passed into *oblivion* (9)

. . . to warn them to desist or *decamp* (12)

. . . adopted the *eerie* disguise (13)

. . . *brazenly* defied the federal authority (14)
. . . *alleged encyclical* commanding the faithful to "exterminate all *heretics*"
(16)
. . . *mainstay* of the Democrats (17)
The first outburst of *zealotry* . . . was a *throwback* (18)
. . . an *erstwhile itinerant* preacher (18)
. . . the *resuscitated* Klan (19)
At its *zenith* the membership . . . embraced (20)
. . . popular *revulsion* to brute force (21)
Communist *infiltration* (22)
. . . *compulsive* desire to win (23)
. . . persons of unblemished *probity* (23)
. . . *pilloried* for disloyalty (24)
. . . *sacrosanct* constitutional safeguards (25)
. . . *indigenous* in origin (25)
Xenophobia and *Negrophobia* received the highest priority (27)
The United States is an *undoctrinaire* country (29) . .

THEME SUGGESTIONS

Where We Get Our Prejudices
Can We Overcome Racial or Religious Prejudices?
Extremists Are Often Patriotic Zealots
How to Detect Propaganda
Hate and Fear as Propaganda Devices
Why X Thinks His Group Is Superior to Other Groups
Why I Am a Conservative (Liberal)
Education Lessens Prejudice

THE DARK OF THE MOON

Eric Sevareid

(*See chapter 11 for biographical data.*)

[1] This, thank goodness, is the first warm and balmy night of the year
in these parts; the first frogs are singing. Altogether this is hardly the
night for whispering sweet sentiments about the reciprocal trade act,
the extension thereof. But since we are confined, by tradition, to the
contemplation of public themes and issues, let us contemplate the moon.
The lovely and luminous moon has become a public issue. For quite a

few thousand years it was a private issue; it figured in purely bilateral negotiations between lovers, in the incantations of jungle witch doctors and Indian corn planters. Poets from attic windows issued the statements about the moon, and they made better reading than the mimeographed handouts now being issued by assistant secretaries of defense.

[2] The moon was always measured in terms of hope and reassurance and the heart pangs of youth on such a night as this; it is now measured in terms of mileage and foot-pounds of rocket thrust. Children sent sharp, sweet wishes to the moon; now they dream of blunt-nosed missiles.

[3] There must come a time, in every generation, when those who are older secretly get off the train of progress, willing to walk back to where they came from, if they can find the way. We're afraid we're getting off now. Cheer, if you wish, the first general or Ph.D. who splatters something on the kindly face of the moon. We shall grieve for him, for ourself, for the young lovers and poets and dreamers to come, because the ancient moon will never be the same again. Therefore, we suspect, the heart of man will never be the same.

[4] We find it very easy to wait for the first photographs of the other side of the moon, for we have not yet seen the other side of Lake Louise or the Blue Ridge peak that shows through the cabin window.

[5] We find ourself quite undisturbed about the front-page talk of "controlling the earth from the moon," because we do not believe it. If neither men nor gadgets nor both combined can control the earth from the earth, we fail to see how they will do so from the moon.

[6] It is exciting talk, indeed, the talk of man's advance toward space. But one little step in man's advance toward man—that, we think, would be truly exciting. Let those who wish to try to discover the composition of a lunar crater; we would settle for discovering the true mind of a Russian commissar or the inner heart of a delinquent child.

[7] There is, after all, another side—a dark side—to the human spirit, too. Men have hardly begun to explore these regions; and it is going to be a very great pity if we advance upon the bright side of the moon with the dark side of ourselves, if the cargo in the first rockets to reach there consists of fear and chauvinism and suspicion. Surely we ought to have our credentials in order, our hands very clean, and perhaps a prayer for forgiveness on our lips as we prepare to open the ancient vault of the shining moon.

QUESTIONS AND COMMENT ON FORM AND CONTENT

1. Like Frost's essay (see "The Figure a Poem Makes," chapter 12), Eric Sevareid's informal essay begins with delight and ends in wisdom. Why is the setting (time and place) appropriate for the theme?

2. What is the real theme?

3. What words or phrases remind us of Sevareid's work as a news reporter and interpreter? Why, for instance, does he speak of "bilateral negotiations between lovers"? Can you identify the source of "on such a night as this"?

4. Why is the essay called "The Dark of the Moon"?

VOCABULARY: WHAT DO THE ITALICIZED WORDS MEAN?

. . . whispering sweet sentiments about the *reciprocal trade* act (1)

. . . *bilateral negotiations* between lovers (1)

. . . *incantations* of jungle witch doctors (1)

. . . *mimeographed handouts* (1)

. . . consists of fear and *chauvinism* and suspicion (7)

. . . have our *credentials* in order, our *hands* very *clean* (7)

THEME SUGGESTIONS

The Man on the Moon

Superstitions about the Moon

With How Sad Steps, O Moon (See Sir Philip Sidney's sonnet #31 in *Astrophel and Stella*.)

Space Travel

The Scientist's Moon

The Lover's Moon

Words Derived from Belief about Heavenly Bodies (Note: include *lunacy, disaster, mercurial, saturnine,* and the like.)

THE UNKNOWN CITIZEN

(TO JS/07/M/378 THIS MARBLE MONUMENT IS ERECTED BY THE STATE)

W. H. Auden

W. H. Auden (1907-   ), Anglo-American poet, was educated at Oxford. In 1939 he came to the United States and later became an American citizen. His poetry is noted for its force, variety, and originality. The Collected Poetry of W. H. Auden *appeared in 1945. His* Age of Anxiety

*(1947), which received the Pulitzer Prize in 1948, shows continued prog-
ress in his art. He was elected Professor of Poetry at Oxford in 1956.*

He was found by the Bureau of Statistics to be
One against whom there was no official complaint;
And all the reports on his conduct agree
That, in the modern sense of an old-fashioned word, he was a saint,
For in everything he did he served the Greater Community.
Except for the War till the day he retired
He worked in a factory and never got fired,
But satisfied his employers, Fudge Motors Inc.
Yet he wasn't a scab or odd in his views,
For his Union reports that he paid his dues,
(Our report on his Union shows it was sound)
And our Social Psychology workers found
That he was popular with his mates and liked a drink.
The Press are convinced that he bought a paper every day
And that his reactions to advertisements were normal in every way.
Policies taken out in his name prove that he was fully insured,
And his Health-card shows he was once in hospital but left it cured.
Both Producers Research and High-Grade Living declare
He was fully sensible to the advantages of the Installment Plan
And had everything necessary to the Modern Man,
A phonograph, a radio, a car and a frigidaire.
Our researchers into Public Opinion are content
That he held the proper opinions for the time of year;
When there was peace, he was for peace; when there was war, he went.
He was married and added five children to the population,
Which our Eugenist says was the right number for a parent of his gener-
    ation,
And our teachers report that he never interfered with their education.
Was he free? Was he happy? The question is absurd:
Had anything been wrong, we should certainly have heard.

QUESTIONS AND COMMENT ON FORM AND CONTENT

1. Why was this citizen unknown? Who is making the report?
2. This is obviously a satire using irony principally to get its effect. What is
the difference between satire and irony?
3. Who or what are being satirized? Is the title a part of the satire? What is
the allusion in the title?

4. How do you account for the unusual use of capitals?

5. What is the meaning of "he held the proper opinion for the time of year"? Would he have been very careful to follow the styles, customs, and hit tunes that are "in" and to avoid those that are "out"? What is the meaning and effect of the next to last line?

6. Is there a regular meter or rhyming scheme in this poem?

THEME SUGGESTIONS

A Normal Citizen
An Average Man (or Woman)
Conformity
Self-Reliance

INDEX TO AUTHORS AND TITLES

Ad and the Id, The   356
Adler, Mortimer J.   227
Anderson, Maxwell   388
Areopagitica   428
Assassination of Lincoln, The   50
Auden, Wystan Hugh   444

Bacon, Sir Francis   218, 247
Battle of the Ants, The   34
Belloc, Hilaire   39
Bennett, Arnold   10
Boll, Eleanor Stoker   311
Bossard, James H. S.   311
Brown, John Mason   159
Browning, Robert   69, 90
But What's a Dictionary For?   139

Campus Marriages—For Better or for
   Worse   311
Cather, Willa   288
Character of Washington, The   79
Chesterfield, Lord   280
Chicago   131
Child, A   76
Chute, Marchette   211
Ciardi, John   238
Clemens, Samuel Langhorne, see
   Twain, Mark
Cliché Expert Reveals Himself in His
   True Colors, The   164
College Athletics: Their Pressure on
   High Schools   341
Commager, Henry Steele   348
Copland, Aaron   397
Courtship through the Ages   318
Cowley, Malcolm   169
Creative Process in Music, The   397
Cub Reporter Becomes Disillusioned,
   A   365

Dark of the Moon, The   442
Davis, Robert Gorham   200

Earle, John   76
Encantadas or Enchanted Isles, The
   59

Evans, Bergen   139
Extremism in American Politics   432

Father to His Son, A   306
Feel, The   25
Figure a Poem Makes, The   395
Fishwick, Marshall   81
Florida, Missouri and the Quarles'
   Farm   104
Four Kinds of Students   221
Frost, Robert   70, 72, 73, 395
Fuller, Thomas   221
Future of Grammar, The   135

Galileo   190
Gallico, Paul   25
General Electric Bulletin   3
Getting at the Truth   211
Gigantic Task Ahead, The   371
Give the Games Back to the Students
   348
Grave, The   62

Hannibal, Missouri   112
Here Is New York   122
Hicks, Granville   154
Hillside Thaw, A   70
Housman, Alfred Edward   417
How to Mark a Book   227
Hutchins, Robert M.   371
Huxley, Thomas Henry   183

In the Laboratory with Agassiz   222

Jefferson, Thomas   79

Kazin, Alfred   256
Keller, Helen   13
Kerouac, Jack   43
Kitchen, The   256

Letters to His Son   280
Lexicographer's Easy Chair, The   151
Logic and Logical Fallacies   200
Loon, The   37
Lucidity, Simplicity, Euphony   174

McGinley, Phyllis   114
Man in the White Marble Toga, The   81
Man Jones, The   323
Maugham, William Somerset   174
Meeting at Night   69
Melancholy Man, A   77
Melville, Herman   59
Method of Scientific Investigation, The   183
Milton, John   428
Miracle of Language, The   16
Modern Architecture: The Cardboard House   404
Morgan, Edmund S.   232
Morgan, Thomas B.   267
Most Important Day, The   13
Mowing of a Field, The   39
Mumford, Lewis   16
My Last Duchess   90

Of Studies   218
Of Youth and Age   247
Old Junior's Progress—From Prep School to Severance Pay   261
On the Road with Memère   43
Orwell, George   421
Overbury, Sir Thomas   77

Packard, Vance   356
Patton, Frances Gray   323
Paul's Case   288
Pleasant Agony   159
Porter, Katherine Anne   62
Prayer for My Daughter, A   307

Reflections on Mass Culture   380
Reik, Louis E.   249
Right Word to Write, The   154
Road Not Taken, The   72
Roberts, Paul   135
Russell, Bertrand   190

Sandburg, Carl   50, 131, 306
Schlesinger, Arthur M.   432
Scudder, Samuel H.   222
Seeing Life   10
Sevareid, Eric   365, 442
Shooting an Elephant   421
Sledd, James   151
Sociological Habit Patterns in Linguistic Transmogrification   169
Suburbia, of Thee I Sing   114
Sullivan, Frank   164

Teen-Age Heroes: Mirrors of Muddled Youth   267
Television: The Lion That Squeaks   374
Terence, This Is Stupid Stuff   417
Thoreau, Henry David   34, 37
Thurber, James   318
Toynbee, Arnold J.   374
Twain, Mark   104, 112

Unfading Beauty, The: A Well-Filled Mind   238
Unknown Citizen, The   444

Van den Haag, Ernest   380

War of the Generations   249
Welty, Eudora   92
What Every Yale Freshman Should Know   232
Whatever Hope We Have   388
White, Elwyn Brooks   122
White, William S.   261
White-Tailed Hornet, The   73
Why I Live at the P.O.   92
Why Study English?   3
Wright, Frank Lloyd   404

Yeats, William Butler   307
Youngert, Eugene   341